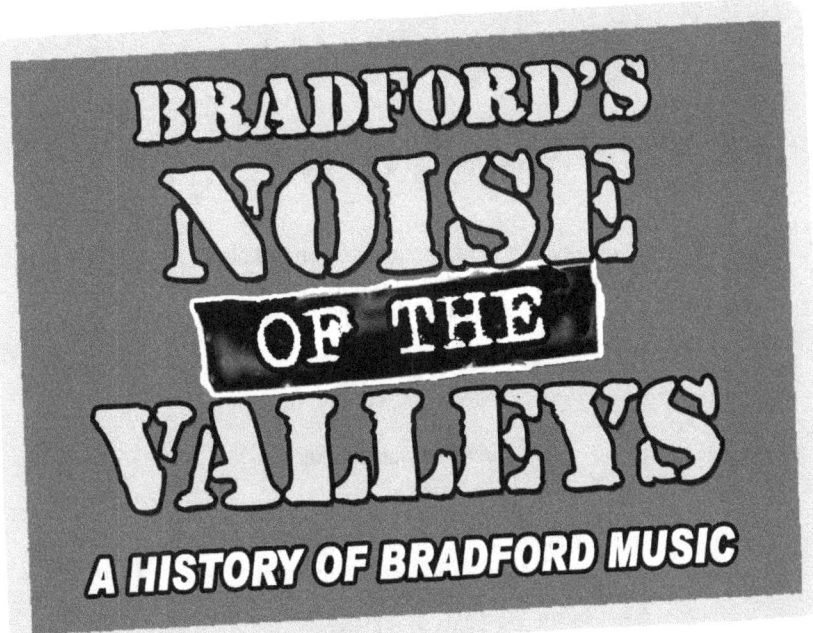

A HISTORY OF BRADFORD MUSIC

VOLUME 2 • 1988 - 1998
GARY CAVANAGH AND MATT WEBSTER

LS ARTS BOOKS
A Bradford Noise Production

Dedicated to all the musicians who are no longer with us, by Gary.

Dedicated to a Hippy, by Matt.

Bradford 2025 Edition

This revised, updated and expanded edition
published in the United Kingdom in 2025 by
LS Arts Publishing
West Yorkshire

Leeds Streets Ltd

www.leeds-streets.uk

First published in the United Kingdom in 2013 by
Mutiny 2000 Publications
Bradford
West Yorkshire

bradfordnoise.com
mutiny2000.com

© 2013, 2025 by Gary Cavanagh and Matt Webster

The Authors hereby assert their moral rights to be identified as the Authors of the Work.

Written and researched by Gary Cavanagh and Matt Webster
Graphic design by Matt Webster
Layout by Matt Webster and Gary Cavanagh
Family trees drawn by Gary Cavanagh

All images in this book are copyright of the original creators.

All rights reserved. No part of this publication may be reproduced, stored in a retrieval system, or transmitted, in any form or by any means, electronic, mechanical, photocopying, recording or otherwise, without the prior permission of the publisher and copyright holders.

British Library Cataloguing in Publication Data
A catalogue record for this book is available from the British Library

ISBN 978-1-7391481-4-0

Printed in the UK by Lightning Source

FOREWORD

When asked if I'm from Bradford, my response is always, "Born and bred". The next question is often, "Didn't you want to move away?" I have to explain then, that Bradford is just a place with some people in it, like anywhere else in the world and your experience of that place is what you make it. You will always meet people you like or dislike and want to work with or not and great music can be created and consumed anywhere.

Bradford has always had its fair share of talent, though never quite had the synchronicity of the fashionable music movements of cities like Liverpool or Manchester. Still, the sonic output of the city is formidable and Gary Cavanagh and Matt Webster's efforts to document this fact have given our music scene a much needed public persona and a well deserved pat on the back, through these impressive books.

Watching Bradford bands in the Vaults Bar in the early eighties, gave me that eureka moment of realisation that unknown bands could be just as good as those you saw on the telly, or heard on the radio. From that moment on, I wanted to be a creator and facilitator, not just a consumer of music and that decision shaped the rest of my life. From becoming a guitarist in a school band, through semi-successful rock groups in the eighties and nineties, starting a record label, building recording studios, running PA and lighting rigs, dabbling in management, promotion, photography, video, album artwork, music journalism etc etc, my existence has been consumed by a Bradford-based music vocation and obsession.

I have had the privilege of realising a huge percentage of my early ambitions, through being a Bradford musician. I have lived a roller-coaster ride of a life, never the same day twice. I have met some amazing, inspirational, gifted and hilarious people, travelled to many weird and wonderful places and hung out with musical legends, all from buying that Hondoll Les Paul in the Shoulder of Mutton in 1980.

Ultimately, I'm secretly glad that Bradford never really had a definitive sound of its own. It's this city's infinite diversity and variety that keeps me interested and shows the full effect of the region's endless talent potential and I am forever grateful to be lucky enough to be a part of it and long may it continue.

I shall read this book with pride.

Tim Walker
Voltage Studios/Voltage Records

Another bloody blustry day...

Bradford is in some ways still a small town, surrounded by a number of smaller townships that all merge into the city as we know it today. Situated at its centre is a natural bowl provided by the great valleys of the rivers Aire and Wharfe.

Since 1974 Bradford has been enlarged to a metropolitan district, taking in the townships of Shipley, Bingley, Haworth, Keighley and Ilkley, making it the seventh largest urban/rural conurbation in the UK.

Nationally, over the last few decades, the City of Bradford has perhaps been perceived in a negative light. Despite this, it has continued to provide a positive and diverse multi-cultural heritage.

The city has also bred giants of contemporary cultural art of the twentieth century such as the unique classical composer Frederick Delius, the renowned playwright, dramatist and novelist JB Priestly and perhaps the UK's most famous living modern artist, David Hockney.

The city's resilience in brushing off the pejorative image that has been foisted upon it is a tribute to its positive nature and the creative power that exists within the people of the area.

Is there something in the water that makes the people of the region, and especially the local musicians, from so many ethnic backgrounds and seeped in the strong radical tradition of social justice, produce an eclectic range of sounds that must easily rank as good, if not better than, some of the bigger cities elsewhere in Britain?

To carry on with the Bradford's Noise Of The Valleys project, we had to remember that we were documenting people's real lives from all across the city's music scene and needed to effectively document their hard-fought artistic and musical accomplishments.

We thought it was important to preserve these memories, images and narratives before they were lost to us all and to espouse, to whoever is interested, the wonderful range of great music our city has produced, and continues to produce, to this day.

When looking back at all this nostalgia, from the dizzy heights of the present day, we are apt to forget and lose sight of how difficult it was for bands 'back in the day' to even produce music and to get equipment, rehearse, find a studio and to release a finished product.

So, this book stands as a document of the endeavours of Bradford folk (and a few off-cumdens who have found themselves drawn into our city's music scene) and will stand as a record for all they have achieved.

And long may it continue...

Gary Cavanagh
Matt Webster
Bradford,
November 2013

www.bradfordnoise.com

How to read the Rock Family Trees

Just in case anybody has difficulties in understanding the Rock Family Trees, below is a basic key on how to read them. Firstly they are read downwards and in chronological order by year date. Year dates in closed brackets indicate the years a band was active, and the rear end open brackets denotes that no information is available as to when the band ceased to be active.

Symbols and abbreviations

#2 etc – denotes the 2nd incarnation of a band
voc – vocals
gtr – guitar
drm – drums
keyd – keyboards
harm – harmonica
hamm – hammond organ
trump – trumpet and so on
- - - ! denotes an occasional guest or studio member
(RIP 2000) – As a mark of respect for the fallen, this denotes the year known of the individual's passinG.

CONTENTS

Preface   1-4
News And Reviews

Chapter 1: 1988-90   5-62

The Godfathers • Miracle Mile • Two Sandwiches Please • The Escapement • The Keep • Bomb Disneyland • Thomas J & The Gangsters Of Soul • Sonando • Talulah Gosh • September Kitchen • Natural Rhythm • Bradford's Alternative Cabaret • Battle Of The Bands 1988 • Hansaid • Jane Mountain • Symphony In X • Gypsy • Little Brother • Vochi • Bradford Recording Studios • Hard Rock • Heavy Metal • Voyager UK • Krakatoa • Foul Play • Diamond Light • Taboo • Carrera • Wicked Rich • Rasa Returns • Third Season • Twice Around The Houses • The Bobby Charltons • Music Venues • Bradford Festival • Dicke Bards • Jane Harrison • Pro Audio • Djibouti Blue • Clocks & Clouds • The Headmen • New Model Army • Battle Of The Bands 1989 • The Orange World Of Titan • Dubh Chapter • The Hollow Men • Sloan Square East • Elsie Moon • The Big Five Record Companies • Zed • Loud • PADD • Poppy Factory • Hyacinth House • The Third Bradford Festival • Futurama 6 • Psycho Surgeons • Pride • Rio's • Mr Meana • Joolz • Architect • The Battle Of The Bands 1990 • BBC • DJ Linda • The Apple Moths • Bedlam • Lost Patrol • Mr Giblet • The Score • The Keighley Scene • Sybil • Thundering Hearts • The Big Bang • The Spurs

Chapter 2: The 1 In 12 Club 1988-90   63-100

Opening The 1 In 12 Club Albion Street Building • The UK Hardcore Scene • Peaceville • Toranaga • Paradise Lost • Sore Throat • Eric Pickles And The Bradford Revolution • The Next World • Kage Engineering • Fulton Street Studios • Wonderful Thing Called Tiddles • Volnitza • The Pickles Papers • Knee Deep In Shit • Generic • Pleasant Valley Children • Disaster • The Poll Tax • Twinned Clubs • Ma Brench Cafe • Cabbage Head Kids • Threshold Shift • Straight Edge • Beer Beast • Doom • Wild And Crazy Noise Merchants • Crisis 1 • ILP Anniversary

Chapter 3: The Dance Scene 1989-98   101-120

Unique 3 • The Mad Musician • No Noise/Pure Noise Recordings • Nightmares On Wax • Rodeo Jones • Push Button Technology • UXL • Underground Swing • Scape • DJ E-Logic • The Rise Of The DJ • Club Nights In Bradford • The Criminal Justice Bill • Stimulations • Miracle Records • Glamorous Hooligan • Rootsman • Dayiah • Third Eye Music • Strongpoint • Pirate Radio Stations • Pianonman • Doctor Man • Usurpa • Janet Jaye • Angeles • Pied Piper Records • Flammable Records • Camp Boyz

Chapter 4: 1991-93   121-190

MacRory's Bar • The Melborn • Metal Mountain 91 • Great Pop Explosion • Music At Myrtle • Bradford Festival • Terrorvision • Primate • Chest • My Dying Bride • Chorus Of Ruin • Solstice • Station West • Pax Records • Royce • Full Colour • For What • Metal Mountain 92 • Slammer • Wasteland • The Edge • Monorail • Hot Spiced Bananas • Bradford Festival 1990 • Bands On The Beck • Tasmin Archer • Lot 49 • Gorgeous • Dawnraiser • Reckless Rhino Records • Mouldy Warp • The Broomdusters • 1 In 12 Club Gigs 1991-93 • Subsonics • Daisy Chainsaw • Therapy? • 1 In 12 Club 10th Anniversary • Bradford Festival At The 1 In 12 • Sons Of Ishmael • Fanzines • Distro • Flat Earth Records • Health Hazard • Armed With Anger • Wartorn • Nailbomb • Voorhees • Mad Dog Ink • Heavier Than Thou • Virtual Reality • Ironside • A Nightmare On Albion Street • Neckbrace • GFA • Claremont The Site • Richard Ingham • Riot Grrrl Movement • Witchknot • Phosphene • The Auxiliary Of Real Men • 1 In 12 AFC • Tom Jones & New Model Army • Simon Ashberry Reviews • Keighley Festival • Mannix • Grain • Mapp • Chaos

Chapter 5: Folk & World Music 1988-98   191-218

Topic Folk Club • Liz Narey • Pre-Moonkyte • Janet Jones • Roger Sutcliffe • Titan • Womad • Kevin Young • The Triangle Club • Old Joe Zydeco • Stony Mountain Trio • Granny Thompsons Big Bald Head • Tok Toki • The Celtic Music Scene • Scarlet Heights • Wild Geese • The City Fleadh • Roger Higgins • The Palladinos • Angelo Palladino • Grace Notes • Los Zimmos • The Bhangra Scene • Saagra • Shahkaar • Naseeb • Karpal Singh • Nachida Punjab • Sansaar • Nation Records • Fundamental • Folk At The 1 In 12 Club • Duffy Gibbons • Egomania • L'Orchestre Du Cafe • Avalon • Shiny Beast • Tooth Fairy • Jazz • Asha Brewer Trio • Milan Lad • Cajun Aces • Crone • Loobie • Jon Harvison • Fiona-Katie Roberts • Phil Gilbert • Milltown Productions

Chapter 6: 1994-96   219-260

D:Ream • Brit Pop • Embrace • Basement Club • The Motorvators • Mr Mak • Psyche • Navaho UK • Nowt • Grim • Tiny Monroe • Summum Bonum • Ripcord • Lional Blairs • The Engine Rooms • Anita Madigan • Nelson's Column • Trip And Stumble • Loco Mosquito • Kill II This • Twister 5 • Lowlife UK • Seal Team 6 • Far Fetched • Serenity • Tropicana • System Records • Screaming Life • Bradford Community Broadcasting • The Bradford Beat • Bullweek • The Pondskaters • Grip • Goodbye Queen's Hall • Blood Orange • Rollercoaster • Comic Book Heroes • Smokie • Blck Bull jam Sessions • John Beck • Sniffa • Detrimantal • Riot In Manningham • Slack • Hardware • Strain • Kiki's New Album • Freaky G's • Headache • Stalingrad • Kito • Local Extras For Film ID • Hannau Tournament • Crisis 2 • Dub Kitchen • Spies At Work • Zapatistas • Endless Struggle • Suffer • Cowboy's Visit • Launch Of 1 In 12 Library • Sure Hand Records • Mayday In Barcelona • Armed With Anger Records Benefit LP • Bad Wisdom Tour • In Yer Face Records • Facelift • Mundane • Slack Elvis • Dragster • Bradford Festival 1996 • Lost Weekend • Green • Homesick • Trotwood's Sunday Sunday • Bands On The Beck • Off The Wall • Dead Celebs • Garden Of Remembrance

Chapter 7: 1997-9   261-282

The Love Apple • Delius Lived Next Door • Marsha Singh • Cecil Zinyuku • Zed Again • The Horton Carpets • Mutiny 2000 • Gardeners Of Eden • Daily Mutiny • Blue Noise Studios • Bias • TV Eye • Radius • Benway • The Blister Factory • Storm Promotions • Reclaiming May Day 1997 • Keith Narey • Purity Cries • Cyber Circus • Bradford Music Week • Worm • Us • Chumbawamba Hit Top Spot • Local Jazz Virtuoso Guitarist • The Empress • The Band Magazine • Incardia • Drench Warfare • Sasquatch • Soulfish • Danbert Nobingo • May Day 1988 • Keighley Scene Tree • John Holmes • InFest • After • The Missing Bands

References/Bibliography   283-288

Index Of Bands On Trees   289-294

From Abiosis to ZX Plectrum

Afterwords   295-301

When's This Bloody Book Coming Out? • Author Profiles • Acknowledgements • The Music 1988-1998 6 CD Set • Missing Music 1 & 2

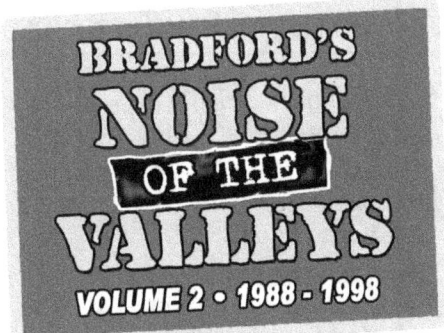

PREFACE

As the title suggests, this book is the follow up to *Bradford's Noise Of The Valleys - A History Of Bradford Rock And Pop 1967 - 1987* (BNOTV1) which was originally published in 2009. The new edition has a revised title and has been considerably expanded, as has this new edition of *Volume 2*.

As a series of books about the passage of time it seems strange that these volumes now have their own history.

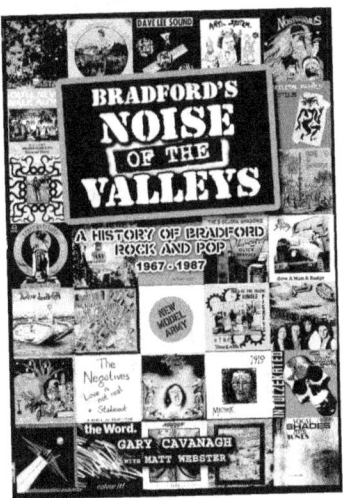

Back in 2009, Bradford was a different place. A large part of the city centre was a building site and we were still wondering how the Forster Square/ Broadway area of town would turn out. Whether Bradford's new layout is an improvement or not you can judge for yourself. Many other iconic areas of the centre were still standing. Marks & Spencer, John Street Market and the Arndale Centre were still thriving. The *Telegraph & Argus* was still made and printed in Bradford on its own printing press, another familiar landmark, now gone.

Thankfully, at the time of writing, the Wool Exchange is still there, housing Waterstone's bookshop. It was here *Bradford's Noise Of The Valleys* first appeared on bookshelves and sold well enough in the last half of 2009 to make the *Bradford's Top Ten Books* list. it even hit the number one spot just before Christmas in a list that included Terry Pratchett (now no longer with us), Bernard Cornwell and *Guiness World Records 2010*!

The book also received critical acclaim in the local press and from many individuals, as well as an excellent review by Nick Toczek in the magazine *R2* (now known as *RnR*).

It also achieved good local sales in record shops

BRADFORD'S TOP TEN BOOKS

Supplied by Waterstone's, Bradford Wool Exchange

1. Bradford's Noise of the Valleys – Gary Cavanagh & Matt Webster (Bank House, £19.99)
2. Longy – Sean Long (John Blake, £17.99)
3. The Gathering Storm – Robert Jordan & Brandon Sanderson (Orbit, £20)
4. Unseen Academicals – Terry Pratchett (Transworld, £18.99)
5. Guinness World Records 2010 – (Guinness, £20)
6. Tempted – PC & Kristin Cast (Atom, £9.99)
7. The Defence Of The Realm – Christopher Andrew (Allen Lane, £30)
8. Family Britain – David Kynaston (Bloomsbury, £25)
9. Thornton – Who'd 'Ave Thought It? – Thornton Antiquarian Society (Bank House, £15.99)
10. Burning Land – Bernard Cornwell (Harpercollins, £18.99)

like Jumbo in Leeds and Wall Of Sound (now Vinyl Tap) in Huddersfield.

The book also had a ten minute filmed TV feature on YTV's *Calendar* news programme in 2010 which can be found on YouTube) and radio featured interviews with Gary on BBC Radio Leeds and Bradford's own Bradford Community Broadcasting (BCB).

In September 2013 we published a new, revised edition of the book, titled *Bradford's Noise Of The Valleys Volume One 1967 - 1987*, followed by the first edition of *Volume 2 1988-1998*.

Below are some of the comments left by people on our website and from letters.

'I was thrilled when looking through it myself to find a photo of the band my brother was in. He passed away two years ago but this would have been the best tribute he'd ever have wished for.' - Gaynor.

'Absolutely stunning piece of work, finding out much info on old mates that they've kept quiet!' - Lindsay Burns Leonini.

'...the research and detail is stunning, varied and comprehensive, and it is carried out with a professional clarity rarely found in monkeys with type writers! well done!' - Griff.

R2 MAR/APR 2010

BRADFORD'S NOISE OF THE VALLEYS: THE MUSIC 1967-1987

Gary Cavanagh with Matt Webster
(BANK HOUSE BOOKS)
ISBN 978-1904408543
Softcover, 278 pages

Some numbers: for twenty-five quid you get a 278-page A4 book (size of a telephone directory) with eighty-five tracks on four CDs. This minutely detailed history of urban music making is the result of years of obsessive research by Gary Cavanagh. As a mainstay of Bradford's legendary 1-in-12 Club, Gary witnessed much of the music he documents. And his remarkable assemblage is the completist's dream.

Assisting him in planning the whole thing, filling gaps, checking details, laying out each page, editing and compiling the CDs and bringing the project from dream to reality was Matt Webster, another ubiquitous figure on the city's music scene.

With photos, rock family trees, press cuttings and detailed histories of even the briefest bands and smallest venues, this publication is surely the most authoritative, comprehensive and exhaustive local music scene history to have been compiled for any British city.

Smokie, Kiki Dee, The Love Affair, The John Verity Band, New Model Army, Southern Death Cult (later The Cult), Skeletal Family and Voyager UK sit alongside the lesser known, and the truly excellent CDs amplify this variety. An absolute benchmark for anyone, anywhere, planning a local rock history, this is a great read for everyone who's every listened to anything sung or strummed from Britain's best city ... and that's without mentioning its beer or its curries!

Nick Toczek

'Excellent book brought back so many memories and, God, Bradford's such a small place!' - Steve Atkins.

'This book is AMAZING and is a must read for all fans of music, particularly those who grew up around the Bradford music scene.' - Gary Kaye.

'Congratulations on all the hard work in producing this book ...amazing detail and a lot of good research gone in to this, well done...' - George Mazur.

'The book is an awesome piece of work!' - Jim Pickles.

'...a magnificent social document, ... i look back with incredible fondness on the whole era.' - Stephen Brown

'Thank you for enabling me to take a trip back in time!' - Helen Varley

'...a stunning piece of work that thoroughly documents the Bradford music scene and all it's prime movers.' - Johnny Lorrimer.

THE MISSING MUSIC

In December 2011, we released a CD of tracks that we did not mange to find in time for the publication of *BNOTV1*. These tracks would have been on the original 4 CD set if we had found them in time, but we didn't, so we put them out on a separate CD. Featuring the likes of The Shakes, Ghost Dance, Barbara Moore, Kiki Dee, Shadowfax, Catch 22 and Dedringer, it received a double-page spread in the *T&A* in January 2011, courtesy of Emma Clayton.

The Missing Music 1 and 2 CDs are the bridge between the first book and this book and are numbers 5 and 6 in our CD collection which continues with the six CDs released with *BNOTV 2*.

THE MISSING MUSIC 2 CD

In March 2013, we released another CD of local tracks that weren't on our previous releases, which got a 3 star review in *Record Collector Magazine* (right) and a good review in RNR.

Bradford's Noise Of The Valleys: The Missing Music 2, 1972-1987

★★★

Bradford Noise BNOTVCD 006
Yorkshire's forgotten musical heroes

Bradford musicians Gary Cavanagh and Matt Webster began their celebration of their home city's pop and rock heritage as a 2009 book containing more than 130 family trees, and covering 5,000 local heroes from the lowliest wannabe to national success stories such as Smokie and New Model Army. However, the accompanying four-disc box set would appear to have left a few stones unturned, hence this supplementary disc.

The intervening years has certainly unearthed some curios, not least Bingley-born Rodney Bewes' own version of the theme to his celebrated sitcom *Whatever Happened To The Likely Lads?*, and striking workers from the Hindle industrial plant covering The Strawbs' hit Part Of The Union. Unfortunately, a lack of biographical detail in the sleevenotes means referring to the original book may be the only way to get the full stories behind these tracks.

Beyond the spirited efforts of parochial stargazers such as Excalibur, The Invaders and the delightfully named Edible Marquetry, there are numbers which allude specifically to the region and its famous sons. A cappella folkies Swan Arcade chronicle bygone skirmishes on The Battle Of Sowerby Bridge, while Midnight Hearse sing of forlorn hope on We're Gonna Have A New World Champion, recalling boxer Richard Dunn's 1976 title fight with Muhammad Ali.

Terry Staunton

PREFACE 1988 - 1998

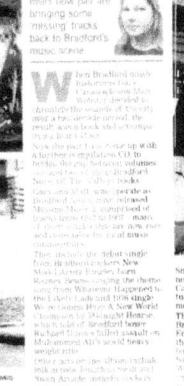

The two centre spreads by Emma Clayton, courtesy of the Telegraph & Argus

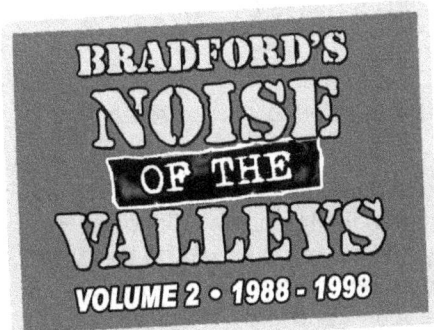

CHAPTER 1: 1988-1990

By 1988, the Bradford local music scene had developed into a healthy, diverse and vibrant music culture. Previous music genres such as rock, prog, punk and new wave had all survived in some form but had also evolved into hybrid crossover styles and sub-genres. So, by 1988, there appeared to be no distinctive new musical genre coming through, more a mixture of all the styles that had gone before.

THE GODFATHERS

Local Bradford drummer George Mazur, formerly of local bands The Scene, Idle Rich and The Cut-out Shapes, had relocated to London where he joined ex-Sid Presley Experience brothers Chris and Peter Coyne in their new band, The Godfathers, in 1985. By 1988, their second LP *Birth, School, Work,*

Death, on the Epic label, had established them as a tough and tight R&B indie rock outfit. A single from the album, *Love Is Dead*, reached No 3 in the indie charts. The title track of the LP got to No 38

in the US Billboard Top 40 singles chart after receiving heavy college radio airplay.

They had previously had two other indie hits from their first LP, *Hit By Hit*, on Homestead

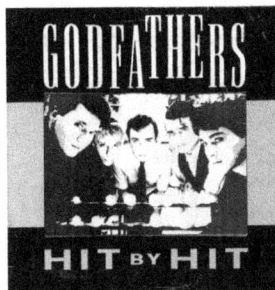

Records, produced by Vic Maile. In April 1986 *This Damnation* reached No 37 and their version of Rolf Harris' 1962 hit *Sun Arise* got as high as No 6 in September 1986.

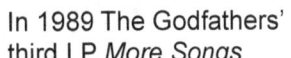

In 1989 The Godfathers' third LP *More Songs About Love & Hate*, again on Epic, reached No 49 in the UK Album charts while the track *She Gives Me Love* reached No 8 in the US Rock charts.

A fourth LP, *Unreal World,* was released on Epic in 1991, followed by a live compilation album, *Dope, Rock'n'Roll & Fucking In The Streets,* on the

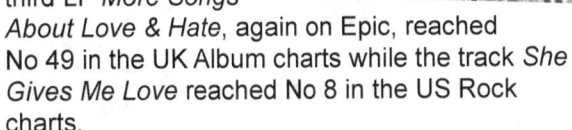

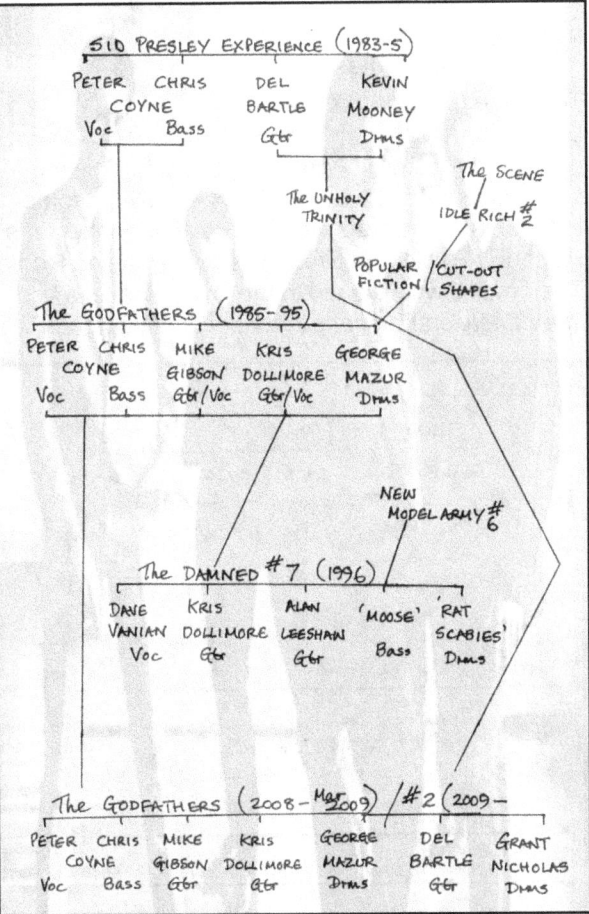

independent Corporate Image label. Two further LPs followed, *Orange,* in 1993 and 1995's *Afterlife,* before the band split.

In 2008, the original line-up reformed and toured and, although George left The Godfathers in March 2009, the band are still gigging today and played at the May 28-30 2010 *Strummercamp Festival* in Manchester which celebrated the life, music and influence of The Clash's Joe Strummer. (1)

MIRACLE MILE

Although hailing from Cleckheaton, Miracle Mile had been based in London since 1985.

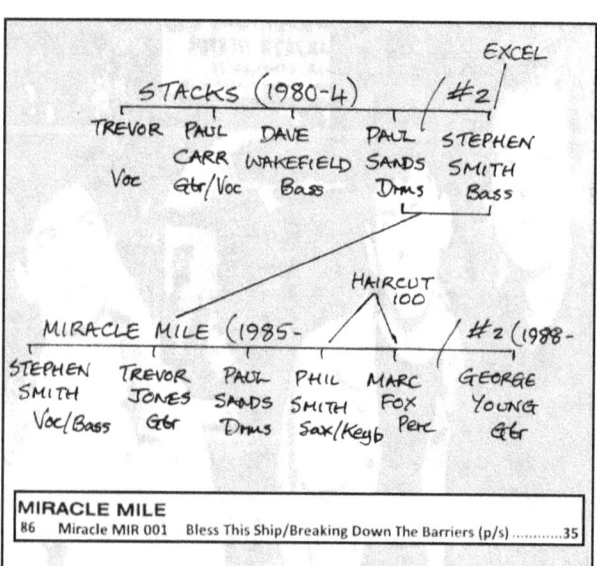

The main trio of musicians had originally been in the band Stacks (1980-84). They added two ex-Haircut 100 side men to the lineup on saxophone and percussion.

Their first single, Bless This Ship / Barriers Of Love, was released on their own label in April 1988, published by the international Zomba Music. It got airplay on some independent radio stations, including Manchester's Piccadilly Radio and Bradford's own Pennine Radio. Their music was likened to the Blow Monkeys and *'their finely crafted songs were in the tradition of Crowded House and Prefab Sprout'.* (2)

Their later releases included the EPs; *Candids, Bicycle Thieves* and the excellent *Heroes & Misfits.*

In early 1988, two new venues sprang up and started putting on gigs - The Yarnspinners at the bottom of Manchester Road and The Cotton Club at the bottom of Leeds Road, while in Keighley Vikki's Bar started gigs on Thursday nights.

TWO SANDWICHES PLEASE

Born out of two 1980s bands, The Violent Carsons and Reefer, Two Sandwiches Please were fans of 1970s glam rock/punk/ new wave. Their first

gig was at the Elephant & Castle at the bottom end of Great Horton Road. After that, every gig 'became a party' and they even supported the late legendary Desmond Dekker at Leeds Astoria in January 1988.

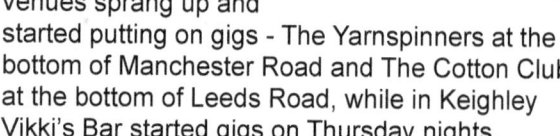

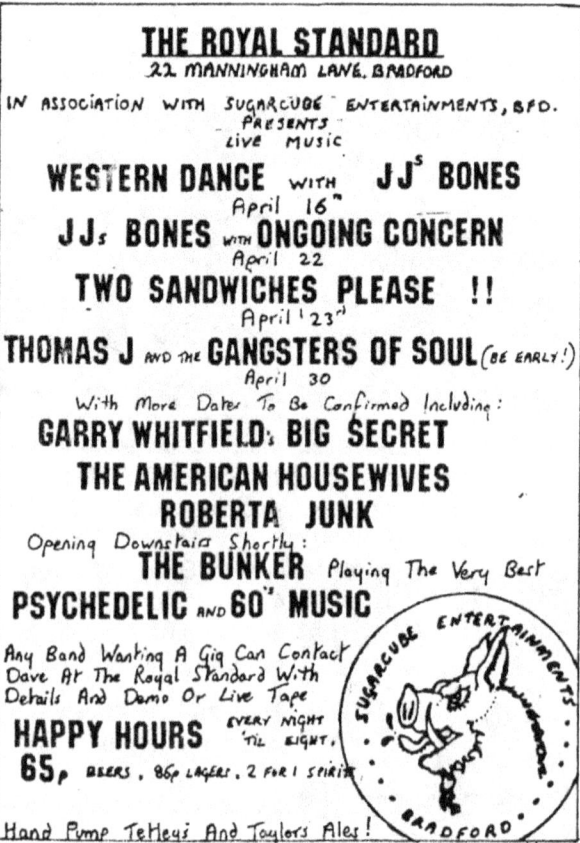

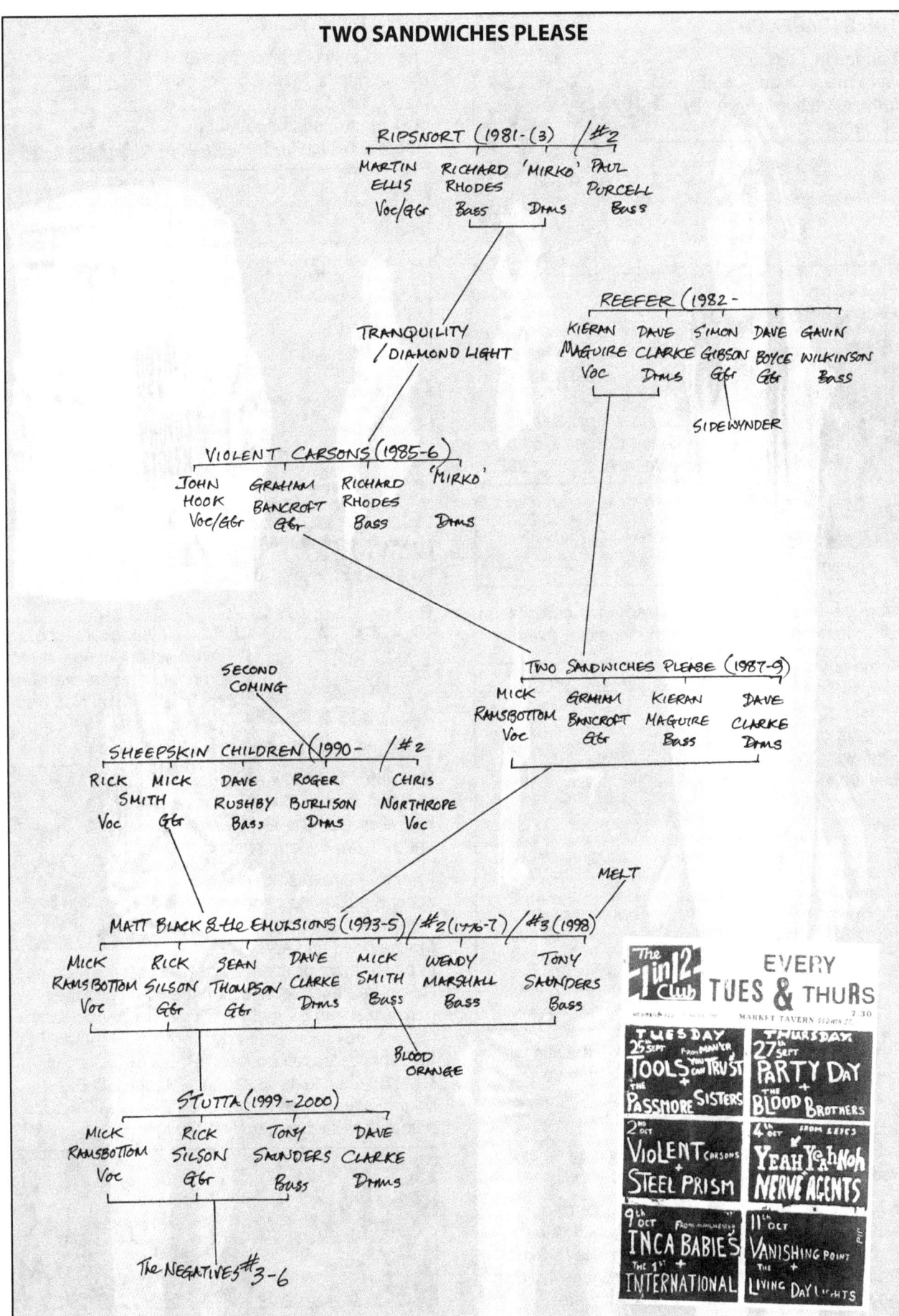

THE ESCAPEMENT

Formed in 1986, they were mainly made up of former Bradford University students.

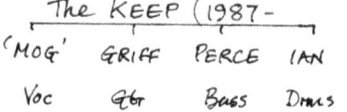

THE KEEP

This Leeds/Bradford indie band formed in 1987 and put out the three track single *Six Silent Years / See My Side / Cockpit B* on their own label in July 1988.

They went on a European tour to promote the single and had a track on a compilation LP which was put out by Italian magazine *Avanti*.

Some other bands around at the start of 1988 were local indie-rockers Seven Dead Americans, soul outfit Thomas J & The Gangsters Of Soul, Latin jazz-funksters Sonando, the psychedelic soul/pop of September Kitchen.

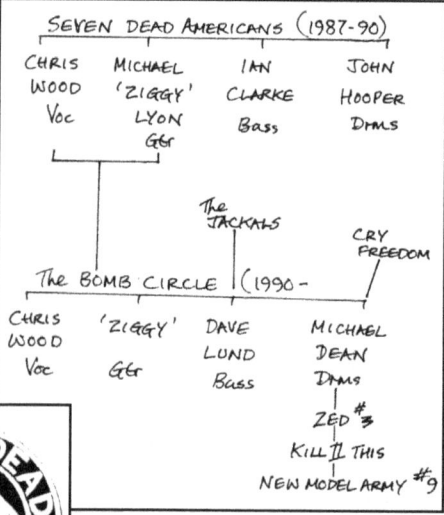

February 5 1988 saw Comic Relief's the first ever *Red Nose Day* charity fund-raising campaign.

In March, Tickles nightspot on Westgate re-opened with live shows four or five nights a week with the first gig, on March 9, featuring Bill Presley's Coat. These events were run by DJ Colin Egan who also ran the discos at The Smithy on Southgate.

BOMB DISNEYLAND

The group was started by two Bradford lads, Mark Cooper and Mark 'Prud' Prytherch, who, after busking around London tube stations, settled in Cheshire and

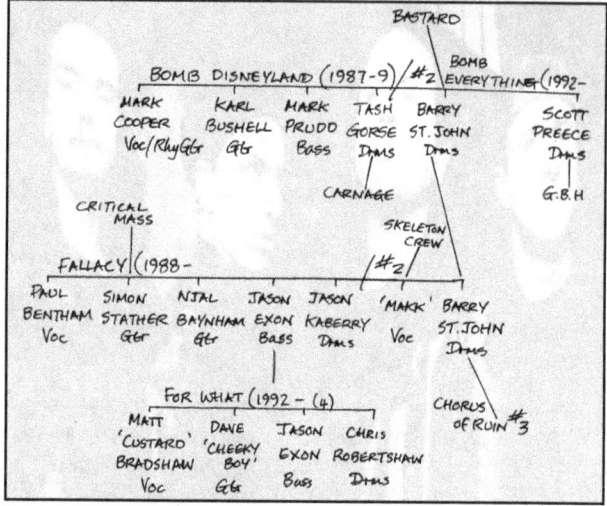

North Wales, before adding two more members.

After sending a demo to London indie record label Vinyl Solution, the band was offered a deal and their first LP, *Why Not*, was released in late 1988 and produced by Justin and Rob of New Model Army.

By 1989, the band was based in Nottingham and later that year supported NMA at Leeds Town & Country Club.

Prior to the release of their second album the band's logo, which featured Mickey Mouse head and ears, began to cause them problems. After lawyers from Disney Corp threatened legal action they changed their name to Bomb Everything. Their record company also had to change the cover artwork of the original LP. They released another LP, *Guess What*, on Vinyl Solution in 1990 and in 1992 the CD EP, *Fountainhead*, was released on Devotion Records before the band split up in 1993.

Fallacy

CHAPTER 1 — 1988 - 1990

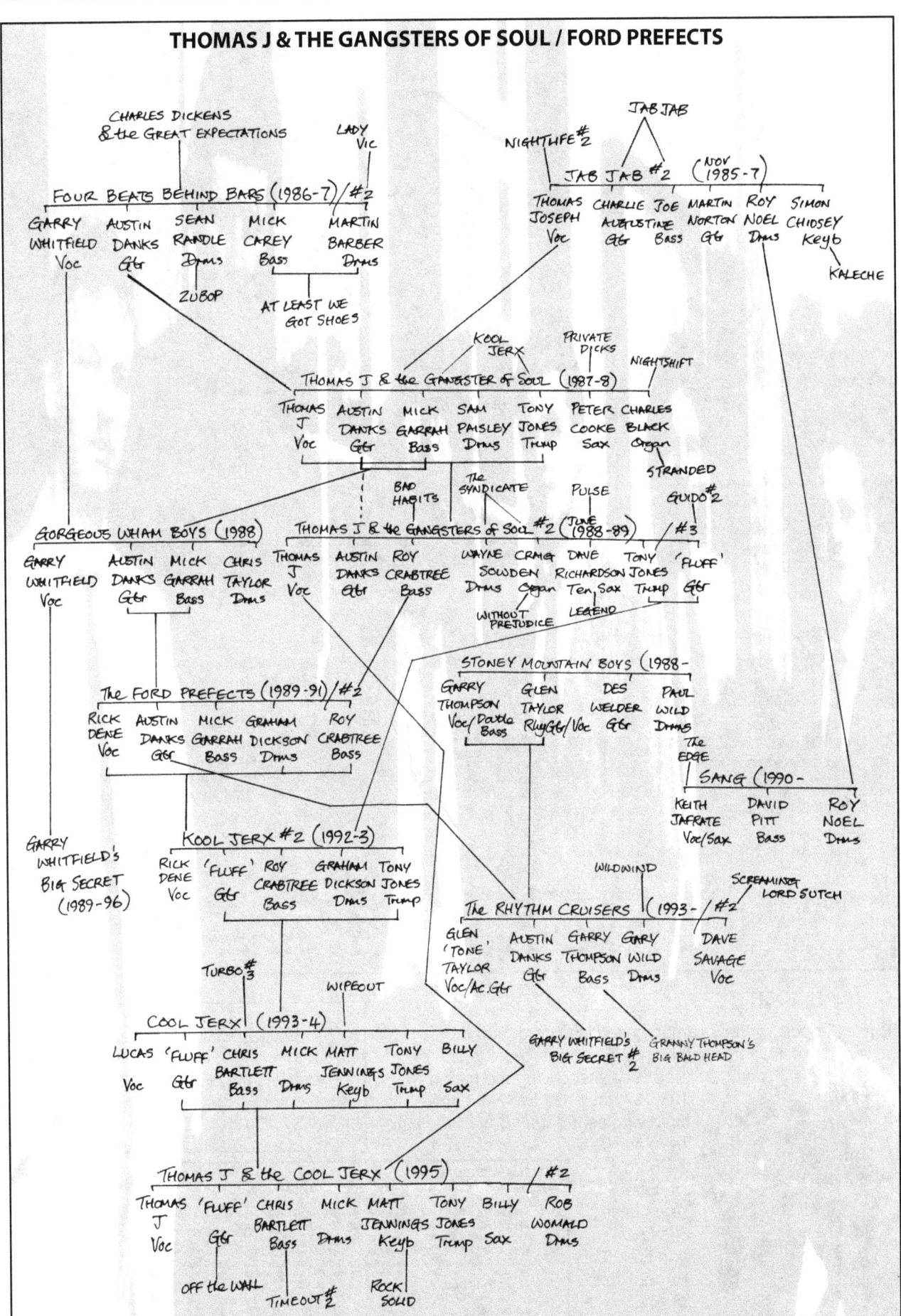

SONANDO / SYBIL BEATS

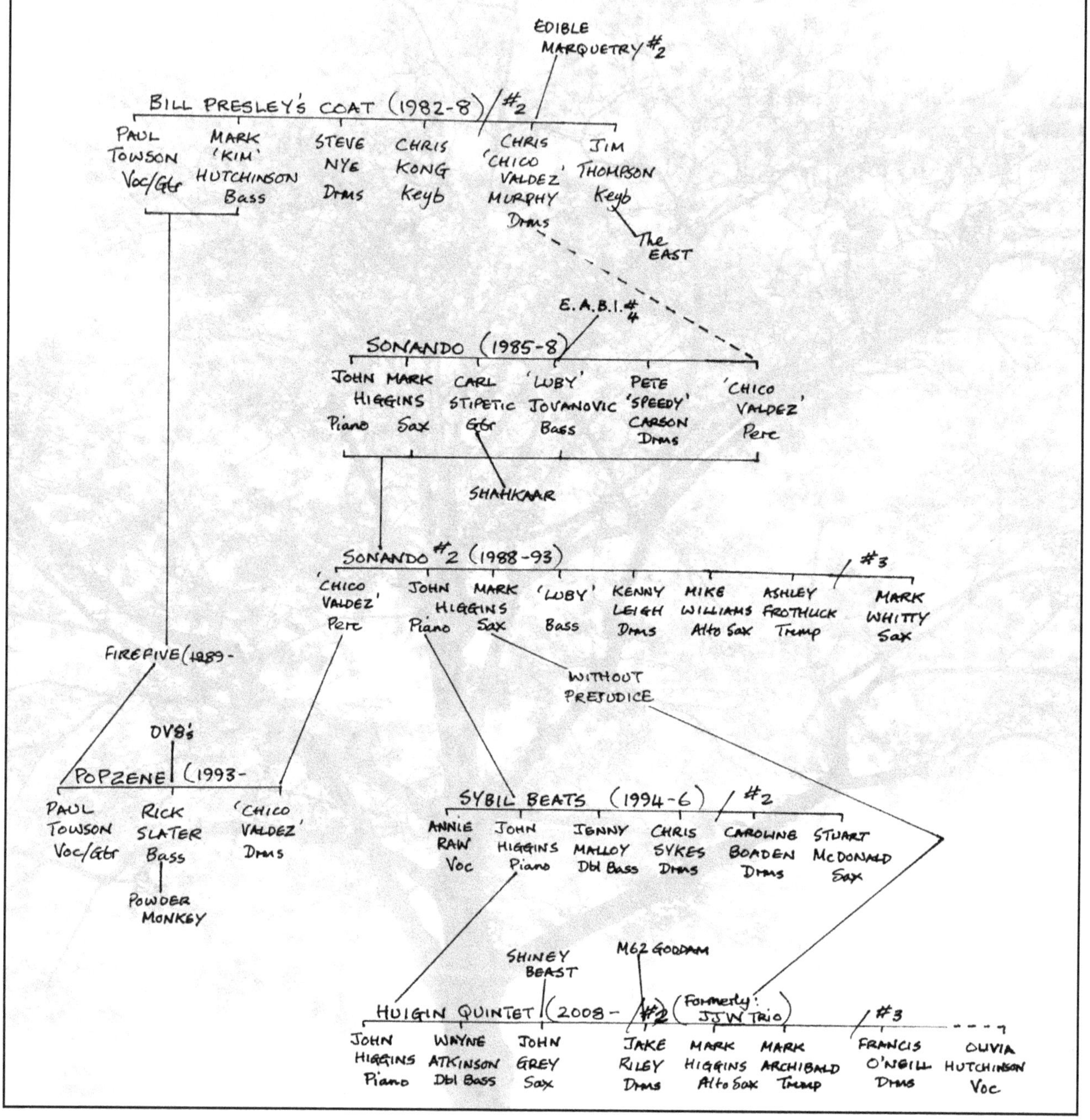

[Family tree diagram showing band lineages:]

BILL PRESLEY'S COAT (1982-8) /#2 → EDIBLE MARQUETRY #2
- PAUL TOWSON – Voc/Gtr
- MARK 'KIM' HUTCHINSON – Bass
- STEVE NYE – Drms
- CHRIS KONG – Keyb
- CHRIS 'CHICO VALDEZ' MURPHY – Drms
- JIM THOMPSON – Keyb → The EAST

E.A.B.I. #4

SONANDO (1985-8)
- JOHN HIGGINS – Piano
- MARK STIPETIC – Sax
- CARL JOVANOVIC – Gtr
- 'LUBY' – Bass
- PETE 'SPEEDY' CARSON – Drms
- 'CHICO VALDEZ' – Perc

SHAHKAAR

SONANDO #2 (1988-93) /#3
- 'CHICO VALDEZ' – Perc
- JOHN HIGGINS – Piano
- MARK – Sax
- 'LUBY' – Bass
- KENNY LEIGH – Drms
- MIKE WILLIAMS – Alto Sax
- ASHLEY FROTHUCK – Trump
- MARK WHITTY – Sax

WITHOUT PREJUDICE

FIREFIVE (1989-)

OV8s

POPZENE (1993-)
- PAUL TOWSON – Voc/Gtr
- RICK SLATER – Bass
- 'CHICO VALDEZ' – Drms

POWDER MONKEY

SYBIL BEATS (1994-6) /#2
- ANNIE RAW – Voc
- JOHN HIGGINS – Piano
- JENNY MALLOY – Dbl Bass
- CHRIS SYKES – Drms
- CAROLINE BOADEN – Drms
- STUART McDONALD – Sax

SHINEY BEAST   M62 GODDAM

HUIGIN QUINTET (2008-) /#2 (Formerly JJW Trio) /#3
- JOHN HIGGINS – Piano
- WAYNE ATKINSON – Dbl Bass
- JOHN GREY – Sax
- JAKE RILEY – Drms
- MARK HIGGINS – Alto Sax
- MARK ARCHIBALD – Trump
- FRANCIS O'NEILL – Drms
- OLIVIA HUTCHINSON – Voc

TALULAH GOSH

This indie-pop, girl/boy combo based in Oxford, had the distinction of having Bradford lass Elizabeth Price as one of their vocalists. During the period 1986-87, they had two No 3 indie chart singles, *Beatnik Boy / Steaming Train* and *Talulah Gosh,* both on the 53rd & 3rd label. Years later, Elizabeth won the 2012 Turner Prize for Art.

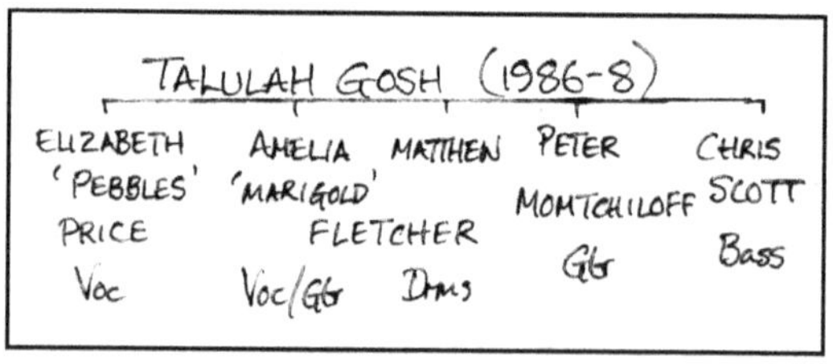

TALULAH GOSH (1986-8)
- ELIZABETH 'PEBBLES' PRICE – Voc
- AMELIA 'MARIGOLD' FLETCHER – Voc/Gtr
- MATTHEW – Drms
- PETER MOMTCHILOFF – Gtr
- CHRIS SCOTT – Bass

TALULAH GOSH

Year	Label	Cat No	Title	Price
86	53rd & 3rd	AGARR 4	Beatnik Boy/My Best Friend (p/s)	8
86	53rd & 3rd	AGARR 5	Steaming Train/Just A Dream (p/s)	5
86	53rd & 3rd	AGARR 4/5T	Beatnik Boy/My Best Friend/Steaming Train/Just A Dream (12", p/s)	8
87	53rd & 3rd	AGARR 8	Talulah Gosh/Don't Go Away (p/s)	5
87	53rd & 3rd	AGARR 8T	Talulah Gosh/Don't Go Away (12", p/s)	8
88	53rd & 3rd	AGARR 14	Bringing Up Baby/The Girl With The Strawberry Hair (p/s)	6
88	53rd & 3rd	AGARR 14T	Bringing Up Baby/I Can't Get No Satisfaction, Thank God/The Girl With The Strawberry Hair/Do You Remember?/Sunny Inside (12", p/s)	8
88	53rd & 3rd	AGARR 16	Testcard Girl (p/s)	5
87	53rd & 3rd	AGAS 004	ROCK LEGENDS VOL. 69 (LP, clear vinyl)	15
91	Sarah	064	THEY'VE SCOFFED THE LOT (LP)	12

CHAPTER 1 — 1988 - 1990

SEPTEMBER KITCHEN

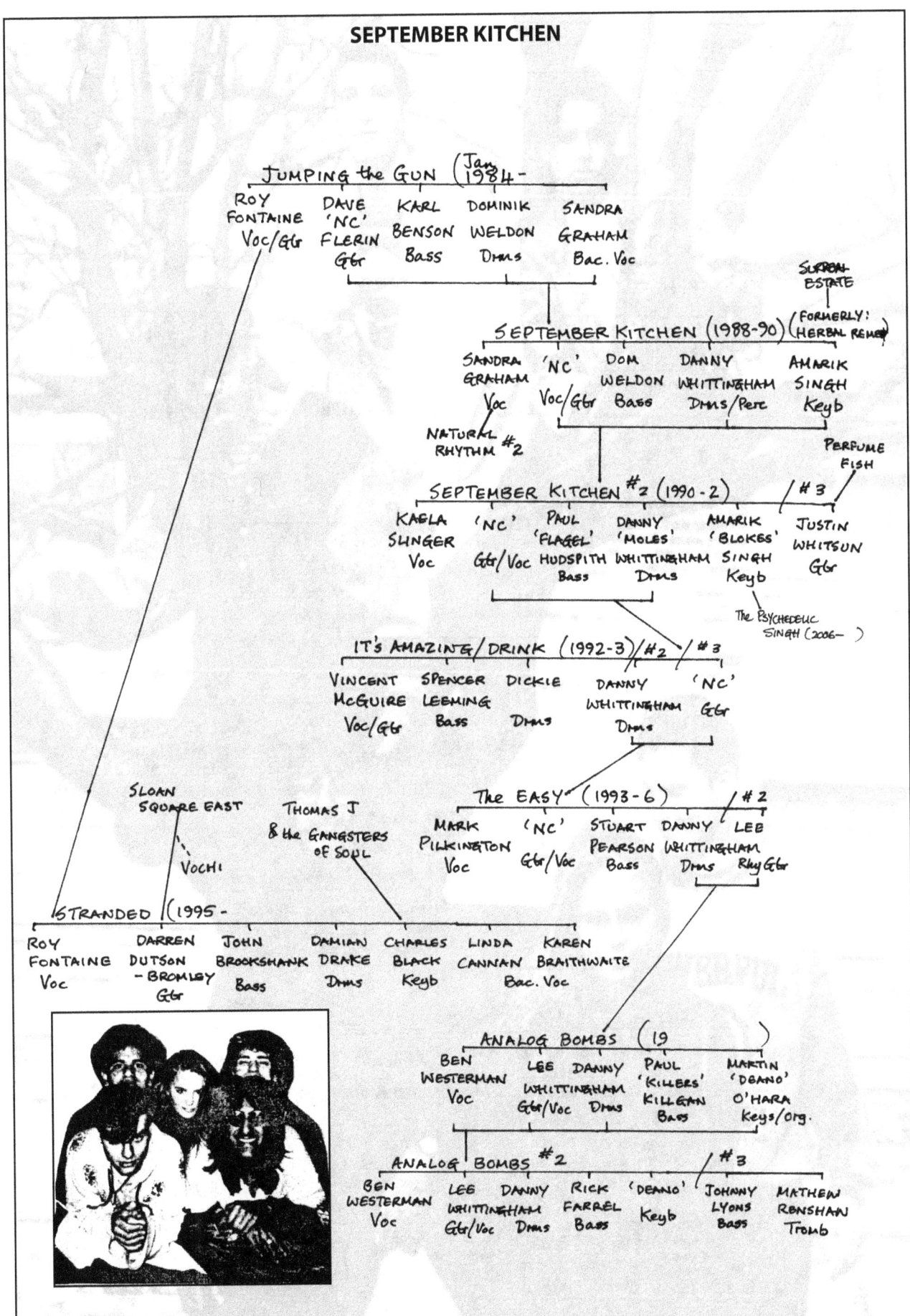

NATURAL RHYTHM

Still going strong in 2025, Natural Rhythm are Bradford's longest established ska/reggae band, performing regularly around the country.

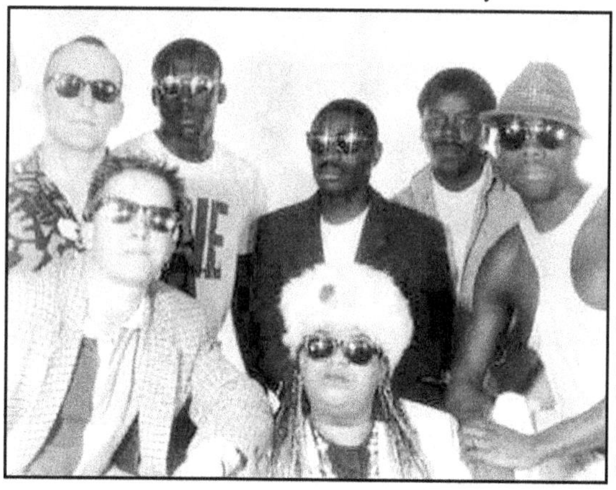

Formed in 1986 from previous local bands, they released their LP, *Bluebeat And Ska,* in 1991 on their own label , produced by Carl Stipetic at In A City Studios.

BLUEBEAT
Natural AND Rhythm
SKA

NATURAL RHYTHM
RaW SKa

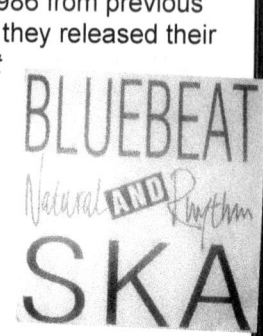

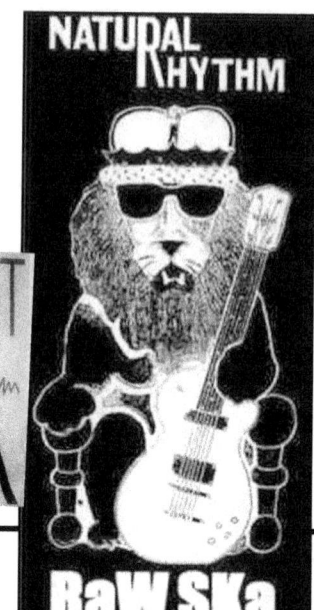

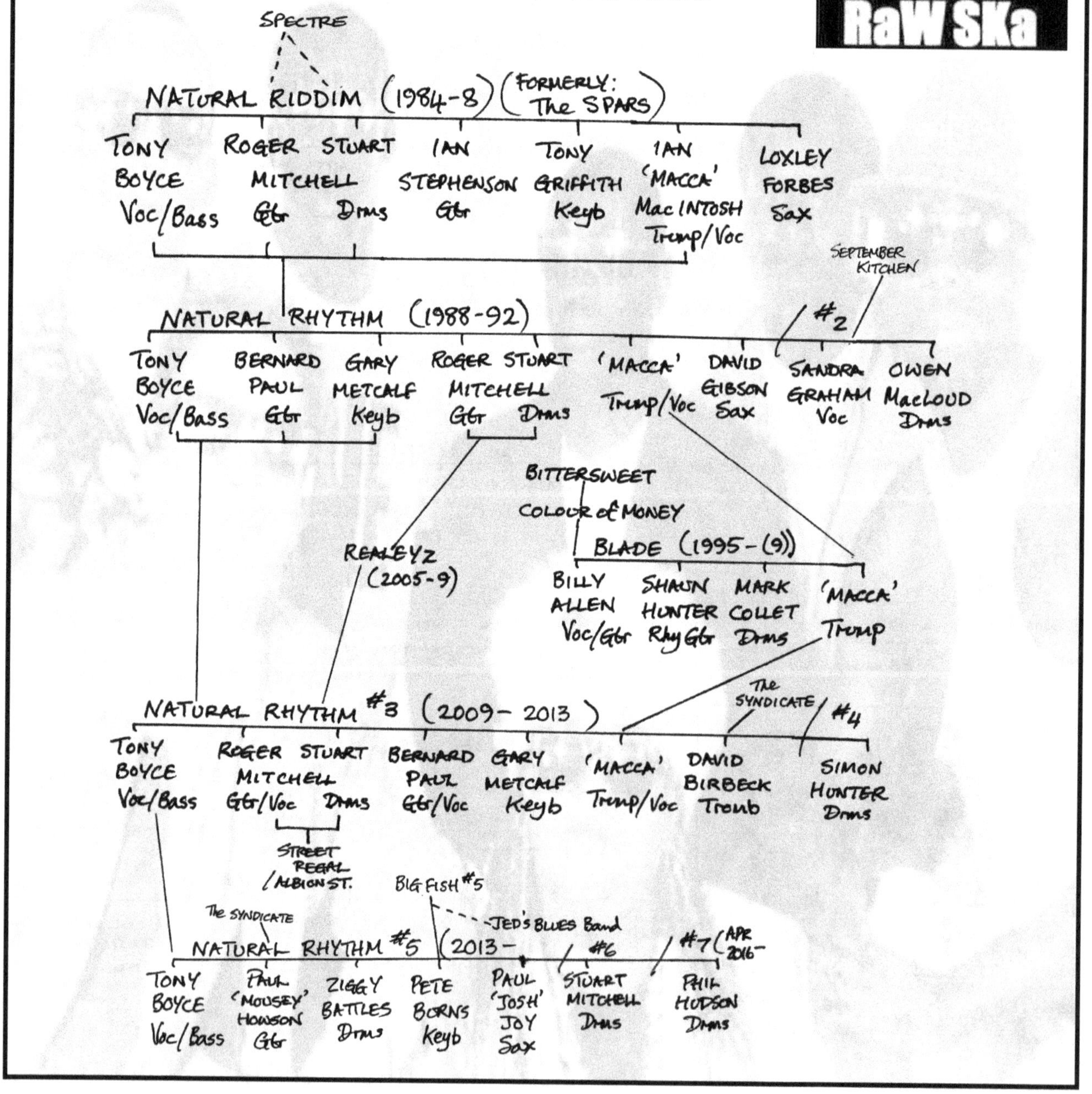

NATURAL RHYTHM / BLADE
SPECTRE
NATURAL RIDDIM (1984-8) (FORMERLY: The SPARS)
TONY BOYCE Voc/Bass
ROGER MITCHELL Gtr
STUART Drms
IAN STEPHENSON Gtr
TONY GRIFFITH Keyb
IAN 'MACCA' MacINTOSH Trmp/Voc
LOXLEY FORBES Sax
SEPTEMBER KITCHEN
NATURAL RHYTHM (1988-92)
#2
TONY BOYCE Voc/Bass
BERNARD PAUL Gtr
GARY METCALF Keyb
ROGER MITCHELL Gtr
STUART Drms
'MACCA' Trmp/Voc
DAVID GIBSON Sax
SANDRA GRAHAM Voc
OWEN MacLOUD Drms
BITTERSWEET
COLOUR of MONEY
BLADE (1995-(9))
REALEYZ (2005-9)
BILLY ALLEN Voc/Gtr
SHAUN HUNTER Rhy Gtr
MARK COLLET Drms
'MACCA' Trmp
The SYNDICATE
NATURAL RHYTHM #3 (2009- 2013)
#4
TONY BOYCE Voc/Bass
ROGER MITCHELL Gtr/Voc
STUART Drms
BERNARD PAUL Gtr/Voc
GARY METCALF Keyb
'MACCA' Trmp/Voc
DAVID BIRBECK Tromb
SIMON HUNTER Drms
STREET REGAL / ALBION ST.
BIG FISH #5
The SYNDICATE
JED'S BLUES Band
NATURAL RHYTHM #5 (2013-
#6
#7 (APR 2016-
TONY BOYCE Voc/Bass
PAUL 'MOUSEY' HOWSON Gtr
ZIGGY BATTLES Drms
PETE BORNS Keyb
PAUL 'JOSH' JOY Sax
STUART MITCHELL Drms
PHIL HUDSON Drms

CHAPTER 1　　　　1988 - 1990

BRADFORD'S ALTERNATIVE CABARET

Local ranting poets Nick Toczek (below) and Wild Willi Beckett started hosting a weekly alternative cabaret night called *Stereo Graffiti* on Sunday, September 28, 1986, at the Spotted House on Manningham Lane, where it ran for a year, then tried various venues (and cabaret names) before settling (as Tumbling Hill Street Blues) at Tumbler's on Tumbling Hill Street from December 1987 until the end of July 1988.

As side projects, they also founded *Bradford Writers' Group* (1987), ran *The Bradford Festival Of European Community Literature* (1989), a nightly cabaret for Bradford Festival (1987, 1988, 1992 & 1993) and a summer poetry season at Bradford Playhouse (1992).

The cabaret resurfaced at Treadwell's Art Mill in Little Germany from September 1991 until July 1992. Re-named *Bradford Alternative Cabaret*,

it returned to The Spotted House (November 1992 - May 1993) before moving to The Sidings Bar at The Midland Hotel for several months. In the mid-nineties, it continued at The Java Café on Great Horton Road, then at Korks Wine Bar in Otley and finally at The Town Hall in Batley.

This pioneering blend of comedy, music, circus, theatre and more - much of it quirky and unpredictable - was the first of its kind outside London and rapidly became one of the most influential.

Drawing on local, national and international talent, it featured many comedians on their way up including Jo Brand, Steve Coogan (paid just £5 for each of his first two appearances), Jack Dee, Jeremy Hardy, Julian Clary, Mandy Knight, Mark Miwurdz, Ross Noble, Peter Kay, Mark Steele and Henry Normal. Musicians included Gene 'Mighty Flea' Connors (USA), Tony McPhee (Groundhogs), Freddy Macha (Tanzania), Huw Lloyd Langton (Hawkwind), Guy Jackson, Labi Siffre, Rory McLeod, Spartacus R (Osibisa), Celso Chavarria (Nicaragua) and Wreckless Eric. Among the featured poets were Benjamin Zephaniah, John Cooper Clarke, Linton Kwesi Johnson, Attila The Stockbroker, Carolyn Cassady (from the US beat poetry scene), Liz Lochhead and Jean Binta Breeze.

13

If you can stand the heat..

THE first 12 heats of this year's North of England Battle of the Bands have been finalised and the first kicks off next Friday in Bradford's Queen's Hall.

Pop bands Boom Or Bust, Wall To Wall and Bill Presley's Coat will be fighting it out for a quarter-final place and a chance to be among the £3,000 prize money on offer.

Applications from bands have come in from as far as Newcastle, Blackpool as well as the East Coast but there are still a few of the 108 places available.

To make sure of your place ring Malcolm Hanson, of Circuit 22, on Bradford 392712.

Wall

The first 12 heats of the battle, sponsored by the T&A among others, are as follows - Jan 22, Boom or Bust/ Wall To Wall/ Bill Presley's Coat (pop); Jan 25, The Carny/ Das Tor/ Sarcasms Kings (alternative); Jan 27, Ethel and The Heroes/ Good Question/ Krakatoa (rock); Jan 29, Big Man Aviators/ The Alligators/ Armadillo Hat Band (pop/ rock); Feb 2, I Conspire/ Tapestry Sky/ Condition Red (alternative); Feb 3, Three Aviators/ From Knowhere/ Sloan Square East (pop); Feb 5, New Market Cross/ JJs Bones/ Little Chief (pop/soul); Feb 8, The Motive/ Collapse/ plus one more (alternative); Feb 10, No Tick/ Beats Working/ Holy Marimba (pop/ speciality); Feb 12, Avarice/ Artemesia/ Gun Law (rock); Feb 15, S.D.A./ Lemon Ice Scream/ Love It To Death (alternative/ rock); Feb 17, Eazy Street/ Rough Justice/ Aurora (heavy rock).

BATTLE OF THE BANDS 88

For the second year running Malcolm Hanson, of *Circuit 22 Promotions*, staged the *North Of England Battle Of The Bands* at Queen's Hall.

The competition was sponsored by the Telegraph & Argus, Bradford College Students Union, Far North Music, Circuit 22 and Bradford Bounce Limited.

The heats began on Friday, January 22, with Bradford's Bill Presley's Coat winning over Leeds' bands Boom Or Bust and Wall To Wall judged by a panel that included Bradford vocalist Carol Neen and journalist Chris Maguire who also wrote regular updates and reviews for the *T&A's Rock On* page.

Early heats were split into genres of pop, indie and rock, with Bradford's Das Tor winning the first indie heat on January 25 and Krakatoa winning the first rock heat on January 27.

Initially, heats were run on three nights a week, downstairs in the Cellar Bar and, later in the competition, five nights a week. From the quarter finals onwards gigs were moved up to the Ballroom to accommodate the larger crowds.

A draw on points between Bradford's JJ's Bones and Leeds reggae band Little Chief in their heat on February 15 led to an additional quarter-final being added, making fifteen in all.

Many locals bands, including Diamond Light, Midnight, Western Dance, JJ's Bones, Spoilt Bratz, Optic Nerve, The Bobby Charltons, Sensai and Halifax's Chinese Gangster Element, made it through to the quarter-finals.

Blue

Feb 19, Central Drive/ Bubbling Vessel/ Upside Down; Feb 20, Insect-O-Cutor/ White Hot and Blue/ Beyond The Shadow; Feb 22, Kama Rouge/ Silence/ The Users; Feb 24, Western Dance/ Witness/ Seven Antelopes; Feb 26, Midnight/ Diamond Light/ Changeling; Feb 27, Purple On The Storm/ Dirty Tryx/ Paint It Black; Feb 29, Harry Wharton & Co/ Aurora/ Spoilt Bratz; March 2, Optic Nerve/ Lady/ Highschool Hookers; March 4, Aphrodite/ A Little Rain/ No Romance; March 5, Enufsed/ The Escapement/ Chinese Gangster Element; March 7, Massacre/ To The Fountain/ Sensei; March 9, The Convulsions/ The Guilt Parade/ Rebecca.

Rock On — by Chris Maguire

A week in the life of...

Western Dance — Happy Mondays?

A HECTIC week in the life of the Battle of the Bands has seen five groups already lay claim to places in the semi-finals.

And Bradford took the honours in the first two quarter-finals. Holy Marimba, the unique acoustic duo of Craig Duckworth and David Wilson, earned the vote over Bill Presley's Coat and The Armadillo Hat Band. Then it was the turn of White Hot and Blue, fronted by that outstanding guitarist Ken Goble. Their musicianship and ability to entertain proved too hot for rivals Avarice and Krakatoa.

Then it was time for other areas to hit back and To The Fountain's trip from York on Monday proved worthwhile. They have been described as a cross between U2 and Simple Minds and singer Alex Halliday earned many plaudits on the night. To The Fountain went through at the expense of Optic Nerve and Spoilt Bratz.

Leeds funk band Enuf Sed stormed through with their brand of soul and funk overcoming the challenge of The Owter Zeds and The Rumble Band.

Wednesday, alternative night, saw Das Tor go through earning the vote over Condition Red and Collapse. Das Tor return for the third semi-final on May 11.

Holy Marimba and Enuf Sed are back for the first semi on May 5 while White Hot and Blue and To The Fountain are two of the bands playing the following night.

Tonight is one of the major soul concerts with Little Chief, Central Drive and From Knowhere coming together. It's back to rock tomorrow with Charger, Love It To Death and Mainframe battling it out.

Holy Marimba — on the beat

Courtesy of the Telegraph & Argus

CHAPTER 1   1988 - 1990

CIRCUIT 22's BATTLE OF THE BANDS 88
Friday, April 22,
Quarter Final 6
From Knowhere
Central Drive
Little Chief
Queen's Hall Cellar Bar, Morley Street, Bradford
Doors open 8 p.m.
£1.50/£2.00

Semi-finals began on Friday, May 6, with reggae act Little Chief winning out over fellow Leeds band Enuf Sed and Bradford duo Holy Marimba.

May 7 saw York's To The Fountain go through at the expense of Charger and White Hot & Blue.

Nexcastle's Eat The Peach scored higher with the judges than Do It (Barnoldswick) and Purple On The Storm (Blackpool) on May 13.

Rotherham's Springheel'd Jack won out over Das Tor and Colne band A Little Rain in the fourth semi-final. The last semi saw Guido grab the remaining spot in the final by beating Beats Crazy (Leeds) and From The Heart (Manchester) in the judge's vote.

The final took place on May 21 at the Queen's Hall Ballroom as over 600 people saw Bradford's Guido (pictured above) grab the first prize of £1,500. Runners up were Little Chief (pictured left). (3)

The final was expanded to an all-day event with the previous year's runners-up Somebody's Brother playing two sets in the Cellar Bar during the afternoon, as well as discos, hot food and various other surprise attractions'.

Overall, the competition featured 114 bands who took part in 36 heats, with 45 of those going on the play in 15 quarter-finals and over 10,000 people had attended the gigs.

CIRCUIT 22s
NORTH OF ENGLAND BATTLE OF THE BANDS
SATURDAY MAY 21st, 1988
GRAND FINAL
DOORS OPEN 12 NOON
All day discos — Bradford's favourite "SOMEBODY'S BROTHER" entertaining throughout the afternoon.
Hot food — surprise attractions.
WAR DECLARED AT 5.59 p.m.
6 p.m. THE BANDS

LITTLE CHIEF (Leeds)
GUIDO (Bradford)
TO THE FOUNTAIN (York)
EAT THE PEACH (Tyne & Wear)
SRING HEEL'D JACK (Rotherham)

£4. CUT OUT THIS AD AND BRING BEFORE 3 p.m. AND ENTRY IS JUST £3
QUEENS HALL BALLROOM, MORLEY STREET, BRADFORD
BD7 1BW

HANSAID

Soul outfit Sloan Square East, ex-pupils of Hanson School, released a 7' single, Hands Reach Out, for the HansAid charity (Bradford's War on Cancer & Leukaemia). The single was recorded with girl pupils from Hanson School at Flexible Response Studios and coincided with a HansAid charity gig at Queen's Hall in April with Sloan Square East, Boom & Bust and The Three Aviators.

A further charity concert for the Lord Mayor's Appeal at St George's Hall followed in May. The gigs were promoted by Malcolm Hanson, who did his own 470-mile sponsored walk from John O'Groats to Bradford to raise money for Bradford's War On Cancer appeal.

Malcolm Hanson was also the promoter at Queen's Hall until after *Battle 88*. He went to put on gigs at the Royal Standard and Rio's and also promoted a series of all-dayers at the Royal Standard, the first of which, on Saturday, August 27, featured White Hot & Blue, Thundering Hearts, Sensei, Asylum, Caught In The Act, McCooney and Warrior Cross.

JANE MOUNTAIN / SYMPHONY IN X

This band appears to have been essentially a vehicle for the singer Jane Mountain. Jane had previously been in the folk/rock band Gypsy with guitarist Stephen Helm and both of them had played in the three-piece Lipsbury Pinfold.

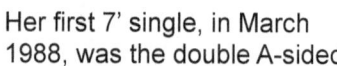

Her first 7' single, in March 1988, was the double A-sided *Dreams Never Die / Shape Of Things To Come*, as Symphony in X, utilizing two ex-members of jazz band Middle 8 on keyboards and guitar as her band.

The single was recorded at Ric Rac studios in Leeds and appeared on the Sowerby Bridge-based label Synthetic Dance Records, distributed via the Cartel with Liverpool's Probe Records.

Soon after the release of the single Jane left the area and joined Birmingham band Tour De Force who hoped to release their own single in June 1988. .

GYPSY

Gypsy were formed in 1986 by Baildon born Stephen Helm. On March 9, 1988, they appeared on *Yorkshire Television's* new programme *It Sounds Good*, a series showcasing young musical talent from the region, playing their composition *Hopeful*.

The track was later used on the opening credits to YTV's *James Whale Radio Show* on Friday nights during 1989.

LITTLE BROTHER

Dave Stockell, aka Little Brother, was one of Bradford's original group of ranting poets of the early 1980s, his style was always witty and insightful.

Dave had previously released two 7' singles during the 1980s, the split EP with Seething Wells and the 1986 *No Relation*

George Mazur, Dave, Tim Beckham

single on the Leeds-based Rouska label. In April 1988, Dave released his now rare *Champion The Underdog* LP, again on the Rouska label. It was recorded at Lion Studios in Leeds, using musicians from Somebody's Brother, and produced by Andy Tillison. Dave went on to present his weird thoughts on *The Open Mind University*, his weekly radio show which ran for many years on the local BCB radio station.

VOCHI

Nigel Smith, aka Vochi, from Heaton, was an obscure individual who was apparently heavily influenced by the late Jim Morrison of The Doors. He was active around Bradford during 1985-95, as a writer, poet and musician. A musical *Haruspex The Harlequin* was written and some songs recorded (with support from Island Records) but the show was never performed.

He released a 7' single *The Loner* in May 1990 with help from Red Rhino Records of York. He formed Naracen Productions to promote the single and his other interests, like the March 1993 Film screenplay of *Teenage Stoned Death Games* about the attitudes expressed by the media towards AIDS and HIV for which he had received funding from both the National Film Institute and Yorkshire Art's Association. Vochi also wrote five songs for the film's soundtrack.

In 1996, a track called *Please* by Vochi appeared on the CD Compilation *Exposed: The Melting Point* on the Fagley-based In Yer Face Records.

CHAPTER 1 — 1988 - 1990

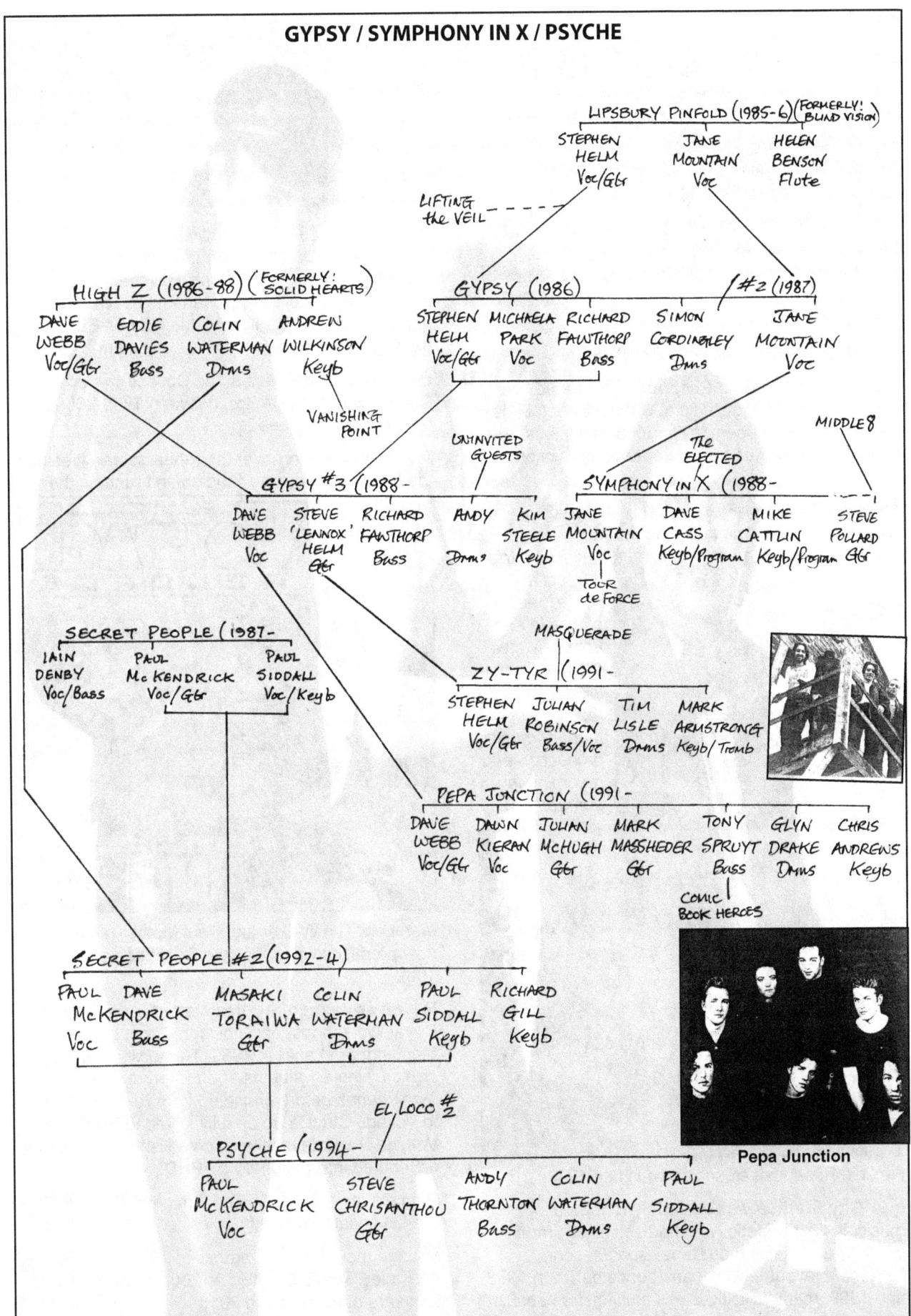

GYPSY / SYMPHONY IN X / PSYCHE

Pepa Junction

PUB VENUES

Besides the city's traditional large-capacity music venues like St George's Hall, Queens Hall and the University's Communal Building, a succession of pub venues started to put on live music nights, including the Brewery Tap (Idle), the Gatehouse and Quarry Arms (Clayton), the Drop Kick (Low Moor) and the Park Hotel (Manningham).

BRADFORD RECORDING STUDIOS

In April 1988, **Flexible Response** celebrated five years as a recording studio at Chapel Street, Little Germany, with an open day for local musicians to check out their upgraded 24-track production facilities.

A spokesperson for Flexible Response said, *"We now feel the time is right to introduce local musicians to the technology and expertise available and hopefully give them a greater insight into the process of modern music production and recording in general."* (4)

Flexible Response closed down in late 1989.

In-A-City Studios was started by Hull-born musician Carl Stipetic (who had settled in Bradford in 1981) at a building on Canal Road. It soon became a favourite with many bands between 1988 and 1998, many utilizing Carl's multi-instrumentalist talents (especially keyboards) as a guest artist on many bands' demo releases.

In December 1989, the studio was burgled with over £3,000 worth of equipment stolen. A benefit gig was organised at Queen's Hall the following January with Spoilt Bratz, Harlequyn, Twice Around the Houses, Single File and Jed's Blues Band all helping to raise funds for new equipment.

He moved to premises at the Council-owned Carlisle Business Centre, between 1999-2009, before moving to Leeds.

After initially taking over the rehearsal facilities in the Flexible Response Studios and running them as The Boiler Rooms in 1986, former Harlequyn members Tim Walker and Paul Mother relocated to new premises when Flexible Response closed in 1989.

Revolver/Voltage Studios started at the Theatre Royal Workshops, on Snowden Street (off Manningham Lane) in 1989. The facility produced demos, singles, albums and pre-production for many bands before changing from Revolver Studios to Voltage Studios, to be fully linked to their own Voltage Records label also established in 1988 and distributed internationally by PHD.

Paul moved on in 1994 and Tim carried on running the studio/label himself.

Voltage moved to new premises at St Stephen's Mill on Ripley Street, Bradford in 2004 and celebrated 25 years of recording in 2013.

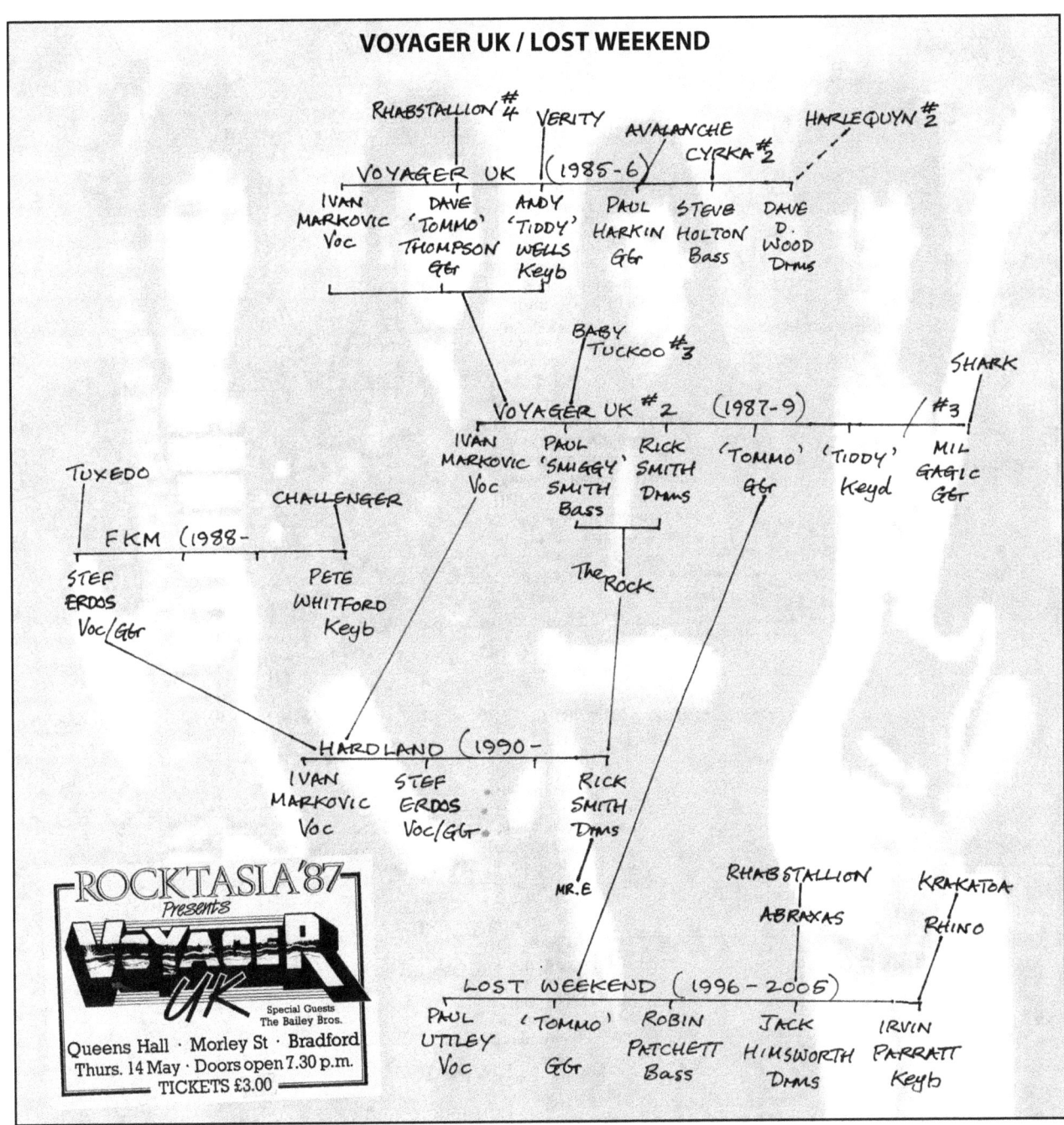

HARD ROCK / HEAVY METAL

The hard rock and metal scene has always been a constant feature of Bradford's local music culture since the late 1960s, so it's no surprise that many new bands were still emerging at this time.

VOYAGER UK

Formed in 1985 from the ashes of a host of bands from the area, Voyager UK mark one never actually got to play a gig, although they did release the classic NWOBHM single *Run Away Heart / Don't Hold Back* on their Fighting Cock label.

By 1987, Voyager UK 2 were up and running and they played their first gig at Queen's Hall, quickly followed by their second gig at the Return Club in Halifax. On September 16, 1988, the band and fellow Bradford metallers Excalibur appeared on the BBC 2 *Pop It's Not* programme, hosted by Radio 1 Rock DJ Tommy Vance.

They recorded a second single, *Rock This Town*, at Studio 2 in Armley, Leeds. It was meant to be released by Javelin Records of London but the band decided to scrap it after an abortive session in London of trying to re-mix the track eight times.

After the demise of Voyager UK in 1989, keyboard player Andy Wells went into solo projects and production, singer Ivan Markovic managed The Westleigh during the '90s before continuing in future music projects and guitarist Tommo formed Lost Weekend in 1996.

KRAKATOA / RHINO / NOISEGATE

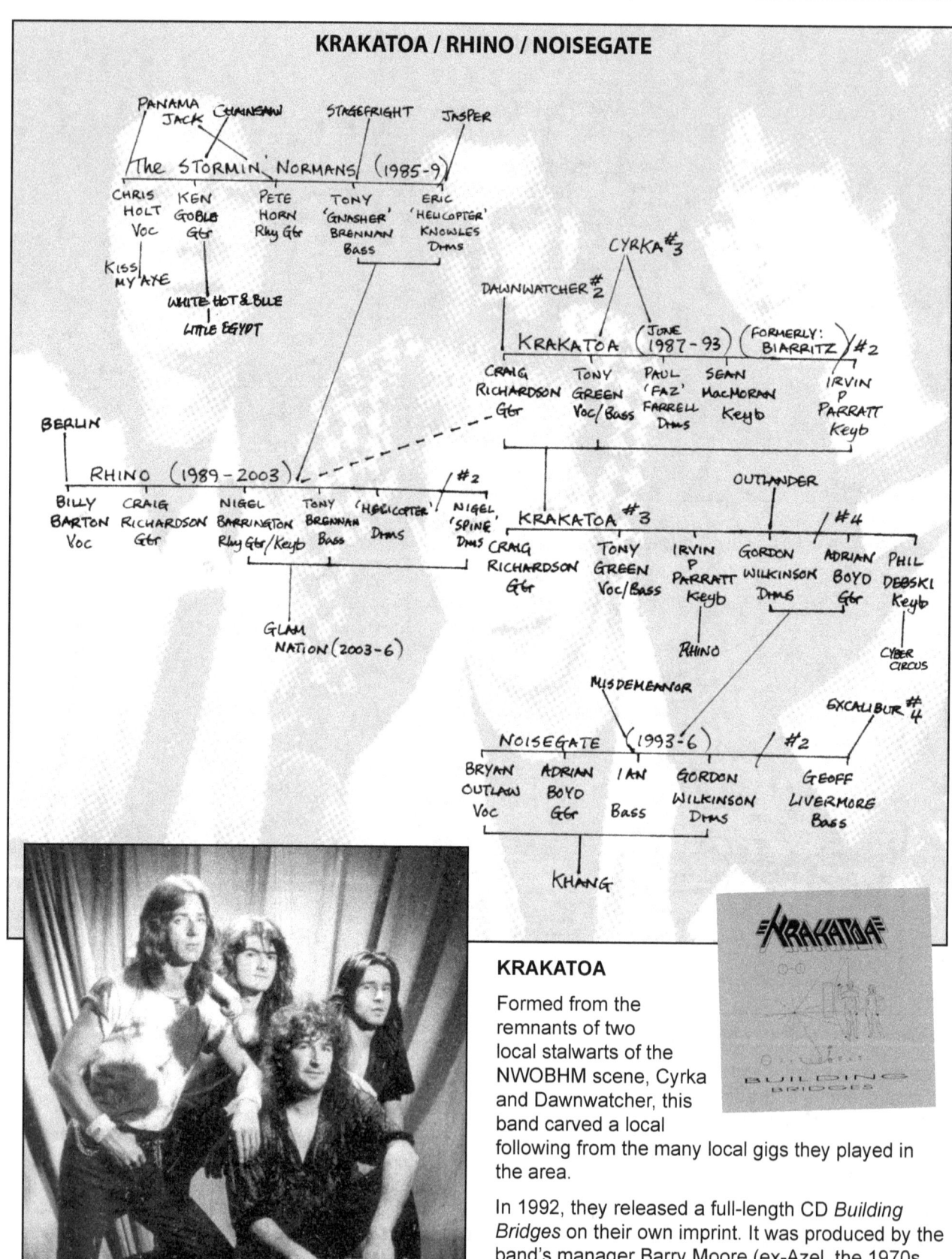

KRAKATOA

Formed from the remnants of two local stalwarts of the NWOBHM scene, Cyrka and Dawnwatcher, this band carved a local following from the many local gigs they played in the area.

In 1992, they released a full-length CD *Building Bridges* on their own imprint. It was produced by the band's manager Barry Moore (ex-Azel, the 1970s metal/prog band) and recorded at the Engine Rooms studio in Bradford.

The band entered the Circuit *22's North Of England Battle Of The Bands* in 1988, 1989 and 1990, reaching the quarter-finals in the latter two years.

CHAPTER 1   1988 - 1990

SIDEWYNDER / FOUL PLAY

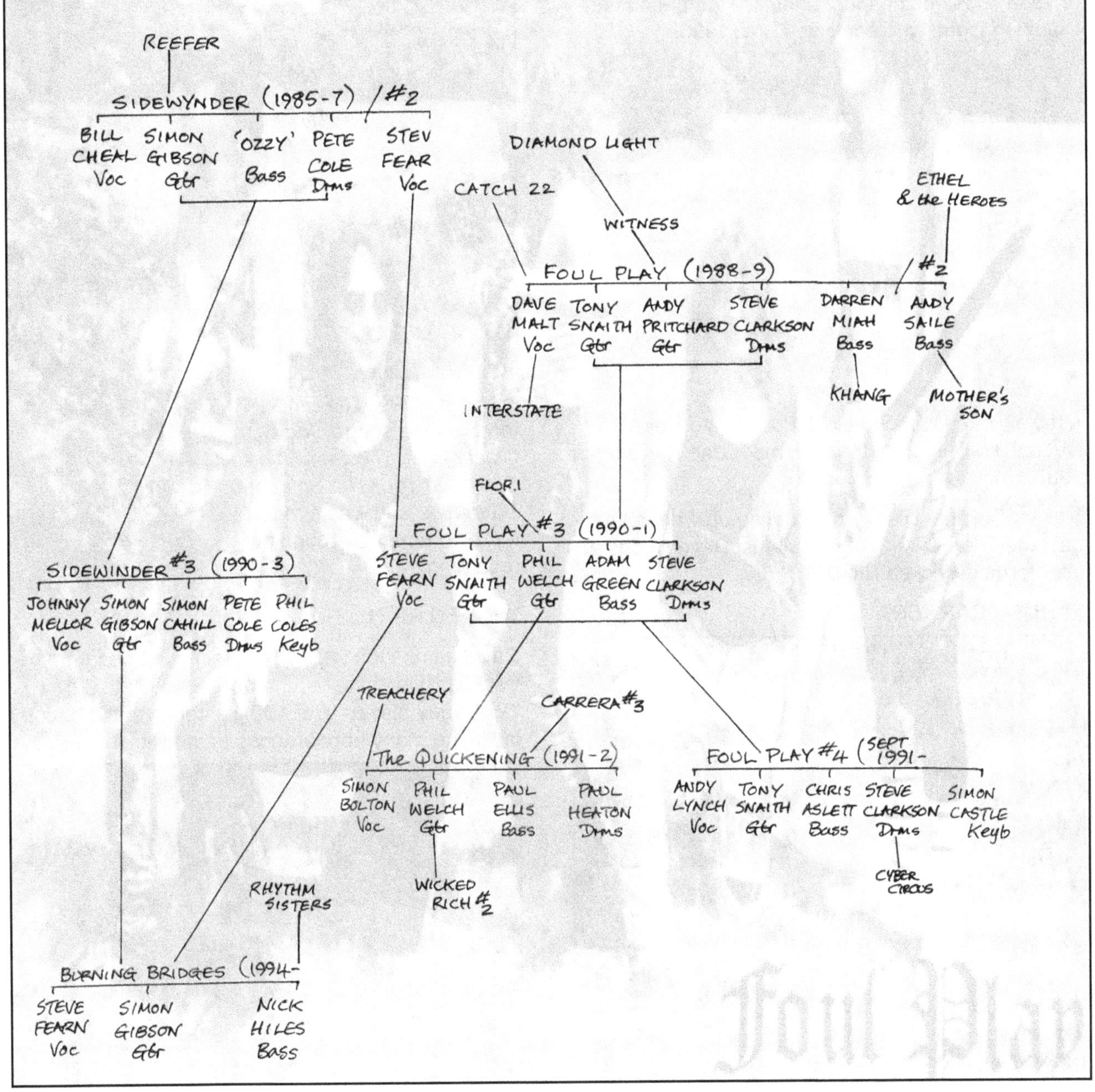

[Band lineage chart]

REEFER
SIDEWYNDER (1985-7) / #2
BILL CHEAL - Voc
SIMON GIBSON - Gtr
'OZZY' - Bass
PETE COLE - Dms
STEV FEAR - Voc

DIAMOND LIGHT
CATCH 22
WITNESS
FOUL PLAY (1988-9) / #2
DAVE MALT - Voc
TONY SNAITH - Gtr
ANDY PRITCHARD - Gtr
STEVE CLARKSON - Dms
DARREN MIAH - Bass
ETHEL & the HEROES
ANDY SAILE - Bass
KHANG
MOTHER'S SON

INTERSTATE

FLOR.I
FOUL PLAY #3 (1990-1)
STEVE FEARN - Voc
TONY SNAITH - Gtr
PHIL WELCH - Gtr
ADAM GREEN - Bass
STEVE CLARKSON - Dms

SIDEWINDER #3 (1990-3)
JOHNNY MELLOR - Voc
SIMON GIBSON - Gtr
SIMON CAHILL - Bass
PETE COLE - Dms
PHIL COLES - Keyb

TREACHERY
CARRERA #3
The QUICKENING (1991-2)
SIMON BOLTON - Voc
PHIL WELCH - Gtr
PAUL ELLIS - Bass
PAUL HEATON - Dms

FOUL PLAY #4 (SEPT 1991-)
ANDY LYNCH - Voc
TONY SNAITH - Gtr
CHRIS ASLETT - Bass
STEVE CLARKSON - Dms
SIMON CASTLE - Keyb
CYBER CIRCUS

WICKED RICH #2

RHYTHM SISTERS
BURNING BRIDGES (1994-
STEVE FEARN - Voc
SIMON GIBSON - Gtr
NICK HILES - Bass

FOUL PLAY

Formed in 1988, from ex-members of Catch 22 and Diamond Light, Foul Play battered their way onto the local scene with a hard gigging attitude. They won the popularity poll for local Pennine Radio's FM show *Off The Record* and received some optimistic advice from visiting EMI A&R man Nick Mander who met them at the station.

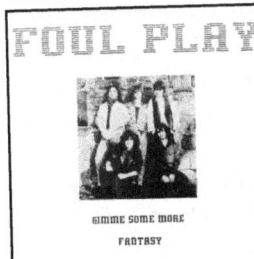

In late 1989, the band released and recorded the 7' single *Gimme Some More / Fantasy* on their own label.

DIAMOND LIGHT

In 1986, local rock band Tranquillity morphed into Diamond Light, who continued until 1990.

A review of a Diamond Light/Thundering Hearts Queens Hall gig from the rock magazine *Kerrang!* in 1988. (5)

Most of the final Diamond Light line-up went on to become The Fear in 1988. Guitarist Dave Hodgson later formed Wicked Rich.

TABOO / CARRERA

Wicked Rich bassist David James was previously in rock outfit Taboo, who gigged between November 1988 and May 1989.

The second lineup of Taboo featured Roger Carbutt on lead vocals, Stuart Crowther on lead guitar, Dave James on bass, Pat Denning on keyboards and Simon Jones on drums. This line-up recorded a demo called *Tastes Even Better* which featured the tracks *Lets Make Some Noise*, *She's So Lonely* and *Doing The Dirty*.

When Stuart Crowther left and Pete Rollings joined on guitar, the band became Carrera. They played live between July and October 1989 including gigs at Rafters in Bradford, Ossett Woburn House, and Queen's Hall, Bradford, on September 2, 1989.

Carrera recorded their four-song *Borderline* tape

in Hull in 1990. The EP featured the songs *One Step Closer*, *May The Sun Shine Down On You*, *The Spirit* and *Borderline* and was a much more commercial-sounding recording.

WICKED RICH

David James left to join The Fear, who became Wicked Rich in the summer of 1990. Up to July 1994, they played over 100 gigs all over the country, including many appearances at the Rio.

Wicked Rich recorded a two-song demo *The Fear / Rebel* at Patchbay Studios in 1990 which was almost released as a 7' single in 1991 on a Falkirk-based indie label, but plans fell through.

The band recorded a couple of demos, including the three-part song *Wargames* in 1992, at In A City Studio which were compiled, along with other tracks, into a full CD album *The Science Of Reasoning*, on the Quarter Eclipse label, followed in 1994.

CHAPTER 1 — 1988 - 1990

DIAMOND LIGHT / WICKED RICH

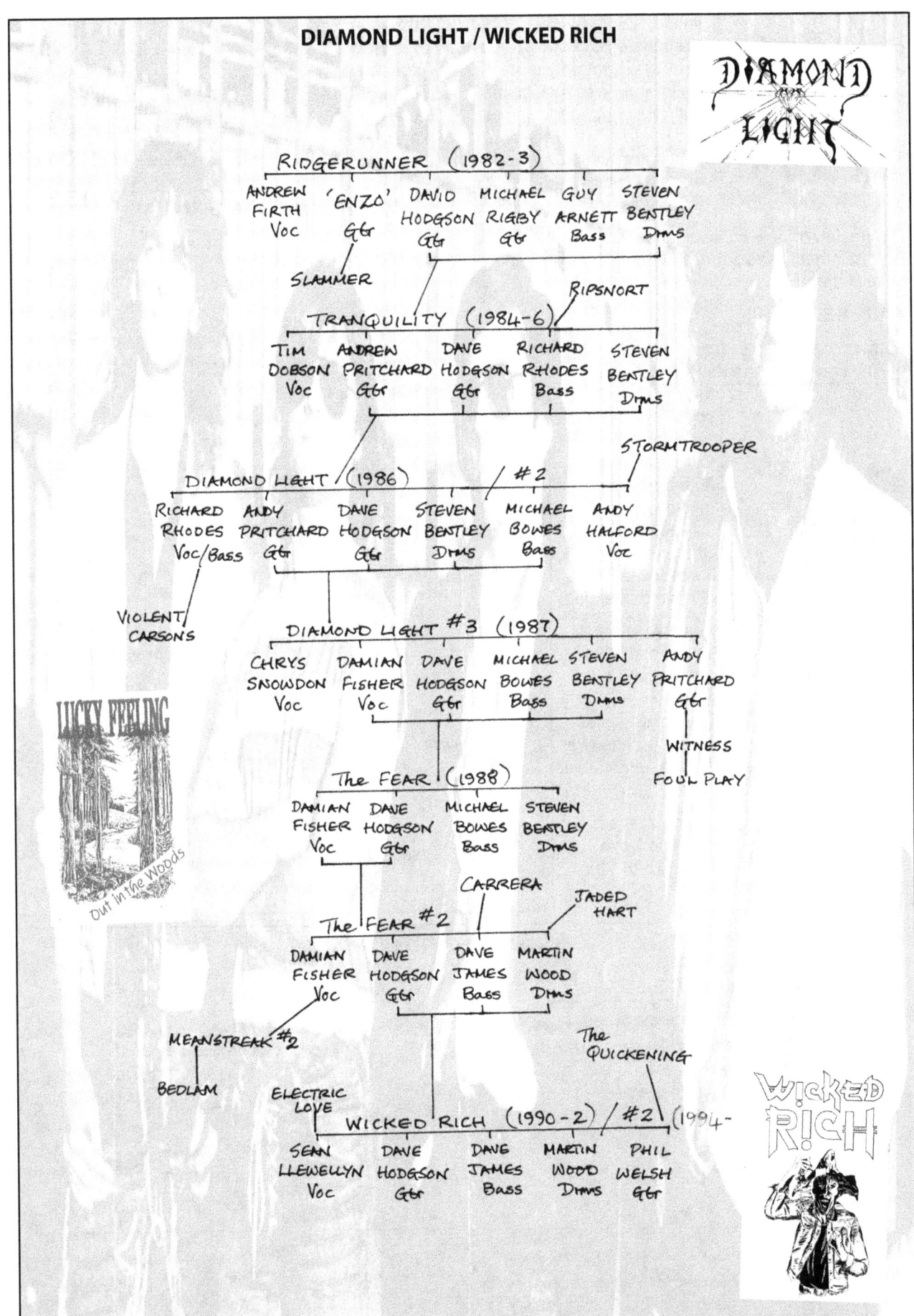

On May 26, 1988, the infamous Macc Lads played their first Bradford gig at the Frog & Toad rock club. With their outrageous lyrics and stage act, the band at that time were the most 'banned' group in Britain.

On September 26, Los Angeles speed-metal rockers Metallica played St George's Hall.

During July, a new music agency, Key Entertainment, was set up in Wibsey by Glen Harland.

RASA RETURNS

Former pupil Rasa Didzpetris, the ex-wife of Ray Davies of The Kinks, returned to the city for the school reunion at St Joseph's College on their 80th anniversary on the weekend of July 15-16 1988. She was among hundreds of 'old girls' who attended.

Rasa had been expelled in 1964 over her affair with the Kinks' songwriter and frontman whom she later married in Bradford. She gave birth to two daughters, Louisa and Victoria, during their seven years of marriage.

Other rock/metal outfits on the scene at this time were **Carrera, Electric Love, Sensei, Aurora, Sidewinder, Byte The Bullet, Kick** and **Premiere**.

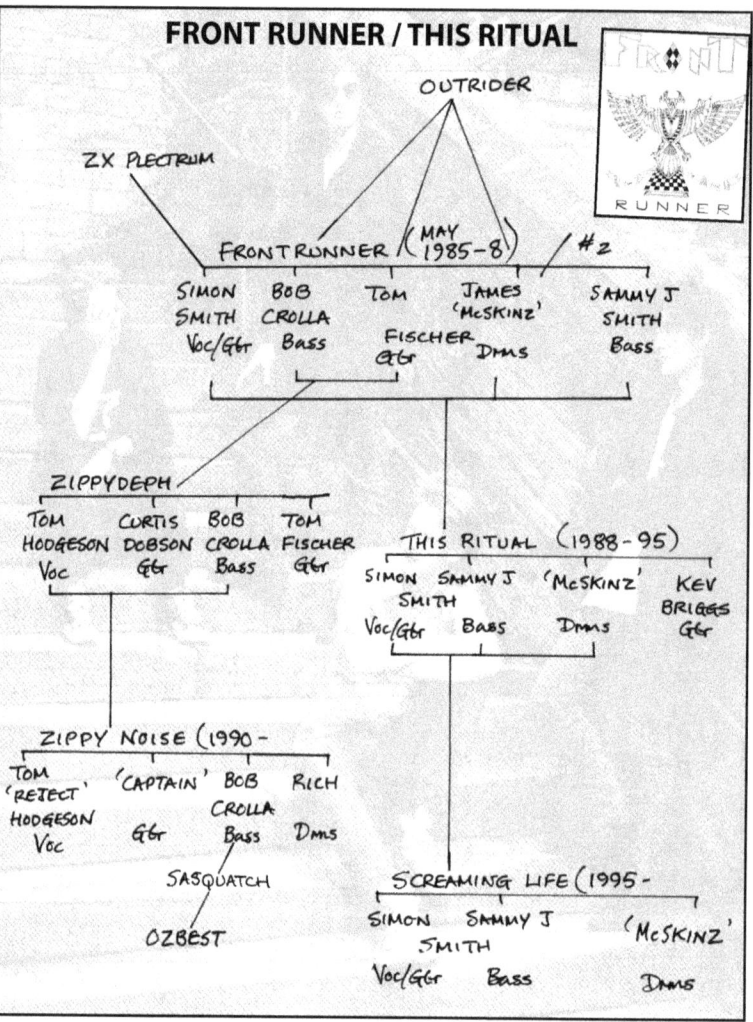

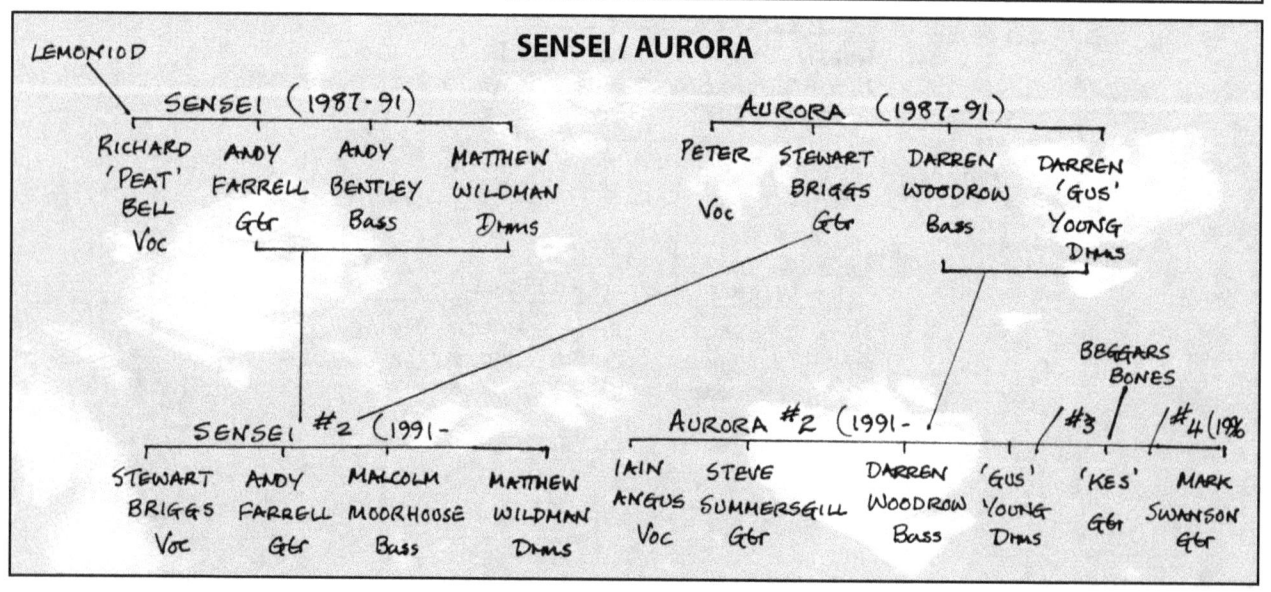

CHAPTER 1 — 1988 - 1990

WHITE HOT & BLUE / BYTE THE BULLET

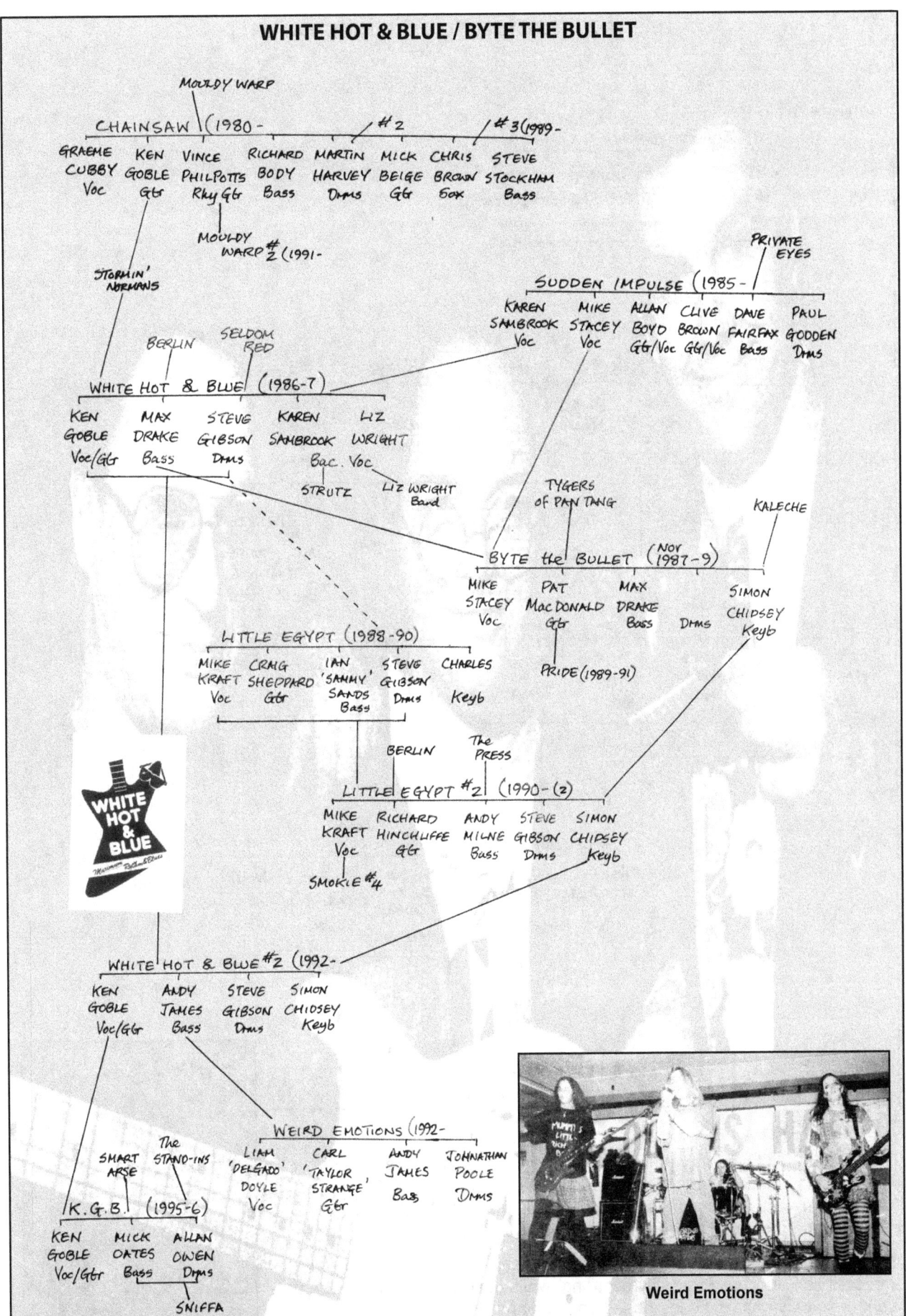

Weird Emotions

DAS TOR / THIRD SEASON / LIVINGSTON DAISY

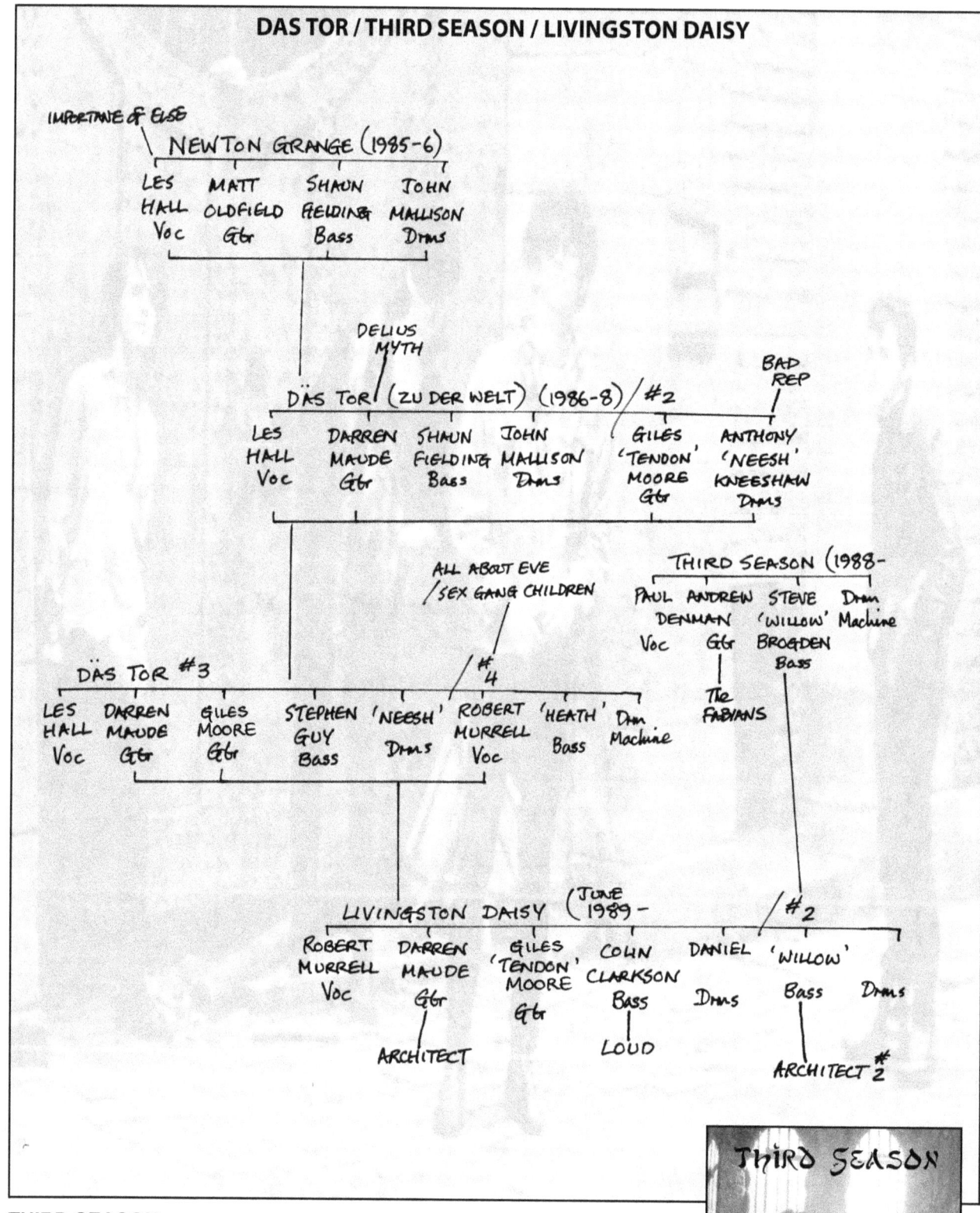

THIRD SEASON

This local band played only a handful of gigs around Bradford and Huddersfield but did record one three-song tape, *Third Season,* which featured the tracks *Wishing Well, Punch Drunk* and *Roll Of The Dice* and was recorded and produced by Darren Maude, in 1991.

Bassist Ste Brogden went on to play bass in Architect, Paul Denman went on to record as Fabric Of Fear (still recording) while his brother Andrew Denman went on to play bass in Leeds-based The Fabians.

CHAPTER 1 — 1988 - 1990

JAVYER / TWICE AROUND THE HOUSES / THE BIG FISH

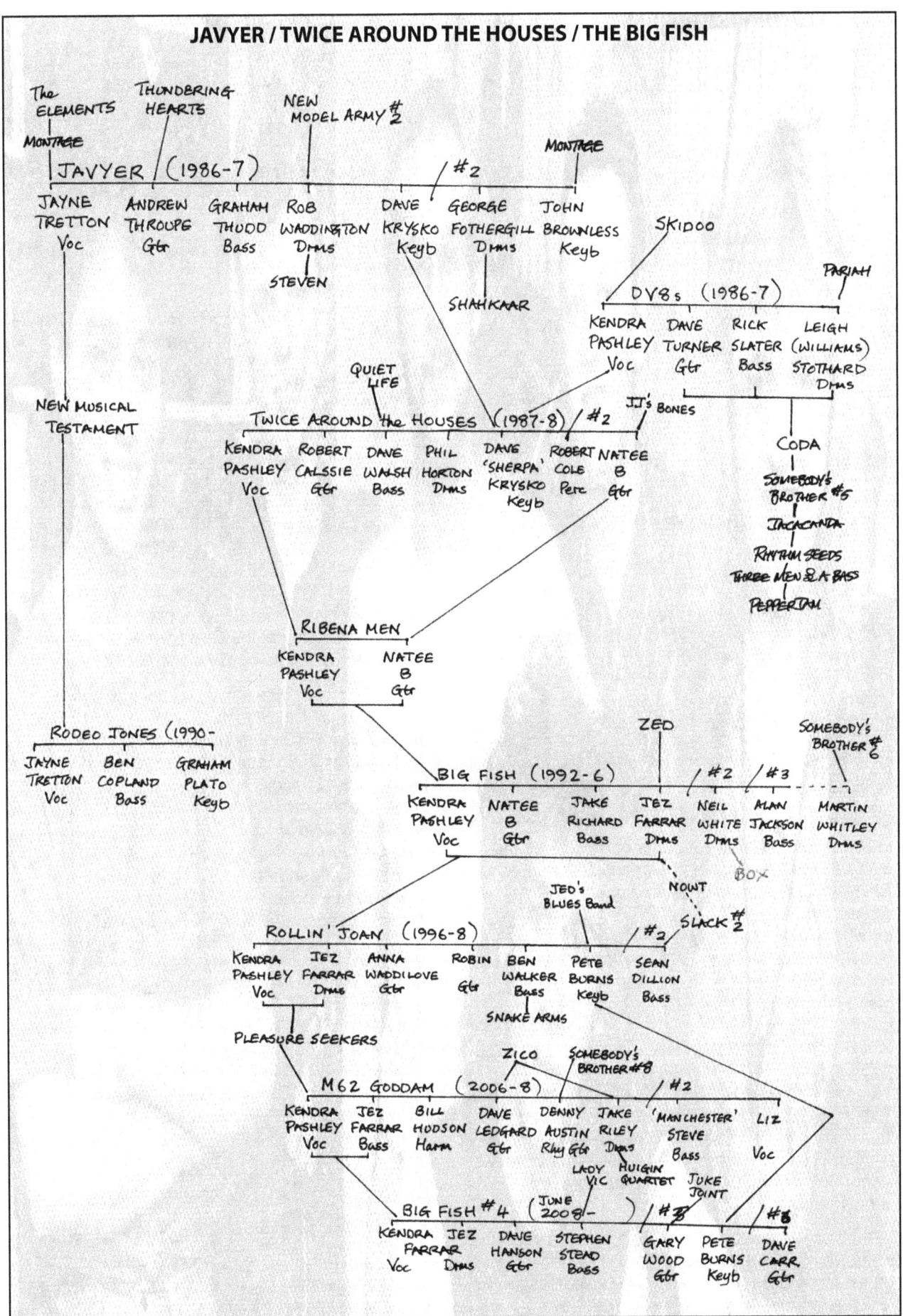

TWICE AROUND THE HOUSES

Allerton-born singer Kendra Pashley started singing in working men's clubs at the tender age of six. At fifteen she was fronting her own club group, Skidoo, and in some circles was touted as Bradford's next Kiki Dee.

She worked with local band DV8s, before joining four Keighley lads to form Twice Around The Houses in 1988. After solidly gigging for over six months the band entered *Circuit 22's North Of England Battle Of The Bands* competition in 1989. During the initial heats the band were approached to record a potential 7' single, featuring the tracks *Learning / One In A Million*, by property manager and backer of BOTB Paul Young, although the single was never released.

In May 1989, they were finalists of *BOTB*, coming a close second to winners Poisoned Electric Head. Despite this, the band broke up soon after, with Kendra forming the busking duo Ribenna Men with former JJ's Bones guitarist Nat

'Natnee B' Brewer. She formed covers band The Big Fish in 1992, a group who played many gigs in the local area during the early and mid-1990s including a gig at The Bradfordian when all the pub's windows were put through during the first Bradford riot in June 1995.

Kendra continued to perform her distinctive vocal style, with her partner Jez (ex-Zed, JJ's Bones) on drums in various new projects. She said *'Good solid drummers are hard to find, so I married ours.'*

THE BOBBY CHARLTONS

Formed in 1986, this near-legendary local band were football-loving funsters who played a mean rock'n'roll with harmonies. Their frontman Gary Quinn had previously been in both local 1970s club band Ocean and new wave pioneers Harsh Words.

The Bobby Charltons gigged and toured extensively around the local area and beyond during the 1990s, including a showcase gig at London's Rock Garden venue in July 1989. They supported the likes of Blur, Squeeze and the late John Martyn amongst many others. In October 1988, they played the Sunday afternoon session at the Quarry Arms public house in Clayton (a private house since 2010).

The band's first release was a double A-sided 7' single *Hole In The Sky / Bastard Town* in 1991, on their own 9 Records label engineered by ex-Donkeys Neil Ferguson. This was followed by a three-track 12' single again on their own label, *A Man From Nowhere / Message From Heaven / Lost In Another Time*, recorded at Patchbay Studios, Leeds.

They tried hard to interest major record labels but, as one record executive Gordon Charlton of CBS said, *'I love the music...but five strands of hair swept across the head was never my idea of handsome.'* (6)

The Bobby Charltons #2 saw local rock-god guitarist John Verity's son join as bassist. The band went on to release two critically acclaimed albums on CD. 1993's *God's Game* and 1995's *Glow*, again on their own 9 Records, before the final whistle blew in 1997.

CHAPTER 1 — 1988 - 1990

THE BOBBY CHARLTONS

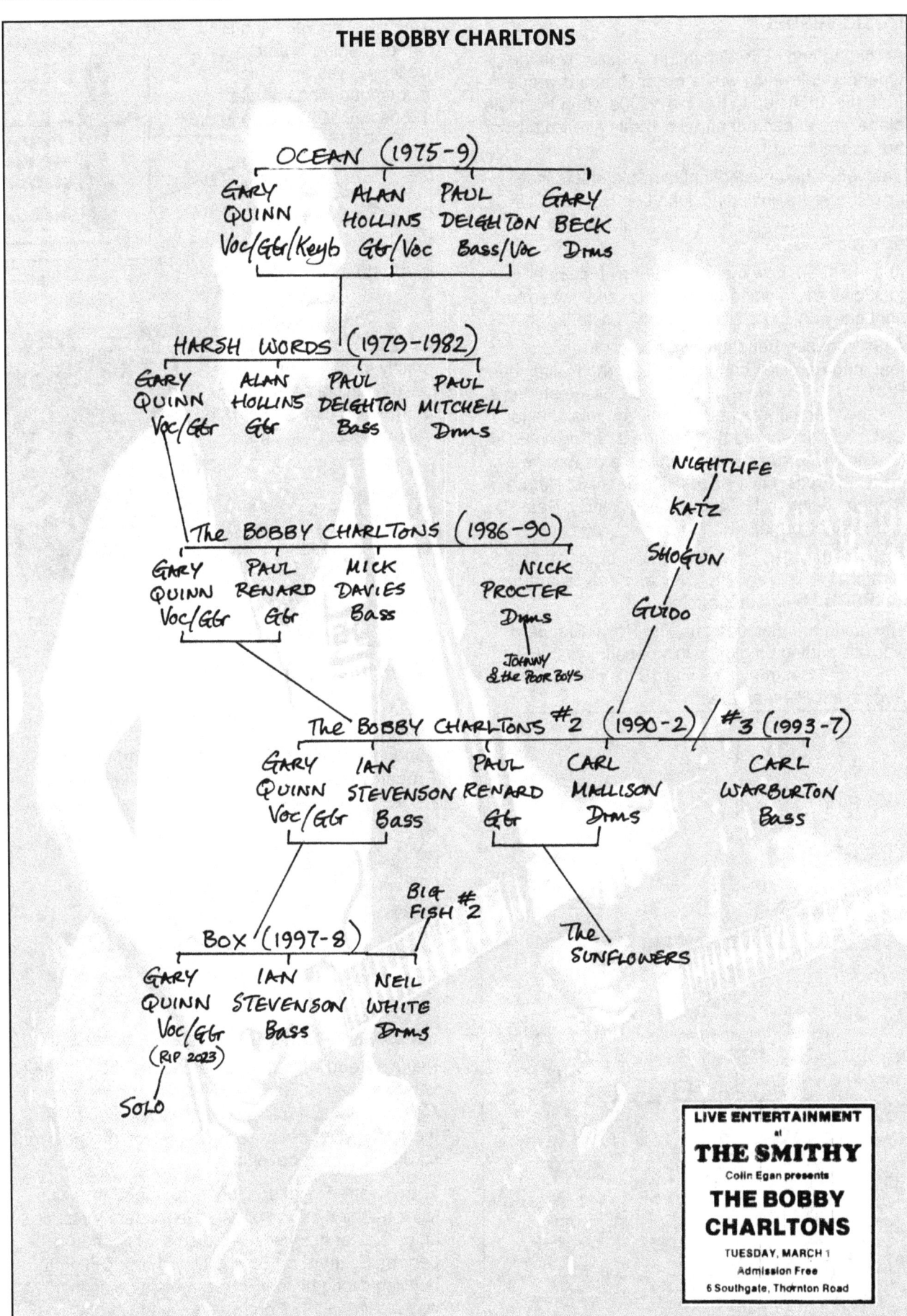

MUSIC VENUES

At the top end of the Alhambra complex was the Queen's Hall which was a major Bradford venue from the 1950s up to the mid-1990s when the main stage was ripped out and a central bar area built on the dance floor.

The venue had hosted innumerable artists there over the years, including John Lee Hooker, Cliff Richards, Medicine Head, Crass, Kirsty MacColl and The Ruts.

In June 1988, new manager Johnny McGhue took over the running of the venue and vowed to continue booking a wide range of artists.

A Greenpeace Benefit took place on June 22, featuring Barnsley band Party Day and Halifax band Broadcast, who were all Bradford College students. Another benefit was held on July 16, this time for CND, which featured two members of Poison Girls (Vi and Richard) as Famousubversa as well as Fartown Fruits, Owter Zeds, Chuffenhals, Natural Rhythm, Danbert Nobacon, Kevin Seisay, Pete Pax and Henry Normal.

A soul club called *Hole In The Wall* organized all-nighters there every Thursday and was featured on the BBC's *People* programme.

The landmark Victorian pub The Royal Standard was still putting on gigs at this period, like the Friday and Saturday gigs and 1960s Nights run by *Sugarcube Entertainment*.

Tumblers, on Tumbling Hill Street (behind Bradford College), was a popular nightspot during the late 1980s and 1990s, putting on occasional gigs but mainly disco nights. These were often linked with drink promotions that incorporated various local DJs. The club was demolished in the 1990s

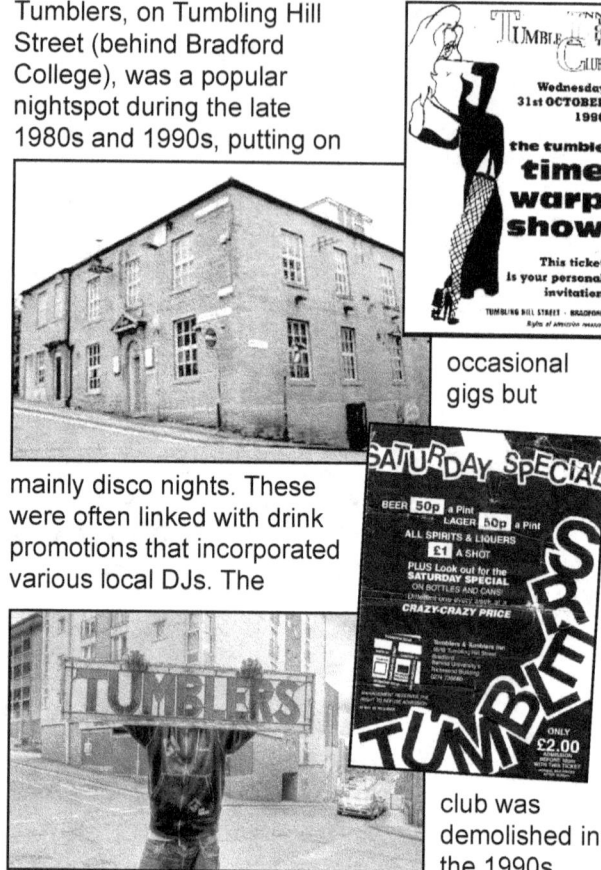

THEATRE ROYAL DEVELOPMENT

In October 1988, plans for the redevelopment of the Theatre Royal, Manningham Lane, were announced by Bradford-based consortium WY Properties, who owned several pubs in the area.

Plans to rebuild the theatre as a live 2,000-capacity venue to rival St George's Hall, with promoter Malcolm Hanson (pictured above) lined up to run the music side, never came to fruition, despite work starting on the redevelopment.

The Theatre Royal opened in 1864 and was said to be haunted by the ghost of legendary Victorian actor Sir Henry Irving, who died shortly after performing there on Boxing Day, 1905. During the building's long history, it became a cinema in 1921, was closed in 1977 and was severely damaged by fire in 1982 before being demolished in 1990.

CHAPTER 1 1988 - 1990

THE SECOND BRADFORD FESTIVAL 1988

Held between September 16-25, this Festival was financed and supported by Bradford Council and various local businesses like the *T&A* and Grattan. Again co-ordinating the festival team was the organiser of the first Festival, Allan Brack.

The Festival boasted something for everyone, with a week-long schools programme of events, an international array of classical, jazz, pop and contemporary music, theatre and dance as well as the ubiquitous street entertainment, which included acts like The Letterman (pictured below), all around the city. It also incorporated a series of new events, such as an Alternative Cabaret week at the Midland Hotel, Visual arts, film and special events, the Lord Mayor's Parade, led by the Red Herrings street band (pictured below), a Poetry day, a festival in the Wool Exchange and the first Asian Mela. (7)

The highlight of the festival was the four-day climax in Lister Park with scores of attractions, a funfair and a string of free concerts on the specially constructed *Stage On The Lake*. Those playing included local acts Ajana and Psycho Surgeons, Tangram (from Germany - pictured), Don Weller Quartet, Brendan Croker & The Five O'Clock Shadows, The Wedding Present and Steeleye Span.

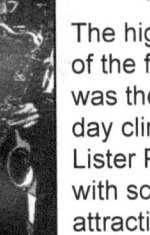

The ultimate finale was a spectacular performance of wild dance and pyrotechnics by the Barcelona troupe Diables Del Clot (The Forces Of Evil). They thrilled the crowds with a show of colour and movement with their 'Dance Of The Devils', using firecrackers and candles.

In October, Chris Maguire left the *T&A's Rock On* column and was replaced by a new reporter, David Ford.

On October 21, at St George's Hall, there was a concert billed as *Night Of The Guitar*s. It featured some of the world's top guitarists, including Randy California (Spirit), Steve Howe (Yes), Robbie Krieger (The Doors), Alvin Lee (Ten Years After), Robin Trower (Procul Harum), Andy Powell, Ted Turner (Wishbone Ash) and Leslie West (Mountain).

DICKIE BARDS

Formerly known as The Seaton Sisters, this dynamic comic duo of Mandy Craig and Jayne Tunnicliffe performed tongue-in-cheek rhyming poetry in a colloquial Yorkshire dialect. Their subject matter was wide-ranging and playful, attacking many of their pet hates including men with beards, mindless marriages, 'Tracy and Kevin's' and tacky nights out in wine bars and discos.

They had spots on Radio Sheffield, YTV's *Calendar* and the late-night *James Whale's Radio Show*.

```
The SEATON SISTERS (1988-
(FORMERLY: The SCREAMING D-CUPS)

MANDY              JAYNE
CRAIG              CLIFTON
Voc/Gtr            Voc/Bass
```

JANE HARRISON

Classically trained singer Jane Harrison, of Wilsden, won the Bob Monkhouse fronted *Opportunity Knocks* in June 1988.

She was a graduate of the Royal Northern College Of Music.

Later that year, she released her first LP, *New Day*, on the Stylus label, with orchestral backing from arranger and conductor David Bedford. (8)

The album included a version of the 1976 Chicago No 1 hit, *If You Leave Me Now*.

It was heavily promoted on TV and in the press, with Jane making many personal appearances, including one at Sunwin House in Bradford on Friday, January 20. Just after Christmas 1988, she began a three-week tour to promote the album with a gig at Halifax Civic Theatre, backed by the Black Dyke Mills Band and the Halifax Choral Society.

She released two singles from the album, the title track *New Day* and *Ave Maria*. A third single, *I Will Protect You*, followed in 1989.

PRO AUDIO

Started in September by three musicians Carl Walters, Paul Siddall, and Brian Lumb, Pro Audio was a new business that installed and hired out PA sound systems.

They said, *'virtually any company of any size will use some form of sound system, anything from background music to paging and intercoms'*. (9)

By December, Pro Audio had undertaken work for Bradford & Bingley Building Society, Bradford University and a major Leeds discotheque. They also installed a new system at Blackpool's Winter Gardens complex for the annual Labour Party conference.

DJIBOUTI BLUE

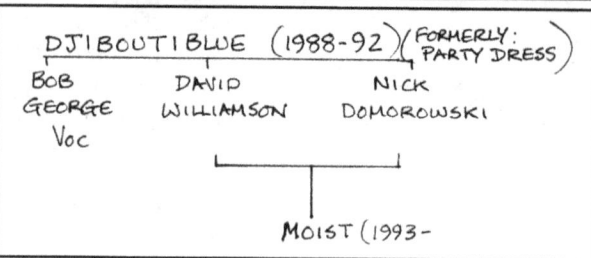

This Heaton-based trio were former members of the band Party Dress. Their name was derived from an East African township called Djibouti. In 1993 two members of the band split off to form the group Moist.

As 1989 began, the news broke in the *T&A* that Scotland Yard were starting a new investigation into the 1966 escape from Wormwood Scrubs of Soviet spy/MI6 agent George Blake. The reopening of the case was prompted by the furious demands of over a hundred MPs and the

right-wing *Freedom Association* after Mike Randle and his fellow peace campaigner Pat Pottle revealed they intended to publish a book outlining their part in Blake's escape. (For a summary of the escape, see page 154 in *BNOTV Volume 1*)

Mike Randle was an anti-nuclear defence expert working as a lecturer at the Peace Studies Department of Bradford University prior to losing his position as a result of the controversy. He stated he would be available for any police interview, but insisted he *'had no regrets'*. (10)

Mike's son, Sean, played drums in many local bands during the 1980s.

CHAPTER 1   1988 - 1990

CLOCKS & CLOUDS

The duo of Graham McAndrew and Martin Griffin were formed by McAndrew, an ex-punk rocker who had caused a stir in 1977 when he wrote the controversial punk musical *Hokum* while he was a student at Bradford University.

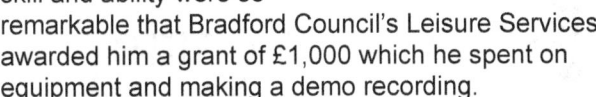

Despite Martin being blind and disabled, his keyboard skill and ability were so remarkable that Bradford Council's Leisure Services awarded him a grant of £1,000 which he spent on equipment and making a demo recording.

The council also sponsored the 1988 release of the *Bradford Music Promotions* 7" single *Christmas Song / Music Is My Life* by the Bradford Kids, a group of local musicians including Martin, Mike Smith and Scott Peters of local Funk band Guido. It was recorded at Flexible Response and produced by Diamond Light guitarist Dave Hodgson.

In February 1989, the duo released a charity 7" single *Have A Heart (For The Children)* which was recorded at Bradford's In-A-City Studios and mixed at EMI's world-famous Abbey Road studios in London. The single also featured a handful of local musicians from the Bobby Charlton, Old Joe Zydeco and Graham's old combo The Pools Winners From Kent.

During the next couple of years, they released two cassette LPs, *Blind Man's Rebuff* in 1990, which sold around 500 at their gigs, and *Launderette Of Desire* which came out in March 1991.

THE HEADMEN

This band, formed in late 1988, were made up of members from Bradford (Wkye) and Huddersfield.

As a four-piece indie group, they put out their debut 7" single *Kissed To Pieces / Roundabout* in November 1990. It was released on the Huddersfield Positive Records label and was recorded at the town's Beaumont Street Studios.

The band gigged regularly over the next two years before releasing a four-track 12' EP, *Reach The Sky*, in 1991, again on Positive Records.

NEW MODEL ARMY

In early 1989, Bradford's most successful band of the 1980s released their fourth album *Thunder And Consolation* on EMI. The album was promoted on a mammoth British tour, including a home town gig at St George's Hall, and reached No 20 in the LP charts.

Three singles from the album (widely regarded as their best) charted in the Top 40, *Stupid Questions* at No 31 in January, *Vagabonds* at No 37 in March, and *Green & Grey* also at No 37 in June.

In September a new single *Get Me Out* reached No 34 and was released on a special 10" disc.

During March, the Lancastrian town of Burnley held its first *International Blues Festival* at the Mechanics Institute. Among the artists on the bill were Bradford band Garry Whitfield's Big Secret and Halifax-based blues legend Champion Jack Dupree.

BATTLE OF THE BANDS 1989

Circuit 22's fourth *North Of England Battle Of The Bands* competition kicked off in January 1989.

Early heats were held at The Windsor pub, on Burrow Street, before problems with the venue meant later heats were moved to The Royal Standard on Manningham Lane.

The event promised £5,000 in prize money with a larger number of bands than before competing.

Over twenty bands from the local area took part with Krakatoa, Spoilt Bratz, The Gospel, The Big Bang, Twice Around The Houses, Pure Motive, NMT, Seven Dead Americans, Tapestry Sky, Fire Five, This Concern and Pulse making it through to the quarter-finals.

Thirty bands made it through to the semi-finals which were moved to Queens Hall, including The Gospel and Keighley's Twice Around The Houses.

Doc to MC band battle

TOP weird singing star The Doctor — kingpin of Psycho Surgeons, left — has been announced as a compere for the Battle of the Bands final.

The Goth hero, alias Wild Willi Beckett, intends to keep the 12 bands firmly in check during the all-day climax to the Telegraph & Argus-sponsored North of England contest at St George's Hall, Bradford.

Said the enigmatic Doc: "I fully intend to enjoy myself among the company of the warm-blooded beings of planet earth."

Organiser Malcolm Hanson, of Circuit 22, said he will also be introducing the Insect-Inspector — described as every band's worst nightmare and too dreadful to contemplate.

Tickets for the band bash of the year on Saturday, September 16, are available at £5 from St Georges box office or by writing to Circuit 22, 6 Old Road, Denholme, Bradford.

The final took place on Saturday, September 15 at St George's Hall and was won by St Helen's band Poisoned Electrick Head with Twice Around The Houses coming in second place.

Battle of Bands

THE North of England Battle of the Bands contest has now reached the semifinal stage with the original 300 groups having been whittled down to just 33.

To cater for the bigger crowds, organisers Circuit 22 have switched the contest to the 800-capacity Queen's Hall venue in Morley Street, Bradford.

And already one band has made it through to the grand final. Bradford rock outfit The Gospel fought off the challenge of Scripture and Kappella in the first semi-final at the weekend to put themselves in with a chance of sharing in the £5,000 prize money.

The rest of the semi-finals are: May 5, Twice Around The Houses, National People's Gang, True Image (pop); May 6, The Raiders, Sweet Fanny Adams, Do It (rock); May 12, Killingbeat, One Man's Medicine, Beat Crazy (pop); May 13, Brasilia, Thieves Forty Thieves, Eat The Peach (pop); May 19, Collapse, Broadcast, Poisoned Electrick Head (alternative); May 20, Krakatoa, Strongheart, Tai Shan (rock); May 26, Springheei'd Jack, Mikey Boy Stiletto, N.M.T. (alternative); May 27, A Little Rain, Dog Soldier, Domain (alternative); June 2, White Hot and Blue, Noussommes, China White (rock).

The last semi-final date is June 23 with Loaded, Mercy, Mercy and Kage.

CHAPTER 1   1988 - 1990

Battle of the Bands 1989

The final call for tickets

TICKETS for the final of the Telegraph & Argus-sponsored Battle of the Bands competition go on sale at St George's Hall today.

Fans of the two surviving local bands, The Gospel and widely fancied Twice Round the Houses, are being advised in true travel-agent style to book early.

The contest's final dozen will tread the St George's Hall boards on Saturday, September 16, as part of the Bradford Festival.

Organiser Malcolm Hanson, back from a fact-finding mission to the USA, is predictably predicting a sell-out.

"Remember, these bands are the final 12 from 200 — their fans have followed them from day one, and in the case of Do It, the whole town of Barnoldswick is turning out!"

Malcolm believes the festival tie-in will boost local interest.

Tickets for the show, which will feature star comperes, are £5 from the box office or by sending an sae to: Circuit 22, 6 Old Road, Denholme, Bradford BD13 4DJ.

Courtesy of the Telegraph & Argus

BOTB 89 runners-up Twice Around The Houses performing in the final at St George's Hall.

Funk band that is twice as good

TWICE Around the Houses are, quite simply, the most entertaining funk-rockers currently playing the Bradford music circuit.

In ten months they have gathered together an envious clutch of upbeat and uplifting tunes which they perform with such energy that a stranger to their set could be forgiven for thinking every gig was their last.

Rock On's profiles of the Battle of the Bands finalists continues with the Keighley-based combo Twice Around the Houses.

They also have a slightly silly name and a logo of a teddy bear holding a group of balloons.

Guitarist and song writer Nat explained: "The drummer, Philip Horton, came up with the name for the band after he got us together.

"He found the name in a children's book

Phil's band brief was simple — he wanted commitment and something with a bit of character.

He found what he was looking with Kendra's hugely powerful voice, Nat's ear for a good tune, the keyboards of David Sherpa Krysko and David Walsh's bass.

A place in the final of the North of England Battle of the Bands competition next month will cap a highly successful and eyecatching first year.

THE ORANGE WORLD OF TITAN

Flautist Colin Whittaker had started out with his brother Mick in the band Lemathus in the mid-1970s. He formed his own group, Titan, in 1981 and they released their only 7" single *Imaginary Lady / Guaranteed You Won't Like It* which has now become very collectable. (11)

In August 1989, after a name change to The Orange World Of Titan, (12) Colin released a new double A-side single *Big Baby* (vocal and instrumental versions) on EMI, on which he plays all the instruments. With a full backing band, they headlined that year's *Pennine Radio Music Festival*.

In 1992, as a group, they released a much delayed second single (again a double A-side) *Walking In The Sea By Mistake / Heaven*. A third single, *Pushing Water Up The Hill*, was scheduled for release in 1993.

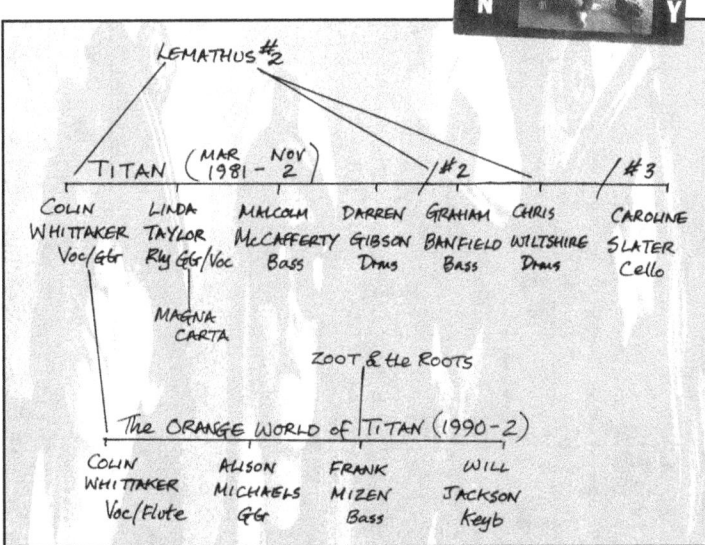

35

DUBH CHAPTER

Dubh Chapter (Dubh in Gaelic means black) were formed by the two Staunton brothers Brendan and Des, Bradford-born lads of parents from the west of Ireland. Before settling in London in the mid-1980s, they had both played in a succession of local bands including Idle Rich, Popular Fiction, Cut Out Shapes and Tea House Camp.

In 1982, as the Cut Out Shapes, they released a four-track cassette after landing a deal with Houndslow agency BPM, a company which had previously handled The Beat and Madness.

As Tea House Camp the lads released a 7" single *To Kill: Stab In Back / Poor Tom* in 1985 and had the track *Redneck Greenbacks* on the Tanz Records compilation *Just Say Yeah* in 1986. Also featured on that compilation were goth/alternative bands such as Bomb Party, Hunters Club, Gaye Bykers On Acid, Play Dead, Chat Show and Crazyhead.

Dubh Chapter formed in 1987 and their first release, after signing to EG records in June 1990, was the single *Happy Is The Bride / Who Decides* which just scraped into the UK's Top 100 singles chart.

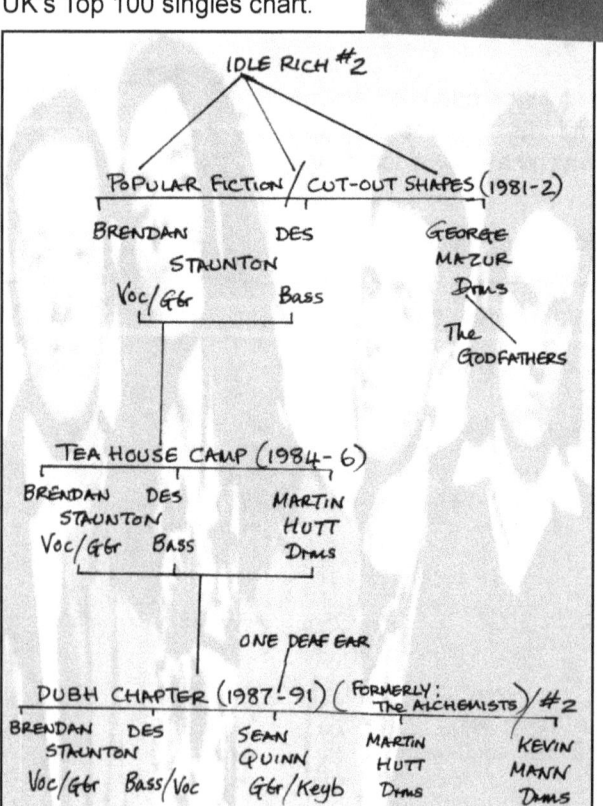

It and their subsequent releases were produced by ex-Gong guitarist Steve Hillage. Their second single *Touch & Go / Sleep & Be Thankful* soon followed, before their debut album *Silence, Cunning & Exile* was released in November 1990.

After a couple of disastrous UK tours and management issues they split just before a European tour supporting Iggy Pop in 1991.

THE HOLLOW MEN

This Leeds/Bradford combo were made up of the ex-Salvation guitarist Choque and later on by members of The Passmore Sisters. Originally a duo, after their first single *Late Flowering Lust* on their own Dead Man's Curve label in 1985, they were augmented by Howi of the Passmores on bass for their self-produced LP *Tales Of The Riverbank* in 1986.

In 1987 they released the 12" single *Gold & Ivory* on their Evensong label, followed by a single *The Drowning Man* on Leeds based label Blind Eye Records in 1989.

For their next release, the album *The Man Who Would Be King* in 1988, the trio added fellow Passmores guitarist Brian Roberts as well as drummer Johnny Cragg.

Signing to Arista Records in 1989, they released the single *White Train,* a remixed version of a track from their second LP.

By the end of 1989, the band were being touted by the *NME* as among the *'stars of tomorrow'* with others like Carter the Unstoppable Sex Machine and The Charlatans.

Their only LP for Arista was *Cresta* in 1990. They released three more singles, *The Moon's A Balloon* (1990), *The Rolling Sea / November Comes* (1990) and *Pink Panther (Pantera Rosa)* in 1991 before splitting up. Arista then released *November Comes* as a single and it reached 16 in the US Rock charts.

THE HOLLOW MEN / FEVER HUT

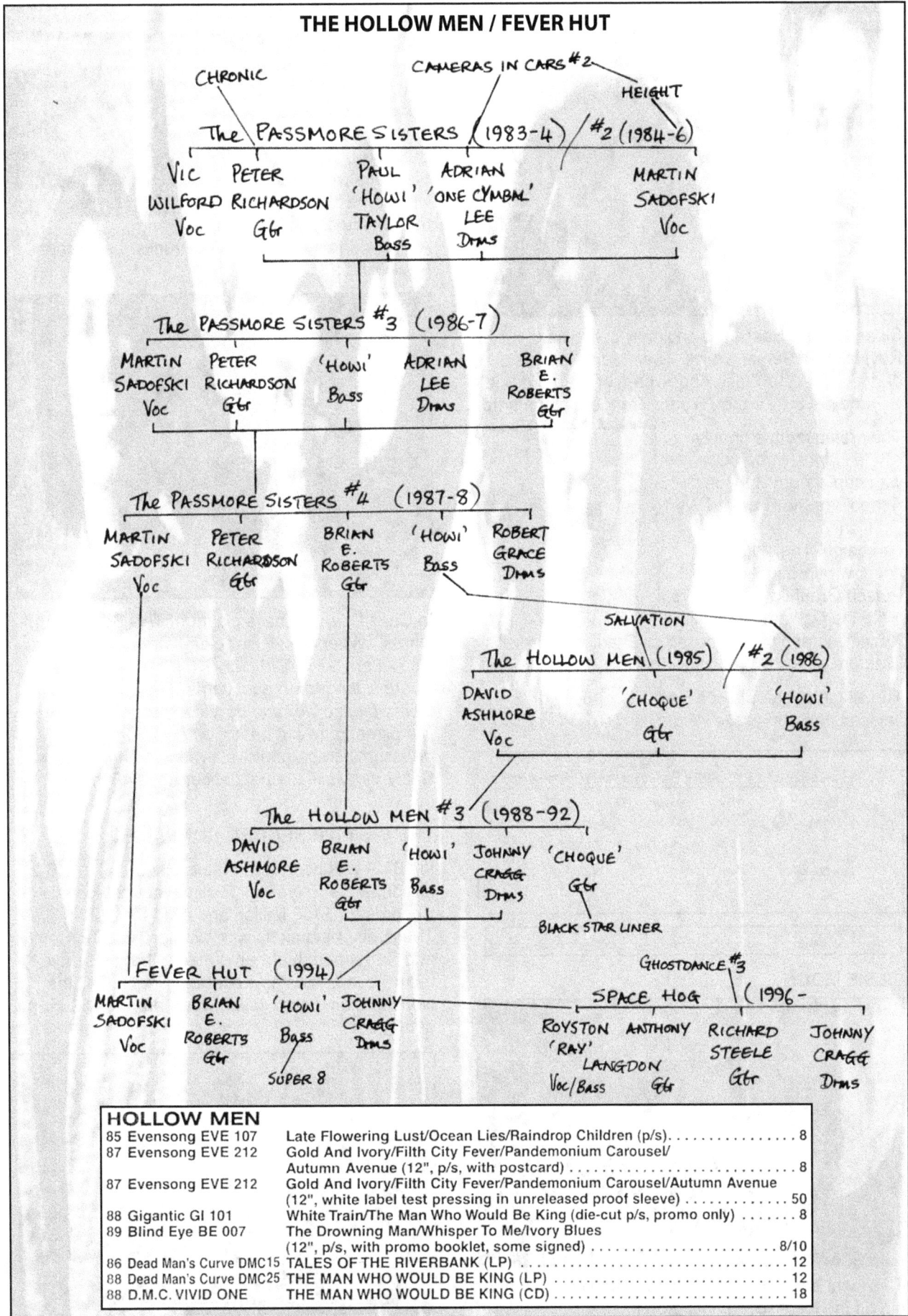

HOLLOW MEN		
85 Evensong EVE 107	Late Flowering Lust/Ocean Lies/Raindrop Children (p/s)	8
87 Evensong EVE 212	Gold And Ivory/Filth City Fever/Pandemonium Carousel/ Autumn Avenue (12", p/s, with postcard)	8
87 Evensong EVE 212	Gold And Ivory/Filth City Fever/Pandemonium Carousel/Autumn Avenue (12", white label test pressing in unreleased proof sleeve)	50
88 Gigantic GI 101	White Train/The Man Who Would Be King (die-cut p/s, promo only)	8
89 Blind Eye BE 007	The Drowning Man/Whisper To Me/Ivory Blues (12", p/s, with promo booklet, some signed)	8/10
86 Dead Man's Curve DMC15	TALES OF THE RIVERBANK (LP)	12
88 Dead Man's Curve DMC25	THE MAN WHO WOULD BE KING (LP)	12
88 D.M.C. VIVID ONE	THE MAN WHO WOULD BE KING (CD)	18

SLOAN SQUARE EAST

Sloan Square East were originally called Jazz Revival then Semai Cruise. Their monicker was derived from the White Abbey area of Bradford and a parody of the London Sloane Rangers of the time.

They released the charity single *Hands Reach Out* with pupils from Hanson School, for the Bradford War On Cancer & Leukaemia campaign. The single's cover was produced by Putsch Graphikz which were 'Fritz the Cat' and Mechelle Hesseltine and was released on Bradford Council's Bradford Music Promotions label in 1988.

The single got air play on Radio 1 courtesy of Janice Long and Steve Wright.

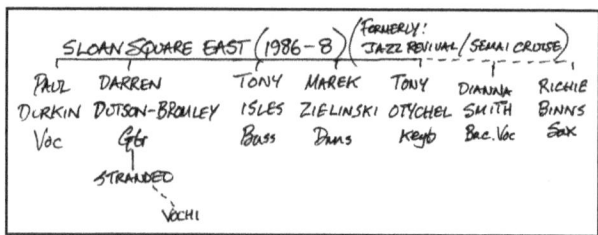

SLOANE SQUARE EAST
88 Hans Aid BMP 010 Hands Reach Out/Hand Reach Out (Remix) (p/s) 15

ELSIE MOON

This local band started life in 1989 and continued to gig on the local scene until around 1995.

THE GODFATHERS

The Godfathers 1989 12" single release *She Gives Me Love* was from their LP *More Songs About Love And Hate*. It was produced by legendary British record producer Vic Maile who had worked with some big names in the music industry, including The Animals, Fleetwood Mac, The Kinks, Led Zeppelin, Hawkwind and Dr Feelgood.

In Chris Coyne's (bass player of The Godfathers) words, *"When we were looking for a producer, we remembered 'Dirty Love' the b-side of 'Ace of Spades' the Motorhead single. The sound was just incredible, so we rang up Vic expecting this Lemmy-like biker figure but he turned out to be a quiet, unassuming sort of bloke a real diamond geezer."* Sadly Vic Maile died of cancer aged 45 in July 1989.

THE BIG FIVE RECORD COMPANIES

In 1989, EMI bought Chrysalis Records for £46.2 Million, while Polygram (Phillips) bought Island Records for £150 Million and A&M for £320 Million. These buy-outs along with Warner/Timelife, Sony and Bertelman (Germany) meant that these five record companies now controled 70% of all the world's retail record sales, worth around £12 billion at that time.

CHAPTER 1 — 1988 - 1990

ELSIE MOON

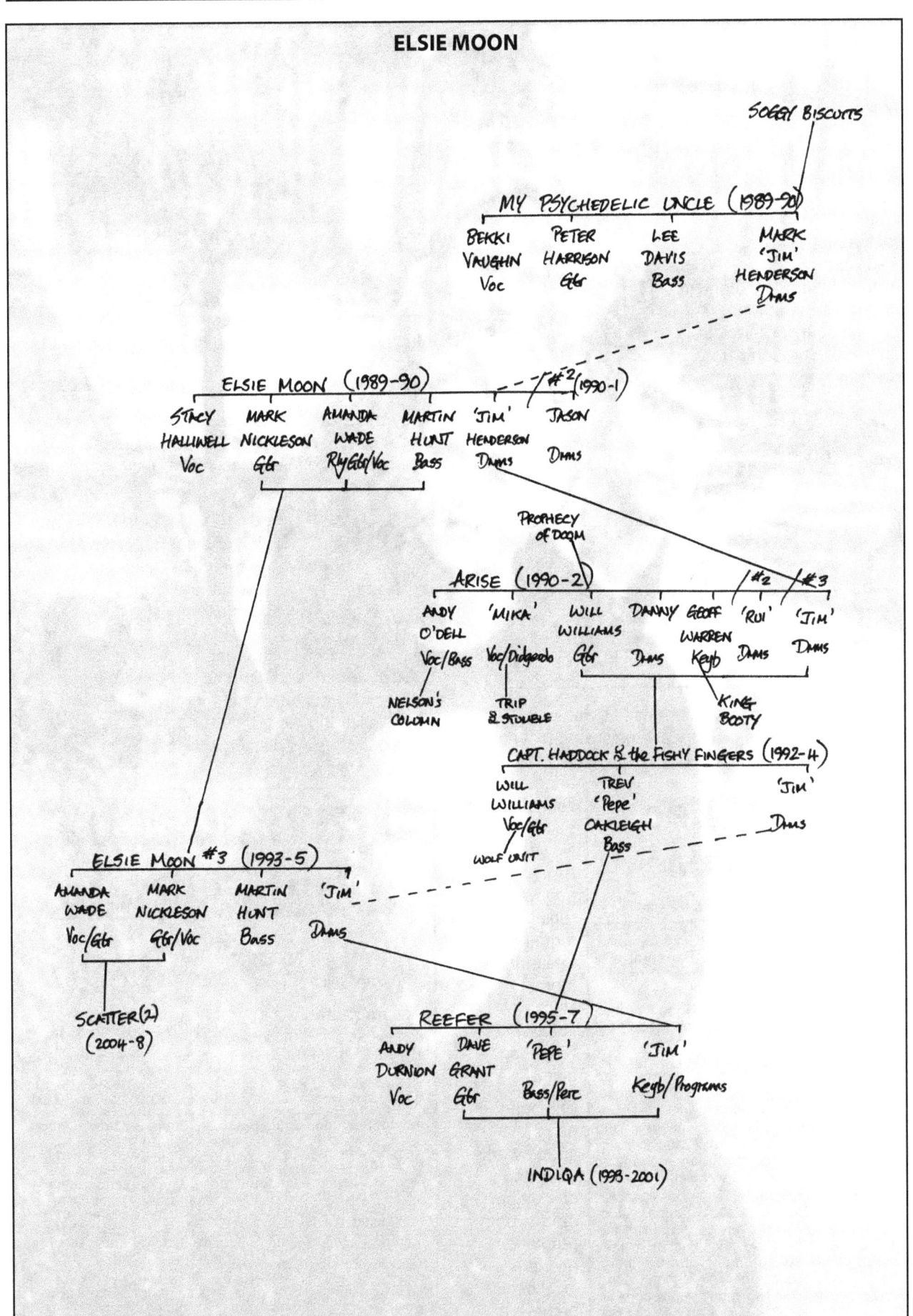

ZED

Said to be 'a cross between Led Zeppelin and The Buzzcocks' indie rockers Zed were formed by former Requiem and Psycho Surgeons bassist Jont, initially with fellow ex-Surgeon Chris McLaughlin on guitar and former JJ's Bones drummer Jez Farrar. Before any gigs were played McLaughlin left and formed his own band Loud, after a stint as live guitarist for New Model Army, and was replaced by former Anti-System/Morbid Humour vocalist Nogsy on guitar.

The band had a strong work ethic and quickly built up a strong reputation on the local circuit before embarking on various European tours, such as the Mad Dogs And Yorkshiremen Tour of 1990, with Wild Willi Beckett and Griff's Magic Theatre, that took them to Czech Republic and Sweden.

They released a 12' single, *Easy Does It / A Dollar And A Dream /Shape Of Things To Come,* which was released on Willi Beckett's QTA Records in 1990.

By 1993 Jez and Nogsy had left and been replaced by Handful Of Dance frontman Harris on guitar and former Psycho Surgeon Bambi on drums and this line up recorded the album *The Articles Of Captain Mission.*

Mighty Zed 'have a do'

AS the smoke clears and the fire eater pauses for breath, three figures appear on the stage. At the back, a wild explosion of hair and drumsticks as the spirit of a thunderstorm possesses drummer, Jez.

With a wah-wah pedal nailed to one foot stands guitarist, Nogsy. In the left corner, Jont, the man with the hat, bass and microphone cries, "Let's have a do!".

The mighty Zed unleashed song after song of relentless, blistering energy on an appreciative audience at the Palm Cove, Bradford, last Friday night.

Songs about life, the universe and 'other' things performed with the force of a controlled nuclear explosion — the after effects will stay with you forever!

The set closed with 'Easy does it', Zed's recently released debut single, and, obligatory encores over, the band left the stage giving Radical Dance Faction a hard act to follow. At the end of April the group head for Europe on their second tour. They return after two months to record an L.P.

Matt Webster

Dynamic debut album should put Zed ahead

Album review

Zed — The Articles Of Captain Mission (Bus Shelter)

WHILE bands like Loud and New Model Army are high up on Bradford's alternative rock roll of honour, lesser lights like Zed rarely get mentioned in dispatches.

Yet after hearing the three-piece's forceful, dynamic and imaginative debut LP, I just can't figure out why.

The band have been purveying their aggressive brand of environment-friendly dreadlock rock for more than three years.

Throughout the music scene's obsession with all things danceable they have stuck to their hardcore roots and deserve more recognition now that American-style grunge is the flavour of the month.

With former Psycho Surgeon Jont on bass and vocals, Harris on guitar and Bambi on drums, Zed are a tight ship and whip up a welter of sound which can be both vicious and acutely emotional.

If you're familiar with the band's last single Easy Does It, which featured in Rock On's 1991 Top Ten, there's plenty more where that came from.

It would be churlish to single out specific tracks on an album which is strong throughout.

Courtesy of the Telegraph & Argus

CHAPTER 1 — 1988 - 1990

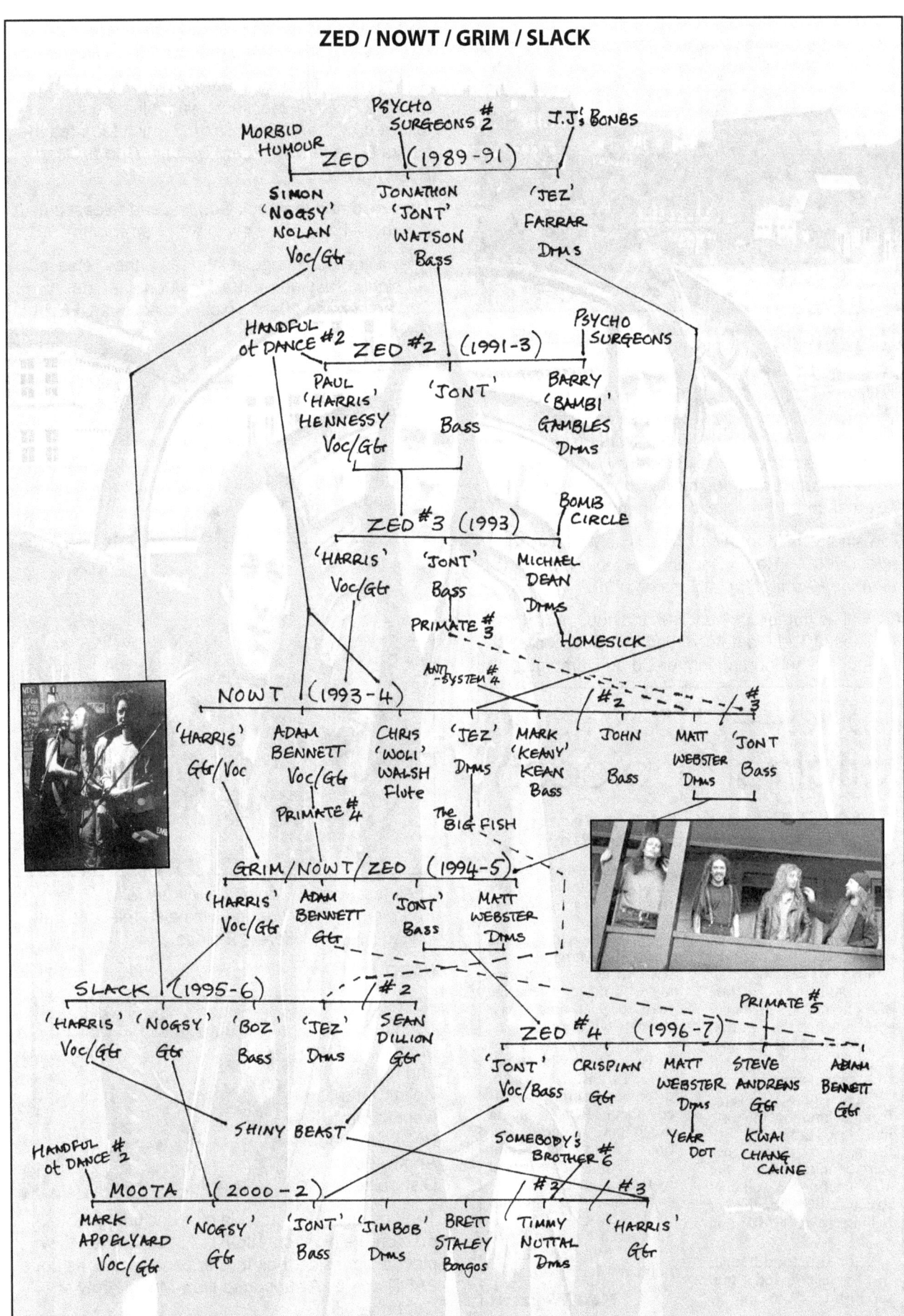

ZED / NOWT / GRIM / SLACK

LOUD

The band were formed by frontman Chris McLaughlin, after his time as New Model Army's live guitarist. They were quickly signed to China Records and recorded their first album, *D-Generation*, produced by J Martin Rex and Jaz Coleman of Killing Joke, with whom they toured.

The single *D-Generation / This Time* was played extensively on Radio One and the album was voted 19 in the *Kerrang!* top albums of 1990.

As well as numerous headline and support slots to the likes of The Godfathers and The Buzzcocks, they toured supporting former Duran Duran guitarist Andy Taylor, who also remixed their second single *Explosive / To Have And to Hold / Black Hysteria*.

A third single from the album, *Song For The Lonely / Geist II / Massacre* was released in 1991, followed by the 12-inch *Sex EP* which featured the tracks *D Generation / Day Tripper / God Is Dead / Resurrection*.

They also had the track *God Is Dead* released as a 7-inch flexi disc given away with *Kerrang!* in 1991.

After a line-up change in late 1991, they released the single *Easy / Give Me The Money / Late September* and 10-inch picture disc version *Easy / Geist III / Psyche 21*.

Their second album, *Psyche 21*, was produced by renowned Queen and Black Sabbath producer Rheinhold Mack and released in 1992 again on China Records.

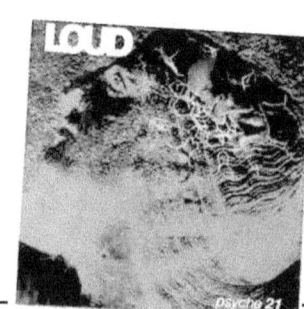

Their last single, *Mary (She Made Me...) / I Want To Be Loved / I Am The Idol*, was also released as a limited EP with different B sides.

PADD

After leaving Loud, bassist Martin Hawthorn and guitarist Colin Clarkson went to form PADD (Powerful And Deeply Disturbing).

They played a few notable gigs, including the memorable night on August 27, 1992, when they played alongside their former band mates, as Loud PADD and GFA supported New Model Army at Queen's Hall.

Loud — a fresh and original approach

LOUD, Happiness Ad, The Shotgun Brides – Queens Hall, Bradford

PLAYING their first gig since the recording of their debut LP 'D Generation', Loud took to the stage with the power and confidence it can take bands years to achieve.

Fronted by Chris McLaughlin, probably best known as the guitarist for New Model Army Loud played with a fresh and original approach.

Their songs, powered from behind by the brilliant ex-Happiness Ad drummer Ricky Howard, were definitely 'loud', but also tuneful and well constructed, with touches of Killing Joke, NMA and Rush.

With an LP and single due for release and a tour support to Fields of the Nephilim, Loud are a band you shouldn't have to strain too hard to hear in the future.

It was good to see the wonderful Happiness Ad back in action, performing with more of an edge than the last time I saw them, two years ago.

Only having time for three practices with stand-in Psycho Surgeon drummer Bambi prevented them from playing much new material, but their 'U2 meets the Damned' style was well received by the audience.

Up next, The Shotgun Brides blasted out their no-nonsense brand of rock 'n' roll - raw, to the point and very good.

Matt Webster.

Courtesy of the Telegraph & Argus

CHAPTER 1 — 1988-1990

LOUD / PADD / HARDWARE / KILL II THIS

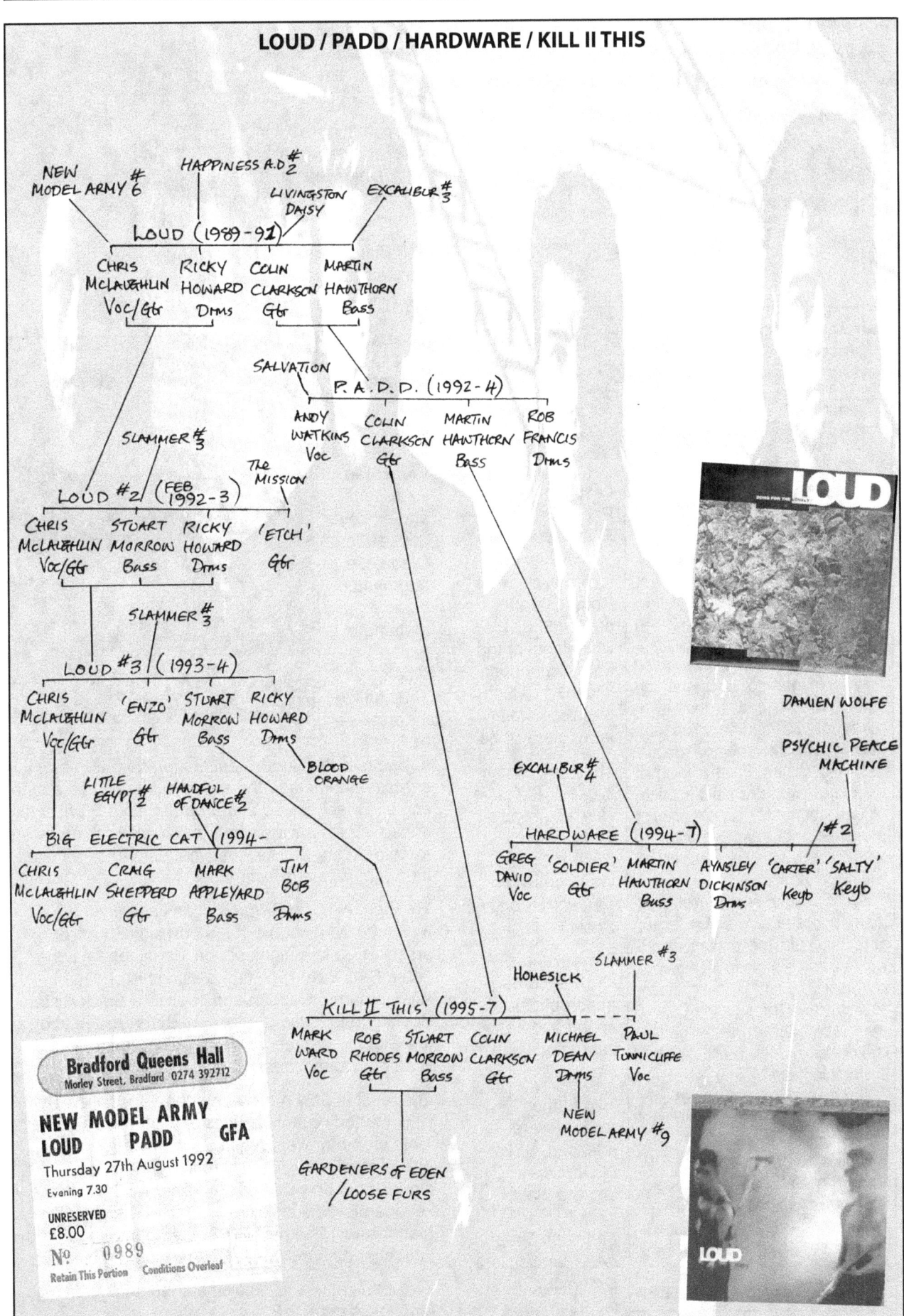

POPPY FACTORY

Ex-Word members Jock Cotton (who is a cousin of The Cure's Robert Smith) and Jon Binns teamed up with future Embrace keyboard player Mick Dale on bass to form Poppy Factory. They were quickly signed to Chrysalis Records and produced a 12' white label of the track *Drughouse* (Poppy 1) which was promoted around the clubs.

Their first proper single, *7x7 / Little Princes* (Poppy 2) became Record Of The Week on Radio 1's *Janice Long Show*.

Their live show featured quadrophonic sound and an integrated light show.

Two further records were released, *Stars / Goodtime* and the three track EP *Fabulous Beast / Acceleration / Dreamsick*, both in 1991.

These singles were from a recorded but never-released album, *Good Time*.

Poppy factory split in 1992. Keyboard player Mick Dale went on to have success with indie rockers Embrace.

Jon Binns moved to France and worked on ambient dance solo projects.

Fabulous Factory
**Poppy Factory
Queen's Hall**

SATURDAY night saw what was only the second gig by new Bradford band Poppy Factory. Unusually for such a new blood they managed to pack out the cellar bar and had at least two-thirds of the audience up and dancing after the opening songs.

Strong on the visual aspect of their show with dramatic lighting, colour patterns and images projected onto a white backdrop, and obscure film clips shown on two large TV sets.

But it is the sheer quality of their songs that is the main attraction. Stirring arrangements with moving rythms to memorable choruses – sometimes comparable to New Order or the Cure – were ably delivered by guitarist/vocalist Jock and Synth players Jon and Mik.

You could close your eyes and stick a pin in their set list to pick a hit single.

Poppy Factory manage to create the elusive atmosphere that make their gigs musical 'events' and elevates them above the masses. Catch them if you can.

Matt Webster.

Bradford Star 1991

HYACINTH HOUSE

Our House - Paul O (left) and Paul B. Photo by Fritz The Cat

The band was formed in 1988 by two bassists called Paul, former-Word man Paul Bahr and ex-Toyz geezer Paul Oladajoye, augmented by an ex-Mammoth guitarist Vince. They hailed themselves as "..of the dawning of the Bomb-Beat Generation, with a mix of rock rhythms and the sound of the 'House' scene' sampling techniques and programming. Promising the sound of Now with music and songs made in the forge of today, after all they intended to be a major part of tomorrow's history." (13)

Through the local BP promotions agency the band were offered a couple of support slots to major artists at Dollars nightspot on Manningham Lane. Later, Paul Bahr reverted to using his original African name, Nagbea and opened a Black History Bookshop for several years on Barry Street, above the Global Beat record shop, before founding the Bradford *Soundshack Records* label in 2010.

In August, a new promotions company called The Club started organising gigs at Queen's Hall. The main promoter was Eileen Verity (nee Fearnley), wife of local rock guitarist John Verity. The first gig they put on was AOR rockers FM (whose keyboardist was local lad Phil 'Dige Digital' Manchester) The next, on September 24, featured Los Angeles band Bullet Boys supported by Shy.

Two new venues in Shipley started putting on gigs, Mr Craig's and Mr Clappers.

POPPY FACTORY / HYACINTH HOUSE

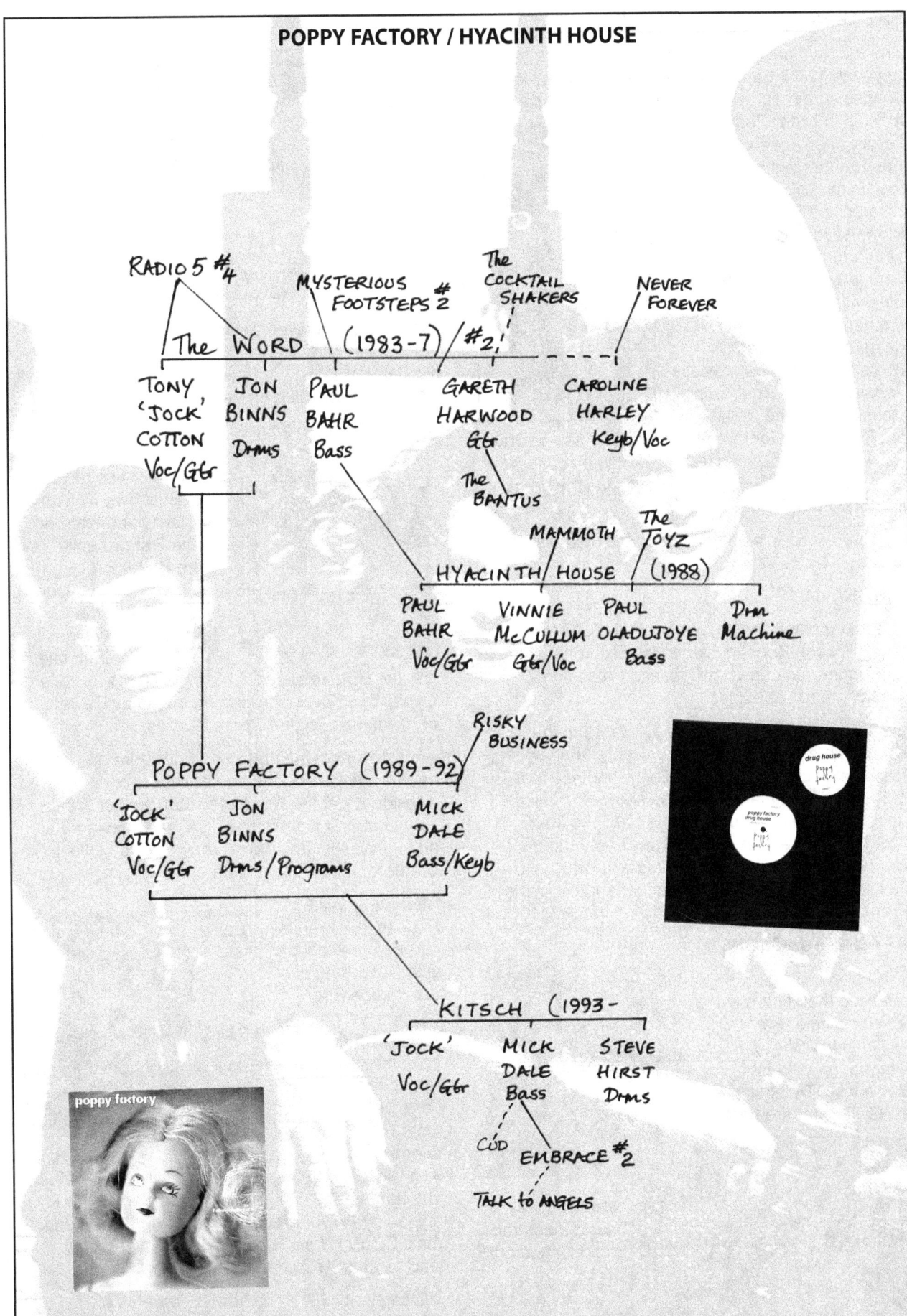

THE THIRD BRADFORD FESTIVAL

The third annual Bradford Festival took place between 12-23 September, with gigs at many local venues, street carnival entertainment, the Mela and a finale in Lister Park. As before, many events on the Festival programme were free to the public. The main difference this year was that the Festival had been re-structured into a non-profit company, Bradford Festival Ltd, with offices in the Wool Exchange. The organisers, despite the £120,000 overspend from the previous year, which the local council picked up, hoped to raise

the £1/4 million for that year's event by asking 600 local firms and businesses for sponsorship, as well as a series of raffles and flag days plus the grant of £75,000 from the council.

Any profits made went forward to the next festival in 1990.

FUTURAMA #6

Leeds promoter and organiser of the *Futurama* festivals John Keenan, staged his sixth one on Sunday, October 1 at Ceaser's Palace on Manningham Lane. (14)

Gary was fortunate to be able to 'blag' into the event with ex-Membranes John Robb, (then writing for the music paper *Melody Maker*) and see four of the nine bands and artists on show. The line-up featured Primal Scream, The Fall, The Man From Delmonte, James (15), New Fast Automatic Daffodils, two Leeds bands - Cud and Bridewell Taxis, the Blackburn band-Bradford and performer Frank Sidebottom (aka Chris Sievey 1956-2010).

PSYCHO SURGEONS

The Pyscho Surgeons released their final vinyl 12-inch single, *Panic On / RD Laing / Chasing The Dragon,* on Wild Willi Beckett's QTA label in 1989. Their entire back

catalogue was later remastered and released on CD by Mutiny 2000 Records in 2003.

PRIDE / ANITA MADIGAN

During the late summer of 1989, a new BBC television drama hit the screens. *The Paradise Club* was about brothers Frank and Danny Kaye (played by actors Don Henderson and Lesile 'Dirty Den' Grantham, fresh from Eastenders), two hardened South London criminals who inherit the club on the death of their mother.

The programme featured 'live' bands playing during

most episodes, including ex-Bradford based band The Best Way To Walk. Another band featured in the first two episodes were Pride, a rock group led by Bradford guitarist Pat MacDonald and featuring lead singer Anita Madigan. In late

'89, the BBC released a 7" single *Mercenary Man / Gypsy* by Pride which was produced by Dave King of Bradford's Engine Room Studios.

Anita was born in Ormskirk, Lancashire and had been singing since the age of fifteen, once having a residency at the Ritz Hotel, Manchester. While doing cabaret work in the USA, she answered an ad in a Washington paper and came to settle in Bradford, thus joining Pride.

After the demise of Pride in 1991, Anita carried on working with Dave King at the Engine Room Studios writing songs and doing backing vocals for the likes of Terrorvision on their first LP. One of the

songs she wrote, *Heart Over Mind* was covered by Kim Wilde in 1992 and charted at No 34. By 1993, she had a new outfit, Big Bang, who were quickly signed by Polydor records, releasing the 12' and maxi CD *Big Bang*, which charted in Germany, Austria and Switzerland.

We catch up with Anita further career later, in Chapter Six.

CHAPTER 1 — 1988 - 1990

PRIDE / BIG BANG

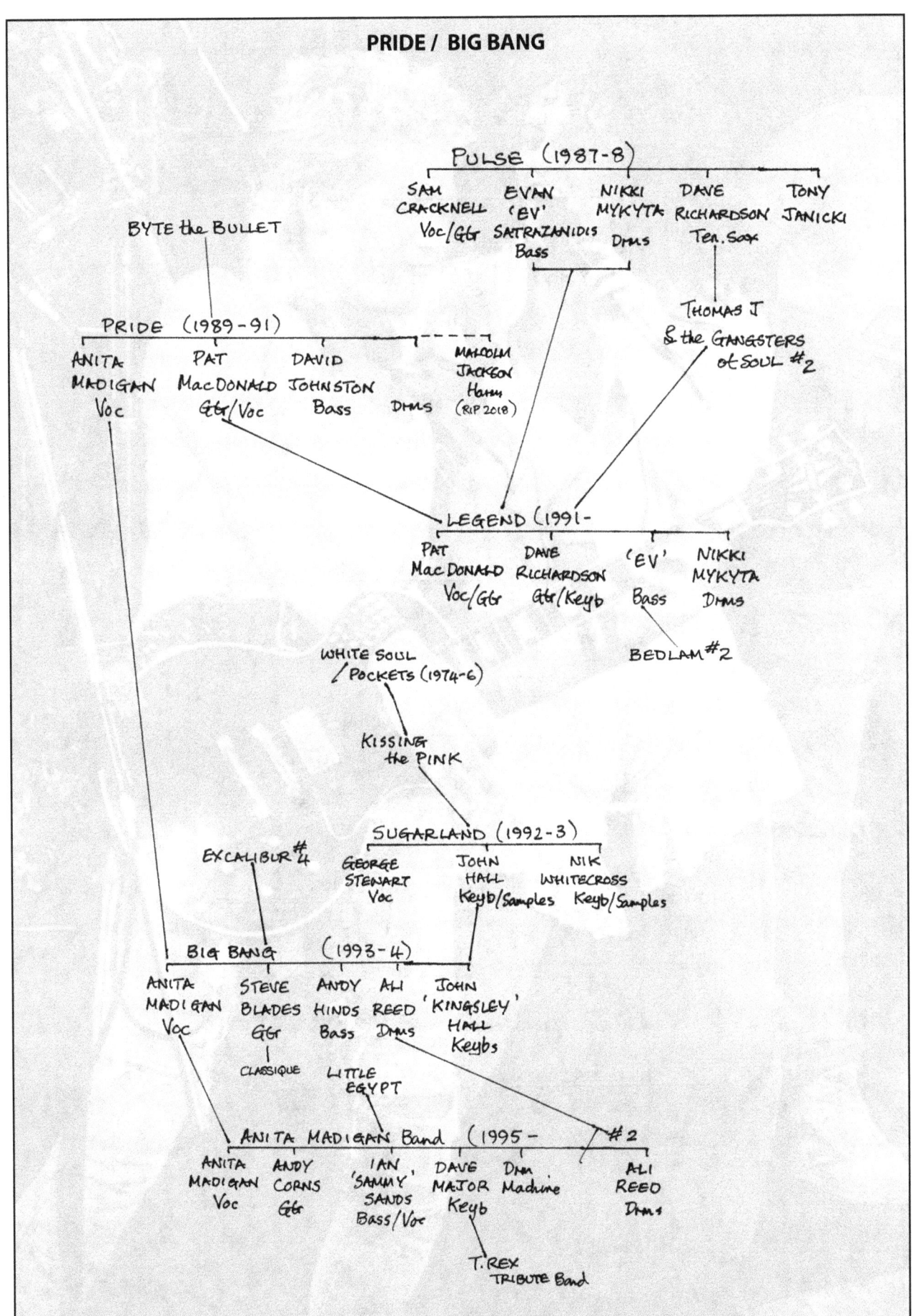

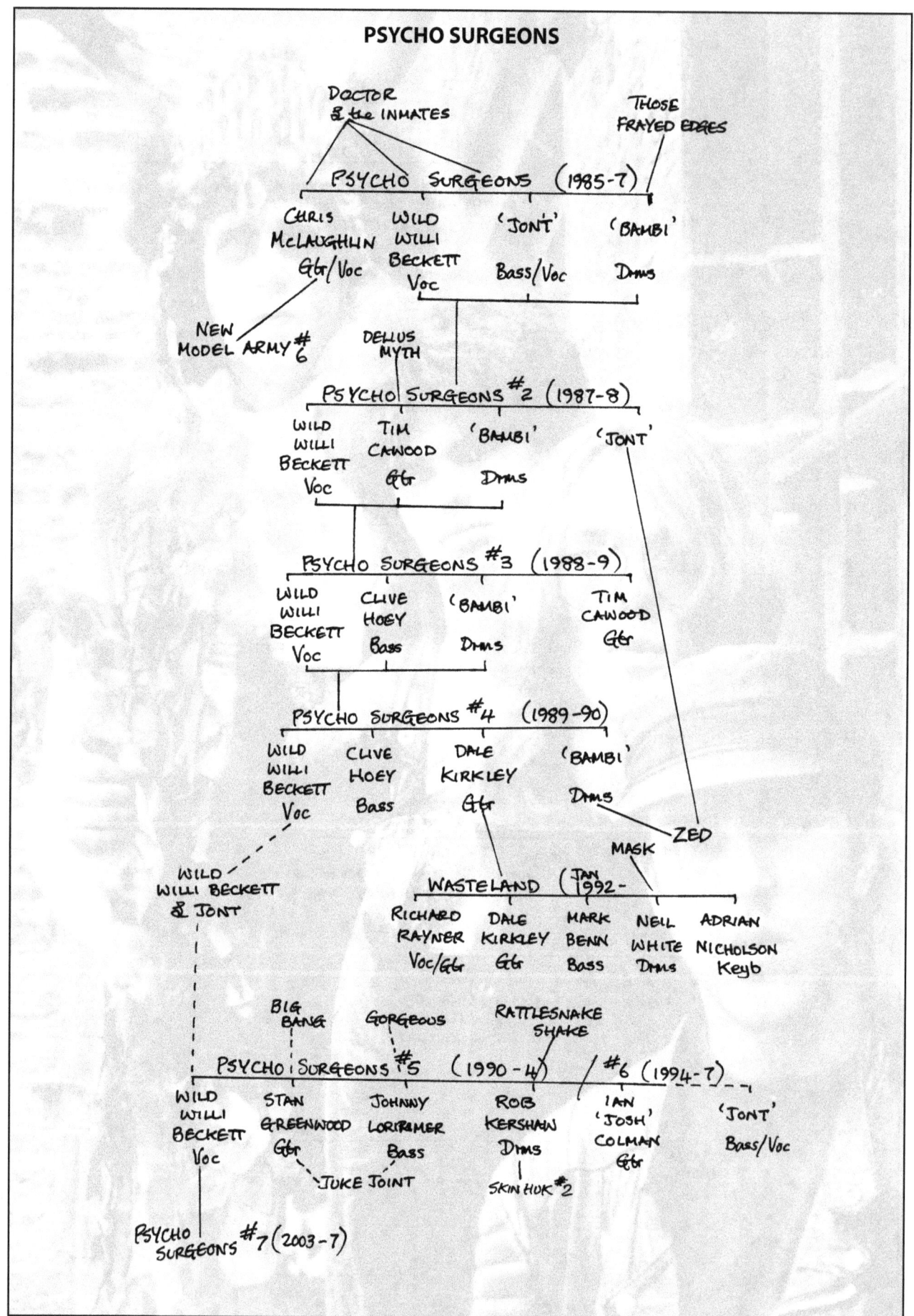

CHAPTER 1 — 1988 - 1990

MR MEANA / SCREAMACHINE / DEAD CELEBS

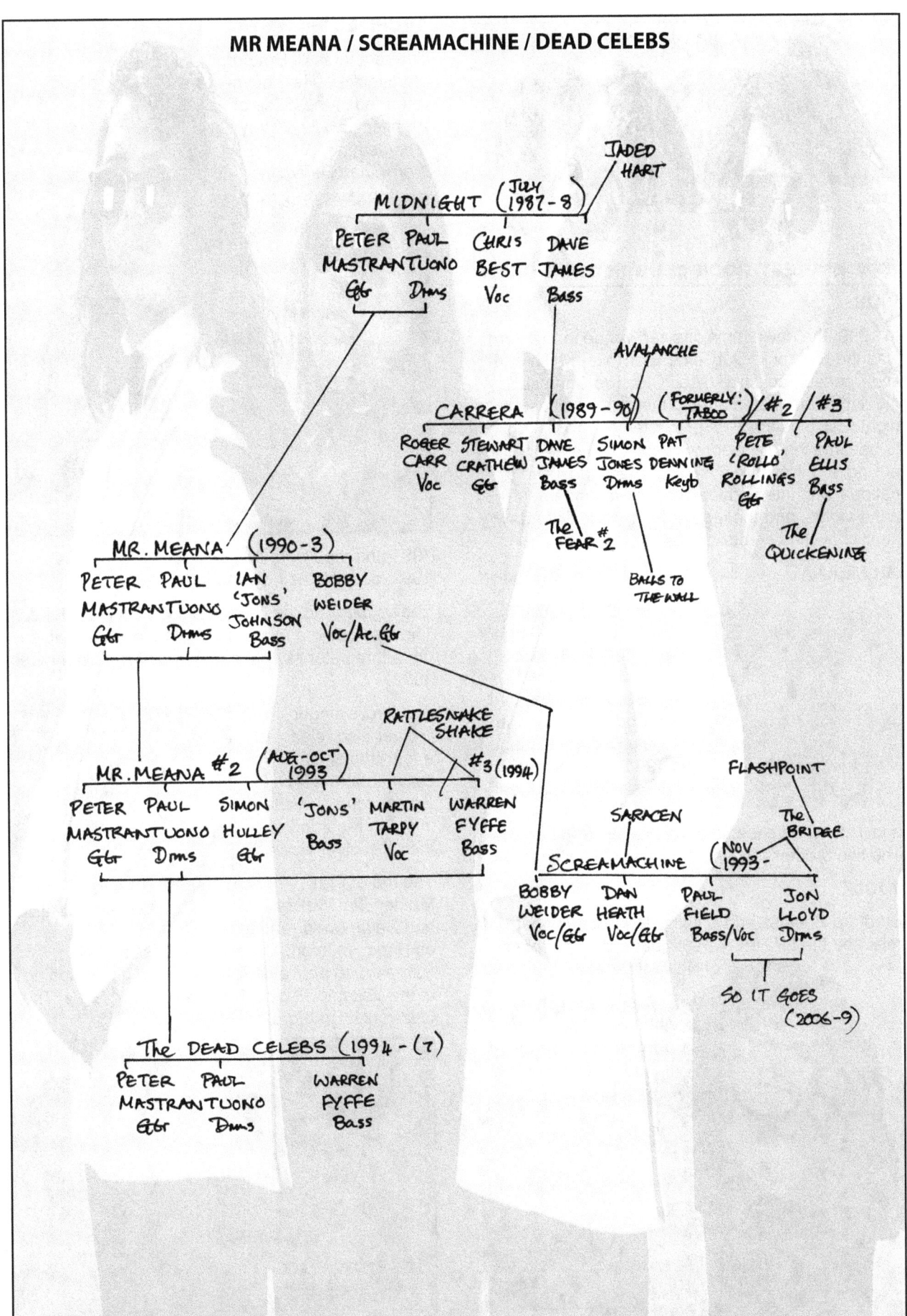

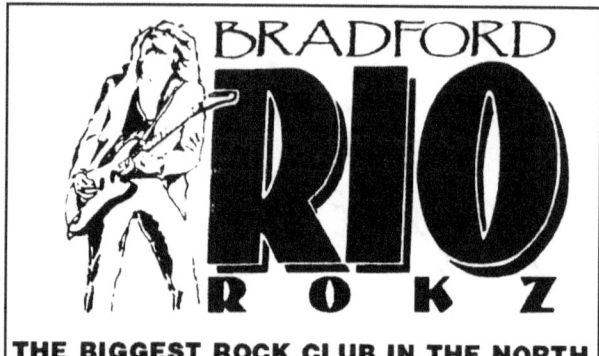

THE BIGGEST ROCK CLUB IN THE NORTH

RIOS

In 1990, the newest major-sized venue in Bradford was the Rio 'rock' Club, later Rio Rokz, which had first opened back in 1987 as Club Rio Campus nightspot, but then started putting on Wednesday night rock gigs from 1988. In later years went on to become the premier rock venue in the north of England. It featured a mix of many local and national and international rock, metal and thrash band nights, and the regular Friday and Saturday after-show heavy rock discos till 2 am.

MR MEANA

Started in 1990 by the Mastrantuono brothers, formerly of local rock group Midnight, they released a self-financed CD, *Social Elite,* on the Royale Recordings label in 1991. They gigged extensively on the local scene, especially at Rio's and The Wheatsheaf pub, on Little Horton Lane. The two brothers formed the Dead Celebs in 1994.

JOOLZ

Bradford Poetess and Britain's leading cult poet released the LP *Hex* in 1990, backed by members of New Model Army.

The ten tracks on the album were some of Joolz's finest pieces of social commentary.

ARCHITECT

The remnants of Bradford glam rockers Harlequyn reformed in the guise of Architect in 1990. They released the 12-inch EP *More Than Before* in

1991 and the *Poets And Thieves* album on CD in 1992, both on their own Voltage label.

They supported the likes of Big Country, Doctor & The Medics on a tour to promote the album, which got a three star review in *Q Magazine* in December 1992.

Architect's singer- Paul Mother also released a four-track Marc Bolan tribute CD called *Bolanesque* on Voltage in 1993, recorded at their Revolver studios.

The trio of Paul Mother, Tim Walker and Dave Wood reunited as Harlquyn, along the their old bassist Phil Sargeant, to play a series of reunion gig, including at the *Voltage Studios 25th Celebration Gig* at The Gasworks, Bradford on October 26, 2013.

CHAPTER 1 — 1988 - 1990

ARCHITECT / BLOOD ORANGE / WORM

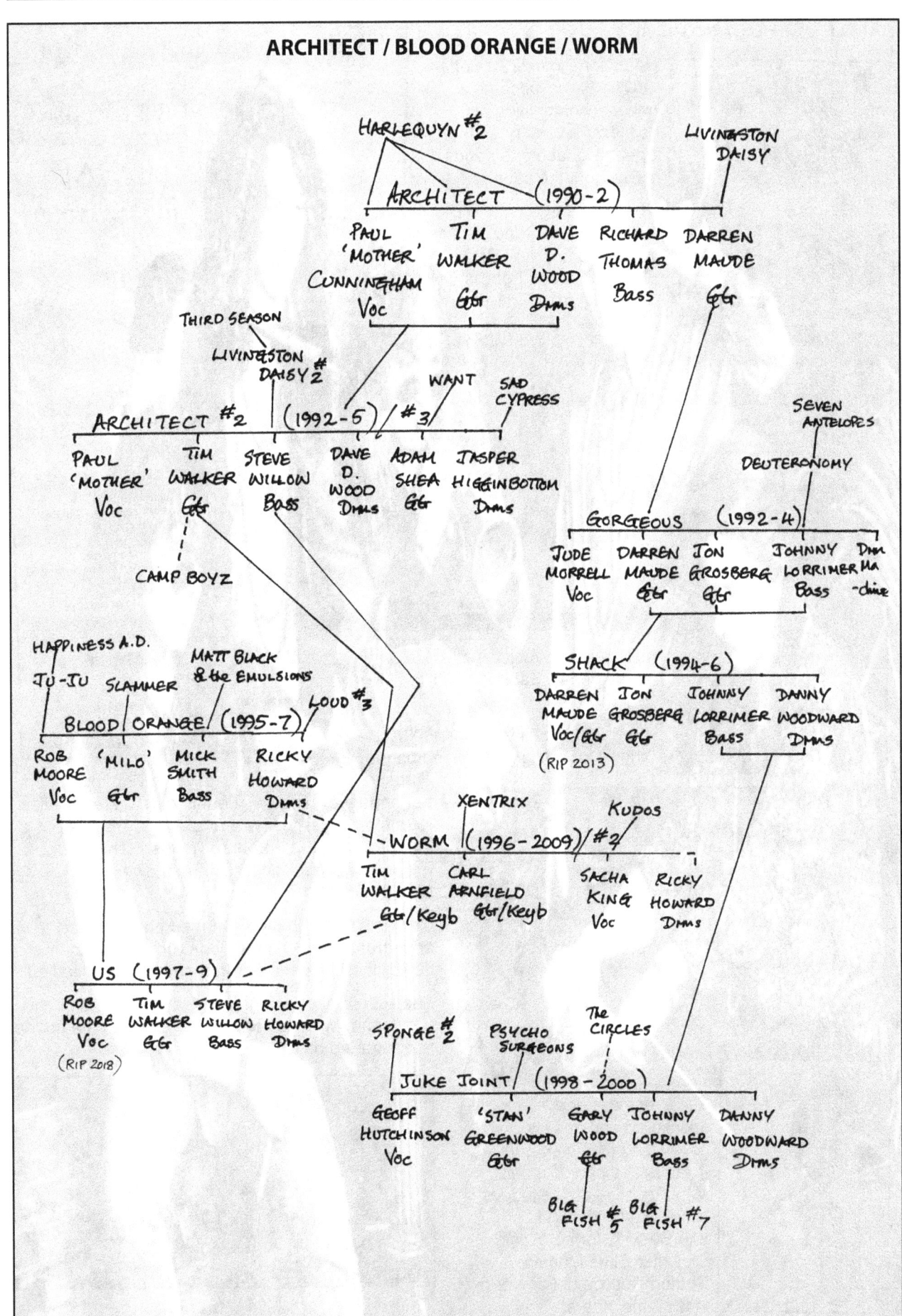

BATTLE OF THE BANDS 1990

Heats for *Circuit 22's Battle Of The Bands* became a national competition on its fifth anniversary and opened its doors to bands throughout the country.

The heats began at the Rio on Woodhead Road (briefly known as the New Rio Dance Club) on February 2 and ran from 7-11 pm, followed by a rock disco, every Friday, Saturday and Sunday.

Over 200 bands took part in 100 shows including local based bands

Threshold Shift (pictured above - giving their debut performance), The Wonderful Thing Called Tiddles, New Morning, The Lively Arts, Fallacy, Krakatoa, The Fear, Big Eyed Beans, Travesty, The Insect, Premiere, Sheepskin Children, All The President's Men (Halifax).

Cameras from Channel 4 turned up to film an appearance by Bradford duo Clocks & Clouds during their heat for a programme for the disabled.

The second round began on May 18 and ran until sixty bands were left to battle it out when the quarter finals started on Saturday, July 14.

The event was again sponsored and heavily covered by the *Telegraph & Argus* and had columnist Mike Priestley on the judges panel, alongside Wild Willi Beckett, former *Rock On* writer Chris Maguire, Gordon Roscoe of Far North Music, and others.

Semi-finalists Fallacy

CHAPTER 1   1988 - 1990

Only three groups from the local area made it through to the semi-final stage, Bradford's New Morning

ROCKBOX
The Battle is on!

Put together ten of Britain's finest unsigned bands, throw in a few judges and watch the fur fly. Yes, it's that **Battle Of The Bands Final** time of year and once again a Keighley band is among the competitors.

As regular readers know, rock-poppers **Premiere** will be playing their original songs at tomorrow's bash. They fought their way past 200 other bands from all over the country for a place in the final. Hopefully Frank's Foursome will go one better than Keighley's Twice Round The Houses who came second last year.

Tickets for the 3-11pm final at Bradford University's communal building cost £6.50 and there's an all-day bar and hot food. Ticket-holders get free entry into the 9.30pm-2am celebration disco party at nearby Club Rio, home of the Battle heats.

and Keighley bands Fallacy and Premiere (pictured above), the latter making it through to the final.

The final was an all-day event held at Bradford University Communal Building on Saturday, September 8. It was won by Liverpool heavy metal band Sian with Harrogate's Brazil coming in second place.

This proved to be *Circuit 22's* final *Battle Of The Bands* as the following year the competition was split into two separate entities, the *Metal Mountain* and *The Great Pop Explosion*.

Finalists 'lack originality'

FOR a competition that boasts to showcase the best unsigned bands in Britain, there was remarkably little originality on display at the Battle of the Bands final on Saturday.

From an original 200 entrants eleven bands remained to slug it out for the £1,500 first prize.

The all day final, which like many all-day events was sometimes more of a toil than a pleasure, was enjoyed by over 600 rock fans.

The predominantly heavy rock orientated final was won by cliched metal merchants Sian, from Liverpool, who claimed the prize money, two days in a recording studio and an appearance at the Stage-on-the-Lake concert that closes the Bradford Festval.

Second place went to similarly competent but predictable rockers Brazil, from Harrogate, and Bowie-influenced Cat Balou who travelled down from Scotland to finish third.

My favourite bands of the day were Napoleon's Piano, from Blackpool, who played tight, powerful soul

With the competition doubling in size next year, and heats being held in Bradford, Ayrshire and a venue somewhere near London, it will hopefully attract a greater cross section of popular music.

Matt Webster

Tonight — SATURDAY, JULY 28
POP QUARTER FINAL 5
featuring
**LOCKS AND CLOUDS/CLEMENTINES
GRASSHOUSE/CAT BALOU**

Tomorrow — SUNDAY, JULY 29
POP QUARTER FINAL 6
featuring
**THAT'S THAT/HEARTLAND
MOONSHIRE/THE EXIT**

BATTLE OF THE BANDS THREATENS TO BECOME THE GREATEST POP PHENOMENON SINCE MERSEYBEAT" — *THE BRADFORD BOOK*

"THE 1990 EVENT IS SERIOUSLY HAPPENING" — *CHRIS MAGUIRE*

Come along and see why 25,000 fans have voted CIRCUIT 22's NATIONAL BATTLE OF THE BANDS the best live music competition in the country.

VENUE: THE RIO, WOODHEAD ROAD, BRADFORD BD7 1PD (REAR OF UNIVERSITY) TEL. 0274 735549

BBC

This Bradford / Leeds band was formed in 1990. Their sound was influenced by the 1960s mod scene. They sent a demo to ex-Jam guitarist Paul Weller who thought it had *"plenty of atmosphere and vitality"*.

BBC (1990 -				
JOHN	SIMON	MATHEW	PAUL	DAVE
HILL	NORFOLK		SCHOFELD	FARRELL
Voc	Gtr	Dms	Gtr	Bass

During the fourth Bradford Festival, Iranian Hamid (a former radio DJ) opened a world music record shop in South Square, Thornton.

DJ LINDA

In July, DJ Linda Sprogis started her *Hellfire Club* discos on Thursday nights at the Function Centre, Salem Street (off Manor Row), then ran a second night on Fridays at the Peel Hotel as well as one-offs at The 1 In 12 Club and other venues.

Alternative disco venue

A NEW disco venue for 'alternative music' has been set up in Bradford by DJ Linda Sprogis called the Hellfire Club.

Linda, who has been DJ-ing in the city for nine years, started the free membership club at the Bradford Function Centre, Salem Street, Bradford, three weeks ago. The disco costs £1 to get in and goes on from 9pm-2am.

Linda said she has started the new venture because there was nowhere playing her type of music in discos in the area and she hoped music followers would support her and help it take off.

Linda was a regular DJ at lots of local gigs and had spells as resident DJ at many pubs and clubs throughout the '80s and '90s, including Benson's, The Spotted House, The Smithy, W's /The Basement.

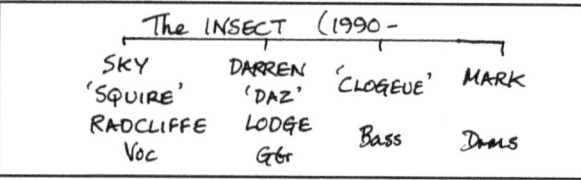

Between August 10-12, a series of free open-air events at Apperley Bridge playing fields were organised by the Heineken brewery.

THE APPLE MOTHS

Formed in the late 1980s by brothers Rick and Matty Bolton, this local Smiths-influenced jangle-pop band were heavily into rehearsing and recording. They only ever played one gig at Raw Nook Community Centre, Low Moor, supported by The Sheepskin Children but they did released a three track 7' EP, *Fred Astaire / Elvis / Miserable Town,* on the German label A Turntable Friend Records in November 1990.

BEDLAM

Rock/metal band Bedlam came together in December 1990 and quickly established themselves on the local metal circuit. The band played their first gig in 1991 at Queen's Hall. They soon produced a few demos, but unfortunately got no interest from

record companies. They put out the CD single *Dear Father* on their own label and were planning an album release. They toured the UK and Europe, including a 30-date tour of the Czech Republic, and also appeared on the late night Yorkshire Television programme *The James Whale Radio Show*.

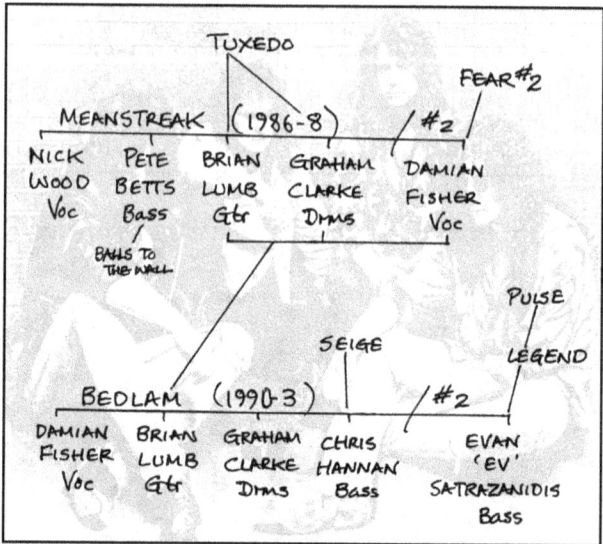

THE APPLE MOTHS / WINDY MILLS / IDIOT BOX

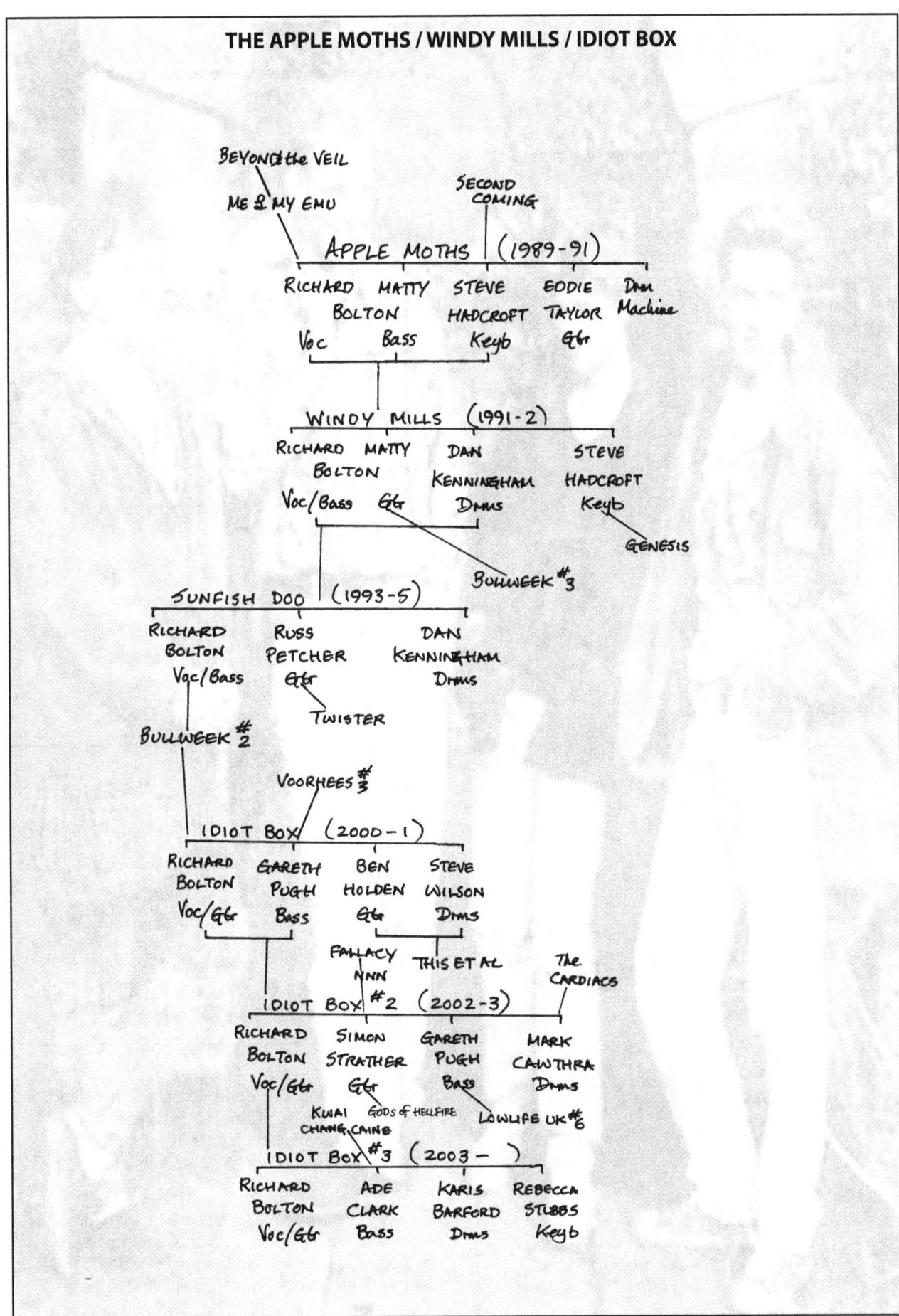

LOST PATROL

The three-piece Lost Patrol formed out of the ashes of The Candidates, a band influenced by Velvet Underground and Iggy Pop.

After a few lineup changes, the band's sound became a fusion of indie and dance with a mod influence.

"We are trying to push indie music to the forefront in Bradford, hot on the heels of local heroes Poppy Factory," said guitarist John Rhodes. (16)

The band were also known as The Liberty Ship under which name they recorded a cassette EP, *Spirit*, at In A City Studios featuring the tracks *Long Since Gone*, *Flowers*, *Ghost Of Shame*.

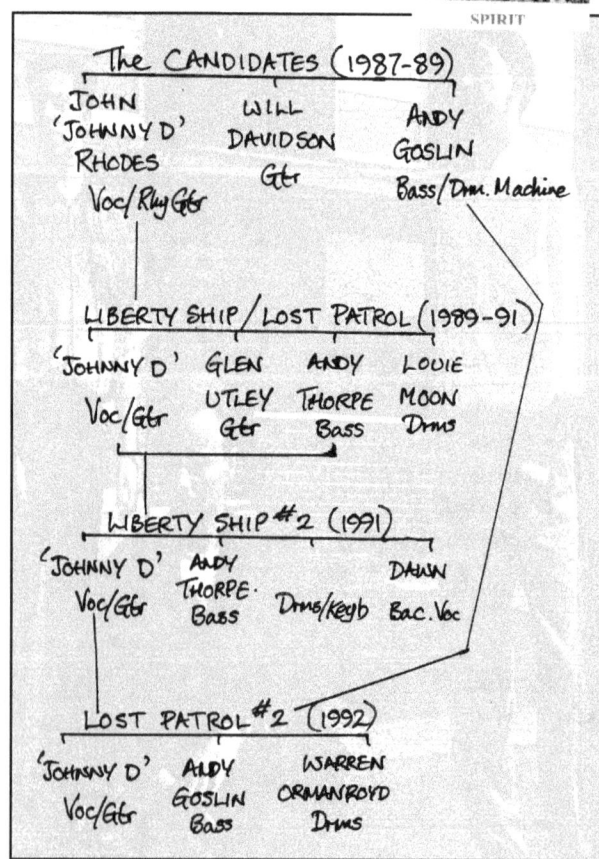

MR GIBLET

Local band Mr Giblet played the usual Bradford venues like Queen's Hall and the 1 In 12, they were later renamed Red Bead Game. Two members of the band went on to be two thirds of the trio Flange in 1993.

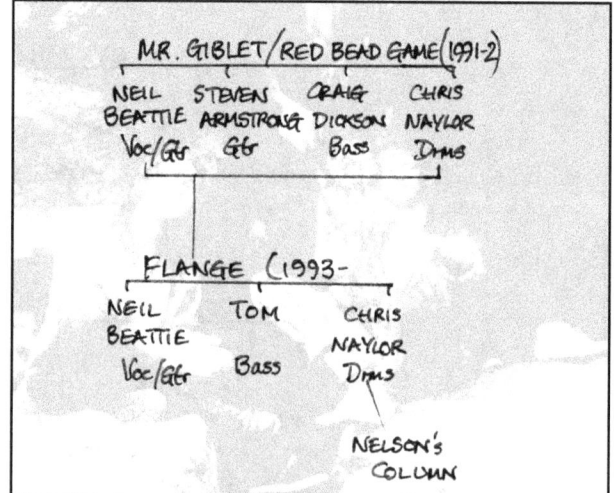

THE SCORE

Local indie band The Score featured Threshold Shift's Tony Fox on drums, Mick Daynes on keyboards/vocals, Jacko from The Le Fleur Brothers and guitar/vocals, and John Holland on bass.

They were only active for several months around 1991 and '92, dabbling with challenging covers and original material, and recorded a demo in 1992 featuring the tracks *Trust To Luck* and *Where I Wanna Be*.

CHAPTER 1 — 1988 - 1990

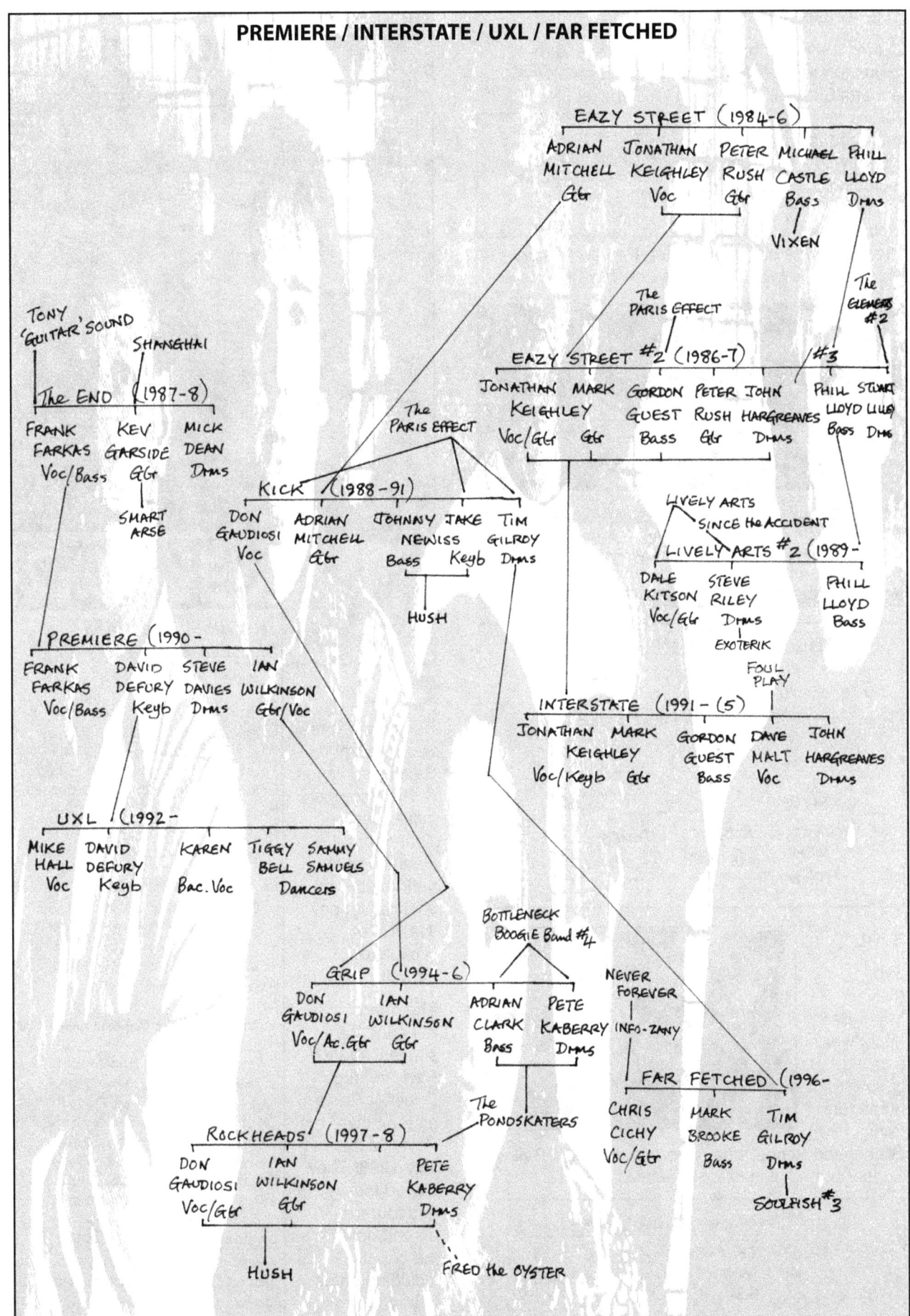

THE KEIGHLEY SCENE

During 1988-90, the Keighley music scene regrouped after the demise of the town's major exports Skeletal Family and The Shakes. New bands emerged to fill the void including the likes of Optic Nerve, Pregnant, Unsuitable Footwear, Premiere, Kick, Interstate, Rattlesnake Shake and The Big Bang.

OPTIC NERVE (1987-
STEVE 'PEE WEE' WILSON — Voc/Gtr
ANDY — Drms
PAUL INGHAM — Bass

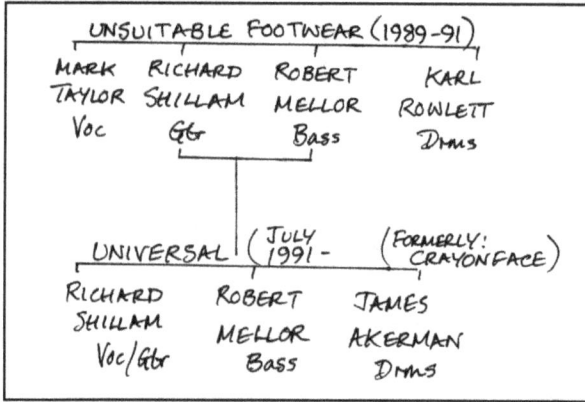

PREGNANT (1989-(91)
IAN GEDDES — Voc
SI LISTER
DAVID LYNCH
GEOFF TALLON

UNSUITABLE FOOTWEAR (1989-91)
MARK TAYLOR — Voc
RICHARD SHILLAM — Gtr
ROBERT MELLOR — Bass
KARL ROWLETT — Drms

UNIVERSAL (JULY 1991- (FORMERLY: CRAYON FACE)
RICHARD SHILLAM — Voc/Gtr
ROBERT MELLOR — Bass
JAMES AKERMAN — Drms

SYBL

Sybl (Seven Years Bad Luck) were a group of six teenagers from Greenhead School who performed in the TSB *Rock School* competition held in Leeds in 1988.

SYBL — SEVEN YEARS BAD LUCK (1988-
SARAH LANE — Voc
STEVEN BROOKS — Gtr
REBECCA HAWORTH — Bass
MATHEN LINK — Drms
GRAHAM CLARKE — Piano
DAMIEN MADDEN — Keyb

THUNDERING HEARTS

Blazing a trail on the Keighley scene were Georgia Satellites / Jason & The Scorchers influenced Thundering Hearts, led by their exuberant vocalist Johnny 'Nashville Hipshake' Gowcho.

The band released the 7' single *Caught Red Handed / Down At Rosie's* on their own Pole Kat label in July 1988. They played locally and toured up and down the country, including dates in London.

KERRANG!

THUNDERING HEARTS
Marquee, London
Sunday 28th, July

THE POIGNANT strains of Doris Day boomin' 'Whipcrack Away' are injected with the electric spurts an' tunings which tell you Bradford buckaroos Thundering Hearts are about to explode bareback onto the Marquee stage. Then YAA-HOO, they hit the ground cunnin', with the impact of Stormin' Norman pilotin' a nuclear bulldozer!

And there he was — sexier than legend and more legendary than sex — 'Hearts' front-rebel Notty Ash Windbreak (He means Nashville Hipshake - Long-Sufferin' Ed.) as the host with the most!

The boys in the band kick out somethin' bouncin' from the Quireboys to the Red Dogs to the Georgia Satellites while content to bathe in the glorious golden shower of their beloved General Smallville Earthquake! And just as I suspected, peroxide mop-topped Nash The Hip was a palpitatin', hip-gyratin' tough-nancy in the Jagger/Stewart mould. Dumb and brilliant (so too the band!).

RAY ZELL

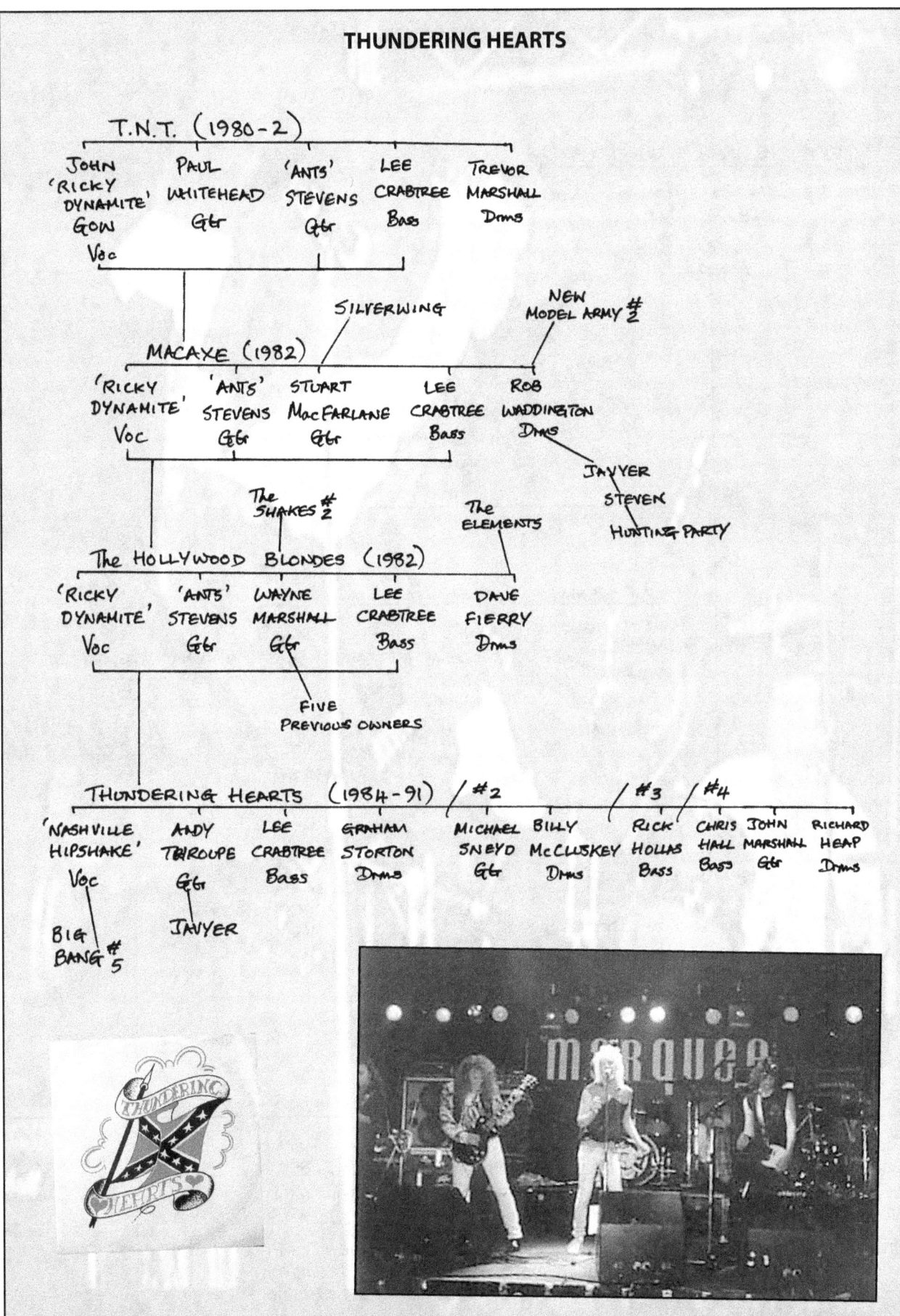

ASYLUM / RATTLESNAKE SHAKE

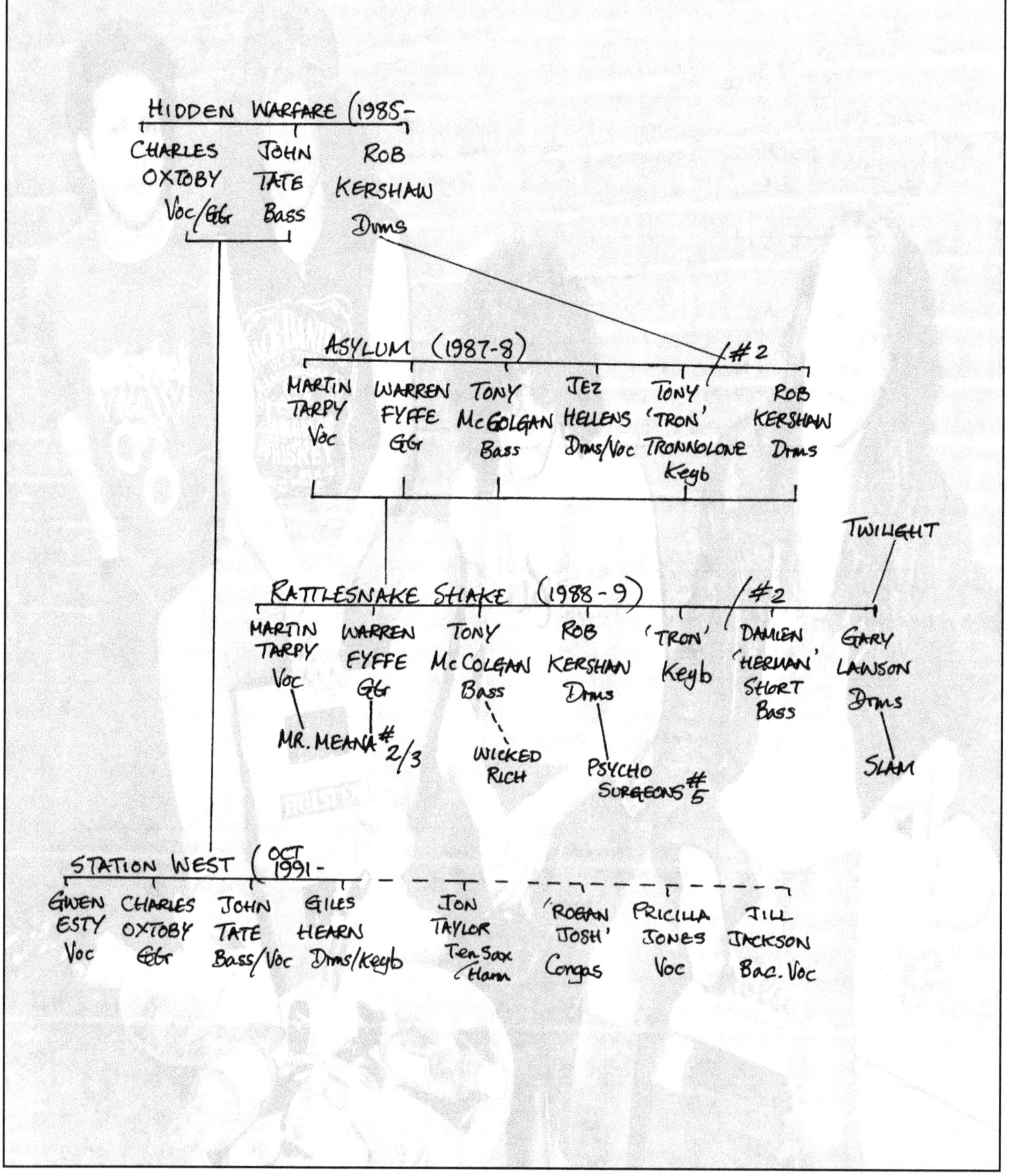

HIDDEN WARFARE (1985-
- CHARLES OXTOBY – Voc/Ggr
- JOHN TATE – Bass
- ROB KERSHAW – Drms

ASYLUM (1987-8)
- MARTIN TARPY – Voc
- WARREN FYFFE – Ggr
- TONY McGOLGAN – Bass
- JEZ HELLENS – Drms/Voc
- TONY 'TRON' TRONNOLONE – Keyb
- ROB KERSHAW – Drms (#2)

RATTLESNAKE SHAKE (1988-9)
- MARTIN TARPY – Voc → MR. MEANA #2/3
- WARREN FYFFE – Ggr
- TONY McCOLGAN – Bass → WICKED RICH
- ROB KERSHAW – Drms → PSYCHO SURGEONS #5
- 'TRON' – Keyb
- DAMIEN 'HERMAN' SHORT – Bass (#2) → TWILIGHT
- GARY LAWSON – Drms → SLAM

STATION WEST (OCT 1991-
- GWEN ESTY – Voc
- CHARLES OXTOBY – Ggr
- JOHN TATE – Bass/Voc
- GILES HEARN – Drms/Keyb
- JON TAYLOR – Ten Sax/Harm
- 'ROGAN JOSH' – Congas
- PRICILLA JONES – Voc
- JILL JACKSON – Bac. Voc

The Keighley Festival was held between August 13-21 1988 at Victoria Hall and Vickki's Bar. The week's gigs featured, amongst others, the local talents of Lively Arts, Hunting Party, Big Eyed Beans, Twice Around The Houses, Asylum and American Housewives.

On Wednesday, July 11 1990, NWOBHM heroes Saxon opened a new Our Price record store in Keighley where they signed copies of their new LP, *Rock'n'Roll Gypsies*. The band's first LP, *Saxon*, was produced and engineered by Bradford guitarist John Verity in 1979.

CHAPTER 1 — 1988 - 1990

THE BIG BANG

This Keighley-based band are a kind of local 'supergroup', made up of former members of various local bands which centred around Skeletal Family guitarist Stan Greenwood.

They emerged in 1988 and lasted until the 2010s, despite various line-up changes, playing a mix of covers and their own material.

They have self-released numerous tapes, CDs and videos of their live sets over the years as well as studio recordings.

Titles of the band's releases include *Fab*, *Wanna Try A Piece Buddy?*, and *Smell Your Budgie*.

The Big Bang were regular faces on the local music scene and have made many appearances at the Keighley Festival over the years.

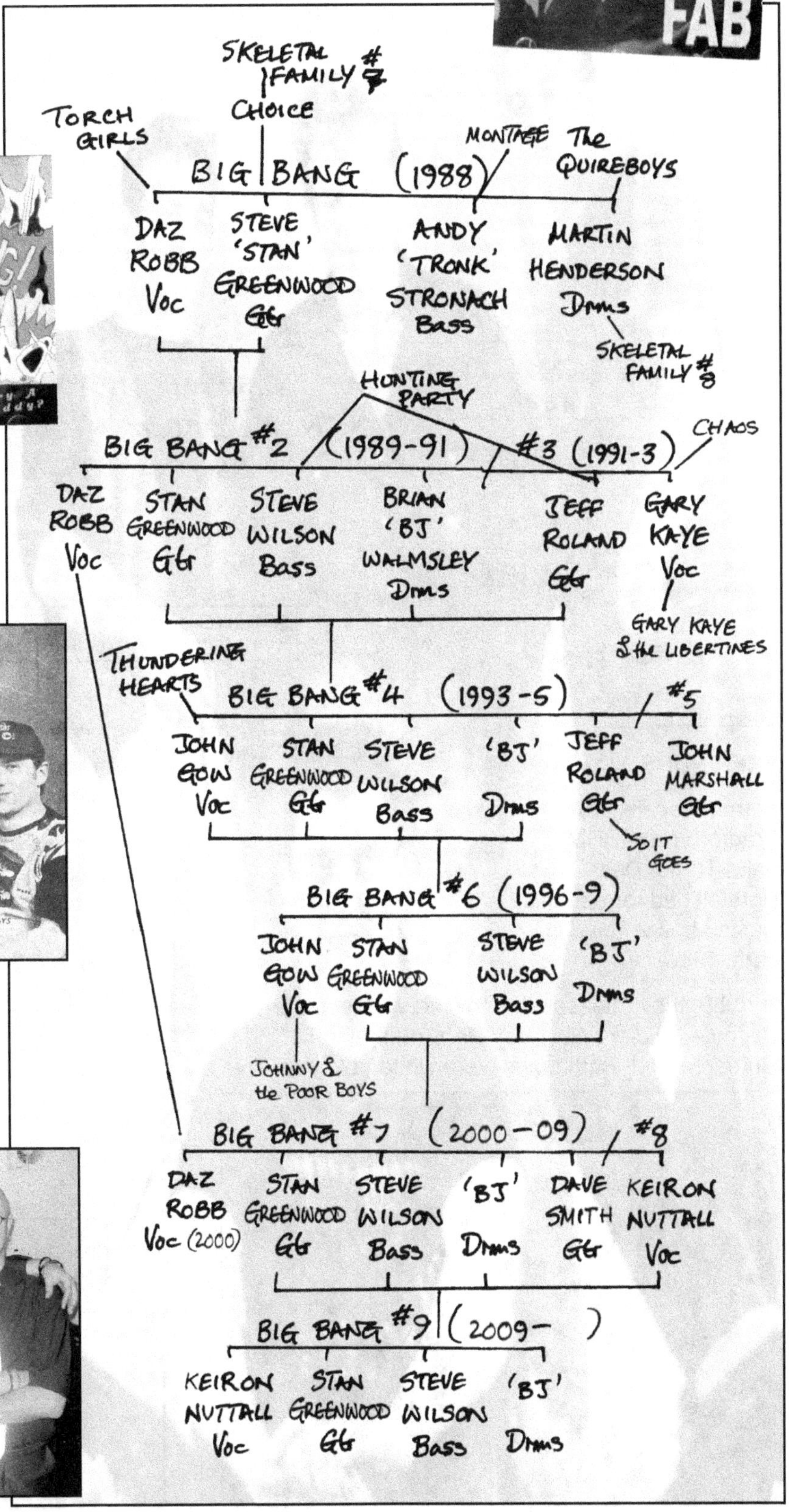

By 2013, the three longest-serving members, Stan Greenwood, Steve Wilson and BJ Walmsley had a combined time of 73 years in the band!

61

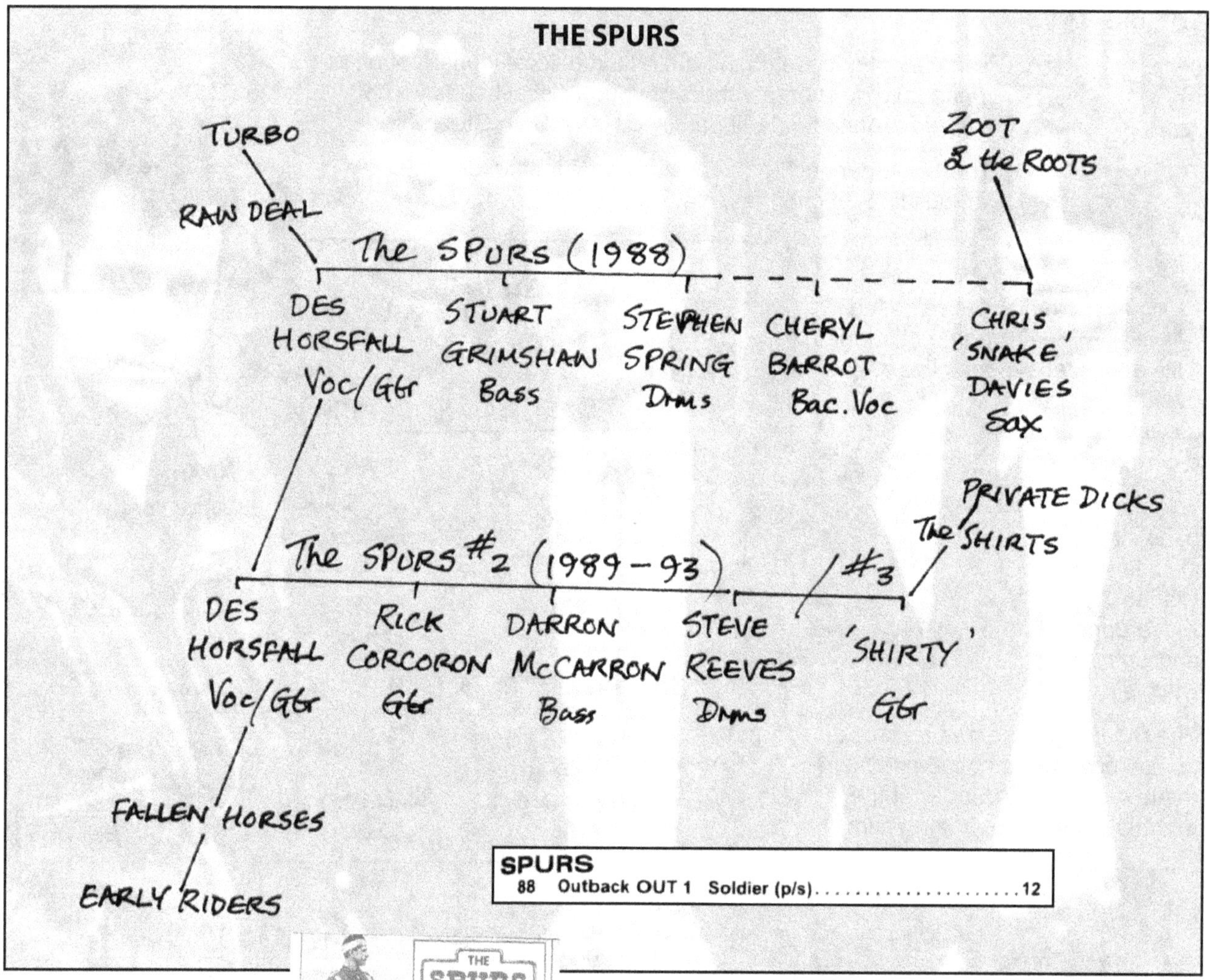

THE SPURS

```
TURBO
RAW DEAL                                                    ZOOT & the ROOTS
         \        The SPURS (1988)                         /
          ┌──────────┬──────────┬──────────┬──────────────┐
         DES      STUART     STEPHEN    CHERYL         CHRIS
       HORSFALL  GRIMSHAW    SPRING    BARROT         'SNAKE'
        Voc/Gtr   Bass        Drms    Bac.Voc         DAVIES
                                                       Sax

                                                    PRIVATE DICKS
                                                    The SHIRTS
          The SPURS #2 (1989-93)       /#3/
       ┌─────────┬─────────┬─────────┬─────────┐
        DES      RICK     DARRON    STEVE     'SHIRTY'
      HORSFALL CORCORON  McCARRON   REEVES      Gtr
       Voc/Gtr   Gtr      Bass      Drms
        /
    FALLEN HORSES
        /
    EARLY RIDERS
```

SPURS		
88	Outback OUT 1	Soldier (p/s) 12

THE SPURS

Former vocalist from Bradford NWOBHM band Turbo, Des Horsfall had formed this Halifax-based band in early 1988.

In 1989, they released the now very collectable 7' single *Soldier / Hey, Hey Baby* on their own Outback label. Both tunes were written by Des. The A-side featured a sax break by future M-People saxophonist 'Snake' Davies. (17)

The single was recorded with a group of Des's friends in the music world but that line-up was unable to tour. A completely different band trod the boards for their live shows, which included their support slot to Climax Blues Band at Queens Hall on March 3, 1989.

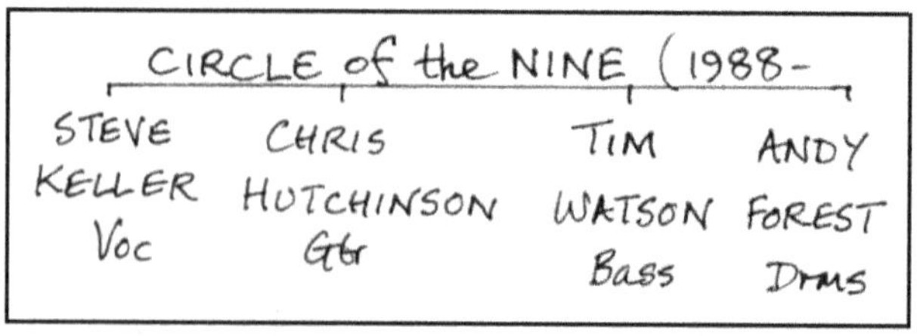

```
        CIRCLE of the NINE (1988-
   STEVE    CHRIS       TIM      ANDY
   KELLER  HUTCHINSON  WATSON   FOREST
    Voc      Gtr        Bass     Drms
```

Also around at this time were Halifax bands **Hx2** and goth band **Circle Of Nine**.

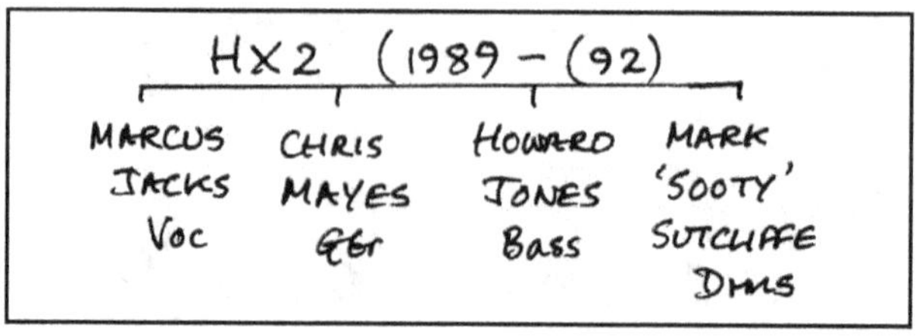

```
          HX2 (1989 - (92)
   MARCUS   CHRIS    HOWARD    MARK
   JACKS    MAYES    JONES    'SOOTY'
    Voc      Gtr      Bass    SUTCLIFFE
                               Drms
```

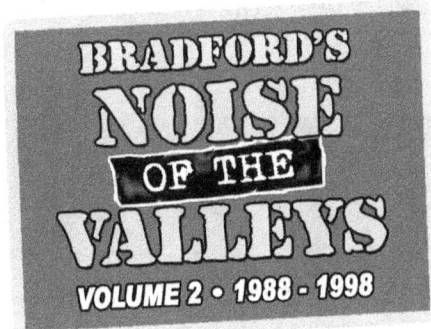

CHAPTER 2: THE 1 IN 12 CLUB 1988 - 1990

Clubs are an essential part of the lifeblood of any city or town's local music scene, so why should Bradford be any different? In the 1960s and '70s, the city had a range of commercial and self-run clubs who gave struggling local groups a platform to express themselves, like The Little Fat Black Pussycat Club, The Dungeon, The Coffin Club, String O'Beads, Jook Joint, The Gorgon, Argonaut, The Tavern In The Town Rock Club and The Princeville Rock Club.

> the little fat black pussy cat
> friday 11th september at 7.45
> straight from london's flamingo club
> **georgie fame and the blue flames**
> admission 6/- with membership card
> next week
> jimmy powell and the five dimensions

By the 1980s, virtually all of these were gone and the emerging young punk/new wave bands found it hard to get a gig locally or even organise one themselves. Made aware of this, after staging a few benefits, the local Claimant's Union decided to organise a regular weekly gig night at The Metropole Hotel on Sunbridge Road, which heralded the start of The 1 In 12 Club.

Since that beginning in April 1981, The 1 In 12 Club had staged over 300 gigs, benefits and festivals in its seven years of nomadic existence, moving from venue to venue, all the time galvanising the local music scene with the Club's principles of self-management and mutual aid, before if found it's own permanent venue.

21-23 ALBION STREET

When the Club negotiated a grant and bought a building in late 1985, it had taken inspiration from two Dutch venues - The Milkveg and the Emma squat in Amsterdam, both of which a group of members had visited and been inspired by their style of organisation and cultural freedom.

HANDYWOMAN, Gemma Stark, can rip a strip off most male plasterers.

The enterprising 18-year-old has been bowing and scraping at ceilings for only three months but already her plastering skills have been recognized from the dizzy heights of workman's ladders.

Professional plasterer, Paul Saxby, 22, from Keighley, rates her work very highly: "She's quicker at picking up the skills than the lads on the YTS he says, adding:

"She learnt plastering very quickly and she's an extremely pleasant and hard-working girl."

Gemma is a regular visitor of the One in Twelve Club, on Albion Street, where she developed her plastering skills. The club, which is a regular haunt of young people, is an old warehouse and in desperate need of renovation.

"We weren't able to get contractors so we were forced to do it ourselves. I got taught by Paul when he came to do our ceiling and started being his labourer." she said.

A satisfied customer in Huddersfield, Mrs Scott, won't have anyone touching her skirting-boards but Gemma.

The petite DIY entrepreneur is unemployed but with her good record she's hopeful about her job prospects.

Young jobless club together

TEAM: Sharing a drink and a chat

HARD-UP Bradford punks, anarchists and ordinary young jobless proved that where there's a will there's a way by opening their own club tailored to their own needs.

The 1 in 12 Club has been running since the early 80s in various venues in the city including the Metropole Hotel, Queens Hall and the Royal Standard, but now a new chapter is beginning with the move into their own building.

The dream of their own club has become a reality for the rag-tag bunch after they tapped into local and national government grants to help with the freehold of their £95,000 city centre building.

A team of volunteers has spent two years working on the new club headquarters in Albion Street where they have converted the dilapidated sweat shop into a venue where they can play their own music at prices which fit their own pockets.

And now they have two bars and a hall for concerts

by Jeremy Cooke

completed and are still working on top-floor workrooms and offices.

The members of the club make no secret of their political views — they are of the Left and proud of it. And people wanting to join the organisation will have to prove they can abide by the 1 in 12 philosophy.

As one founder member put it: "This is to be a an alternative social scene for those of us with little or no money. It is free from sexist, racist, statist hassles and from bouncer intimidation and violence and dress regulation. Anyone who can't get on with that will be asked to leave."

The young people of the 1 in 12 know that Bradford, like any other city, has a drugs problem.

But even with their libertarian views one rule which must be totally inflexible is No Drugs — and organisers reckon that means anyone smoking cannabis or high on anything else will be shown the door.

Another rule is that the 1 in 12 is a members club so punters wanting to attend gigs will have to sort out the paperwork at least two days before the event.

An opening night gig on Friday includes a strong West Yorkshire line-up with The Three Johns, Brendon Croker and the Five O'Clock Shadows and Little Brother.

Work on the Club's building took over two years and was undertaken by a dedicated core group of members plus hundreds of volunteers, local and from all over the country, some even moving to Bradford permanently.

Many members' skills in woodworking, painting and decorating, plastering and electrical know-how were utilised in renovating the four storey building as it was completely stripped, with floors removed and walls demolished then, with painstaking effort,

rebuilt to new specifications, incorporating all the recognisable fixtures and fittings you would expect in any social club.

Samuel Smith's Brewery in Tadcaster agreed to be the Club's brewery. They fixed the barrels and pumps in the cellar and installed the taps on the two bars, ready for opening.

The Club building would add to the existing collectives; for gig booking, records, publications and Solidarity Fund, with new maintenance and bar collectives, which meant the Club's first paid staff were Dave Groper and Gemma Stark as bar staff.

In late April 1988, The 1 In 12 Club celebrated its seventh birthday with a disco and membership enrolment night at Checkpoint. (1)

1 in 12 Club open — official

WITH poetic oratory, and the lightest sprinkling of pomp, 'Wild Willi Beckett', Bradford's decibel doctor, pronounced the 1 in 12's backstreet palace officially opened. It was, he said, a dream fleshed out. The central event of last Thursday's reception was the dedication of the main bar to the memory the Keith Campbell, a long-standing member who died last year at the untimely age of 23.

Pictured above is Keith's brother (right) presenting an Irish crystal bowl to Wild Willi on his and his parents' behalf in memory of Keith.

New centre for unemployed

BRADFORD'S famed 1 in 12 Club will shortly be opening it's new three storey club building after magistrates granted a one-year registration certificate last week.

The certificate was finally awarded after drawn out negotiations with police. Clarification of club rules about committee membership and general membership was achieved without 'compromising the club's intentions' said a club organiser.

The 1 in 12 building is expected to be opening in mid-June.

It has taken two years of concerted hard work and effort by club members to convert the three storied ex-textiles sweatshop into an all purpose music and social club.

Stripped down to a shell, the building's interior was redesigned, refitted and rebuilt by a core group of around 20 people using the technical skill of club members and the services of a builder employed to co-ordinate and train members.

The "1 in 12" grew out of Bradford Claimants Union in the early 80's, and after a number of years hiring venues for gigs and co-ordinating meetings, applications were made to the Department of the Environment and Bradford Metropolitan Council for grants to buy and rebuild a suitable building.

They were sucessful. £95,000 has secured the freehold for the city-centre building and paid for it's full internal rebuilding. Sam Smiths recently signed up as their beer suppliers and now people are invited to join what augers to be one of the area's prime venues.

The club's motivation is to be a social club for young, unemployed and working class people, to have fun, as one member said, in a "libertarian atmosphere".

The new club building, at 21/23 Albion Street, off Sunbridge Road (near Sunwin House) in Bradford's city-centre, (telephone Bradford 734160), has two bars, gig floor and an as yet unfinished top floor for workrooms and offices.

The 1 in 12 Club is a *members' club*, and it's organisers appeal to those interested to sign up as soon as possible. Yearly membership is £2 for low or unwaged, £5 for waged people. (Phone the above number for further details).

Meanwhile, work continued on completing the final stages of renovating the building and preparing for the opening. Despite ongoing financial worries, and the police opposing the registration certificate (Bar Licence), the building finally opened in the second week of June, with a members-only first night.

The 1 In 12 Club, which since 1983 had around 700-1,000 regular members, finally had its own premises.

The official opening and the first-ever gig was on June 17, featuring long-time stalwarts and supporters The Three Johns and local ranter/poet Little Brother. As one member commented, *"I walked down to the club on the opening night... I was stunned. It was actually working. All of a sudden it hit me, fuckin' hell we did it. And if the club closes down tomorrow, we still did it."* (2)

Around this time, 1 In 12 Publications produced a new book. *Against Democracy*, by Dirk Spig was a brilliant in-depth history of the

right-wing *Economic League*, who compiled and sold lists of trade unionists and left-wing activists to employers.

After the huge success of the first gig night, over the next few summer months, leading into autumn, a succession of local Bradford bands and others graced the stage on gig nights, including the band Bradford, Manchester's Vee VV, Rubella Ballet and, from the midlands, Giant Treads Clean. It also played host to the Nottingham band Every New Dead Ghost, Lincolnshire's The Hoverchairs, and old comrades The Ex from Holland (3), supported by Middlesbrough's Shrug, the Canadian band Rhythm Activism and the American band Die Kreuzen, from Milwaukee.

By October, Huddersfield's Another Cuba (formerly Dry Ice, pictured above) were playing, supported by the Club's own Pete The Poet, and, on October 27, there was a return gig for the Three Johns, who were promoting their latest LP, *The Death Of Everything*.

The Dirty Dozen

UNDER THE shadow of the skyline dominating Yorkshire Bank HQ, Bradford's edifice of credit and consumerism, musical and social independence has a new stronghold... the 1 In 12 Club.

It's seven years since the Rayner Report announced that one in 12 social security claimants were defrauding the state. There was a derisory snarl from the city's unamused and disenfranchised claimants, and the club was formed.

There's been seven years of flitting from pub to pub and weekly gigs giving Bradford the likes of Rubella Ballet, Poison Girls, Big Flame, a new born and native New Model Army, Leeds neighbours and stalwarts The Three Johns and Chumbawamba and Red Lorry Yellow Lorry.

There has been burning hot free Summer festivals and a catalogue of live compilations.

But with £95,000 extracted from local and central government, two years' sweat, muscle, thought and determination, the 1 In 12 now has it's own building and a rapidly swelling membership.

Housed in a slim, three-storied converted textiles factory, the club that refreshed West Yorkshire with indie vigor is back in business.

It's two gigs a week in Bradford's heartland, with advance bookings and a queue of bands for the Summer. Two bars and a gig floor, fresh paint and old furniture. It's a musical and social resource.

"Anything that requires four walls round it, we've got it," said Peg, a long serving member. "That's what it is here for."

The 1 In 12 Club is at 21/23 Albion Street, Bradford.

IAN CHEEK
SOUNDS July 16 1988

THE UK HARDCORE (UKHC) SCENE

The UK's underground hardcore punk scene had existed since the mid-1980s, inspired by the faster, harder and more metallic sounds emanating from US punk groups. British bands absorbed this crossover sound and created their own scene, setting up gigs, trading tapes, fanzines, forming record labels and organising distribution to mail order outlets and merchandise stalls at gigs.

Labels like Earache, Meantime, Loony Tunes, Peaceville, Manic Ears and Words of Warning released singles and albums that helped promote these bands. Sub-genres and offshoots emerged, like grindcore, stenchcore, doom, death, gothic, speed metal, emo and straight edge.

The Radio One DJ John Peel championed the scene by giving many bands sessions on his show. The international nature of the scene was covered by many US fanzines, most notably *Maximum Rock'n'Roll (MRR)*. (4)

The 1 In 12 had been putting on hardcore gigs for a number of years prior to the building opening and it continued to do so during those early gigs in 1988. Debauchary (pictured left) / Aural Corpse / Active Minds, Thatcher on Acid / Feed Your Head, all played in August, Shrapnel / Life Cycle, The Instigators / Sink, in September, then Doom / Insurrection, Hotalacio / 2000DS / Radio Mongolia and Decadence Within played during October.

PEACEVILLE

Peacevelle began life as a DIY tape label in Dewsbury in 1981 created by Paul 'Hammy' Halmshaw, one of the singers in Civilised Society and then drummer in The Instigators, both Huddersfield bands. The label's first release was a 7' flexi, *Will Evil Win*, featuring Civilised Society, Desecrator, Annihilated, and Lord Crucifier, in 1987.

The first few vinyl releases in 1987-88, started to move away from anarcho-punk towards a more metal-influenced type of hardcore punk, which incorporated the Doom, Thrash and Gothic metal sub-genres. Besides releases of bands like Deviated Instinct, Doom, Atavistic, Electro Hippies and Decadence Within, the label signed two Bradford bands Toranaga and Paradise Lost.

With its two sub-labels Deaf and Dreamtime,

Peaceville expanded and became one of the UK's leading extreme metal labels, including on its list of bands some of the world's most prominent modern doom metal artists; Autopsy, Darkthrone, Liverpool's Anathema (formed by the Cavanagh brothers) and Bradford's My Dying Bride.

Peaceville's logo changed to the star image around 1990, designed by 'Mid' of Deviated Instinct.

In 1995, due to being over-extended and owing the bank £20,000, a deal was struck with Music For Nations, effectively making Hammy lose total control of his own label. By 2006, Hammy had left the label following the label's sale to Snapper Music,. Peaceville continued as the home for My Dying Bride releases.

TORANAGA

Along with Slammer, this Bradford band were the premier local exponents of thrash metal. Formed in 1986, they released their debut LP *Bastard Ballads* on Peaceville in June 1988. This was after a successful BBC radio session for rock DJ Tommy Vance.

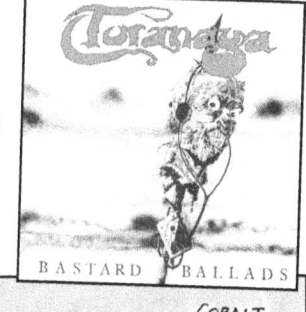

In March 1990, they signed to Chrysalis Records and released the single *Psychotic /The Shrine* and their second LP, *God's Gift*, followed by the EP *Beauty And The Beast* in 1991.

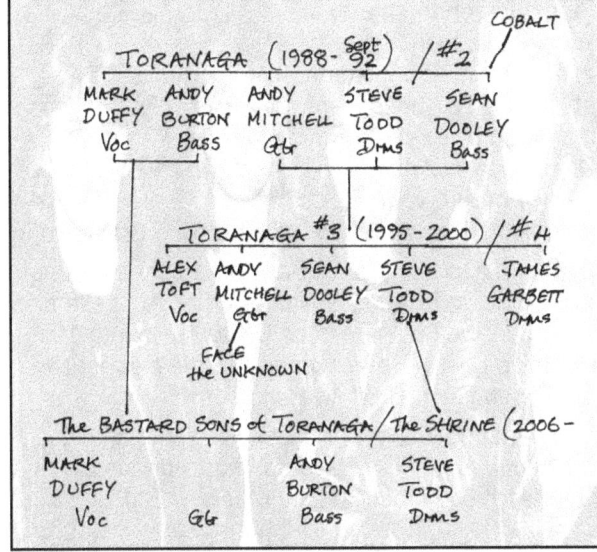

PARADISE LOST

This Bradford / Halifax band, formed in 1988, are one of the pioneers and best exponents of the sub-genre in the UK's gothic metal scene. They are Bradford's longest-surviving doom/death/gothic

metal act. An early signing to Peaceville Records, their first releases were the *Lost Paradise* LP/CD (Vile 15), in February 1990, and in April of the same year, the *In Dub* 12" EP (Vile 19T).

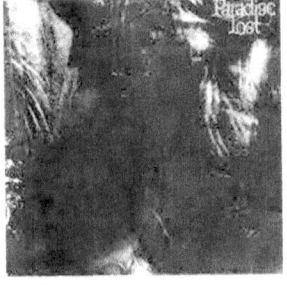

Their next release was the 1991 Gothic LP/CD (Vile 26), which was their last output for the Peaceville label. This album has become a classic, helping to put gothic metal into a range of styles in extreme metal circles worldwide.

The band then signed to the Music For Nations label for their next four albums, *Shades Of Gold* (1992), *Icon* (1993), *Draconian Times* (1995) and *One Second* (1997).

Icon and *Draconian Times* solidified the band's reputation on the metal scene, with Icon hitting the German album charts at No. 31. The band were managed by ex-Living Dead vocalist Andy Farrow of *Far North Music*

(later *Northern Music Co Ltd)*, based in Bradford.

By the mid to late 1990s, Paradise Lost had toured worldwide, in Europe, South America, Australia and Japan, as well as numerous UK tours. In late 1995, Paradise Lost were described as, *'the biggest UK metal band since Iron Maiden'*.

The band moved labels to EMI Electrola in Germany, then GUN Records, then signed with German metal label Century Media in 2007.

In 2008, to celebrate their 20th anniversary, they released the live DVD *The Anatomy Of Melancholy*, with key tracks covering their whole career. Bonus material on the DVD included a promo video of *The Enemy* (from their 11th LP, *In Requiem*), shot on location in the Crimea by avant-garde Russian director Edward 209.

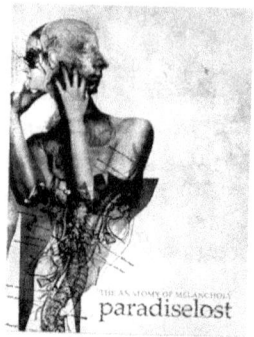

They topped the release off with two special shows in September, at the Bataclan in Paris on the 18th and the next day at the Forum in London, supported at both venues by fellow Bradfordians My Dying Bride and Liverpool's Anathema.

Paradise Lost were nominated in the *Metal Hammer Golden God*s award for 2008 Best UK Band.

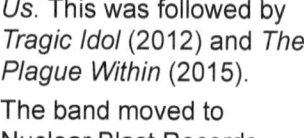

2009 saw the release of their twelfth album, *Faith Divides Us, Death Unites Us*. This was followed by *Tragic Idol* (2012) and *The Plague Within* (2015).

The band moved to Nuclear Blast Records for their next two albums *Medusa* (2017) and *Obsidian* (2020).

In 2023, the band decided to do a complete re-recording of their 1993 album, *Icon*, for its 30th anniversary. It was released, with new artwork, as *Icon 30*. They toured to promote the album with guests My Dying Bride.

Despite, in true Spinal Tap style, wearing out a succession of drummers, Paradise Lost's front foursome have remained unchanged since their formation.

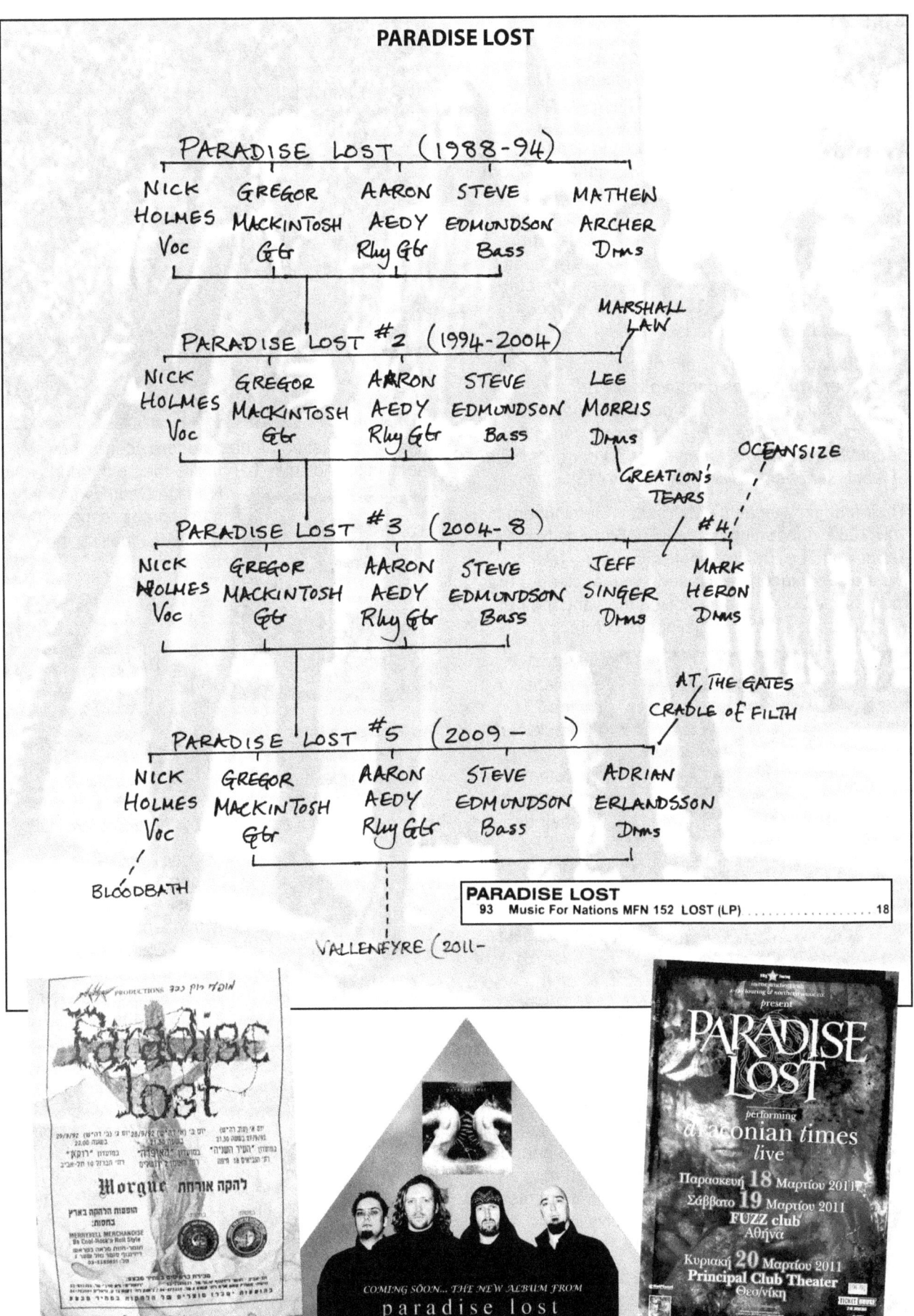

SORE THROAT

Formed by Huddersfield lads Rich Militia and Nick Royles with Bri and Jon from Birmingham's Doom, Sore Throat took their basic sound from the Japanese / Scandinavian punk scene and created their own type of noise.

As Rich and Jon said, '..*their objective was to piss off as many people as possible while drinking as much scrumpy (cider) as possible... become a vehicle for all of us to freely annoy and insult people/bands while still remaining, in our own minds at least, seriously political to the core*' (5)

Their first gig was at the Mermaid in Birmingham in July 1987, supporting Bolthrower, Extreme Noise Terror and The Electro Hippies, playing a twenty minute set of incoherent fast-noise that cleared the room of the 200 punters but won the band the bet with the bar staff for two gallons of scrumpy.

14. SORE THROAT
'Death To Capitalist Hardcore'
(Acid Rain 1987)

It's fitting to hoist these scallywags onto the podium of grindcore-in-*excelsis* on the strength of a Xeroxed bootleg – the original pressing was limited to 1,000. But 'Death...' was an explicit ejaculation of crusty spite, training an erratic crosshair on rapists and the US government, while sluicing some bile in the direction of DRI and Suicidal Tendencies in the fashion of an irreverent 'Scum'. [JHo]

After releasing the 27 track *Aural Butchery* demo, they recorded their debut 7" EP single, the 44-track *Death To Capitalist Hardcore*, on the Acid Rain label at Leeds' Lion Studios in 1988.

The band's sound would be dubbed 'grindcore'; a mix of hardcore punk with a metallic gore, speed and distortion, with the savage gnarled sound of screaming, yelling, growls, gargles and abusive vocal delivery.

By 1988, three-quarters of the band (Rich, Nick and Bri) were based in Bradford and were all heavily involved with activities at The 1 In 12 Club. When Nick left to form Withstand, in stepped Hammy, formerly of the Instigators, on drums.

Hating what they saw as the commercialisation of the hardcore scene, they mercilessly ridiculed bands like their old friends Napalm Death, with the music press (especially the *NME*) fuelling the feud.

As Rich said later, '*Looking back, it was a load of bollocks really, and it got blown out of proportion. But it fizzled out by the end of the '80s.*' (6)

During 1988-89, they released three albums; *Unhindered By Talent*, on the Darlington label Meantime, run by Ian of Sofa Head, the benefit album for the 1 In 12, *Disgrace To The Corpse Of Sid,* on the Earache label, and the concept album, *Inde$troy* (as Saw Throat), on Manic Ears.

By the end of 1990, the band had split with each member moving on to other projects, but still leaving an influential legacy on the UKHC scene, and their 7"/LPs and t-shirts are still being bootlegged today.

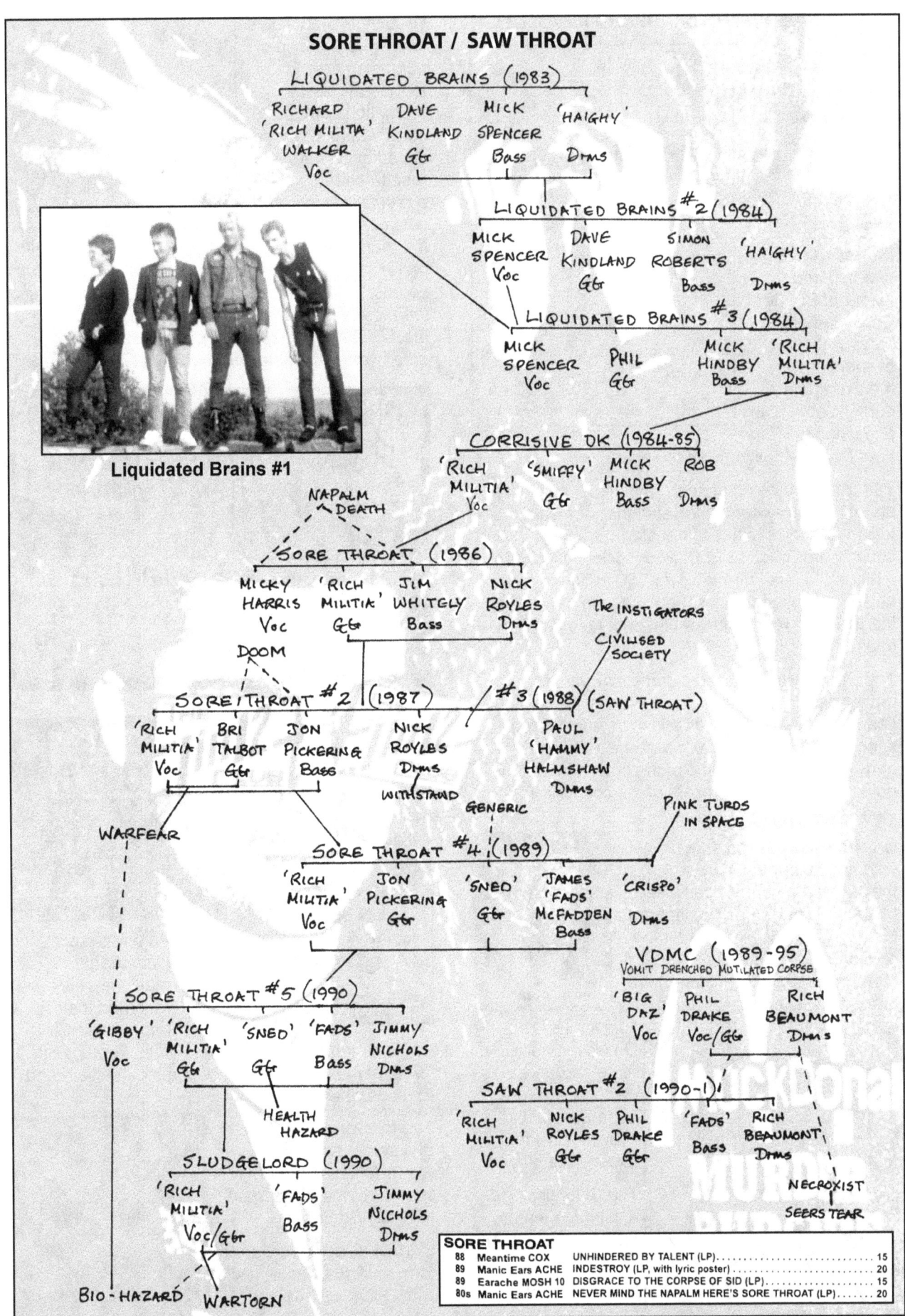

ERIC PICKLES & THE BRADFORD REVOLUTION

In late October, the Club's publications collective issued a free double-sided A4 KDIS Special Bulletin entitled *The Secret Life of Eric Pickles*. Pickles had become leader of Bradford Council after the Torys won two by-elections in the Odsal ward during September and using the Tory Lord Mayor's casting vote to secure victory.

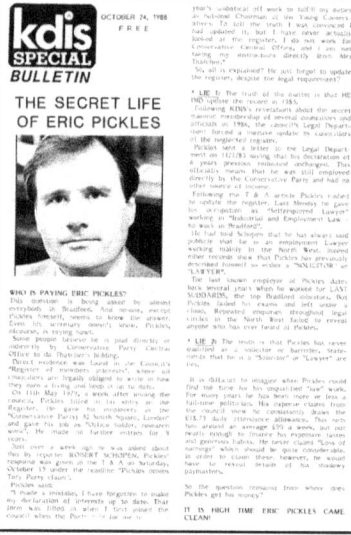

With Bradford being the only large inner city to fall under local Tory control, revelations soon came to light of radical plans to transform Bradford council into Bradford PLC. Eric Pickles, as leader, intended to push through over £50 million in cuts and privatisation policies, heralding the dawn of the Bradford Revolution, a blueprint for every Tory council in the land.

The Special Bulletin asked some awkward and embarrassing questions about Pickles' personal finances and his status as a lawyer. Another four special bulletins would follow in late 1988 and early 1989, profiling some of the other scandalous goings-on of other members of the council's Tory leadership. (7)

On November 2, The 1 In 12 Club went truly international when the Japanese band Rose Rose played, supported by Nottingham's Heresy. The following night, the original guitarist of Hawkwind, Huw Lloyd-Langton (pictured), graced the Club's stage doing a solo acoustic set. On November 9 more hardcore was on show as Generic / The Next World / Joyce McKinney Experience played.

The Club also had a full-page feature article in *Maximum Rock'N'Roll* magazine that month.

Within the Club at this time were a bunch of punk members who formed their own promotions group, *Metal Faeces*, whose stated aims were to *"put on cheap gigs on a regular basis. Bands who offer more than the third rate-heavy metal and vacuous right-wing capitalistic crap that seems to make up much of the hardcore scene at the moment. We make no profit, and all the money made over band expenses goes to the 1 In 12 or other worthy causes. Our music, get involved."* (8)

Club members Kev and John

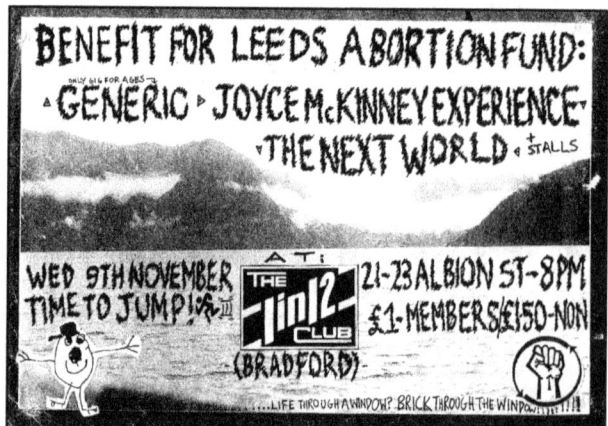

THE NEXT WORLD

Brothers Steve Roue and Darron Ward moved to Bradford from Kettering to help work on the 1 In 12 building, then settled here.

As a two-piece (with drum machine), they recorded their debut three-track single *Branded / Public Order / Safe Territories* in 1988, at In A City Studios, becoming the first band to record there.

The following year, they released their LP *Resurgence*, again on Bradford Music, recorded In A City Studios.

In 1994, Steve and Darron formed Virtual Reality (VR) with Doom's Bri Talbot.

On reading about the Gilman street project in S.F., we here in Bradford, West Yorkshire thought you might be interested in hearing about a similar project to Gilman street, which is only now coming to fruition after several years hard work. The 1 in 12 club (named after a government report that stated that '1 in 12 dole claimants were defrauding the state) was set up by members of Bradford claimants union and others as a collective (based loosley on anarchi principles) with the aim of providing an alternative social scene for those of us with little money, free from sexist, racist, statist hassle, bouncer hassle, violence and dress regulation. Sure, a lot of 1 in 12 club members are anarchist punks into hardcore, but there are different interests represented within the club musically, culturally and politically (to a certain extent). The one uniting factor is a desire to control the way we enjoy ourselves, seeing as so much has been taken away from us and handed back at a high price. For nearly 7 years the 1 in 12 club has been putting on gigs regular fearturing mostly independent bands, all of whom have to conform to our standards—no racist, sexist rockstar shit. We keep entry prices down, it was one pound (70p for members) to see BGK last year, and this is possible because we have our own PA System. And now we have our own center, a converted four story factory in Bradford's city center. It has a bar, a gig room and we hope to expand to accomadate other political and social activities. Like Gilman, the building has been converted mostly through the voluntary efforts of club members (except specialist jobs). The whole project been financnd by the then Tory (extreme right wing) Bradford council (they got the wrong end of the stick when we talked about 'Self management').

Hopefully, the 1 in 12 will provide a focal point for the currently fragmented counter culture in West Yorkshire, and break down a lot of barriers that exist between the little cliques that have formed (even in the 'Punk/Hardcore' 'scene') due to the lack of any central meeting point.

The practical problems have been and still are immense, money being a factor. Also, trying to get people involved in doing something that is inevitably in their own interest instead of sitting around and waiting for other people to do things for them and then moaning about how shit everything is when nothing happens. The club aims to have no elite hierachy or leaders, but this of course could happen if people let others do all the work and just consume.

Like I said, the club is run on a collective basis and tasks are alloted to smaller collectives which are open to all members. We have a building collective and in the past had a record/publishing collective (which may be revived). There is also a solidarity fund. All these different groups came together at weekly Sunday meetings open to all members where administrative details are thrashed out and issues concerning the club and other social/political activities are bough up for discussion. If you live in the area or are just passing through come and visit us or get involved. Also any foreig bands (especially hardcore bands who aren't capitalist wankers) interested in playing here get in touch.

The 1 In 12 Club/ 21-23 Albion St (off Sunbridge Rd)/ Bradford, West Yorkshire/ BD1 2LY England/ telephone # Bradford 734 160)

LIBERTY EQUALITY SOLIDARITY

Review from Maximum Rock'N'Roll magazine, November 1988

KAGE ENGINEERING

Kage Engineering were a five-piece band from Skipton who appeared at the Club a couple of times in the early years.

In 1988, they released the five-track *Flight* 12-inch on their own Ascension label. They also were featured on two compilation LPs, *1988's Grit In The Oyster* and a 1991 The Clash tribute album covering *Charlie Don't Surf*.

KAGE ENGINEERING (1988 – (90)
K   GRAHAM
BINNER   SHAW   SADDINGTON

A packed end-of-year monthly gig roster kicked off with the UK Subs and Dutch band Neuroot supported by Default (right).

Then a gig featuring HDQ / Pleasant Valley Children / The Abs / Incest Brothers, a triple bill of The Instigators (again) / Mega City Four / Vee VV (again), Archbishop Kebab / The Hoverchairs (again) and to see the year out, a special Xmas show on the 23rd by Danbert Nobacon with Chumbawamba.

WORLD EVENTS 1989

The year 1989 would become a tumultuous one, as events unfolded leading to shocking re-alignments in international relations that would change the world forever and begin the process of creating a new world order.

The publication of Salman Rushdie's novel *The Satanic Verses* (a fictitious account of the sexuality of the Prophet Muhammed and his wives) trod on the most sensitive areas of the Qur'an and enraged large numbers of British Muslims, some of whom exploded with rage onto the streets of many cities, demanding the book be withdrawn and claiming that it was blasphemous.

In Bradford on January 14, a large group of local Muslim protesters burnt a copy of Rushdie's book in front of the law courts, fuelling the controversy further within the international media's spotlights. Photo images of the burning were beamed around the world. By February 14, Iran's Ayatollah Khomenimi had issued a 'fatwa' (death sentence) on Rushdie which still stands to this day. (9)

Between 3-8 June, 1989, in Beijing, China, the army cracked down on millions of pro-democracy protesters in Tiananmen Square who were pleading their communist leaders for change.

The most enduring image shown to the world was of the lone man (nowadays dubbed 'Tank Man') who stood in front of a line of tanks.

During the protest the Chinese army massacred an estimated 7,000 unarmed citizens.

FULTON STREET STUDIOS

On the street adjacent to The 1 In 12 Club, a brand new recording studio opened. Fulton Street Recording Studios was run by Dave Culling, the former keyboardist of Psychic Wardrobe / Karma Rouge. It soon became like a second home to many bands based in and around the 1 In 12, as over the next few years, they would use Dave's facilities to make demos, record material for release or simply rehearse.

Dave had self-built the studio and sunk most of his redundancy money into the business and, although it was a little cramped, it was very cosy. On many gig nights, when the Club's PA members needed an extra microphone or two, they could be seen scuttling across to the studio through the arch to borrow one.

During the first months of 1989, the Club was putting on around two to three gigs a week, as well as disco nights and a regular pop quiz night every Thursday. A team from the Club would soon join the Airedale Quiz League and bring honour and trophies to the 1 In 12 for many a year.

Because it would be too lengthy to list every single gig, from now on we will only highlight key or very important ones, a full list can be obtained elsewhere. (10)

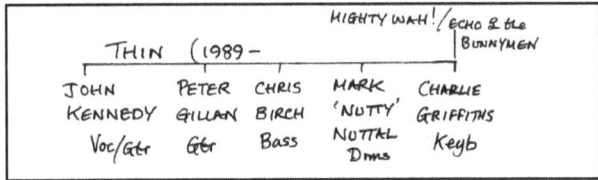

A series of Halifax-based bands came to play who were linked to a venue there called The Return Club. These included; Thin, Broadcast - all Bradford College students, and Inky Pig who included former members of Chinese Gangster Element. (11)

Other notable gigs were Leeds indie band Greenhouse, The Attic (below), from Pudsey, who played a couple of times, Harlow's ranting poet Attila the Stockbroker, Hull's Pink Noise and Planet Wilson (ex-Red Guitars), and Sheffield's The Honkies.

Another Hull band, Penny Candles, led by original Housemartins drummer Hugh Whittaker, also played the 1 In 12 twice that year.

On the punk/hardcore front the Club hosted gigs by Thatcher on Acid, Edinburgh group Political Asylum (12), Leeds band Nerverack, Active Minds (again), PVC, Dog Faced Hermans, Thrilled Skinny (again), Senseless Things, the Dutch band Vernon Walters, HDQ, from Germany Pullerman, Blyth Power, Darlington's Sofa Head, City Indians and the notorious punk band The Exploited in early June.

In June, the 1 In 12 had a visit from the scouse band The Farm (pictured above), who were linked to the newly emerging but short-lived 'Madchester' scene. The dominant look for this scene was the football/casual street look and the music a mix of pop, rock and rave / Acid house. The Farm would go on to have two top ten hits in 1990, *Groovy Train*, No 6 in September, and the anthem *All Together Now* No 4 in December. Two of the most important bands on this scene were The Happy Mondays and The Stone Roses. (13)

On July 21, local band Zed were supported at the Club by Carter The Unstoppable Sex Machine, who then came back on November 3 to headline with support from local boys The Wonderful Thing Called Tiddles. Carter USM played their next gig in Bradford at Queens Hall in February 1991 promoting their *Something* LP on Island Records.

THE WONDERFUL THING CALLED TIDDLES

Formed in 1989, this trio were led by vocalist Mick Cartledge, who had been in a few indie/goth bands in the early 1980s. The band played the Club a few times in 1989 and produced a demo which they sent

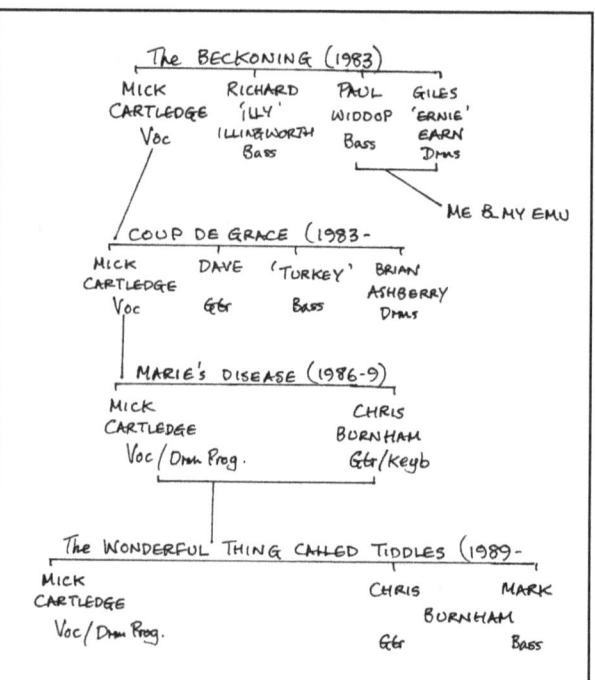

to Neneh Cherry due to having covered her No 3 hit *Buffalo Stance*. She wrote back to the band saying she loved their version. (14)

The 1 In 12 Club gig room

VOLNITZA

WORST OF THE 1 IN 12 CLUB VOLUME 6/7

At the end of June 1989, the 1 In 12 Record Collective released the Club's first LP showcasing bands who had played at their Albion Street home. *Volnitza* (15) was a double album which featured 29 bands and artists who had played the Club between June and December 1988.

The album had a gatefold sleeve and included an A4 booklet with band's artwork and inner sleeve notes were written by Boff of Chumbawamba. It was edited at Fulton Street Studios and cut at Porky's in London.

Volnitza contained tracks by Bradford based bands; Old Joe Zydeco, The Next World, Western Dance, Seven Antelopes, Heart of Darkness (pictured right), The Everly Sisters, Kage Engineering and Sore Throat, whose epic twenty-second ditty *Eric Pickles Is A Fat Tory Bastard* caused much consternation with the local council leader. (16)

Copies of the LP were sent out via mail order to various countries in Europe, also Japan, USA and Ukraine. The LP sold out within months, probably due to airplay on John Peel's radio show (he played The Hoverchairs track on July 12) and positive reviews in *Sounds*, *House Of Dolls* #23, *MRR* and Ben Sick 'o' War's *Raisin' Hell* #21.

VARIOUS
'Volnitza – Worst Of The 1 In 12 Club Vol 6/7'
(1 In 12 12006/7) ***½

BY THEIR nature most compilations suffer to a degree from incestuous affinity, inherent fabrication and mediocrity. 'Volnitza', while far from perfect, is guilty only of the latter.

Released by Bradford's 1 In 12 Club and featuring 29 bands over four sides, 'Volnitza' opens with Shrug's 'Fear And Violence', a haunting keyboard affair. The Whiskey Priests follow with the furious, accordion-driven, beauty of 'Shut Down The Wagon Works', while PMT and Thrilled Skinny offer frenetic rushes with 'Video Monster' and 'Tec Buff'.

Elsewhere, admirable efforts come from Seven Antelopes, Kage Engineering (who sing in German... curious, since they come from Skipton!), Vatican Shotgun Scare and the quirky Volunteers.

Redressing the balance somewhat are the mildly annoying Giant Treads Clean, the punk-by-numbers tedium of Default and the 20 seconds of noise that constitutes Sore Throat's 'Eric Pickles Is A Fat Tory Bastard' (come on lads, say what you mean).

Unremarkable in places, inspiring in others, 'Volnitza' has the courage to marry the onslaught of Doom with the melodic charm of The Everly Sisters and, for that at least, it's worth your time.

IAN CHEEK
SOUNDS August 26 1989

V/A - "Volnitza - The Worst of the '1 in 12' Club" 2LP

Tracks by THIS PERFECT DAY, SHRUG, DOOM, PRE-MENSTRUAL TENSION, and the great THRILLED SKINNY highlight this varied effort from the '1 in 12 Club" UK music collective. The best songs range from punk to thrash, but mid-tempo post-punk predominates. (SS)

VARIOUS "Volnitza-Worst Of The 1 In 12 Club Vol 6/7"double LP-With a double LP including 29 bands who've played at the 1 in 12 over the last year or 2 its bound to be pretty varied.Theres stuff on here from punk bands,thrash bands,crappy pop bands,predictable goth bands,merry Irish type jiggs,studenty indie type bands and a whole fuck of a lot more that would be impossible to go into detail about here.Theres just over one side of punky stuff and no doubt theres something on here for everybody,it also co mes with a booklet.

SORE THROAT/THE HOVERCHAIRS
Bradford 1 In 12 Club

THRUST MERCILESSLY before a Sore Throat audience in Bradford's hardcore headquarters, Scunthorpe's Hoverchairs were always going to wish they'd stayed at home.

Their breezy, reverberating guitar harmonies may well flourish in a more accommodating venue, but here they were met only by indifference. Leaning at times towards Wedding Present-style cacophony, they quickly secured my vote but sarcastic calls for an encore shortly after they appeared didn't help morale.

Later, the current animosity between certain hardcore factions – not least Napalm Death and Sore Throat – were charmingly put in their own ridiculous context when the mother of Throat vocalist Rich Militia confided to me how proud she was of her little Richard. In fact, the nearest we came to actual physical contact was when one irate customer alleged the raffle had been fixed.

Sore Throat's anticipated and much-vaunted pummelling attacks never fully materialised, while their staccato bursts of mayhem were too few to ever be enthralling. But their slower, Swans-like rhythms showed a far more stimulating, confrontational side to their psyche, and their brooding cover of Black Sabbath's 'Iron Man' dispelled a few more preconceptions.

Until petty wrangling is cast aside, the hardcore scene will remain its own worst enemy. A band like Sore Throat, with their horizons forever broadening and their vision clearly unclouded, are its hope.

IAN CHEEK
SOUNDS   July 29 1989

1 in 12 Klub

Ezt a klubot néhány elszánt zenélni és politizálni egyaránt szerető fiatal alapította 1981-ben az angliai Leeds közelében lévő Bradfordban. Az alapelv egyszerű volt: olyan klubot kell csinálni, ahol minden olcsó és ahol mindent szabad csinálni, érdekes és jó élő zene mellett. A klub hamarosan igen népszerű lett. 1983-ban már több, mint ezer tagja volt. Végre egy klub, amely a hét 6 napján nyitva áll, a belépti díj mindössze két és fél font és sok jó zenét lehet hallani szép felsőkéntjét!

Tulajdonképpen már a klub alapításakor felmerült az a gondolat, hogy kazettaválogatásokat adjanak ki a fellépő legkeresebb számaikból. [...] Worst Of The 1 in 12 Club lett a címe arra, hogy ebből a klubból "minden szép" zenét játszó. Ezen mindenem albumhall is saját zenekarunk is, a rendes fejes, zenekarok...

The album *Volnitza* was launched at the 1 In 12, with a few promotional gigs during July and August, and one gig received another fine review from Ian Cheek in the national music magazine *Sounds* and a review in a Hungarian magazine.

THE PICKLES PAPERS

In August, The 1 In 12 Club produced its fourth publication. *The Pickles Papers* by Tony Grogan is an intriguing tale of Eric Pickles's rise to power in the local council. The book was mentioned in Parliament by local Bradford MPs, and Mr Pickles sought legal advice with a mind to halt publication.

T&A, Saturday August 5, 1989

Song strikes wrong note with Pickles

BRADFORD Council leader Eric Pickles is becoming a big name on the underground music scene.

by DAVID FORD
T & A Rock On writer

A controversial song about the Conservative group leader is featured on a new compilation album being distributed all over the world by a Bradford nightclub.

The title of the song, by Bradford-based hard core thrash rock band Sore Throat, is unprintable.

Coun Pickles said today he was unlikely to take any legal action against Sore Throat or the record label because they had little or no money to pay any damages.

He said: "It is the work of a bunch of eccentric weirdos. The title of the song is just a gratuitous insult — and no doubt the LP will flop as all their other stuff has done in the past."

The specially recorded song, which has no decipherable lyrics and lasts for just 22 seconds, is one of the tracks on an LP put together by The 1 in 12 Club Records, a co-operative label based in Albion Street, Bradford.

Album tracks have already been played on John Peel's evening show on Radio One.

Backwards

Orders for the £7 double-LP, called The Worst of The 1 in 12 Club Volume 6/7 — Volnitza, which means Free Life in Russian, have been received from as far away as Poland and Japan. A booklet accompanying the record includes a photocopied picture of Coun Pickles with £-signs instead of eyes.

Sore Throat vocalist Eddie Cochran said: "There are lyrics on the song, but we recorded them backwards.

"Hopefully the moral majority will find them if they play the record the right way."

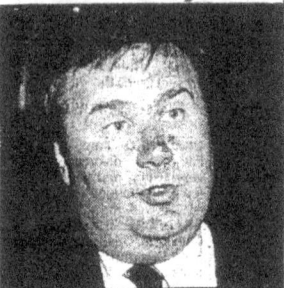

INSULT: Coun Eric Pickles

More hardcore gigs during August and September featured Slum Turkeys (pictured below), Chaos UK and Japanese band Gauze, Scotland's Oi Polloi (their first gig in a long association with the Club), Satanic Malfunctions / Paradox UK and an all-dayer on September 2. Also in September, Irish band Pink Turds in Space, Snuff / Wat Tyler / Sofa Head, Filler with Chicago band Spongetunnel and another Irish band Fual / Sledgehammer / Crow People on the 28th.

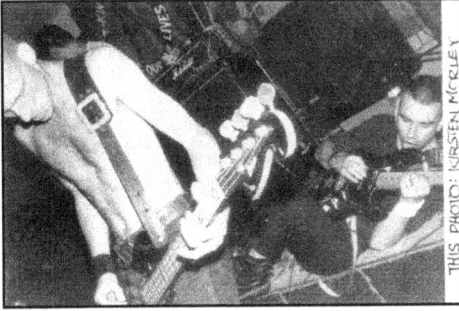

1989s Bradford Festival held a series of gigs at The 1 In 12 in September, starting with Post-Glasnost / Dickie Bards (who had played in April) and Suitcase Circus on the 14th, two 'gay' bands, Leeds' Fartown Fruits / Shades Of Pink on the 15th. On the 16th there was a 12 hour all day indie extravaganza with many local acts, such as Frontrunner, Anorexia, Trashtown, Warfear, Sad Cyprus, Call Me Legion, Proud Flesh, The Undecided, Pete The Poet, Chris & Mary, all compared by Psycho Surgeons frontman and 1 In 12 chairman Wild Willi Beckett. The Hogwash Theatre Co supported by Danbert Nobacon (pictured) provided the entertainment on the 17th.

Between October and December '89, the Club put on around 28 gigs that were a mix of hardcore, folk, indie-pop and ska. Key gigs in October were Doom / Next World, Fudge Tunnel / Nerverack, the second visit of Dutch comrades The Ex with Houndgod / Pete The Poet and London friends and Club stalwarts Rubella Ballet / M4Alice.

Also that month, local heroes The East (formerly Boys From The East), The Clearing / Greenhouse (again) and the London-based guitar-pop quartet Bob, who had an indie hit single *Esmerelda Brooklyn* at No 12 at the time.

In November, gigs by Attila The Stockbroker (the book, *Cautionary Tales From Dead Commuters*, co-authored with Seething Wells, came out around this time) with support from ex-Adverts frontman TV Smith's Cheap, the second appearance of Chaos UK on the 11th, and on the 15th, Trottle (from Hungary) / Saw Throat / Slum Children.

THE BERLIN WALL

On November 19, the East German people dismantled the Berlin Wall and flooded into the west of the city. This momentous event signals the collapse of the Communist system and heralded the end of the Cold War. Spurred on by Gorbachev's reforms in the USSR and their total withdrawal that year from Afghanistan (their Vietnam), Hungary had opened its borders to the West, Solidarity had reformed in Poland, and the Czech's had their *Velvet Revolution*. By the end of December 1989, the Rumanians had ousted Ceausescu in a violent revolution and the whole eastern map of Europe was to change. (17)

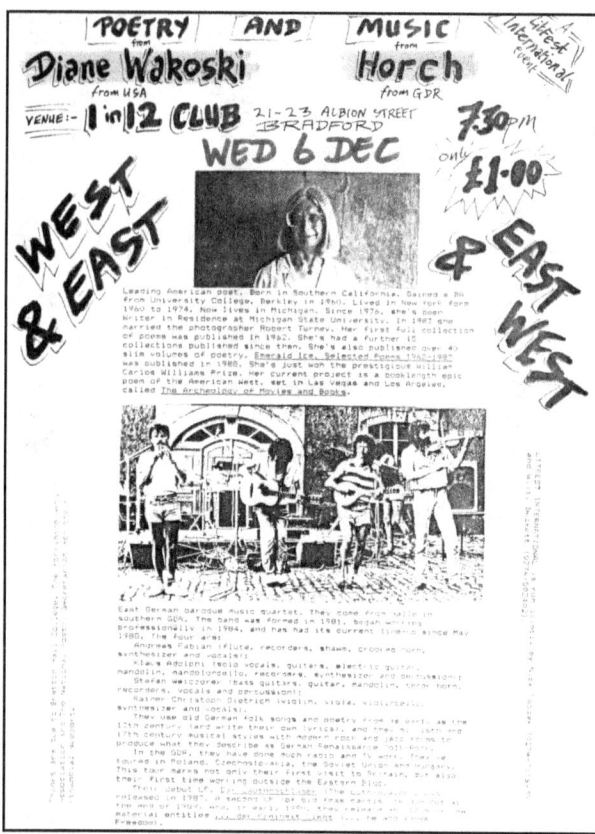

At The 1 In 12 Club, December started with the annual Chumbawamba gig on the 3rd, followed by the East German band Horch on the 6th. Two ska gigs on the 8th and 9th with Thomas J and the Gangsters Of Soul and Skaboom / Natural Riddim. On December 19 it hosted Dr & The Crippens, whose stage antics and projectile cabbage bombs left a stink in the Club for days.

The final gig of the year on December 30 saw Doom headline their third gig at the 1 In 12, supported by Holland's Mushroom Attack, Ireland's Fual, Warfear, Pleasant Valley Children and The Psycho Flowers.

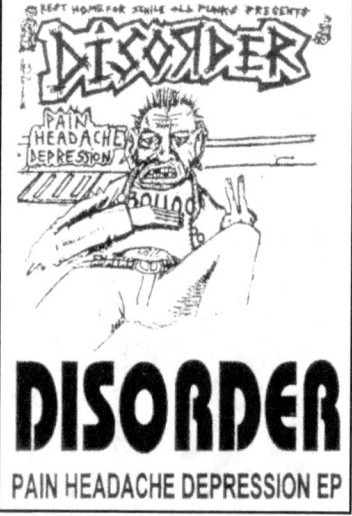

At the start of 1990, The 1 In 12 Club's January gig programme began with The Jaybirds / Not Precious on the 5th, followed by Disorder / Night Terror Syndrome / Saw Throat on the next day.

The 1 In 12 was featured in a new publication, *The Musician's Gig Guide UK* - a directory of UK venues with details of capacity, admission, fees, room hire, PA specs and other facilities that any young aspiring band needed to know before booking a tour. Besides the Club, other local venues such as St George's Hall, Bradford University's Communal Building, Queen's Hall, Rio's and the Warehouse and Duchess in Leeds were also listed.

February began with the news that Anti-Apartheid leader Nelson Mandela had been freed from his 27-year-long prison sentence at Victor Verster jail in Cape Town, South Africa. Walking free, hand in hand with his wife Winnie, to meet his supporters and greet the ranks of the world's media. Within hours of being freed, he told an ecstatic crowd of supporters at a rally, *'The armed struggle against Apartheid would continue.'* (18)

All through the late '80s and early '90s, local promoters *Red Notes* had put on many Anti-Apartheid events at venues like Checkpoint on Westgate.

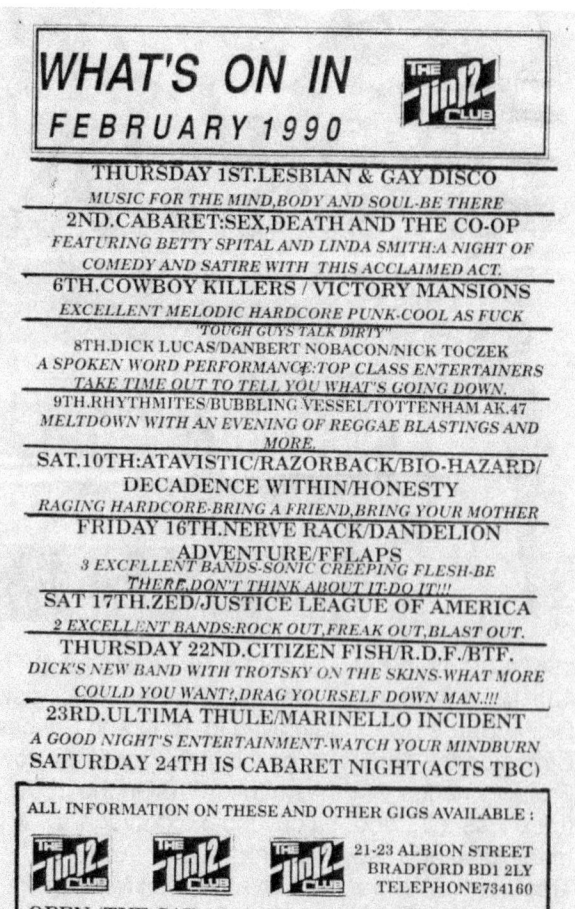

KNEE DEEP IN SHIT
WORST OF THE 1IN12 CLUB VOLUME 8

The 1 In 12 Club's Record Collective produced the second compilation LP of bands/artists who had played at the Albion Street venue, this time between January and June 1989.

Named in honour of the Club's long-running fanzine, *Knee Deep In Shit* (KDIS) *Worst of... Volume 8* was a fourteen-track LP. It came with a large A4 poster of the band/artists lyrics and artwork and featured five local acts; Uncle Ted Grundy (the alias of Pete The Poet), Not Precious, The Attic, Inky Pig and Danbert Nobacon. Other bands included Scotland's Political Asylum and Archbishop Kebab, Sheffield's The Honkies, Hull's Pink Noise and The Planet Wilson (ex-Red Guitars) and Atavistic, Thought Police, Alienation and Virus Insurrection. The LP was distributed nationally through the Cartel by APT (formally Red Rhino) of York.

Positive and complimentary reviews were forthcoming from the *T&A, MRR, Raisin' Hell #22* and the Dutch magazine *Opscene*.

Four promotional gigs were organised to promote the LP; on February 28, with Inky Pig / The Attic / Danbert Nobacon, on March 15, with The Planet Wilson / Pink Noise / Uncle Ted Grundy, on March 28 with The Honkies / Not Precious and on April 24, Archbishop Kebab / Virus Insurrection / Thought Police.

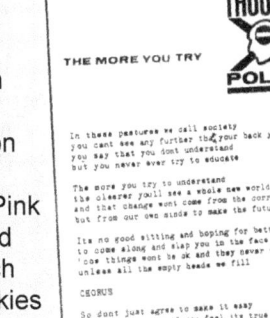

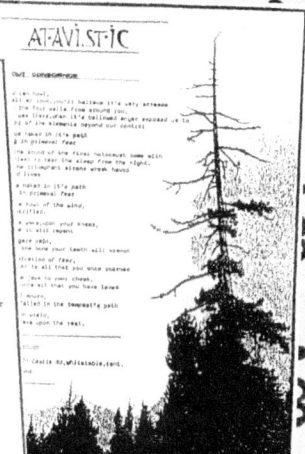

Weird music is only knee deep

THE latest volume of alternative music history from one of Bradford's least celebrated clubs is now in a trendy record shop near you.

KDIS — The Worst of the 1 in 12 Club Volume 8 — features 14 tracks by some of the weird and wonderful bands who graced the converted warehouse in the latter half of last year.

The title is an acronym of four words, 'knee', 'deep' and 'in' and a word which is unsuitable for publication in a family newspaper, folks.

It features: Political Asylum; Alienation; The Honkies; Thought Police; Uncle Ted Grundy; Pink Noise; Danbert Nobacon; Atavistic; The Attic; The Planet Wilson; Virus Insurrection; the wonderfully named Archbishop Kebab; Inky Pig; and Not Precious.

The album sleeve has a moody shot of the Albion Street home of the city's most experimental and, yes, controversial club.

The album, distributed by APT, is available from the club or Rocks Off in Westgate, Bradford, for a bargain £4.50.

T&A, Friday March 16, 1990

Key gigs during February and March were; Atavistic / Razorback / Bio Hazard / Decadence Within / Honesty on the 10th, Zed / Justice League Of America on the 17th, Citizen Fish (Dick Lucas of The Subhumans new outfit) / Radical Dance Faction / BTF on the 22nd, Thrilled Skinny / The Keatons on March 2, Dutch band Moengo Taope /

PVC / Anything But That on the 12th, Blyth Power / Sofa Head on the 13th, AC Temple on the 17th, Soar Throat / Bio-Hazard / Disaster / No Way Out / Feeding For two on the 24th and The Astronauts / Decadent Few on March 30.

GENERIC / PLEASANT VALLEY CHILDREN

The drummer in both these Leeds-based bands was Sned, who had moved down from Newcastle to settle in 1988. He set up Flat Earth Records / Distro around this period and when he moved across to Bradford he became instrumental in organising key gigs and all-dayers at the 1 In 12 over the forthcoming years as well as forming

new Bradford-based bands like Health Hazard and Suffer.

PVC released their early material on Welsh label Words Of Warning, including the EP *What The World Needs Now* and the LP *Fuck, Kill, Destroy*.

DISASTER

Halifax-based Disaster, heavily influenced by the Midland's band Discharge, played the 1 In 12 four times during 1990.

Although the band were short lived they managed to release an LP *War Cry* on their own Tone Deaf label in 1991. It was recorded at Fulton Street Studios and produced by Bri Talbot of Doom. The LP had a *Pay No More Than £2* on the cover and over the years has now become very collectable.

The band's guitarist 'Browny' also played in Wartorn, another band started by Rich Militia of Sore Throat.

GENERIC / PLEASANT VALLEY CHILDREN / HEALTH HAZARD / SUFFER

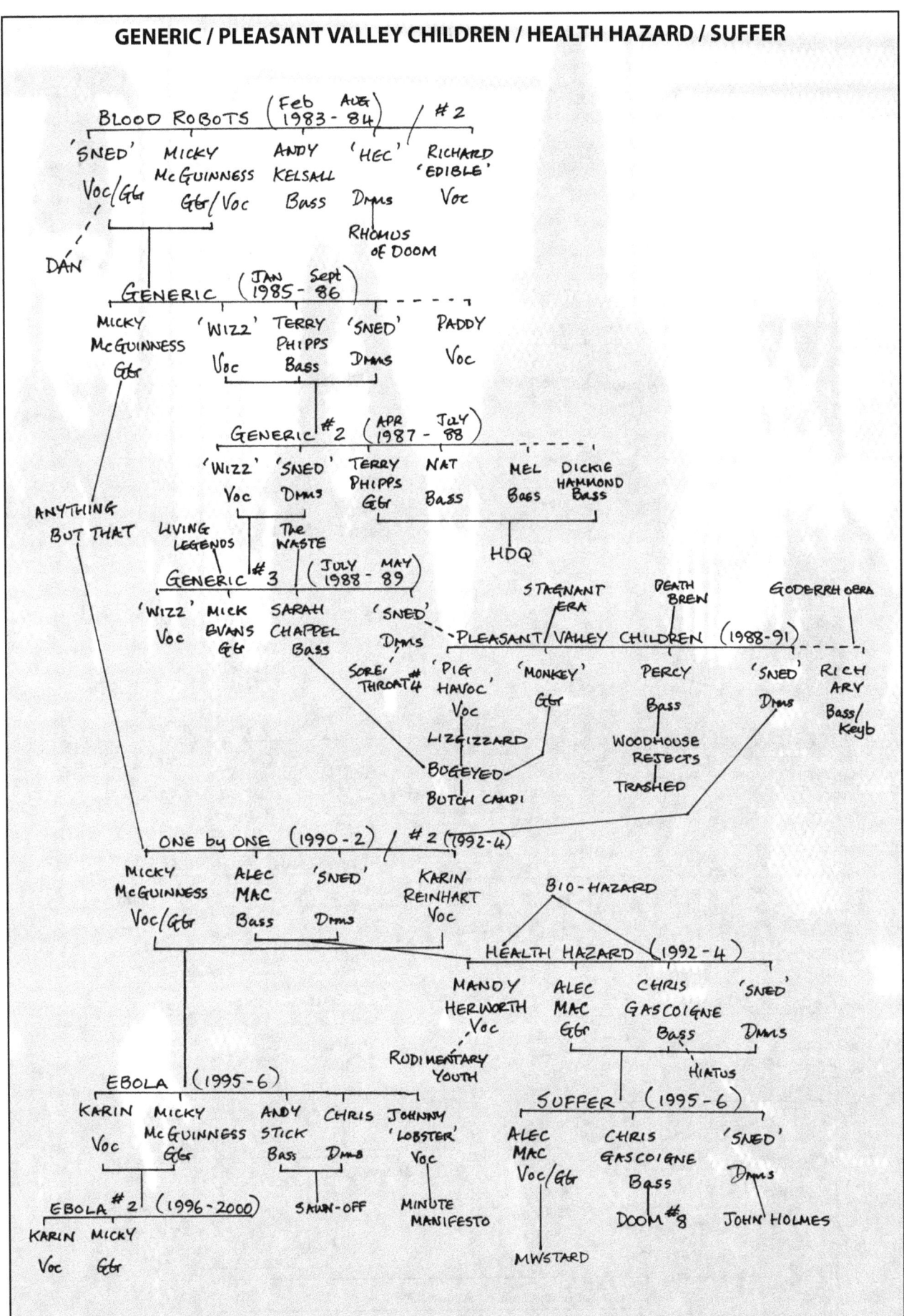

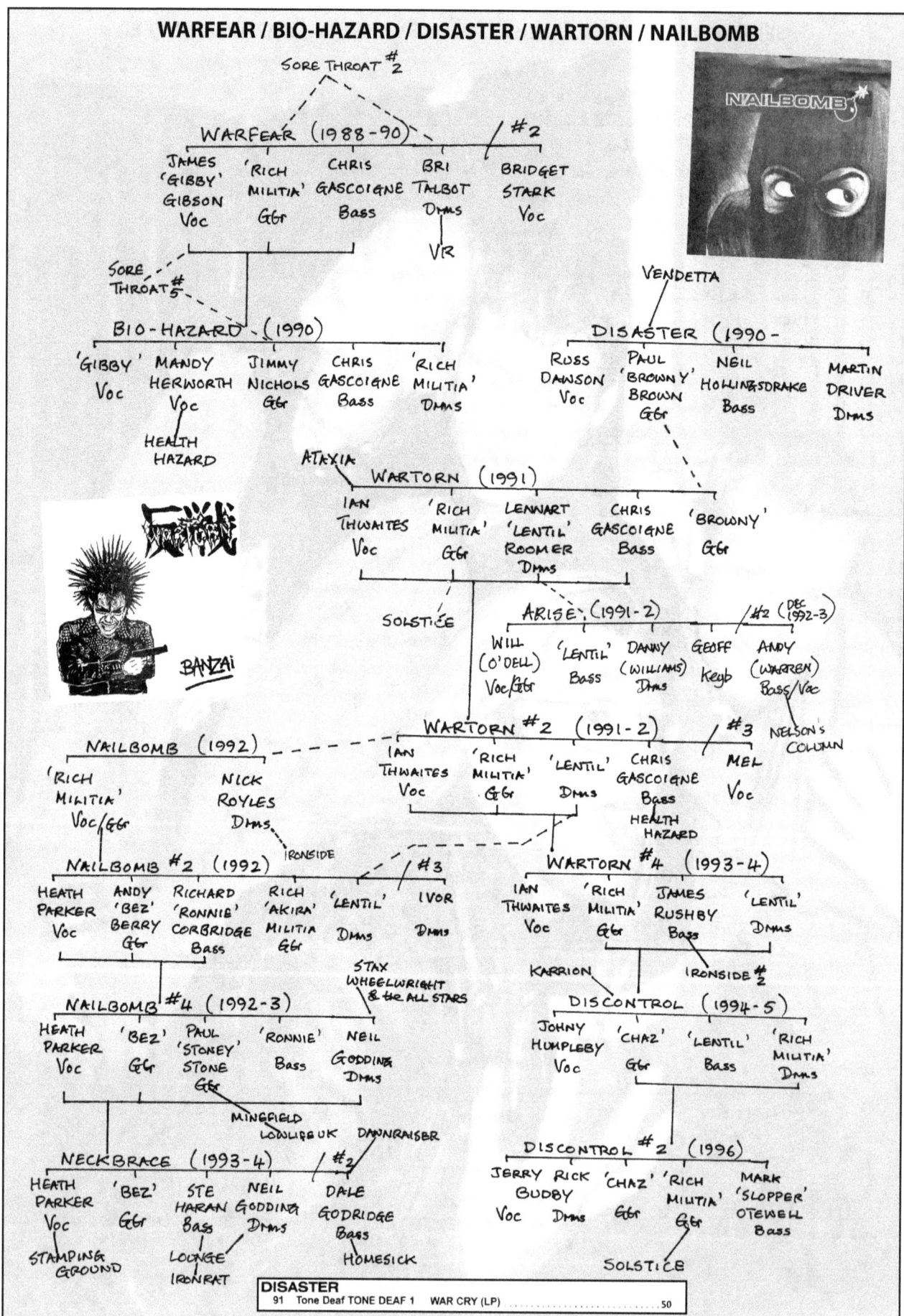

THE POLL TAX

Margaret Thatcher's Tory Government brought in the flat rate *Community Charge* to replace the rates, first as a trial in Scotland in 1987 where it met massive popular resistance and non-payment. Dubbed the *'Poll Tax,'* after the Great Peasant's Revolt of 1381 led by Wat Tyler, the tax didn't distinguish between people's ability to pay and demanded the same rate for rich or poor.

When it was implemented in the rest of the UK in 1989, the financial burden on the poor led to a nationwide Anti-Poll Tax movement that refused to pay, following the earlier Scottish resistance. A massive campaign of non-payment ensued, *Can't Pay, Won't Pay*, sending many defaulters to prison. (19)

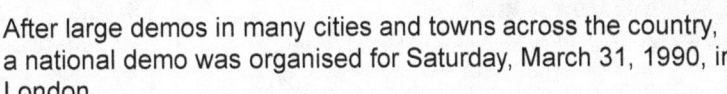

After large demos in many cities and towns across the country, a national demo was organised for Saturday, March 31, 1990, in London.

An estimated quarter of a million people turned up to protest, including many families with children, old age pensioners and trade unionists as well as opportunists of the far-left like Militant and Socialist Workers.

The peaceful march set off, intent on reaching 10 Downing Street, but heavy-handed Policing forced the march to split in two. In Trafalgar Square, two police vans drove straight into the crowd, followed by a mounted police charge.

The ensuing riot was the biggest and most violent the UK had ever seen. The demonstrators fought back against the police violence, set fire to South Africa House and damaged over fifty police and other cars. Over three hundred and sixty shops and offices were smashed up including banks and West End 'elite' shops.

Over 500 police were injured, 60 hospitalised and 396 people were charged with various offences from over 30,000 media photos and 90 hours of video evidence. Despite the media and government outcry, the riot forced a U-turn in policy and helped undermine Thatcher's position as Prime Minister, leading to her eventual resignation. (20)

TWINNED CLUBS

During The 1 In 12 Club's first two years with its own venue, new alliances were made with other autonomous social centres and venues across Europe.

Firstly, through Petesy Burns of Belfast's Youth & Community Group and Northern Irish bands Fual and Pink Turds in Space, the Club was twinned with Belfast's Warzone. Their centre strove to diminish the sectarian divide among the Northern Irish youth. Belgian's Vort 'N' Vis (Rotten Fish) club based in Leper (known as Ypres to us Brits and the site of many horrendous battles in WW1) ran a reciprocal membership scheme with the 1 In 12, as many local Bradfor-based bands toured there and across Europe, uniting the underground HC scene.

The Next World's Darron Ward twinned the Club with The Metzenstrasse in Hannau (Near Frankfurt) in Germany as well as Villa Barbara in Thessalonika & Villa Amelius in Athens, Greece while on his travels.

1 IN 12 CLUB GIGS 1988/89

JUNE 1988
17 - The Three Johns / Little Brother
21 - Bradford / Upside Down
24 - Rubella Ballet / The Next World
28 - The Hill Bandits / Malcolm's Interview

JULY 1988
1 - Adams Family / Chinese Gangster Element
5 - Tapestry Sky / Mr Morality
8 - Vee VV / Seven Antelopes
12 - Heart Of Darkness / Seven Dead Americans
15 - Old Joe Zydeco / Black Spot Champions
19 - You Slosh / Whisky Priests
22 - The Cateran / We Free Kings
29 - Giant Treads Clean / States Of Unrest

AUGUST 1988
2 - The Filth Sisters / Pete Pax
5 - Debauchery / Aural Corpse / Active Minds
9 - Bloo & The Crazy 9 Mile Flares
16 - Front Runner / Everly Sisters
19 - Natural Riddim
23 - Berserker Joe / Bomb Disneyland
26 - Thatcher On Acid / Feed Your Head
30 - From Knowhere / The Volunteers

SEPTEMBER 1988
2 - Shrapnel / Life Cycle
9 - The Keep / The Abs
13 - Every Dead New Ghost / Purple Eternal
20 - The Instigators / Sink
21 - The Ex / Shrug
23 - The Blisters / The Hoverchairs
27 - The Motsons / The Postcards
30 - Wolverines / The Recliners / Alligators

OCTOBER 1988
4 - Jackdaw With Crowbar / Rhythm Activism / Red Letter Day
7 - Die Krezen
8 - Doom / Insurrection
11 - Hotalacio / 2000DS / Radio Mongolia
14 - The Motive / The 3 Aviators
18 - The Owter Zeds / Kevin Seisay
21 - Another Cuba / Pete The Poet / Collapse
22 - Decadence Within / Pete Pax
25 - Seven Dead Americans / Death By Milkfloat
27 - The Three Johns / Danbert Nobacon / Anhrefn
28 - Sadistic Death / Psycho Flowers

NOVEMBER 1988
1 - Whip Me Harvey / PMT
2 - Rose Rose / Heresy
3 - Huw Lloyd Langton
4 - Altered States / Thrilled Skinny
9 - Generic / The Next World / Joyce McKinney Experience
11 - Vatican Shotgun / Beautiful Suit / The Wendies
17 - Alex / Pete The Poet
19 - Perjury / Sore Throat
22 - Kage Engineering / Wardance
25 - Western Dance / Jellyfish Kiss

DECEMBER 1988
1 - UK Subs / PMT
2 - Bastard / Paris In The Fall
3 - Neuroot / Default
6 - HDQ / The Abs / Pleasant Valley Children / Incest Brothers
9 - Strange Folk
14 - The Instigators / Mega City Four / Vee VV
16 - Brewster Bovis Combo / Old Joe Zydeco
17 - Karma Sutra
21 - Archbishop Kebab / Hoverchairs
23 - Danbert Nobacon / Chumbawamba

JANUARY 1989
6 - Carol Neen / Little Brother
7 - Disturbed / Aargh / Chaotic Subversion
14 - Concrete Sox / Mulch / Tomorrow's Alcoholics
20 - Broadcast / Trashtown
25 - Penny Candles / Not Precious
27 - Berserker Joe
28 - The Futons / Wild Willi Beckett

FEBRUARY 1989
7 - Thatcher On Acid / Danbert Nobacon / Political Asylum / Nerverack
10 - Cryfreedom
11 - Active Minds / Pete Pax / PVC / Atavistic Default
15 - Bloo & The Crazy Nine Mile Flares
17 - Dog Faced Hermans / Thrilled Skinny / Senseless Things

1 IN 12 CLUB GIGS 1989

22 - Inky Pig / Pop Pigs
24 - Thin / Shark Taboo

MARCH 1989
3 - Kage Engineering / The Attic
10 - Virus Insurrection / Thought Police / Scatwailing
17 - Rosetta Stone
22 - Penny Candles
23 - Generic / The Next World / Vernon Walters / Hate That Smile
25 - Atilla The Stockbroker / Steve Drewett
29 - Shrug

APRIL 1989
7 - Vagabond / Middle Earth
8 - Life Cycle / BTJ / Pete Pax
11 - Blyth Power / Sofa Head / The Volunteers
14 - The Planet Wilson / The Postcards
15 - City Indians
21 - The Motive
29 - The Dickie Bards / Alex / Pete The Poet

MAY 1989
5 - The Crowmen / Thin
6 - The Honkies / Not Precious
11 - The Volunteers / Slopdosh
12 - The Radium Cats / The Wendies
16 - HDQ / Pullerman
19 - Strange Folk / Black Spot Champions
20 - Feed Your Head / Thought Police
27 - Old Joe Zydeco / The Onset

JUNE 1989
1 - Alienation / Incest Brothers
2 - Pop Pigs / Jump The Gun
3 - The Farm / Bounce The Mouse
7 - The Exploited / Skitzo / The Crumps
8 - Rosetta Stone
10 - Revolution / Des The Miner / The Recliners / Foam
16 - Archbishop Kebab / Heavy Discipline / The Next World
17 - Hogwash Theatre Co / Jonathan Hall / Uncle Ted Grundy / System Casualties
23 - Pink Noise / Jump The Gun

24 - Legion Of Parasites / Geod / Life Cycle / Twerp
30 - Natural Rhythm / Bubble Head

JULY 1989
1 - Karma Sutra
3 - Slum Children / Scraps / Obligatory
7 - Bloo & The Crazy 9 Mile Flares
14 - Bliss / Crow People
15 - Sore Throat / Hoverchairs / Heart Of Darkness
20 - PVC / Godarrea
21 - Zed / Carter USM
22 - Tubilah Dog
28 - Dawn Of Liberty / Decadence Within / Drudge / Insurrection

AUGUST 1989
3 - Hotalico / Everly Sisters / V.S.Sisters
4 - Slum Turkeys
11 - Western Dance / 12 Angry Men
12 - Nitro Puppy / Salad From Atlantis
17 - Chaos UK / Gauze / Incest Brothers / Warfear
22 - Oi Polloi / Telic Tribe / City Indians / GGF
25 - Satanic Malfunctions / Paradox UK / Slander

SEPTEMBER 1989
1 - Out Of The Blues Band / The Wonderful Thing Called Tiddles
2 - Saw Throat / PVC / GFDD / Yeah God / Drudge / Warfear / Psycho Flowers / Sedition / Nerverack / Bounce The Mouse / Active Minds / Slum Turkeys / Flea
8 - The Clearing
13 - Pink Turds In Space / Indian Dream / Scorched Earth
14 - Post Glasnost / Dickie Bards / Suitcase Circus
15 - Fartown Fruits / Shades Of Pink
16 - Wild Willi Beckett / Call Me Legion / Pete Pax / Revolt
17 - Hogwash Theatre / Danbert Nobacon
19 - Snuff / Wat Tyler / Sofa Head
22 - Filler / Spongetunnel
28 - Fual / Sledghammer / Crow People

1 IN 12 CLUB GIGS 1989/90

OCTOBER 1989
6 - Doom / Next World
7 - Fudge Tunnel / Nerverack
10 - The Ex / Houndgod / Pete The Poet
14 - Rubella Ballet / M4 Alice
17 - Rory McLeod
18 - Life Cycle / Sharon Tate / Rectify
20 - The East / Rainy Days
21 - Greenhouse / The Clearing
25 - Bob / Penny Candles
27 - Groove Farm / 3 Men Gone Mad

NOVEMBER 1989
2 - Crazy Pink Revolvers / Turbo Rockets
3 - Carter USM / Wonderful Thing Called Tiddles
4 - Head In The Heavens
9 - Atilla The Stockbroker / TV Smith's Cheap
10 - The Da Vincis / Archbishop Kebab
11 - Chaos UK / Incest Brothers / Carnage / Leatherface / State Of The Nation
15 - Trottle / Saw Throat / Slum Children
18 - Smoking Mirror / Slum Turkeys / Flea
24 - Kage Engineering / Alienation

DECEMBER 1989
3 - Chumbawamba / Seize The Day / Shrug
6 - Horsh / Diane Wakowski
8 - Thomas J And The Gangsters Of Soul
9 - Skaboom / Natural Riddum
15 - Rubber Leather Plastic / Burning Skies Of Elysium
16 - Po! / Not Precious
19 - Dr And The Crippens / Delusions Of Grandad / Strawberry Girl
20 - Rev Rev / Mary Johnstone & Chris
30 - Doom / Mushroom Attack / Warfear / Fual / PVC / Psycho Flowers

JANUARY 1990
5 - The Jaybirds / Not Precious
6 - Disorder / Night Terror Syndrome / Saw Throat / Linda Smith / Betty Spital
26 - Heart Of Darkness / Glass Hammers
27 - Johnny Dangerously / Alex
31 - Idiot Gods / Pram

FEBRUARY 1990
2 - Sex, Death And The Co-Op
6 - Cowboy Killers / Victory Mansions
9 - Rhythmites
10 - Atavistic / Razorback / Bio-Hazard / Decadence Within / Honesty
16 - Dandelion Adventure / Fflaps
17 - Zed / Justice League Of America
22 - Citizen Fish / RDF / BTF
23 - Ultima Thule / Marinello Incident / Jackdaw With Crowbar
24 - Clare Mooney / Chris And Mary / Little Brother
28 - The Attic / Danbert Nobacon / Inky Pig

MARCH 1990
2 - Thrilled Skinny / The Keatons
3 - Roy Bailey / Steve Graham
7 - Tottenham AK47 / Rhythmites / Bubbling Vessel
8 - Creaming Jesus / Rubber, Leather, Plastic
9 - Planet Wilson / Pink Noise / Uncle Ted Grundy
12 - PVC / Moengo Tapoe / Anything But That
13 - Blyth Power / Sofa Head
16 - Nick Toczek / Danbert Nobacon / Dick Lucas
17 - AC Temple
20 - Bastard Kestral / Nutmeg
22 - Idiot Box (Primate) / Dawson
23 - Hash & Thrash / Vatican Shotgun Scare
24 - Soar Throat / Bio-Hazard / Disaster / No Way Out / Feeding For Two
28 - The Honkies / Not Precious
30 - The Astronauts / Decadent Few
31 - Wild Willi Beckett & Jont / Paul Cookson / Andy Darlington

APRIL 1990
4 - Oi Polloi / Beyond The Pale
5 - Toxik Ephex / Active Minds / Full Of Shit
6 - Hotalacio / Nerverack / Visions Of Change
7 - Leatherface / Dan Dares Dog
10 - Thatcher On Acid / Target Of Demand
12 - FUAL. / Headcore / Next World
14 - Roy Bailey / Robb Johnson / Political Asylum
21 - Wonderful Thing Called Tiddles / Thin

1 IN 12 CLUB GIGS 1990

24 - Archbishop Kebab / Virus Insurrection / Thought Police
26 - UK Subs / Bo-Hazard
27 - Threshold Shift
28 - Henry Normal / Pete The Poet

MAY 1990
2 - The Driscolls / Mousefolk
9 - The Reckoning / Rev Rev
11 - The Bollweevils / Glass Hammer
19 - Cabbage Head Kids
25 - Anarcrust / Doom / Sedition

JUNE 1990
2 - Peter Plate / Nick Toczek / Michael

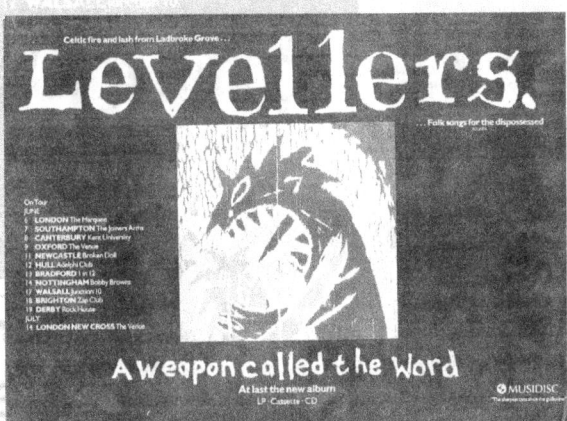

5 - Corrosion Of Conformity / Next World / Disaster
13 - The Levellers / Mary & Chris
15 - Idiot Gods / The Jerks
16 - Disaster / Hellbastard / Trash / Senile Decay
21 - Langfield Crane / Protagonists
30 - Walter Mitty's Head / Knights Of Passion

JULY 1990
3 - GI Love / Zowtovit
7 - September Kitchen / Ruby Tuesday
8 - Citizen Fish / Salad From Atlantis / Since The Operation
20 - Cracous Rock n Roll
21 - Shutdown / Tallman / Steadfast / Stepone
26 - Medicine Factory / Gentle Ihors Devotion
28 - Sabot / Leatherface

AUGUST 1990
7 - Goober Patrol / Vehical Derek / Damage
10 - Chaos UK / Psycho Flowers
11 - Deutronomy / Sheepskin Children
16 - Dr & The Crippens
17 - Knights Of Passion / Walter Mitty's Head
23 - Telic Tribe / Trashed
24 - Natural Rhythm / Skaboom
26 - The Ex / Chumbawamba

SEPTEMBER 1990
1 - Intense Degree / Nitro-Puppy / Kalus / Disaster / Virus Insurrection
8 - FUAL / Headcore / Feed Your Head
13 - Blyth Power / Salad From Atlantis / Cabbage Head Kids
14 - Inside Out / Totalitar / Trashed
21 - Doom / Paradox UK
23 - Linda Smith / Henry Normal

OCTOBER 1990
4 - Guana Batz
11 - False Prophets / PVC
12 - Nosferatu / Every New Dead Ghost / Vlad
19 - Beer Beast / Razorback
27 - Stretcheads / Magic Bastards
28 - Extreme Noise Terror / Antic Hay / Kluster Bomb Unit

NOVEMBER 1990
9 - Head Of David / PVC
10 - M4Alice / Slander / WTCT / Paradox UK
16 - Adams Family / The Threads
24 - Fartown Fruits

DECEMBER 1990
2 - Heavy Plant Crossing / Fuller Vale
8 - Threshold Shift / Criminal Damage
9 - Chumbawamba / Greenhouse
14 - Chaos UK / Trashed / Active Minds
15 - Silverfish / Sofa Head / Crane / Milk
16 - Senseless Things / Nerverack
18 - Citizen Fish / Hash N Thrash
22 - The Three Johns / The Big Bang
29 - Kulturo / Force Fed / Kings Of Oblivion / Nailbomb

MA BRENCH / 1 IN 12 CAFE

Picture by Marie Bennett

On April 8 1990, half of the top floor of the 1 In 12 Club building was converted into Bradford's first vegan/vegetarian cafe. The mother of a club member Pat Brench invested over £3,000 into stocking and equipping the kitchen and dining area. *Ma Brench's Cafe* was strictly vegan/vegetarian and would promote and stock only fair trade products where possible. At gig and all-dayers it did a roaring trade and became famous for its delicious veggie burgers. (21)

After running the cafe with the help of volunteers for over a year, Ma Brench then handed the whole operation over to the Club. Since then, the cafe has been run as another Cub collective by a dedicated ever-changing role-call of volunteers. They have provided superb quality dishes for all Club events and have even done many outside catering jobs for various festivals, conferences, seminars, etc.

From April to July, key 1 In 12 Club gigs were an eclectic mix of folk, stand-up, indie-pop and hardcore acts like Oi Polloi, Toxic Ephex, Hotalacio, Leatherface, Target of Demand from Austria with early punk legends UK Subs playing in April.

On April 28, the Club's long-standing member, Pete Chapman (alias Pete The Poet) performed his stand-up Poetry supporting Henry Normal (pictured right).

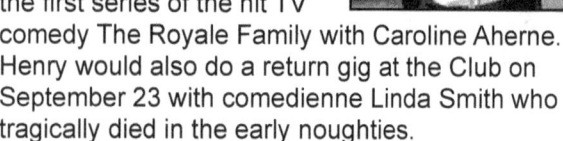

Henry Normal would later rise to prominence as co-writer of the first series of the hit TV comedy The Royale Family with Caroline Aherne. Henry would also do a return gig at the Club on September 23 with comedienne Linda Smith who tragically died in the early noughties.

May gigs kicked off with The Driscolls / Mousefolk on the 2nd, The Reckoning / Rev Rev on the 9th and The Bollweevils / Glass Hammer on the 13th. On May 25, Dutch group Anarcrust played, supported by Doom and Scottish band Sedition.

Two local bands Cabbage Head Kids and Threshold Shift played at the 1 In 12 at this point..

CABBAGE HEAD KIDS

Anton Shaw, the drummer of this locally based band, also produced the short-lived *Ugly* fanzine. He organised a series of gigs at the 1 In 12 under the promotional title *Club Ugly Presents*.

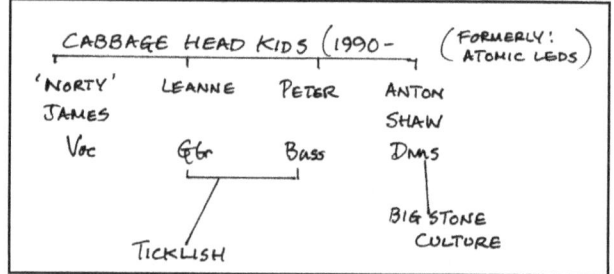

June and July gigs included the American band Corrosion Of Conformity on June 5, The Levellers

/ Mary & Chris on the 13th, an all-dayer on the 16th followed by Halifax's Langfield Crane / Protagonists on the 21st, Citizen Fish / Salad From Atlantis / Since The Operation on July 8, and the American/ Czech band Sabot (pictured) / Leatherface on the 28th.

THRESHOLD SHIFT

Formed by vocalist Mick Barrett and ex-Negativz drummer and guitarist Tony Fox and Daz Keighley, the band started gigging in 1990.

Their song *Power Games* was recorded live at The 1 In 12 Club and released on the Club's compilation LP *Nightmare On Albion Street* in 1991.

Former Convulsions bassist Kenny Armitage joined on bass after a spell as the band's manager in 1991 and the four-piece brought their brand of high energy punk rock to venues around the country.

They released their first LP, *Threshold Shift*, in 1992, recorded at In A City Studios in Bradford and mastered for vinyl at Abbey Road Studios in London.

Threshold Shift played the punk gig circuit up and down the country during the early 1990s.

The band were briefly renamed Jinx after guitarist Daz Keighley left in 1993 before splitting for the first time in 1994.

In 2002 Mick Barrett and Kenny Armitage reformed the band with former Convulsion Phil Hey on guitar and Paul 'Chillo' Child on drums.

The re-formed band released a number of CDs on their own label, inlcuding the album *'65* on CD (2005), *...Another Fine Mess!* in (2007), as well as appearing on numerous compilation LPs.

They supported Stiff Little Fingers at the Bradford Rio in 2006 and released a live CD of their set from the night.

The band called it a day in 2012 after the departure of Kenny Armitage, although Mick, Phil and Chillo carried on for a while with a new sound as Chutzpah. Threshold Shift briefly returned in 2019.

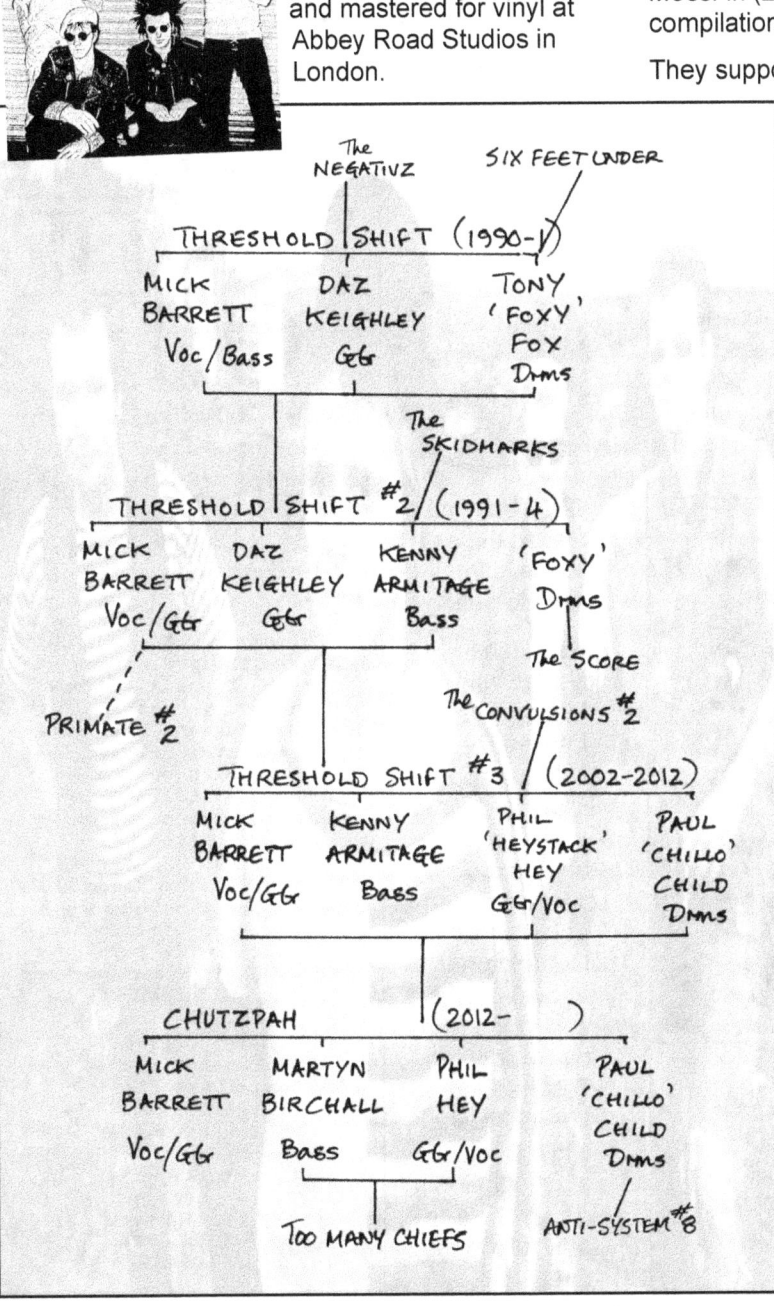

> THRESHOLD Shift's first gig could hardly have been more successful.
> For this Bradford band decided to enter the Battle of the Bands, based in their home city, and ended up being one of the heat winners.
> Now Threshold Shift, who describe their music as rock punk, are looking forward to June 8 for their quarter-final bash.
> The band formed in August last year with 'Sir' Mick Barrett taking bass and vocals, 'Lord' Daz Keighley, guitar and vocals, and The Marquis Foxy, drums. Their first meeting took place on the unlikely setting of Ilkley Moor.
> Foxy said: "It was one lazy summer afternoon and Mick and I got together with a load of other musicians and, along with a generator, we indulged in a jam.
> "In short we hit it off and decided to stick together. After this moorland escapade I was reunited with Daz, whom I had not seen since our days together in The Negativz, and subsequently a band was formed."
> Now Threshold Shift, who already have a tape out, are on the lookout for more gigs — and more success.

STRAIGHT EDGE (SxE)

A sub-genre of the hardcore scene, straight edge (SxE) originated in the USA as a reaction to the age of consent being 21 for the consumption of alcohol. Youth who abstained from alcohol use on the HC gig scene also embraced the life choices of being strict vegans, they didn't smoke and refrained from casual sex. The movement grew on both East and West coasts where bands like Quicksand and Sick Of It All were major players.

The casual dress code of SxE was generally shirt/t-shirt/sweatshirt, baggy combat trousers and Converse sneakers with an X mark on their hands at gigs. The first all-SxE gig at the 1 In 12 was on July 21, 1990, when Shutdown / Tallman / Steadfast / Stepone played. This was followed over the next few years with a range of SxE bands from the UK and abroad playing at gigs and all day festivals and labels like Nick Royles' Sure Hand Records released vinyl 7-inch singles by UK local groups such as Ironside.

On August 2, 1990, Iraq, under its dictator Saddam Hussein, invaded the Gulf state of Kuwait. Despite the overwhelming forces, the Kuwaitis defended their capital Kuwait City, before it was finally overrun. Iraq soon announced the annexation of Kuwait while the world watched. (22)

Gigs at The 1 In 12 Club in August and September included the thrash-punk of Chaos UK from Portishead, Bristol, on August 10. They had been spearheading the UK hardcore scene since 1979, and their self-titled LP had reached No 16 in the indie charts in April 1983. Local bands Deuteronomy and Sheepskin Children played on August 11, two bands making their second appearance that year, Walter Mitty's Head and Knights Of Passion played on the 16th and on August 26 The Ex and

Chumbawamba played the club for the third time since opening.

September started with Mansfield's Intense Degree / Nitro-Puppy / Disaster / Virus Insurrection, and on the 14th American girl trio Inside Out (pictured above) played, supported by Sweden's Totalitar and Leeds' Trashed, while Doom played their 5th gig at The 1 In 12 Club on the 21st.

BEER BEAST

Comedy-edged hardcore band Beer Beast were regulars at The 1 In 12 Club.

They released their *Homebrew Session* tape in October 1990, and had tracks on a split tape with Immortal Dead called *3 Go Big Spit* in 1992.

Beer Beast had two tracks, *Governmental System* and *Ilkley Moor (You Twat)*, on the compilation album *Endless Struggle - The Worst Of The 1 In 12 Club Volume 12/13*.

The band were re-branded 'Beer Beast: Warriors Of Piss' when they released their *Abuse Of Technology* album on CD and cassette, which was recorded June 2001.

Peter 'Skinny' Finan went on to sing for new wave covers band Plastic Letters.

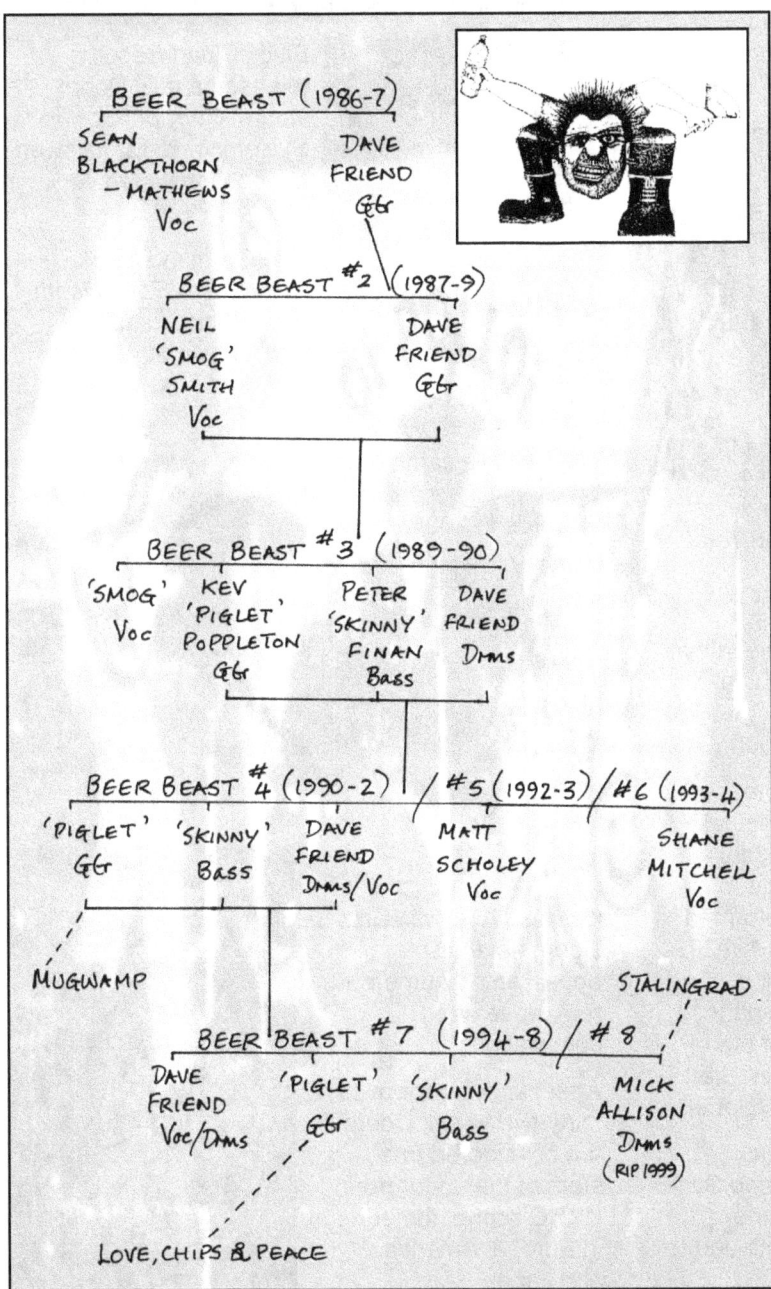

DOOM

Doom are the UK's most influential and near-legendary crust/hardcore band. Formed in Birmingham in 1987, their distinct crusty sound was influenced by Discharge and a crossover thrash style.

They joined Peaceville Records in 1988 and their debut 21-song album *War Crimes (Inhuman Beings)* was recorded at Rich Bitch studios.

This was followed later that year by a split album release *Bury The Debt - Not The Dead* with Swedish band No Security, which got into the Indie charts at No 16 for two weeks.

In 1989, Peaceville released the compilation *Total Doom* of all their recordings up to this point.

By 1989, Bri Talbot, the band's guitarist was based in Bradford, but left the band after a lengthy European tour, the others carried on but split in August 1990.

The original Doom #2 lineup reformed in 1992 for a Japanese tour and released the LP *Doomed From The Start* on the Vinyl Japan label,

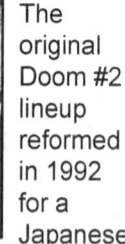

There were various lineups, with Bri and Stick as constant members, but the band continued to tour and record.

In 1993, Flat Earth released the split 7" *Lost The Fight* single with Belgium's Hiatus. In 1995, the double album *Fuck Peaceville* came out on the US Profane Existence label, followed by 1996's album *Rush Hour Of The Gods* on Flat Earth.

Their *World Of Shit* LP came out on Vinyl Japan / Discipline Records in 2001, engineered by Carl Stipetic.

Doom played regularly, at least twice a year, at The 1 In 12 Club. After the death of vocalist Wayne Southworth in 2005, they put on an annual *Sozzfest* to commemorate his memory.

Black Cloud Records released a new Doom album, *Corrupt Fucking System*, in 2013, followed by the *Consumed To Death* EP (2015).

The German split 7' EP *They Love (Fear) Death* with Electrozombies appeared on the Angry Voice label in 2017.

Their limited edition four-track 7" EP *If Oceans Die, We Die* came out on Global Resistance Records in 2021.

Doom have also appeared on numerous re-releases and compilations.

After surviving for over thirty five years, Doom are considered true stars of the underground UKHC scene, famed in Europe, America and Japan.

THE 1 IN 12 CLUB — 1988-1990

DOOM / NEXT WORLD / VR

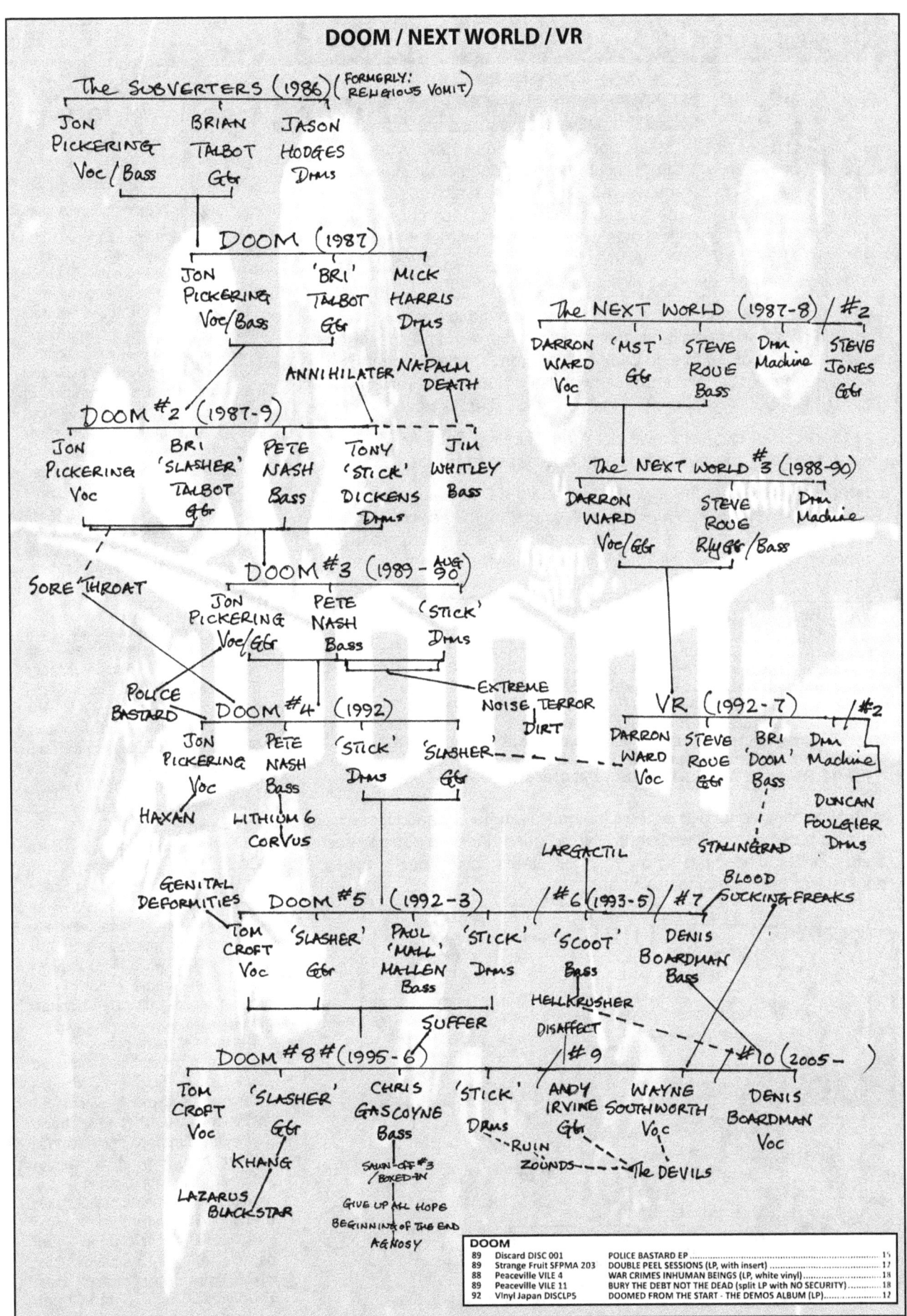

WILD & CRAZY "NOISE MERCHANTS"...

....INVADE A CITY NEAR YOU
WORST OF THE 1 IN 12 CLUB VOL. 9/10

The second LP released in 1990 by the 1 In 12 Club's record collective came out in late October and was a 22 track double album. All artists had played between July and December 1989. Five local acts were featured: Warfear, The Clearing, The Wonderful Thing Called Tiddles, Chris Halliwell & Mary Johnston and Wild Willi Beckett & Jont.

Leeds-based Greenhouse and Chumbwamba, whose track *Bradford Bad Lad* (23) was specially recorded for the album and has never been released since, joined foreign contributions from Trottle (Hungary), Spongetunnel (USA), Northern Irish bands Fual and Pink Turds In Space, Telic Tribe (Guernsey-Channel Islands) and Scotland's Psycho Flowers.

The LP received excellent reviews by Ian Cheek in *Sounds*, *MRR*, *UK Resist*, the *T&A*, and *All For Noise* #5 zine based in Hanau, Germany.

On receiving his copy, this is what the late John Peel said on his Radio 1 show on November 4, "Here's a nice letter from the people at 1 In 12 Records...with another LP in their series, here's Godorrhoea with Garble...(plays it)..admirably succinct. I'll be playing more from the LP no question."

V/A - "Wild & Crazy 'Noise Merchants' " LP

One of the best comps I've heard in a while. For three of the four sides it's one of the most consistent and powerful collections of punk styles, including such bands as GODRRHOER, PSYCHO FLOWERS, PARADOX UK, ACTIVE MINDS, CHUMBA, PINK TURDS IN SPACE, FUAL, SOFA HEAD and lots more. I kept waiting for the interspersed "arty" tracks that seem to freqent these large comps, but they never came. They saved them all for side 4, which was quite thoughtful. (TY)
(1 In 12 Records, 21-23 Albion St., Bradford, BD1 2L4, UK)

With two promotional gigs at the Club on November 10 and December 9, the album began to sell well and within a year it had sold out and has not been repressed as yet. It is now very collectable, mainly due to the rare original track from Chumbawamba.

VARIOUS
'Wild And Crazy Noise Merchants Invade A City Near You – Worst Of The 1 In 12 Club Vol 9/10'
(1 In 12 Records) ***½

WHEN BRADFORD'S 1 In 12 Club release compilation LPs they don't do things by halves. This time they've managed to cram 22 bands into four sides of vinyl, accompany it with a 24-page booklet and maintain their laudable policy of including only previously unreleased tracks.

Of course it's only to be expected that with such a concentration of bands, the odd track will poke out like a sore thumb through its sheer mediocrity. Psycho Flowers and Slander fall conveniently into that category with their regressive Discharge impressions; Indian Dream and The Clearing offer pleasant yet pedestrian affairs while Paradox UK, Godorrhoea, Tiddles and The Incest Brothers are all hugely uninspiring.

Marginally more palatable are Warfear, who incorporate an impressive array of tempo changes into a standard format; the powerful aggression of Active Minds; the folk-roots of Halliwell And Johnston; M4 Alice's swirling rhythms and FUAL's scathing lyrical attack on the situation in Northern Ireland which, frankly, warranted better musical accompaniment.

Then there are the gems, of which indeed there are many. The grossly-named Pink Turds In Space cover 'Teenage Kicks' with wholesome fury; Greenhouse are rhythmic and muscular on 'This One's For Me' while Nitro Puppy's 'Bubblegum Burnout' wallows in the glory of severely distorted buzzsaw guitars.

The three absolute pearls, though, are Chumbawamba's inspired skank-cabaret 'Bradford Bad Lad'; Sofa Head's typically venomous 'Invitation' and the final track, 'Averagely Surprised' by Wild Willi Beckett And Jont which couples poignant verse with dazzling bass in an unusual combination that takes the honours for the entire LP.

(Available for £8.00 inc P&P payable to '1 In 12 Records' from 21-23 Albion Street, Bradford, West Yorkshire BD1 2LY).   **Ian Cheek**

October gigs at The 1 In 12 Club included psychobilly rockers Guana Batz on the 4th, False Prophets / PVC on the 11th, Beer Beast / Razorback on the 19th, Stretcheads on the 27th and Extreme Noise Terror / Antic Hay and German band Cluster Bomb Unit on the 28th, while on November 9, Head of David / PVC (again) played.

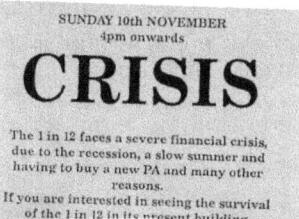

November 1990 saw the resignation of the Tory Prime Minister Margaret Thatcher. The 'Iron Lady' had won three consecutive general elections and had dominated British political life for eleven years (1979-1990). She had been elbowed out by her cringing cabinet, who replaced her on the 27th with John Major after winning the election for leadership of the Conservative Party and became Prime Minister.

CRISIS #1

On Sunday, November 10, 1990, the 1 In 12 held a meeting to discuss the future of the Club, which was advertised in the local alternative paper, *Leeds Other Paper*. (24)

Since opening nearly two years earlier, the Club had inevitably struggled to tackle the many difficulties of running its own building, not helped by the ongoing Tory recession, having its PA system stolen and the general financial worries of meeting day-to-day bill payments.

The meeting was divided into 'working sessions' to debate areas like general finances, gigs, events and the cafe etc, in order to decide on the implications of either cost-cutting or raising money in some other way. Above all, it was not going to be another 'talking shop' meeting, where no real decisions were reached by consensus.

At the same time, one of the bar stewards' jobs was up for grabs, as Tammy (Bri Doom's then-wife) was leaving on amicable terms.

In the end, the crisis was eased by a long-term loan from Sam Smiths Brewery, which tided the Club over and helped to keep the place running and galvanized a more focused and committed approach by the Club's membership.

November 27 saw the sad passing of Buttershaw playwright Andrea Dunbar, whose play *Rita, Sue And Bob Too* had made her famous when made into a movie in 1987.

Bradford's famous libertarian social centre **The 1 in 12 Club** is holding an emergency meeting to reassess the organisation's structure. The meeting will take the form of a half day conference, breaking into groups to discuss such aspects as finance, gigs and events, security and membership.

The event, which takes place from 12 noon to 4.30pm this coming Sunday, follows financial difficulties caused primarily by the theft of the Club's PA equipment in September.

All Club members willing to input ideas and follow them through into action are urged to attend. A draft document states "This must not be just another talking shop."

The Club is approaching its 10th anniversary and members are determined to outlive the Thatcher regime.

Club chair Matt Hannam said; "If membership of this Club means anything, then it's now we need more than words. Self help and mutual aid have been the foundations of this Club; they have helped us survive so many external attacks that to go under through complacency would be unforgivable. The situation is that urgent."

The December gigs worth noting were; Chaos UK on the 4th, then on the 9th was the annual Chumbawamba gig, supported by another Leeds band, Greenhouse.

London's Silverfish played on the 15th. These noise merchants included 'Fuzz' on guitar who had previously played the 1 In 12 back in 1984 when he was with The Instinks. Silverfish were signed to Wiija Records at the time but later moved to Alan Magee's Creation Records.

The Senseless Things played the Club for a third time on the 16th, as did Citizen Fish on the 18th.

On December 22, the Club's old comrades The Three Johns made it a trio of gigs at the building with a pre-Xmas show. 1990 ended with a gig by Kulturo (ex-AntiSect) / Force Fed / Kings Of Oblivion / Nailbomb on the 29th.

A couple of end notes for 1990:

On December 20, the Channel Tunnel was finished, soon giving quick rail travel between the UK and mainland Europe.

```
BULLS HEAD
GREAT HORTON ROAD
Presents
BLUES NIGHT
TUESDAY, MAY 3
JEDS BLUES BAND
FULL NIGHT OF BLUES WITH BLUES DJ
```

Page 28 SOUNDS January 19 1991

LIVES

THE THREE JOHNS
Bradford 1 In 12 Club

MY FIRST ever encounter with The Three Johns occurred when, strangely, they played Leeds Polytechnic on a weekday afternoon more years ago than I care to remember. As any sane young schoolboy would surely do, I missed and therefore failed my French 'O' level and of course blame them to this day.

Many years later, The Three Johns are thankfully still with us, albeit somewhat sporadically. Their recent 'Eat Your Sons' LP sold two and a half copies, inspired little critical acclaim – other than in this august journal – and general consensus would have us (wrongly) believe they are something of a joke band.

Three days before Christmas they're here in Bradford, charming the very pants off a packed 1 In 12 Club. Hyatt looks ravishing in leather trousers; Brennan has grown his hair at the back to compensate for its imminent withdrawal at the front and Langford, well, Langford looks the same as always. He also looks pissed. But it is Christmas.

To celebrate they combine a series of classic oldies with the better moments from 'Eat Your Sons'. The pervasive atmosphere and escalating bassline of 'Key Largo' is perhaps the better moment of that LP, elevated further by Hyatt's exaggerated and self-derogatory vocal manner. 'Blind Heart', building from subtle beginnings to majestic crescendo, is equally fine.

It's several years since 'AWOL', 'Lucy', or, joy upon joy, 'English White Boy Engineer' were heard, but tonight our desires are wholly fulfilled, each performed with the sparkling dexterity that characterised their original appearance. They've lost none of their rapier-like wit either, nor the ability to waffle endlessly between songs. 'Kick The Dog Right Out' is dedicated to John Major ("That man who lives happily in 10 Downing Street with his wife and three suits") while Langford confesses "It's two years since I've played guitar and you've made me feel at home".

Too frivolous to be taken seriously, too genius-like to be dismissed. Thank you Three Johns, you made my Christmas.

Ian Cheek

ANNIVERSARY OF THE INDEPENDENT LABOUR PARTY AND THE MANNINGHAM MILLS STRIKE

Bradford's radical political history was celebrated on December 20, with the centenary of the Independent Labour Party (ILP).

A free lunchtime programme of music and comedy was performed at the Wool Exchange, where there was also an historical talk by local Labour Historian Tony Jowitt. The event also commemorated the great Manningham Mills strike of 1893, which in turn led to the eventual formation of the ILP. (25)

MANNINGHAM MILLS STRIKE AND FORMATION OF THE INDEPENDENT LABOUR PARTY
1890-1990 1893-1993
CENTENARY CELEBRATION
12 noon - 3pm with food & bar
THURSDAY 20th DECEMBER
FREE LUNCHTIME ENTERTAINMENT
6.30pm
TALK WITH SLIDE SHOW BY AUTHOR TONY JOWITT ON THE HISTORY OF THE EVENT
8pm food & bar adm. £3/£1.50
THE HANK WANGFORD BAND & THE CHUFFINELLES
WOOL EXCHANGE, BANK ST. BRADFORD
information tel: 0274 309199

After the dispute, the strike leaders saw the need for their own political party and, in 1891, set up the Bradford Independent Labour Party at Laycock's Tavern off Kirkgate.

Two years later on January 13, 1893, the Independent Labour Party was born at an inaugural conference at the Labour Institute on Peckover Street in Little Germany, Bradford (pictured right).

Amongst the 120 delegates, chaired by Keir Hardie (MP for West Ham South) were local Labour councillors Fred Jowett and Willie Leach, playwright George Bernard Shaw for the Fabians and Karl Marx's daughter, Eleanor.

By 1900, a loose socialist group of MPs, Trade Unionists, the ILP, Fabians, Co-Operativists, etc, were representing the working class to Parliament as the Labour Representative Committee (LRC).

In the 1906 election, seven Labour MPs (including Bradford's first ILP Labour MP, Fred Jowett) plus eleven union-endorsed MPs entered Parliament as a bloc, but not as the LRC but renamed as the Labour Party at the suggestion of Fred Jowett, thus starting the modern day party.

A Century for Socialism

ILP

Socialist greetings from the ILP
"The early ILP preached a socialism parliamentary in character but revolutionary in intention and radical in practice."
We still do!
Today we also campaign for a socialist rethink and socialist renewal.

For a free information pack about the ILP, past and present, contact the ILP, 49 Top Moor Side, Leeds LS11 9LW, Tel: 430613

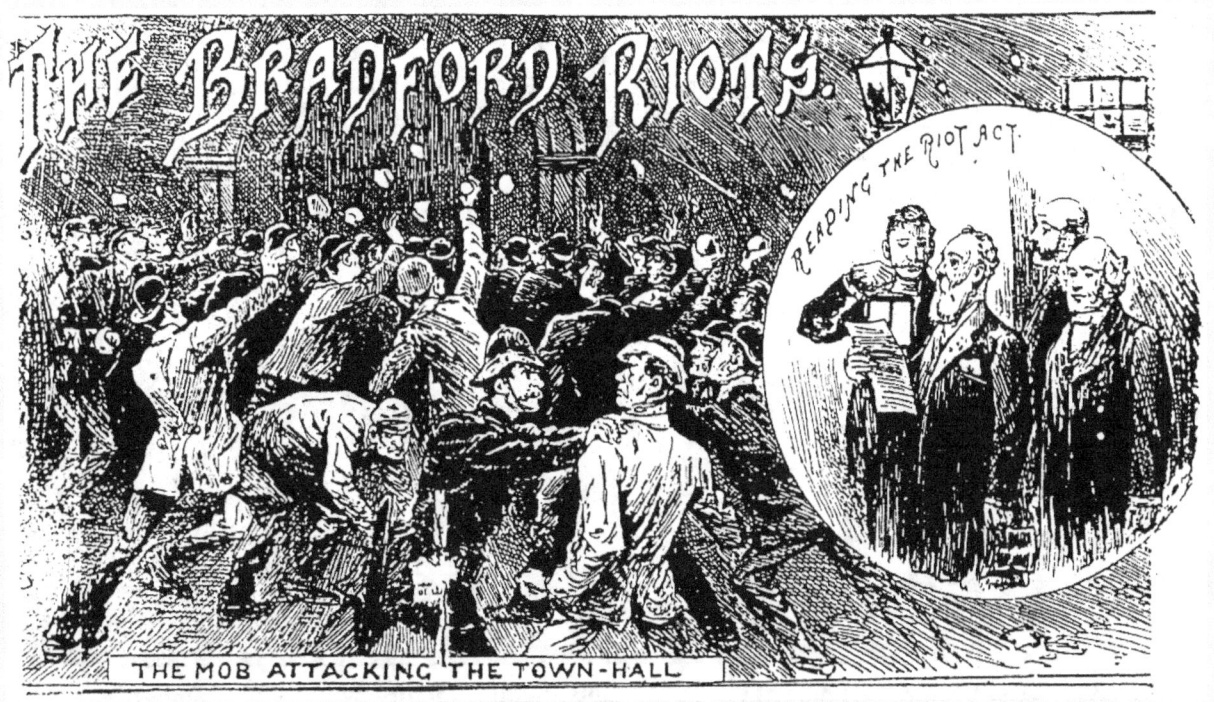

Albion Street, Bradford, home of the 1 In 12 Club building. Picture by Giuseppe Lambertino.

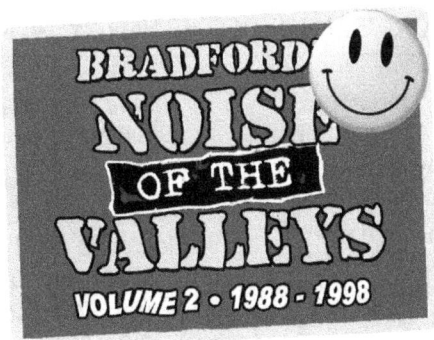

CHAPTER 3: THE DANCE SCENE 1989 - 1998

Dance music has always been part and parcel of popular culture, from the boppin' & jiving to jazz, boogie-ing to the blues, laying down some moves to Northern Soul, steppin' out to funk based disco music or just hitting the dance floor at the local pop/rock weekly disco night.

Dance music as a new musical genre emerged in the late 1970s in America, originating from the Bronx with local DJs who blended snippets of records and different tracks together to form new songs, with people rapping over the top. Using anything at hand to keep the punters dancing, DJs like Kool Herc, Africa Bambatta and Grandmaster Flash played cuts from James Brown Live albums, obscure soundtrack LPs, heavy rock and German electronica.

Defined as hip hop and rap, it had its origins in the debut LP by the Last Poets in 1969 and the late great Gil Scott-Heron in his 1970s album *The Revolution Will Not Be Televised*, as well as German based Italian producer Giorgio Moroder's 1977 electro-pop number one hit *I Feel Love* by Donna Summer. From the Hip Hop block parties, groups like Public Enemy (pictured) and Run DMC became the first superstars of Rap, while on the West Coast NWA (Niggers With Attitude) and Ice Cube produced the harder more aggressive 'Gangsta rap' scene.

US record companies would soon sanitize and de-politicise the music, Chuck D's (of Public Enemy) analysis was: *'..it suited record companies to sell Gangsta rap, it made big money while promoting a negative stereotype, it helped to keep the black people down and the white superior, like it's a music business conspiracy to promote the negative side of hip hop culture to the exclusion of all those who have a positive voice.'* (1)

By the late 1980s, Black America had *'generated four distinct and fully formed genres of electronic dance music; Detroit techno; the deep house/ garage sound of Chicago and New York: acid house and minimal jack tracks; breakbeat and sample-based hip hop.'* (2)

When it transplanted to the UK and Europe, these musical styles would mutate into a hybrid of sub-genres over the forthcoming years. The term 'house' would be an all-encompassing general term for 'rave' music, with its array of pre-fixes like Deep, Hard, Tribal, Progressive and Handbag House. Then there were the other emerging dance styles- Belgian Hardcore, Jungle, Electro-Funk, Trance, Big Beat, Trip-Hop, Drum'n'Bass, Ragga, Dubstep etc., all named in order to define the precise stylistic trends. (3)

In the UK, underground clubs, started in London, promoting this new style of dance music, fuelled by the new designer drug Ecstasy (MDMA). The scene was soon dubbed 'acid house' using the smiley faced logo from Alan Moore and Dave Gibbons' Watchmen graphic novel as their symbol. These events became known as 'raves' - a term first used in the 1960s to describe the all-night gigs and happenings of the nascent psychedelic scene.

By 1989/1990 the British dance/rave scene was in its second wave. It had begun to take on the cultural phenomenon of a 24-hour party weekend, with police chasing ravers en route to the home counties' illegal raves and mega-raves like Sunrise and Energy. The scene soon spread into a thriving circuit, moving from illegal sites to commercial venues, as the relaxation of licensing laws allowed the growth of all-night rave-style clubs. This led to an increase in the consumption of the drug Ecstasy. (4)

In Bradford, the scene took a while to emerge in the clubs. Artists such as the US vocal/disco group Tavares were still playing gigs and appeared at the Cloud Nine club (Manor Row) on September 22, 1988.

Tavares had featured on the soundtrack LP of the 1977 disco film *Saturday Night Fever* and had seven top 30 hits in the UK between 1976 - 78, their most familiar being *Heaven Must Be Missing An Angel*, a number four hit in July 1976, which reached No 12 as a remix in 1986.

Although the dance scene locally was mainly about DJs and producers, it did produce a few dance acts, like the all-girl trio Desire in 1988, and others between 1988 and 1994, some of whom are mentioned below.

UNIQUE 3

A trio of Bradford guys who trailblazed the 'bleep'n'bass' style of Northern hardcore house, Unique 3 had their roots in the old 1970s reggae sound-system culture mixed with hip hop and electro.

They began as DJs at the *Soundyard* based at Club Rio Campus in 1989 - a melting pot for future Bradford dance artists, playing a mix of deep house and post-acid house beats. The all-nighters (10 pm-6 am) at *Soundyard* had a membership of around 3,000, from as far as Manchester, Hull and Birmingham, and was filmed by the BBC show *Behind The Beat* on August 26, 1989. (5)

As Unique 3 And The Mad Musician, they cut their first floor-quaking sub-bass track *The Theme* as a B-side to *Only The Beginning* on their own Chill label in 1988, it's now a very collectable 12-inch.

A white label copy got heard at Manchester's Hacienda nightspot. Virgin Records' dance label, 10 Records, home to Jazzie B's Soul II Soul, whose album *Club Classics: Vol 1* included the hit No 1 single *Back To Life* in June 1989, signed the crew to a three-single, one-album deal.

The re-release of The Theme as a 12" came out on November 4, with the street art cartoon cover by System and the legendary graffiti tag 'Yo! Bradford Massive, Chill Posse' and reached No 61 in the charts.

The crew's second 12", *Musical Melody / Weight For The Bass*, came out the following year in April. The 'Original Soundyard Dubplate Mix' of *Musical Melody* reached No 6 in the Dance Chart and No 29 in the singles chart and was described as *'..brutal house with a Jamaican twist, heart-palpitating B-line which jabs and judders in sync with the cardiac-arrhythmia inducing pattern of the programmed drums and ultra trebly piano vamp...'* (6)

In May 1989, the trio were poised to launch their new dance club night Energy at the Palm Cove Club on Hollings Road. The guys would perform and spin platters of different styles of house on two dance floors every other Saturday from May 26.

THE DANCE SCENE 1989 - 1998

UNIQUE 3 / MOMENTUM / GLAMOROUS HOOLIGAN

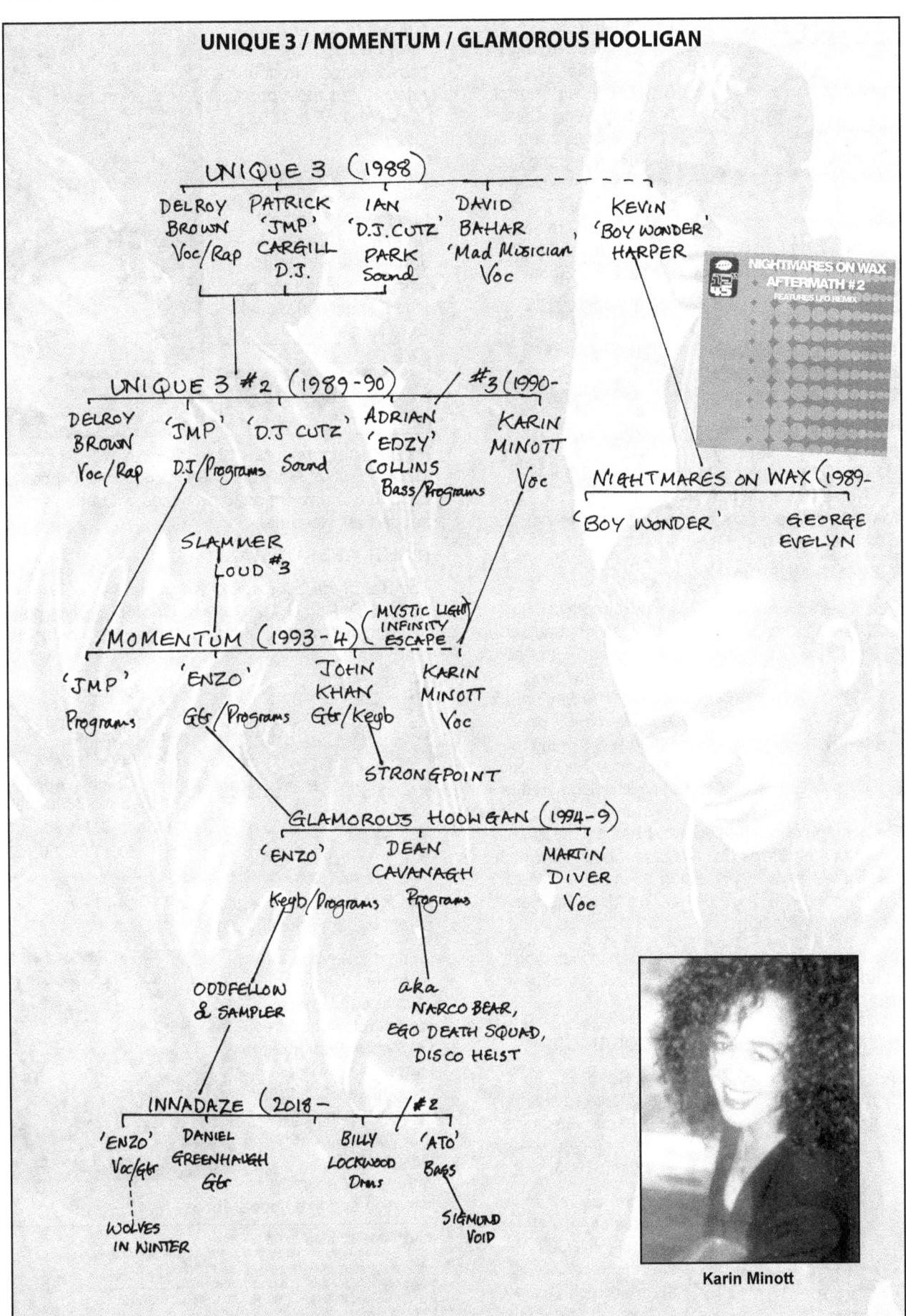

Karin Minott

103

Their album *Just Unique* was released in August 1990. Another 12", *Rhythm Takes Control,* featuring Karin Minott (7) on vocals, came out in November, and got to No 41 in the charts. A further two 12-inch singles were released in 1991, *No More*, was released in November, reaching number 74, followed by *Activity,* both on 10 Records.

In 2007 they came back with their *Rock The Bass* 12" and *I'm The...* CD single, both on Fat! Records.

The team then moved on to other projects. Eddyz, DJ Cutz and Delroy set up No Noise Recordings and JMP formed Miracle Records with Enzo formerly of Slammer and Loud.

THE MAD MUSICIAN

David Bahar, aka The Mad Musician, had set up Chill Records with Patrick Cargill and released the *Only The Beginning / The Theme* 12" prior to Unique 3 signing to Virgin. After being bought out of all writing credits by Virgin, he set up Tribe Recordings and released two 12-inch singles. The first was *Braek Out / Jazz In / Jazz Out* which had three tracks by X-Plosion on the other side. The second was *Together* as The Mad Musician Featuring X-Plosion.

He worked with many other musicians including sound engineer and keyboard whizz Carl Stipetic and guitarist Yoggy.

NO NOISE / PURE NOISE RECORDINGS

Set up at Try Mills, 237 Thornton Road, Bradford, by members of Unique 3, this hardcore rave label released at least nine 12-inch singles between 1992 and 1993.

The first was *I Know I'm Rushing*, by No Control (NNDJ001) and the second was the four-track *Victim Of Obsession / Feel Like Running / Astral Trance / Who Do You*, by local boys Escape. The fourth release was the *Open Up Your Mind EP* in 1993 by Unique 3.

Other releases were by acts like Mo2vation and the Huddersfield drum'n'bass rapper Lee Johnson aka L-Double, who also helped run No Noise and its sub-label Pure Noise.

Pure Noise put out five 12-inches in 1993, by DJ Trix, L-Double, Mo2vation, RTR and Zone Tripper. L-Double later went on to be based in London and set up Flex Records..

NIGHTMARES ON WAX

The Bradford/Leeds duo of Kevin Harper (cousin of Unique 3's Patrick Cargill) and George Evelyn, put their first 12" release *Dextrous* out on the Sheffield Warp label.

Their following release was the dance classic *Aftermath / I'm For Real*, in 1990, which reached No 38 in the charts and it is still heavily sampled to this day.

An LP, *A Word Of Science: The First And Final Chapter*, came out in 1991.

George Evelyn went on to run *The Headz Club* in Leeds and continued Nightmares On Wax without Kevin Harper, who went on to have a DJing career. Kevin released the album *Smokers Delight* in 1995, with further sporadic releases and live appearances.

NIGHTMARES ON WAX			
91	Warp WARPLP4	A WORD OF SCIENCE (THE 1st & FINAL CHAPTER) (LP)	20
95	Warp WARPLP 36	SMOKERS DELIGHT (2-LP)	20
99	Warp WARPLP 61	CARBOOT SOUL (2-LP)	20
06	Warp WARPLP 133	IN A SPACE OUTTA SOUND (2-LP)	25
08	Warp WARPLP 159	THOUGHT SO (2-LP)	12

RODEO JONES

The group was formed in London by Ben Copland and Graham Plato, who were faces on the rave scene in 1988, with original vocalist Michelle Jones. Their first release was *Desire* on the indie label G&M. The track became an underground club hit as well as being a hit in the New York charts.

After a band fallout, Michelle was replaced by local Keighley lass Jayne Tretton in 1990. Jayne had moved to London after leaving the Bradford band New Musical Testament, who'd had their track *Shamiso* featured on the *RISE* dance compilation cassette put out by Leeds-based Sunshine & Thunder Records.

With Jayne on board, the Rodeo Jones sound became a fusion of house and Ms Tretton's love of Northern Soul. They re-vamped the previous single as *Desire II* and it was a pirate radio hit and a bigger hit in the clubs than the original.

Their next release on their own label was *Natural World,* before being spotted and signed by A&M Records. The group's first release for the label was *Get Wise* which included a re-mix by E-Smoove & Steve 'Silk' Hurley of *Jack Your Body* fame.

Next came a re-release of *Natural World*, which became a club classic, then *Shades Of Summer* before their final release, *Ain't No Sunshine In The Rain / Surrender*.

An album was mooted but fell through as they left A&M.

Jayne went on to supply vocals on tracks by Brit Pop bands Suede, James and Placebo.

PUSH BUTTON TECHNOLOGY (PBT)

Formed around 1992, this local combo was led by Paul Janetta and were considered Bradford's answer to Germany's Kraftwerk. They did at least one personal appearance at an *Activate* all-nighter at Queen's Hall on May 2. In November 1992, they released a white label 12-inch *Just For You* coupled with a 'mash-up' B-side, *I'm Your Exstasy*. The original 12" and its re-mix have since become very collectable.

PUSH BUTTON TECHNOLOGY (PBT) (1992-			
PAUL JANETTA	CRAIG SUGDEN	MARK	DAVE NIETCHE D.J

UXL / UNDERGROUND SWING

PREMIERE				
UXL / (1992-				
MIKE HALL Voc	DAVID DEFURY Keyb	KAREN Bac.Voc	TIGGY BELL Dancers	SAMMY SAMUELS Dancers

These two local dance acts both appeared at the Maestro's nightclub (the old Mecca) on March 26, taking part in the regional heats of the *Sony Dance Music Search Of 1993*.

UXL (pictured above) went on to win the heat, performing their own composition, *I Gave You Love*, despite never before playing live. This qualified them forward to the competition's national final that May in London, where a recording contract was on offer by the RAL group part of Sony Records. The group's keyboard player Dave Defury had previously been in the Keighley band Premiere.

One of the members of Underground Swing was a cousin to Tasmin Archer.

UNDERGROUND SWING (1993-		
SIMONE Voc	'MR.FROSTIES' Voc	'RAD'

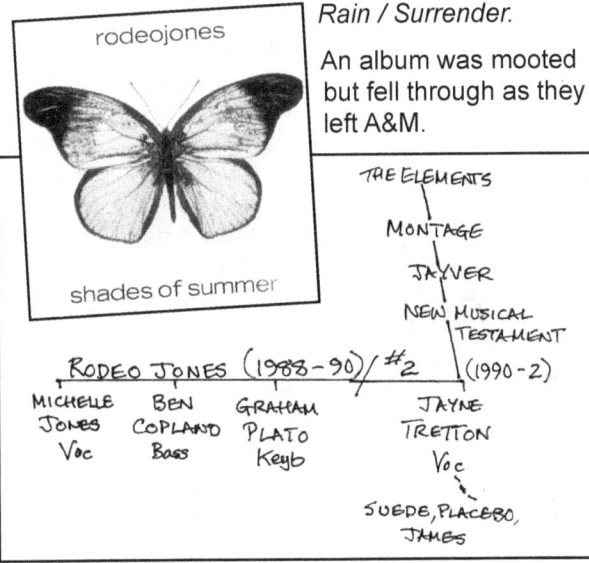

THE ELEMENTS			
MONTAGE			
JAYVER			
NEW MUSICAL TESTAMENT			
RODEO JONES (1988-90) / #2 (1990-2)			
MICHELLE JONES Voc	BEN COPLAND Bass	GRAHAM PLATO Keyb	JAYNE TRETTON Voc
			SUEDE, PLACEBO, JAMES

SCAPE

Formed in the early 1990s, Scape were Jason Laless and Les Simpson. As this combo they released the single-sided white label 12" *In Control* on the Time2Move label, which featured the sampled vocals of Chaka Khan, the singer in the 1970s funk band Rufus. This 12" is now very collectable on the Dance Scene.

DJ E-LOGIC

Local DJ Bahram Nikfar aka DJ E-Logic / Ill-Logic had started playing Italian Piano House after being a punter at the early dance nights at the Capricorn Club (Bibi's) in the early 1990s.

He released his first 12" *More Control / Musical Mayhem (featuring Defender)* in 1992, which was a Sanctuary Recording for JNS and had a '*Thanks to PBT*' etched into the runout grooves.

His next release, in 1995, was the 12" *Unreel Vibes Vol 1*, followed in 1997 with a version of Simon & Garfunkel's *Bridge Over Troubled Water / Get On Up* which included DNA featuring Deanna for Infinity Records. The same year he put out the 12" *Heat Is Jumped (DNA mix) / Going All The Way* on New Essential Platinum. A further two 12" releases for Infinity records followed in 1999, *Run to Me / Give Me All Your Love* and *The Gate / Nu Skool Jam*.

In 2000, he set up his own label, Elasticman Records, whose first release was the 12" *Want To DJ / Cooking Up Yer Brain*, credited to ILOGIK & Bazooka Joe. Further releases over the next years besides his own were by artists such as Testube Babies, Dom Demure & M Ramone and Marc Johnson & Dave Holmes. Bahram carried on DJing and travelled the world from Russia to Ibiza to New Zealand.

In 1994, another new dance act formed, called Ethos, which included Karl Hamilton the former drummer of the 1980s band From Knowhere.

THE RISE OF THE DJ

In the year 1943, at the height of World War II, in a room above a Working Men's Club in Otley, West Yorkshire a young (and future Sir) Jimmy Savile started playing 'dance' records on a rudimentary Gramophone linked to an amplification system. By 1946, he was working for the Mecca organisation in ballrooms where he commissioned a 'twin deck' system built by Westrex. (8)

Savile was probably one the world's first club Disc Jockeys (DJs) as well as being the first presenter on the TV pop programme Top Of The Pops in 1964.

From the 1960s to the 1980s, the DJs of the BBC's Radio 1 were either held in high regard, such as independent music champion John Peel, or considered larger-than-life characters, such as Dave Lee Travis, aka The Hairy Cornflake.

The stereotypical Radio 1 DJs of this period were later derided as 'Smashie 'n' Nicey' caricatures, based on Alan 'Fluff' Freeman, with corny catchphrases and sound effects as part of their presenting style.

Even provincial local radio DJs and the thousands of mobile DJs working in pubs and clubs all around the country were not taken very seriously by the public or musicians.

This all changed with the arrival of the dance/rave scene, as the DJs who spun the discs and segwayed into the next track using faders and mixers became artists in their own right, with the aim to seamlessly continue the beat and keep people dancing.

Soon the scene had its own specialised dance magazines, like Mixmag and Muzik, which framed their reviews of raves, not about the atmosphere and the punters, but around the DJs as cult figures, thus projecting DJs as 'stars' akin to rock and pop stars.

Some of the early top DJs were Danny Rampling, Paul Oakenfold, Nicky Holloway and Carl Cox, who worked in London-based clubs, while at Madchester's Hacienda Club, Mike Pickering and Dave Haslam were the key DJs. Initially very few women DJs breached the scene, but some like Judge Joolz and Liza Pinup (Lisa Chilcott - pictured) gained iconic status.

THE CLUB NIGHTS IN BRADFORD

Bradford's after-hours nightlife had always been diverse and vibrant, with night clubs like Bibi's, Palm Cove, The Mayflower, Sugarcane, W's and The Function all playing a mixture of soul, disco, reggae and Lovers Rock, to late-night drinkers and dancers. Even in 1992, new clubs were opening, like New Edition (see below).

MONEYSPINNER ... Floyd Peltier, left, and brother Chris hand over £400 to nurse Anne Walmsley

REVELLERS danced the night away at a nightclub to raise money for a hospital ward.

Brothers Chris and Floyd Peltier, owners of the New Edition nightclub in Worthington Street, Bradford, held an all-night cabaret and disco, which raised £400 for Ward 15 at Bradford Royal Infirmary.

The money from the nightclub will go towards buying special mattresses as relief for patients' bed sores, and pain relieving equipment which costs between £2,000 and £3,000 each.

Christine Barratt, secretary of the Ward 15 Home from Home Appeal at the hospital, said: "Chris and Floyd saw the ward and wanted to help raise money for the patients.

"It is a very nice gesture and we are very grateful to them."

But, with the advent of the emerging dance scene, a host of new dance nights began to appear in the early 1990s, run by an eclectic range of people and promoters, each offering different styles at various venues from the University's Communal Building to Queen's Hall.

One of the earliest was *Tolerance* started in 1991 by Dean Cavanagh (more of whom later) whose nights first started at Rio's. He was even able to bring over from the US top Detroit techno DJ Juan Atkins in February 1991. With the help of fellow DJs 'Slim' Mark and Tony Ross, the *Tolerance* nights later moved to the University's Communal Building and continued through to 1992.

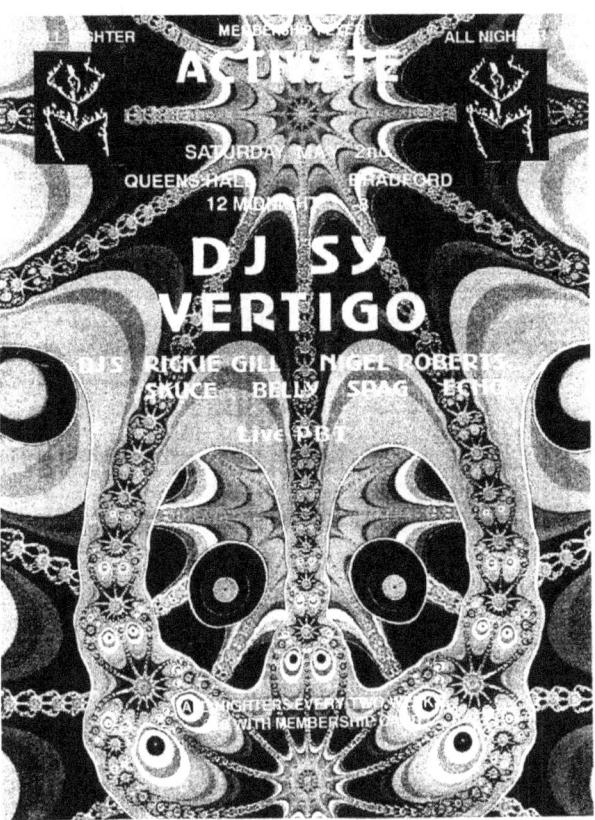

Another early dance night was *Activate*, organised by the posse of Gary Holdsworth, Richard 'Gilly' Gill and others, who had late-nighters at Queen's Hall during 1991. At one event in May, they had a live performance by dance combo Push Button Technology.

Gary and Richard were also involved in both of the local dance specialist record shops that opened in Bradford during this period; *Happy House Records*, on Southgate, and *Global Beat*, on Barry Street. When both these concerns closed, Gary started *The Disc* in 1994 on Barry Street, later moving to Sunbridge Road.

There were also events at the Capricorn Club (Bibi's) in Manningham and *Escape* at Champagnes nightclub, near the university. Mainstream dance nights were also held on weekends at Bradford's regular nightspots like Maestros and Cloud 9 and Mackenzie's in Bingley.

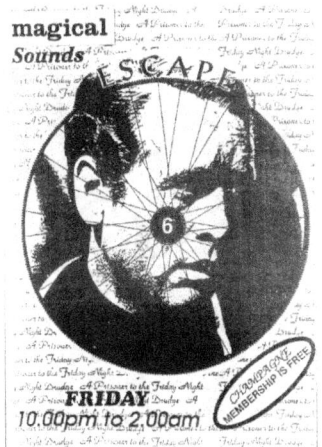

As the dance scene grew, there was a constant search for that ultimate disco experience. As the Queen's Hall acquired a late license more dance nights appeared, like **Qix,** a monthly event originally started at the University's Subway Bar. This funk phenomenon was a collection of DJs whose "primary aim was to support the Colin Reid Countryside Trust (CRCT), an explorer who died tragically on an expedition in the Himalayas in September 1991. In his memory, Qix intends to raise money for CRCT - an environmental conservation group mirroring Colin's concerns. All door money goes directly to the Trust and a door to door recycling project in BD7 has been totally funded by the Qix events" (9).

Throbbing to the sounds of classic 1970s disco was the **M&M's** nights at the University's Communal Building. Started in May 1991, by Munsor and Malcolm (hence the name), these 'search for Love' nights re-lived the sounds of private parties that no clubs were playing at the time.

"After rave more people are willing to go out and dance, and not worry that they are wearing the right clothes or making the right moves! There is so much freedom at M&M's – you do your own Thang!!" (10)

Global was another monthly event held at Queen's Hall's cellar bar, which attracted many dance fanatics with their slogan, *'Music is the Drug. The Future is ours to Party'*.

In late 1992, **Spice** hit the scene, developed from a collaboration of Bradford College and University entertainment groups. They staged impressive events every Thursday night at Queen's Hall, using some of the same DJ's as Qix and also inviting guest DJs and bands to play live. This all added to an unique atmosphere that was emphasised by their rather impressive decor.

Then there was the Underworld (formerly W's) under the world famous Bombay Stores on Great Horton Road, who had trance and techno nights by **Floating Bong** and **Eternal Smile**.

Onwards from 1993 were events like **Pump** and **Planet** at Queen's Hall, and others like **Universe**

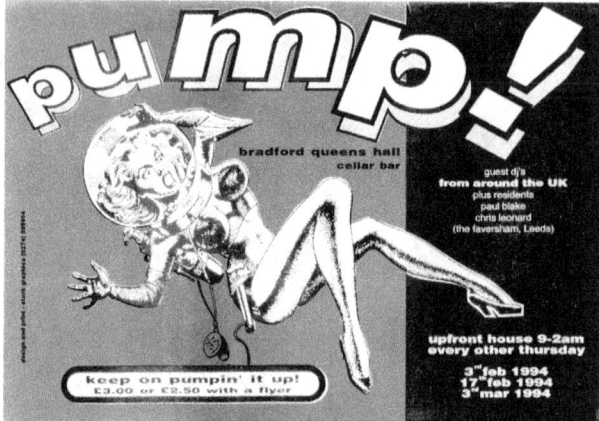

and **Her Majesty's Service**, but none could compete with the two biggest dance nights in the North both in Leeds, **Ark** and **Back To Basics**.

By late 1995, Mark and Matt, owners of *System Records*, the second hand record shop on Barry Street, were DJ-ing at the Beehive's cellar bar as

The Underground Set, and were also guest DJs at Leeds' **Lava Lounge**.

This is only a short snap shot of the range of dance events during the period under investigation and is in no way is meant to be definitive, and to list all the individual DJs who were working locally would also be too numerous to mention.

THE CRIMINAL JUSTICE BILL

On the Bank Holiday weekend of May 29, 1992, Castlemorton Common, near the Malvern Hills in Worcestershire, became the site of the biggest illegal outdoor rave in history, with an estimated 20-40,000 ravers attending. The free party was organised by the Spiral Tribe, a bunch of 'Crustie' anarcho-hippy-punk type travellers, who had been running free parties in old warehouses and at disused air fields for a couple of years.

These New Age Travellers were nomadic, visiting the dozen or so annual free festivals around the country during the summer months. By the beginning of the 1990s it was estimated that there were around 40,000 travellers inhabiting converted coaches, buses and various other motor vehicles.

When urban ravers first encountered the 'crusties' at previous year's festivals, there was a mutual suspicion, until they discovered some common ground. The rave scene was all about drugs, dance and having a wild time dirt cheap. This alliance brought the feeling of freedom in these temporary autonomous zones. (11)

"During the five days of its existence, Castlemorton inspires questions in Parliament, makes the front page of every newspaper, and incites nationwide panic about the possibility that the next destination on the 'crustie' itinerary is your very own neighbourhood. Tabloids like the Sun stoke the public fear and resentment of 'the scum army' of dole scrounging soap dodgers having fun on your tax money. In the quality papers, commentators line up to fulminate against the malodorous anarcho-mystics. A local resident in Castlemorton complains ' There's something hypnotic about the continuous pounding beat of the music, and it's driving people living on the front line into a frenzy'. On the last day, after hanging around rather than attempting to sneak a getaway, thirteen members of Spiral Tribe are arrested, and several sound-systems are impounded. Police forces across rural Britain start collaborating in Operation Snapshot: the creation of a massive database with names of ringleaders and licence numbers of travellers' and ravers' vehicles. An intensive campaign of surveillance and intelligence work is mounted to ensure that any future Castlemortons are nipped in the bud. And the Conservative government begins to hatch the ultimate death-blow to the free party scene: the Criminal Justice and Public Order Act." (12)

In the summer of 1994, the Tory party presented to Parliament Part 5 of the Criminal Justice and Public Order Bill (CJB). With extra police powers to stop and search, it targeted squatters, travellers, illegal raves and free festivals.

The act defined a 'rave' as a crowd of people, as small as a hundred, playing amplified music-emitting a succession of 'repetitive beats'. (The average rave tune ran at 125 bpm.) Failure to comply with any dispersal order by the police would result in a three month prison sentence and a fine of £2,500.

Before long, organised resistance to the bill, to the soundtrack of the Beastie Boys rallying cry, *Fight For The Right To Party*, began with a 15,000 people demo on May 1, in London. Organised by SQUASH (Squatters Action for Secure Homes) and the Advance Party (an alliance of sound systems) the demo converged on Trafalgar Square. Two bigger demos in July and October caused some disruption of the capital, but nothing like the Anti-Poll Tax riots of 1990.

Amongst the various protest EP 12 inches released to support opposition to the bill was *Repetitive Beats* by Retribution (a mixed bunch of members from The Drum Club, System 7 and Fundamental).

On November 3, 1994, the CJB was passed in Parliament and became law. Yet, the scene didn't die, it just went underground, organising smaller and less annoying parties with the tacit tolerance of the police. (13)

STIMULATIONS: RAVES AT THE 1 IN 12 CLUB 1993-98

Although The 1 In 12 Club's reputation would always be linked to the punk and hardcore scene, it had always promoted gigs and events by a range of bands and artists, showcasing a whole range of musical styles from indie and ska, through to folk and world music. So, at the height of the dance scene, it was no surprise that certain Club members decided to form a dance collective to promote all-nighters.

The *Stimulations* collective formed in early 1993 and soon started organising monthly events. They made use of the Club's three floors, transforming each into a distinct space with backdrops, projections and spectacular lighting.

Two floors were designed as areas for different

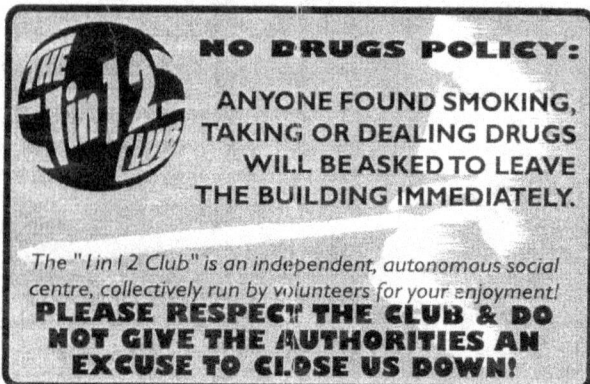

Jon Langford (Three Johns / The Mekons) enjoying a rave at The 1 In 12 Club

dance styles while the top floor was the 'chill out' room.

Long-time members Emma Marshall, Marek Skoczylas (Fritz The Cat), Dave Lizard and former Figures From The Cold bass player Padee Singh were, with 'Badger' Brock, Kelvin Edwards and other more recent members, instrumental in ensuring that these events ran smoothly and the Club's 'no drugs' policy was rigorously enforced.

Of course, The 1 In 12 Club had previously played host to various disco nights before the Stimulations

crew, DJ Padee had put on one of the first club raves back in February 1991.

Many other promoters and members organised similar nights like *M&M's, Going Back To My Roots, Glad* (a lesbian and gay night), *Tune In/Turn On*, Back To Bradford, Quantum, Rebirth, and various dub nights. (14)

1 In 12 Club All Nighter 23-10-93

I knew it was going to be a good night because Stork's very own Custard was doing security. The 1 In 12 Club has a reputation for putting on good events and this one was no exception. There was a bit of trouble with the p.a. at first but when things got going I was in for a kicking night (and day). On the top floor we had the 'chill out' room which played ambient trance and had some excellent visuals. Downstairs on the middle floor was Spice, which again was cool although it was a while until it got going, (due to technical difficulties). Downstairs on the gig floor the D.J.'s were playing some of the best sounds in the world of Techno/Break beat. The 1 in 12 Club has a very sensible policy about no trouble and no bullshit and is proving once again that it's just not out to rip people off. This was the best all nighter I've been to.

DAVE BERG   STORK #10

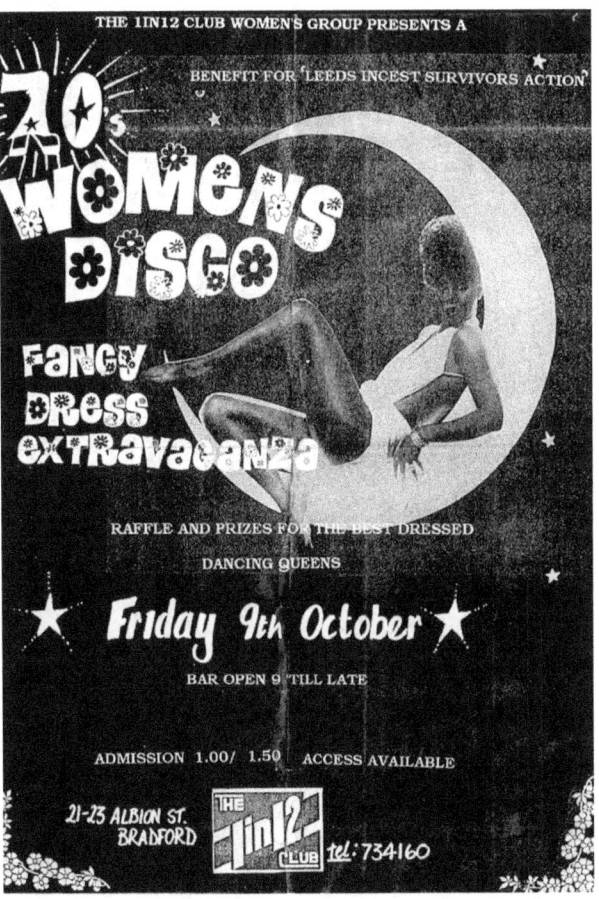

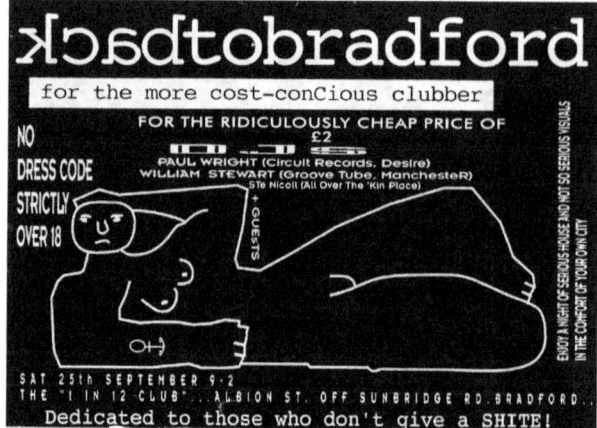

But it was the monthly *Stimulations* events that were the most popular, with membership growing as crowds queued around the block to attend the nights.

This first wave of dance all-nighters at the 1 In 12 by the *Stimulations* collective took place between February 1993 and March 1997.

MIRACLE RECORDS

Funded with a grant from the Prince's Trust, ex-Unique 3 member Patrick Cargill and former Slammer/Loud guitarist Enzo Annecchini formed Miracle Records. Based in Enzo's 'rat loft studio' at Flat 7, 5 Oak Avenue, Manningham, Bradford. They produced four 12-inch singles during 1993-94. The duo soon became a trio, when John Khan got involved, and as Escape they released the *Victim Of Obsession EP* on local label No Noise in 1993.

Miracle's first release was a 'white label' only 12" entitled *Take Me I'm Yours* by their incarnation Momentum and featured the vocals of Karin Minott (ex-Unique 3) who was also John's partner.

The trio's next release was the five-track *Feel Your Love* 12" EP (as Momentum), followed by the four-track *In Casa Bella* 12" (as Mystic Light), then the five-track *Judgment EP* (as Infinity).

GLAMOROUS HOOLIGAN

'*Glamorous Hooligan were formed in the Young Lion Cafe, a seedy back street hostelry in the red light district of multi-cultural Bradford. Amid the sound of Prince Jammy, deep lovers rock, drug bartering and drunken rows between hookers and their pimps a conversation was struck off between Enzo Annechini (late of major league thrash metallers Slammer and live guitarist for UK techno pioneers Unique 3) and Dean Cavanagh (late of Her Majesty's Jobclub, Armley and Leeds seminal dance club Soundclash) that resulted in the unholy alliance that is Glamorous Hooligan.*'

'*The two found they both shared an avid interest in low-life activities, football, dub, guitars, old skool hip hop, cult movies and hard-core porn finding common ground in Public Enemy, Steinski and the Mass Media, Debbie Does Dallas, Mad Professor, The Revolting Cocks, Freddy Bastone, Led Zep and Italia League TV coverage.*' (15)

Enzo's partner in crime, Dean Cavanagh, was a local Clayton lad, DJ and founder of *Tolerance* dance nights who, whilst having the same illustrious surname as the co-author of the fine book you hold in your hands right now, is no relation.

The duo's first release as Glamorous Hooligan was the 12" EP *Research & Destroy*, in 1995, on the London-based indie label Delancey Mass Of Black. The EP's back cover was an iconic photo of the 1929 St Valentine's Day Massacre in Chicago.

Their second EP, *Viva Negativa*, also came out that year. The following year would see them release their first LP, a ten-track double vinyl affair called *Wasted Youth Club Classics*.

The lads were then picked up by Warner Brothers sub-label Arthrob for their next EP, *In Absentia*, in 1997. Their second LP, *Naked City Soundtrax*, came out in 1998 on Arthrob.

Another 12", *Jump*, was released in 1997 on the Leeds Cooker label. Two more 12-inches, *Needle 23* and *Stone Island Estate* followed in 1998, again on Arthrob. A further 12", *Unusual Suspects*, was released on the Armadillo label before Dean started to produce music under the pseudonyms of Narco Bear, Ego Death and Disco Heist.

In 1999, Dean, as the frontperson for Glamorous Hooligan, was interviewed by John Peel in the derelict Manningham Mills Complex as part of Peel's *Sound Of The Suburbs* TV series on Bradford.

Another sideline for Dean during this period was freelance journalism. He wrote articles for magazines such as *The Face, ID, NME, Melody Maker* and *The Guardian* and founded his own club culture 'zine *Herb Garden*.

Since then, Dean has progressed to writing theatre plays, film scripts and sceenplays, usually in collaboration with Scottish author Irvine Welsh (of *Trainspotting* fame).

Some of their plays have won critical acclaim, like *Babylon Heights*, and their 2004 BBC 3 short film *Dose*, which was nominated for a *BAFTA* award. The team of Dean and Irvine had many simultaneous projects in development for film and TV.

In the 1970s and 1980s, besides the commercial disco scene, the UK's biggest dance scenes were Northern Soul and Dub Reggae, the latter had been long established at venues like the Palm Cove Club in Bradford. Most weekends at this time were 'battles' between rival Sound Systems pumping the bass-heavy vibes to 'toasters' (early rappers) voicing their narrative, to a room heaving with bodies dancing in oblivion.

When the new rave scene appeared in the early 1990s, it also revitalised the old Dub scene and there were soon DJs and nights to exploit the renewed interest.

One of the first, starting in 1991, was *Dub Me Crazy*, appearing first at Palm Cove, then Checkpoint, then Queen's Hall between 1992-4, before finishing at Bradford College's Sound Gallery venue (next to the University) on Great Horton Road.

ROOTSMAN, DAYIAH AND THIRD EYE MUSIC

After settling in Bradford in 1983, John Bolloten immersed himself in the local reggae scene. He worked for over two years at Roots record store on Lumb Lane, where he became known as Rootsman.

As a DJ he had been doing sound systems since 1985, before founding the highly successful club night *Dub Me Crazy*, promoting roots and dub music and giving a platform to up-and-coming artists to play their own material.

Dean Cavanagh worked a residency at the *Sounclash* event nights in Leeds and Rootsman for over two years. *'My year zero came in 1992, after sucking up a skinful in Scruffy Murphys, I happened to stagger into the gothic Queens Hall, Morley Street, Bradford. Up until then my skooling in all things Dubular had taken place in low-rent terrace dwellings in Manningham where the sound of coke rocks popping was louder than the system. That night was my road to Damascus, The Rootsman was at the helm of his Dub Me Crazy session and the vibrations were like nothing else I'd heard: original, inspiring and above all fresh. After that initial fix, I was hooked.'*

'I got to know the Rootsman and before long the seeds of the legendary Soundclash Club were sown, we joined forces and soon after we were

inviting the likes of Adrian Sherwood, Dr Alex Patterson, and Andy Weatherall up to the monthly audiophonic mish-mash at the Music factory in Leeds'.

'We believe it set a precedent. Sadly due to getting fucked about and losing our income support giros on the night, we had to put it to bed in late 1994.' (16)

Rootsman's debut 10" white label EP *Koyaanisqati* was released in May 1994 on the Soundclash label to critical acclaim in the music press. After another EP, *Soundclash City Rockers*, he left to continue his career on his own label, Third Eye Music.

The debut release was the *Storm Clouds* LP by his first wife Dayiah, subtitled Dayiah Meets The Disciples. A follow-up LP, *Urban Jungle*, was released in July 1997, by Dayiah And The Disciples. The Disciples were a London-based bunch of roots and culture musicians, who had previously released several killer singles, like

Prowling Lion, as well as six dub albums and were famous for having their music featured on the legendary Jah Shaka Sound System.

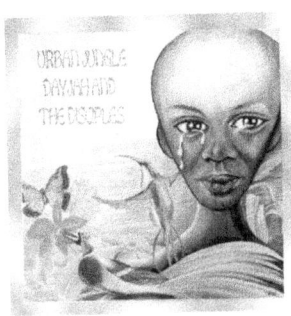

The label's next release, in 1995, was his own *Natural Born Thrillers* EP, which was the first UK roots release to successfully marry the steppers and jungle styles. In the same year, he released his debut album *In Dub We Trust*. The myriad diverse samples, beats and African, Arabian and Asian sounds, all tied to a heavyweight rhythm section in the mix, made this album one of the most original releases that year.

CLUB OF THE WEEK
DUB ME CRAZY : BRADFORD
SATURDAY JUNE 10

The Sound Gallery, Great Horton Road. 01274 604831. 9-late

BRADFORD'S Rootsman is one of the most prominent artists on the UK's reggae roots scene, having had a good handful of years at its core, but, like so many on the UK's reggae scene, it's only recently that he's become a recognised name, helped by the melting barriers within the leftfield side of the UK's underground music scene.

His monthly 'Dub Me Crazy' nights have become legendary on the Sound System scene where his characteristic hard digital steppers rhythms are relayed via DAT-plate, and it now regularly plays host to guests like Boom Shacka Lacka (The Disciples), Iration Steppas, Mixman, Mannasseh, Dub Judah, Jah Works, Rod Taylor, Paul Fox and Joey Jay.

Last year, The Rootsman issued his first two singles, 'Koyaanisqatsi' and 'Soundclash City Rockers' on Leeds' Soundclash label, and has just set up his own outlet on which his third 'Natural Born Thrillers' – featuring experimentations in jungle/dub – appeared earlier this year. This will be followed soon by 'International Language Of Dub'. His first steps into the world of remixing were interpretations for The Woodshed and Blue, and his debut album, 'In Dub We Trust', is ready to be launched in July.

Tonight's guests are London's Jah Warrior – who have been regulars on the circuit for a number of years and have released a number of records under the name of Zulu Warriors – with a new single (as Jah Warrior again) ready to roll. The night promises to be another well-attended session with plenty of dub-hungry followers commuting from all over the country.

1. Shangri-la/Dayiah & The Disciples/Dat
2. Babylon/Splash/Dee Jay
3. Morocco/Bud Alzir/Virgin
4. Thanks & Praises/Frankie Paul/Marshalls
5. Psalms 72/D-Maximillion/DAT
6. Acting Solemn/Ahlam/Barbarity
7. Judgment Morning/Sizzla/Xterminator
8. Set El Banat/Magdy Gazoly/Pardees
9. River Nile Dub/El Jathoor/DAT
10. In Dub We Trust (CD)/The Rootsman/Third Eye

Chart compiled by The Rootsman

Melody Maker review

Next came the CD album *International Language Of Dub*, a compilation of Rootsman's tracks remixed by a range of local and non-local artists. It featured Bradford artists like Glamorous Hooligan, Dayiah, Strongpoint, Sansaar, King's Highway, DJ Nigel Parker and Dave McT, plus The Disciples and Leeds rockers Black Star Liner. It reached No 26 in the UK's independent album charts and was declared one of the top 100 dub albums of all time by the UK's *DJ Magazine*.

Other artists who released 12" EPs on Third Eye were Grounation (from Frankfurt, Germany), Oochi (from Leeds), Winston McAnuff and Daddy Freddy.

Over the years, Rootsman continued to release EPs, LPs and CDs on Third Eye, as well as for other European labels, like *Realms Of The Unseen* (1999), *Roots Bloody Rootsman* (2001) and *New Testament* (2002).

He has also collaborated with artists such as medieval folk group Celtarabia and has done remixes for Soulfly, a band led by ex-Sepultura frontman Max Cavalera.

While travelling the world to do DJ sets, Rootsman concentrated more on running his Tales From Bradistan Blog site.

He also became a renowned photographer. In November 2011, he had an exhibition at Gallery II in the University's Richmond Atrium. Bradford Raw was a collection of portraits of ordinary folk who call Bradford home.

STRONGPOINT

A collaboration of ex-Momentum DJ/artist John Khan and Simon Manger, who worked at one time selling electronics at Wood's music shop. Besides their track on the *International Language Of Dub* CD, they also released on Third Eye a 12" EP entitled *Product Of Imagination* in 1996.

John Khan would later take a break for a few years to concentrate on DJ-ing at clubs like Planet Venus, Boilerhouse and Conners Nightspot in Bradford. He honed his mixing, mastering and production techniques to start writing and producing a new vibe, alongside his partner Karin Minott's vocal skills, on two singles by Earl Tu Tu and DJ Dera.

In 2003, he wrote *The Hitter* for former Bradford WBO Champion boxer Junior Witter (pictured right), which featured Karin and JMP (Patrick Cargill), both ex-Unique 3.

He produced material and collaborated on projects with various artists such as Tariq Sheikh (aka DJT).

PIRATE RADIO STATIONS

Pirate radio stations have been around since the 1960s when off-shore stations like *Radio Caroline* played the latest new sounds. In the early 1990s, when mainstream radio stations like the Bradford-based commercial *Pennine Radio* were only playing the chart hits of the day, a new breed of local underground dance-orientated pirate stations emerged.

These pirate stations were organised by local DJs and supporters to play the latest dance 12-inches that were hitting the scene.

Three stations that were broadcasting during this period were *Emergency 99.9* (originally run from a flat in Allerton), *WKLR*, and *Paradise City Radio* which was one of the first in Yorkshire.

Emergency 99.9 FM started broadcasting twenty hours a day, seven days a week. It played a wide variety of music, all types of dance, plus reggae, jazz and even heavy metal slots at the weekend.

The station even organised regular under-18s raves called *Voyage* on Thursday nights for £2 entry at Berlin's nightspot on Manor Row.

IF I RULED THE WORLD

ROOTSMAN, WKLR 107.5 FM, BRADFORD

#	Artist	Track	Label
1	DENNIS BROWN	PROMISED LAND	SHALOM
2	LUCIANA	POOR AND SIMPLE	GREENSLEEVES
3	JAH WOOSH	ISAIAH	BLAKAMIX
4	FRANKIE PAUL	RECESSION	OBSERVER
5	HORACE ANDY	WHO SAY JAH JAH DEAD	HORACE ANDY
6	ZION TRAIN	KING OF THE MOUNTAINS	ZION TRAIN
7	WINSTON SMITH	MR BOSS MAN	BUFFALO
8	DAYJAH & THE DISCIPLES	GATHER TOGETHER	THIRD EYE MUSIC
9	DREAD ZONE	AFRICA	CREATION
10	YAMI BOLO	REMA AND JUNGLE	BUFFALO

Rootsman's set list for local pirate station WKLR published in Echoes Magazine

JAMES 'PIANOMAN' SAMMON

Local Bradford lad James Sammon started DJing on the local pirate radio station *Paradise City Radio* in his late teens and continued there and on other Yorkshire stations like *Dream 107.6 FM* for around ten years. During his time as DJ Sammon and while working at Happy House Records on Southgate, he gained his nickname 'Pianoman' due to his love of uplifting piano-based tunes.

In November 1993, he started Piano City Productions (PCP) with fellow Bradford DJs Richard Copley and Housey G.

After releasing a disc called *PCP Vol 2*, which included the track *That Whitney Tune* (featuring the chorus from Whitney Houston's smash hit *I Wanna Dance With Somebody*) the PCP crew started to get noticed. So much so, that they were invited to Moscow to play at a 12,000-capacity rave organised by *AZ-Art DJ Corporation* in September 1994. The three DJs flew out to Russia accompanied by Leeds dancer Fiona Day.

DJ Sammon, DJ Coply and dancer Fiona Day

Courtesy of the Telegraph & Argus

James' other releases in 1994 included the 12-inch singles *Revelation*, on Steppin' Out Records, and *Tribute To Asha*, on Disco Magic UK and then, in 1995, *Cast a Spell*, on Reach Records.

He hit the singles chart at No 6 in June 1996 with *Blurred* which sampled a section of Brit Pop band Blur's song *Girls And Boys*.

'I'll bet there are dozens of people in Bradford who own a record with DJ Sammon's name tag on it. He seems to have sold off his music collection at some point or another and it's filtered through time to various music shops and car boot sales.' (17)

As well as his own releases, he has done remixes and recorded with a host of musicians such as ex-Stone Roses frontman Ian Brown, Craig David and Donna Air.

In October 2009, he wrote the single *Eternity* for X Factor reject Danny Antenbring of Heaton. In December 2010 he directed his first video, for female rapper Michela Mac Bromley's debut single *Told You So* at the Move nightclub in Bradford.

Besides his 'Pianoman' moniker, James also uses the aliases of Bass Boyz, Service Crew, Hidden Agenda and Serious Business.

DOCTOR MAN

Local West Bowling rap artist Mohammed Sajid, aka Doctor Man, released his first single *Comin' In Style* in 1996, on his own record label, DMP. It was released on cassette and featured toaster Dady Rizla helping out. The cassette single was distributed through Virgin, HMV and Asian outlets.

Former Grange Upper School pupil Doctor Man had started rappin' and writing material back in 1993 when he was only seventeen.

He released a second self-penned double-A sided single, *Natural / Feelings*, which introduced the new vocal talents of Michelle on backing vocals.

In November 1998, Luke Singh interviewed Doctor Man for a full-page article in the first issue of the new magazine, *The Voice of Manningham*.

USURPA

This dance act consisted of two guys, Rick and Bruce, who formed around 1996. They produced at least two singles, one a cover of Denice William's 1984 No 2 hit *Let's Hear It For The Boy* and the electro tracks *Together / Burning Desire*.

These last two tracks featured the vocal talents of Sally Dawson from Stoney Ridge, Bradford, and gained some interest from certain record companies interested in re-mixing the tracks.

```
USURPA (1996-
RICK          BRUCE         SALLY
              Keybs/Programs DAWSON
                             Voc
```

Rhythm & Blues (R'n'B), or soul music, has been part of the dance scene since the early 1960s and has always had a large following in the UK. Especially popular are US labels like Motown, Stax and Atlantic, with top artists like Aretha Franklin, Diana Ross, Curtis Mayfield, Marvin Gaye, The Four Tops and The Temptations.

Soul singers and groups had always been around on the local Bradford scene, and some still performed during the modern dance scene 1988-98.

JANET JAYE

Bradford-born soul diva Janet Lewison had originally performed with her two sisters Rose and Christine, as the trio of vocalists fronting the band Sanction (1978-79) which also included their brother Sam on drums.

By 1993, as 'Janet Lewis', she was fronting a Midland-based band who played at Ronnie Scott's in London and had signed to FM Records.

Using the stage name 'Janet Jaye', Janet had worked as a backing singer for Ruby Turner and The Drifters amongst others. She performed as a Whitney Houston sound-alike/look-alike for two years which took her to Berlin, Switzerland, France and Spain.

Although she was approached by people from

the recording industry on more than one occasion, she has never been signed.

Janet performed locally in clubs and pubs, covering the classic soul standards like Whitney Houston's *I'm Every Woman* and Sister Sledge's *We Are Family*.

On Saturday, November 12, 2011, she attempted to recreate the 1970s and 1980s nightclub scene at a special concert entitled *Disco Inferno* at Bingley Sports Centre.

"There used to be many nightclubs in Bradford City centre to choose from, back in the day, when people would dress to impress and you could dine and dance to the best music," recalled Janet in a T&A article promoting the event.

ANGELES

Formed around 1996 by Jay Welsh and Martin Cartledge, this local dance duo released six 12-inch singles between 1996-99. *It's Alive / Shine* came out on the Perfecto/EastWest label in 1996, followed by *Keeper Of The Dream* on Concept Records later that year.

The duo's third release, *High Horse & Sunset Sky*, appeared in 1998 on the local Pied Piper Records and was re-released that year on Night Flight Records. Their final two 12-inches, *Hit Zero* and *It's Over Now*, were both released on the local label Flammable Records in 1999.

Angeles also performed and recorded under a string of aliases such as Black Ice, Blind Faith, Fatheads, Sisko, Sleepwalkers and The Unknown.

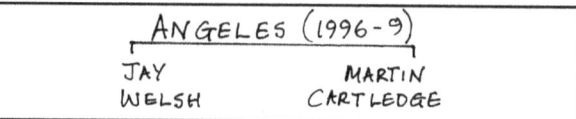

PIED PIPER RECORDS

This local dance label was started in 1997 by Jay and Martin of Angeles, Richard Gill, and Nathaniel Cook. The first release was a 12" by Sunset Sky, which was an alias of Martin from Angeles.

His other aliases were Kid Scientific, Darkside, Cirque, Sneaker, Siren City and Skydiver Sloshi.

Sunset Sky released a further two 12-inch singles on Pied Piper in 1998, *Blackout* and *Built To Burn*.

Pied Piper's second release was the white label *Hi Horse* by Angeles. The fourth was the *Full Circle* EP by Darkside (Martin again!), and the fifth and sixth were *Anathema* by Scott Ruthford and *Walkaway* by Seafield, all in 1998.

Jay, Martin and Nathaniel broke away to form Flammable Records, while Richard continued to release 12-inches by artists such as X-Trax, The Arc, Tom Cole, Blue Noise, Odysseus and Northface between 1999 and 2001 before shutting the label down.

FLAMMABLE RECORDS

After breaking away from Pied Piper, the three lads were based in Bingley and their first two releases were by Angeles; *It's Over Now* and *Hit Zero*, both in 1999.

The next three releases were by Sunset Sky (alias Martin) *Rock It*, and *Back To Future*, both in 1999, followed by *A New World* in 2001.

By the end of 1998, Bradford's dance scene was flourishing, with labels, artists and new dance nights appearing regularly, but this was not without some controversy.

In November 1996, a twenty-two-year-old Jason Ali from Rochdale died at a Windsor Baths dance event from a toxic cocktail of drugs, including Ecstasy. (18)

On Sunday, February 16, 1997, there was even a rave-style worship called *Eternity* at Bradford's St Peter's Cathedral. The Reverend David Banbury led the service with electric guitars, fancy lights and projectors. (19)

In March 1997, Matthew Perry and Trevor Malcolm, the owners of *The Core* nightclub on Leeds Road, were charged by the police after a dawn raid which ejected over 200 clubbers after finding a quantity of drugs.

They were charged with allowing the supplying of drugs and not having a drinks or entertainment licence. (20)

House/dance music would continue to grow in the 21st century. Events like *Gatecrasher*, *Cream* and various club nights all around the UK became the all-pervasive sound of the modern popular charts. In Bradford, new crews continued to set up all-nighters.

CAMP BOYZ

The outrageous dance act Camp Boyz formed in 1994 with members named Crispin Quent, Titus Aduxas, Susan Winterbottom, Brutus Maximus and Jo-Jo (featured).

They released their first 12" white label single, *Camp Boyz Do It*, in 1994, recorded at Tim Walker's Voltage Studios.

Their first gig was an event called *Hell For Leather* at Manchester *Gay Pride* in 1995. They later performed at *London Pride* in 2000 with pop acts Steps and Hear'Say.

They released a further 12" single Hot Pants (which came on a pink label), and a CD album called *Our Soul*.

Their CD single *Richard & Judy* was banned by ITV for using a sample of the *This Morning* theme tune and with lyrics including, *'I want a threesome with Richard And Judy...'* Perhaps it wasn't surprising!

The single became an underground hit and almost led to an appearance on Channel 4's rival morning magazine show, *The Big Breakfast,* which fell through at the last moment.

The story of the *Richard And Judy* affair made the front page of the *T&A* on Saturday, March 18, 2000.

Their final release was the *Millennium Buggers* CD EP before the band split up in 2001.

The original Camp Boyz singer was Mark who appeared as a member of the drag duo Bosom Buddies on *Britain's Got Talent* in 2013.

Bradford band's cheeky single is stopped in its tracks!
RICHARD AND JUDY SONG ROW

EXCLUSIVE
by SIMON ASHBERRY
T&A Reporter

TV's husband and wife team Richard and Judy have come under fire from outrageous pop group the Camp Boyz after they blocked the release of their cheeky new record.

The Bradford four piece had already recorded their latest single, which pokes fun at the daytime TV presenters.

The song, called Richard and Judy, incorporates the theme tune to the couple's programme This Morning.

But when they contacted Granada Television, which owns the copyright to the tune, they were told they could not use it. In a fax to the group, sent when the dispute broke out, Granada said Richard and Judy had not given 'clearance' for the theme tune to be used. But today a spokesman for the company said the decision had been made by Granada and not the celebrity couple.

Camp Boyz founder member Tim Walker, said: "They're really taking themselves a bit too seriously by stopping us from releasing this.

"What really annoys me is that it's not as if we've been really nasty about them. We could have said a lot worse. We're making fun of ourselves as much as anything."

Bosses at the Camp Boyz' publishing company Sherlock Holmes were convinced they had a potential hit on their hands when they heard the Richard and Judy song.

Ian Volke, of Sherlock Holmes

● Continued on Page 3

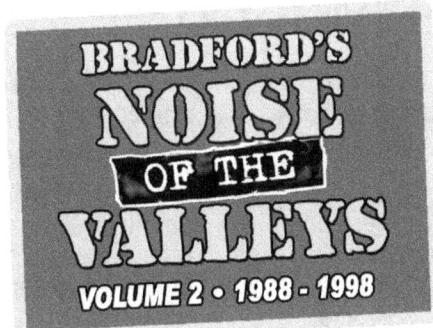

CHAPTER 4: 1991 - 1993

Every decade up to the 1990s had produced a distinct new genre of music style and the nineties was no different. Coming out of Seattle, USA, was a small indie label called Sub Pop, where a range of bands developed a brand new sound termed 'grunge'. This sub-genre of rock music revolved around bands like Tad, Soundgarden, Mudhoney

(pictured left) and, perhaps the most well known and influential of the era, Nirvana.

Nirvana would catapult grunge onto the world's stage in a short space of time with their 7" single *Smells Like Teen Spirit*, which reached No 7 in the UK charts in November 1991, from what was probably the most influential album of the early 1990s, *Nevermind*, before having a further six top thirty hits up to December 1993,

By the time of the tragic suicide of frontman Kurt Cobain in 1994, the grunge sound had moved on after influencing a whole range of new bands.

Nirvana played a memorable show at Bradford University's Communal Building on Tuesday, November 26, 1991, supported by Captain America.

Bradford at this time was still rocking to an eclectic mix of heavy rock and indie-style outfits like Aurora, Sensei, Wicked Rich (pictured right),

The Quickening (above), Station West, Zy-Tyr, China

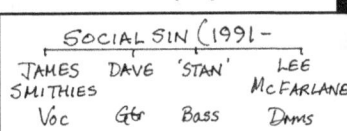

Doll, Loud, Primate, Mr Giblet, Social Sin (pictured above, from Bingley, whose crowd pleaser was entitled *Shotgun Mountains*), Elsie Moon (pictured left), and

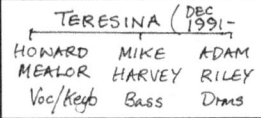

Teresina, a Bradford / Leeds three-piece combo who played jazz funk fusion.

These are only a small sample of bands that were playing live at the time.

In March 1991, Simon Ashberry took over the *T&A's Rock On* column from David Ford and would prove to be the last compiler of the paper's long-running weekly music piece.

While there was the still thriving Queen's Hall, Bradford University's Communal Building and St George's Hall, Bradford needed other venues. In in the early 1990s, a handful of music-orientated pubs like MacRory's on Easby Road, The Melborn on White Abbey Road, The Peel, The Park Hotel in Manningham and The Brewery Tap in Idle provided the much-needed venues for the scene.

Other pubs like The Fighting Cock, The Smithy, and The Quarry in Clayton, put on music less regularly, with bands playing original music and the cover versions.

These same pub venues often held jam sessions, run by one or two established local musicians, where people could turn up and join in. For example, Denny Austin, of Somebody's Brother, ran jam sessions at a number of pubs including The Peel, The Biko Bar (a Bradford University bar), Macrory's and The Black Bull in Clayton.

MACRORY'S BAR

On Easby Road, opposite Bradford College's McMillan Halls of Residence, this cellar bar below the Beechfield Hotel, a traditional, intimate hostelry became the hub for a whole range of local musicians and put on regular gigs on Wednesday and Sunday nights.

The bar was run by Ian Austin, who took over ownership in 1991 after running the place for the previous three years.

Ian tried to book a range of bands and have music of various genres. Several bands played on a regular basis, but the bar played host to a number of one-off visitors.

Some of the bands playing regularly were; country blues band The Horsemen, Jazz swing blues group Still Jumpin', blues and Doors cover band Sponge/Jukejoint, country band The Whitfield Family, psychedelic skiffle trio Trip & Stumble (which featured new Model Army's Nelson), weird acoustic mayhem rabble Nowt, indie rockers Slack, country blues rock from The Palladinos, psychedelic world music exponents Elephant Talk, R&B man Brendan Croker, solo blues and folk man Duffy, songwriter John Gibbons with Dillon & Gibbons and his band Egomania, original songwriter Jason Feddy, electric folk band Free Sandwiches, the eclectic Lost T-Shirts Of Atlantis, Legs Bisto, acoustic four-piece Shiny Beast and The McRory Brothers, otherwise known as the FOS Bros (Full of Shit).

Another regular performer was Ian's Brother Denny Austin who played in several bands there, including Somebody's Brother, two Grateful Dead tribute bands New Speedway Boogie and Laffin' Bones and country band Howling Whippets.

Along with yearly St Patrick's Day and New Year's Eve gigs, MacRory's also hosted annual outdoor charity events in the large car park, in aid of MIND, after the death of his best mate 'Mad Phil'. The first of these featured The Lost T Shirts Of Atlantis and took place in 1991.

In 1998 the outdoor event was christened 'The Ginger Fringe Festival' and changed its focus to supporting Cancer Research.

MacRory's changed hands in 2004 and closed a year later but The Ginger Fringe continued for a few years at Delius Lived Next Door.

THE MELBORN

Run by 'Brother' Eamonn Halloran (pictured singing below), this warm and friendly pub venue on White Abbey Road was putting gigs on several nights a week, featuring mainly blues, folk and traditional music, with a Sunday afternoon jam session run by Denny Austin from 1993, originally with The Howling Whippets as the house band.

Bands who played there regularly included Rent, Duffy Gibbons, Jeds Blues Band, Last Orders, Midnight Train, Somebody's Brother, The Big Fish, Nowt, Shiny Beast, Buzzard and Avalon.

The Melborn closed in January 2006.

THE PEEL

This pub venue was just above the University and put on regular gigs on Saturdays and Thursdays. When Betty Casey took over in the mid-1990s gigs were less regular but still hosted many local bands and had the occasional outdoor gig in the car park, like in 1997 when Dragster, Zed and Shiny Beast played there.

And, you guessed it, Denny Austin ran a legendary weekly jam on Tuesday nights.

The Peel was closed in 2007 and later demolished.

THE BANDS: Top — Rattlesnake Shake; second row, Suffrajets and (Fleetwood) Roadhouse; third row, Sarajevo; Boneyard; bottom row, Frontier

METAL MOUNTAIN '91

After criticism about *The Battle Of The Bands 1990* being too rock-orientated, promotor Malcolm Hanson decided to hold a dedicated rock band competition called *The Metal Mountain* alongside the Battle. In the event, there was no Battle Of The Bands 1991, instead, Malcom's *The Great Pop Explosion* took place later in the year.

Heats for the *Metal Mountain* began at the Rio Rokz on Saturday, January 13. Prizes offered were £1,500 cash, studio time, a produced video and a spot at the Bradford Festival.

Gigs were every Thursday, Friday and Saturday and took part before the Rio's usual rock disco which was from 11 pm - 2 am.

After the heats, twenty-five bands remained to take part in the semi-finals, including only two surviving local bands Rattlesnake Shake, who played in the semi on June 14 semi, and Mr Meana, who performed on the 15th.

Rattlesnake Shake made it through to the final although the event was won by Doncaster's Boneyard, with Sarajevo (Manchester) and Roadhouse (Fleetwood) coming second and third.

1991 - 1993   BRADFORD'S NOISE OF THE VALLEYS VOLUME 2

THE GREAT POP EXPLOSION 1991

The more commercial alternative to *The Metal Mountain* was *The Great Pop Explosion*, which featured 40 bands playing at heats that took place at various venues around the City. Bradford acts taking part included Shane Eastman, Cabbage Head Kids, Peppa Junction, Royce, Cats Eyes, Chaos and Timeless Thoughts.

UNTER power is to be the judge of success at Bradford's biggest live music event.

Organisers of the Great Pop Explosion competition are to allow the audience to have their say in deciding which bands are the best.

The event, backed by the Telegraph & Argus, kicks off at the end of the month and reaches its climax during the Bradford Festival.

Former Psycho Surgeons front man Wild Willi Beckett, who is helping to mastermind the contest, said special T&A voting cards would be distributed at all heats and semi-finals to allow the fans to vote on the winners.

Entries for the contest closed at the end of July and 40 bands from all over the north of England are lined up for the ten first round.

The competition starts with two heats at the Sunny Bank Social Club in Silsden and the Morley Carr Working Men's Club on August 30.

Further heats take place on August 31 at the Hightown Liberal Club, Liversedge, and the IDL Club in Rebecca Street, Bradford; Ms Leisure Centre in Saltaire on September 1; Jericho's in Thornton on September 2; the Club Rio on September 3; Dudley Hill and Tong Working Men's Club on September 4 and at the Idle and Thackley Conservative Club and Great Horton Working Men's Club on September 5.

Four bands will take part in each heat, with the top two qualifying for the five semi-finals, to be held on September 6 at the Morley Carr Working Men's Club, on September 8 at Ms Leisure Centre, on September 12 at Great Horton Working Men's Club and Bingley Working Men's Club and on September 13 at the Victoria Hall in Keighley.

Five bands will take part in the grand finale at Myrtle Park, Bingley, on September 14.

For up-to-date details of line-ups for the Great Pop Explosion, check out Rock On.

The competition took place over two weeks, starting on August 30 and culminating in a five-band final held at Myrtle Park, Bingley, on September 14 as part of *Music At Myrtle* and the Bradford Festival.

Bradford seven-piece Pepper Junction were the only local band to make it to the final. The eventual winners were Fools And Kings from Dewsbury.

MUSIC AT MYRTLE

In September 1991, the Bingley Music Festival was started at Myrtle Park. Over the next few years, this free event featured headline acts,

Bands storm to success

by ALUN PALMER

STORMY weather couldn't dampen the final big bang of the Great Pop Explosion.

Bingley's Myrtle Park was the setting for the all-day festival of Northern musical talent, backed by the Telegraph & Argus, and each of the five bands brought along their own fan clubs. Hundreds of pop fans in the city also turned up to lend their support.

In the face of fierce competition, Dewsbury-based band Fools and Kings came out on top and walked away with a cheque for £1,000, free promotion and a gig at the end of the Bradford Festival in Lister Park next week.

A special stage was built in the centre of the natural amphitheatre with an impressive sound and light system.

A brief shower of rain, just after Bradford band Pepper Junction had finished their set, sent everyone scurrying for cover into the beer tent.

After the five bands, from all over the North of England, had finished their sets, the winners of Bradford's rock version of the Explosion took the stage while the judges deliberated.

Just before Boneyard began thrashing, the heavens opened but their faithful fans braved the weather to cheer them on.

The announcement was made and the winners cheered and the losers drooped.

Fools and Kings' lead singer Terry Gill, 29, was overjoyed at the result.

He said: "This is a great leg-up for us. We wanted to win when we sent in the form, but we didn't think we would win.

"The competition was very good but I think when we are playing well, we are excellent."

Judge Nicholas Smethurst, 20, said the panel had reached a unanimous decision.

He said: They were very taut and professional. They were very good, as were the rest."

Co-promoter Willi Beckett, of Psycho Surgeons fame, said the hectic four-week series of heats and semi-finals, culminating in the Explosion's final big bang, had been an unqualified success.

He said: "We have been invited back to all the venues, which were packed out during the whole competition.

"This event will go from strength to strength."

including Bradford's own Smokie, Alvin Stardust, Hot Chocolate, Suzi Quatro, Boney M and Motown legend Edwin Starr.

By 1998, it had become a two-day affair, with the addition of the *Pulse Party In The Park*, organised by local radio station Pulse FM. It featured such contemporary pop acts as McFly, Busted, Liberty X, Rachel Stevens and Bradford's own Gareth Gates.

It continued successfully in this format until 2006.

BRADFORD FESTIVAL 1991

The fifth Bradford Festival kicked off for seventeen days of music, fun and entertainment from September 5 to 22. With artists and performers from all around the world, the Festival was bigger and began to put Bradford on top of the league of arts and cultural development in the UK.

Bradford was rightly proud of its multicultural community, putting on events for most if not all the ethnic groups resident in the City, from daily street performers doing comedy and music, regular lunchtime gigs in the Wool Exchange, the schools programme, to the host of performing arts and film events.

The main top stars that year were All About Eve, Labi Siffre, Carmel, Desmond Dekker and Bad Manners, Beverly Craven and jazz from Andy Sheppard and John Surman's Brass Project.

The Festival climax was the Mela weekend in Lister Park, which had grown in size and stature over the preceding years to become the most important event of its kind in the UK. (1)

Dusty Rhodes, one of the festival directors, stated that the artistic vision was one of community ownership and celebration: *"It was a giant artslab of fellow travellers doing these things together. We used to go into the park a week or two before the event and start building the thing, and people that we didn't even know would come with huge tubs of curry and feed us because we were working to build the Mela. These were spontaneous gestures. There was just a real sense that the event was by and for the community, and anybody who had an idea could come along and join in."* (2)

Skinning The Cat

During September a new venue for Saturday and Sunday rock gigs started at AJ's on Hubert Street, organised by Lloyd Spencer of Ozone Promotions.

TERRORVISION

After three years of hard gigging, *Battle Of The Bands* competitions and three demo cassettes as Spoilt Bratz, the band moved on with a new name; Terrorvision.

The band signed to EMI Records after doing the rounds of London-based record companies in October 1991.

Their debut release was the EP *Thrive*, in February 1992, which the band promoted with a support slot on a UK tour with Zodiac Mindwarp.

Their debut album *Formaldehyde* was released in December 1992, reaching number seventy-five in the album charts.

The band won the *Best Band* category in the *Kerrang! Readers Poll* for two consecutive years; 1995 and 1996.

They released another three LPs; *How To Make Friends & Influence People* (1995), *Regular Suburban Survivors* (1996) and *Shaving Peaches* (1998), all reaching the UK album charts at numbers eighteen, eight and thirty-four respectively.

y late 1996, singer and frontman Tony Wright, with his down-to-earth and media-friendly sense of humour, was fast becoming a minor celebrity, appearing on numerous episodes of BBC2's *Never Mind The Buzzcocks* music quiz as well as presenting the BBC's longest-running music programme *Top of The Pops*.

Terrorvision released over twenty singles, sixteen of which reached the UK pop charts, including three Top 10 hits; *Perseverance* (1996), *Bad Actress* (1996) and *Tequila* (1999), which reached numbers five, ten and two.

In 1999 the band left EMI and signed a new deal with Papillon Records with whom they released the LP *Good To Go* in 2001.

The band first called it a day after a farewell tour and a 'final' concert at Pennington's Nightclub (the old Mecca Ballroom) on Manningham Lane on the 4th of October 2001.

Bass guitarist Cluey soon started his own band, Malibu Stacey, in 2003, playing at The 1 In 12 Club in September of that year.

Singer Tony Wright performed with his band, Laika Dog, when not involved in his dry stone walling business in the local area.

Terrorvision re-formed in 2005 to play two tours, including a 'last ever' gig is Scarborough on September 17.

The band got together again to play more shows in 2007.

TERRORVISION			
90	(own label)	TERRORVISION: Brand New Toy/Human Error/Pain Reliever/ The Pilgrims Rest (cassette, private issue)	20
91	(own label)	PUMP ACTION SUNSHINE: Urban Space Crime/My House/Jason (cassette, private issue)	20
91	(own label)	TERRORVISION: Blackbird/American TV/Pain Reliever/Human Being (cassette, private issue)	20
92	Total Vegas 12VEGAS 1	THRIVE EP (12" EP)	12
92	Total Vegas CDVEGAS 1	THRIVE EP (CD EP)	20
92	Total Vegas CDVEGAS 2	My House/Coming Up/Tea Dance (CD)	20
93	Total Vegas CDATVR 1	Problem Solved/Corpse Fly/We Are The Roadcrew/Sailing Home (CD)	25
93	Total Vegas CDPVEGAS 3	American TV/Psycho Killer/Hole For A Soul (CD)	15
92	Total Vegas ATVRLP 1	FORMALDEHYDE (LP, 14 tracks, green vinyl, 500 only, stickered sleeve)	30
92	Total Vegas ATVRCD 1	FORMALDEHYDE (CD, 14 tracks, 1,000 only)	15
93	Total Vegas VEGASLPS 1	FORMALDEHYDE (reissue LP, 12 tracks, 1,000 copies with 12-page booklet, stickered sleeve & lyric inner)	20
93	Total Vegas BOOT 1	LIVE AT THE DON VALLEY STADIUM (CD, picture disc, 250 promo copies only)	30

TERRORVISION

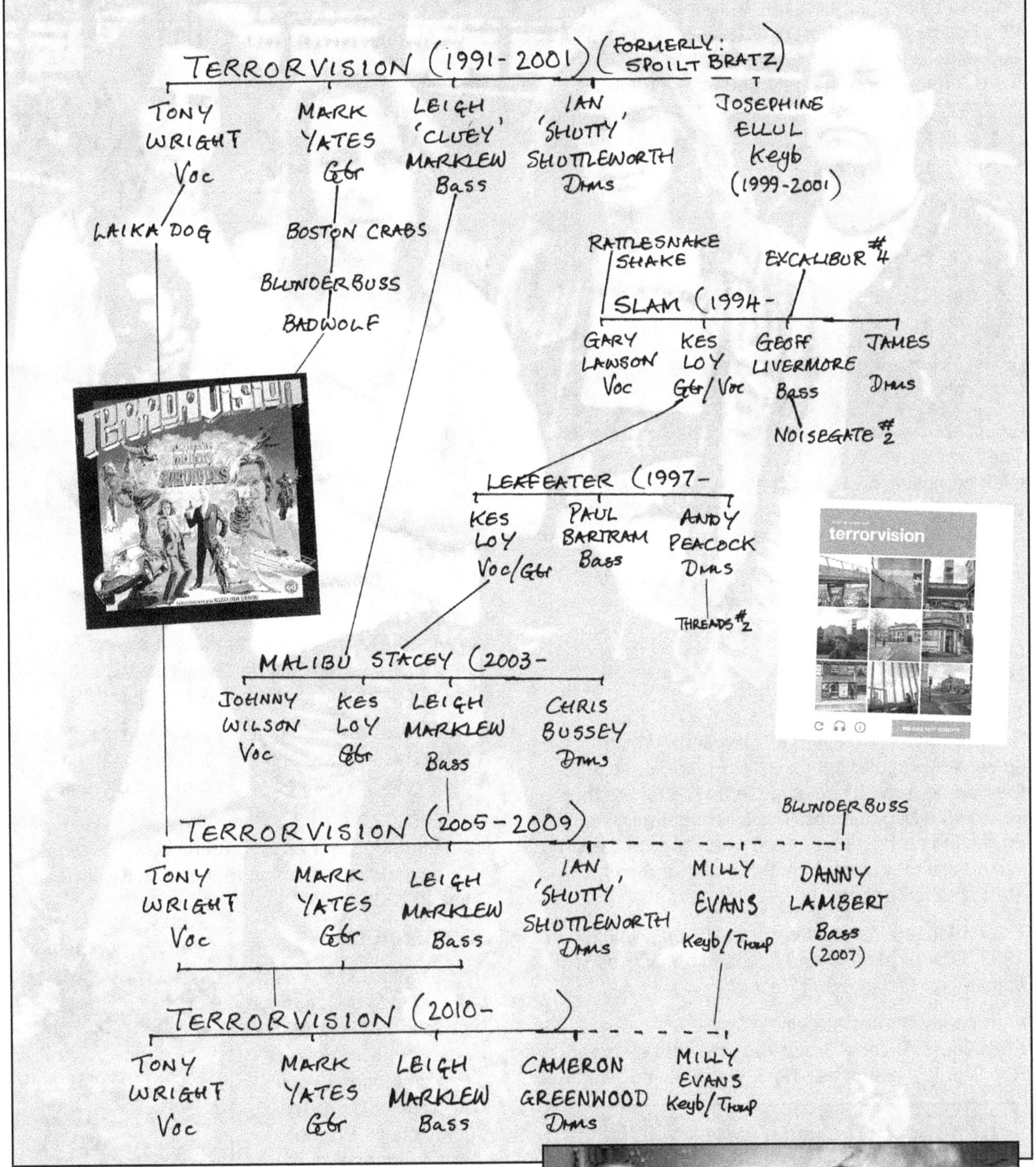

TERRORVISION (1991-2001) (FORMERLY: SPOILT BRATZ)

- TONY WRIGHT — Voc
- MARK YATES — Gtr
- LEIGH 'CLUEY' MARKLEW — Bass
- IAN 'SHUTTY' SHUTTLEWORTH — Dms
- JOSEPHINE ELLUL — Keyb (1999-2001)

Tony Wright: LAIKA DOG
Mark Yates: BOSTON CRABS, BLUNDERBUSS, BADWOLF

Ian Shuttleworth: RATTLESNAKE SHAKE, EXCALIBUR #4

SLAM (1994-
- GARY LAWSON — Voc
- KES LOY — Gtr/Voc
- GEOFF LIVERMORE — Bass
- JAMES — Dms

NOISEGATE #2

LEAFEATER (1997-
- KES LOY — Voc/Gtr
- PAUL BARTRAM — Bass
- ANDY PEACOCK — Dms

THREADS #2

MALIBU STACEY (2003-
- JOHNNY WILSON — Voc
- KES LOY — Gtr
- LEIGH MARKLEW — Bass
- CHRIS BUSSEY — Dms

TERRORVISION (2005-2009)
- TONY WRIGHT — Voc
- MARK YATES — Gtr
- LEIGH MARKLEW — Bass
- IAN 'SHUTTY' SHUTTLEWORTH — Dms
- MILLY EVANS — Keyb/Thmp
- DANNY LAMBERT — Bass (2007)

Danny Lambert: BLUNDERBUSS

TERRORVISION (2010-
- TONY WRIGHT — Voc
- MARK YATES — Gtr
- LEIGH MARKLEW — Bass
- CAMERON GREENWOOD — Dms
- MILLY EVANS — Keyb/Thmp

Drummer Ian Shuttleworth left in 2010, to be replaced by Cameron Greenwood who played on the band's, *Super Delux* album which came out on Townsend Records in February 2011.

In 2025, Terrorvision toured in support of their *We Are Not Robots* album, released in 2024.

PRIMATE

Formed by ex-members of Western Dance, the band came back with a harder-edged sound in 1990 and, after a first series of gigs as Idiot Box, they were renamed Primate and began recording.

Their track *Overwound* appeared on The 1 In 12 Club compilation LP *A Nightmare On Albion Street* and received airplay on Mark Radcliffe's *Out On Blue Six* Monday night Radio 1 show.

Their first gig wasn't until March 1992, now with Mick Barrett on bass, when they supported Claytown Troup at Queen's Hall. The band then played all the local rock venues like the Rio and Leed's Duchess of York.

Their track *Break My Fall* was played on Mark Radcliffe's Radio 5 *Hit The North* show which spawned a regular spot, *Easter Eggs Please*, after their demo arrived packaged in an Easter egg box sent with a bag of chips. The tape went missing prompting co-host Mark 'Lard' Riley to sing the song live before they rang drummer Matt live on air to request another copy.

They released the cassette compilation Evolution in 1993, later expanded and released on CD as Mad Monkey on Mutiny 2000 Records.

A proposed three-track single *Liquid / My Passionate Friend / Brutal*, recorded at Leeds Ric Rac Studios in summer 1993, was shelved after the band were unhappy with the mix.

After playing numerous gigs up and down the country, including the outdoor stage Bradford Festival in 1993, Matt left to live and play in the Czech Republic with

former band members Jont and Adam Bennett, both of whom had played bass for the band.

Primate continued with Threshold Shift's Mick Barrett and Tony Fox joining the line-up, playing numerous gigs, including a benefit for the Manorlands Hospice at the Rio in August 1994.

In 1995, ex-Western Dance bassist Ade Clark rejoined his former band mates, along with the returning Matt Webster, to play and record until the band folded later that year.

Liam and Ade went on to form the band Bullweek, and the core line-up again reunited as Kwai Chang Caine in 2000.

BOOZE CRUISE '92

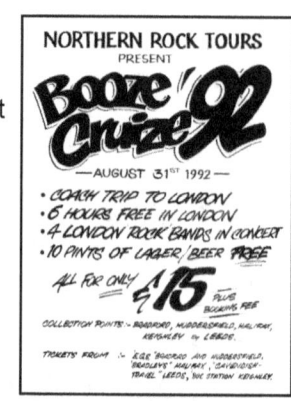

This 'Bradford showcase' was meant to be a support to headliners Nirvana at a mystery English Holiday Camp on Monday, August 31. Promoter Dave Mumby chose Bradford bands Primate, Weird Emotions, and Hybrid. However, the gig changed venues several times, and Nirvana disappeared from the bill! First, it was moved to London's Marquee, then to another London club, The Venue, and finally, as the bands and two coaches of supporters were halfway down the M1, to a pub in London. The bands ended up playing support to Paddy Goes To Holyhead, who were unaware of the arrangement, much to the disappointment of all concerned..

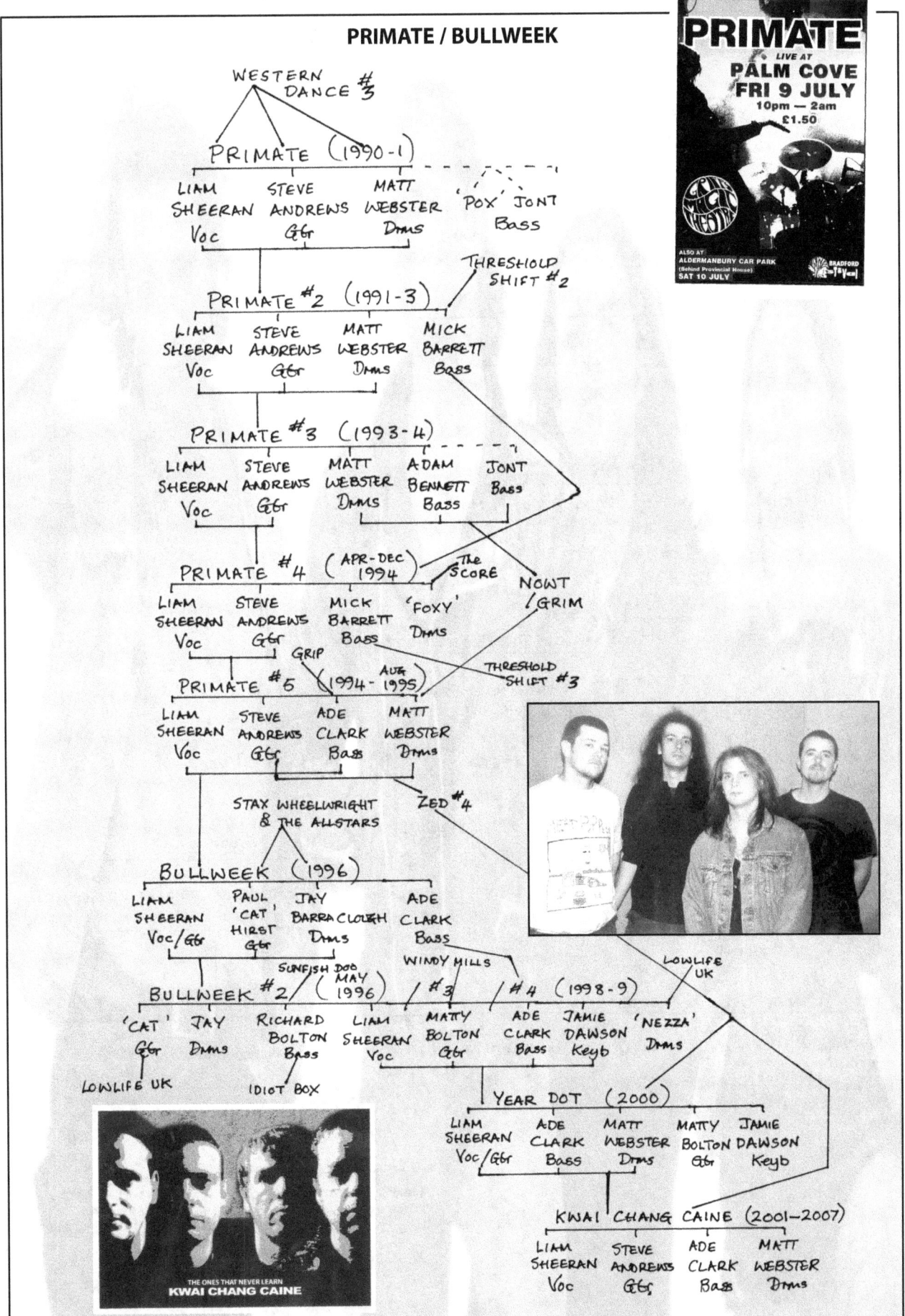

WIPEOUT / ROCK SOLID / TIMEOUT

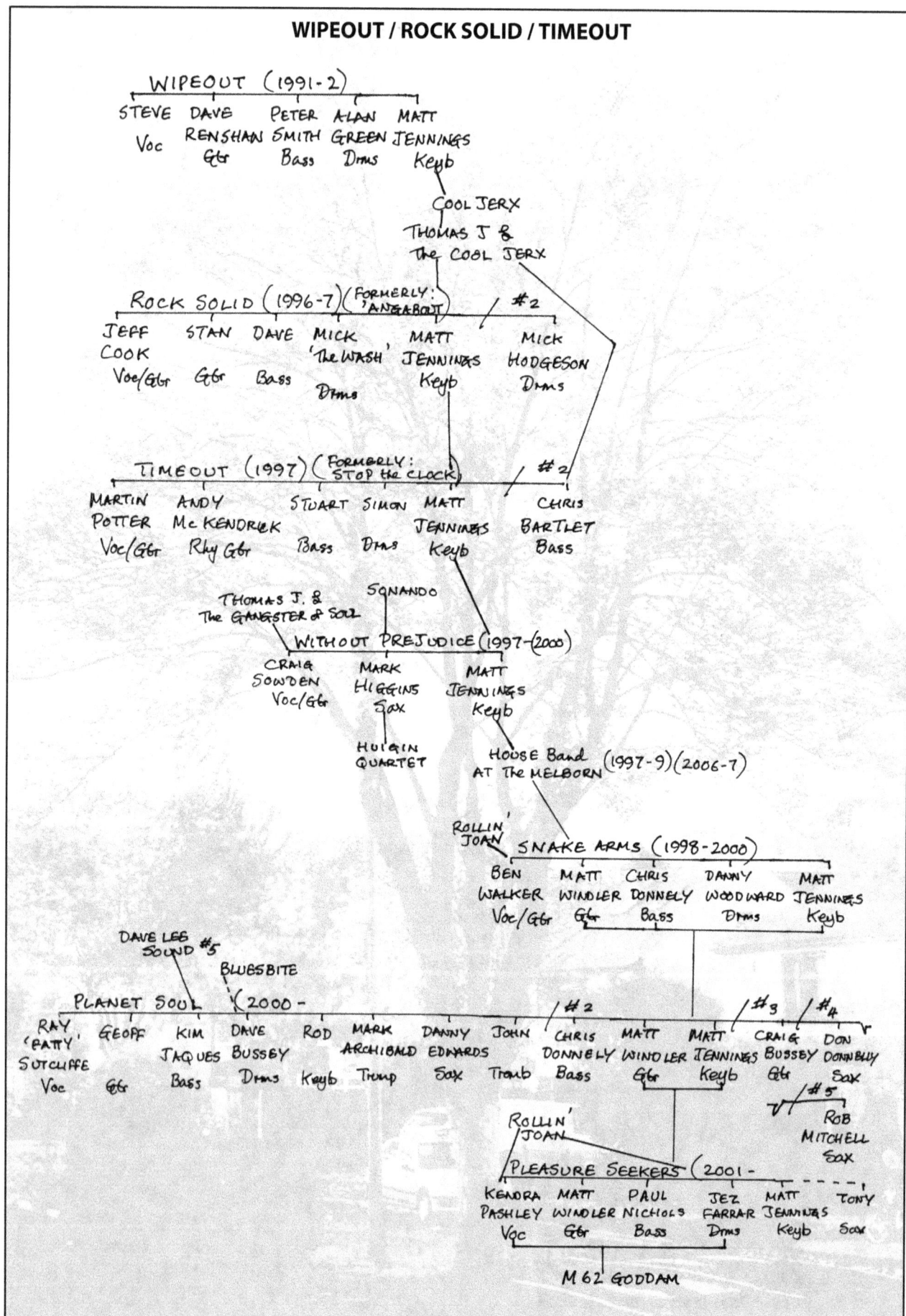

CHEST / FALCONETTI

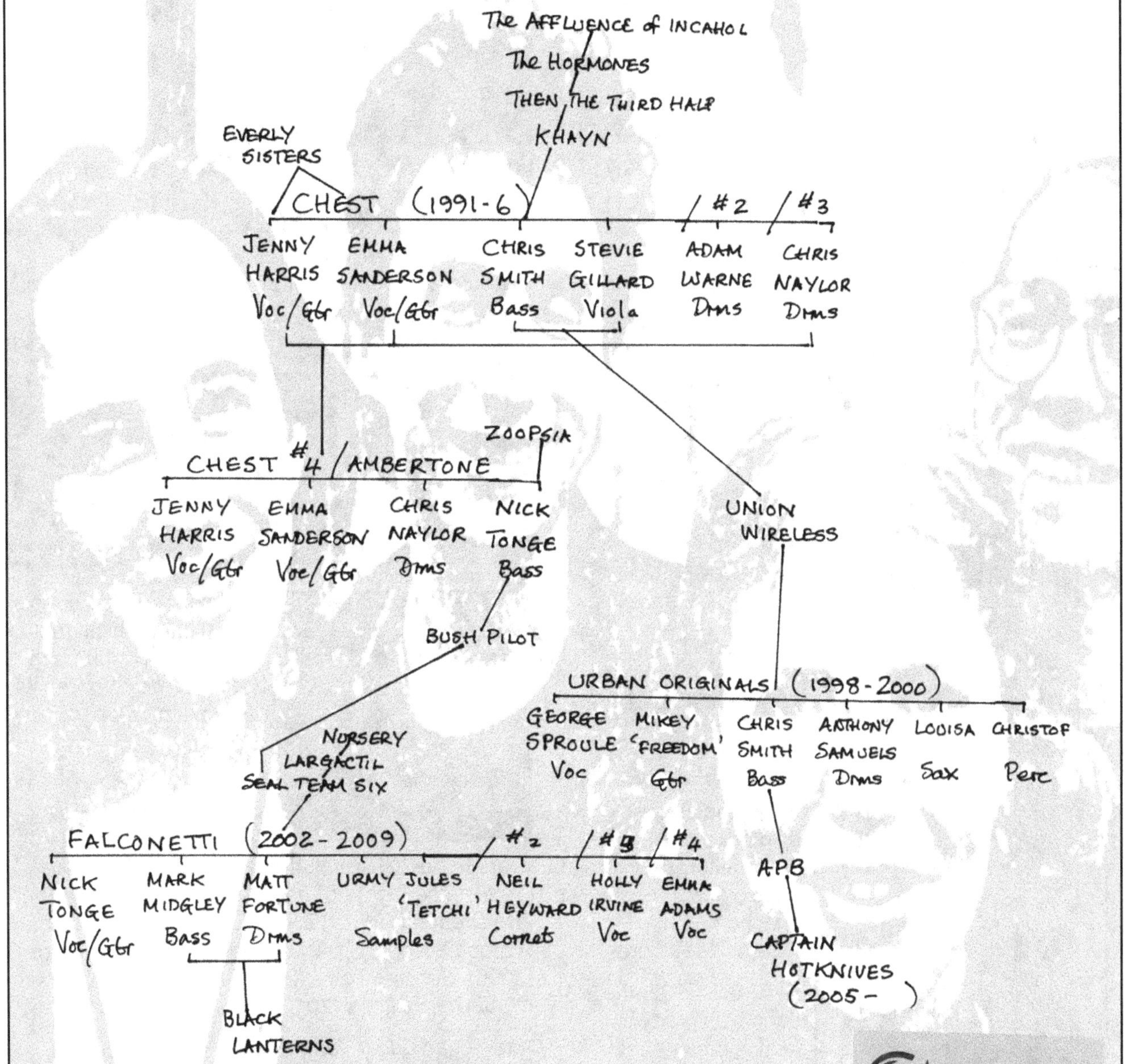

[Hand-drawn band genealogy chart:]

The Affluence of Incahol
The Hormones
Then, The Third Half
Khayn

Everly Sisters

CHEST (1991-6) / #2 / #3

Jenny Harris	Emma Sanderson	Chris Smith	Stevie Gillard	Adam Warne	Chris Naylor
Voc/Gtr	Voc/Gtr	Bass	Viola	Dms	Dms

Zoopsia

CHEST #4 / AMBERTONE

Jenny Harris	Emma Sanderson	Chris Naylor	Nick Tonge
Voc/Gtr	Voc/Gtr	Dms	Bass

Union Wireless

Bush Pilot

Nursery
Largactil
Seal Team Six

URBAN ORIGINALS (1998-2000)

George Sproule	Mikey 'Freedom'	Chris Smith	Anthony Samuels	Louisa	Christof
Voc	Gtr	Bass	Dms	Sax	Perc

FALCONETTI (2002-2009) / #2 / #3 / #4

Nick Tonge	Mark Midgley	Matt Fortune	Urmy 'Tetchi'	Jules	Neil Heyward	Holly Irvine	Emma Adams
Voc/Gtr	Bass	Dms	Samples		Cornet	Voc	Voc

APB

Captain Hotknives (2005-)

Black Lanterns

CHEST

Chest were a Bradford / Leeds outfit formed in 1991 by Jenny Harris

and Emma Sanderson (formerly The Everly Sisters - above) with Chris Smith on bass. His previous band, Affluence Of Incahel, had played a gig supporting 1970s rock gods Argent.

In 1994, they put out the 3-track cassette *Bovine Behaviour*.

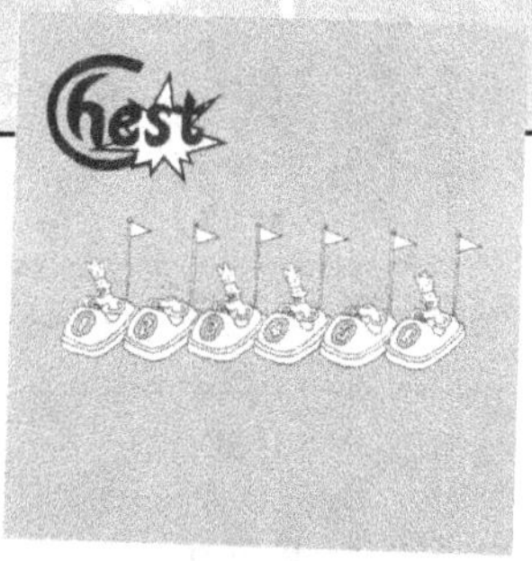

The band's first vinyl was the four-track 10-inch EP *Destiny Phones*, released in 1995 on the Leeds label Mook, run by Phil Mayne. Their next release was the 7-inch single *Angels / Panic* (1996), also on Mook.

Chest then signed to Fierce Panda Records, owned by ex-*NME* journalist Simon Williams. They put out two 7" singles on the label in 1997, *Feel The Same / Better Now* and *Aniseed / Nosebleed*. Both singles were taken from their *Mystery Superette* album..

During the early 1990s, the doom/death/black metal underground scene was very big in the UK, and Bradford had its share of influential local bands and promoters, like *Heavier Than Thou* who promoted gigs at The 1 In 12 Club and Queen's Hall.

MY DYING BRIDE

This long-surviving band were formed in June 1990, from the ashes of local band Abiosis, by key members Andy Craighan and Ricky Miah.

After six months of rehearsals the band recorded and released the *Towards The Sinister* demo, before releasing their first 7" single, *God Is Alone*, on the small French label Listenable in 1991.

When the single sold out almost immediately they were quickly snapped up by Peaceville Records.

By March 1992, the band was ready to launch their debut one-track 12-inch *Symphanine Inferius Et Spera Empyrium*

for Peaceville, soon followed by the album *As The Flower Withers*.

Both releases were supported by big tours of the UK and mainland Europe where, with Liverpool's Anathema and fellow Bradfordians Paradise Lost, the band gained the reputation of being at the forefront of the death / doom metal scene.

The band's 1993 album *Turn Loose The Swans* is

considered a classic example of the genre, with its *'weeping melodies, spoken word, growls and clean vocals full of despair and woe...'* as reviewed retrospectively by Juha Raivio in the September 2010 edition of *Terroriser*.

They continued their epic themes of mythical realms on their 1996 album *Like Gods Of The Sun* with its haunting, string-heavy sound.

They continued to release albums on Peaceville Records every couple of years up to 2015, including *34.788%...Complete* (1998), *The Light At The End Of The World* (1999), *The Dreadful Hours* (2001), *Songs Of Darkness, Words Of Light* (2004), *A Line Of Deathless Kings* (2006), *For Lies I Sire* (2009), *Evinta* (2011), *A Map Of All Our Failures* (2012), *Feel The Misery* (2015).

After a gap due to family issues and lineup changes, My Dying Bride signed a new deal with Nuclear Blast Records for their 2020 *The Ghost of Orion* album.

The band's 14th album. A Mortal Binding, came out in 2024. After its release it was announced that singer Aaron Stainthorpe would be absent from the 2025 tour supporting the album. Aaron and guitarist Andrew Craighan are the only two members to appear on every release up to this time.

My Dying Bride are regarded as one of the most influential pioneers of the gothic/death/doom metal genre. (3)

CHAPTER 4 — 1991 - 1993

MY DYING BRIDE

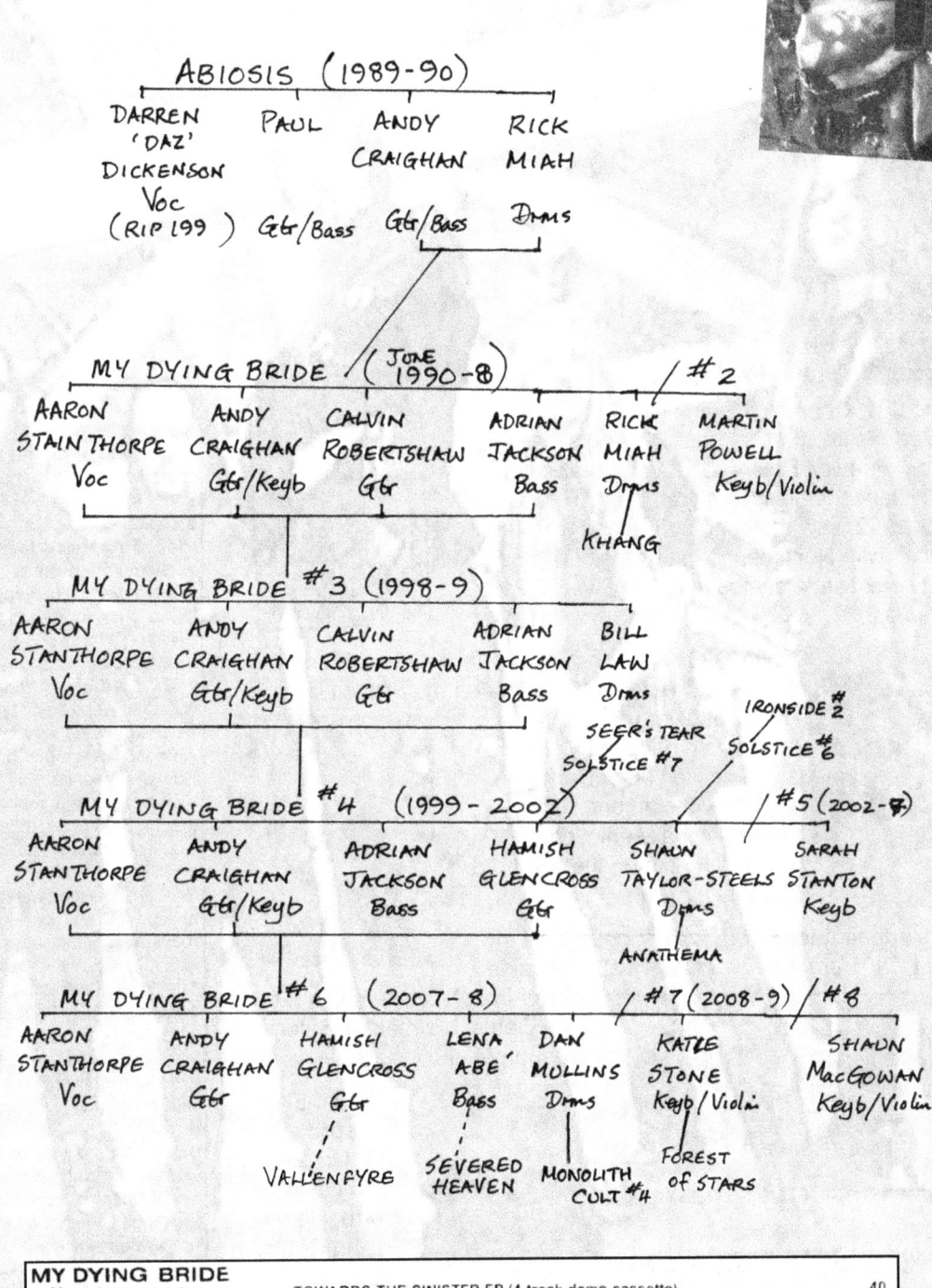

ABIOSIS (1989-90)
- DARREN 'DAZ' DICKENSON — Voc (RIP L99)
- PAUL — Gtr/Bass
- ANDY CRAIGHAN — Gtr/Bass
- RICK MIAH — Drms

MY DYING BRIDE (June 1990-8) / #2
- AARON STAINTHORPE — Voc
- ANDY CRAIGHAN — Gtr/Keyb
- CALVIN ROBERTSHAW — Gtr
- ADRIAN JACKSON — Bass
- RICK MIAH — Drms
- MARTIN POWELL — Keyb/Violin

KHANG

MY DYING BRIDE #3 (1998-9)
- AARON STANTHORPE — Voc
- ANDY CRAIGHAN — Gtr/Keyb
- CALVIN ROBERTSHAW — Gtr
- ADRIAN JACKSON — Bass
- BILL LAW — Drms

SEER'S TEAR
SOLSTICE #7
IRONSIDE #2
SOLSTICE #6

MY DYING BRIDE #4 (1999-2002) / #5 (2002-7)
- AARON STANTHORPE — Voc
- ANDY CRAIGHAN — Gtr/Keyb
- ADRIAN JACKSON — Bass
- HAMISH GLENCROSS — Gtr
- SHAUN TAYLOR-STEELS — Drms
- SARAH STANTON — Keyb

ANATHEMA

MY DYING BRIDE #6 (2007-8) / #7 (2008-9) / #8
- AARON STANTHORPE — Voc
- ANDY CRAIGHAN — Gtr
- HAMISH GLENCROSS — Gtr
- LENA ABE — Bass
- DAN MULLINS — Drms
- KATIE STONE — Keyb/Violin
- SHAUN MacGOWAN — Keyb/Violin

VALLENFYRE
SEVERED HEAVEN
MONOLITH CULT #4
FOREST OF STARS

MY DYING BRIDE

Year	Label	Title	Price
90	private pressing	TOWARDS THE SINISTER EP (4 track demo cassette)	40
92	Peaceville VILE 27	Symphonaire Infernus Et Spera Empyrium Act 1/ Symphonaire Infernus Et Spera Empyrium Act 2 (12", p/s)	25
92	Peaceville VILE 27	Symphonaire Infernus Et Spera Empyrium/God Is Alone/ De Sade Soliloquay (CD)	15
93	Peaceville VILE 37T	The Thrash Of Naked Limbs/Le Cerf Malade/Gather Me Up Forever (12", p/s)	25
93	Unbridled Voyage	Unreleased Bitterness: The Bitterness And The Bereavement (1-sided flexidisc, fold-out p/s in poly sleeve, 1150 only)	20
93	Peaceville VILE 44T	I Am The Bloody Earth/Transcending (Into The Exquisite) (12", p/s)	20
93	Peaceville VILE 44	I Am The Bloody Earth/Transcending (Into The Exquisite)/ Crown Of Sympathy (Remix) (CD)	12
94	Peaceville CC5	Sexuality Of Bereavement/Crown Of Sympathy (Remix) (p/s)	25
92	Peaceville	AS THE FLOWER WITHERS (LP, gatefold sleeve)	15
93	Peaceville VILE 39	TURN LOOSE THE SWANS (LP, double)	25
94	Peaceville VILE 45	THE STORIES EP (box set, 1000 only)	75
95	Peaceville VILE 50	THE ANGEL AND THE DARK RIVER (LP, picture disc)	15

CHORUS OF RUIN

Formed in 1991, Chorus Of Ruin played many gigs locally at venues like the Bradford Rio and some promoted by *Heavier Than Thou*, during their three years of existence. One such gig at The 1 In 12 Club on May 15, 1992, saw the band supporting Gorefest, from Holland, with Necrosanct and Korpse. The band produced two cassette demos in 1992, *Swan Dive* and *Les Miserables*.

In 1993, they released a 7-inch single *Ocean Of Sins / Dreaming Of Indigo*, on the French label Avant Guard Records. It was produced by Gene Hoglan of Dark Angel/Testament, who occasionally enjoyed hanging out on the Bradford metal scene.

Also in 1993, their track *Headstone* appeared on the Peaceville *Deaf Metal Sampler* (Deaf 12), alongside tracks from Vital Remains, At The Gates, Maimed, Impaler, Baphomet and others.

In 1994, they released a split CD EP with Iceland's Sorrocide on Rising Realm Records. Their two tracks were *Last Dance* and *In This Church*.

Members of Chorus Of Ruin went on to other local bands like Ironside, Purity Cries, Silverburn and The Enchanted.

In 2009, the band's original lineup reformed for a one-off gig at the Mannville Arms pub.

Chorus of Ruin/Malediction/ Arise/Lone Wolf.
1 in 12 Club.
16/10/92.   STORK #7

Lone Wolf got the night off to a flying start with their humorous set. They appeared on stage dressed as hippies, wearing incredibly vile flared trousers and false beards. The bassist was also wearing a Hawkwind t-shirt. Their songs, (all 3 of them) were humorous but occasionally did have a serious side to them. The first song was imaginatively titled 'Lone Wolf' but after a couple of minutes seemed to turn into a very dodgy rendition of 'Smoke On The Water'! When the chorus came round it sounded very much like "Lone Wolf ooowooooh!". the next song in the set had the catchy title "We Take drugs For Satan", which had a number of weird licks that were probably written under the influence of illegal substances.

They finished with a cover version of Hawkwinds classic "Silver Machine" which they introduced as "Silver Washing Machine". They went down pretty well and even came back for an encore.

Arise were next up on stage with their weird hippy type music. The keyboards were very 1970's and they sounded like another bunch of Hawkwind wannabe's. That aside they played some really good music that had alot of depth and groove. It would of helped if I'd been able to see them in all that smoke.

Malediction were next to literally appear on the smoky stage. This band brought a new feel to the gig with their aggressive Death Metal. They played material from their demo's and also from a new demo which is apparently surrounded by a lot of secrecy. Malediction played an excellent show of Brutal aggression with songs that stood out. They are regarded as one of the top underground bands, and anyone at the gig would understand why.

Chorus of ruin were last to take the stage and after a lengthy tuning up session they kicked off with "In This Church". They then got to the second song "Eclipse" but half way through the vocalist stormed off the stage after damaging some of the bands equipment. The sound went off and it seemed as though Chorus Of Ruin's big moment as headliners had ended. I managed to get a few words withthe bass player Issac after the gig and apparently the singer had been a asked to leave the band follwing his little display on stage. Oh well, these things do happen. See you next time!   Paul Jacques.

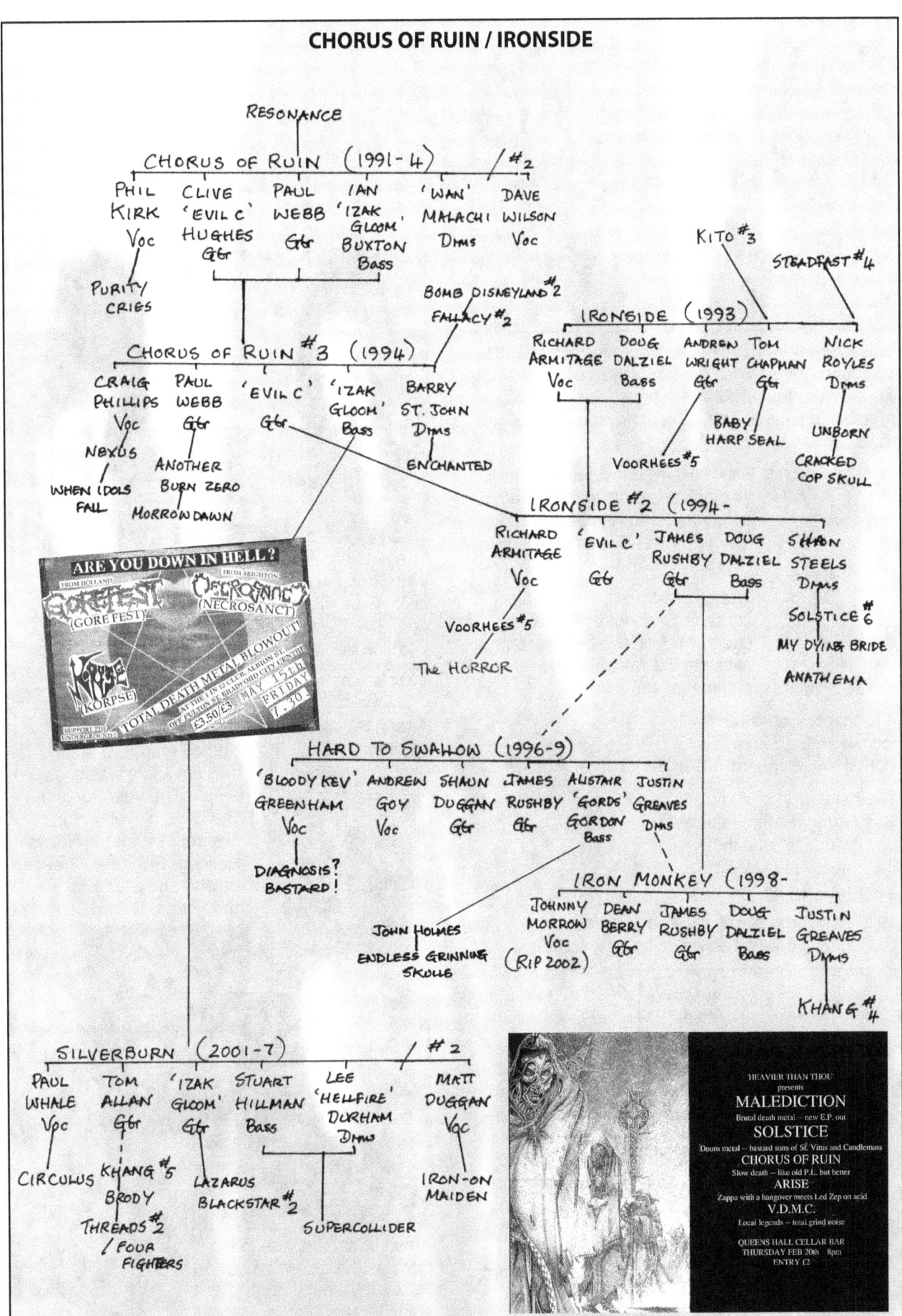

SOLSTICE

This long-surviving five-piece were formed in 1991, by Bradford-born Rich 'Militia' Walker, of Sore Throat / Warfear / Biohazard fame, as his doom metal side project. The band professed a devotion to paganism.

Solstice played locally, as well as gigs up and down the country and toured with Anathama. Their first gig was at Queen's Hall in February 1992. (4)

Their three-track *Lamentations* cassette demo was released in late 1991, followed by a second cassette, MCMXCII, in the summer of 1992.

A further two cassettes followed, *As Empires Fell* (1993) and *Ragnarok* (1994).

Their first proper studio album was *Lamentations*, released on CD in 1994 and that year they toured the UK with Sweden's Count Raven.

1996 saw the release of the band's *Halcyon* CD EP on Godhead, followed by *New Dark Age* (1988) on Misanthropy Records.

They released their track *Englander* as a limited cassette and white label 10-inch in 2000. That same year Solstice played the WOA Festival in Germany, alongside Venom and Twisted Sister.

They headlined the Headbangers festival in Germany in 2002.

Solstice also shared two split picture discs, the 10" *The Sleeping Tyrant* in 1998 (with Twisted Tower Dire) and the 7" *Gloves Of Metal* in 2001 (with Slough Feg).

After several CD reissues, *Lamentations* got a vinyl release in 2006 as a gatefold-sleeved double album on the German label Metal Supremacy.

The double album *Only The Strong* in 2008 collected earlier Solstice demos and recordings into one package.

```
SOLSTICE
08   Iron Kodex IK 003  ONLY THE STRONG (2-LP).............20
```

After a Solstice split in 2002, a new lineup got together in 2007. In 2013 they produced another mini album. *Death's Crown Is Victory* was released on Into The Void Records. The band played live in Sweden, Denmark, Norway, Holland, Germany, Greece, Ireland and the UK to promote it.

After yet another lineup change, the album *White Horse Hill* album came out in 2018.

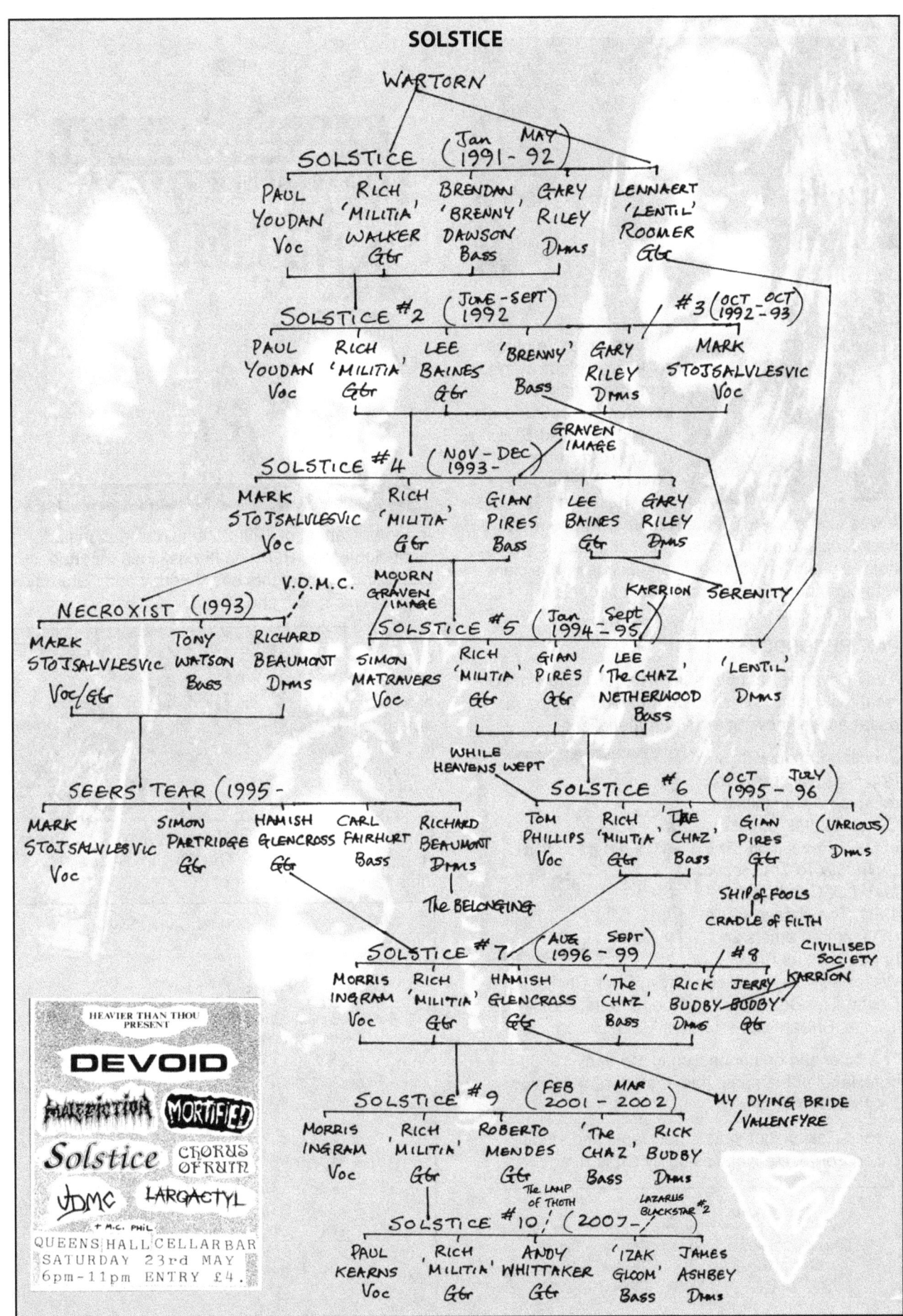

STATION WEST

This progressive blues-rock three-piece combo from the Bradford/Leeds area recorded a CD album called *Blues In The Red House* at Square One Studios in Manchester in 1991. It was released on T-Bone Records, whose motto was *'Music to get your teeth into'* and the trio were helped out in the studio by various guest musicians who contributed extra vocals, saxophone, harmonica and percussion.

PAX RECORDS

Andy Edwards set up this label in 1991 and signed local rock outfit Silence to do an album, although, as far as we know, this never materialised..

In collaboration with Pop God Records, Pax released a Compilation CD of Beatles' covers, entitled *Revolution No 9 (A Tribute To The Beatles In Aid Of Cambodia)*, in 1991. The sixteen-track CD featured artists and bands such as Paul Weller, Billy Bragg, Mega City 4, Pooh Sticks, John Otway, The Driscolls, The Moonflowers, Senseless Things, Brilliant Corners, Frank Sidebottom.

The label had no connection to the early 1980s punk label of the same name, started by Marcus Featherby in Sheffield.

Also in Halifax that year, a new label and studio called Forget Me Not was up by Chris Birch.

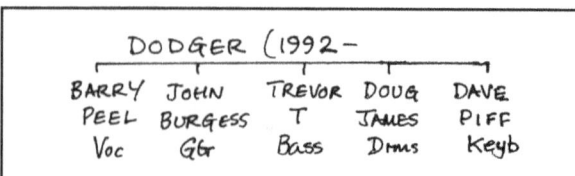

At the beginning of 1992, a new rock and indie night club called ROX, on Leeds Road, opened, promoting event nights every Friday and Saturday, but it seems it was short-lived.

A new bunch of local bands emerged in 1992, including hard rockers  Flashpoint (pictured), rock'n'roll revivalists Dodger, Hump, The Dead Dogs, The Rhythm Seeds and indie rockers Bob Got Shot.

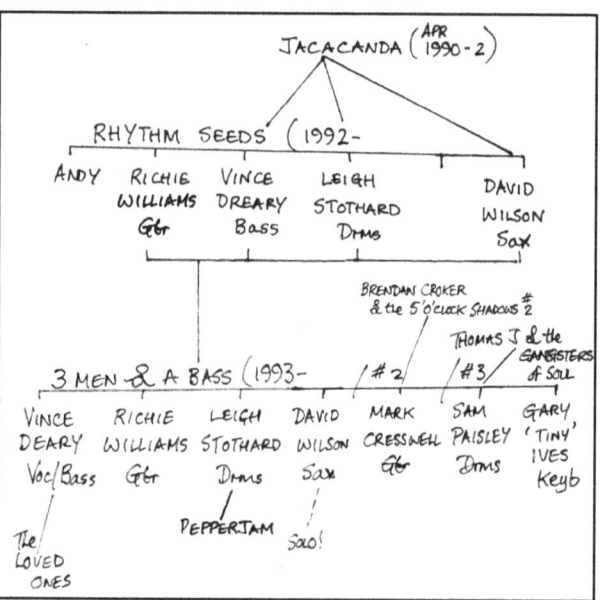

CHAPTER 4   1991 - 1993

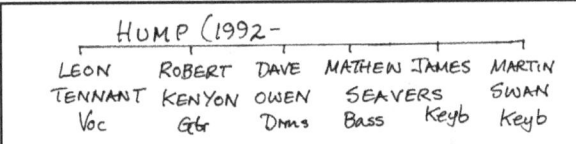

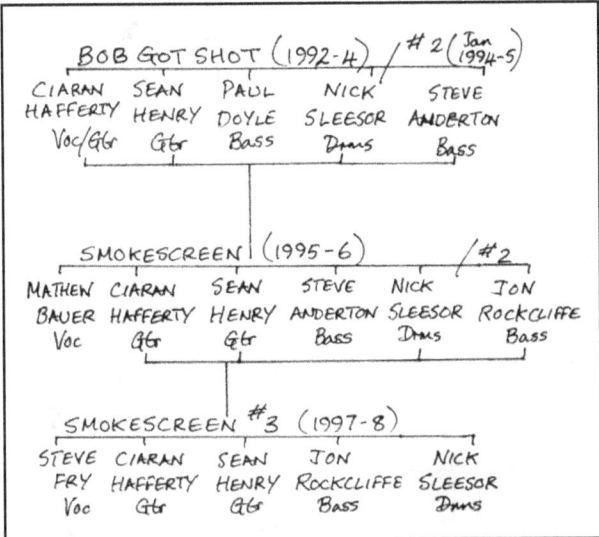

During these early months of 1992, Queen's Hall played host to an eclectic range of American acts like sub-pop style rockers Pearl Jam, Motown's Edwin Starr (supported by Bradford's Thomas J) and the superb Southside Johnny & The Asbury Dukes.

On Sunday, May 17, the American hardcore band Fugazi played at Bradford University's Communal Building. The gig was organised by *Flame In Hand*, run by Karen of Leeds fanzine Ablaze.

Two pop/rock groups who appeared in 1992 were:

FULL COLOUR

Full Colour were a six-piece pop outfit who wrote their own material but also did the odd cover version of songs by Alison Moyet and Tears For Fears.

ROYCE

Three-piece Royce morphed from the earlier Voyce. In February 1995, the group featured in the second part of the BBC 2 television drama *Blood & Peaches*. Set in Bradford, it tells the story of four young people growing up together.

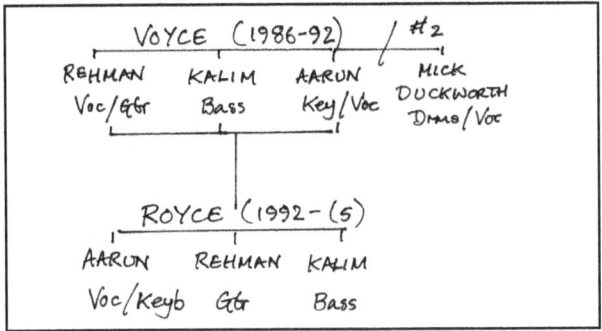

Local band Secret People were in their second incarnation, having been a three-piece back in 1987, when they released their 7" single *China / Evergreen* on the Jive Records label.

They also appeared on the cult Channel 4 '80s music show *The Tube* twice.

FOR WHAT

This local band, who gigged extensively around the region, released the four-track CD EP, Some Other Time, on the local Voltage label in July 1992. The tracks were Clear / Where Are We Now? / Tribute / Moodswing.

When For What finally split up, their vocalist 'Custard' went on to work at Jumbo Records in Leeds.

139

METAL MOUNTAIN 92

The second, and what turned out to be the final, *Metal Mountain* rock band competition had begun at the Rio (Rio Rokz) in February, with Keighley thrash metal band Mannix performing at the first heat.

The event ran into difficulties in May after promotor Malcolm Hanson got into a legal wrangle with the venue over ticket sales and crowd numbers.

The *T&A* cancelled its sponsorship and the competition remained stalled until December, when the remaining 20 bands got to play for a place in the final. The semi-finals were held at Queen's Hall.

PROGRAMME

Queens Hall
Morley St, Bradford
23rd January 1993
Price £1

The final didn't take place until 1993, on Saturday, January 23. Ten rock bands performed at the all-day gig at Queen's Hall.

Doncaster band Boethius Saul won on the day, with Bradford/Leeds grunge rockers Weird Emotions (pictured), the only local interest remaining, coming fourth.

Organiser Malcolm Hanson left Bradford for Northampton and, although co-promoter Wild Willi Beckett had intended to continue both competitions in following years, that was the end of the line of this type of competition that had begun with the *North Of England Battle Of The Bands* in 1986.

SLAMMER

Slammer were one of the first UK thrash metal bands to sign to a major record label when they released their first LP *The Work Of Idle Hands* on WEA Records in 1989. The band went on to release the EPs

Born For War (above) in 1989 and *Insanity Addicts* in 1990. Their second and final LP, *Nightmare Scenario*, was released in 1991 on Heavy Metal Records and featured a sleeve with artwork by Bradford artist Koot.

WASTELAND

This local five-piece band, formed in 1992, included the ex-Psycho Surgeons guitarist Dale Kirkley. They released their debut CD, *Heroes And Villains,* in May 1999.

THE EDGE

The Edge formed in 1992 after the five lads met at school. They played a set at that year's Bradford Festival.

They recorded a demo tape which included the tracks *Justify* and *Where Were You*.

In September 1994 they supported local rockers Terrorvision.

Another band around at the time was Thee Athenaeum (1991-94). They were led by Tony Lee and played The 1 In 12 Club during March 1993.

MONORAIL

Formed in 1992 as a 'mod-style' band originally called Funky Monorail, they released an EP entitled *Stars In Their Cars* before dropping the 'Funky'. This was followed by another self-released 7", *Blind Valentine*, in 1993 on Numb Productions.

Now firmly re-named Monorail, the band's style moved into the Britpop vein as they signed a deal with German label Edel Records in 1995. Their debut release, in February 1996, was the three-track CD single *I Can See You In The Mirror / What Do You Get / Between Here & Somewhere*, soon followed that year with another three-track CD, *Like I Do / You Look How I Feel / Hang Reality Bo*.

The band played live on the first BBC broadcast of Camelot's *National Lottery* programme.

In September 1997, fresh from a rip-roaring week of fun in the sun on the *Radio One Roadshow*, they released another CD single, *Do Better / Repeat To Fade / I've Gotta New Name*. Like all their previous singles, it was produced by Giles Martin (the son of The Beatles' producer Sir George Martin) and appeared on Edel's Facedown imprint.

A fourth CD single *I Think I Feel It / Forget It / I've Gotta New Name* was released only in Germany.

There was an Anti-Nazi League benefit at Queen's Hall on Friday, May 20, 1992, featuring The Big Bang, Primate, Threshold Shift and Criminal Damage.

Another ANL gig at The New Beehive with Primate and The Big Bang took place a week before.

HOT SPICED BANANAS

This poppy rock combo played a mixture of original and covers around the local gig scene with bassist Mark Cranmer being the only constant member.

They recorded a three-track demo, *Sitting Pretty / In And Out Of Love / The Human Show* at guitarist Mick Smith's 8-track studio, which he had built under Spectre Sound music shop in Bingley.

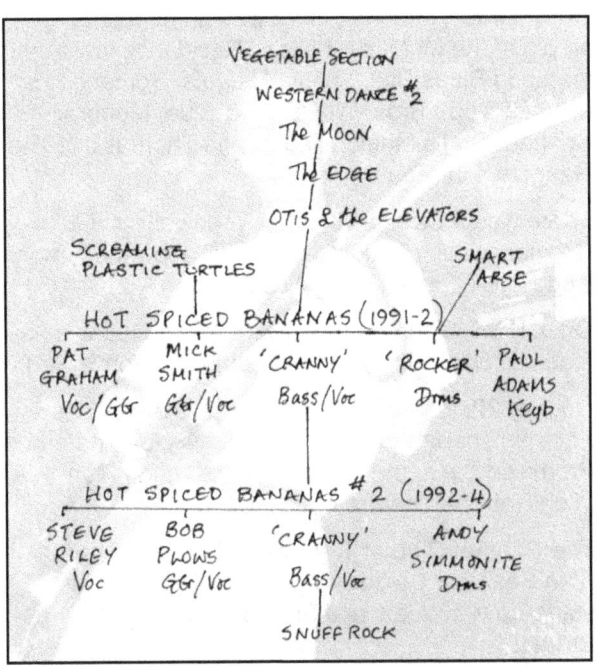

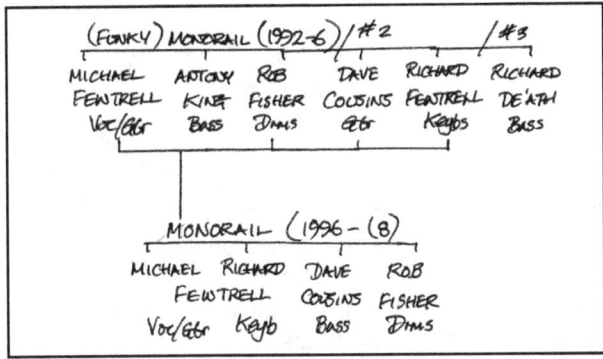

BRADFORD FESTIVAL 1992

This year's Bradford Festival took place between June 19 and July 5.

The City was awash with entertainers as jugglers, musicians, mime artists, and dancers took to the streets. With events taking place each lunchtime and every evening, there was a wide variety of entertainment to be found. A large number of venues held events and the Wool Exchange put on daily lunchtime gigs.

Musical highlights of the festival included;

On July 19: Milan Lad's Jazz Fuse played the lunchtime slot at the Wool Exchange, Somebody's Brother supported Stan Webb's Chicken Shack at Queen's Hall and The Brass Hoppers played at the Festival Launch Party at the Wool Exchange.

On Saturday, June 20, there was an all-day open-air gig at the McMillan Halls of Residence lawn, featuring Blues Bite, Scarlet Heights, Somebody's Brother, Repo Bros, White Hot & Blue, Monorail, Sponge, Griff's Magic Theatre and Thomas J & The Gangsters Of Soul.

There was a Cabaret Club at Treadwell's in Little Germany which featured Clash collaborator Tymonn Dogg, Nick Toczek, Chris Wright and TAS.

On July 21, a summer solstice party at Queen's Hall featured Ozric Tentacles, RDF and Bradford's Zed.

On July 22, local playwright Keith Narey and his Pheonix Theatre group produced his play The Promised Land, the final part of his Union Man trilogy, at The Theatre In The Mill.

The Cabaret Club at Treadwell's had blues from Alan Seaman, Celtic swing from Quicksilver and stand-up from Alex, and Bradford's own Little Brother.

July 23 saw Monorail support The Boo Radleys at the Wool Exchange.

On July 25, Bradford's Arise played with Hope Springs Eternal at The 1 In 12 Club.

On Saturday, July 26, a MAPA People's Day was held at Mapa Community Centre in West Bowling, featuring music from Creation Roots, New Musical Testament and Klymax Band, while The 1 In 12 Club put on a punk all-dayer.

Sunday, July 28 saw a concert in Bell Dean Fields in Allerton with bands including Scarlet Heights, Invaders and Creation Roots.

This year also saw the creation of Festival Radio, set up by former Pennine Radio presenter Nigel Schofield, which would later become Bradford Community Broadcasting (BCB).

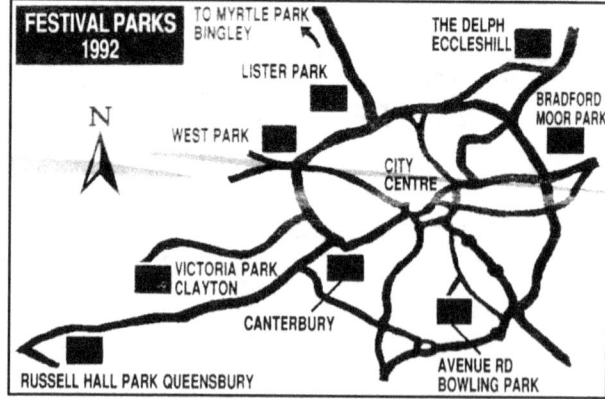

Bands On The Beck took place on Friday, July 3 and Saturday, July 4, outside the Theatre In The Mill, while the Bradford Mela was held over Saturday and Sunday at Lister Park.

HOW WAS IT FOR YOU?

BANDS ON THE BECK- JULY 3rd &4th BRADFORD UNIVERSITY.

Typical Bradford. It's been sunny weather for weeks, then on the day of "Bands on the Beck" the heavens open and it pisses it down for 2 days solid. The powers that be decided to move the venue inside to the Commy building to prevent the possibility of no audience and the bands playing in 3 feet of water. I just feel very sorry for the those people who spent the whole of the previous week building a magnificent outdoor stage.

FRIDAY

Black Angel Blues started Fridays proceedings but I was too busy sheltering in the Mainline with a pint to be bothered to make the effort. I don't think I missed anything mindyou.

Rattle Snake Shake, oh dear, what a sad attempt at a band. Glam Metal at it's most nauseating. Riddled with cliches including the now standard acoustic song where the drummer plays the tambourine. My only advice to this band is to hang up your cowboy boots and get proper jobs.

By the time **Blind Mole Rat** (stupid name) graced the stage, I had discovered that the makeshift bar, and with Newcastle Brown at a quid a time things were beginning to look promising. (F**kin Student -Ed). The group had obviously attempted to jump on the Folk/Rock bandwagon popularised recently by bands like The Levellers, but missed the mark by a long way. The usual hint of 'right on' lefty politics made me hate this band even more. ("Oh you fascist bastard "I here you cry).

4 Millions couldn't be more different. I always thought that when you reached 35 you have to lead a 9 to 5 existance and watch a lot of television. how wrong I was ; you form a retro-punk covers band in a last chance to capture your lost youth. At least this band had the honesty to openly admit onstage that they were shit.

Arise were next, a blend of 70's psychedelic reggae - easily the best band on tonights bill. The fact that Arise a mainly an intrumental band found me occasionally loosing concentration but that was probably

PHOTO: KEV BRIGGS

the whole idea. The hippy playing the Digeridoo was an original touch!

I was getting pretty fucked off with the whole do by now and **New Musical Testament** drove me to the point of thinking that there must be better places to go. Their blend of Soul, Funk and Reggae made a few people get down and boogie an equal number thought it a good opportuinity to leave.

Fridays choice of bands was in my opinion uninspired at best and dire at worst.

SATURDAY

Yes it was still raining. After Fridays disapointing state of affairs I was in no hurry to rush back for more especially as todays ten band line up started at 3pm. Hey I've got to eat you know! As a result of my unenthusiasm I missed the **Rhythm Seeds**, Price of Ivory, Sliante, Jubilee and 2 Memphis, some reporter I am! Out of the five bands I did manage to see, three of them were amazingly similar. **Swerve, The Headmen** and **Monorail** represented the Manchester type Indie guitar band and as a whole showed nothing to make them stand out from the crowd. The Headmen were probably the best with a rousing version of the Monkeys "I'm a believ

Trip & Stumble w made up of the bass player from New Model Army an some other bloke with a si hairdo. Obviously this duo didn't take themselves very seriously playing covers ar original material using a variety of strange instrume including a cazoo. Taken v a rather large amount of sa this band were reasonably enjoyable.

Ap'l stood out like a sore thumb. A rave keyboa band sounding like an electronic instrumental version Sisters of Mercy. You have got to give this band credit, they did there own thing and made people sit u and listen unlike nearly eve other band that was on offer. This difference alone made me enjoy Ap'l more than any other band on the bill.

On paper the idea of event like this would look l an exiting prospect. In reali it takes more than good idea to pull it off. I know that technically speaking the eve was totally sound. The outdoor stage constructed in the University Ampitheatre was a magnificent achievement that was ruined by tha old bastard the weather. I sa half a dozen pissed off looking people sitting on the stage in the pouring rain while the gig was going on inside.

The sound and lights were handled extremely wel by the great TSA as usual - well done guys.

Unfortunatly the ever was let down by the most important aspect - the bands. Whoever was in charge of booking the bands deserves t be beaten with a very large stick! They didn't have much imagination and obviously settled for the first band to volanteer. If your going to pu on a gig of this magnitude make sure you book some decent bands. The event was run as part of the Bradford Festival, maybe this was it's kiss of death?

Tom Fisher.

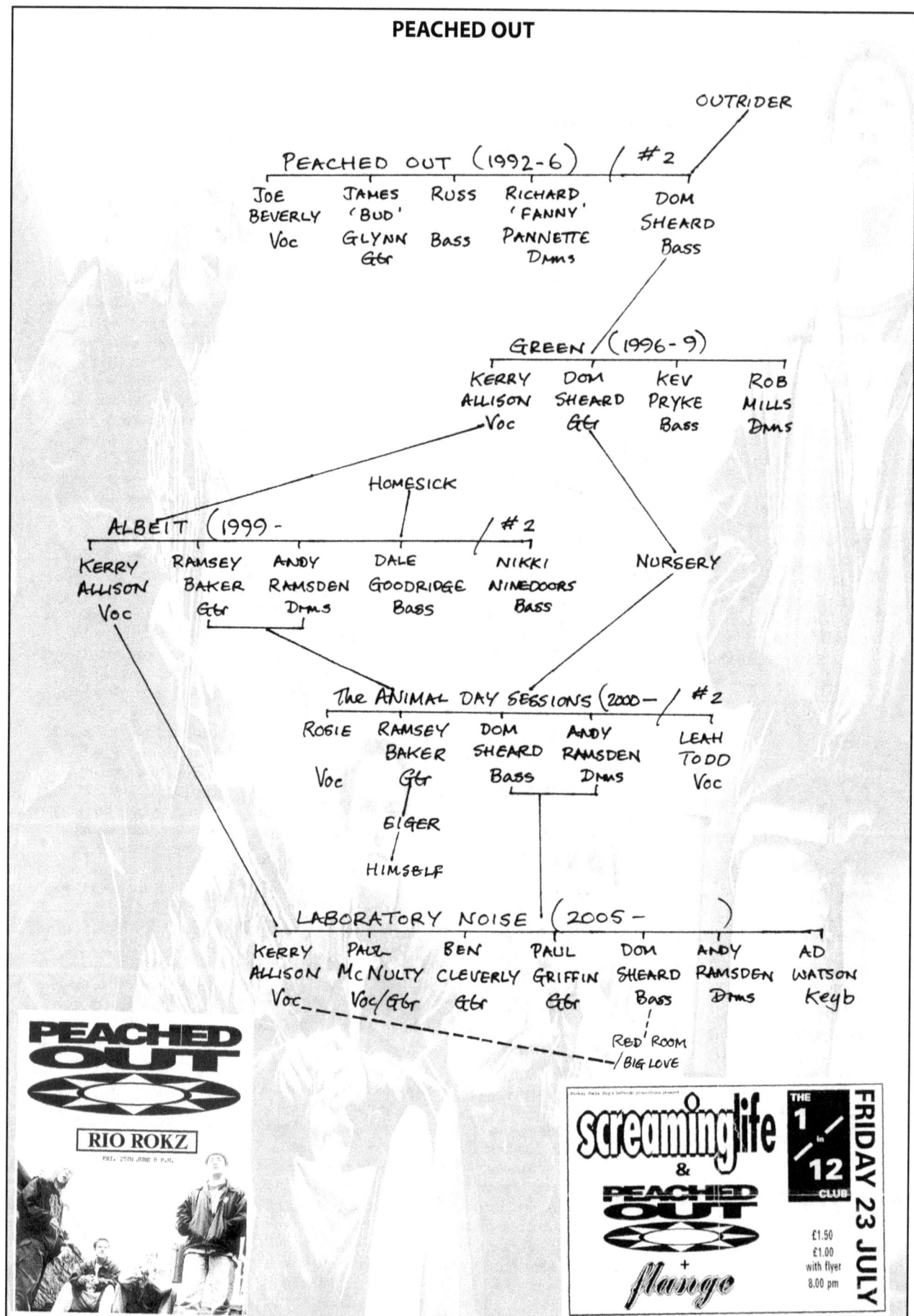

CHAPTER 4 — 1991 - 1993

TASMIN ARCHER

On September 12, 1992, Tasmin Archer went straight to No 1 in the UK single charts with her first single *Sleeping Satellite*. The haunting ballad, written by Tasmin and her two writing partners John Beck and John Hughes, stayed in the charts for another sixteen weeks.

She became the first UK woman in over a decade to have a solo number one hit, and that year she won a Brit Award for Best Newcomer.

Tasmin was born locally and had gone to Grange Upper School. She started her musical career as a backing vocalist in the local group Dignity while working as a clerk in Bradford Magistrates Court in 1977. She later worked at Flexible Response Studios. She met her future writing partners, John Hughes and John Beck, and formed the band The Archers after a spell singing for Somebody's Brother. After the usual slog around record labels, Tasmin signed to EMI in 1990, spending the next few years honing her sound.

Her LP *Great Expectations* came out in October 1992. It spawned another three hit singles; *In Your Care*, No 16 in February 1993, *Lords Of The New Church*, No 26 in May and *Arienne,* No 30 in August 1993. (6)

In January 1994, Tasmin's version of Elvis Costello's *Shipbuilding* (a hit for Robert Wyatt) got to No 40 in the charts. The 7-inch vinyl EP contained three more Costello penned songs, including *New Amsterdam*.

In March 1996, she released her last charting single, *One More For The Boys*, reaching No 45.

Her second album, *Bloom*, released in May, was produced by legendary country producer Mitchell Froom. Later that year she decided to quit the music business but continued to write songs with her partner John Hughes.

After a gap of ten years, a new Tasmin Archer album appeared on her own Quiverdisc label.

2006's *On* was produced by John Hughes and featured bassist Bruce Thomas, of Elvis Costello & The Attractions fame.

Tour slot crowns Tasmin's success

by SIMON ASHBERRY

SINGING sensation Tasmin Archer has landed a support slot on a UK tour by Curtis Stigers.

The Bradford-born star will be playing live dates across the country next month in the wake of her overnight success.

Her debut single Sleeping Satellite has already rocketed to number 13 in the Gallup chart in just three weeks since being released - and record company EMI is hoping it will smash into the top ten at the weekend.

Tasmin, 25, who now lives in Guiseley, is expected to play a full series of headline live concerts in the New Year.

But meanwhile she has been specially asked to open for soulful American heartthrob Stigers at five major venues next month.

The mini-tour opens at Nottingham Royal Centre on October 8, followed by dates at Wolverhampton Civic Centre (October 9), St Austell Colosseum (October 1), London's Town and Country Club (October 12) and the Leas Cliff Hall in Folkestone (October 13).

After the gigs, Tasmin has an album called Great Expectations released by EMI on October 19 and a follow-up single is likely to be taken from it.

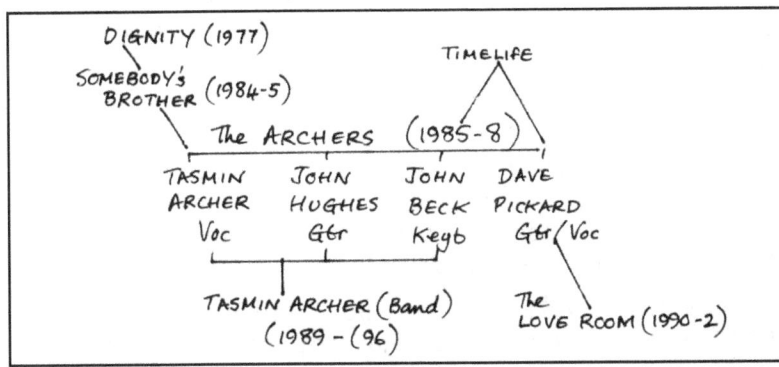

LOT 49

Local three-piece Lot 49 formed around the summer of 1991 and musically were influenced by REM and It Bites as well as trying to define their own sound. They played locally often as well as far as Manchester and Leeds.

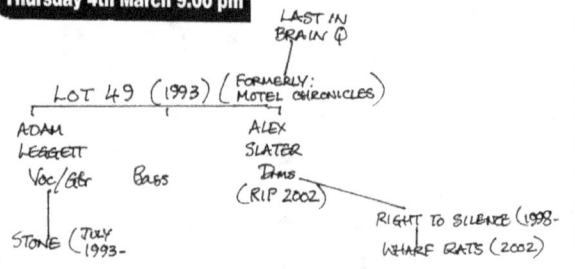

The Motel Chronicles   1 in 12 club 21/8/92

There is something about going to a gig at the 1 in 12 Club that sets it apart from anywhere else. Maybe it's the unsual surroundings of the place with its bizzarre wall sculpture, or the great tasting Sam Smiths Bitter. It could be the fact that the audience of about 30 made more noise than a room of 100 people at the Queens Hall. I'd never heard of tonights band the only reason I went was because I didn't fancy yet another night sat in the Biko Bar.

The band were reminiscent of REM at times, the guitar was in extra ringy-jingy mode, the bass and drums kept the songs ticking over. I did find my attention was drifting occasionally during the set, but the lone dancer, a crazy pissed up bloke at the front was dancing around trying to keep the audience's attention.

The band played about 10 songs, most of them in the same tempo, and looked incredibly suprised by the rousing applause of the audience. They left the stage to yet more cheering and were soon back after our pissed up dancer ran around the audience shouting "play on, play on."

They came back and guess what? Straight into coversland. They played "Allright Now" (you know - the chewing gum advert), which got a few people up to dance.

All in all I enjoyed this gig. It's reassuring to know that somewhere in Bradford people are still appreciating live music.

Tony Dillon.
Stork # 5

GORGEOUS

Formed in November 1992, around Darren Maude (ex-Architect) and guitarist Jon Grosberg, after toying with a sampler.

They were soon joined by Harrogate singer Jude Morrel after she replied to an advert in Melody Maker. The quartet was completed by ex-Seven Antelopes / Deuteronomy (pictured below) bassist

Johnny Lorrimer. After a couple of years, Darren and the two Johns formed the new band, Smack in 1996.

DAWNRAISER

This local rock outfit strutted their stuff for a couple of years before its members typically split up and went off to form other bands. Most notable of these were Dark Embrace, a gothic/doom metal band, and Neckbrace, a straight-edge punk band.

By June 1995, twin guitarists Alex and Paul had re-convened and started Dawnraiser II, with a more heavy metal/thrash style to their sound. Again, they only lasted a couple of years, before all moving on to other projects.

In April 2009, a line-up of Dawnraiser reformed and played a one-off charity gig.

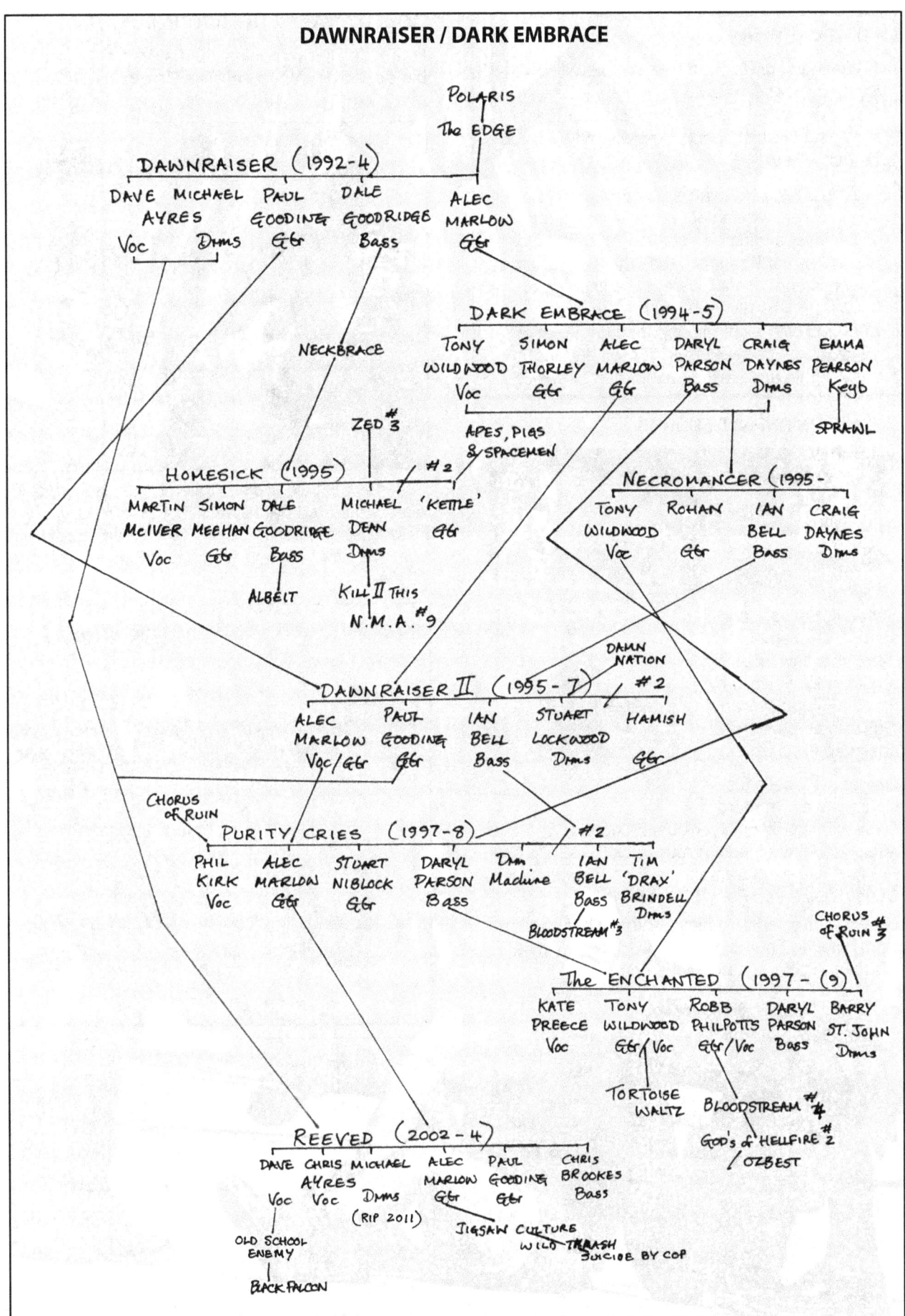

THE GULF WAR

On January 16, 1991, four months after Saddam Hussein's invasion of Kuwait, the Allies (USA, Great Britain and some EU countries) finally started the 'shock and awe' of *Operation Desert Storm*.

The re-taking of Kuwait by the Allies, and subsequent invasion of Iraq, only lasted forty-three days, ending on February 28 with the capitulation of Baghdad. The UK's casualties from this brief conflict were; seventeen dead (nine from 'friendly fire') and forty-three wounded with eight missing, at a total cost to the taxpayer of over £3,000 Million and the terrible pain and loss for families on both sides.

RECKLESS RHINO RECORDS

Based in Baildon, and set up in November 1992, this new local record label was run by ex-1919 guitarist Mark Tighe as an outlet for unsigned bands.

One of the label's first signings was Bradford / Halifax melodic hard rock band Legend, who released a limited edition four-track CD single *Cry For Me*. The other tracks were *Blue Bullets / How Does It Make You Feel / Can't Wait*.

Legend launched their single with a gig at the Northcliffe, in Thornton, on April 10, 1993, while planning a UK tour later that summer.

MOULDY WARP / THE BROOMDUSTERS

In the 1990s, two original 1960s Bradford blues bands, Mouldy Warp and The Broomdusters, reformed.

At Leeds Irish Centre on November 3, 1994, Mouldy Warp supported Paul Jones' The Manfreds, which included original members of Manfred Mann - a band they had supported at Leeds University in the 1960s.

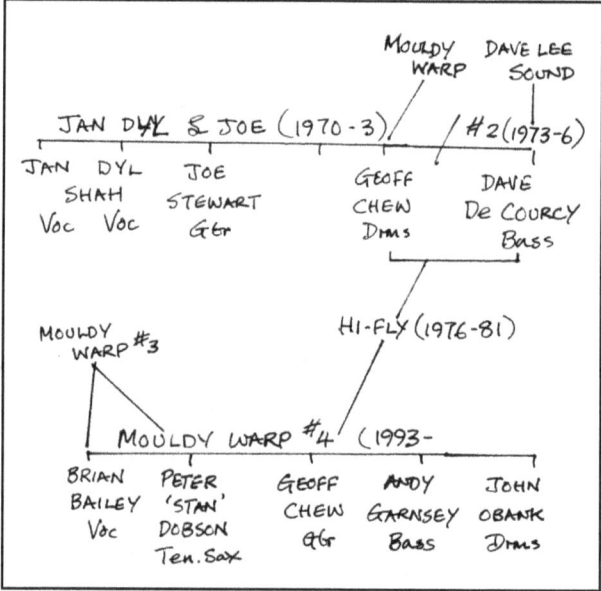

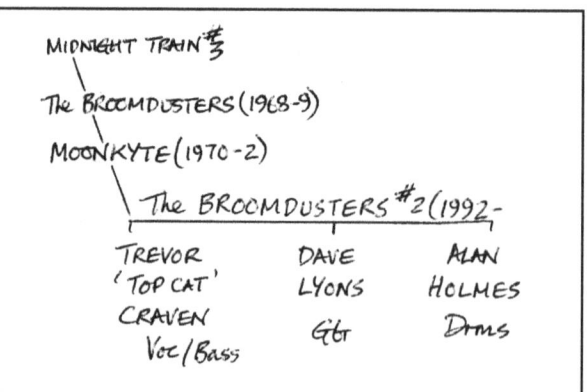

CHAPTER 4 — 1991 - 1993

THE 1 IN 12 CLUB 1991-1993

The 1 In 12 Club started the fourth year of existence in its new converted home at 21-23 Albion Street. The first gig of 1991, on January 28, was a rare appearance by Leeds early punk legends The Mekons, some of whom were long-standing members and supporters of the Club.

Some members of the band would later relocate to the USA to settle, have families and continue to perform The Mekons newly developed folk-Americana sound on the alt-country circuit.

Many regular gigs followed, between 1991 and 1993, by local acts and groups from all over the

Thursday, April 18, 1991 Bradford Star.

BRADFORD's famous 1 in 12 Club decided to celebrate it's tenth anniversary in style recently by asking local artist Tom Cousins to brighten up the bar.

The result, an imaginative design featuring lion-faced figures floating downstream, reflects the relaxed, Bohemian atmosphere of the Sunbridge Road bar, which enters its second decade next month.

Club members Paddy Shanks and bar steward Dave Gropper are seen here admiring Tom's work, and holding some of the recordings of numerous artists who have appeared at the night-spot over the years.

Tom, 29, a former London arts student, from Neal Street, in Bradford, says: "It is supposed to be quite a happy scene and make you feel like being happy in our club. Reaction has been mixed so far."

Bradfordians will be able to make their own minds up about the flowing art work by joining the club — ring Bradford 734160 for more details.

More proof that Mekons deserve a lucky break

THE Mekons are one of those enigmatic bands who have been plying their trade for eons without unearthing the commercial success they deserve.

They have a small but loyal following, a nice line in daft humour and some fine pop-rock songs, but try as they might that elusive hit has evaded them.

The nearest they came was three years ago with the majestic Ghosts of American Astronauts, one of their lilting, simple, guitar pop songs with the

REVIEW The Mekons, at the 1 in 12 Club, Bradford — T&A, Tuesday, January 29, 1991

striking opening salvo: "Up in the hills above Bradford, outside the Napalm factory."

It was sung by the hugely energetic Sally Timms, one of the Leeds-based band's three lead singers, who is still the main focal point for a Mekons show.

Her bleached, vogueish haircut, which repeatedly ruffled as she danced and grinned through the set, could be seen bobbing up and down even from the back of the crowded room for the combo's more Celtic numbers.

For the slower ones, Sally, sporting cut-away-jeans over her woolly tights, took up the familiar study in concentration — both hands gripping the microphone for dear life, eyes tightly shut and wonderful voice resonating amid the mushy guitars and beautiful violin playing.

It was the virtuoso violin of Susan — sometimes classically stroked, sometimes splayed with the abandon of the fiddler, and sometimes delicately plucked to great effect — that sprinkled a touch of stardust over the six-piece band packed on to the little stage.

Guitarist-singer John's laddish reference to her as Bogienose — justified, it seems, only by Susan's thin-nosed attractiveness — earned a stiff rebuke from Sally, but such chumminess is all part of a Mekon.

They were really excellent — there is still time for their rocking dreamboat to come in.

David Ford

UK. The Club also played host to thirty-two foreign bands, twenty-two from the USA, two Canadian, plus Dutch, Swiss, Belgian, Swedish and Norwegian groups.

These gigs are documented here with examples of some of the flyers and posters that were produced at the time, and the odd short profile.

1 IN 12 CLUB GIGS 1991/92

JANUARY 1991
28 - The Mekons

FEBRUARY 1991
9 - Lizgizzard / Trashed / Beer Beast
20 - Quicksand / One By One / Nailbomb
27 - Stretcheads / Tse Tse Fly / Lizgizzard

MARCH 1991
2 - Duma Yuma / Asylum
15 - Milk / Prophecy Of Doom / Deviated Instinct
16 - Pregnant / Sheepskin Children
28 - MDM / Threshold Shift / Beer Beast

APRIL 1991
3 - Oi Polloi / Jimmy Savilles Wheelchair
6 - Jailcell Recipes / Sofa Head / Concrete Sox / Exit Condition / Flame On / Sleep / Pitch Shifter
12 - Blyth Power / Pram
14 - Kulturo / Trashed
20 - Crane / Slum Turkeys / Cabbage Head Kids
28 - Inside Out / Nerve Rack / Frogs Of War

MAY 1991
2 - Therapy?
18 - The Blaggers / Disaster / Indian Dream / Active Minds / Sundance / Earth Citizens / Sanctions / Kismet HC

JUNE 1991
3 **1 In 12 10th Anniversary Gig at Bradford University** - The Wedding Present / Chumbawamba / Wild Willi Beckett
6 - Nausea / Hellkrusher / Attaxia
13 - Sally Barker And The Rhythm
29 - Kulturo / Pitch Shifter / Inside Out / Thought Police / Sedition / One By One / The Rise

JULY 1991
13 - Immortal Dead / Cataclysmic / Subsonics / Saucepan Spasm
16 - Econochrist / Knucklehead

AUGUST 1991
3 - Sofa Head / Adversary / Speed Hippies
8 - Harmony As One / MTA / Older Than Dirt
10 - Blitzgrieg / Threshold Shift

SEPTEMBER 1991
5 - September Kitchen / Soft Black And Blue
6 - Old Joe Zydeco / Black Spot Champions / Alex / Eric The Heretic / Chris & Mary
8 at Queen's Hall - Flux Of Pink Indians / Little Chef / Citizen Fish
11 - Kulturo / Stockwell
14 - Oi Polloi / Concrete Sox / Drill / Sofa Head / Wordbug / Immortal Dead / The Losers
19 - Scarlet Heights / Benjamin Zephaniah / Little Bro' / Wild Willi Beckett
21 - Architect / Big Bang

OCTOBER 1991
12 - Bobby Charltons / Cabbage Head Kids / Sheepskin Children / Mugwamp
13 - One By One / Disaster / Search Party
17 - Sons Of Ishmael / Nessun Dorma
26 - Blaggers / Terminus / Codename Fadge / Space Monsters
27 - Faith Healers / Pram
31 - Daisy Chainsaw / Sunshot / Frogs Of War

NOVEMBER 1991
15 - Dog Faced Hermans / The Ex / Nerverack
17 - Dawson / Tunnel Frenzies / Mr Giblet

DECEMBER 1991
6 - Chumbawamba / UV Pop
18 - Sofa Head / Gan
21 - Threshold Shift / MDM / Chaos / Search Party / Wartorn
28 - Sedition / Monks Of Science / Disaffect / Dirty Headed Bastard / Threshold Shift / Disturbed

JANUARY 1992
17 - Dragonflies / Arise / MDLF

FEBRUARY 1992
2 - Threshold Shift / Voorhees / Sore Throat / Immortal Dead / Beer Beast / Wartorn / Nailbomb / Cataclysmic
21 - GFA / Arise
22 - Blaggers ITA / Threshold Shift / Harmony As One / Frogs Of War / Disaffect / Kickback / Wartorn / Vomithead
27 - Back To The Planet / Under The Gun

1 IN 12 CLUB GIGS 1992

MARCH 1992
3 - Herb Garden / Active Minds
13 - Creaming Jesus / Yardstick / Arise
18 - Blyth Power / Atilla The Stockbroker
28 - Sick Of It All / Harmony As One

APRIL 1992
4 - Terminus / Monks Of Science / Substandard
11 - Doom / Anaemia / Sarcasm
18 - Slunk / Lizgizzard
26 - Active Minds / Kito / Submission / Burst Of Silence

MAY 1992
2 - Tribe 8
7 - Hiatus / Mushroom Atack / Disaster
9 - Headcleaner / Yardstick / Cactus Juice
15 - Gorefest / Necrosanct / Korpse / Chorus Of Ruin
16 - Pig Ignorance / Virtual Reality
17 - Ironside / Nailbomb
30 - Hell No / Decline / Kito

JUNE 1992
3 - Rorschach / One By One / Wartorn / Voorhees
13 - Nadir / Honeyfungus
25 - Hope Springs Eternal / Arise
26 - Under The Gun / Tequila Girls / Blind Mole Rat
27 - No Use For A Name / Downside / Soricide

JULY 1992
4 - Resist / Hellkrusher / Kismet HC / Largacty / Woodhouse Rejects
9 - Emily Playground / Cactus Juice
18 - Oi Polloi / Terminus / Threshold Shift
24 - Crane
31 - Phineas Foam / Us

AUGUST 1992
7 - MDC / Nailbomb
15 - Codename FADGE / Bugeyed / Disaster Unit
16 - Onward / Strength Alone / Understand / Stand Off
27 - Sedition / One By One / Active Minds / Generic / PVC

SEPTEMBER 1992
5 - Virtual Reality / Lizgizzard / Horror
11 - Spinewrench / Oil Seed Rape / Largactil
24 - Sofa Head / Gan / Downside

OCTOBER 1992
2 - Dirt / Hellkrusher
16 - Incarcerated / Malediction / Chorus Of Ruin / Decomposed / Lone Wolf
17 - Neurosis / Yardstick / Skindrill
21 - Arise / Low / Trip & Stumble
23 - Disaster / Threshold Shift / Biohazard
24 - Arise / Kava Kava
25 - Low
30 - Integrity / Downcast
31 - Oi Polloi / Sublime / Swine Flu / Rub The Buddha / Indian Dream / In Anger / Doom / Beer Beast

NOVEMBER 1992
13 - Sawtooth / Bug Eyed / One By One / Largactil
28 - Terminus / Endemic / Bug Eyed

DECEMBER 1992
11 - Blyth Power / Lizgizzard
19 - Farside / Supertouch / Woodhouse Rejects / Extinction Of Mankind / Sedition / Disaffect / Vomithead

1 IN 12 CLUB GIGS 1993

JANUARY 1993
30 - Dread Messiah / Pissed

FEBRUARY 1993
11 - Immortal Dead / Beer Beast
12 - AS03 / 7% Solution
17 - Dick Gaughan / Danbert Nobacon
18 - Get Monk
19 - Yardstick / Skink / Bugeyed
26 - Mad Halibut

MARCH 1993
2 - Life....But How To Live It / Active Minds
3 - Snarling Horses / Mugwamp
17 - Bikini Kill / Huggy Bear
20 - Glue / Health Hazard / Dog On A Rope / Immortal Dead / Nihilist Reality / Slum Gang / Body Bag
25 - Thee Anthenaeum / Cody Beach
26 - GFA
28 - Spinewrench / Largactyl / Discordance

APRIL 1993
2 - Terminus / Herb Garden / Decadence Within
10 - Oi Polloi / Rub The Buddha / Sublime
18 - Slapshot / Voorhees / Nailbomb
24 - Witchknot / Toxic Shock Syndrome / Chest / Frantic Spiders
28 - Sedition / Extinction Of Mankind / Body Bag

MAY 1993
14 - Big Stone Culture / Ticklish
20 - The Rub / Imago
26 - Blyth Power / Phosos Demos
28 - God Is My Co - Pilot / Disaffect
29 - Mambo Taxi / Chest
31 - Ship Of Fools / Mugwamp

JUNE 1993
3 - Blind Mole Rat
12 - Bender / Beer Beast / Immortal Dead
17 - FOS Brothers / Mushroom Attack
23 - Disaffect / Jap's Eye
30 - UK Subs / Truth Decay

JULY 1993
4 - Econochrist / One By One / Kitchener
15 - Hiatus / Extinction Of Mankind / Manfat
24 - Bugeyed / Dead Wrong / Slum Gang
29 - Nessun Dorma

AUGUST 1993
21 - Oi Polloi / Excrement Of War / Terminus / Active Minds / Spithead / Substandard
28 - Sarcasm / Brawl / Japs Eye / Slander / Contempt

SEPTEMBER 1993
4 - The Auxiliary Of Real Men
5 - Dawson / Archbishop Kebab / Witchknot
8 - Blyth Power / Ye Fungus / Thistle Fairies
10 - GFA / Ship Of Fools
18 - Armed Relapse / Bob Tilton

OCTOBER 1993
16 - Tribe 8 / Witchknot
22 - Chest / Oozy / Babyglide
30 - AOS3 / Bender / Thistle Fairies / Lianne / Frog

NOVEMBER 1993
6 - Blindfold / Ironside / Spirit Of Youth / Fingerprint / Understand / Disrupt
7 - Kito / Health Hazard / Dead Wrong / Bob Tilton / Fabric / Hypocritical Society / Grip
11 - Threshold Shift
12 - Primate
20 - Doom / Kitchener / Health Hazard / Four Past Midnight / Distorted Truth

DECEMBER 1993
4 - Citizen Fish / AOS3 / Recusant / Health Hazard
11 - Linus / Sister George / The Gr'ups / Delicate Vomit / Witchknot / Thistle Fairies / Coping Saw / Profound Victims
15 - Doom / Hiatus / Unhinged / Manfat / Headache

SUBSONICS

This young local band, who played the 1 In 12 on July 13, seem to have not lasted very long. Guitarist Jools Anderson is pictured left.

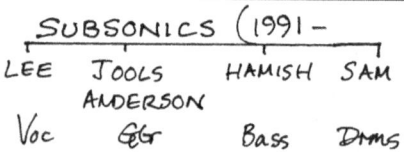

DAISY CHAINSAW

This London band, led by Katie Jane Garside, whose voice could *'send shivers down your spine'*, played at the 1 In 12 on October 31, just prior to the release of their three track *Love Your Money* CD single on Deva records.

The single then got to No 26 in the charts in January 1992. They claimed another chart entry with the No 65 single *Pink Flower / Room Eleven* in March.

Former Skyritch and JJ's Bones bass player Tom Currie joined at some point.

THERAPY?

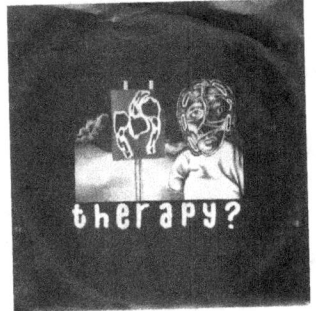

In late 1990, the Club's booking collective received the demo and debut 7" single *Meat Abstract* from an Irish band called Therapy? asking for a gig.

On hearing their stuff, most of the collective were so stunned by the brilliant barrage of punk/metal aggression of the three-piece group, that they were quickly invited to play at the Club asap. Therapy? graced the 1 In 12 Club stage, on May 2, 1991, playing to a small crowd of people who gave the band's excellent show enthusiastic acclaim, as they were very impressive.

At the gig there was surely closer to twenty people there that night, not twelve and a dog as the band's singer/guitarist Andy Cairns told the Bradford University Communal Building crowd a year later, when they returned to the city, now riding high on their success. (7)

THE CLUB'S TENTH ANNIVERSARY

On Monday, June 3, 1991, The 1 In 12 Club celebrated a decade of existence. A gig was organised at Bradford University's Communal Building, with two top Leeds bands, The Wedding Present and Chumbawamba, compered by Wild Willi Beckett. The gig was a sell-out. Both bands presented storming sets of their indie hits. The Wedding Present played most of their new Seamonsters album for an appreciative and wild crowd. (8)

T&A, Friday, April 26, 1991

Rock On
BY SIMON ASHBERRY

Ten-up 1 in 12 Club lays on birthday bash

One of Bradford's top alternative music venues celebrates its tenth anniversary this week. The 1 in 12 Club marks its completion of a decade of live music with a lunchtime buffet and karaoke evening at its Albion Street base tomorrow.

Promoters have announced the club will be moving for one night in June up to Bradford University for a bash to celebrate. Leeds-based guitar monsters The Wedding Present will be headlining the gig at the university's communal hall on June 3 with Chumbawamba and The Levellers supporting.

The 1 in 12 Club started with humble beginnings, putting on gigs once a week in the former Metropole and then spent several years as a nomadic enterprise, using Tickles, the Royal Standard, the Queen's Hall and the Market Tavern.

The club eventually bought its own building in Albion Street with a grant from Bradford Council.

1 in 12 Club founder member Gary said: "We're realy proud of what the club has achieved over the past ten years.

"Nobody outside the members ever believed we'd be running our own building and offering music, a games night, a vegetarian cafe and so on."

T&A, Tuesday, June 4, 1991

A Present to keep as a punk souvenir ...

SOME wedding presents turn out to be yet another pop-up toaster bought with trading stamps.

But West Yorkshire's favourite guitar-totin' post-punk mop tops proved last night they are a gift worth treasuring as they celebrated the tenth anniversary of Bradford's 1 In 12 Club.

TWP mix in equal measure dollops of ringing powerchord pop (Pete Shelley claimed recently the band were still rehashing the first Buzzcocks album), hardcore riffing, sweet-bitter street lyrics and crunching bass and drum rhythms.

Their changes of pace were quite breathtaking, as Gedge cranked himself up after moments of quiet jangling for

REVIEW The Wedding Present at Bradford University

oldies (apart from a storming Everyone Thinks He Looks Daft from the George Best LP), the Weddoes interspersed many of the favourites from the last couple of years with material from their heavy-sounding new album Seamonsters.

The blistering Brassneck and vicious Don't Talk, Just Kiss were highlights, though at times Gedge seemed to swap his guitar just once too often without having the sound balance readjusted properly.

The Wedding Present — savour them,

KARAOKE NIGHT AT THE 1 IN 12 CLUB

Prior to this celebration, the Club had held a members' Karaoke night on Saturday, April 28, where many members present got up to strut their stuff and sing various classic songs. A great night was had by all concerned, as no doubt many headaches testified to the next day.

CHAPTER 4   1991 - 1993

BRADFORD FESTIVAL 1991 AT THE CLUB

As part of that year's Bradford Festival, The 1 In 12 Club organised sixteen events as part of the two weeks of the celebrations, starting with a gig by local psychedelic funk/rock combo September Kitchen, on Thursday, September 5. This was followed by a five-act *Cabaret Night* featuring Old Joe Zydeco, Chris & Mary, Black Spot Champions, comedian Eric Heretic and feminist poet Alex on September 6.

On Saturday 7, a thirteen-hour celebration of lesbian/gay sexuality, part of the *Deviate & Celebrate Week*, started with Lark After Dark, featuring Huffty The Crimplene Comic (9) and Irish reels and jigs from Hangin's Too Good For Them, which was followed by a late disco.

On Sunday, the Club transferred across town to Queen's Hall for a special one-off, 10th Anniversary gig with London anarchos Flux Of Pink Indians, Leeds band Little Chief, and Bristol's Citizen Fish.

Other highlights of the festival at The 1 In 12 Club included;

On Tuesday, September 10, a guest night organised by Leeds' *Termite Club*.

A women's only night with Newcastle act All Because The Lady Loves, on the 12th.

On Friday the 13th there was a fancy dress *Abba Nite* (appropriately dressed partygoes pictured left).

Popular local punk and indie DJ Linda Sprogis' *Hellfire Club* disco night,

```
CARRY ON THE PARTY
TONIGHT
AT THE
1 in 12 Club
with
THE HELLFIRE CLUB
Only One Pound In-Bar till 1am
1 in 12 Club, 21-23 Albion St.
```

and a Bhangra performance from Dhanak, playing Hindi film songs on the 18th.

Thursday, September 19, saw Liverpool Rastafarian poet and philosopher Benjamin Zephaniah (pictured left) perform, supported by Psycho Surgeons frontman and 1 In 12 Club chairman Wild Willi Beckett and the Bradford Irish folk roots group Scarlet Heights.

In the noughties, Benjamin refused an OBE (Order Of The British Empire). *'Me? I thought, OBE me? Up yours, I thought. I get angry when I hear that word "empire"; it reminds me of slavery, it reminds of thousands of years of brutality, it reminds me of how my foremothers were raped and my forefathers brutalised... Benjamin Zephaniah OBE - no way Mr Blair, no way Mrs Queen. I am profoundly anti-empire.'*

The last event, on Sunday, September 22, was a women-only event with American charismatic comedienne, singer and caricaturist Janice Perry (aka Gal) dubbed as, *'Vermont's most dangerous comic'*.

SONS OF ISHMAEL

Canadian punk band, who played the Club on October 17, with Bristol's Nessum Dorma. Sons of Ishmael had been around since the mid-1980s and had released numerous 7" singles on small labels.

FANZINES

Fanzines are usually a non-professionally published phenomenon, produced by fans of a particular genre, such as certain types of music, bands, TV shows, film series, or about certain authors, artists, etc.

The term 'fanzine' first appeared in an 1940s science fiction publication by Russ Chauvenet.

They are produced by fans of a certain genre, with contributions by like-minded, interested people and produced cheaply and sold for a nominal fee with the aim being to reach as many people as possible, and sold at gigs, conventions or via mail order.

With the emergence of punk, fanzines became the voice of fans who were passionate about their particular scene or band and became an example of the DIY culture.

The punk rock fanzine **Sniffin' Glue**, by Mark Perry, set the template for such publications, a prime example of which was **Strangled**, a fanzine produced by fans of The Stranglers, which included gig reviews, pictures and interviews and often included contributions by the band themselves. It also occasionally was sold with rare early recordings and specially produced records by the band.

Other fanzines also put out flexi-disc releases by featured bands.

Bradford's first fanzine was **Wool City Rocker**, started in late 1979 by Ulterior Motives singer, poet and author Nick Toczek, initially with Kay Russell.

This was soon followed by a flurry of local Bradford and Leeds zines in the 1980s, like **Apathy**, **Molotov Comics**, **Attack On Bzag**, **Tongue In Cheek**, the 1 In 12 Club's **Knee Deep In Shit** (**KDIS**), and many others.

Of special note was Ben Sik'o'War's Leeds based **Raisin' Hell**, sold at first for 10p and by the last edition, in the 1990s, was priced at 30p. When Ben moved to London his new zine was entitled **You're So Hideous**.

By 1988, in Bradford, besides the intermittent **KDIS**, the band The Headmen had their own zine called **Roundabout**, costing 25p, and there was also **Swipe**, who produced at least two issues.

In 1991, there was **24 Hours** by George Obradovic, a Yugoslavian punk based at the 1 In 12, Jane Graham of Witchknot's **Shag Stamp**, which did a few split zines with Leeds zine **Duhhh**, written by ex-Embitted singer Anth Palmer, Chris Banks' **Noisefest**, which then changed to **Aversion** and later **Agitate**, and **Armed With Anger** and **How We Rock**, by Richard Corbridge and Nick Royles respectively.

Dean Cavanagh's **Herb Garden** which covered all the main info on Bradford's burgeoning dance scene.

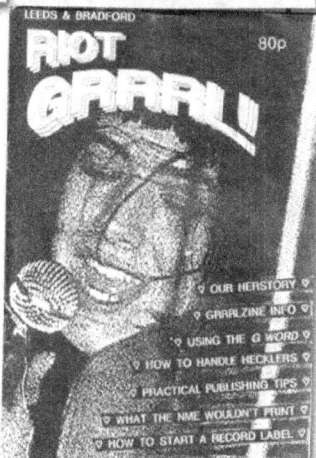

By 1992, Bradford had a new zine, **Stork**, set-up by Thornton based Tom and James Fisher, from local combo This Ritual, and scene commentator Dominic Devereaux. The first issue appeared in April and continued for eighteen issues before folding in February 1994.

Also around at this time was **Riot Grrrl**, produced by a collective of women from Bradford and Leeds, then there was Leeds based **Clowns Laughing** and **Bald Cactus** plus the free Duchess Of York pub's listing guide.

UK Resist from Surrey covered the national underground punk and hardcore scene, as did Cardiff's **Fracture** starting in 1997.

In April 1997, Richard Bolton of local band Bullweek started **Bratford** for a couple of issues, while in Leeds there was **Panic** run by Richard Rouska and the free live music magazine **Backbeat**.

Numerous international zines featured bands from the local punk/HC scene, such as **Voyageur** (France), **All The Noise** (Germany), **Masodik Latas** (Belgium), and **Mac Parazk** (Poland), while in the USA **Maximum Rock'n'Roll**, Minniapolis' **Profane Existence** and **Heartattack** also ran regular UK scene reports.

CHAPTER 4 — 1991 - 1993

IMMORTAL DEAD / MUGWUMP

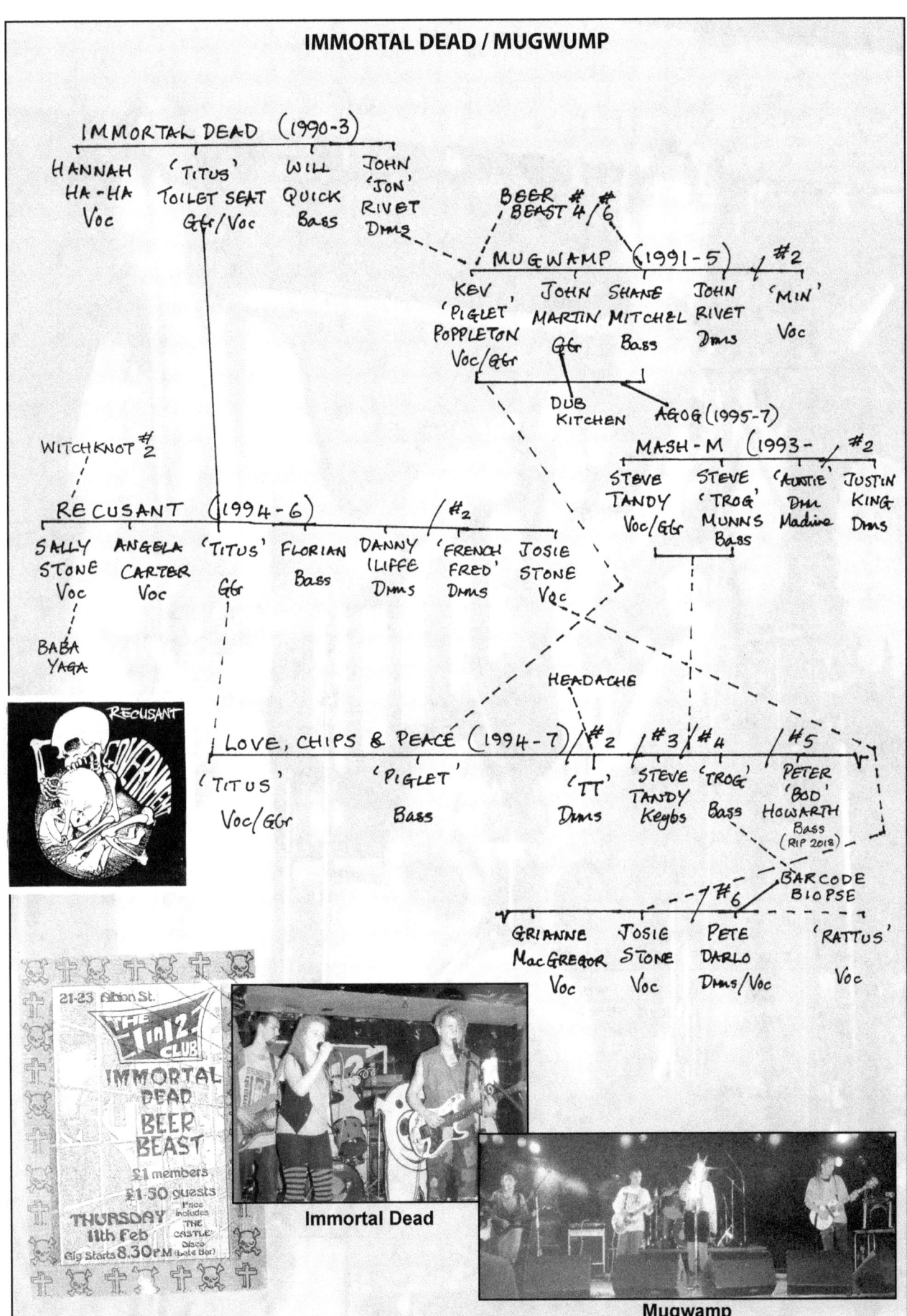

Immortal Dead

Mugwamp

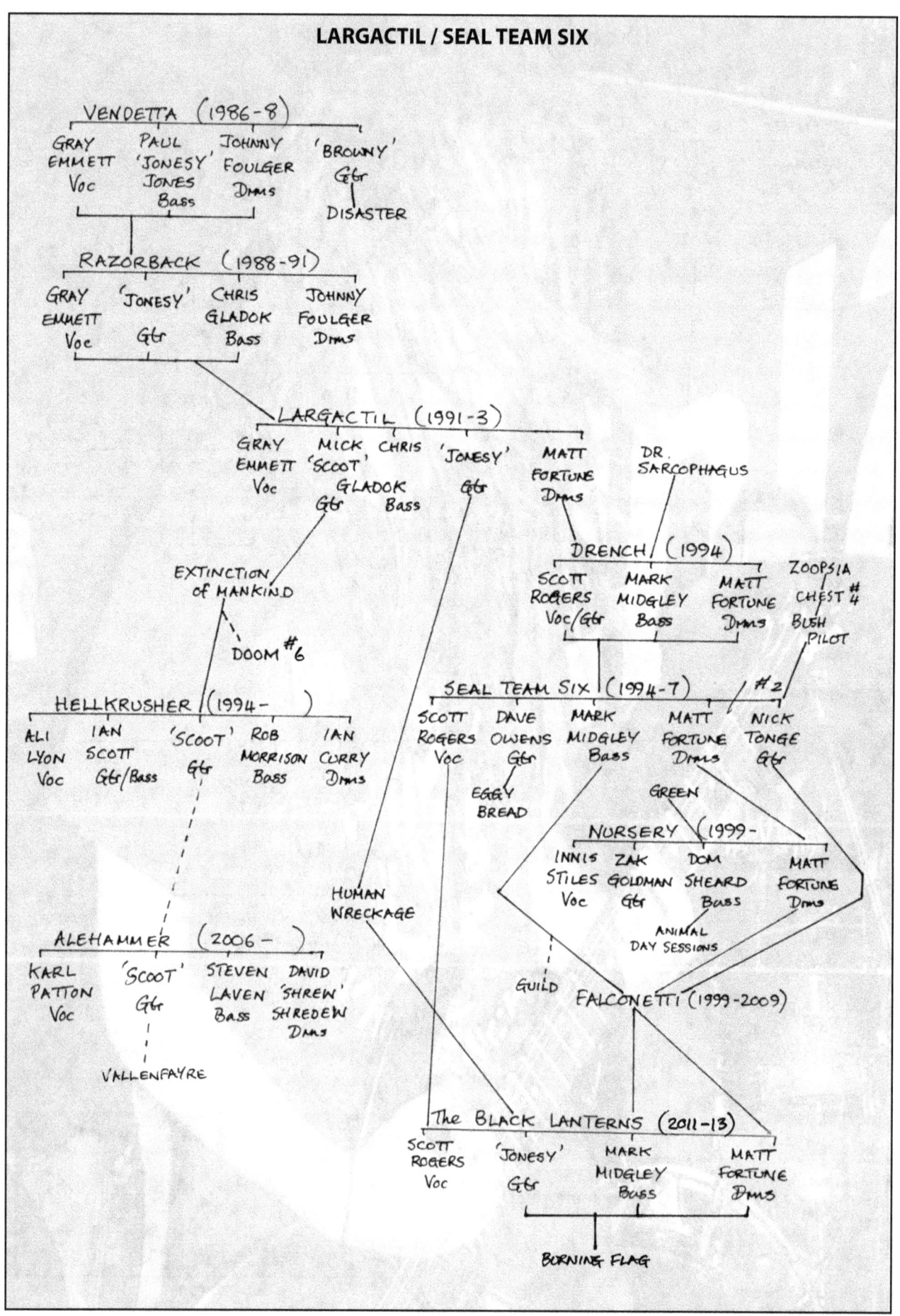

At the start of 1992, The 1 In 12 Club's international reputation was enhanced when *UK Resist* voted it the best self-managed venue in Europe in a reader's poll.

BEST SELF MANAGED VENUES IN EUROPE (Sned, Leeds)
1) 1 in 12 Club, Bradford, England.
2) AK47, Dusseldorf, Germany.
3) Vort 'n' Vis, Ieper, Belgium.
4) Blitz Club, Oslo, Norway.
5) WNC, Groningen, Holland (RIP)
6) Forte Prenestino, Rome, Italy
7) FriedensGasse, Zurich, Switzerland.
8) L'Asilo, Portenza, Italy
9) Breenuys, Leiden, Holland.
10) De Kerk, Breda, Holland.

That year's first gig was on January 17, with local combo Arise and support from The Dragonflys. Arise would play the Club again later in the month with another local act, GFA, on February 22.

Later in the year, GFA played a series of gigs in Moscow, Russia at ex-underground rock clubs, all sponsored by a grant from Bradford Council.

Two local bands around at this time and closely associated with the Club were Immortal Dead and Halifax's Largactil.

DISTROS

Hundreds, if not thousands, of mail-order distribution enterprises (distros for short) of DIY punk/hardcore products sprung up like mushrooms during the 1980s and 1990s in the UK.

```
How We Rock Zine presents
    A Benefit Show For The 1 in 12 Club
******** ALL AGES AFTERNOON SHOW ********
********* SUNDAY 2ND FEBRUARY 1992 *********
+++++++++++15 minute sets from+++++++++++
SORE THROAT * First gig in a longtime, new EP out soon.
  DISASTER * Discharge clones, debut 12" out now, ep out sometime.
NAILBOMB * Terrorist Hardcore, split 7" out soon.
 IN TOUCH * Bradford sXe,reformed from '88,split 7" out in March/April.
IMMORTAL DEAD * Anarchist christian punk,early 80's influence.
 WARTORN * Mix manic Jap hc with siege/Infest. split 7" out soon.
CATACLYSMIC* Frontman Graham of CRAPP fame.
THRESHOLD SHIFT* Melodic punk, 77 style, recording LP soon.
*******************************************
     **ORDER OF LINE UP DECIDED ON THE DAY**
***** HARDCORE ***** THRASH***** PUNK*****
*** 3pm - 7pm, Bar and food from 1pm-3pm ***
************ at The 1 in 12 Club Cafe ************
*** 21-23 Albion St.Bradford BD1.Tel.734160 ***
**1.00 + donation. Bands pay 2.oo to play **
 Record and zine stall, Lucky Dip, Raffle and
other attractions.
Promoter selling record collection, loads of rare wax ( Minor Threat 7s, Iron Cross
Judge,SSD,DYS, GI 7,loads of sXe, Scandanavian,UK hardcore,thrash,punk,Oi!).
       **THIS EVENT IS BEING VIDEOED**
               DRESS TO SWEAT
```

They were usually run by lone individuals from out of their bedrooms, selling and trading C60/C90 cassette tapes, fanzines, T-shirts and patches, then moving into DIY vinyl releases from UK labels.

Many produced free lists or catalogues and the products sold were at low 'cost' prices, following the DIY rejection of rip-off corporate record label prices.

These 'distros' were the UK's network between all the various regionally  located underground punk/HC scenes. Some were also labels, like *Full Circle* (Huddersfield) run by ex-Instigators vocalist Tez (11), *Flat Earth, Words Of Warning* (Newport, Wales), *Looney Tunes* (Scarborough) - run by Set & Bob of Active Minds, *Meantime* (Darlington), run by Ian of Sofa Head.

RANDOM DISTRIBUTION
Punk Rock Mailorder

PO Box 59 · Hazel Grove · Stockport · SK7 4JY

Others were run in conjunction with their 'zines, like *Bald Cactus*, *Armed With Anger* and *How We Rock*, or by individuals Squally (Bradford), Random (Stockport), Land Of Treason (Manchester), DS4A (Bristol) and Active (London).

Most also stocked many European and US /Canadian releases, not available in your local record shop, due to the international trading networks set up by bands who regularly toured Europe and the lucky few who got to America or Japan.

Some key European and North American distros were *Nabate* and *Genet* (Belgium), *New Wave* (France), *K-Baal* (Holland), *Don't Belong* (Spain), *Sacro* (Austria), *Trujaca Fala* (Poland) - run by Filip from Sopot near Gdansk and *Blacklist* (San Francisco, USA), *Vacuum* (USA) and *Still Angry* (Canada).

FLAT EARTH RECORDS

This label and distro was a classic example of the type of UK mail order set-up working at this time, run with passion and a dedicated DIY ethic that produced high-quality material and packaging at very reasonable prices to customers.

Originally started in Newcastle in 1986 as a collective by members of the band Generic, the label's first four releases were 7" singles by that band. By July 1988, the band's drummer Sned had moved down to Leeds and was the sole person left running the label/ distro. In 1991, now settled in Bradford and heavily involved with The 1 In 12 Club, Sned single-handedly continued to release product, sometimes in conjunction with the Belgian labels Nabate and Genet.

Besides 7" /10" vinyl from his own bands (One By One, Health Hazard, Suffer) there were releases from Scottish bands Sedition, Disaffect, Scatha, Hiatus and Unhinged (Belgium), Los Crudos and Drop Dead (US), Submission Hold (Canada) and many local bands too, like Witchknot, Doom, VR, Recusant and Kito.

In all over a twenty-year period (1986-2006) the label released 46 products, thirteen LPs, twenty 7", four 10" and nine CDs, quite a feat for a cash-poor tiny DIY enterprise.

CHAPTER 4   1991 - 1993

HEALTH HAZARD

Formed in late 1992, from the split of One By One (Sned and Alec) and Biohazard (Mandy and Chris), the band were defined on the UK scene by Mandy's incredibly intense vocal style and the band's raging sound.

They played their first gig on March 20 1993, at The 1 In

They recorded and released the 7" single *Not Just A Nightmare* on French Minstrel label.

The band toured regularly, in France, Spain, Portugal, and Greece and even did a 1 In 12 tour of the UK with fellow Bradford bands Mash M, Headache and Rescusant.

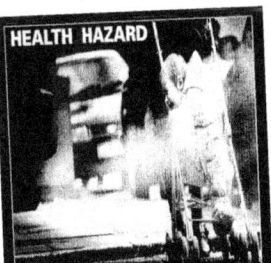

The band's second release was the self-titled 10" fourteen-track mini-album for Flat Earth (FE13) recorded at In A City Studios and produced by Bri Doom.

12 Club, the band's spiritual home. As bassist Chris explained, *'Bradford was a pretty happening place at the time, lots of bands and active people, the catalyst being the 1 In 12, which was a magnet for disaffected types beyond the usual punk crew, so it was a meeting point for ideas and sparks flew in all directions.'* (12)

It came in a large fold-out poster-style cover, which in the middle had an 'anti-car' montage entitled Stop The Madness.

Unfortunately, Mandy left soon after the 10" release so the other three members re-grouped to form the three-piece Suffer.

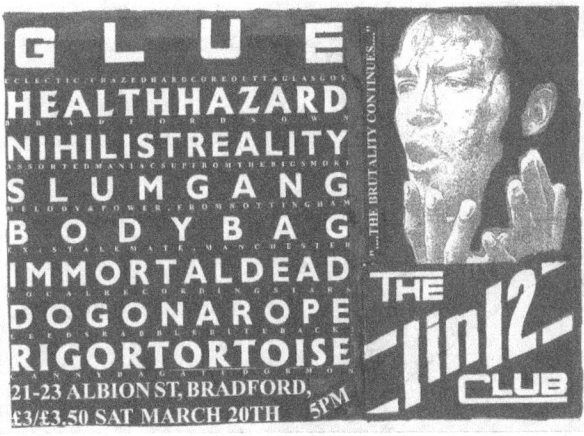

165

On May 2 the all-girl 'dyke' group Tribe 8 from San Francisco did their thing, followed by Hell No at the end of that month.

On June 3, coming out of New Jersey, was the band Rorschach (pictured below), who were on a European tour and were working on material for their second album.

Their LP *Protestant* came out the next

year just prior to the band splitting up in August 1993. It has since gone on to be a highly influential example of the crossover of hardcore with metal, and is considered a classic by many current bands still around on the scene.

Between March and June 1992, The 1 In 12 Club played host to no less than five top US hardcore bands, cementing it as a venue at the epicentre of the UK's underground scene.

First, on March 28, was New York's Sick Of It All (pictured left), playing to a packed house, who went into a frenzy of stage diving. (10)

At the end of June, the oddly named No Use For A Name became the fifth American band to play, supported by two UK bands Downside and Submission.

CHAPTER 4   1991 - 1993

BRADFORD FESTIVAL 1992 AT THE 1 IN 12 CLUB

For the second year running, the Club played host to Deviate & Celebrate a series of events in support of the local gay and lesbian

community. On Saturday, June 20, an all-day extravaganza included Huffty (again) and the Camp Vamps, an eight-piece women's band plus a late disco.

Other venues around the city also participated, like Checkpoint, The Bavaria and the Wool Exchange (nowadays Waterstones) who saw Liverpudlian drag queen Lily Savage (Paul O'Grady, pictured left) perform her quick-witted, foul-mouthed barbs on Tuesday, June 30.

The last event, on July 11, was a benefit disco at the 1 In 12 for the *Pink Paper*, the UK's only free weekly Lesbian & Gay newspaper. The paper was facing bankruptcy after being fined £20,000 for libel.

Many other gigs and events were staged at the 1 In 12 as part of the festival, including a gig on June 26, by Swedish band The Tequila Girls (who were all boys!) supported by Under The Gun and Blind Mole Rat.

ARMED WITH ANGER

This was another local Bradford record label, which emerged from the fanzine of the same name, releasing its first split 7" by Nailbomb / Wartorn in 1992.

The label was run by Richard Corbridge (original bassist in Nailbomb) who stated his aims as, *"Recognising the comparatively unproductive UK Hardcore scene that exists, sought to stimulate some life back into it, by the release of the Consolidation compilation 7" (AWA02) showcasing a rising fresh and enthusiastic network of bands and an affiliated scene."*

The compilation single contained seven tracks

AWA01: NAILBOMB / WARTORN split 7"

AWA02: Consolidation v/a 7"   AWA03: VOORHEES 7"

AWA04: UNDERSTAND 7"   AWA05: VOORHEES flexi

AWA05.5: Nothing New v/a 7"   AWA06: KITO 7"

AWA07: DEAD WRONG 7"   AWA08: VOORHEES LP

AWA09: STALINGRAD picture disc   AWA10: A Means To An End v/a LP

by Voorhees, Kito, Stand Off, Nailbomb, Ironside, Submission and Understand.

Over the next ten years, Richard tirelessly championed the hardcore DIY scene, by releasing in total nine 7" singles, five LPs and one CD of bands as diverse as Voorhees, Kito, Dead Wrong, Stalingrad and Schema.

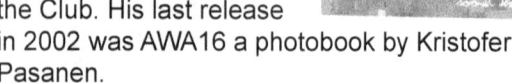

He also organised many gigs at the 1 In 12 to promote bands and in 1997 he released the compilation LP *A Means To An End*, which was a benefit for the Club. His last release in 2002 was AWA16 a photobook by Kristofer Pasanen.

WARTORN / NAILBOMB

Both of these bands were started by ex-Sore Throat vocalist Rich Militia. Wartorn were a raging Japanese influenced band who recorded five tracks for the split 7" single, while Nailbomb recorded four tracks. All were recorded at In A City Studios, Bradford. Nailbomb (pictured left) had a changed lineup by the time they recorded the track *One World* for the *Consolidation* 7" compilation.

Wartorn released their 12-track 7-inch *Banzai* EP in 1994 on Crust Records.

In 2015, FOAD Records released the *Destroy All Monsters* compilation vinyl album comprising the EP, the split 7, compilation tracks and a 1991 demo.

Other later compilations featured live sets from 1992.

VOORHEES

Formed in Durham in 1990, from the ashes of Steadfast and False Face, Voorhees became a raging, intense SxE hardcore band, taking their name from Jason Voorhees, the serial killer character in the 1980s *Friday The 13th* films. When vocalist Lecky moved to Bradford, and later two Bradford lads joined the band, they were considered to be based there. (12)

Their debut release on the Bradford label AWA, was the ten-track 7" EP *Violent* in April 1993, soon followed by the flexi disc single *Everybody's Good At Something....Except Us* again on AWA. This was followed in 1994, by an LP called *Spilling Blood Without Reason*, after which the band toured Europe for the first time.

In early 1995, the band recorded a session for John Peel's radio programme, which was later re-recorded in Pots'n'Pans studio in Bradford for a split 7" with Stalingrad, put out on Lecky's own Thinking Smart Records. (13)

In 1996, the band toured North America, organised

by Nausea's vocalist Neil who ran Tribal War Records. After the tour, a new lineup ensued with Bradford lads 'Arms' from Ironside and James 'Atko' Atkinson joining. The new line-up, toured America again with US band Drop Dead before returning home to record their next LP *13* released on AWA in collaboration with US label Six Weeks in 1998.

The band split in 2001, having released four LPs, one split 12", and nine 7" singles (three splits), but re-grouped for reunion gigs in 2004, 2010 and 2013.

CHAPTER 4 — 1991-1993

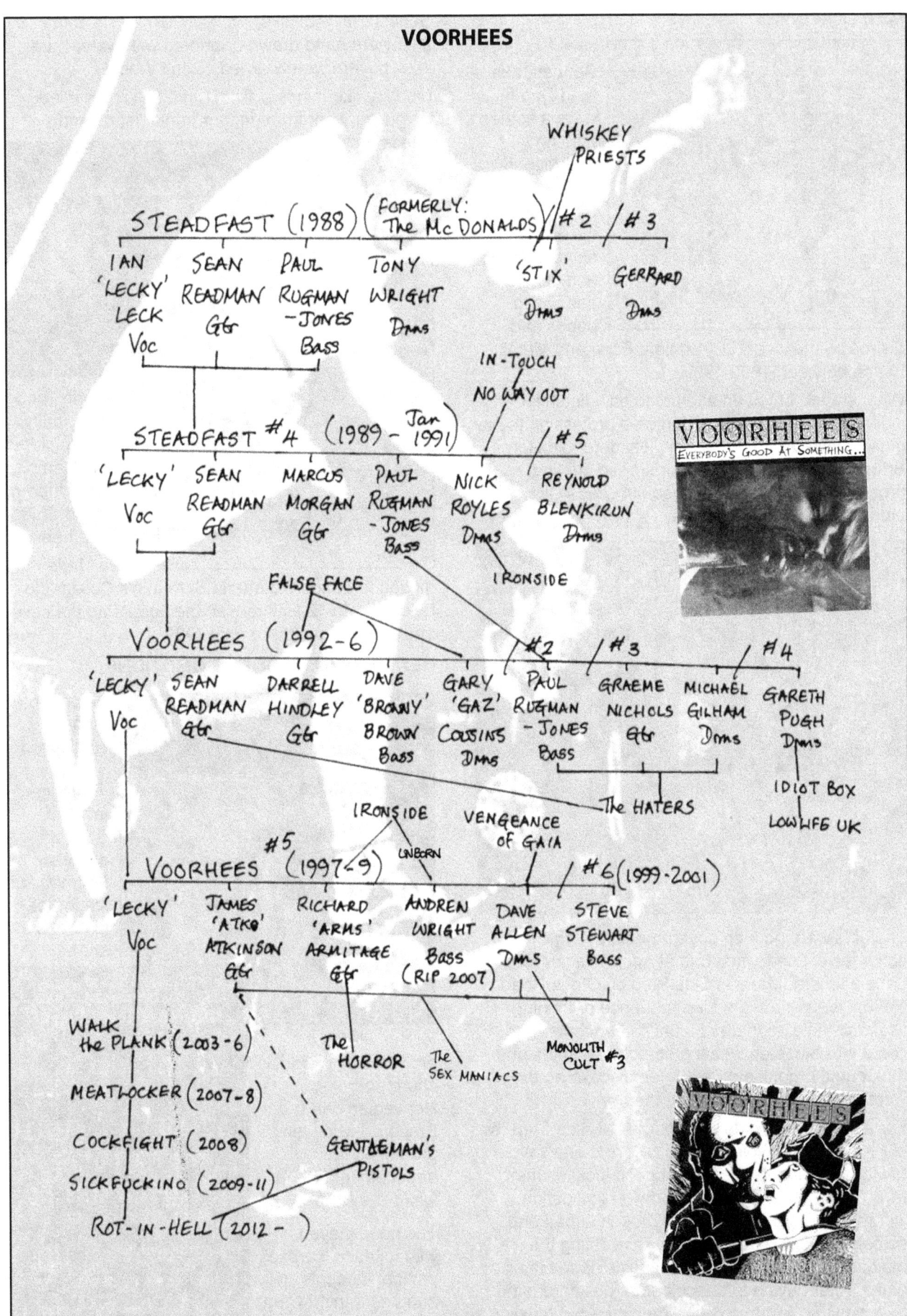

169

MAD DOG INK

Britt & Marie Bennett, aka Mad Dog Ink, were a screen printing / promotions outfit supplying quality band shirts, bootleg and original designs to bands and distros on the local H/C, Straight Edge and Metal Scene between 1990-1999.

What started out of an attempt to gain financial independence in a male-orientated profession these girls achieved with no backing just determination. Britt found a description of the screen printing process in a 1960s fine art book in Leeds City Art Library and learnt from there.

Picture by Marie Bennett

The girls were both on government training schemes in Leeds, first Britt at Apex Trust on Call Lane and later Marie at Side Step on Globe Road. Neither were offered work experience or training like their male counterparts until a band member came into Sidestep wearing one of their shirts and the course organisers Paul & Ian discovered they were already producing shirts themselves.

For a short spell shirts were printed at Side Step, as were the 1 In 12 *Volnitza* album covers as a favour to Gary Cavanagh. A stroke of good luck led them to walk into Apex Trust on the day of liquidation, where they purchased a small broken airbed and screens for £40. Gradually - by reinvesting the majority of what they made - the girls upped their game. After buying a four-colour carousel from the Exchange & Mart and Spot Dryer, they could use Sericol Plasticol inks. Typically DIY shirts at this time were hand drawn or printed with water-based inks, buyers were warned, 'Don't Wash!'

Meeting like minds at The 1 In 12 Club Cafe led to regular work from underground distros and bands on the local scenes. Clients included: Rich 'Solstice', Ron 'Armed with Anger', Nick Royles, Sned

'Flat Earth', and bands including Wartorn (pictured left), Nailbomb, Solstice, Unborn, Threshold Shift and Voorhees.

When Marie moved to London to attend St Martin's College, to help the 1 In 12 Britt moved their gear into the cellar and printed from there until 1999.

HEAVIER THAN THOU PROMOTIONS

As promoter of the *Heavier Than Thou* gigs in 1993, Solstice guitarist Rich Walker staged at least two shows for the ultra-fast black metal, pagan, church-burning Norwegian band Emperor, who were promoting their debut album *In The Nightside Eclipse*.

The band played with full-face 'corpse' paint at Queen's Hall and The 1 In 12 Club during 1992/93.

"HEAVIER THAN THOU"
Presents
Unholy Black Metal
From Norway
EMPEROR
True warriors of the Anti-Christ
CRADLE OF FILTH
Twisted UK Black/Death Metal
THE FALLEN
The UK's Black Metal Warlords

MONDAY JULY 12th
QUEENS HALL CELLAR BAR
ADMISSION £4   DOORS 7.30pm

"I deny Jesus Christ the fucking deceiver"

VIRTUAL REALITY (VR)

This locally based rock-noise trio, which consisted of the brothers Darron and Steve of Next World and Bri Talbot of Doom.

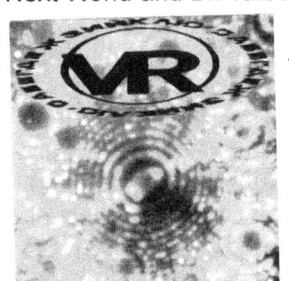

Their debut track *Take It Or Leave It* was released on a split 7" single, with Belgian band Neuthrone, in 1993 by Genet Records. One of the band's first gigs was at the 1 In 12 on September 5, 1992, with support from Lizzgizzard and The Horror.

During 1996, the band's album *Dreamstate* was released in a joint venture between Flat Earth and Genet Records.

The second half of 1992 saw another wave of five US bands play at The 1 In 12 Club, while on tours of Europe. First, on July 4, came Resist from Portland, Oregon, who were followed on August 7 by the political hardcore band Millions Of Dead Cops (MDC). Based in San Francisco, MDC were one of America's most radically political bands in the same vein as Jello Biafra's Dead Kennedys.

The night MDC played, supported by local HC band Nailbomb, The 1 in 12 Club was totally packed out, rammed with folk who had travelled from all over to see them, in fact there has never been a gig at the 1 In 12 like it before or since. (12)

Millions Of Dead Cops live at The 1 In 12 Club (pictured above) and Bradford's Nailbomb (below).

Live pictures courtesy of Tony Woolgar.

Then, in early October, another Californian band, Neurosis, came and blew away those who saw them play their material from their excellent *Souls At Zero* album. Next, at the end of October, was the noise of Integrity from Cleveland, Ohio, playing a set from their classic 1991 album *Those Who Fear Tomorrow* which had been put out on Overkill Records.

In between the fourth and fifth US bands, came Saw Tooth from Quebec, Canada, on November 13, before, on December 19 (the last gig that year) came Farside from Orange County, California, who headlined an all-dayer.

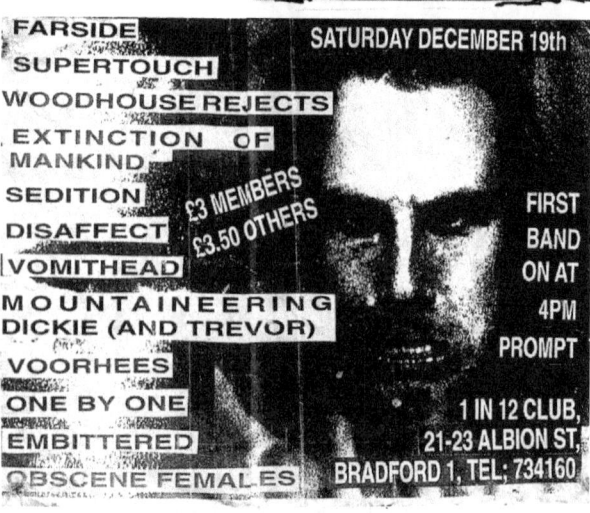

IRONSIDE

A Bradford band playing brutal metallic SxE hardcore, who played their first gig supporting Sick Of It All at the 1 In 12 in 1992. They then got invited to play at the first Ieper festival in Belgium at the Vort'n'Vis, which has since become an annual staple of the international underground HC scene.

In August 1992, they released a five-track cassingle *Neutered Innocence* on the drummer Nick Royles' Sure Hand label. Then they went to In A City Studios in September to record their track *Modern Myth* for the *Consolidation* 7" compilation for the Armed With Anger label.

In 1993, they released their debut 7" single *Fragments Of The Last Judgement*; a six-track EP, released on Helene and Ian's Darlington-based label, Subjagation. The tracks had again been recorded at In A City over a two-day period in February.

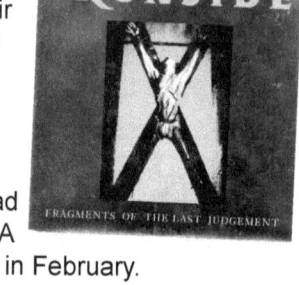

A change of musical style to a more metally sound overall caused lineup changes in 1994, before the band released the single *Damn Your Blooded Eyes* on Stormstrike, a German label.

The band split in 1995, with its members moving on to other projects, but, while short-lived, their influence on the development and the cross-over of styles in the underground HC scene is still felt today.

A Nightmare on Albion St

WORST OF THE 1 IN 12 CLUB • VOL. 11 ....

The 1 In 12 Club's seventh vinyl compilation release, *A Nightmare On Albion Street, The Worst The 1 In 12 Club Volume 11* was released in late October 1992.

The LP's front cover design was specially commissioned from local artist Jayne Allen and contained a lyric/artwork sheet.

Amongst the thirteen bands/artists appearing on the album were five local bands, Biohazard, Disaster, Threshold Shift, Primate and Rubber, Leather, Plastic. Other tracks were supplied by Nerverack (Leeds), Citizen Fish, Dutch band Mushroom Attack, Canadian band Rhythm Activism, BTF, Idiot Gods, Justice League Of America, and folk troubadour/activist Robb Johnson.

The album was mixed and edited at the nearby Fulton Street Studios and was cut for vinyl at Porky's in London like all the previous 1 In 12 releases.

Some very positive reviews appeared in *MRR, Profane Existence #19, Angry Thoreaun #5,* and *You're So Hideous #3.*

The album received airplay on John Peel's Radio One show, some US College radio stations and on the Italian radio station Attaco Sonoro, based in Rome.

A NIGHTMARE ON ALBION STREET Worst of the 1-in-12 Club, Vol. 11 comp LP

This is the 1st in this series that i have had the pleasure of hearing. On it are BIO-HAZARD, B.T.F., DISASTER, THRESHOLD SHIFT, CITIZEN FISH, NERVERACK, IDIOT GODS, MUSHROOM ATTACK, PRIMATE, ROB JOHNSON, JUSTICE LEAGUE OF AMERICA, RHYTHM ACTIVISM, & RUBBER.LEATHER. PLASTIC. Pure thrashy punkrock dominate one side in the vein of that raw DOOM/ENT/ICONS & early DISCHARGE style. There are also a couple with a more straightforward melodic punk sound (such as THRESHOLD SHIFT). Side two is more refined (but not commercial, mind you) & has a bit more variety. A pretty decent comp, but it's too bad there was nowt more than a big insert w/ lyrics & little else on it. Other than that, this is a good comp, & it is benefiting an remarkable club/label/distro as well. (£6 or $12 ppd: 1-in-12 Records / 21-23 Albion St / Bradford BD1 2LY / UK)

— ANGRY THOREAUN #5

PLAYLIST JUNE '93

1. AMEBIX - "The power remains" LP
2. CONCRETE SOX - "No world order" LP
3. INFEZIONE - "Religione oppio dei popoli" LP
4. FUGAZI - "In on the kill taker" LP
5. SIEGE - "Drop dead" CD
6. CCC CNC NCN - "Proclami/Suicidio" 7" + TAPE
7. ETERNAL TORMENT - "Downfall of human existence" 7"
8. CORPUS VILE/MAGGOT SLAYER OVERDRIVE - SPLIT LP
9. A NIGHTMARE ON ALBION STREET - "Worst of the 1 in 12 club - vol.11" LP COMPILATION
10. COUCH POTATOES - "Excess all areas" LP

— ATTACCO SONORO

V/A A Nightmare on Albion St. LP
The 11th installment of "The Worst of the 1 in 12 Club" compilatoin album series. All the bands here have played live at the club between 1988 and 1990 and there's an impressive line-up indeed. This starts off with BIO-HAZARD (a Sore Throat spin-off that's better than the original??) and goes to more varied styles from there with the likes of RHYTHM ACTIVISM, CITIZEN FISH, MUSHROOM ATTACK and tons more.

V/A - "A Nightmare On Albion St." LP
I'll admit it. I thought this album was going to suck shit.'I hate comps and I'd never heard of half of these bands. But, oh how wrong I was. BIO-HAZARD rip it up and I almost thought it was old E.N.T. when I first put it on. In fact great tracks by new names (to me, anyway) like BTF, DISASTER, THRESHOLD SHIFT, etc. as well as my old faves NERVERACK, CITIZEN FISH and RHYTHM ACTIVISM. Great stuff. (LH) — MRR

At the start of 1993, the 1 In 12 had a mention in that year's Bradford University handbook advising students on the best and worst pubs and venues in the city.

> The "One in Twelve" is the one true alternative club in Bradford. Sticking very much to its cooperative roots, with its colourful membership responsible for Bradford's only all nighters, a strong riot grrrrl scene, punk and hardcore gigs, seventies nights, gay, lesbian and women's only events. It serves excellent cheap beers, superb veggie and vegan food, has pool tables and the world's best jukebox. Pound for pound, Bradford's best club!!

While the Club continued to strive to survive, in an internal newsletter, containing info on gigs, etc, there was a piece called *The Boring Bit* which explained how the Club worked and how it relied on the numerous behind-the-scenes members who gallantly did all the mundane and dirty jobs.

> **THE BORING BIT !**
> The Club relies on the work and enthusiasm of its members and there are many ways to get involved. Decisions are made at the Sunday meetings to which all members are invited. These are held at 8.30pm in the bar every week and are not as dull as you might imagine. Also if you're not there you don't have any influence in the direction the Club takes.
> The booking collective meets on a Wednesday night and is a loose group of the people who put on gigs, events etc. More help is needed to organise a more varied gig list. So if you have any interest in organising gigs come along and we'll do our best to help you.
> Finally some good news about the financial situation. Although we are still very much in debt we seem to be slowly breaking even. This years bar takings are nearly 20% up on the same time last year. We cannot afford to be complacent but if things carry on as they are there is some light at the end of the tunnel.

The first Club gig of the year, on January 30, was American band Pissed, from Minneapolis, who had members of the zine *Profane Existence* in their line-up.

NECKBRACE

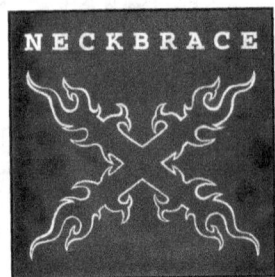

Another short-lived SxE band from Bradford, formed from the ashes of Nailbomb #4 in 1993.

They managed to record and release one 7" single, the four-track EP *Neckbrace* on the German Label X No Cruelty. The single came with an enclosed booklet called *Why Vegan* (in both English and German), which espoused the merits of veganism, a central tenet of the SxE scene.

The band split up in 1994, as their vocalist Heath went to join the band Stamping Ground.

GFA

While working as a tech with the Psycho Surgeons, guitarist Dave Fields started to put the trio together in 1992 with former Skeletal Family and Ghost Dance technician Pogs and TSA PA company engineer Noka.

They supported New Model Army at Queens Hall and were the first British band to play the Moscow clubs the Bunker and Club Sexton while on a Russian tour in September 1993.

CLAREMONT 'THE SITE'

During 1991, some empty waste land on Claremont (near Bradford University) was 'squatted' by people living in their vans, coaches, etc.

A few local musicians were among those who settled on what became known as 'the site', like Paul Arron (ex-Vegetable

Section), John Gray and Bela Emerson (Tooth Fairy -pictured below, Shiny Beast) and Jez (Zed, Big Fish) with artist Moray, and Lianne Hall of Hiphuggers and Witchknot.

RICHARD INGHAM

During the 1990s local photographer Richard Ingham took many photographs of local bands, from publicity shots to photos from gigs and events at Bradford's popular pub venues like The Melborn and MacRory's Bar, where his shots of local bands adorned the walls.

His shots were used on album covers and for publicity shots for many local bands including Tooth Fairy, Nowt (above), Shiny Beast (below),

Zed, Grim, Moota, Somebody's Brother (bottom), jam sessions (below) and the early *Ginger Fringe Festivals* at MacRory's Bar.

THE RIOT GRRRL MOVEMENT

"For girls to pick up guitars and scream their heads off... in a totally oppressive, fucked up male dominated culture, is to seize power... we recognise this as a political act" (15)

So spoke Tobi Vali, drummer in US band Bikini Kill, who pioneered, with other all girl groups in the 1990s, the movement of women playing rock as a form of direct action, thus making Riot Grrls agents of revolution.

Started around 1991, by young radical feminists in America, like Bikini Kill (vocalist Kathleen Hannna pictured left) from Olympia, Washington State, whose first EP was produced by Ian MacKaye of Fugazi, and who featured on the Riot Grrl compilation *Kill Rock Stars* LP.

This movement, not musical genre, was steeped in the creative DIY culture, and was overtly political and directly attacked the male dominated punk / HC scene with the attitude of *women who take no shit!*

It soon transferred across the Altantic to the UK, where young women rallied, picked up guitars and formed bands. Some of the first were London / Brighton based Huggy Bear (pictured left) and another London band Mambo Taxi (pictured below).

These UK acts drew inspiration from the 1970s/80s punk and indie bands like The Slits and The Raincoats, as well as mixed groups like The Au Pairs, The Passions and the Leeds band Delta 5. They re-claimed 'girl power' from the commercial sound of the Spice Girls and formed powerful gangs of girls, creating an underground network of highly charged and empowered females that became known by the loaded term, Riot Grrrl.

It wasn't long before young, radical feminists up North started to organise and it was no surprise that women involved with the 1 In 12 Club were amongst those who formed the Leeds / Bradford Riot Grrrl Collective (pictured below) in late 1992.

Originally set in motion by Karren of *Ablaze!* Fanzine, there was soon a core of around twenty women who began holding regular meetings on Wednesday evenings at the 1 In 12. Soon they were organising 'workshop days' on zine writing, banner making, DJ-ing, sound mixing, etc.

The first Riot Grrrl event at the Club was a Disco on Saturday, January 23, by the 'Docs and Frocks' collective, where there were prizes for the best frock, worn by girl or boy!

After a few 'fast zines' single sheet publications espousing their message, the grrrls were soon producing local full zines like *Angels Of Anarchy* and *Shag Stamp*.

The Riot Grrrl message was clearly laid out in those early 'fast zines':

"We're the cool rock chicks, no longer willing to be misconstrued. We are going to explain ourselves, if and when we feel like it. We deny stereotypes used to limit women who are involved in the indieworld, stereotypes that allow people to say 'she's only into it because her boyfriend likes it' or 'she's only here cos she fancies one of the band', stereotypes that perpetuate the ideas that we can only be singers, NOT musicians and we don't write music; generally, that we are illegitimate and should be patronised.

"And we destroy the myths that support boyrock-like, that you have to spend your developing years alone in your bedroom playing along to the records of your heroes; that stage diving and aggressive displays at gigs are cool; that hierarchies and leaders and idols are necessary. We attack misogyny in all its guises, from body fascism to rape. We're cutting the tripwires of alienation that separate girls from girls. We're forming bands together, writing things together, having meetings and planning events.

"We've got miles to go but it's gonna be so exciting getting that there. We might be called RIOT GRRRL, but we're aware of the media deadtime deadlines that crush anything it discovers by treating it as trend and the old hype mechanisms that tire us with an endless churning up of novelty approaches to the same old structures. Seeing all that, we use their media whilst we sneakily construct girl lines of communication.

Secret things that only we know........"

(From the 'fast zine' sheet *Girl Power Explosion*)

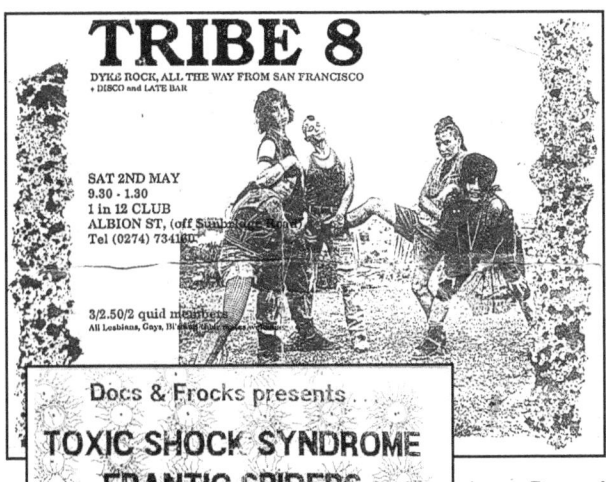

Although the US all girl queercore band Tribe 8 had played the 1 In 12 the previous May, the first Riot Grrrl gig was on March 17, 1993, with Bikini Kill and Huggy Bear. This was soon followed by a *Docs And Frocks* extravaganza of bands on April 24, then God Is My Co-Pilot, from New York, played on May 28 and the next day there was a gig by Mambo Taxi, supported by local girls and boys with attitude Chest.

Three members of the Leeds / Bradford RG collective, Lianne, Jane and Sarah, quickly formed a band aptly named Witchknot.

Huggy Bear / Bikini Kill / 1 in 12 Club / 17th March 1993

'Riot Grrrl' bands aren't really my cup of tea. So okay I know it's stupid to classify all bands in one scene together, but I honestly came to the conclusion that I'd be in for a night of boring and crap bands especially after seeing the abysmal all girl band the Mambu Taxis. However tonight I was surprised.

The first band Bikini Kill could only be described as fucking brilliant. It's patronising to say that they were like a female version of another band so I'll use The Replacements as a reference point. As someone stood next to me said 'They've restored my faith in rock 'n' Roll'. Top banana indeed!

Next up were Huggy Bear and as they began to churn out their material I was was impressed by the fact that they were actually quite talented musicians, dispelling the myth that they're just another all girl puppet band. Half way through the set a guy wearing a white hood climbed onto the stage and began ranting about art. What a wanker! Put your self in Huggy Bear's position; someone interrupting your set wearing a mask can be pretty unnerving especially if you happen to be the vocalist who has been assaulted on stage before. Fortunately the bloke left the stage peacefully on this occasion.

I tried to get some idea what the bands and the Riot Grrrl thing is all about through listening to their lyrics and this prompted me to talk to the both bands after the gig. Half expecting to be slagged off for being male I ended up having an interesting conversation, giving the bands a chance to set a few matters straight. Firstly it's not just a scene, it's more a cry for equality. Secondly both bands firmly believe in themselves and thirdly both bands consist of 'normal' non-male hating people. So thanks to Bikini Kill and Huggy Bear for giving me half an hour to express their ideas without biting my head off!

CUSTARD

Review from Stork Magazine #11

Docs and Frocks Extravaganza
The 1 in 12 Club,
24/4/93

Things got going at about 6.30pm, when the first act took to the stage in the form of a lone girlie with an acoustic guitar and a good voice, who warbled through her set saying little, if anything to the crowd. She was warmly received by those people who like that sort of thing.

The first band up was Bradford's own 'Witchknot', and bugger me if the woman with the acoustic guitar wasn't back on stage, only this time with an electric one. This all female trio (drums, bass, guitar/violin) played a highly original bunch of songs. I can't describe the sound so I won't bother, but go and see them when they play next (or be an asshole all your life).

Chest, another Bradford band (ex-Everly sisters: girlie acoustic guitar duo), started their performance by playing the theme from Grange Hill (yay! A band with a sense of humour!) A pretty energetic and vibrant performance from this lot. Surreal too - I swear the guitarist is a red-haired version of Lewis Carroll's Alice. Chest play the 1 In 12 Club again on Monday 3rd of May - go and see what I mean.

The next band up was Suzie Never Barks. Though admittedly plagued by PA/vocal problems and a broken string in the first song which held everything up in for five minutes, what they did play was unbelievably tedious. Dullness personified, I fear.

The next band, Frantic Spiders spent a long time fucking about on stage before getting going. My hopes were high for the second all girl band of the evening, with their two guitarists and gobby attitude. It looked as though they were going to kick a little ass. Alas, my hopes proved unfounded; a mainly indie-ish set had little power. Their only redeeming feature's were the drummer who was cool and they knew all the best put-down lines.

Final band of the night was Toxic Shock Syndrome. Comprising guitar, bass, vocals and unfortunatly a drum machine (arrgh)! Although this did not hinder their performance with some impressive stuff from the singer, wearing what looked like a butchers apron. Still no butt being kicked though. This may have had something to do with the fact that quite a few people had pissed off for their last bus home making the gig room quieter for the band, which was a pity.

A varied evening at the 1 In 12 Club - the bands had little in common other than the presence of female members. If such thing as a "Riot Grrrl" scene exists it did not make itself apparent, as no common Riot Grrl feeling or style came through, though there were a lot of rope heads about. But that's the 1 in 12 Club after all.

Mr A

Review from Stork Magazine #13

WITCHKNOT

This band started out as a trio and used the 1 In 12 as a base to create their unconventional, quirky sound, which was a little bit weird on first hearing.

Drummer Sarah had moved to Bradford from Telford to join her partner Alec (of Health Hazard), while Lianne had arrived at Bradford University from Peterborough to do Interdisciplinary Human Studies before 'dropping out' and doing some busking around the town while Jane of Sowerby Bridge had been a regular at the Club for many years.

After their first gig at the April 1993 *Docs And Frocks* do, they did a European tour with Health Hazard and Doom, before augmenting into a six-piece.

This new line-up recorded the 7" *Suck*, a four-track EP, in September 1994, at the ubiquitous In A City Studios which was produced by Des Butler. The EP came in a fold-out poster-style cover and was released by Flat Earth Records.

Members of the band were very active in all Docs And Frocks and Riot Grrrl activities at the 1 In 12 and formed two side project bands; The Hip Huggers and Baba Yaga.

In 1996 Witchknot recorded the LP *Squawk*, again at In-A-City, where the final mix was by Jer Reid of Scottish band Dawson. Released again on Flat Earth, it was globally distributed by (Jon) Active of London.

The band played their last gig in 1998, at the 1 In 12, supporting Canada's Submission Hold.

Docs And Frocks events were organised regularly during the 1990s, as were the annual *Witch Fest* dos, with many strange and wondrous bands performing at The 1 In 12 Club.

The impact of these women in the Riot Grrrl movement meant that in the following years, more and more women

CHAPTER 4　　1991 - 1993

WITCHNOT

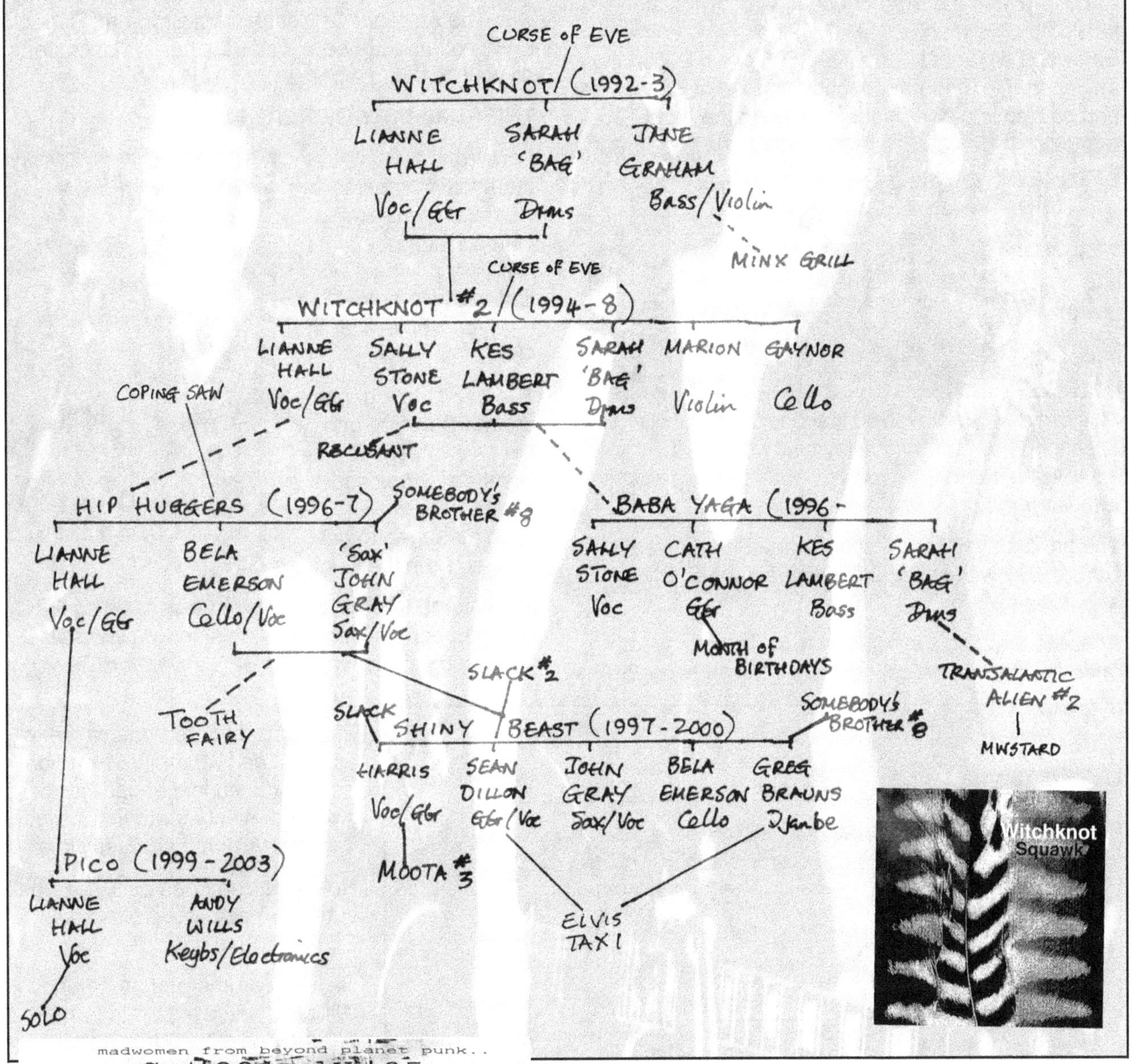

WITCHKNOT (1992-3) — CURSE OF EVE
- LIANNE HALL — Voc/Gtr
- SARAH 'BAG' — Drums
- JANE GRAHAM — Bass/Violin → MINX GRILL

WITCHKNOT #2 (1994-8) — CURSE OF EVE
- LIANNE HALL — Voc/Gtr — COPING SAW
- SALLY STONE — Voc
- KES LAMBERT — Bass — RECUSANT
- SARAH 'BAG' — Drums
- MARION — Violin
- GAYNOR — Cello

HIP HUGGERS (1996-7) — SOMEBODY'S BROTHER #8
- LIANNE HALL — Voc/Gtr
- BELA EMERSON — Cello/Voc — TOOTH FAIRY
- 'SAX' JOHN GRAY — Sax/Voc — SLACK #2

BABA YAGA (1996-
- SALLY STONE — Voc
- CATH O'CONNOR — Gtr — MONTH OF BIRTHDAYS
- KES LAMBERT — Bass
- SARAH 'BAG' — Drums — TRANSALANTIC ALIEN #2 — MWSTARD

SHINY BEAST (1997-2000) — SLACK — SOMEBODY'S BROTHER #8
- HARRIS — Voc/Gtr
- SEAN DILLON — Gtr/Voc — MOOTA #3
- JOHN GRAY — Sax/Voc
- BELA EMERSON — Cello
- GREG BRAUNS — Djembe
- ELVIS TAXI

PICO (1999-2003)
- LIANNE HALL — Voc — SOLO
- ANDY WILLS — Keybs/Electronics

Witchknot Squawk

madwomen from beyond planet punk..
Sat 29 July '95
The cherries
witchknot
1 in 12 Club
Albion St.
Bradford
8pm
£2/£2.50
dress: pointy hat/shoes/nose/quiff etc!

were inspired to form bands and attendance at gigs became more equitable than the previous male-dominated crowd.

Ultimately, their legacy *'...created a platform for multiple female voices to be heard and actively encouraged women to start bands as a means of cultural resistance.'* (16)

This message is still important today, as the Russian all girl band Pussy Riot (a collective of more than ten radical feminists, pictured below) took on the might of their president Vladimir Putin in 2012. Their Anti-Putin protests included singing their song *Putin's Pissed Himself* and exposing the moral bankruptcy of his regime, which resulted in three of their members being jailed.

PHOSPHENE

Another all-female Bradford band were Phosphene, formed by two friends, Naomi Calhoun and Lorna Eastwood who got to know each other while working as bar staff in a number of pubs on Morley Street and drafted in other bar maids to form the band.

Musically a sound evolved that could be broadly described as *'punk with flutey bits'* with lyrics expressing *'feminist hardcore righteous indignation, with laughter'*.

The band played their first gig at the Biko University Car in 1992 with subsequent gigs around Bradford and further afield.

After the band split in 1994, Naomi Colhoun went on to perform on an adhoc basis with a number of Bradford groups including # Crime and Loom, Jilly formed Halo in Brighton, and Lorna went on to play with The Auxiliary Of Real Men in Bradford, Birdog in Bristol, and appearances as a performance poet as well as being a presenter on BCB.

THE AUXILIARY OF REAL MEN

Formed in 1993 by theatrical frontperson Noel Baxeton, aka Lynda Baxta, the Auxiliary played their first-ever gig at the 1 In 12 on September 4, 1993.

The band played mainly around Bradford and Leeds and venues like Scruffs'n'Snobs and MacRory's Bar. They even managed to get banned from the Duchess Of York in 1995.

In September 1995, they played a session on BBC Radio Leeds' Steven Le Ferve's show. Lynda also appeared several times on BCB's *Bradford Beat* show, playing solo.

The band recorded one cassette album, *The Weight Of Vermillion*, and produced leaflet updates of gigs and events for their fan club, *The Free Church Of Pestilence*.

Noel also cameoed as 'Drab Noel' in the comedy group *Gradually Stirring* during this time.

He later re-emerged as 'Shandy Williams' and went on to form a band called Dogs That Walk In Milan.

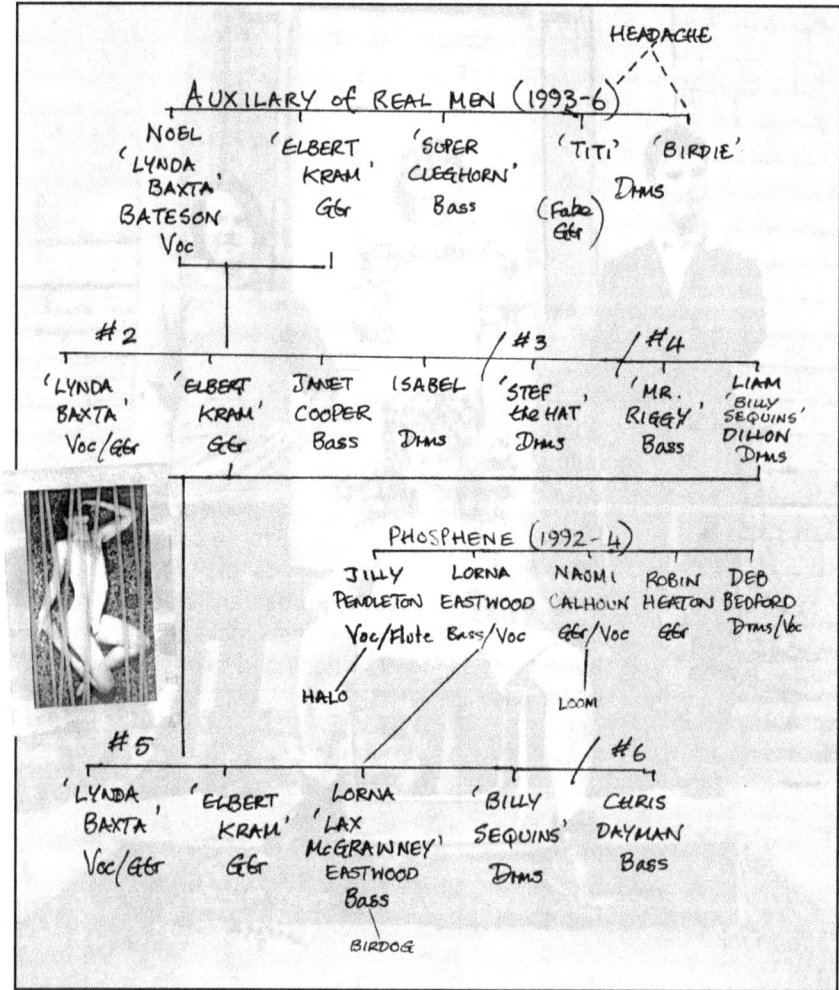

The Auxiliary of Real Men

During the early months of 1993, a series of gigs was organised at the Club under the banner of *Club Ugly Presents...*, promoted by Anton, the drummer from Cabbage Head Kids.

On March 2, the Club played host to its first Norwegian band, Life... But How To Live It?

The next month saw the return of two bands who had played at the Club a few times before, Terminus and, from Ledbury, Herefordshire, Decadence Within, who had released their 1990 LP *Soulwound* on Peaceville Records. Their bass player Ian 'Slug' Glasper went on to write several books about the UK punk and HC scene. (16)

Sixteen days later, the Club played host to that years first touring US band, the Boston-based SxE HC band Slapshot, supported by local acts Voorhees and Nailbomb. The band were promoting their latest album, *Blast Furnace*, on We Bite Records, and played the 1 In 12 on their day off from playing more lucrative dates, thus ensuring the Club's name on their CV.

During May and June, the Club celebrated five years of running the UK's only self-managed venue with a week or two of celebratory gigs.

Gigs at the Club during June and July included the return of the UK Subs on the 30th,

for their third gig at the 1 In 12, and, on July 4, US band Econochrist for their second appearance.

In August, another review of a gig at the Club appeared in the latest issue of *Stork Magazine*.

In September, the Club was looking forward to the visit of legendary Polish band Dezerter, playing on their first UK tour, but Custom Officials refused them entry into the UK.

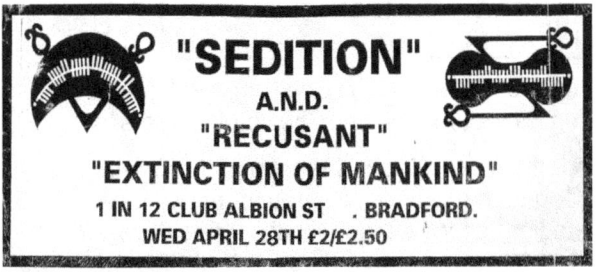

1 IN 12 AFC

Although The 1 In 12 Club was seen primarily as a music venue, it always tried to join in with the more social side of the community of the city, joining local games and quiz leagues.

In 1993, the 1 In 12 formed its own football team. The origins of the team lay in a six-a-side team of members playing friendlies with local and touring bands back in 1989/90.

These six were Matt Hannam, Dominic Watts, Darron and Steve of The Next World, Pete Pax and Seb 'Wolf' Kelly (goalie), and this nucleus, with other members centring around veteran player Steve Jackson, began training regularly at Scholemoor's all-weather astroturf on Tuesdays and arranging friendlies during 1992. (18)

1 In 12 A.F.C. joined the local Grattan League for the 1993-94 season, playing their first game against A.E. Autoparts (losing at home 3-2) on September 4, 1993. Their next game was away to Grovsnor FC playing on Green Lane, when the club won 2-1, and later in February 1994 reached the Quarter-Finals of the local Grattan League Cup, losing 3-0 to Bradford Celtic.

During the summer of 1994, the team played in two tournaments, the first in Hannau, Germany (some team members pictured below), as guests of Werder Bremen FC supporters, losing in the quarter-finals to arch-local rivals Werder Woodhouse. The second tournament was in Bristol, organised by close friends and

comrades Easton Cowboys who held annual summer tournaments in the coming years.

For the team's second season in the Grattan League they had a new ground, the Al Halal Stadium on Woodhead Road, where the team's fans sometimes ranged from 30-40 Club members and friends, all supporting the team by buying a programme which was full of stats and irreverent humour, generally at the team's skill (or lack of!) on and off the pitch.

The team's strength lay in its mixed ability, with some brilliant and experienced players, some mediocre and frankly some enthusiastic but not very good players. They always played with lots of heart and passion, and generally battled against more experienced and superior opponents in conditions of northern winters, with icy winds, water-logged pitches, always trying to play fluent and skilful football, but most seasons finishing mid-table.

Over the years, there was a continued influx of new players, strengthening the squad, this included two members' sons Che Grogan and Michael Cavanagh. (19)

Also, many players were members of local bands, such as Heart of Darkness, Anti-System, Sore Throat, Next World, Mash-M, Beer Beast, Auxiliary Of Real Men, Psycho Flowers and Dog On A Rope.

Team members entered a competition in *90 Minutes* football magazine, and won second prize - a new full strip for the team.

In 1995, a return to the Hannau tournament saw the team avoid the 'pink peril' of Werder Woodhouse and reach the final, beating German side FC Banana 3-0.

The next year they were runners-up in the Bristol tournament.

In 1997, seven team members made it over to the Lunnatics tournament in Antwerp, Belgium, to finish 6th out of ten teams with players borrowed from other teams helping them field a team.

The 1 In 12 team's history continues...

1 IN 12 FC - NEVER SAY DIE!

AS THE mist clears and the last desperate cries from the Spencer Road faithful rise up into the cold Bradford air, and then drift away into the cobwebbed calm of footballing history books, a new dawn of hope emerges from the ashes of a brave but terrifying battle, the scars of which can still be found, deep cuts in that hallowed, lopsided turf.

Half way into their inaugural season, One in Twelve FC have relocated and with them are surely blowing the winds of good fortune. This move follows a series of diabolical hammerings at the hands of such notables as Dale Farm, by such humiliating scorelines as 7-1, 9-1, 4-3 and so on. Only one win, significantly away to Grosvenor, had left them languishing in the foggier reaches of Grattan League Division Two. Since the much publicised move to their new Legrams Lane ground, or "multi-stadia complex", as the board of directors prefer to describe it, the club has only notched up a single point. But how.

The first match at Legrams Lane was an 8 goal thriller against Menstone Rangers. 4-2 down at half time, despite the sweetest football you're ever likely to see on a cold Sunday afternoon in the mud, One in Twelve clawed their way back into the match with a display not of this earth; and when they finally netted that stubborn ball, the mud-bath celebrations resounded through a crowd which included one supporter who had travelled from as far afield as Reading.

THE FORMIDABLE 1 IN 12 IN ALL THEIR GLORY

The second of these games, and the team's most recent to date, was a narrow defeat which can be attributed in no small part to their continual slow starting. A goal conceded within the first five minutes was enough to sink the club's hopes, and snatch a fortunate victory for the outclassed and outrun home side, U-Save DIY. The lads spilt blood, but nothing could reward the anguished cries of the travelling contingent (which, as ever, far outnumbered the home support).

Nevertheless, having finally adopted the sweeper system, whilst also looking for a new regular first team goalkeeper, this is surely the turning point in One in Twelve Football Club's season. Mid-table respectability is no longer a dream. Rather, it is a mere hurdle to be gracefully assailed with characteristic skill, hard work and sheer, gut-spilling determination. Faith in maverick manager Steve Jackson looks at last to be paying dividends, as the Red and Black Army go marching gloriously on to take the Grattan League by force, or is that storm?

Noel Batstone 16/1/94
Article from Black Flag magazine

At The 1 In 12 Club, during the final months of 1993, were a series of gigs including, on November 6 and 7, a two-day, fourteen-band Hardcore festival, with two SxE Belgian bands, two Czech bands, and a French and German band.

Local regulars Doom played twice, in November and December, supported by two more Belgian bands, Hiatus and Unhinged, and Citizen Fish returned for a gig on December 4.

The final event of the year, on December 23, was a benefit cabaret and disco organised by friends of Sarah Terry, a Club member who had unfortunately recently passed away. All monies raised from the event went to her son Todd.

TOM JONES & NEW MODEL ARMY

Tom Jones has had a long association with Bradford. In the early 1960s, his manager, Gordon Mills, would visit

his pal, Bradford singer Ray Kennan, of Bingley, often with Tom in tow.

In 1993 Tom recorded a version of the Rolling Stones classic *Gimme Shelter* as part of a project to promote the charity Shelter, called *Putting Our House In Order*, which raised money and awareness for homeless people.

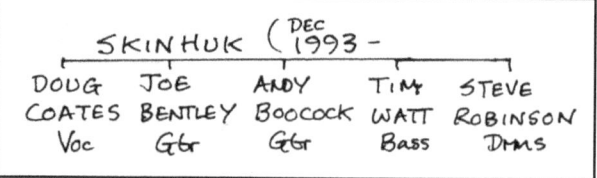

On July 24, The free *Heineken Music Festival* in Leeds Roundhay Park featured bands with a Bradford connection when Embrace, Chumbawamba, Senseless Things and Jellyfish Kiss played.

In August, a new recording studio opened just off Manchester Road. Pots'N'Pans was run by guitarist Steff Eros, who went on to work as a tutor on the Bradford College Music Technology BTEC course alongside Midnight Train vocalist Grom Kelly.

 During the late summer months of 1993, the local *T&A's Rock On* columnist Simon Ashberry, in conjunction with Queen's Hall's new promoter Joe Blencowe, organised an initiative called *Level Out*.

It promoted up-and-coming local acts by showcasing them on Friday gigs at Queen's Hall. The first such event was on September 17, featuring local bands The Bobby Charltons and Blood Orange.

CHAPTER 4 — 1991 - 1993

FRIDAY LEISURE — Rock On
T&A, Friday
CONTACT SIMON ASHBERRY ON ILKLEY 608602

DIE-HARDS... Threshold Shift, Mick Barrett, Tony Fox, Daz Keighley and Kenny Armitage

A rockin' good year for talent

THIS time last year the name Tasmin Archer meant very little to most people.

She could just as easily have been a new character on the Radio soap The Archers as a budding pop singer.

But after the success of her number one hit Sleeping Satellite, Tasmin has made a real name for herself.

The Bradford-born star is a contender for all kinds of music industry awards for 1992 — from Single Of The Year to Best Debut Record and Most Promising Newcomer.

With the album Great Expectations having sold solidly, Tasmin is poised to become Bradford's most successful ever pop star in 1993.

Watch out for a follow-up single in the New Year and a high-profile UK tour — which visits St George's Hall, Bradford, in March — before Tasmin sets off to "crack America."

The past 12 months have seen mixed fortunes for other Bradford acts. New Model Army shrugged off any disappointment in splitting from record label EMI by signing up to Michael Jackson's outfit Epic — and played to a packed house at a fund-raising gig at Queens Hall.

Poppy Factory's Mick Dale and Jock Cotton will want to forget this year pretty quickly, though.

Releases

The excitement generated by their 1991 single releases has long since evaporated and they are back to square one on pop's great snakes and ladders board.

But Terrorvision have been gathering momentum and enter the New Year on the verge of a breakthrough.

Other Bradford bands who have enjoyed varying degrees of success with album releases in 1992 include metalcore foursome Loud with Psyche 21; punk die-hards Threshold Shift, who brought out their self-titled LP; mellow rockers Architect, who released Poets And Thieves, and crusty trio Zed with their cassette-only meisterwerk The Articles Of Captain Mission.

West Yorkshire also gained a major new rock venue when the Town and Country Club opened in the former Leeds Colosseum.

Bookings so far have varied wildly from progressive hippies Asia to funk maestro George Clinton and wilful Americans Sonic Youth.

While Leeds hosted the county's biggest concert of the year — jet-packing Jacko at Roundhay Park in August — Bradford had its fair share of star-name appearances.

The Cure, The Stranglers, Crowded House, Manic Street Preachers, Thunder, Black Crowes, Take That, Snap, Smokey Robinson, Dionne Warwick and Joan Armatrading all graced the St George's Hall, Queens Hall, university or Maestro nightclub during 1992.

There is much to look forward to in 1993 including a promised CD from the Bobby Charltons (who've been strongly denying rumours they are to be re-named the Eric Cantonas) and New Model Army's first offering for their new label.

Rock 'n' roll on the New Year.

T&A, Friday, December 31, 1993 — FRIDAY — Rock On
CONTACT SIMON ASHBERRY ON ILKLEY 608602

Go underground for best sounds

THE national pop music scene may have stagnated somewhat in 1993 but Bradford's is positively burgeoning.

Quite apart from the commercial success of acts like Tasmin Archer, New Model Army and Terrorvision, this year's bumper crop of demo tapes is evidence of a healthy and diverse underground.

From the post-modern punk of Mr Giblet and rollicking Irish anthems of Scarlet Heights to Info-Zany's mild-mannered indie pop and the funky psychedelia of Kava Kava, there's a very broad spectrum of sounds emanating from West Yorkshire.

Rock On has been sifting back through the mountain of cassettes it has been sent over the past 12 months and has chosen this selection of the best of them:

1. Scarlet Heights — **St Patrick's Day.**
2. The Crossing — **I Will Lose Your Mind.**
3. Info-Zany — **Worst Night Out.**
4. Elsie Moon — **Who's Smiling Now?**
5. GFA — **Radio Friendly.**
6. Gorgeous — **The Chill.**
7. Oktober — **Falling.**
8. Big Bang — **Freakshow.**
9. Light Red Bead (aka Mr Giblet) — **Being Me.**
10. Kava Kava — **Feek.**

Keep them coming in 1994. Demo tapes can be sent to the Telegraph & Argus at 8 Wells Road, Ilkley LS29 9JD.

ROCK ON REVIEW OF THE YEAR

During Simon Ashberry's time as the T&A's Rock On columnist, he did a year-end round-up of the local music scene and sometimes a top ten of local releases. As with the two articles featured here, from 1992 and 1993.

Simon wrote the column for most of the nineties. He played in local band Loom and later became a presenter on Bradford Community Broadcasting as a host of the Bradford Beat local music show from 2001.

THE KEIGHLEY SCENE 1991-1993

More new bands emerged on the town's scene during the period 1991-93, and The Keighley News followed their exploits in the *Rock Box* column, edited by David Knight.

In 1991, the Grinning Rat pub started rock nights in the Rat Trap bar on Tuesdays and Thursdays, while at Champers on North Street, every Thursday was *Masters Of Rock* night between 10-2; live music and disco run by York-based promoter Mark Brayshaw.

```
TIMELESS THOUGHTS (1991-
JIMMY          PAUL         PETER
SUMMERS        HIRD         SUTCLIFFE
Voc/Gtr        Bass         Dms
(RIP 1990s)

STAMPEDE (1991-
JOHN    GAV        JAY       DALE     SEAN
HIGNALL HORSHAM              SILK     STORTON
Voc     Gtr        Rhy Gtr   Bass     Dms
```

Bags of Humph and almost everything else at KEIGHLEY FESTIVAL

Long-established Keighley rock band **The Big Bang** is joined by leading Bradford combos **P.A.D.D.** and **Primate** on Wednesday. Their gig at Victoria Hall, replaces the annual Festival Rock Competition cancelled through lack of entries. P.A.D.D., or Powerful And Deeply Disturbing, have pulled out of a prestigious London Marquee appearance to play Keighley. These renegades from Loud and Salvation have signed to Island Records and received praise from top rock mags like Rock Power and Kerrang. "A worthwhile alternative to much of today's production line metal" was the verdict of Raw magazine.

The Big Bang have achieved increasing success since switching style from punky rock 'n' roll to "indie" last year. Regional rock journalists claim

PRIMATE ...Mick, Matt, Liam and Steve

Primate "veer deliciously between gutsy post-punk riffing and classic pop melody." The band's acclaimed tape Feel was described as electrifying, dynamite, excellent and power-packed. Admission to the 7.30-11pm show costs £3 (£2 concessions).

> Rock 'n' rollers from around the world descends on Victoria Hall tomorrow (7pm) for the five-hour Summer Ball. Topping the bill is US rockabilly legend Ronnie Dawson whose three decades in the business has seen regular work with top stars. Freddie Fingers Lee, Britain's "wildman of rock 'n' roll," slaughters his keyboard in true Jerry Lee Lewis style. The Tin Star Trio Plus One, one of the top 50s bands in the Netherlands, cross the water to complete a jive-packed evening. Late bar, record stalls, 50s gear and the Tom Ingrams Rock 'n' Roll Show add to the fun.

Almost 45 years in the business and leading what's reckoned to be his best-ever band – that's **Humphrey Lyttelton**. "Humph" arrives at Victoria Hall on Sunday (8pm) for a jazz extravanganza featuring both glittering music and his witty and informative commentaries. Expect a repertoire ranging from early traditional to moderns by way of Ellington, Basie and other Swing giants.

Bradford's Triangle Club comes to Keighley on Monday (8pm) and brings with it the best of local cajun bands. The sound of the Louisiana swamplands fills up Victoria Hall through the music of **Old Joe Zydeco and the Bearcat Cajun Playboys**. Tickets £5 (£3 concessions).

The annual Feast Of Folk concert features a diverse selection of folky-type music at Victoria Hall on Tuesday (8pm). Local stars **Jim Woodland and The Salami Brothers** are on the bill plus Grinning Rat favourites **Rhythm Rascals** with their 1920s/30s mix of US blues, ragtime, gospel and Hawaiian music. Topping the bill are current folk favourites **Chris Wood and Andy Cutting**, accordion and fiddle duo extraordinaire, praised as one of the most compelling acts for many a

FOLK ...Wood and Cutting

year. There's also **Sid Kipper**, "the rising son" who injects a large dose of comedy into his act.

> The Yorkshire Dales Bluegrass Festival comes to Dales Bank Farm, Silsden (July 17-19), and features concerts by some of the UK's best bluegrass bands together with informal sessions, instrument instruction, band contest, children's entertainments, stalls, restaurant and bar.

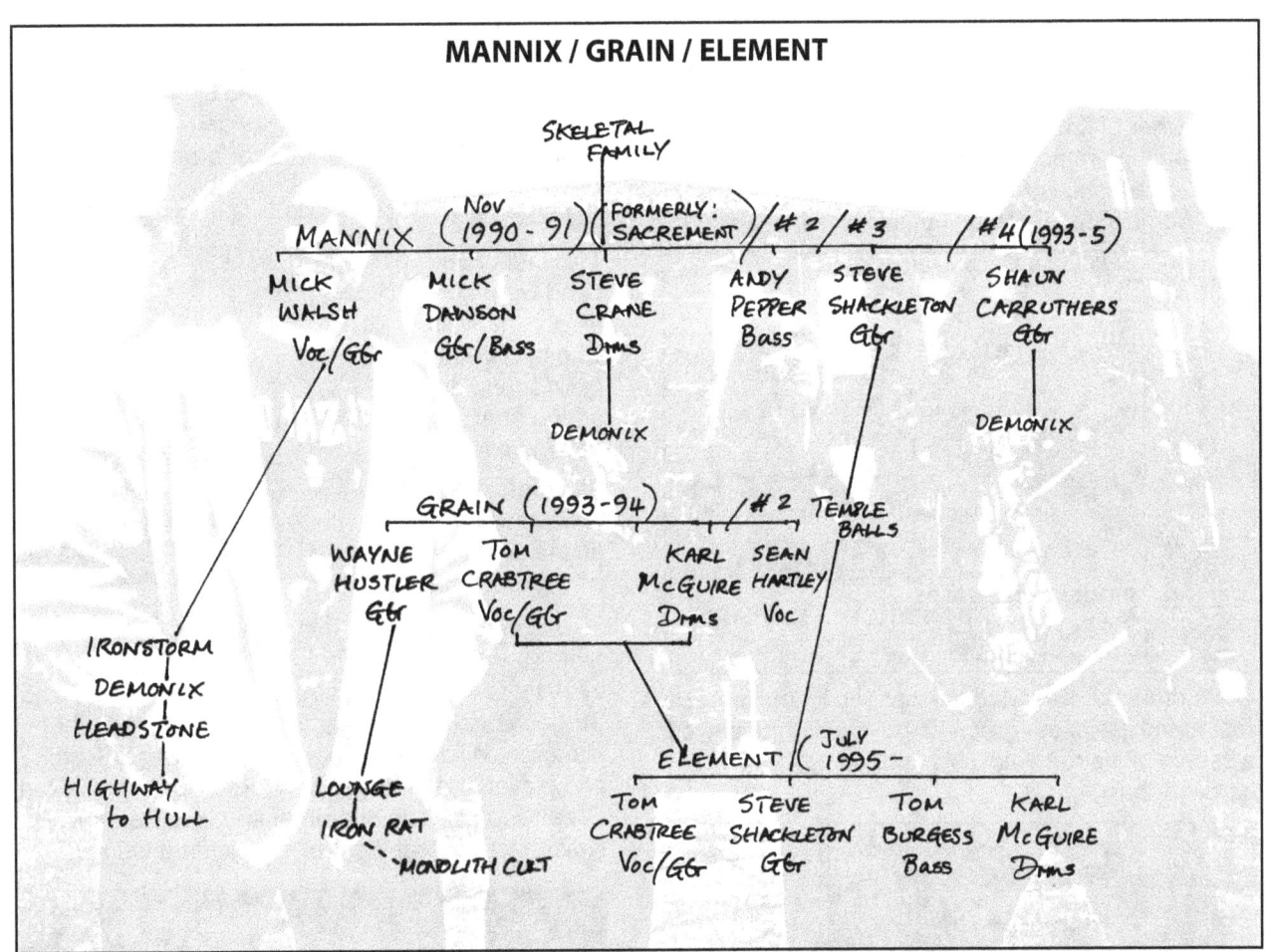

MANNIX

Mannix were Keighley's premiere thrash metal band. Originally known as Sacrement, they were a three-piece with Mick Walsh on vocals and guitar, Mick Dawson on bass and former Skeletal Family drummer Steve Crane.

They played around the local scene, supporting bands like Bolt Thrower, My Dying Bride and Lawnmower Deth, including a gig at the Rio on August 13, 1992.

They got a few positive reviews of their four-track demo EP *Visions Of Sickness* in rock magazines like *Kerrang!* and *Terrorizer*.

They also released the seven-track cassette album *Suffer*, which was recorded at Keighley's RMJ Studios in 1995. In 2011, the album was remastered by Kurt Wood at Jam On Top Studios and released online.

GRAIN

This short-lived rap/hardcore (rapcore) band started out in 1993. They were managed by Dave Wynne, joint owner of the *Wisdom Skateboard Boutique*. The band informed the *T&A* that they had been given an advance of £5,000 for a one-album deal with Warner Bros Records but this was just a scam.

Grain drummer Karl Maguire went on to join forces with members of the group Kingpin, who had played a couple of instrumental sets supporting Grain at a hardcore bash at Rios.

After guitarist Tom Crabtree took on vocal duties, the band evolved a new sound and changed their name to Element (pictured above). They went on to record an EP on their own label.

MAPP

Formed in 1993 around the brothers Nick and Richard Burns, all five members had previously served time in key Keighley bands like Skeletal Family, Teenage & The Wildlife and Class Type Bees. The band's sound was very complex and experimental, using unusual time signatures and incorporating visual elements (video, slides and backdrops, etc) into their live performances.

CHAOS

This indie-rock band were a trio of local musicians, whose original indie sound drew on their bassist's pagan beliefs.

Although short lived, they made an instant impact on the local scene.

Vocalist/bassist Gary Kaye joined other local boys The Big Bang as their new singer in 1995.

In 2011, Gary joined a tribute version of the Psycho Surgeons, taking on the mantle in memory of the late great Wild Willi Beckett's persona The Doctor, and played their first gig with former Surgeons Stan Greenwood, Johnny Lorrimer and Rob Kershaw in November 2011 at the 1 In 12 (pictured below).

Drummer Rob Kershaw joined the second lineup of the band Skinhuk as they reduced from a five-piece to a four-piece.

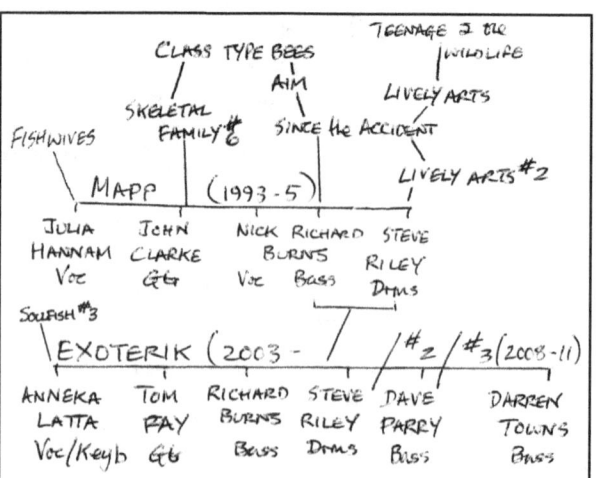

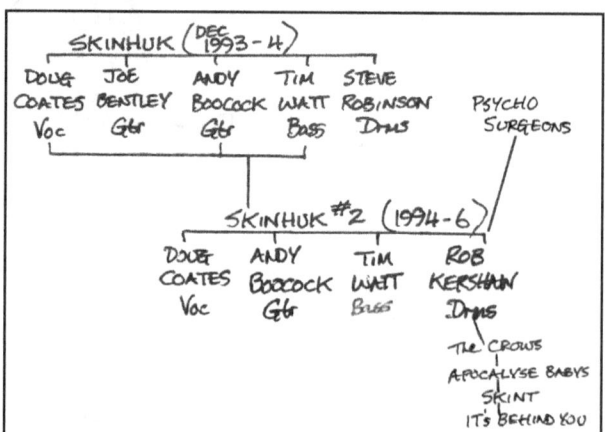

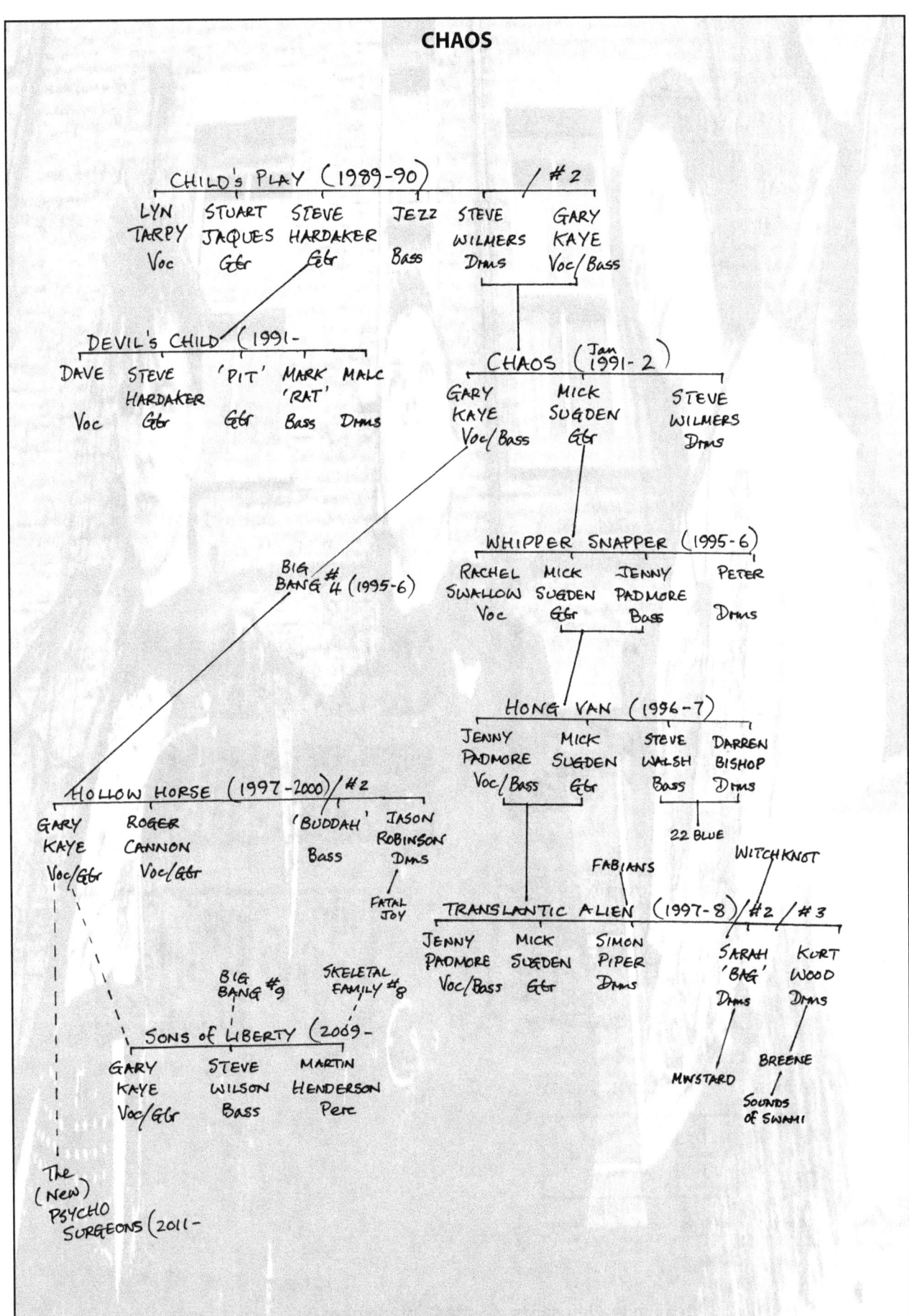

1 in 12 Club membership cards, courtesy of member 007, Gary Cavanagh!

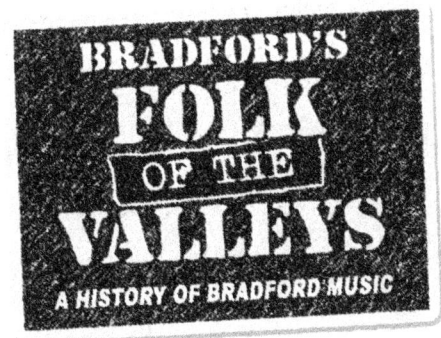

CHAPTER 5: FOLK & WORLD MUSIC 1988 - 1998

Folk music can be expressed universally as the traditional/ethnic music of any country, developed into the 'folk' idiom and passed down through the years. Thus, this 'world' music of various styles and approaches is essentially each country's folk heritage, be it the jigs and reels of the Irish, the zither sounds of the Magyars, the Bhangra style of India, or the drummers of Burundi.

In the UK, folk music had a revival from the 1950s onwards, and today's modern scene is an eclectic mix of old traditional forms, new folk-rock and world music interpretations.

Progressive folkies now take influences freely from the global template of ethnic music and it's now more accessible and create new forms, expressing their own variation on the various styles themes. The following narrative will incorporate local folk artists, world music acts and jazz artists into the story of Bradford's folk scene from 1988 to 1998.

Firstly, this chapter must revisit the local folk scene of the 1960s and '70s, to update information on artists from that period.

In 1975, Island Records released a four-disc vinyl boxed set called Electric Muse: The Story Of Folk Into Rock. It featured many of the UK's key exponents of the changes in folk at that time and was compiled and edited by Karl Dallas. Karl, at

75 Island/Transatlantic ELECTRIC MUSE - THE STORY OF FOLK INTO ROCK (4-LP box set)........40

that time, was a renowned writer on popular music for the music paper Melody Maker, and later became a resident of Bradford. He was active as a 'human shield' during the Gulf War, and is still, in his old age, a fine performer of his material on the local scene today.

During the 1970s, major folk artists like Lindisfarne, The Strawbs, Fairport Convention, Steeleye Span and Ireland's Planxty would all gig at Bradford's biggest venue, St George's Hall.

TOPIC FOLK CLUB

Established in 1956, the Topic Folk Club is still the world's longest-running and surviving folk club, despite moving from venue to venue over the years. From 1969 to 1991, the Club was based in the upstairs room of the Star pub on Westgate, where an impressive list of folk artists, from Ewan McColl to June Tabor, all performed, as well as many local groups and artists, such as Bradford's Swan Arcade (pictured below on the streets of Haworth).

After leaving The Star, the Topic Folk Club was based at The Peel Hotel on Richmond Road from 1991 to 93. It moved to The Melborn, on White Abbey Road, in 1994 and continued there for the remainder of the period this book covers.

LIZ NAREY

Although name-checked on a couple of 'trees' in the previous book, this Bingley-born local folk singer had been a stalwart of the areas folk scene since the early 1970s. Her brother is Steve Narey of Crystalized Anthem.

Liz started as a classical singer at an early age, trained by Joan Coulton. In 1964, at the tender age of twelve, she came second at the *Holmfirth Musical Festival*.

By the following year, influenced by the US singer Buffy St Marie, she was making appearances as a 'floor-singer' at Bingley College's *Folk Club* (1964-69) before working with Paul Keene & The Folk Weavers (1966-68) (pictured above).

In the 1970s she worked with Quiet Farm, Maidenhead Farm and Ragnarok and appeared twice on Arnold Loxam's Radio Leeds folk programme.

Since then she has guested with many other bands, most notably with Alien Sex Fiend in the 1980s when she sang backing vocals on two of their albums, *Evolution* and *Nocturnal Emissions*.

Bringing things up to date, Liz was still performing and producing new music in the mid-2020s.

Her 2023 album, *Nerves Of Green*, was released through Bandcamp and featured guest musicians including, Gill Driver, Conor McMahon, and Jon Harvison, On her next album, *Happens To Be* (2024), she collaborated with producer/guitarist Dicky B (Oliver Sudden).

Telegraph and Argus, Tuesday, September 14, 1971

new
BY CHARLES KEIGHLEY

Three guys and a girl in a band to watch

The odds were against Maidenhead Farm doing well at the Syon Park Folk Festival. For a start they were without the equipment they needed and having only formed a few weeks before were competing against groups who had been established a long time.

But despite these drawbacks the Bradford-based group were placed second out of the 50 groups taking part, a clear enough indication of the potential which lies within this three man, one girl line-up.

Maidenhead Farm consists of Liz Narey (vocals), Mick Reynolds (flute, trumpet and mandolin), Josh Grundy (guitar and mandolin) and Mick Whitaker (bass). They've been together about six weeks now and are rehearsing for what the group considers is an important gig at Bradford University on October 18. They are playing there with an east coast progressive-cum-heavy band called Red Dirt.

Josh is well-known on the local folk circuit and the two Micks will be remembered from their Scorched Earth days. Mick Whittaker formed the group and it lasted 18 months.

He remains as active as ever musically and is dividing his time between Maidenhead Farm and the two other bands he plays with—Ragnarok and Electric Eon.

"The Syon festival sounded like a good idea. We went down and all was well at first apart from the fact that the organisers didn't have any equipment when they had told us they would have," said Josh.

The group managed to borrow some but when it came to the final they found they were the only "electric" band — the rest were playing acoustic. They rushed round trying to get equipment but it ended up with Mick Whittaker having to drop out of their final set and the remaining three playing stand-by numbers.

"They went on feeling despondent, not expecting to do well at all," he said.

The group sound is very Pentangle-ish at first hearing but the mood changes completely when Mick Reynolds comes in on flute or trumpet. The result is a fusion of jazz with folk which is well worthy of development.

Maidenhead Farm also have the added advantage of being able to come up with their own material. A group to watch out for.

Second Dales National

FOLK
CONTEST
GARGRAVE VILLAGE HALL
Saturday, November 13th, 1971
7-30 p.m.

Adjudicating Panel — THE JOVIAL CREW

Comperes — THE TWO DAVIDS

Trophies to be presented by
Austin Mitchell
of Yorkshire Television "Calendar"

Entries to Linton Residential School. Closing date for applications November 10th 1971

TICKETS **30p**
Proceeds for Linton Residential School Recreation Room

Obtainable from
Linton Residential School, Linton Nr. Skipton Yorkshire,
Gifts & Craft Shop, Burnsall Nr. Skipton, Yorkshire

PRE-MOONKYTE

Prior to the formation of Moonkyte in 1970, two of the band's key members, Dave Stansfield and Dave Foster, had cut their teeth in two earlier bands. The Jack Bentley Blues Band (pictured above and below) had formed in 1967 and played regular gigs at The Farmers, at the top of Leeds Road, and at an infamous little-known venue in Bingley called The Turret.

When that band folded, they formed the delightfully named Silas Warthelmet's Battering Ram, an *'art fuelled visual musical installation of miced up vacuum cleaners with improvised poetry, fused with Cecil Taylor style avant-garde piano in an atmosphere of general mayhem.'* (1)

After Silas' demise came Moonkyte, rising phoenix-like from its ashes to produce the strange sound of fusing folk rock with the Delta blues, while the lyrics were about the band's experimentation with LSD and hashish.

Their only released LP, *Count Me Out*, in 1971, with sleeve notes from the legendary DJ John Peel, is nowadays seen as a lost gem of British acid folk and is very collectable. It was reissued on the Sunbeam label in 2006

JANET JONES

Keighley lass Janet Jones was a remedial teacher who began practising on an old guitar in 1970. By the next year, she felt proficient enough to play her first gig at the Fleece pub in Addingham. She soon started to take the local folk scene by storm and became female champion at the 1971 *Dales National Folk Contest*.

In 1972, she appeared on Hughie Green's TV talent show *Opportunity Knocks*. She released two LPs for the folk label Midas, the self-titled *Janet Jones* and *Sing To Me Lady* in 1974.

Janet released the 7" EP *A Fresh Wind Waves* on the Folk Heritage label in 1976, a collection of five poems by Emily Bronte, set to music. On this recording, her beautiful voice was accompanied by Derek Horsfield on piano.

After living for nearly thirty years in Oakworth (Keighley), a mile from Haworth, she finally retired from teaching and now lives quietly near Leeds.

In 2011, her EP was re-released on CD by Aire Valley Music as a part tribute to Janet and to commemorate the life and work of 19th-century Thornton-born novelist Emily Bronte. The original five tracks were digitally re-mastered, and Janet chose to add the cello of Joanna Twaddle to further enhance the mood of the poems.

JANET JONES			
74	Midas MR 005	SING TO ME LADY (LP)	200
74	Midas MFHR 059	JANET JONES (LP, released on Folk Heritage label)	200

JACK BENTLEY BLUES BAND / SILAS WARTHELMET'S BATTERING RAM / MOONKYTE

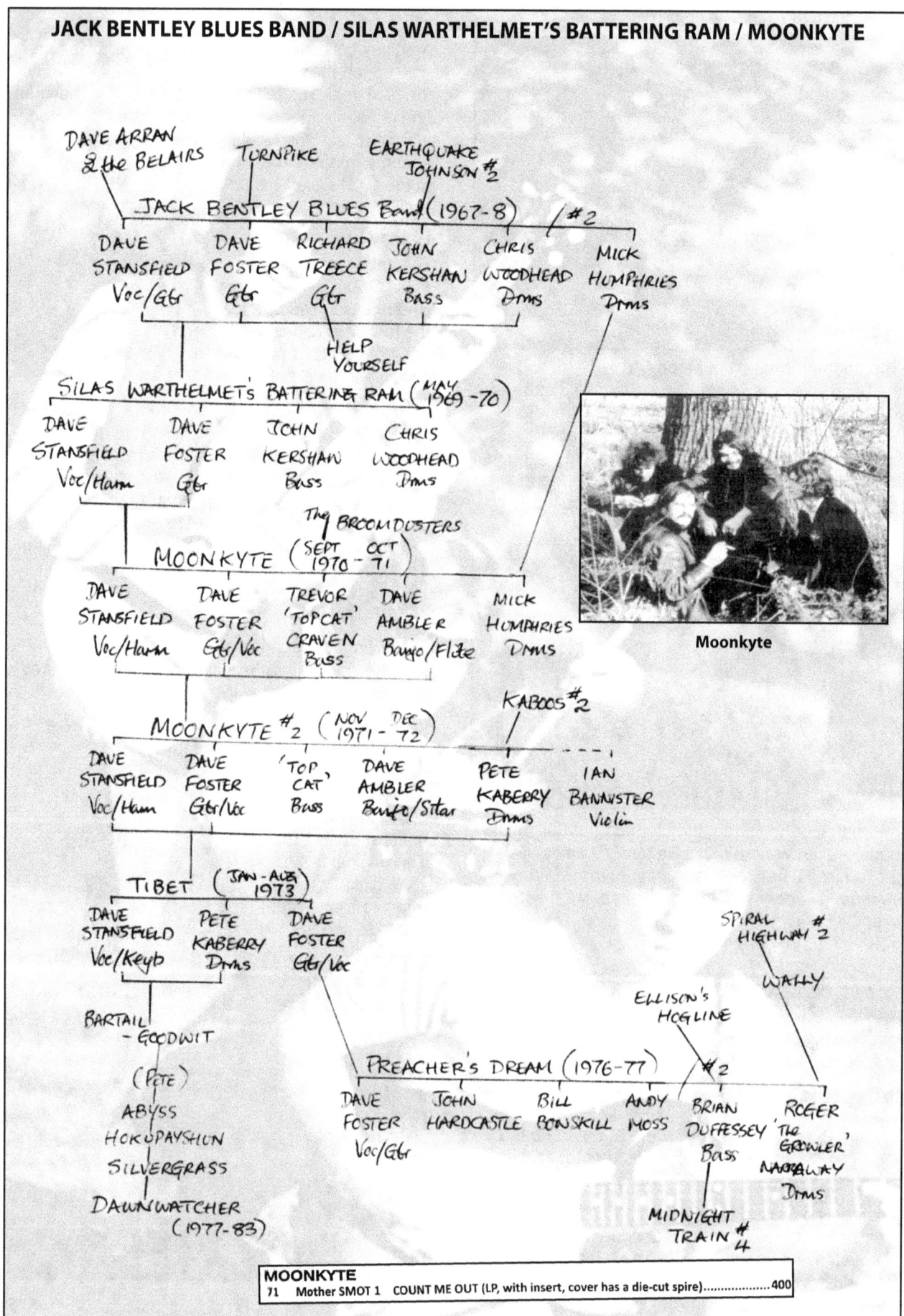

Moonkyte

MOONKYTE
71   Mother SMOT 1   COUNT ME OUT (LP, with insert, cover has a die-cut spire).................. 400

ROGER SUTCLIFFE

In 1963, Roger played his first 'floor session' at the Topic Folk Club, after learning three chords and practising for months. From these humble beginnings, this local Bradford lad was brought up in the Lidgit Green area. He strove to soak up the blues and learn more chords and techniques, becoming something of a folk-blues legend.

His hard-to-find 1976 LP *Death Letter*, on the small Huddersfield Look Records label, is a classic example of his intricate style of playing and the LP is highly sought after.

In 1984, he recorded another album, Under *The Rubber Eagle*, due to be released on Mike Harding's record label, which unfortunately didn't happen. Roger managed to retrieve the master tapes years later and released it himself in 1994 on his Low Ash Music label. The album had fellow Bradford lad Brendan Croker guesting on guitar on three of the tracks, *Living With The Blues*, *I'm Sober Now* and *Troubled Mind*.

After relocating to Whitby, he continued to wow audiences and periodically released music on his Low Ash Music label. He made an annual pilgrimage to his spiritual home, the Topic Folk Club. His appearance on July 11, 2024, marked 61 years since he first hit the stage there.

TITAN

Folk rock band Titan were arranged around main man Colin Whittaker in 1981. Colin had previously played in local 1970s group Lemathus with his brother Mick. In 1982 they released the 7" single *Imaginary Lady / Guaranteed You Won't Like It* on their own Mistic River Music label.

The band were then signed to a two 7" and one album deal with CBS subsidiary After Hours, who then re-released a re-mixed version of *Imaginary Lady* as a single in 1983 (both 7" are now very collectable).

A line-up change brought in ex-Lemathus members Graham Banfield on bass and Chris Wiltshire on drums.

In 1989, Colin went solo under the name The Orange World Of Titan and released three singles for EMI, the first being *Big Baby*.

TITAN			
83	After Hours AFT 09	Imaginary Lady/Tooty Flutey	30

WOMAD

Many folk artists of the 1960s and '70s had experimented with the ethic styles and sounds of world music in their recordings. In 1980, ex-Genesis vocalist Peter Gabriel helped to develop the modern interest in world music by organising the first *WOMAD (World Of Music, Arts And Dance)* festival at Shepton Mallet, in 1982.

The global mix of artists appearing included himself, US jazz trumpeter Don Cherry, The Drummers Of Brunudi, UK acts The Beat, Simple Minds and Echo & The Bunnymen, Irish band The Chieftains and African artists Ekome and Prince Nico M'banga, amongst many others.

Since that festival, the Womad organisation has championed the global/world music scene by encouraging musical collaboration of artists when invited to perform. They also strive to present music of excellence, passion and individuality, regardless of geographical origin or musical genre.

In 1982, there was an eight-piece folk group from the Allerton area called The Row Behind.

1988-1998

1988 started with a Sunday night residency at the Fighting Cock real ale pub in January for Cajun/polka band Car Boot Cowboys & The Sidekicks.

In February, the East/West country music duo So So were led by Richard Dover.

Telegraph & Argus, Saturday, May 7, 1988

Music in store

SHOPPERS had a trolley good deal at their local supermarket when real music replaced the canned variety.

Buskers Dave Sheriff and Nicki Clarke played and sang outside the Asda superstore in Knowles Lane, Bradford, doing requests to raise money for their own charity Cancer Aid, started when they lost members of their families through the disease.

The two troubadours (above) set a world record last year when they played three musical instruments each at the same time for 100 hours and 20 minutes.

Dave and Nicki are on a tour of 40 supermarkets playing for between six and ten hours non stop. They are hoping to raise £50,000 this year for cancer hospices.

July 1-4, 1988, saw the start of the first *Cleckheaton Folk Festival*, which was sponsored by Yorkshire Arts, Kirklees Council and Theakstone's Brewery. (2)

Amongst the acts playing that first year were Scarlet Heights, Witches Bane, Rogues Gallery, Black Velvet, Gringogs, The Doonan Family and The Nook Band.

During Thursday nights in October 1988, the nine-piece Latin-jazz outfit Conjunto Fuego ran salsa/samba nights at Rio's on Woodhead Road.

KEVIN YOUNG

Self-employed painter and decorator Kevin Young began backing his first wife Barbara in the late 1970s with fellow guitarist Jeremy Wolstenholme. Barbara Young had been a singer/songwriter on the local folk circuit since 1971. She released *No Game At All*, a thirteen-track album recorded at Bingley's JSG studios in 1981, and released on their own Corridor Records.

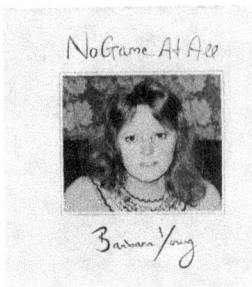

By 1988, Kevin was ready to release his own LP on Corridor Records. *Pick Of The Bric-A-Brac* included Barbara and Jeremy as well as other guest musicians like ex-Gygafo guitarist Charlie 'Speed' Staniforth.

In 1994, Kevin was working during the day as a decorating lecturer at Bradford College, and at night playing with his new band, Collen's Fancy.

His parents were originally from County Kerry, so his Irish roots made the group naturals to perform two songs; *The Fields Of Athenry* and *Strawberry Beds*, on that year's YTV's *Calendar* news programme's St Patrick Night celebrations.

Kevin's band were three times winners of the *International Buskers Festival* and, in 1995, played a four-night residency at the Irish theme pub Scruffy Murphys in Bergen, Norway.

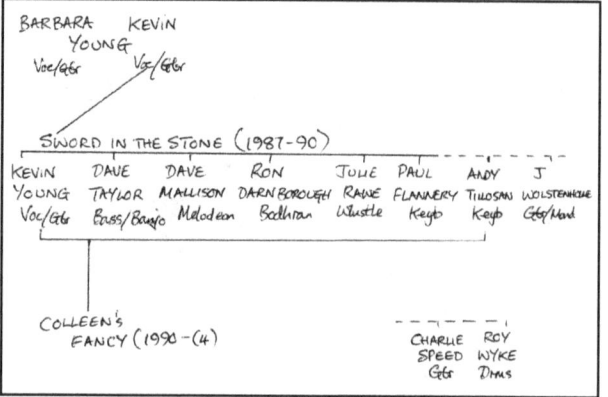

THE TRIANGLE CLUB

A regular weekly Cajun-influenced folk night was organised at the Royal Standard pub from 1988 until late 1991, when the pub mysteriously burnt down.

The nights promoted traditional bluegrass-style Cajun fiddle music, a regular Cajun hootenanny.

The Triangle Club even had its own fanzine *The Cajun Echo* promoted up-and-coming bands at the Triangle and info about other UK cajun clubs, like Derby's Swamp Club and Liverpool's Mons club, alongside the occasional song lyric.

The Triangle Club moved to Queen's Hall from January 1992 until October 1994. It was then based at Pennington's Midland Hotel for monthly Sunday night gigs.

OLD JOE ZYDECO

Formed in 1988, this local Cajun band included Malcolm Manning who had set up Manning's Musicals on Westgate in 1987, after settling in Bradford. Malcolm had come to West Yorkshire to study Fine Art at Leeds Polytechnic and had been one of the people who helped start the Triangle Club.

The band sang in English and Cajun French, gigged regularly all around the country, appeared on TV slots on the BBC and YTV and supported Cajun greats like DL Menard and Eddie Lejeune at the London Cajun Festival.

They self-produced three cassette albums, *Let's Go Two-Stepping*, *Acid Joe* and *Eight Hours From Lafeyette*, the first two selling out several times.

Old Joe Zydeco also contributed the track *Zydeco Gris Gris* to the 1 In 12 compilation *Volnitza* in 1989.

They played their swansong gig at the Triangle Club in September 1992, before certain members reformed as the Cajun Aces.

STONY MOUNTAIN TRIO

This 1950s-style rockabilly trio played their third gig at the Yarnspinners pub at the bottom of Manchester Road on October 13, 1989.

They also played a gig supporting the Meteors in Leeds.

GRANNY THOMPSONS BIG BALD HEAD

After a spell with the Rhythm Cruisers in 1993, bassist Garry Thompson formed Granny Thompson's Big Bald Head. They released an eight-track cassette album on their Then Music label based in Allerton.

MANNINGS MUSICALS

71 WESTGATE
BRADFORD
BD1 2SP

All acoustic musical instruments bought and sold

Telephone
0274-725539
or
663473 evenings

OLD JOE ZYDECO / CAJUN ACES

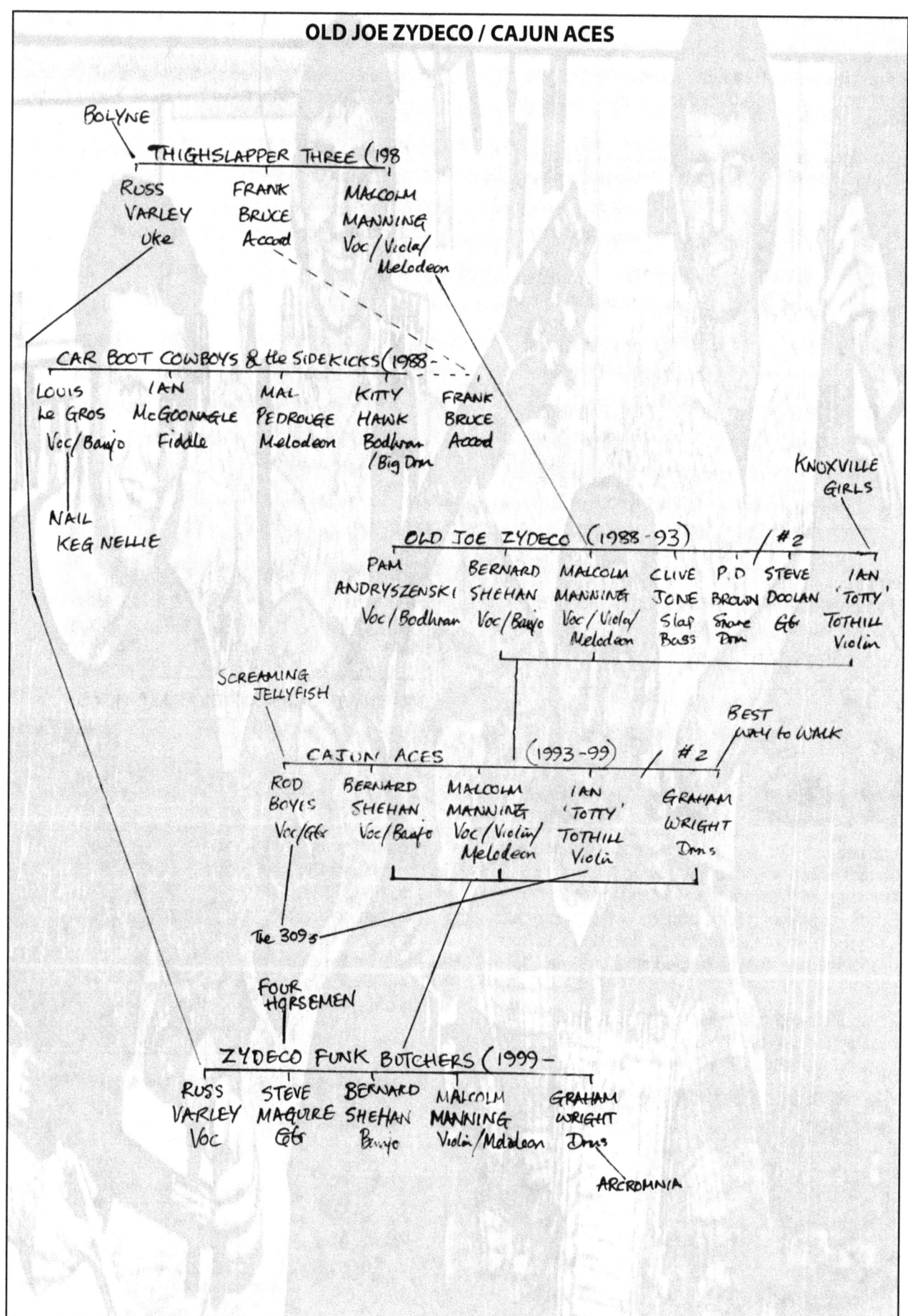

TOK-TOKI

Seven-piece Afro-Latin roots band Tok-Toki were based in West Yorkshire. Their Argentinian singer lived in Bradford during 1991-92.

'Their mainly original songs were arranged around their four percussionists, rooted in the subtle but powerful interplay of congas, djembe, timbales and bass mixed with piano and brass accompanying the strong, impassioned Spanish vocals.' (3)

Tok-Toki live shows provided music for head, hands and feet as audiences soon got up to dance the samba, salsa or just wild jiving.

In February 1993, a new folk club at the Top Oak pub on Leeds Road was started by Dave Vermond of Ilkley.

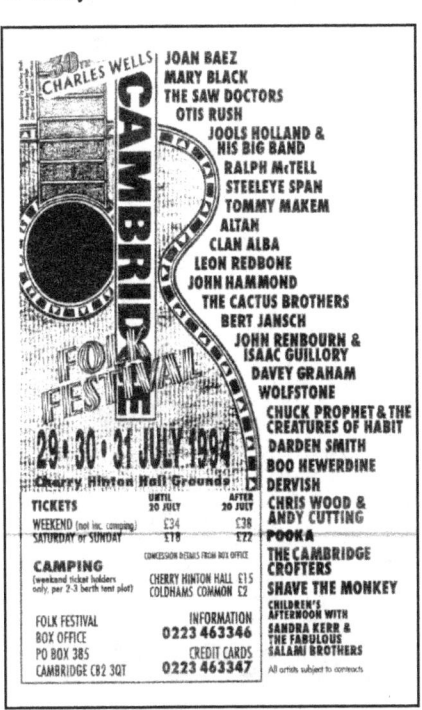

By the mid-1990s, folk/world music was enjoying a renaissance. A wider range of people flocked to annual folk festivals like the *Cambridge Folk Festival* and Fairport Convention's *Cropedy* folk festival as well as a host of smaller gatherings around the UK in the summer.

THE CELTIC MUSIC SCENE

The Irish people were the first immigrants to relocate to the growing industrial city of Bradford in the early 1800s, mainly to work in the mills (some as 'strike' breakers, initially).

As the Irish community grew, the contrast of coming from rural peasant environments to an urban industrial centre meant that they sought companionship and cultural security by forming their own distinct areas in Bradford, like Wapping, Adelaide Street (off Manchester Road), Goitside and Longlands (lower and upper Sunbridge Road and behind Westgate) where their language, culture and music were retained.

These Irish enclaves were amongst the worst living conditions in the city. Overcrowding intensified the squalor and disease as large families usually occupied single rooms. The 1845 *Woolcombers' Report* into these housing conditions showed, that of the 350 houses covered (nearly all Irish), the average number of persons per room was 5.5 and in one building ninety-five people shared eight rooms, with as many as four to a bed. (4)

It is no surprise then, that very many of the Irish were prominent in the activity of the Chartists in the local area. During the Chartist revolts of 1848, in Bradford, they contributed large numbers to mass meetings and military-style processions in the town. Singing Chartist hymns, they fought the police and militia to a standstill in the no-go area of Adelaide Street, led by a huge blacksmith called Issac Jefferson. (5)

By 1851, Irish immigrants made up 8% of the population; 9,581, and this average continued up to World War One. By 1882, there were two Catholic churches in the city. (6).

From those earliest days, informal Gaelic gatherings of music and dancing, known as Ceilidhs, were organised on a regular basis, strengthening shared heritage.

The Bradford Irish Club (formerly The John Dillion WMC) was set up on Rebecca Street (off Westgate) in the early 20th century and is still today the central hub in the city, keeping Irish music and culture alive.

Ceilidh bands were part of the local Irish scene well before the late 1980s-90s popularity of everything Irish, and the growth of Irish theme bars and pubs like Scruffy Murphy's and renewed interest in Irish music.

SCARLET HEIGHTS

This Celtic folk band began around 1990 when Pat Sherry and Nigel Broadbent were joined by Mal Laws on banjo/mandolin for a gig at Benny Maguire's Royal pub in Girlington. Pat and Nigel had until then gone out as a duo, performing since 1983, singing close harmonies and acoustic songs, eventually getting residencies at pubs and building up a following.

Now, as the band Scarlet Heights (named after an area just before Queensbury), they recorded a five-track demo cassette at In A City Studios, using a fluctuating list of guest members from the local folk scene.

With a new lineup, they played larger venues like Queen's Hall and MaGuires on City Road.

After members left in 1993, with Brian joining the band Wild Geese and Dawn moving to Spain to run an internet cafe, they recruited ex-Hedgehog Pie multi-instrumentalist Ian Fairbairn from the Northeast region. Because Ian was mates with Lindisfarne, the band ended up playing support when Lindisfarne did their then annual gig at St George's Hall on July 3, 1995.

That same year, after doing a tour of Ireland, this lineup became regarded as the quintessential Scarlet Heights unit when they recorded the *Kicking And Screaming* CD album at Pots'n'Pans Studios.

After a couple more lineup changes, the band continued to function in a fluid state and played the odd gig now and again.

WILD GEESE

This six-piece Bradford traditional Ceilidh band were formed in the early 1990s and specialised in playing contemporary Irish music.

While touring Ireland in 1994, the band recorded a live 90-minute tape called *Where's My T-Shirt ?*, in the courtyard of Matt Molloy's bar in Westport, County Mayo. Matt Molloy, the flautist with The Chieftains, joined the band on stage during their set, which was part of the Wild Geese annual tour of the West of Ireland. The tape was sold for £3, with £2 going to the local homeless charity CHAS (Catholic Housing Aid Society)

The band's manager, Brendan Hafferty, said the tape's title came about, '*...because a member of the Westport audience kept shouting the phrase throughout their three-hour concert. His persistence paid off; he was given a T-shirt in the end and now is the honorary secretary of the band's fan club in the town.*' (7)

THE CITY FLEADH

Over Saturday and Sunday, June 19/20, 1993, the Maguires pub on City Road held a two-day Fleadh or festival. Many local acts like Scarlet Heights and Roger Sutcliffe played, as well as UK and Irish artists who were a little more well known.

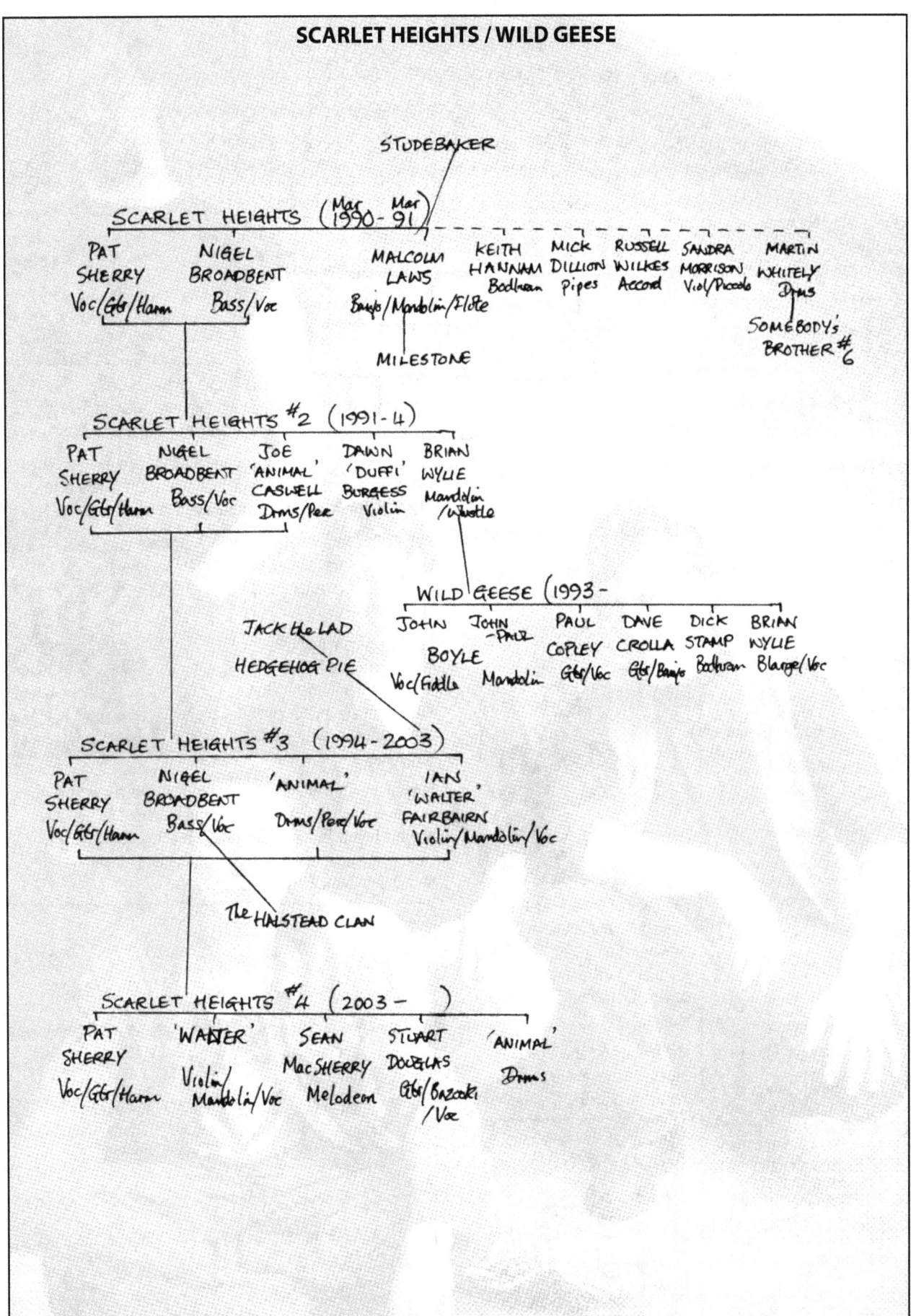

ROGER HIGGINS

Roger, originally from Manchester, moved to Bradford in the 1970s. He played in Bradford bands The Sheds and False Claims, who played the first ever 1 In 12 Club Gig in April 1981.

By 1990, Roger was playing venues all over the North of England, both solo and with his three-piece blues-rock group, The Bottleneck Boogie Band (pictured above).

In the early 1990s he clocked up hundreds of appearances a year, playing regularly at Blues festivals, beer festivals, pubs and clubs, including several appearances at the prestigious *Burnley Blues Festival*.

Roger recorded an album called *Ain't Nothing...*, released in 1994, featuring different lineups of the Bottleneck Boogie Band.

He released the solo album *Straight From The Heart* in 1999.

From the late nineties, Roger was usually accompanied by Big Eyed Beans bassist Tony Evans, who played his hand-built fretless bass.

He also played regularly with his three-piece Roger Higgins Band which featured Tony on bass and Mark Bannister (later Matt Webster) on drums.

In 2000, Roger released a live recording of the band as the CD album *Keep On Drivin'*.

He spent part of the early years of the new millennium living in the USA where he recorded a live album with guitarist Art Steele.

Roger continued to perform solo and as a duo with renowned guitarist Gary Boyle of the 1970s jazz fusion band Isotope. He also hit the road with a new lineup of the Roger Higgins Band, which also featured Gary Boyle.

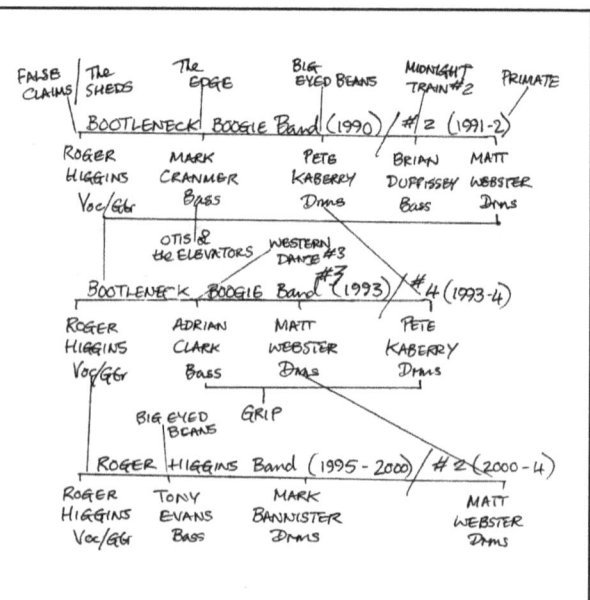

Best of blues

THE FRONT man of The Bottleneck Boogie Band, Roger Higgins, began the evening's entertainment at Bradford's Park Hotel last Friday with a selection of acoustic blues songs from the 20s and 30s, showing himself to be a fine exponent of the slide guitar.

Then joined by the excellent rhythm section, the band played a mixture of original songs and blues classics.

Two 50-minute sets incorporated 12 bar standards, funk rhythms, searing slide guitar and slower melodic numbers that held the attention of the audience. Highlights included storming versions of Dylan's All Along The Watchtower, Freddy King's Love Her With A Feeling, and The Higgin's composed Welfare and Lost and Lonely.

The band have been gigging extensively around Britain for the past year, building up a good reputation on the blues circuit. And they are looking for a permanent drummer for gigs and recording work. Anyone interested can ring Roger on Bradford 574196.

Pete James

THE PALLADINOS

Angelo and Alice Palladino came to settle in Rawdon in 1989. They relocated from Deptford, South East London, where their previous band, The Barflies, had a very loyal following in the 1980s.

After widespread label interest, The Palladinos signed to Miles Copeland and Sting's Pangaea Records label in late 1993. They released the *Travelling Dark* album in 1994.

One song from the album, *(I Won't Be) Going South For A While*, was included on the soundtrack of the film *Leaving Las Vegas*.

Bradford musician Sean Dillon played on one track and was pictured on the album sleeve driving a car, a feat he never managed in real life! Sean played in the touring Palladinos band and later with Angelo until 2002.

The Palladinos supported Sting for two nights at the Albert Hall and played two American tours the same year, including further dates with Sting, at Paramount Theatre, New York.

Over the next couple of years, they supported many internationally known artists, including Sheryl Crow, Squeeze, Jools Holland, Steeleye Span, David Gray and Squeeze.

ANGELO PALLADINO

Singer/songwriter/guitarist Angelo played with numerous Bradford musicians and in local venues after The Palladinos ended.

He recorded a solo album, *Outsiders*, featuring Sean Dillon on guitar and Lee Abbott on double bass, at Mutiny 2000 in 2002.

Although the album remains officially unreleased, the tracks *Just Can't Sleep* and *The Restless Road*, produced by Matt Webster, appeared on the Mutiny 2000 compilation CD *White Abbey Road* in 2000.

Following a lineup change in his live band, Angelo recorded another album, *Blood, Blues & Bad Dreams,* in 20024. Produced by Rob Heaton, it featured various Bradford musicians. *Rolling Stone* gave the album a 3 1/2 star review.

By 2007, Angelo had put together a new backing band, The Skeleton Crew. They released the live five-song CD/DVD *Live At Hall Place* in 2007.

2015 saw a new lineup, Angelo Palladino & The Streethawksm with the album *Streethawk Diaries Volume 1*. His band did a UK tour to support the album in 2016. Another solo album, *This Be Blue*, appeared on iTunes in 2018.

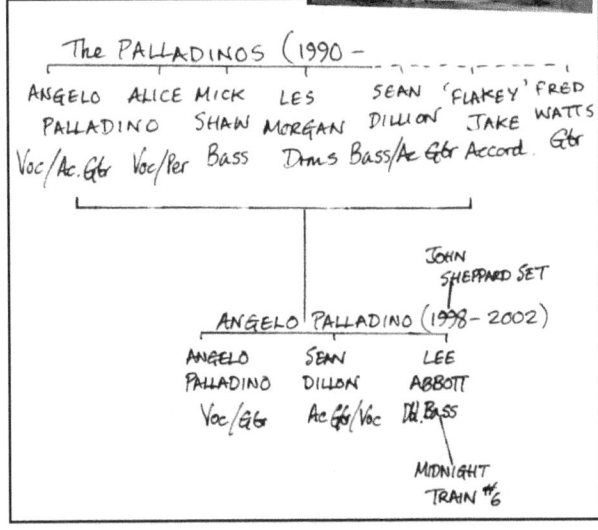

GRACE NOTES

After twenty years together as a trio, Maggie Boyle, Helen Hockenhull and Lynda Hardcastle released the twentieth-anniversary album, *20*, in 2002.

Maggie had performed with The Boyle Family in the 1970s. Her vocals have adorned film soundtracks of major Hollywood films including *Patriot Games* and *The Legends Of The Fall*. She has also worked with some great folk artists like The Chieftains, Bert Jansch, John Renbourne and Steve Tilston.

Lynda had previously been in the 1970s folk band Mountain Ash, and Helen had been a founder member of Muckram Wakes, with whom she made three albums.

Grace Notes's three-part harmonies are the main feature of their songs alongside their instrumental talents on mandolin, flute, bodhran, recorder and keyboards.

Their first album, *Down Falls The Day*, came out in 1993 on their own label. It featured guest musicians Mike Hockenhull, on banjo (who also produced the album), and guitarists Alan Rose and Steve Tilston.

It was followed by *Red Wine And Promises* (1998), *Northern Tide* (2001), and *Anchored To The Time* (2008), all on the Cumbrian-based Fellside Recordings folk label.

LOS ZIMMOS

Cleckheaton born mandolin wizard Andy Higgins formed the duo Los Zimmos with Ronnie Forster while based in the North East in 1991.

The band's name comes from them both loving Mexican food and their catch phrase -*Hey Zimmy* (pet name for Bob (Zimmerman) Dylan).

During 1991, the duo toured Holland, Belgium, Norway and Sweden before releasing their debut album *Raw Fish And Sisters*.

Andy had also released a solo album called *Cartwheels In The Sand*.

The duo did a home town gig at the Topic Folk Club on Friday, January 10, 1992.

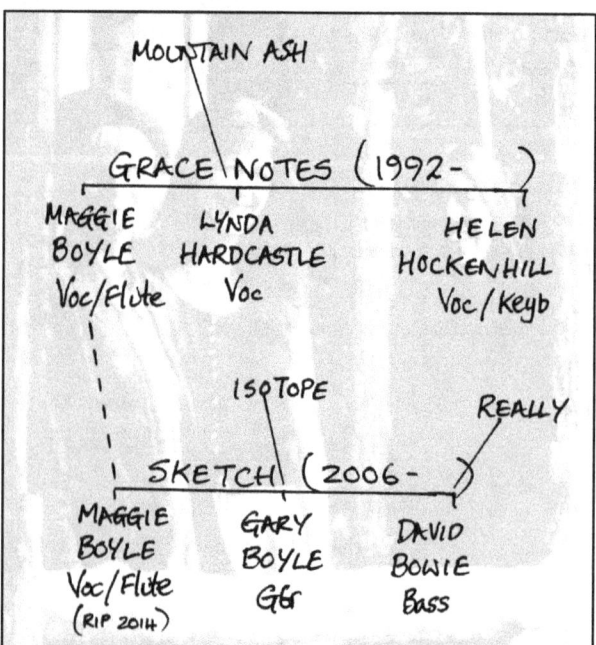

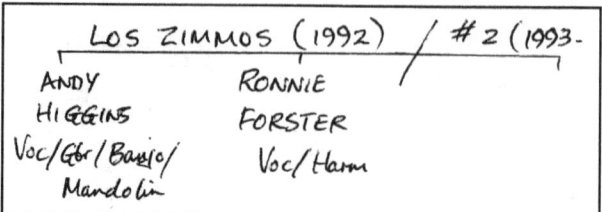

THE BHANGRA SCENE

The Commonwealth immigrants from South Asia (India, Pakistan and Bangladesh) arrived in Bradford during the 1960/70s to settle and work, bringing with them their religion, rich heritage culture and, of course, their traditional music.

Soon, Asian cuisine via the dozens of curry restaurants that sprang up, became very popular with Bradfordians. Over the next few decades curry replaced fish'n'chips as the UK's favourite meal. (8)

Asian folk music also had an impact on British cultural life in the regions where large numbers settled and went on permeate the world music scene.

Bhangra was a form of dance and music originating from the Punjab region of India and Pakistan. It dates back to the eleventh century and is an expression of the rural communities (mainly Muslim and Sikh farmers) celebrating the seasonal harvests and their social life.

The main traditional instruments of Bhangra are the single stringed iktar, the tumbi and the chimta, with the percussive sound of the dhol drum and its smaller cousin the dholki, both used to provide the main beat.

Early Punjabi Sikh bands developed in the UK and made Bhangra a form of music instead of just a dance. Against a cultural backdrop of alienation, tension and racism in British society, this music created a positive identity of their culture.

Bhangra music has become an aspect of South Asian culture, and it is evident in many different styles from film soundtracks to modern pop music.

From the 1980s onwards, Bhangra music became very popular, the period between 1985-1993 is seen as a golden age amongst 'bhangra-heads' and even produced the first bhangra boy band The Sahotas, from Wolverhampton.

As the music progressed it used more keyboards, fusing Bhangra with rock sounds and moving away from the simple and repetitive traditional style.

Most Bhangra artists released their music on the cassette format and, in the 1980s, some acts were selling as many as 30,000 tapes a week in the UK. (9)

ANJANA / ANJAANA

Probably Bradford's first Bhangra band, now known as Anjaana, formed in 1975. They performed all over the UK and were considered one of the best bands around.

They released their *Nachina Pia* LP in 1985 on the SSTV label. It was recorded at Flexible Response Studios in Little Germany and produced by local jazz keyboardist Dave Cass of Middle 8.

The album's music was a new direction for Bhangra, a mixture of the Asian sound with disco they called *The Pangra Sound*.

The title track was a hit in the *Bhangra Beat* charts, the Asian version of *Top Of The Pops*, and featured the guest vocals of the late great Punjabi singer Kuldip Manak (RIP 2011). The song is played at Punjabi weddings all over the world.

This was quickly followed up by a second LP with Kuldip Manak featuring the hit *Gidhe Wich Nachdi*

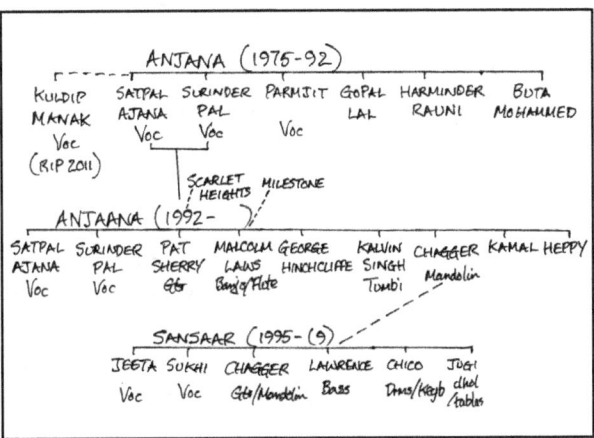

Da. The band had another hit with *Tere Laung Mare Lishkaray*.

From 1992, Anjaana incorporated some new members, including members of local Irish folk group Scarlet Heights.

As part of the local world music scene, the band played the Bradford Festival Mela stage in 1988, playing their rustic village music, rhythmic dance songs, using traditional Punjabi folk instruments.

SAAGRA

Saagra were another local Bhangra band who formed around 1988. They were in demand for weddings, parties and other gatherings and travelled to play all over the UK.

The band included former 1970s bassist Colin Hingston from the local band Dirty Work.

Unfortunately one night, after returning from a gig and when Saagra were having a late curry, the band's van containing all their gear, including the band's backdrop, was stolen.

SHAHKAAR

Formed in 1987, this local Bhangra band were of Asian and white backgrounds and included multi-instrumentalist/producer Carl Stipetic and former Jayver drummer George Fothergill in their lineup.

They got signed to EMI Records and their 1988 cassette album *Pyar De Nasha*, meaning 'addiction of love', was a seven-song affair. It soon began to sell very well in Asian outlets in Bradford as well as in the rest of the UK, Europe, Canada and India.

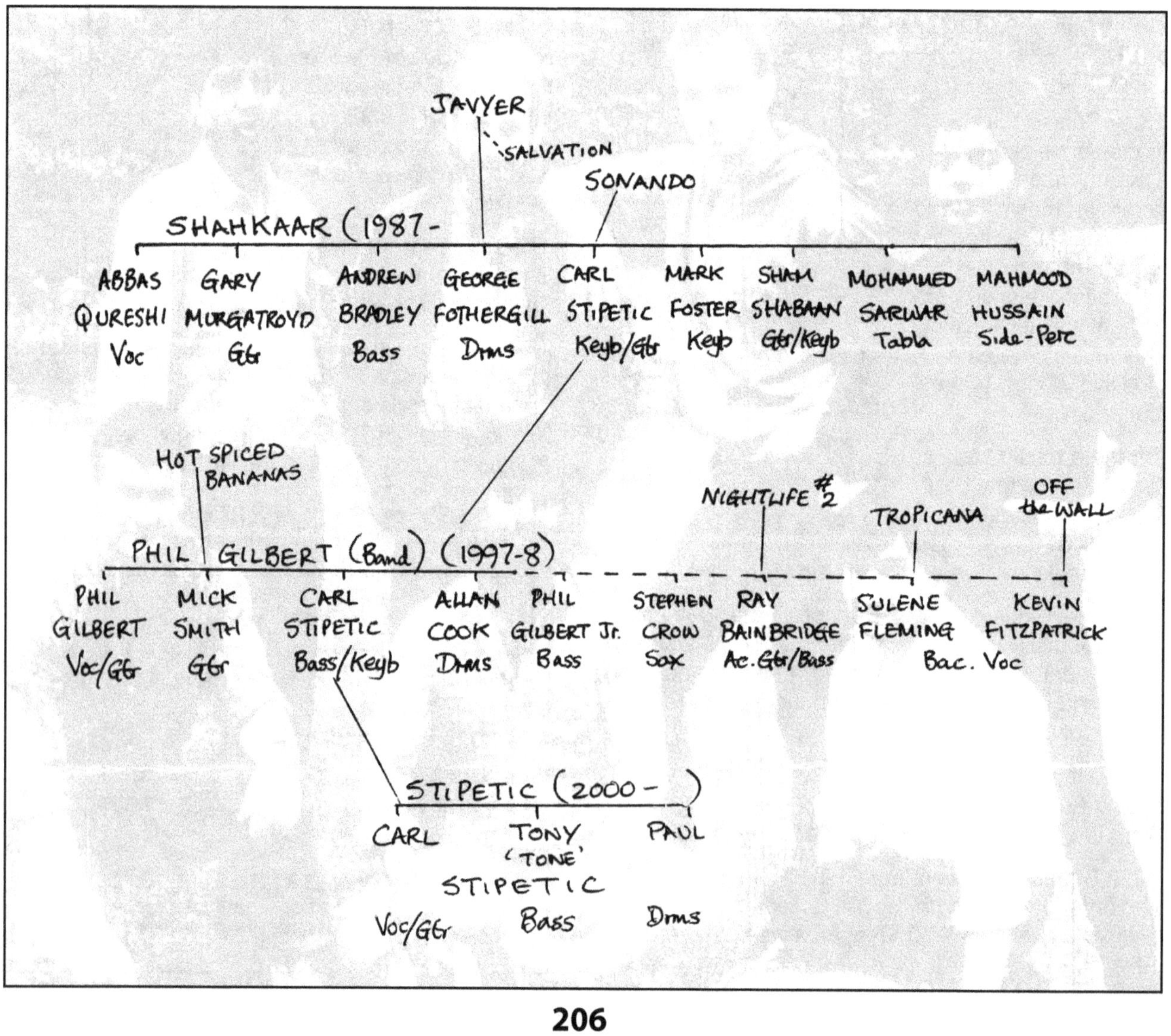

NASEEB

Naseeb were formed in 1990. They were originally a six-piece act which included four school friends, Maky, Malik, Saj and Sundeep, all from Lidget Green.

Their debut cassette album, *Break In The City*, became a best-selling cassette in Canada and topped the *Bhangra Beat* charts for eight weeks in 1992. Despite being very big in Bradford, they broke up that year due to family commitments.

In 1996, the original four Lidget Green lads reformed the band. They shot straight into the Bhangra charts with their new album, *Time*, after signing to Birmingham-based label Music Box.

They were soon working on a follow-up third album. They played a re-launch gig at the Horton Park Festival in August 1996, a celebration of Pakistan's Independence.

KARPAL SINGH

This local Bhangra musician, better known as 'Cowboy Karpal' was a self-employed furniture distributor.

In August 1991, Karpal invested £4,000 of his own money to produce the song *Bhangra Helps The Poor* for the *Save The Children* charity, after watching a news programme on the deprivation in India, Pakistan and Bangladesh.

The fundraising cassette song and accompanying video were played on Bhangra Beat and was available in local Asian outlets.

NACHDA PUNJAB

Performing for over thirty years, since 1977 this eight-piece Bhangra dance troupe were led by Dhol drummer Mangal Singh

As well as playing at a host of weddings and other events, the troupe played at most Bradford Festival Melas during their time.

With local group Royce, they appeared in the BBC2 drama Blood & Peaches which was set in Bradford. In 1999, Mangal was interviewed by the late DJ John Peel for his *Sounds Of The Suburbs* TV series on the Bradford music scene.

SANSAAR

This nine-piece Bradford/Leeds Bhangra band formed around 1995 and rehearsed at the Saathi Centre on Hallfield Road, off Lumb Lane.

In 1995, they released their debut 12" *Bind Us Together* on Rootsman's Third Eye Music label.

During the summer of 1996, besides playing that years Bradford Festival, the band appeared on television three times.

They performed live at the Royal Armouries

Museum in Leeds on June 14 for BBC's *Breakfast News Extra* and had previously been shown twice rehearsing and playing as part of the BBC's *Young Musician Of 96* series.

In 1999, a slimmed-down seven-piece lineup released the *Born And Bred* CD album on their own AMC Promotions label, based on White Abbey Road.

During the 1990s, Spice Entertainment, based at Sunrise House at the bottom of Leeds Road , promoted itself as *'the*

North's leading Bollywood entertainment company' and started the Asian Spice radio station.

Other Bhangra/Asian bands around Bradford in the 1990s were Naya Saaz, Spondon Shilpi Gusht, and Dhanak.

NATION RECORDS

Former Southern Death Cult drummer Aki Nawaz and local Bradford promoter Kath Canoville began the label in 1988, with offices in Notting Hill, London.

The label had been started because major record labels declined to release their *Fuse* compilation LP, a fusion of world music (including Bhangra) and dance music, and featured renowned UK Asian artist Talvin Singh.

Early signings to the label included Transglobal Underground, Loop Guru, Natacha Atlas and the London-based trio Asian Dub Foundation, whose debut LP *Facts And Frictions* came out in 1995.

The fusion of the sounds of Bhangra with hard rock/ heavy metal or dance, meant Asian artists could feel true to their own culture while being open to musical change.

Most of the UK's alternative Asian music scene would pass through Nation's offices at some point, and the label was at the forefront of creating the global world music scene.

Their encompassing attitude of *'no border controls at Nation'* gained them staunch support from the late DJ John Peel for their output of releases.

Kath left the label in 2001. It continued for several more years before it became an online entity, selling old stock.

FUNDAMENTAL

In 1991, Aki Nawaz formed the world music act Fundamental, taking musical influences from Asian Bhangra and Aki's punk rock past mixed with the new dance sound. From the outset, the band had a radical political message, with Aki's outspoken rants against Western Capitalist Imperialism being a strong feature of their material.

Fundamental's first releases on Nation Records were the 12-inches *Janaam / Righteous Preacher* and *Ghandi's Revenge / Azaan -The Calling*, both in 1992. The following year came two more 12"s; *Sista India / Wrath Of The Black Man* and *Countryman / Tribal Revolution*, before the release of their debut double LP *Seize The Time*.

While living with his young family in London, Aki still visited his home town of Bradford on a regular basis to see his parents and other family and friends.

Fundamental played the Bradford Mela at least twice and between 1994 and 2004. The band gigged all over the world and released eight more 12-inches and three LPs. These included *Dog Tribe* (1994), *Ja Sha Taan* (1997), *Why America Will Go To Hell* (1999), The *Last Gospel* (2002) and the LPs *Erotic Terrorism* (1998), *There Shall Be Love (2001)* and *Voices Of Mass Destruction* (2003).

DETRIMENTAL

A split-off from the original Fundamental in late 1991 brought Detrimental to life with the addition of Raj and Mian, the former rhythm section of local band (Boys From) The East. This new combo were firmly based in Bradford and managed by Stuart Firth.

Their debut 7" single/CD *Babylon* on Debt Records became the NME's single of the week in 1995. The single's controversially worded cover was banned and had to be covered up for sale in major retail record shops like HMV and Our Price.

FOLK & WORLD MUSIC 1988 - 1998

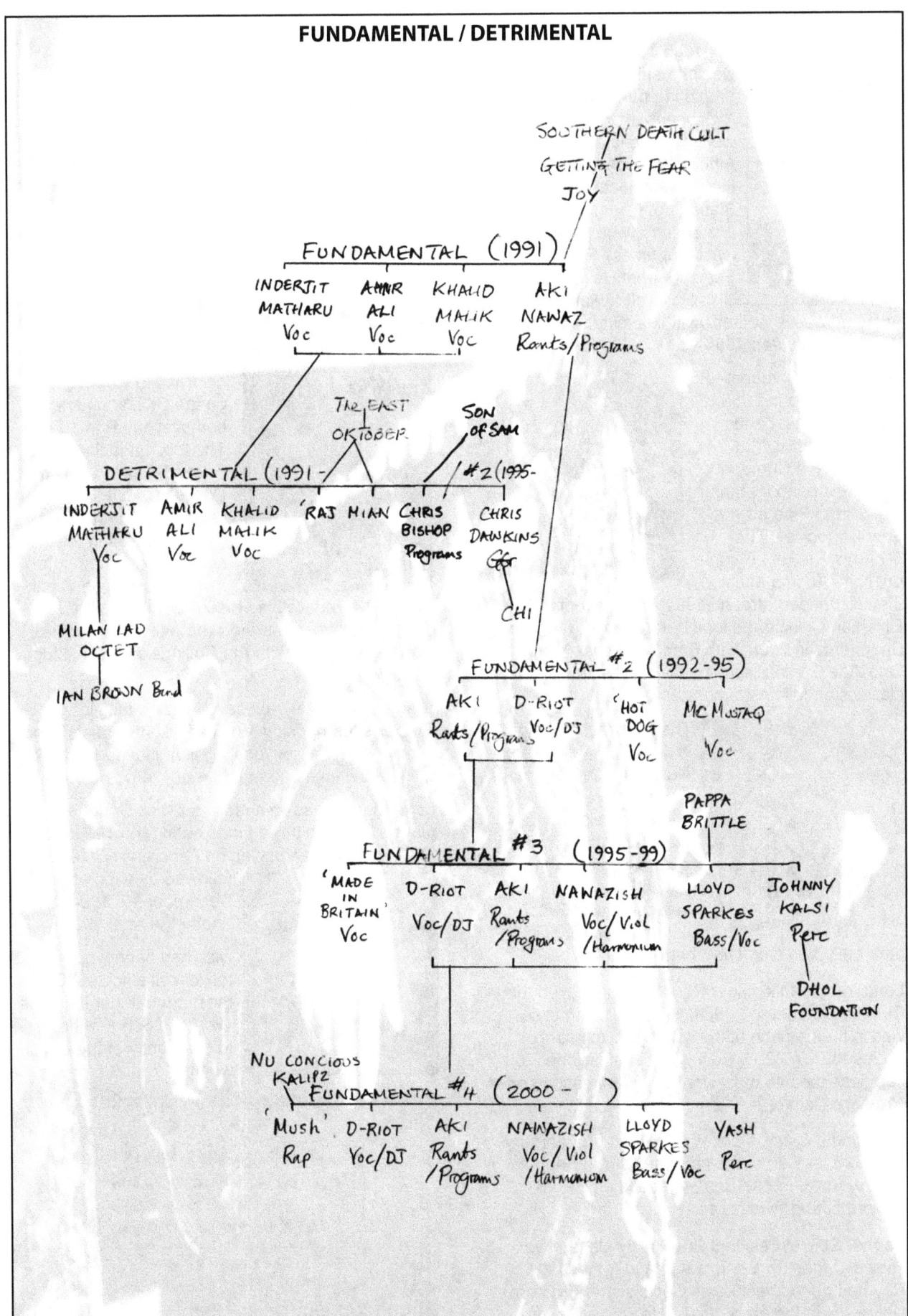

FOLK AT THE 1 IN 12 CLUB

Although The 1 In 12 Club was primarily known for promoting punk and indie-rock bands, many folk nights were organised at its new Albion Street building. Besides, the range of local acts like Black Spot Champions, Old Joe Zydeco (who played at least four times), The Dickie Bards, Scarlet Heights and Chis Halliwell & Mary Johnson (pictured above), other UK folk luminaries graced the stage between 1988-98.

During the first month of the building in 1988, two North-East bands played together. You Slosh were a Cumbrian Celtic folk band featuring the Uillean Pipe player Troy Donockley. Their Glorious Racket LP came out in 1989, and after they disbanded, around 1991, Troy first joined the Christian Celtic band Iona before forming The Bad Shepherds in 2008, with Bradford's own 'Young One' Ade Edmondson, to play punk/new wave classics on folk instruments.

The other act that night in July 1988 were from Durham. The Whiskey Priests played lively jigs and reels with lyrics about the mining communities of their North East. They released two 12 inch singles before their debut LP, Nee Gud Luck, came out in 1989.

London-born folk singer Rory McLeod played the Club on October 17, 1989. His storytelling style was in the tradition of the wandering minstrel or troubadour. In 2003, Rory was commissioned to compose the title music for the TV animation series Creature Comforts.

Folk singer Claire Mooney appeared on February 24, 1990, as part of the promotion for her debut album, Rocking The Boat, released on Big World Records the previous year.

Former Shipley resident Roy Bailey played two shows at the 1 In 12, in March and April 1990. Roy had been a lecturer in Sociology at Bradford University in the early 1970s. He was a regular performer over the years at the Topic Folk Club and his 1971 self titled LP on the Trailer folk label was very collectable.

Roy, as a renowned singer with a social conscience, played a gig on the theme or 'resistance' at the New Beehive in August 2000. The event was jointly organised by Bradford Resource Centre and the Topic Folk Club..

Robb Johnson was a regular visitor to the 1 In 12 during the 1990s and his track El Chorillo was on the Club's Volume 11 compilation LP in 1990. The folk magazine Rock N Reel (R2) called him 'the English Christy Moore', remarking on his gifted lyricism rooted in the heritage of contemporary England. His type of folk equally played well in traditional folk clubs or at any alternative gathering, whether playing solo or working as a duo with Pip Collings or with his full band.

Bradford's own two-piece folk/jazz outfit Not Precious, comprising Monica Hill on vocals/sax and Heather Bayliss on vocals/guitar, played the Club quite a few times during the early 1990s.

Legendary Glaswegian folkster Dick Gaughan played the Club three times during the 1990s. His first appearance was on February 17, 1993,

followed by a gig on December 10, 1994, and another in April 1998.

Dick had been working the folk circuit since 1970. His most popular number was Worker's Song - a homage to the dignity of the British working class.

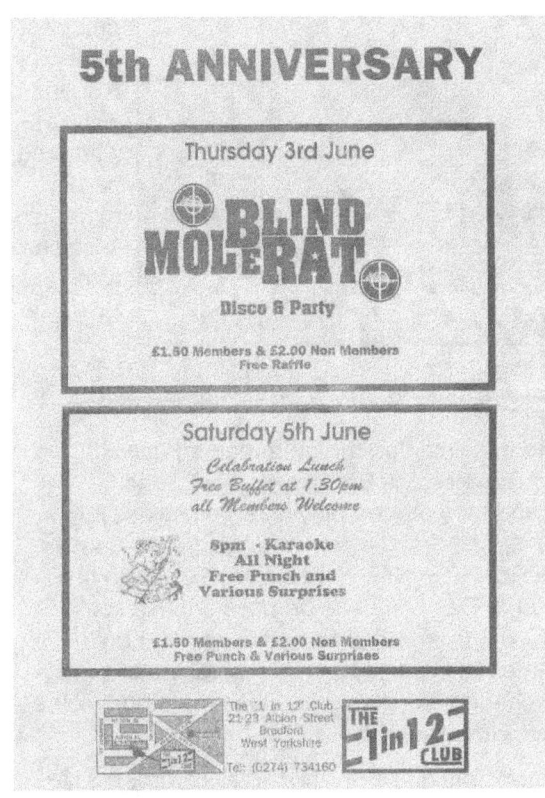

Sheffield's folk/ska-punk band Blind Mole Rat were regular visitors to the Club during the mid-1990s and their *Viva Zapata* cassette album is now very rare.

Swedish folk-punkers The Tequila Girls played at the Club a couple of times during the 1990s.

American folk singer Si Kahn played the 1 In 12 during September 1995. He was an influential activist in American civil rights and labour movements from the 1960s onwards.

Another American, Eugene Chadbourne, a free jazz guitar improviser, played on Monday, February 26, 1996.

Judy Small was an Australian folk singer who played the Club in November 1997, promoting her latest album *Out And Proud*.

JUDY SMALL Thursday 13th November 1997
Tickets £4 non-members £3 members
Australian singer and writer of some of the most powerful and political songs of our time, Judy pays Bradford a visit after headlining at the Raise Your Banners Festival in Sheffield. Having performed with Pete Seeger, Arlo Guthrie and Holly Near to name but a few, Judy is now promoting her first ever album of lesbian and gay songs tentatively entitled Judy Small - Out and Proud

Former Kitchenware Records artist Martin Stephenson and his new outfit The Toe-Rags presented *'an evening of stories, poems and hot music'* on February 27, 1998.

Punky London rockers The Men They Couldn't Hang, who had strong folk/country roots to their music, played on May 15, 1998.

Bradford lad and guitar virtuoso Brendan Croker (picturd above), with the help of drummer Roy Wyke, started regular monthly folk-jam sessions entitled Adventures In Rhythm (And Blues) on Wednesday nights during the late spring-summer of 1998.

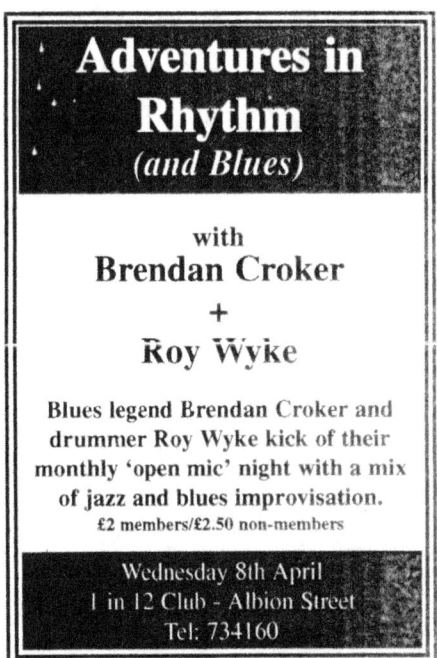

In October 1994, Thornton's *Bluegrass Club* celebrated its tenth anniversary at the Rock & Heifer Inn, with the Bronte Mountain Bluegrass Band.

DUFFY GIBBONS / EGOMANIA

Jon Gibbons came originally from Saddleworth but moved to Bradford in 1991.

He had been playing solo since 1983 and later in a folk band called Kashmir.

In 1989 he recorded an album called *9 Songs* at Thamesmead Studios in London before working with a couple of Irish musicians from London, James McNally (later of Afro Celt Sound System) and Tom McManamon (later of The Popes) in their band Storm.

In 1990 he returned to Saddleworth to play solo and in a garage band called Bikini Luv with a group of school friends.

While visiting a mate at Bradford University he ventured into The Peel and encountered a jam night where Denny Austin and Sean Dillon were playing. Jon and Sean then teamed up to play as a duo throughout 1992 as Dillon & Gibbons before Sean left to join The Palladinos.

In summer 1992, Jon met Nottingham

guitarist Ben Roberts with whom he began recording sessions with Ben's school friend Martin Cooper, who had his own 8-track studio, Sideways Sound, in Nottinghamshire.

Around this time Jon met and teamed up with former Somebody's Brother member John Duffy and they started playing together as Duffy Gibbons. The first gig with a full band line-up was at MacRory's on New Year's Eve 1993, with the addition of Dan McGlade on bass and Nelson of NMA on drums. The same lineup went on to complete the initial recording sessions and, with a name change to Egomania, finish the album *Paris Or New Orleans*.

The band continued alongside Duffy Gibbons as a duo, with various line-up changes, playing on a regular basis at local venues and further

re-view

DUFFY & GIBBONS DUO
MacRory's, Bradford

Duffy and Gibbons, a Bradfrod based duo who play on a regular basis at MacRorys Bar, surpassed all and their own high expectations on Old Year's Night by inviting potential band members, musician Dan McGlade on bass, Ben Roberts on lead guitar and Nelson on drums, who altogether managed to well and truly kick out 1993 and bring in 1994 with effusively expressed heart and soul felt music.

John Duffy, who is a proficient and barnstorming Bazouka player, also provides backing vocals which added the icing to John Gibbons' music. Gibbons, who is an overtly competent songwriter, singer and guitarist, tends to write songs which sound far too optimistic and balanced for some of the pessimistic punters down at MacRorys, yet by the end of the night the most hardened revellers were enthused by the energy and enthusiasm of the band. A couple of the songs written by Gibbons sit inside your head long after hearing, nagging away in that have heard it on an old Van album or Dylan tape feeling; then later you realise this is not the case and that Gibbons deserves more credit than he gets.

Although Duffy and Gibbons are excellent musicians, they plan to have the above band members alongside them for early '94 and I cannot envisage them continuing to play free entry pub gigs for long after, so while you can, get down to one of their sessions and find yourself listening to music that you will soon be wanting to pay to hear.

M O'Murchadha

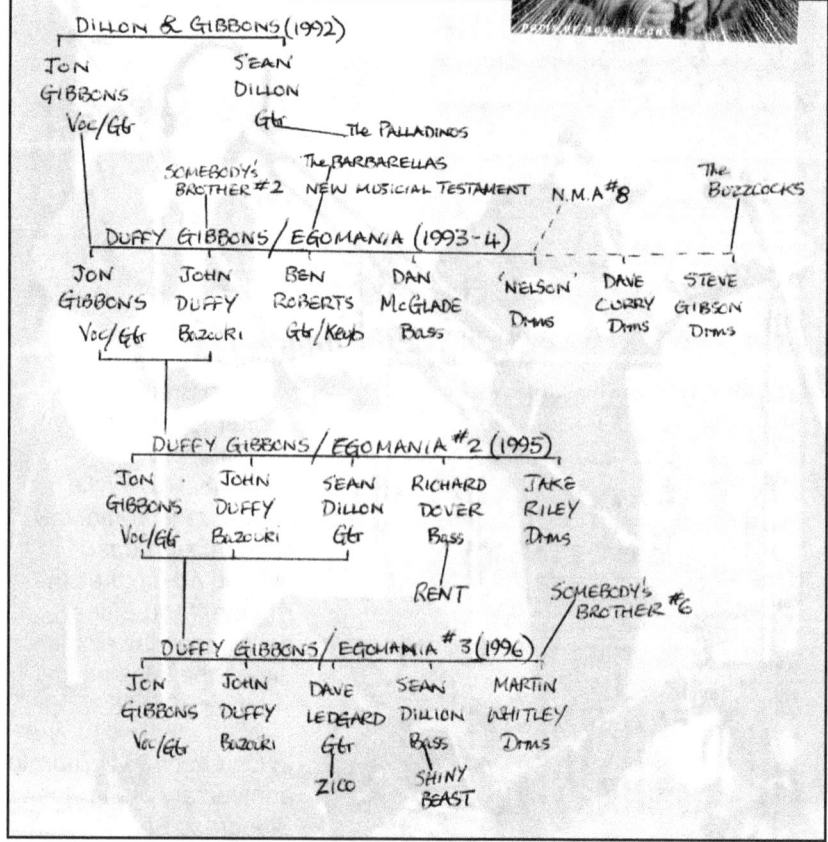

afield, including gigs in London and a support Dr Feelgood at Cleckheaton Town Hall in March 1996.

In October 2003, Duffy Gibbons reunited to play at the Melborn in honour of Liz from The Whitfield Family.

In April 2013 Duffy Gibbons played at a wedding reception and were joined on stage by Sean Dillon and Jake Riley, with Greg Brauns on guitar, after which they agreed to get together for some new recordings.

L'ORCHESTRE DU CAFE

L'Orchestre du Cafe was formed in 1996, and featured John Duffy on bouzouki and vocal, Yves Dumont on double bass and Martin Bond, who played accordion and violin and tarragot.

The group played a mixture of East European tunes and original compositions all around West Yorkshire.

The trio made a CD album, *The Old Cafe*, in 1998, which was recorded by Rob Heaton, partly live at MacRory's Bar and partly at Rob's attic studio, Righteous Sound.

John now fronts his own group, Duffy's Gypsy Band, based in Scotland and plays many festivals in the UK and Europe.

AVALON

Duffy also played in folk band Avalon during the 1990s. The four-piece was fronted by Liz Bray, with Mel Speak on vocals, Mags Fearne on accordion and Yves Dumont on bass.

SHINY BEAST

A band formed around the songs of singer/songwriter Paul 'Harris' Hennessy who played material largely from his previous bands Handful Of Dance, Nowt and Grim, along with new songs. Harris was joined by his cousin Sean Dillon on acoustic guitar, Bela Emerson on cello and John Gray on saxophone, sometimes accompanied by Greg Brauns on Djembe.

Beginning life as Sick Note, the band played an acoustic set at pubs and venues like MacRory's Bar where they were filmed and appeared interviewed and performing their song Your Paradise on the late-night ITV music show *Young Gifted And Broke* in March, 2000.

Shiny Beast had two tracks, *Ed Wood* and *Watching Rain*, featured on the first Mutiny 2000 compilation album, White Abbey Road, in 2000.

TOOTH FAIRY

The duo of John Gray on saxophone and Bela Emerson on cello were well known around the Bradford music scene when they were based here, from the mid-90s onwards, as part of, or guests with various bands. They played instrumentals of various classics like *Eleanor Rigby*, *Take Five* and *It's Only A Paper Moon* around bars and cafes and clubs.

In February 1998, they recorded a cassette album of songs, *Tooth Fairy*, at In A City Studios.

JAZZ

Jazz, and its close relation, the blues were the only 'original' folk music forms that developed in the USA just before the beginning of the 20th Century.

Blues had emerged from around the Mississippi Delta. The descendants of black slaves imported the syncopated rhythms and vocal resonances of their West African heritage and mixed them with the sound of the field workers in the South's cotton fields. By the time it filtered down to the city of New Orleans, it had blended with the existing European musical sounds and military brass band noises to metamorphosise into the early 'Dixieland' jazz sound that could be heard in the riverside brothels and bars around Basin Street, New Orleans.

Through the growing expertise of local musicians like Jelly Roll Morton, Bunk Johnson, King Oliver and a young Louis Armstrong (pictured), this new music form moved north to Chicago, Kansas City and New York, and from the 1920s to the 1940s became the dominant and highest form of cultural expression of North America.

In the UK, jazz first appeared in 1919, just after the Great War, in the form of the all white American Original Dixieland Stompers. By the end of World War Two, big band jazz (Glen Miller/Tommy Dorsey/ Benny Goodman etc) was fast becoming the accepted sound of the British dance hall bands like Henry Hall, Jack Parnell, etc.

During the 1950s, while local rock'n'roll outfits were first starting out, Bradford was already part of the nationwide network for one-nighter jazz combos. As the late George Melly recalls in his 1965 book *Owning Up*. (10)

From the 1960s onwards, there were always a few traditional jazz ensembles in and around Bradford, seemingly playing regular weekly gigs, such as the Gordon Tetley Band and the Hammond Chop Sauce Band, at venues like the Dubrovnik Hotel in Manningham.

Bradford's own little-known jazz vocal diva, Barbara Moore, had grown up surrounded by jazz as her father played in many of Yorkshire's big dance bands during the 1940s/50s. Barbara became an in-demand session singer and was acknowledged as *'one of the UK's wickedest scat jazz vocalists around,'* during the 1960s/70s. She appeared on numerous albums, and also released a few highly collectable Music Library LPs, like *Headline* and *Vocal Shades And Tones*.

In May 1988, on Monday nights, jazz gigs were organised by Four Square Jazz at the Steelers pub in Thornton village.

Around early 1994, there was a trio of jazz swingers based in the Keighley/Skipton area called Swing Parisienne.

SWING PARISIENNE (1994-		
MARTIN LITTLEWOOD Gtr	CRAIG JOHNSON Gtr	KURT HARPER Bass

The New Bradford Jazz Club, organised by Dudley Firth, was putting on concerts at the Pennington's Midland Hotel in Forster Square during the summer of 1995. On Saturday, August 19, Bristol's highly rated Tulane Jazz Band appeared there, led by Pete Child, who had formed the initial band back in 1960.

On October 22, 1995, a new Bradford modern jazz club, The Blackhole Club, opened at Windsor Baths with opening act saxophonist Andy Sheppard..

ASHA BREWER TRIO

Talented Menston saxophonist Asha Brewer was the youngest (at 15) to get to the semi-finals of the Yorkshire TV *Jazz Player Of The Year* in 1994. By 1996, she was fronting her own trio and playing with older musicians. That Easter Sunday, they did a 'brunchtime' gig at the Farsyde Cafe in Back Grove, Ilkley.

ASHA BREWER TRIO (1996-		
ASHA BREWER Voc/Sax	WAYNE CLARKE Gtr	GARY SIMON Bass

MILAN LAD

Bradford's pioneering jazz fusion guitarist Milan Lad released his debut CD album *Dreams* on the Small World Records label in 1995. It was recorded at the Red Fort Studios in London and included some of Britain's greatest exponents of jazz fusion at that time, like Leeds-born drummer Gary Husband (who'd played in Bradford guitarist Alan Holdsworth's I.O.U. band), saxophonist Andy Shepard and fellow guitarist Jim Mullen of Morrisey-Mullen.

The album was also co-produced by former Simply Red bassist and band member Sylvan Richardson Jr.

The tracks *Dreams, No Entry/No Exit,* and *Rainy Season,* from the album had originally been commissioned by Yorkshire & Humberside Arts and Kirklees Cultural Services.

Despite suffering from muscular dystrophy and being in a wheelchair, Milan toured the UK in 1996 to promote the album. He and his band played at Bradford's Windsor Baths on March 13, 1995.

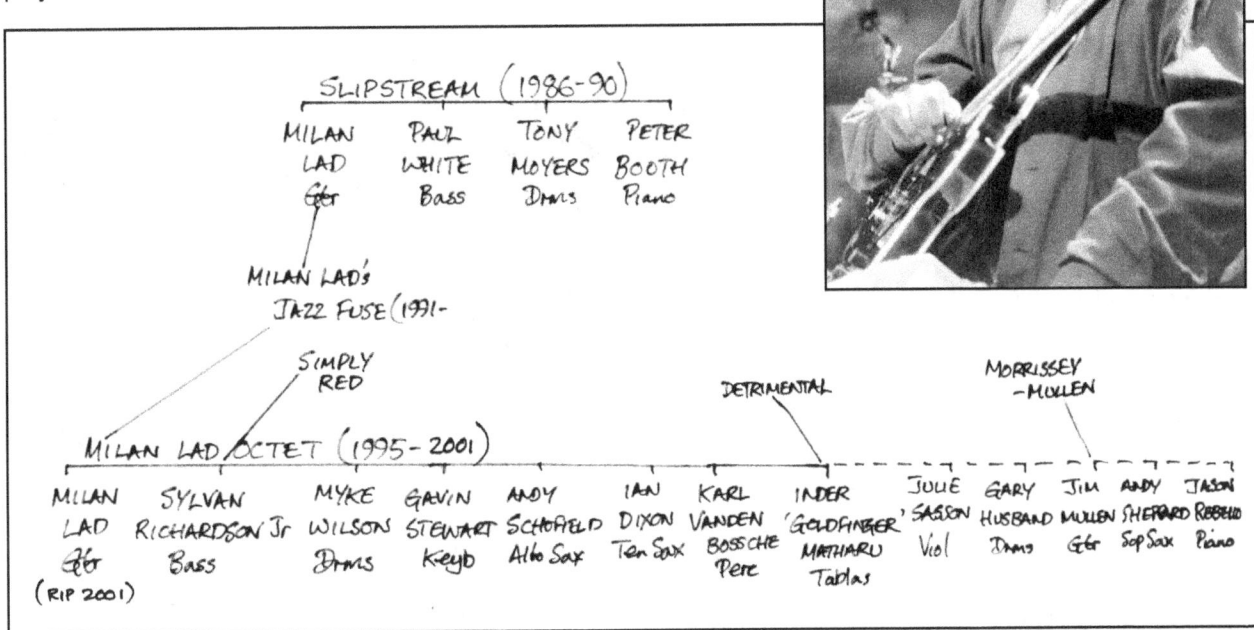

CAJUN ACES

Formed after the demise of Old Joe Zydeco, the Cajun Aces were the first British band to play the famous Liberty Theatre in Eunice, Louisiana, where the band sang in French to a capacity crowd who erupted in wild aclaim. That show was also broadcast live on the local radio station.

Their first release was the 1994 CD *Chere Joues Roses*.

It was followed in 1997 by the release of *Full Hand* on their own Pinegrove Records label in CD and cassette formats, which got a favourable review in the folk magazine *Rock'n'Reel (R2)*.

Besides gigging locally and around the UK, they played in the US and France and appeared at the Shetland Folk Festival in 1999.

CRONE

A Bradford four-piece who recorded their debut album Talk To Me in 1994, before performing their first ever live performance at that year's Glastonbury Festival. They played the festival's green field site, where all power was from alternative energy sources; wind, solar and pedal power.

The group were *'not really a gigging band, we will be doing one-off special gigs, but we don't just want to get on the pub scene playing background music,'* said guitarist Dominic Brown. (11)

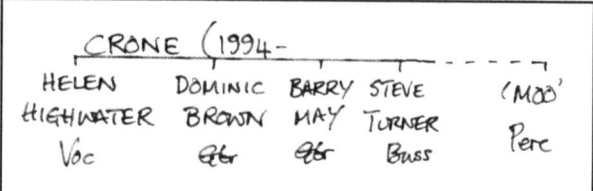

LOOBIE

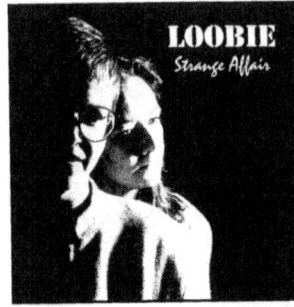

An Ilkley based folk outfit who released a CD called *Strange Affairs* in 1996, which was recorded at Leeds' Tube Studios and co-produced by the band and Jon Strong.

They had started out as an informal two piece of Lorna and Mairead, before augmenting to a trio then a five piece.

Lorna, who hails from Liverpool originally, had previously sung with the folk-rock blues group Joe's Cafe, while Mairead had a background in Irish folk, having played with Oisin for several years.

They performed at the Topic Folk Club as well as various colleges and festivals, including *Edinburgh Festival Fringe Club* in 1994 and 1995.

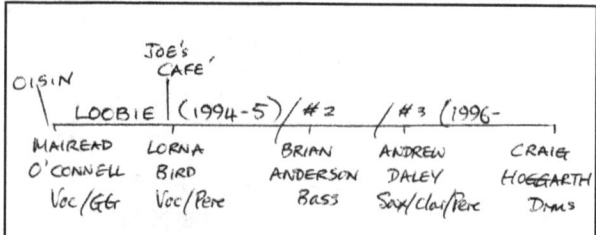

JON HARVISON

Keighley singer/songwriter Jon Harvison played the Topic Folk Club at its latest venue, The Melborn on White Abbey Road, in September 1995. He started writing his own compositions in 1975 while at college but didn't resume his singing career till 1988.

Influenced by English traditional music, he recorded a cassette of his own material called *Dance With Me* and was compared to folk troubadour Roy Harper.

FIONA-KATIE ROBERTS

A multi-talented harpist from Oxenhope who had a unique style of playing and took audiences by storm whenever she performed. Fiona-Katie had started out as a pianist, playing everything from Genesis to opera in pubs, before her husband found her a small harp. Within a few weeks, she had mastered it and was making her first public performance.

Since 1995, she has performed with a wide variety of artists from East Morton pianist John Briggs, to folk groups Alchemy, Loobie and Maggie Boyle, Steve Tilston and Irish band Wild Geese.

'She does not simply pluck the strings, she hammers them, strums them and drums them, her fingers on the harp's sound box her fast-moving hands almost a blur at times.' (12)

As well as performing at events all over the country, she went on to perform with the likes of Led Zeppelin and Guns 'n' Roses. She played in Benjamin Till's *Symphony For Yorkshire*, which was broadcast by the BBC on *Yorkshire Day* in 2010.

PHIL GILBERT

Singer-songwriter Phil Gilbert, from Austin, Texas, USA, was so in love with Bradford that he recorded an album here, named after his favourite Bradford cafe.

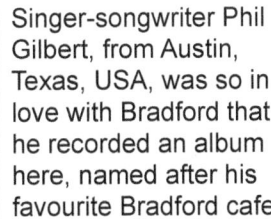

The album, *Britannia Coffee Lounge*, was named after the well known coffee shop (sadly now a mobile phone shop) and was recorded at Carl Stipetic's In A City Studios.

He used experienced guest musicians who had previously played in Bradford bands including Hot Spiced Bananas, Nightlife, Off The Wall and Tropicana, including Ray Bainbridge (above, left), former lead guitarist of Fresh Garbage, who were the winners of the *T&A* sponsored *Now Group Of 1970*.

Carl Stipetic played keyboards and other instruments on the album and Phil's son, Phil junior played on bass on some tracks.

The album was co-produced by Phil Gilbert and local guitarist Mick

Smith, who also played on the album (pictured above).

Released in 1997, on the Texas label Voodoo Children Records, the album featured songs ranging from blues and country to full-on rock, including the track *Gideon Here* which is on CD 8 of the CD box set that accompanies this book.

MILLTOWN PRODUCTIONS

A Bradford promotions company based in Little Germany in 1996, who were *'trying to promote New Country and get away from the old image of Country'n'Western. We're using the concert at Ilkley's King's Hall on Saturday July 6 entitled 'The Other Side Of Country' as a pilot and if all goes well, we hope to get an American band over and go on tour,'* said Milltown's Ian Smith (13).

Headlining the gig was rising Pudsey country-rock performer Stu Page and his band, soon to release the album *Can't Sing The Blues*. Supporting acts on the night were the Harrogate group The Dean Brothers and Glasvegan singer Janette Sommers.

Saturday, June 7, 1997, saw the start of a nine-day-long Keighley Festival Feast Of Folk, which featured former 1960s Incredible String bands's singer/guitarist Robin Williamson at the town's Victoria Hall, with support on the night from local Silsden-based singer Janet Russell.

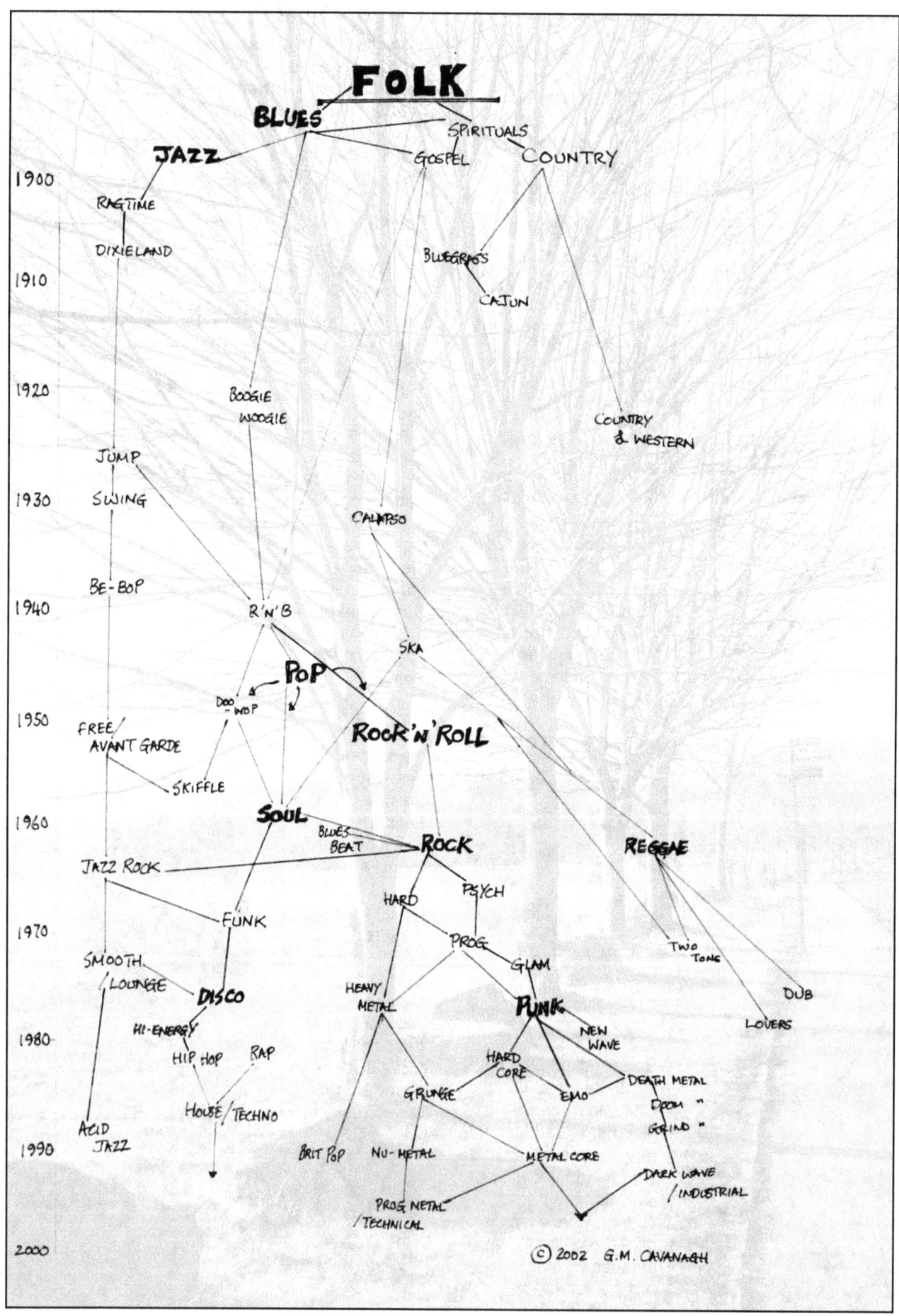

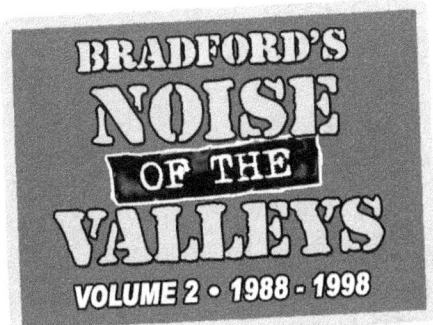

CHAPTER 6: 1994 - 1996

Gigs are the lifeblood for any band starting out. As the mid-1990s approached, there was a change in the number and style of venues available for original bands to play. Long-lived venues like The Royal Standard, the Queen's Hall and the University's Communal Building either disappeared completely or fundamentally changed their focus from live music to nightclub-based events.

The only regular live music venues around at this time, apart from the pub and club circuit, were The 1 In 12 Club, the fading Queen's Hall and the live venue and rock club Rio's, which had a strong focus on the night club side as well.

D:REAM

Bradford lad Simon Ellis joined the second incarnation of this dance-pop outfit in 1993, then, in January 1994, their re-released single *Things Can Only Get Better*, shot straight to the top of the charts. It charted again in may 1997 at number nineteen, when Tony Blair's 'New' Labour Party used the tune as the theme to their general election campaign.

During February, American singer and drinking buddy of the late John Lennon, Harry Nilsson (below) died, within a week his 1972 UK number one single *Without You* was back at number one with a version by Mariah Carey, and Harry's original re-issue got to number forty-seven. The song had originally been written by UK songwriters Pete Ham and Tommy Evans of the band Badfinger, tragically both men hung themselves in 1975 and 1983 respectively.

BRIT POP

Perhaps the last new genre to emerge in the 1990s was Brit Pop, a term coined by *NME* writer and future Radio 2 DJ Stuart Maconie

to explain the likes of Blur, Oasis, Pulp, Elastica, Catatonia, Supergrass, Suede and Menswear's assault on the British pop charts during the mid-1990s.

In 1995, the two heavyweights of the scene, Oasis and Blur, battled it out for the number one spot with Blur's single *Country House* winning out over Oasis's *Roll With It*.

The majority of the Brit pop bands had been around on the Indie scene for a few years, prior to having mainstream chart success, such as Sheffield band Pulp who had been around since 1978 and had played in Bradford at The 1 In 12 Club in the 1980s.

Brit Pop encompassed the sound of sixties bands like The Kinks, The Small Faces, with a heavy dose of The Beatles and the sensibilities and attitude of seventies punk and new wave bands and the more recent Madchester scene.

NORTHERN MUSIC CO

Local promoter and former Living Dead vocalist Andy Farrow parted company with Far North Music to form his new company Northern Music in 1994.

Amongst the bands under his management were Paradise Lost, and Slammer, and later he had big international acts like Opeth and Katatonia.

EMBRACE

Wyke brothers Danny and Richard McNamara brothers started rehearsing in 1990 and played their first gig as Embrace in 1993.

The band recorded two demo tapes prior to releasing their first single. The first contained three tracks, *Sooner Than You Think / Say It With Bombs / Overflowing*.

The second demo contained a track which was given a compilation tape with a Leeds fanzine.

Their first single was *All You Good Good People*, released on Fierce Panda Records in February 1997.

The followed a series of EPs including *Fireworks, One Big Family, Come Back To What You Know*, tracks from which went on to appear on their debut album *The Good Will Out*, which came out in June 1998 and reached number one in the UK album charts.

Former Poppy Factory, Kitsch and Cud keyboard player Mickey Dale officially joined Embrace after the first album was released although he had been playing live and on record with the band before that.

In March 2000 their second album, *Drawn From Memory*, got to number 8. On the tour to promote the album they were supported by Coldplay.

After their third LP, *If You've Never Been*, was released in 2001 and, despite it reaching number 9 and going down well with the critics, the band were dropped by EMI's Hut Records.

In 2004 Coldplay's Chris Martin, who had become friends with the band since supporting them years before, gave them the song *Gravity* which they released as a single that became a number 7 hit in the UK charts.

The subsequent album, *Out Of Nothing*, came out on Independiente Records, owned by former Go! Discs Records founder Andy McDonald, and went on to become the bands second UK number one album.

Their 2006 album, *This New Day* became their third to top the charts and the lead single, *Nature's Law* entered the charts at number two and was the band's highest-charting single.

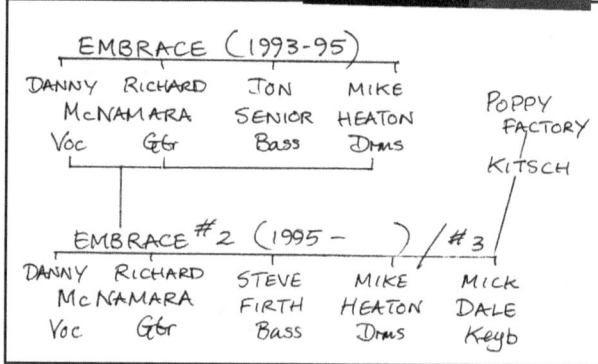

The next single from the album was England's official song for the 2006 World Cup, *World At Your Feet*, which reached number 3.

To date Embrace have had 16 top 30 singles and five studio albums, three of which reached number one in the UK.

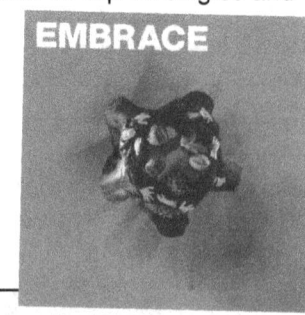

The band returned to recording in 2013, working on their first new album for seven years.

EMBRACE

96	Fierce Panda NING 29	All You Good Good People/My Weakness Is None Of Your Business (p/s, 1,300 only, not numbered)	10
96	Fierce Panda NING 29	All You Good Good People/My Weakness Is None Of Your Business (p/s, 1,300 only, numbered)	15
98	Hut HUTLH 128 103	My Weakness Is None Of Your Business/Feelings Through You Shared (Jukebox issue)	5
98	BBC BOX SET	EMBRACE EP'S (6 x 12"s in black box, numbered, 100 only)	100
99	Hut HUTDX 103/CD 109	ABBEY ROAD SESSIONS (2xCD gatefold, one CD mail-order from fanclub)	30

THE BASEMENT CLUB

Previously known as W's, the Basement Club, on Great Horton Road, put on various nights during the early to mid-'90s, including Griff's Magic Theatre on Tuesdays, a rock/punk/indie night by DJ Linda Sprogis, a punk rock gig night on Thursday nights as well as various other gigs.

THE MOTORVATORS

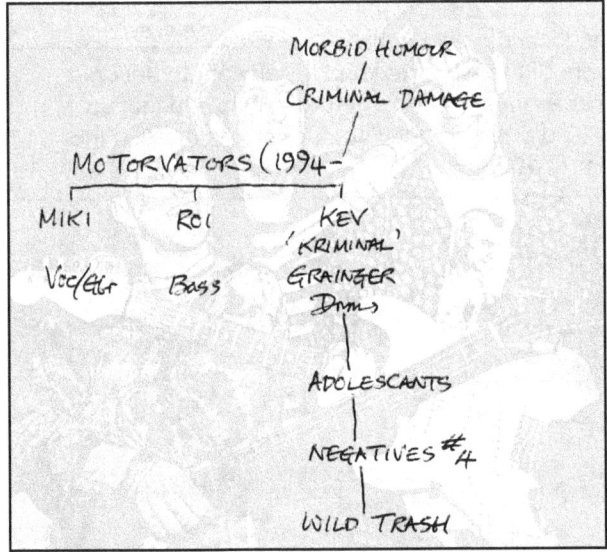

Former Morbid Humour drummer Kev Grainger was joined by mates Miki and Roi on guitar and bass to form this local 'old skool' style punk rock band. They played an early gig at The Basement Club's Thursday punk night.

Kev later had a spell as vocalist in a lineup of the reformed Bradford punk legends The Negatives from 2003 and 2004. He later sang for Wild Trash.

MR MAK

Pop group Mr Mak (pictured right) had within their line-up three ex-pupils of Buttershaw School, so they played a gig especially at their old school to raise money to help buy musical equipment for the pupils.

In 1997, the group changed their name to Daisy Cutter.

PSYCHE

Psyche formed in 1994, after the demise of local pop act Secret People, who had a 1987 single, *China*, on Jive Records. This new band had a more rock-oriented sound.

In late 1994, they self-released the *Psy Complex* CD on their own Flux Records label, a twelve-song affair recorded partly at the Pots'N'Pans Studios, off Manchester Road.

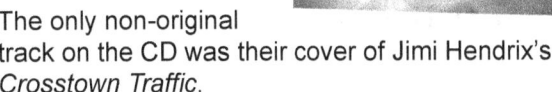

The only non-original track on the CD was their cover of Jimi Hendrix's *Crosstown Traffic*.

NAVAHO UK

This rock quartet from Ilkley were a bunch of students who beat more than fifty other school and college bands from all over Yorkshire to qualify for the *Vicious Sound Competition* of 1994.

They played at the finals in July, held at Leeds' Town & Country Club.

NOWT / GRIM

Nowt were formed by previous members of Handful Of Dance. They had a quirky mix of guitars, mandolin, flute, bass and percussion and delivered original songs with a wry look at life.

After well-received gigs on the local circuit Nowt played a 'final' gig at Palm Cove on May 21, 1994, supported by Primate and Dub Kitchen, although different lineups of the band would play again in 1995.

Having become disillusioned with the local gig circuit three members of the band decided to relocate to become based in Prague in the Czech Republic and join up with former Zed bassist Jont who had moved there in the summer of 1993.

The four would actually perform as two bands with two different sets, as Zed in the bigger venues and Nowt for smaller clubs and acoustic sets.

NOWT LIVE AT MacRORY'S BAR

LAST Wednesday MacRory's Bar played host to one of Bradford's newest and most orignal groups - Nowt.

At first I was wondering where the band was until a bunch of dodgy looking characters who were cluttering up the bar pick up their instruments and begin to play.

Their unasuming stance hides a wide array of talent; the five-piece outfit features Mark Keane on bass, Jeremy the Thug on drums and vocals, Walshy plays flute and sings, and the lead vocals, guitar and mandolin are shared between Harris and Benson.

Formed by ex-members of Handful of Dance and Zed, Nowt are difficult to pigeonhole, moving from plaintive ballads like His Eyes to funky dance or folk influenced tracks such as Your Paradise or Dance Police.

Their songwriting and performance is confident and entertaining, the lyrics are generally wry comments on life seeped in black humour, - as in Dino Rod, a song about serial killer Dennis Neillson, 'Killing for company, what a nice man, boils up the bodies in bits in a pan, hope I don't know what goes on in your brain, didn't get caught 'til you blocked the drains.' - all of which ads up to a band well worth going to see.

So next time Nowt's happening - be there!

PETE JAMES

They band played many gigs in Czech, including a support to Therapy? at the packed 2,000-capacity Tam Tam Club in June 1994. They were based and rehearsed at the notorious Repre Rok Klub, in the heart of Prague in a cellar bar beneath a famous landmark building, Obecne Dum. When the club was shut down, guitarist Adam Bennett broke several ribs after falling from a DJ stand at the closing night party and had to play their next few shows in agony!

As the band were planning a relocation to Croatia drummer Matt Webster broke his foot and the band were forced to cancel shows and return to the UK.

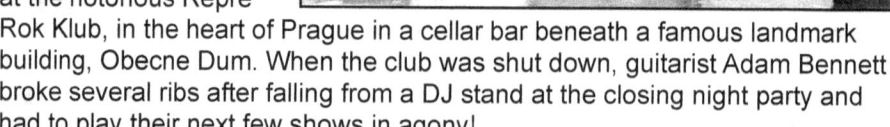

After their return to Bradford they reformed as Grim in 1995. With a new set they started playing gigs in London and around the local area until vocalist Harris left to join former Zed members Nogsy and Jez, and former Nowt bassist Boz in their new band Slack. The last Grim gig was a New Year's Eve warehouse party in 1995, in Amsterdam, as a three-piece.

The band teamed up infrequently after that for various recording sessions although a proposed Grim album was left unfinished Their track Grim appeared on the White Abbey Road compilation album in 2000.

The various members teamed up on numerous future recording and live projects, including a new version of Zed, The Horton Carpets, Moota, The Psurgeons, Signia Alpha and others.

Tragically, Adam Bennett died in 2012.

CHAPTER 6   1994 - 1996

Wednesday, April 6, 1994
Telegraph & Argus

WEEKEND *Planner* — 5

ROCK & pop

Why three rockers are quitting the city music scene and heading for Prague

LIVE DATES: *Guitarist Adam Bennett, drummer Matt Webster and guitarist Harris who are heading for Prague in May*

Czech mates to band together

by SIMON ASHBERRY

Three rock musicians are quitting the Bradford music scene for a new life in Prague.

They have left their old bands to form a new outfit in the Czech capital in May.

Drummer Matt Webster and guitarist Adam Bennett, formerly of the group Primate, and ex-Zed guitarist/vocalist Harris will be teaming up with former Zed frontman Jont who is already in Prague setting up tours of the Czech Republic and Germany for the summer.

The new group will be called God.

"I went over to Prague in January for a couple of weeks and found it a fascinating place to be," said Matt.

"The music scene here is dead at the moment. There's much more of an audience for live music in Czech, and due to the success of the Zed and Psycho Surgeons tours over the past few years we are set up with a lot of gigs to play as soon as we get there."

Adam, Harris and Matt also make up three fifths of popular Bradford band Nowt who will continue to play locally until the trio's departure.

● Vocalist Liam Sheeran and guitarist Stephen Andrews, the remaining members of Primate, are now looking for new recruits after deciding to continue with the band in Bradford.

Primate, who have been featured several times on Radio 5's Hit The North show, are on the look-out for a new bass guitar player and a drummer. For the moment they have enlisted the services of temporary members Mick Barrett and drummer Tony Fox.

Anyone interested should contact Gina Lambert on Bradford 621609.

● Primate's next live appearance will be at Scruffs and Snobs in Listerhills Road, Bradford, on April 27.

IN PRAGUE: *Ex-Zed vocalist/bassist Jont*

Aurora play in the sun

Don't be surprised if rockers Aurora look more tanned than usual — they have just returned from a five-week stint performing in Lanzarote.

The band played six nights a week at the Hard Rock Cafe, where the audience was made up of a mixture of locals and largely German and British tourists.

There was also a guest appearance by Def Leppard singer Joe Elliott — on drums!

But Aurora are now looking for a permanent new guitarist to replace Kes, from Beggars Bones, who has been filling in for about a year. Anyone interested should ring Iain Angus on Bradford 634885.

NEW LOOK: *Maguires*

Gig marks 25 years

Veteran folk musician Vin Garbut has chosen Bradford as the venue for a gig celebrating 25 years in the business.

He will be performing on May 29 at Maguires in City Road, Bradford, which has recently been refurbished with the theme of Irish music and Irish writers.

Sound of silence

A new Bradford band is struggling to make itself heard because of a deafening silence from rock venues.

Five-piece Vengeance, who play mostly light rock cover versions including songs by Bryan Adams and Bon Jovi, are now on the look-out for any pubs or clubs who will give them a booking.

"A lot of places have come back to us and said we should try again when we've done five or six gigs but we can't get those first bookings," said Mick Kevern.

Anyone who can help should ring him on Bradford 619741.

Hi-tech switch

Electronic music fan Graham Spence hopes to generate interest in bands like Kraftwerk, Tangerine Dream and Jean Michel Jarre in West Yorkshire.

The Harrogate-based musician used to be in a conventional rock group but has now switched to synthesiser sounds and is trying to gauge how much interest there is in his style of music in the Bradford and Leeds area. He can be contacted on (0423) 771440.

ALBUMS: *Loud was fronted by Chris McLaughlin*

Pair make a move

Two former well-known musical colleagues on the Bradford rock scene are launching new band projects.

Bassist Martin Hawthorn and vocalist Chris McLaughlin, who played together in Loud are both looking to recruit new musicians.

Chris, who also brought out two albums as frontman of Loud, has teamed up with drummer Ricky Howard and written an album's worth of new material.

The new band — as yet without a name — sounds like quite a change in direction for Chris, who has previously been associated with hard-edged alternative rock.

His latest stuff is influenced by the Beatles, Jellyfish, Wonder Stuff and Crowded House.

"I'll be playing acoustic guitar. The power is still going to be there but it's a bit more melodious," said Chris.

Any bass players interested in joining the line-up should contact him on Bradford 835481 or Ricky on Bradford 882558.

Meanwhile, Martin has linked up with drummer Ainsley, live keyboard player Carter and guitarist Paul Solynskyj to form a new band following the demise of PADD.

He is now on the look-out for a vocalist for the group, which is also unchristened.

"It's a bit like PADD but it's moved on a lot. The new sound has got a lot more keyboards in it," he said.

Anyone interested in auditioning can ring Martin on Bradford 664660.

223

TINY MONROE

Former Skrytch and JJ's Bones singer Norma 'NJ' Wilow moved to London in 1988 and played guitar for indie band Thrill, before forming Tiny Monroe in 1993.

Their first single *VHF855V / Under The Skin* was named after the registration plate of NJ's first car and released on limited edition vinyl in 1994 by manager Howard Gough's Laurel Records label.

The band featured heavily in the NME and Melody Maker and were vaunted as part of the female fronted indie band explosion at the time, alongside the likes of Sleeper and Elastica.

The Cream EP (Cream Bun / Jealousy / Brittle Bones / Sonic Blue) followed, also on Laurel, and reached no 7 in the indie charts.

That summer Tiny Monroe played the festival circuit including Hultsfred Festival in Sweden, as well as at Reading, T In The Park and Glastonbury, where their live performance impressed DJ John Peel.

'For much of the weekend I was playing the platters that matter on the NME stage, so missed most of the big names. Heartbreaking, but my pain was eased by the music I heard on the final day of the festival. The bands featured in the early part of the afternoon were what I think of as Radio 1 Evening Session bands: hard and new staples of the music weeklies' gossip pages, image conscious, fashionable, confident and pretty, sometimes even good.'

'The singer with Tiny Monroe, the first of these bands, strolled past our dishevelled caravan. She is, she told me when the spirit of research sent me flying across the grass, called NJ. NJ is, let me tell you, a wildly charismatic performer and Tiny Monroe live are much more robust than Tiny Monroe on record.'

They also supported Curve, Radiohead, The Pretenders and Suede.

After a gap in releases and line-up changes Tiny Monroe finally released their debut album *Volcanoes* in 1996, also on Laurel. The album included the two earlier singles and offered two more releases; *She / The Party's Over / Really Happy* and the final single, *Open Invitation / Another Station / Mirror*.

NJ also played the part of an alien in the BBC film *The Traveller*.

Norma moved to the Canary Islands where she formed an international group and had several solo releases including the CD albums *Indian Ocean* (2004), *Goodbye Rock'N'Roll* (2005) and *The Cyber Cafe* (2006).

She also worked on a cultural magazine for the Canary Islands, called *Ruido*.

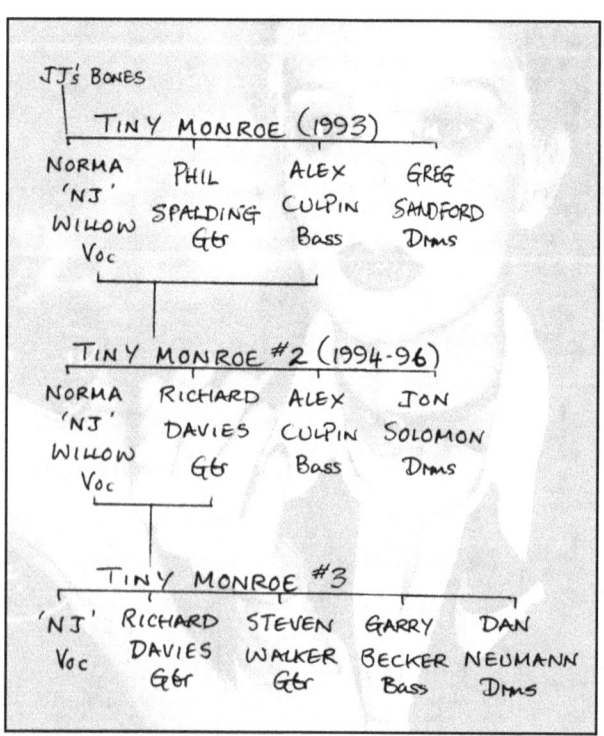

SUMMUM BONUM

This band were another young Bradford four-piece, who formed in early 1994. Their name was from the Latin, *summon bonum* - meaning blessedness or height of goodness.

After sending a demo to London-based Freek Records, they were offered a one single/one album deal.

As vocalist/guitarist Nick recounts, *'I just saw an advert by this label in called Freek Records in Melody Maker and I was very impressed because they had some underground bands that we thought were really good. It was like a dream, until we saw the artwork for the single we didn't believe it was happening.'*

The band's debut 7-inch single, *Song For Gary*, came out in July 1994 and the label reckoned the band sounded *'...like Sonic Youth, Pavement and Nirvana shaking hands with The Smiths while smugly scoffing at the New Wave of New Wave. Some of their stuff is pop, some of it's punk. It's a real mish-mash of experimental styles.'* (1)

Their *David Danson* album was recorded at Woodhouse Mobile Studios in Leeds and came out on CD in that year's late summer. It included a guest appearance by The Ukrainians (side project of members of Wedding Present) mandolin player Peter Solowka on the track *Sniper*.

Summon Bonum (Jan 1994 -
Nick Mitchell	Richard 'Billy' Bailey	Richard Corney	Dave Patel	Peter Solowka
Voc/Gtr	Drums	Gtr/Voc	Bass Sax	Mandolin

Scaramanga

RIPCORD

This young Britpop outfit formed in July 1994. They released their own three track *Ripcord* CD EP: *Runaways / As Funny Folk Might / You (Anytime, Anyplace, Anywhere)* in 1995.

Ripcord had some major record company interest from two

RIPCORD (July 1994 - 2000)
Hayden Berry	Bryan Cooper	Simon Newby	Robert Smith
Voc	Gtr	Bass	Drums

US labels, Sire and Warner Bros, and recorded an album in 1999 produced by ex-Donkeys guitarist Neil Ferguson, but it wasn't released.

LIONEL BLAIRS

A pop duo consisting of Simon Stubbs (pictured right) and Chris Pickard who formed while at College in 1994.

Their mutual admiration for the twinkle-toed entertainer Lionel Blair was the inspiration for their band name. They met their idol when the duo appeared on the Sky TV show *1 To 3*, where he was the surprise guest. The show's host Paul Ross (brother of Jonathan) asked them to take part after liking their debut cassette album *Ugly As You*.

Lionel Blairs (1994 -
Simon Stubbs	Chris Pickard
Voc/Gtr	Bass

THE ENGINE ROOMS / ANITA MADIGAN

The Engine Rooms Studio was 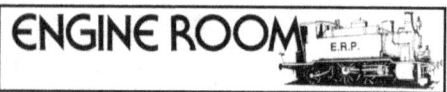 built in the Try Mills complex on Thornton Road.

While working on tracks for his band Pride, who had twice appeared on the BBC drama show, *The Paradise Club*, and released a single of a track featured in the show, engineer Dave King was approached by a friend at EMI who had just won the contract to produce laser discs of backing tracks for electronic giants Pioneer for the newly emerging karoake craze.

After initially hiring a studio in Dewsbury to do the work, the trio of Dave King, Anita Madigan and Pat McDonald leased part of the Try Mills complex on Thornton Road, and converted it into the Engine Rooms Studio in April 1990.

They re-recorded hundreds of classic tracks, using session musicians to re-create the sound as close to the originals as possible, for use on karaoke machines all over the world.

Anita had the single *Heart Over Mind / More Than You Know / What In The World* released on the Polydor label in 1994. It was recorded and produced at the Engine Rooms..

In 1995 Anita Madigan released the single *The Dalai Lama (Loves You All)*, which featured a mix by Detrimental, on Dave and Anita's On The Floor records label.

The Engine Rooms also got funding to run a three month training course in 1996, teaching recording and editing skills to a group of 12 trainees.

In 1996 the studio released the CD *Run With The Bulls* which featured Anita Madigan and Bradford Bulls players and included a rap performed by New Zealand born Bulls captain Robbie Paul.

They built on their Bradford Bulls connections by supplying a PA for half time entertainment.

Anita went on to performed at many UK sporting events including the Rugby Super League Grand Finals in 1998 and 1999, The World Club Super League Finals in 1999 and the Australia versus Great Britain Test match in 1998.

In 1996 they recorded a single by *Emmerdale* star Malandra Burrows (who played Kathy Tate in the ITV soap).

Summernight Love was released on Dave King and Anita Madigan's DKAM Records and featured backing vocals by Anita. The single only reached number 185 in the singles chart although Malandra Burrows had previously reached number 11 with *Just This Side Of Love* in 1990.

Anita's next single was *I Love Him Too / More Than You Know / Meet Me In The Darkness*, released in 1996, also on their On The Floor Records.

In 1997 Anita won the Jonathan Ross Show *Best Band* and songwriters competition and her song *Wish You Were Here* reached the last eight of the 1998 *Great British Song Contest*, the winner of which went on to appear in the *Eurovision Song Contest*.

Anita also sang backing vocals on the *How To Win Friends And Influence People* album for Terrorvision and has sung on a large number of adverts as well as appearing with her band on many shows including *Calendar, Look North, The Jonathan Ross Show, Grandstand* and *Bushell On The Box*.

```
Live Gig Video Shoot
ANITA MADIGAN
DAMN NATION
QUEENS HALL, BRADFORD
Wednesday June 22nd
Doors open 7.30 p.m. - On Stage 9.00 p.m.
Tickets £3.00
```

CHAPTER 6   1994 - 1996

NELSON'S COLUMN

In 1994, while New Model Army took a year off, their bassist Nelson formed a new band, Nelson's Column, with former Arise bassist Andy Warren and Mr Giblet drummer Chris Naylor, with Nelson taking on guitar and lead vocals.

Nelson's Column played their first show, a last-minute benefit gig at The 1 In 12 Club, then went on to play around West Yorkshire.

Nelson, real name Peter Nice, was originally from Colchester. He was good friends with Blur and had played on the same gig circuit. He had joined New Model Army in 1989, replacing Jason 'Moose' Harris. His first appearance on record was their 1990 *Impurity* album.

Nelson rejoined NMA in time to record their 1998 *Strange Brotherhood* album.

TRIP AND STUMBLE

This quirky, light-hearted three-piece played around the local area in the mid-1990s and featured New Model Army bassist Nelson on vocals, mandolin, banjo and bass drum, John Rigby on vocals and guitar, and Micah on didgeridoo, saw, harmonica, coconuts, bongos, pennywhistle, swanny whistle and other things!

Their cassette album was called *Plums And Bitter* and featured their original take on covers of songs such as *Urban Spaceman*, *Delilah* and *The Ovaltinies*.

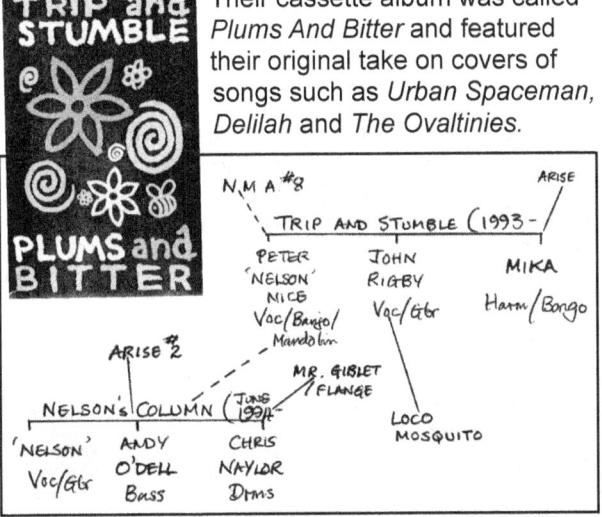

LOCO MOSQUITO

This short-lived band featured Trip And Stumble's John Rigby. They recorded a four-song cassette, *Nutso Strange / Falling Down / For Richer For Poorer / Pushing*.

Loco Mosquito featured John, John Slater, Andy O'Dell and various drummers, including Nelson for a couple of gigs. They evolved from the band Bigfoot, whose line-up was Indica Akashi, John's Rigby and Slater, and Martin McGyver.

John went on to play in another short-lived band, Loom, which featured former *T&A* scribe Simon Ashberry.

KILL II THIS

Former New Model Army/Loud/Slammer bassist Stuart Morrow teamed up with future NMA drummer Michael Dean, guitarist Rob Rhodes and singer Marc Ward to form the grungy metal band Kill II This in 1994.

The band signed to Northampton-based label Horse's Mouth to release their LP, *Everything All the Time*, which was recorded and produced by another NMA man, drummer Rob Heaton.

Kill II This played a Lord Mayor's charity for multiple sclerosis gig with Terrorvision, Liquid Head, The Edge and Mr Mak on September 15, 1994.

During a gig in Lisbon on the band's tour of Portugal, there was a riot outside the converted tram shed where the gig was taking place. Everything outside was badly damaged, except the band's tour bus, which was miraculously left untouched!

TWISTER 5

Based around the harmonising vocals of brothers Jerrad and Nathan Barraclough, this Bradford band played a jangly pop-rock style with a sound reminiscent of The Housemartins.

They recorded a demo called *Pre-Trial Tensions* in 1995.

After a name change to Twister 5, the band released the cassingle *Barbara / Sick And Tired*, which was recorded at Lion Studios, Leeds.

The band played regularily on the local scene and also played a live acoustic session on BCB's *Bradford Beat* show in 1996.

After the departure of guitarist Rusz Petcher, and with the addition of former Bloom member Dave Grant and guitarist Andrew Busby, the band were renamed Flat Back Four and moved into slightly heavier musical territory.

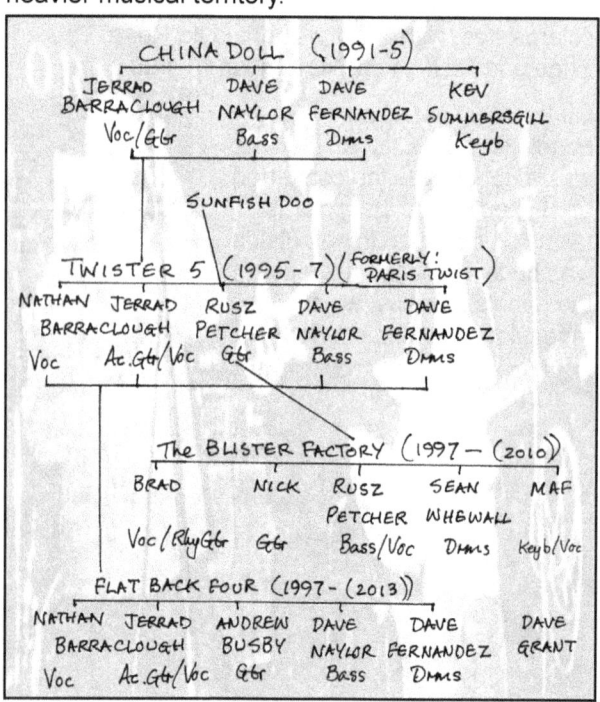

LOWLIFE UK

Formed from the ashes of Stax Wheelwright & The All Stars in 1994, the band played their debut gig at The New Beehive Cellar Bar in March 1995 with The Motorvators.

They then played regularly locally and all over West Yorkshire and released two demo tapes.

In 1998, Lowlife UK released their first CD ...*On Your Knees* on their own Punks For Profit label. That year they had a two-week jaunt in the USA supporting New York HC legends Murphys Law.

The longest-serving members of Lowlife UK were vocalist Darren 'Beaker' Dowson (the only constant member), and guitarists Paul Stone and Paul Mason. At various times the lineup has included ex-members of Anti-System (Mick Teale, Mickey Knowles) and IdiotBox drummer Gaz Pugh.

The band went on to release more self-prodced CDs including *Born To Booze* (2002), *Barstool Preaching* (2004), *That's Just How It Is* (2006), *Desert Island Dicks* (2007), and *The Hypnotized Never Lie* (2009).

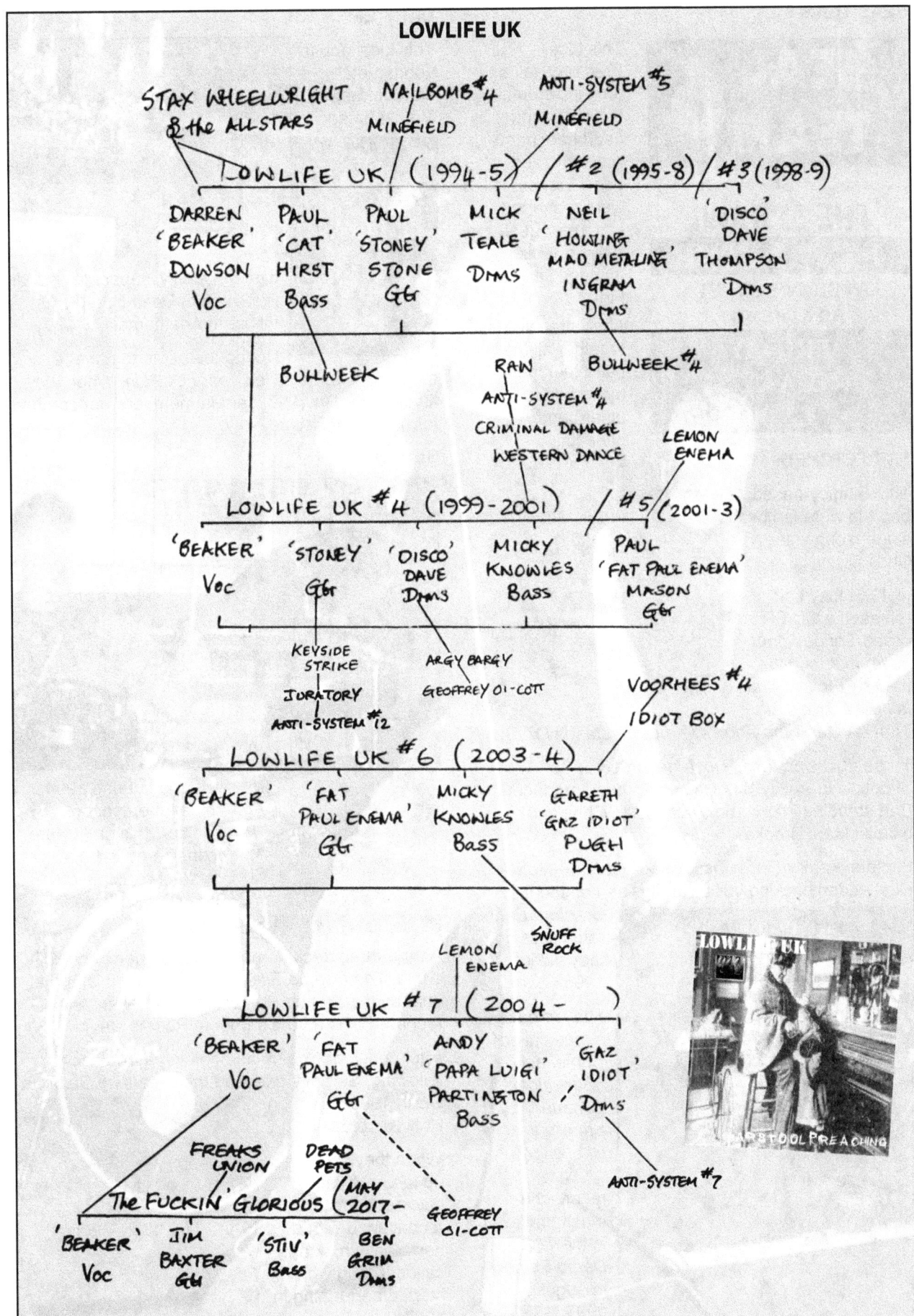

SEAL TEAM 6

This local Bradford/Halifax rock-indie outfit, three of whom had been in the Halifax based band Drench, were managed by former Best Way To Walk manger Stuart Firth.

After three years together all the band members moved on to other band projects.

FAR FETCHED

This Bingley-based pop trio were led by singer/songwriter Chris Cichy.

In 1994 they self-released a CD EP called *Songs About Love,* featuring the tracks *Clumsy / She Is Lost / Love's All That / A Man Who Knows And Understands (You)*.

Three tracks on the EP were recorded at Carl Stipetic's In-A-City Studios and featured producer Carl standing in on drums, alongside Chris and bassist Mark Brooke.

Skeletal Family/Ghost Dance vocalist Anne-Marie Hirst added backing vocals at gigs and on the BCB *Bradford Beat* radio session they did in 1995.

They released a tape called *Comeback / Sunshine Summer / Supermen Challenge* which received a much praise in the *T&A Demo Review* in August 1997.

DARK EMBRACE

This local gothic/doom metal band formed in May 1994 and

gigged heavily, supporting bands like Napalm Death, Cradle Of Filth and Anathama.

During their time together they released a demo called *Tears Of Pain*. When they finally folded in 1997, certain members went on to form The Enchanted.

SERENITY

Formed during 1994, by ex-members of Soltice, this outfit were considered to be a brilliant example of heavy melodic doom metal.

After a three track demo release, their debut CD album *Then Came Silence* was released later that year on the French Holy Records label and was recorded at Bradford's Engine Rooms studio.

After constant gigging and gaining a loyal local following, Serenity released the *Breathing Demons* CD in 1996, again on Holy Records.

When they broke up the next year, key members reconvened with a new heavy rock act called Khang who started performing in 1997.

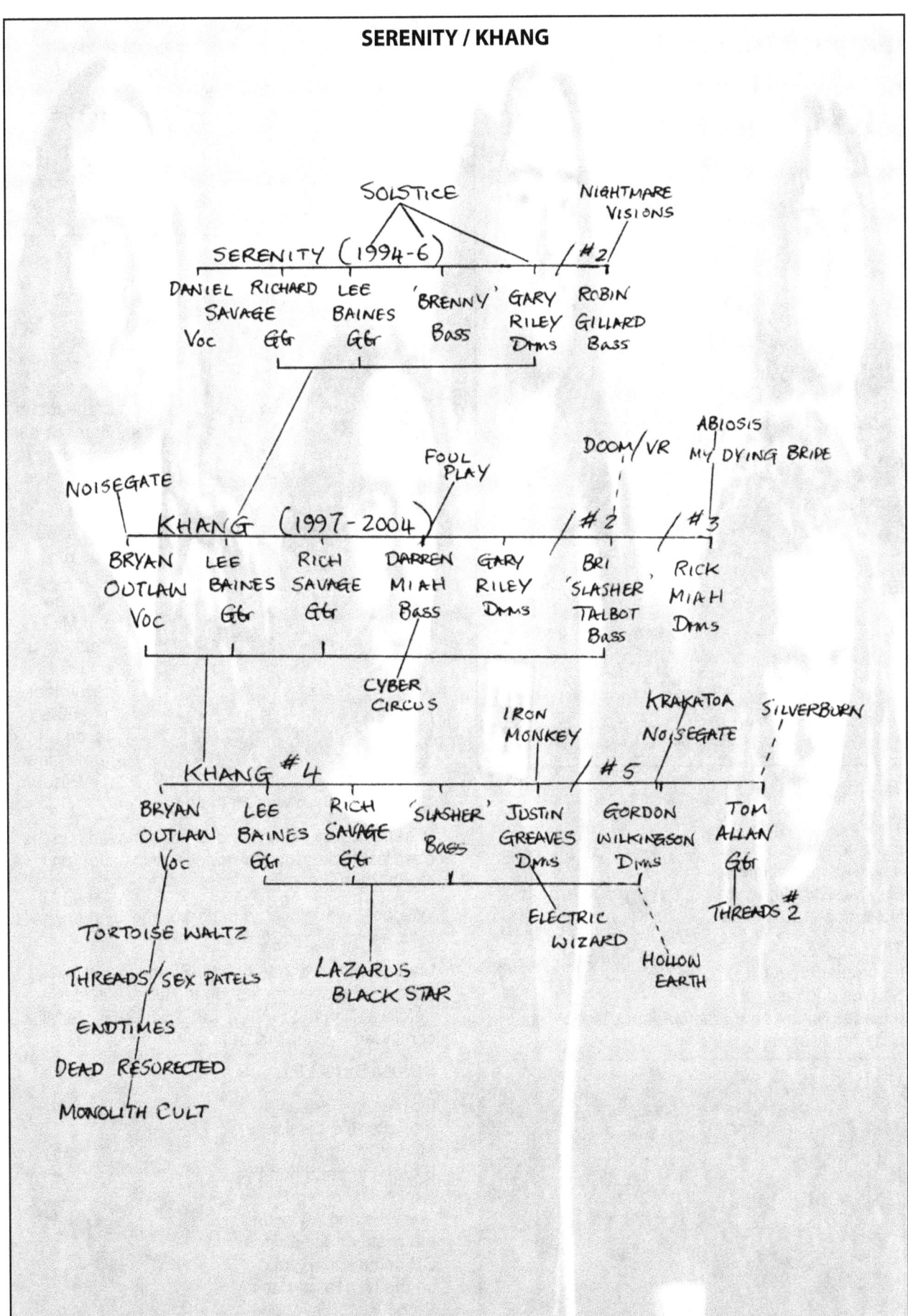

1994 - 1996 BRADFORD'S NOISE OF THE VALLEYS VOLUME 2

Primate rockers say: Ape our aid concert

Friends Gina Lambert and Stephen Andrews are hoping to stage a musical extravaganza to help cancer sufferers.

Gina and Stephen, both from Bradford, are already planning the event for August Bank Holiday Monday, August 29, at the Rio Rokz.

Now Gina — who manages popular rock band Primate — and Stephen, the band's guitarist, hope many other musicians and entertainers will come forward to perform in the event, all proceeds from which will be donated to the Sue Ryder Manorlands hospice at Oxenhope, near Keighley.

Anyone who can help should contact Gina on 0274 621609.

TROPICANA

This local pop five piece released a novelty Xmas single, *Reggae Christmas,* in November 1994.

The song was recorded at In A City Studios and was released on the new Bradford label, Neon Records, based in Allerton.

The single was released on 12" and CD formats and had a Don Lizard doing gruff ragga vocals. A video was filmed with local youngsters at ACW Garden Centre on Canal Road.

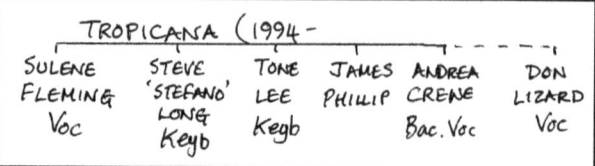

TROPICANA (1994 -
| SULENE FLEMING Voc | STEVE 'STEFANO' LONG Keyb | TONE LEE Keyb | JAMES PHILIP | ANDREA CRENE Bac.Voc | DON LIZARD Voc |

SYSTEM RECORDS

This local music shop opened in 1995 and was situated at the top of Barry Street, next door to The Castle pub.

The shop was run by Mark Kershaw and Mick Hebburn and sold 50% new releases and 50% second-hand gems, and the Wisdom skateboard shop was on the upper floor.

In 1998, both Wisdom and System moved into the basement of a recycled leather goods shop on North Parade.

Wisdom then relocated to Leeds and System finally stopped trading in 2003.

Mark went to work at Wall Of Sound in Halifax (who then moved their shop to Huddersfield, before selling out to Vinyl Tap in 2012), while Mick continued System Records as an online store.

SCREAMING LIFE

Formed in 1995 as a trio, after the demise of local quartet This Ritual, the band had two tracks, *Handstands In The Sea* and *Away* on the twenty track *Gringo* CD compilation, put out on the Nuneaton-based Purge Records label.

BRADFORD COMMUNITY BROADCASTING (BCB)

Mary Dowson came to do Peace Studies Bradford University in the 1970s and decided to make her home in the city.

Mary and Rob Walsh, a former manager of the HMV Shop in Bradford and later a publicity officer at Bradford festival and a long-running DJ and presenter of *Blowin'* on BCB, first mooted the idea of a community radio station in 1991 after meeting on a radio production course.

New legislation was introduced that enabled licenses to be awarded to non-profit-making stations to broadcast for limited periods.

Bradford Festival organiser Dusty Rhodes helped them to broadcast as Bradford Festival Radio for the first time in 1992.

They were based at Treadwells Art Mill for the period of the 1992 festival and in 1993 they set up base at the Wool Exchange for another broadcast.

In 1994 Bradford Community Broadcasting (BCB) was established as a successor to Festival Radio and set up a permanent home at 2 Forster Square, Bradford, where it remained until the whole Forster Square area was demolished and the infamous city centre fenced-off wasteland appeared in 2006.

The station then moved 1 Rawden Road, Bradford.

BCB began broadcasting after receiving a series of temporary licenses which permitted the station to broadcast on FM and the Yorkshire Cable Network for two 28-day periods a year.

The station also broadcast as *On Course Radio* for two further 28-day periods with a focus on the educational and promoting courses and qualifications at local centres of learning and colleges.

BCB also ran training courses for aspiring presenters and engineers and some of those who attended the early courses became long-running presenters or administrators at the station.

Rob and Mary were joined by a long list of people including Ian Sunderland (former 1919 singer), Lloyd Spencer, Jonathan Pinfield and former Violation vocalist Mick Yeadon. Local playwright and Militant activist Keith Narey co-presented a politcal show with young DJ Chris Stephenson.

The station broadcast a wide and multi-racial range of programming including political discussion, sports, women's issues and music programmes.

Presenters of the music-based shows included former promoter Lloyd Spencer, folk musician Tim Moon, Lorna Eastwood, Nigel Lambert and the ubiquitous *Griff's Magic Theatre*.

THE BRADFORD BEAT

After meeting on the BCB radio production course Matt Webster and Craig Williams joined forces to present the BCB events show, *The Guide*, a show all trainees took turns in presenting, in December 1994.

Having a shared interest in local music the pair came up with a new show, *The Bradford Beat*, which ran for the next five years, from 1995 to 1999.

The format of the show was to play exclusively Bradford or local-based music and feature live semi-acoustic sessions by local groups and artists, sometimes featuring two acts per night.

The show ran for either two or three hours and once or twice a week over the four BCB or *On Course Radio* 28-day broadcasts per year from 1995 to 1999.

The pair were often joined by Wild Willi Beckett (left, with Craig Williams) who added witty comment, poetry and general bonhomie to the proceedings.

They even managed to get Captain Sensible of The Damned to appear on their jingle for the show.

During the life of the show, Matt and Craig broadcast live sessions from many local acts, including; Bullweek, Blood Orange, Lynda Baxta,

The Pondskaters, Far Fetched, Slick 50, Moonpump, Nowt, Zed, Grim (pictured), Slack, Trip And Stumble, Shiny Beast, Twister, Ripcord and many others.

In December 1996 they held a demo competition, in conjunction with the Windsor Baths, judged by Matt and Craig and promoter Pat Manning. Winners Slick 50 won a support slot at the venue.

The show was also sponsored at times by Queen's Hall and, on May 22, 1996, they put on a *BCB Benefit Gig* to raise money for a proposed *Bradford Beat* compilation CD. The gig featured Slack, Ripcord, Bullweek and The Auxiliary of Real Men and was compered by 'the incomparable' Wild Willi Beckett.

A further BCB benefit followed on July 14 that same year, featuring Blood Orange and Twister 5 with music from fellow BCB stalwart Griff with his Magic Theatre.

Due to a change in policy at BCB the proposed CD was never compiled although a lot of the bands slated to appear on it can now be found on the CDs available with this book.

A version of their show continued, with presenters including former *T&A* scribe, Simon Ashberry.

BULLWEEK

When rock band Primate folded in summer 1995, singer Liam Sheeran and bassist Ade Clark formed the band Bullweek.

They recorded a self-titled 6-song cassette at Revolver Studios in December 1995, featuring the tracks *New Twist / Pickaside / Mother Earth Mover / Retro / Cruella / Here From Nowhere*.

For the next four years, with various lineup changes, the band recorded more tracks and played their post-punk Britpop style at many local venues like Queen's Hall and Rios, where they supported Stiff Little Fingers in 1998.

Remnants of the band morphed into the short-lived Year Dot in 2000. One-time bassist Rick

Bolton went on to form Idiot Box in 1998, joined in various lineups by other former Bullweek members, including his brother Matty and, later, Ade Clark.

THE PONDSKATERS

This was an occasional band who played around the local area on and off from 1991 until around 1997, featuring two members of Big Eyed Beans, Pete Kaberry on drums and guitarist Stuart Marshall, alongside former Western Dance/Bullweek bassist Ade Clark.

They recorded a seven-track tape called *Heaven Can Wait* and played a live session for BCB's Bradford Beat show in 1996.

GRIP

In 1995 Ade and Pete were also part of indie four-piece Grip, with Donald Gaudiosi and Ian Wilkinson on vocals and guitars.

They recorded a three song tape, *West Yorkshire Coast Music*, which featured the tracks *Technology / Cruel World / Place I Know*, and was recorded at Revolver Studios.

THE WINDSOR BATHS

Originally Bradford's public baths, the building was opened in 1905 as the Central Baths and offered swimming, saunas, slipper baths and various medical treatments as well as a laundry. Despite the addition of a modern sauna suite in the 1970s the building was closed in 1983.

In 1995, after being told they wouldn't be able to use the Wool Exchange as a venue for the 1995 Bradford Festival, organiser Dusty Rhodes asked Bradford Council if the Windsor Baths could be used as a temporary venue.

After months of restoration during which the baths were cleared of old Alhambra props and thousands of dead pigeons, with fire doors, stages and bars added, the Windsor Baths was refurbished and open as a venue in time for the 1995 Bradford Festival, on June 22.

With two large gig rooms and a central bar, the building was an ideal venue. Amongst the first acts to play there were Ruby Turner, New Model Army and D:Ream.

After the Festival, the Windsor Baths continued as a venue until after the following years festival before being transformed into the soulless franchise bars that stand there today. A great loss of what could have been a great attraction for Bradford.

GOODBYE QUEEN'S HALL

In 1995 the main Ballroom of the Queen's Hall was redesigned, putting a bar in the middle of what was the dance floor and removing the stage, which effectively ended its history as a venue.

The cellar bar still continued to put on gigs for a while after a redevelopment which moved the position of the stage from the end of the room to opposite the bar.

Another massive loss for the Bradford music scene.

The venue was been known as Flares nightclub for a while before closing its doors.

BLOOD ORANGE

Former Happiness Ad duo Rob Moore and Ricky Howard reunited in the rock band Blood Orange, joined by bassist Mick Smith and ex-Slammer guitarist Milo Zivanovic.

In 1995 they recorded their album *Middle End Beginning* at the Engine Rooms Studios, on Pulsiv Rock Records.

They had a four-album deal with a Brazilian

record company in 1995 which never came to fruition.

Rob and Ricky also had an acoustic version of the band under the name Moorzart which also played a lot of acoustic gigs. They also played a couple of live sessions on BCB's *Bradford Beat*.

Blood Orange played a *BCB Benefit Gig* at the Rio on July 15, 1995.

In October 1995, Blood Orange arranged a showcase gig at St George's Hall, billed as *Bradford's Best* and featuring themselves, alongside The Bobby Charltons and Mr Mak.

ROLLERCOASTER

This indie-rock band were initially formed by John and Baz when they were both at school. The lads got together again after they both finished University and reformed Rollercoaster as a proper, gigging band.

They recorded their Modern Man demo in 1995 and appeared on BCB's *Bradford Beat* radio show after winning their heat in the Forster's *Icebreaker* band competition. Their vibrant songs like *Aunty Pat and Gypsy Queen* never got, perhaps, the recognition they deserved and major record company interest from labels like Sony and Polydor never bore fruit.

Two more local bands around at the start of 1995 were State 'O' Mind (pictured left) and Comic Book Heroes.

STATE 'O' MIND (1995 -	(FORMERLY: VENGEANCE)		
'NIDGE' TAYLOR Voc	JAMES WILLIS Gtr	DANNY WATERWORTH Bass	MICK MILECKI Drms

COMIC BOOK HEROES

Formed in June 1995, this young local band were managed by the singer's dad. Their musical influences ranged from pop to funk and Acid jazz.

They had composed a song called *Forbidden Peace* about the conflict in Bosnia (formerly part of Yugoslavia).

In 1996, the band took part in a town twinning exchange with The Tragic Comics from Hamm, Germany, Bradford's partner city.

The German band came over for a week in March 1996 and played two gigs at the New Beehive and Queen's Hall, while the Heroes went to play in Germany in June.

COMIC BOOK HEROES (June 1995 -				
NATHAN DAVIES Voc	TOM HALL Gtr	TONY SPRUTT Bass	PHIL YEADON Drms	CHRIS ANDREWS Keyb

WHO THE F**K ARE SMOKIE?

Local 1970s pop/soft rock legends Smokie returned to the singles chart after an absence of fifteen years when a re-recorded version of their hit *Living Next Door To Alice* got to number three in the charts in May 1995. During their 1970s heyday, the band had eleven top twenty hits, three at number five. Their first single, *If You Think You Know How To Love Me*, reached number three in July 1975.

Smokie's original version of *Living Next Door To Alice* reached number five when released in December 1976 and became the song most associated with the band. Written by songwriting duo Chinn and Chapman, it had been a minor hit down under for Australian harmony trio New World in 1972.

The popularity of Smokie's re-recorded version of the song was helped by having the blue comic Roy 'Chubby' Brown add the extra hook line, 'Who the fuck is Alice?' after each chorus.

The additional line came about after Smokie fans in Germany started chanting it every time the band played the song live.

Only two months before the single's release, in March 1995, the band's tour bus went off the road in a freak hailstorm en route to Dusseldorf airport during one of the band's many European tours. Three of the band were injured in the crash, founder members Terry Uttley and Alan Silson received cuts and bruises but singer Alan Barton's injuries were far more serious and resulted in his tragic death after five days in intensive care.

Before joining Smokie in 1988, Barnsley-born Alan had been in West Yorkshire act Black Lace who had a number two hit with *Agadoo* in June 1984.

Smokie released several albums while Alan was lead singer, including *All Fired Up* (1988), *Boulevard Of Broken Dreams* (1989), *Whose Are These Boots?* (1990), *Chasing Shadows* (1992), *Burnin' Ambition* (1993) and *The World And Elsewhere* (1995).

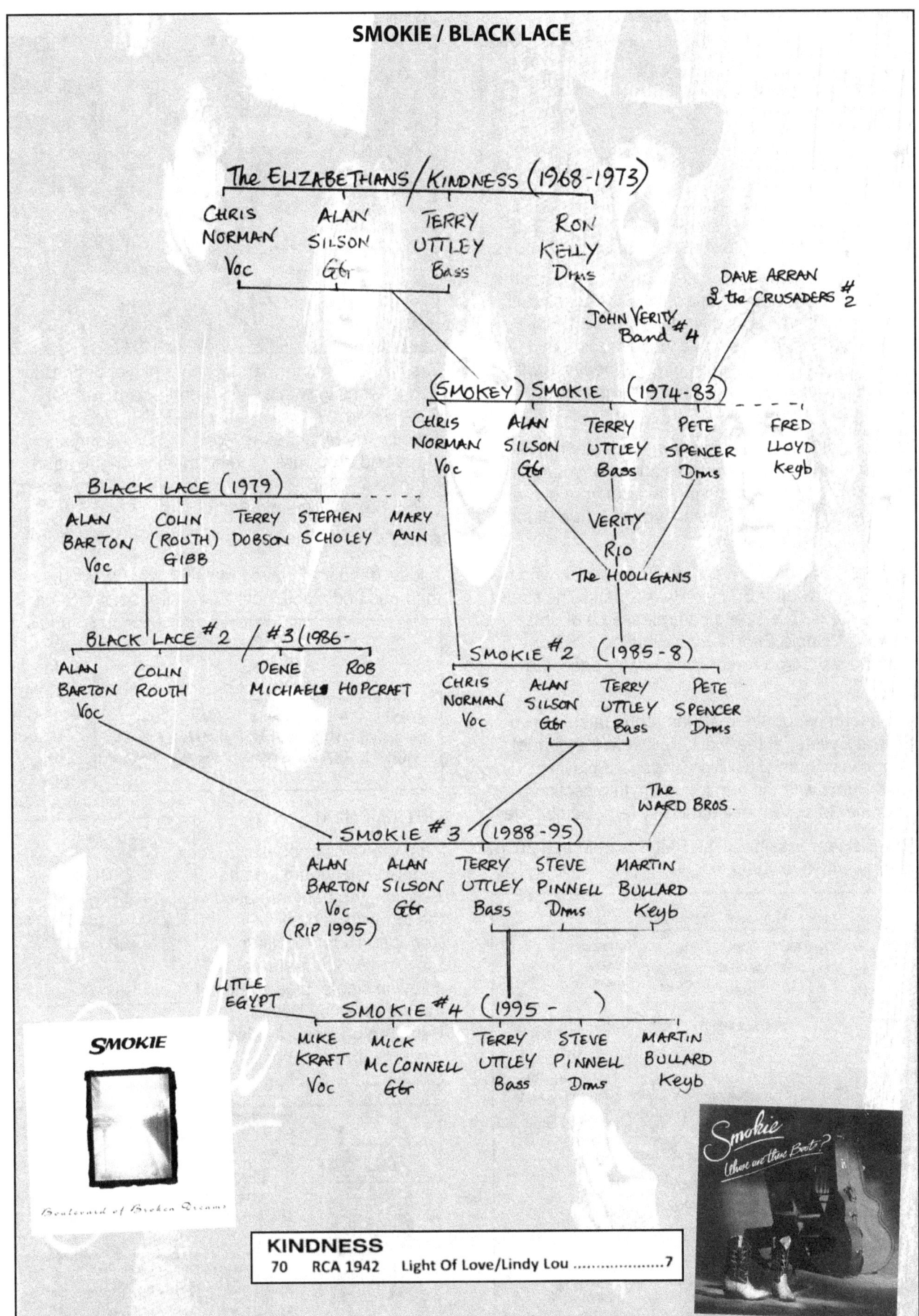

THE BLACK BULL JAM SESSIONS

Over the years many pubs ran 'jam session' nights, but the longest running one was at the Black Bull in Clayton. It was set up initially by pianist Ray Bainbridge in 1993 as an acoustic session and was supported by Denny Austin of Somebody's Brother who helped set-up many jam sessions around the town.

Many local musicians attended these Monday night sessions at the Bull as well as a host of young up and coming players learning the licks from older musicians. An example was a young future Blues guitarist Chantel McGregor.

One regular was drummer Ian 'Tosh' Ward, who had played in Sowerby Bridge / Halifax band The Breed in the 1980s. The Breed had released a double A sided 7"single *Effort / Jeans* in June 1980 on Rochdale's Cargo Records. Ian sadly passed away in 2015.

For a long period the main jam band (also known as The Bullets) at the Black Bull were the quartet of guitarist Sean O'Sullivan, keyboard player Pete Burns with the formidable rhythm section of drummer Mick Wake and bassist Terry Bainbridge.

The last jam session at the Bull was in March 2018, after twenty-five years.

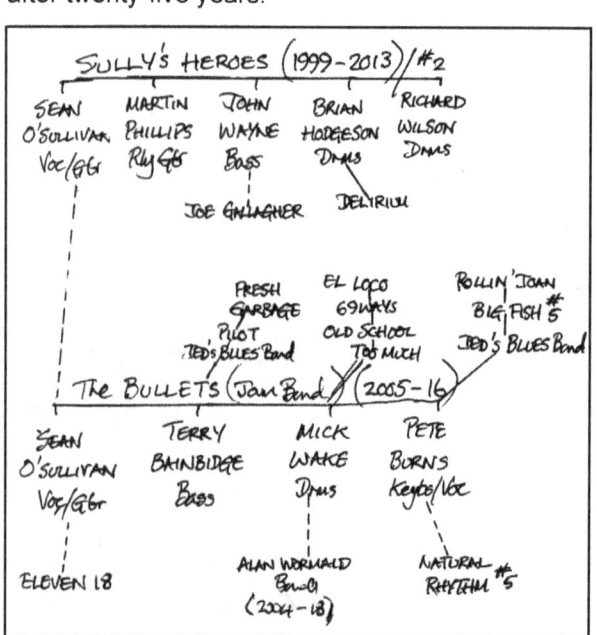

JOHN BECK

Tasmin Archer's former keyboard player John Beck began working with ex-Vex/Fatal Charm guitarist Dave Pickard on material at the Pots'n'Panz Studios, off Manchester Road in 1994. John and Dave had previously worked together in the band Timelife in 1982, and had both been in The Archers (1985-88) with Tasmin Archer.

SNIFFA

A local band that played mainly covers around the pubs and clubs, until they morphed into Elmer Fudd's Wild Ride with the addition of singer Sarah Collins.

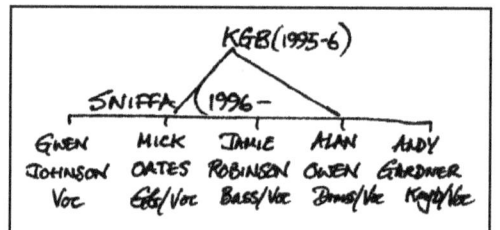

DETRIMENTAL

After the release of their controversial debut single *Babylon*, the band released the ten-track album *Xenophobia* on Cooking Vinyl in 1995. It featured the *Babylon* single, plus guest appearances by Devon Bara-Tan on *Bangra Attack* and New Model Army's Justin Sullivan on vocals on the band's cover of the Clash's *Bank Robber*.

THE BLACK AGENDA
More than a Bookshop!
A MASSIVE Selection of Black, Radical, Afrikan, Asian and Left Wing Books!
Politics, History, Art, Culture, Race & Class, Children's Books, Fiction, Autobiography and More!
Open tues-thurs 10-5, fri-sat 10-6, closed monday.
24 Barry Street, Bradford 1.

RIOT IN MANNINGHAM

On the night of Friday, June 9, 1995, an insensitive and overzealous police force from the nearby Lilycroft station raided a house off Oak Lane, Manningham in response to a domestic violence call.

The initial spark that started the two-day riot was when, *'a mother and her young child were allegedly caught in the middle as police dragged a man from the house, after trying to break up a group of youths.'* (2)

The Lilycroft Police station (with its anti-ram raid ramps) was soon under siege by an angry local community which over that weekend burned down businesses in Oak Lane causing hundreds of thousands in damages, fought police with petrol bombs and stones and left a trail of havoc from Manningham down to Westgate in the city centre, ten people were arrested but no one was convicted.

Bradford band The Big Fish were playing at The Beehive when the windows of the pub were put through, causing panic and chaos within. A number of other Bradford pubs in the area were gutted by fire and never re-opened after the riot.

The Tory Home Secretary at the time, Michael Howard, refused a judicial inquiry into the causes, which involved allegations of Police heavy-handedness before and during the riots. A separate community inquiry by the Bradford Commission published its findings in November 1996. It reported on public order of the mainly Muslim youth in the area, showing that they were disaffected and frustrated by Police aggressiveness, the 'anti-muslim' backlash to the Iraq War and the absence of youth facilities or a community centre locally, all adding to the tensions unleashed on the nights of June 9-10, 1995.

On June 14, 1995, Irish blues-rock guitarist Rory Gallagher died of a chest infection following a liver transplant at King's College Hospital London. His remains were returned to Ireland, for burial in his home town of Cork

He began performing in 1968, with his three-piece blues-rock outfit Taste, before going solo in 1970 and releasing fifteen albums over the next twenty five years.

SLACK

This short-lived but vibrant mid-90s funkjunkpunk rock combo featured former Zed members Jez, Nogsy and Harris alongside former Nowt bassist Boz.

The band adopted the moniker, Slack, as a description of their approach to rehearsing - as singer Harris would often declare from the stage, *'We're called Slack coz we are!'*

In 1996 the band recorded a three-track demo, In *Our World / Ed Wood / Gone* at Revolver Studio with Tim Walker at the controls with a fourth track, *Hat On Backwards*, taped live at the band's appearance at the BCB benefit gig at Queen's Hall.

During their short-lived stint on the local scene, Slack played gigs at Queen's Hall Cellar Bar, The Biko Bar, MacRory's, Leeds Duchess Of York and Windsor Baths where they supported Anita Madigan.

On June 15, 1997, Slack played alongside the latest Zed lineup, Ozric Tentacles, Poison Electric Head and other bands at an all-day festival in Todmorden Centre Vale Park.

HARDWARE

This techno-metal band, who formed in the summer of 1994, with members formerly of Loud and PADD, were managed by the local Northern Music agency.

In May 1996,

 the band signed a five-album deal with the record label Intercord, the German-based division of EMI. Later that year, they released their mini-album *Race, Religion & Hate* which was simultaneously released throughout Europe, including a gig at Prague's Rock Cafe with Amorthic and Therion on September 9, 1996.

STRAIN

A five-piece thrash-rock outfit, originally from the Scottish Shetland Isles, who moved down to Bradford because they had relatives in the area, and thought they would get more gigs.

KIKI'S NEW ALBUM

Bradford's original 1976 number one single hit maker, Kiki Dee, released her latest album *Almost Naked* in October 1995.

The year before, Kiki had met her musical partner Camelo Luggeri and began working on songs and performing as a duo. Her last top ten single was in 1993, a number two hit *True Love*, another duet with (Sir) Elton John.

FREAKY GS

A young local band, who played their debut gig at their local, the Blue Pig in Fagley supporting The Lionel Blairs.

THE 1 IN 12 CLUB 1994-1996

As a self-run autonomous social centre/venue, The 1 In 12 Club had been a base and authentic haven for many of the socially disaffected individuals and band members who relocated to Bradford and got involved in its running, thus creating a strong sense of unity that helped to nurture the 1990s UK's Hardcore scene.

A few quick quotes illustrate the general attitude in the UKHC scene to the Club:

'.....that place was always awesome and it just had such a great vibe.' (3)

'..we played a couple of great shows at the 1 In 12, which was my personal favourite venue.' (4)

'...it was like a second home, I used to travel up to all the festivals and always received a warm and friendly welcome, it was the heart of the DIY scene at the time.' (5)

The first 1 In 12 Club gig of 1994 was on January 22, which included the French band Filthy Charity. This was followed by a series of gigs in the months leading up to June by mainly locally based bands, UKHC scene bands and the occasional touring

European band like Fleas & Lice (Holland) and Warcollapse (Sweden).

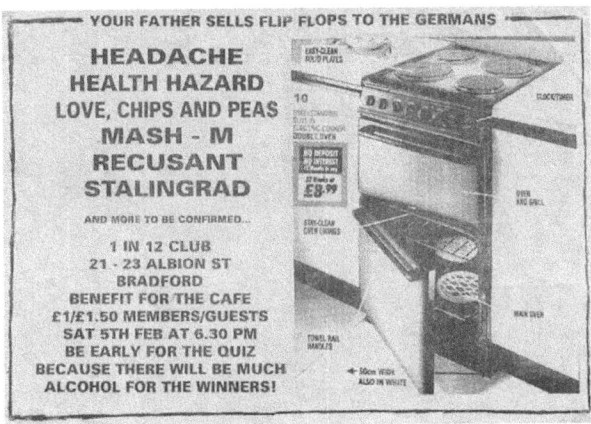

Two local bands who formed in early 1994 and were also heavily linked to the 1 In 12 were:

HEADACHE

This band consisted of a loose bunch of mainly French/French-Canadians who'd settled in Bradford and got active in the Club before eventually moving across to Leeds to set up the 120 Rats squat.

They released a split 7" EP with another local Club band Recusant in 1995. It came in a fold-out cover with a sixteen-page booklet and poster on Flat Earth Records. Headache also released a cassette on Flat Earth, called *Live In Slovenija*, from their final European tour.

STALINGRAD

A brutal metallic hardcore band who made two early demo tapes before their debut *The Politics Of Ecstasy* 7" EP picture disc vinyl release on AWA Records in 1996.

During the band's lifetime, they gigged regularly around the UK, becoming one of the most popular hardcore bands at that time.

They released their debut LP *Patty We Kind Of Missed You On Your Birthday* in 1998, on AWA Records, recorded at In A City Studios.

The LP included guest vocals by Lecky of Voorhees and Wayne of Doom. One track *Hanged Man Will Repent* was remixed by the noise group Smell & Quim.

KITO

A band half in Leeds and half in Middlesbrough, but their vocalist Rob was from Halifax. After a couple of cassette demos, their debut 7" single *Mary Johnson* came out in 1994 on AWA Records.

The band played many gigs and all-dayers at the 1 In 12 over the years and were one of the most original UKHC bands on the scene. Their self-titled LP *Kito* came out on Flat Earth Records in 1998, again recorded at Bradford's In A City.

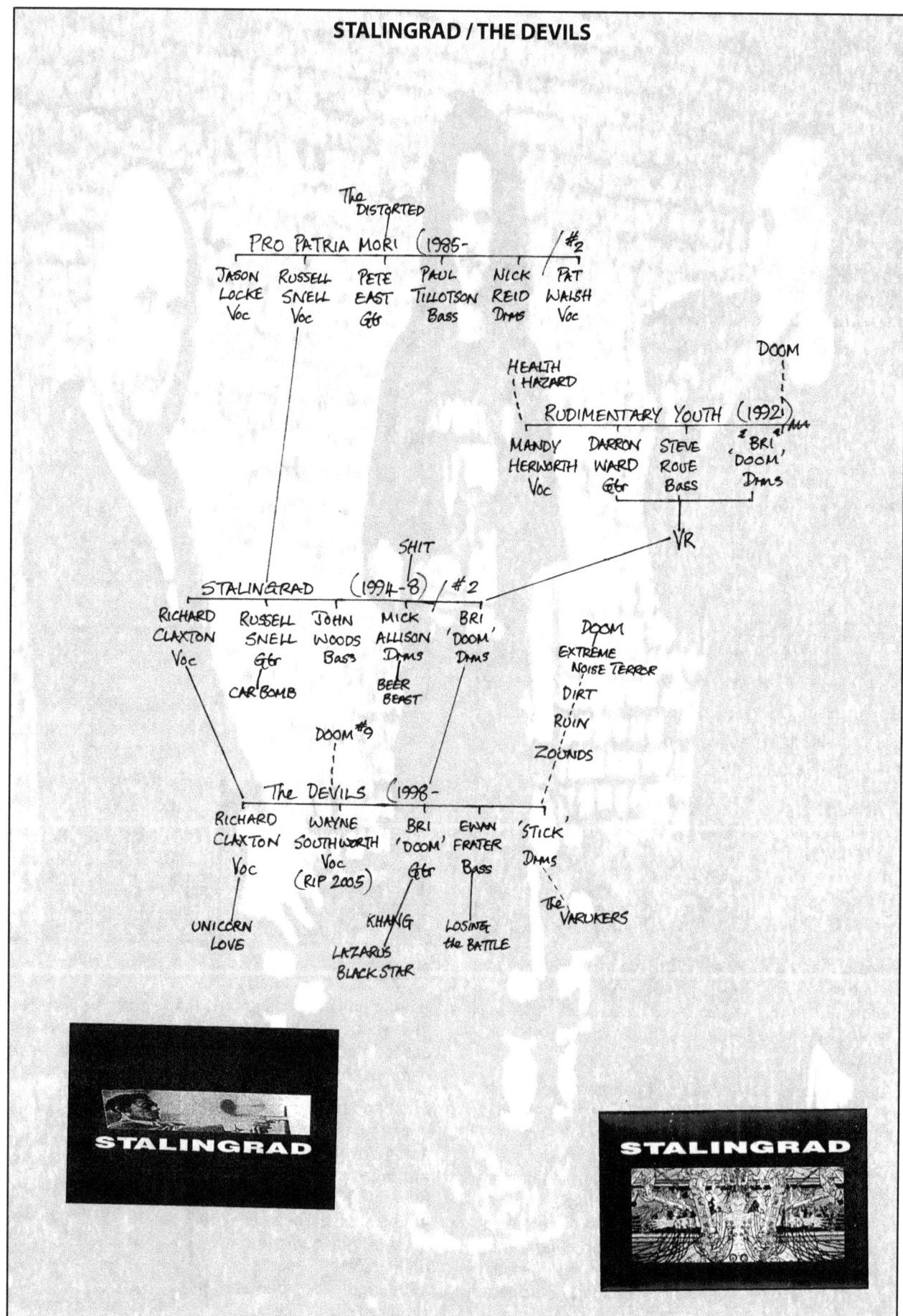

CHAPTER 6 — 1994 - 1996

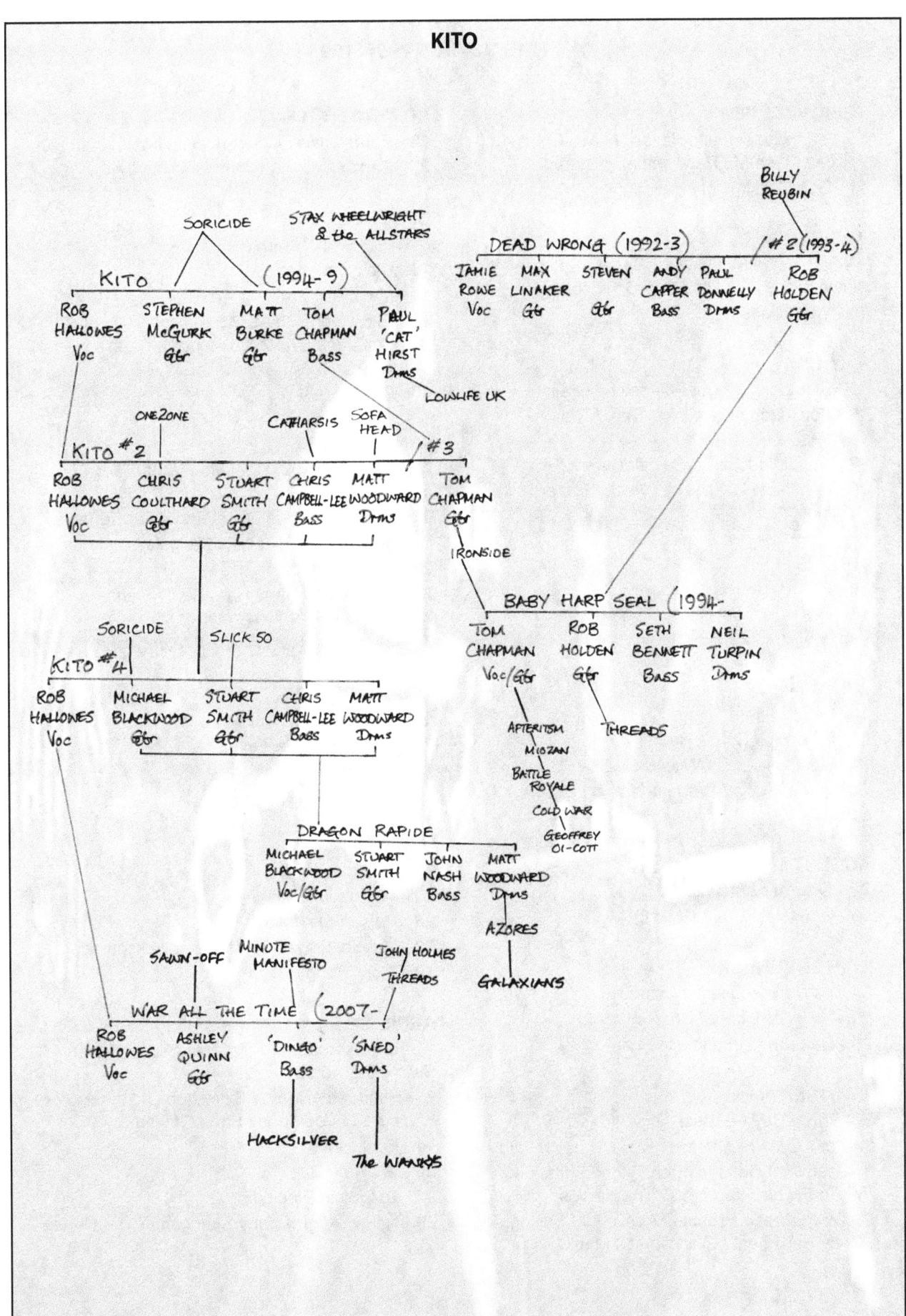

1 IN 12 CLUB GIGS 1994/1995

FEBRUARY 1994
5 - Headache / Health Hazard / Love Chips And Peace / Mash-M / Recusant / Stalingrad
11 - Gag / Witchknot / Headache

APRIL 1994
2 - Glue / One By One / Kitchener / Sarcasm / Active Minds / Nerves / Dog On A Rope
28 - Warcollapse

MAY 1994
13 - Slumgang / Pigpile / Stretch / Grain
15 - Bob Tilton / Baby Harp Seal / Tribute / Voorhees
1? - Coitus / Fleas & Lice / Decadent Few
20 - Disaffect / Headache / Health Hazard / Recusant / Mash-M

JUNE 1994
10 - Blind Mole Rat
18 - CDS / Maggot Slayer Overdrive / Bloodsucking Freaks

JULY 1994
1 - Oi Polloi
6 - Brittle Hip / Space Heads
22 - Health Hazard / Witchknot
27 - One By One / Ex-Cathedra / Where's Rachel

AUGUST 1994
?? - Disorder / Stalingrad
19 - Iconoclast / Dead Wrong

SEPTEMBER 1994
3 - The Nerves / Health Hazard
?? - VR / Stalingrad / Grain
25 - Dawson / Longfinkillie / Lag

OCTOBER 1996
7-9 Three Day Festival
7 - Lash Out / Neckbrace / Kito / State Of Filth
8 - Jasmine / Undone / Bob Tilton / Spithead / Will To Power / Voorhees / The Nerves
9 - Dead Wrong / Tribute / Above All / Stalingrad / Baby Harp Seal / Extinction Of Mankind

NOVEMBER 1994
26 - Earth Crisis / Doughnuts
27 - Earth Crisis / Abhinanda / Above All

DECEMBER 1994
8 - Witchknot / Headache
10 - Dick Gaughan
15 - Mash-M / Grain
17 - Excrement Of War / Ex-Cathedra / Health Hazard / Japs Eye / Rudimentary Youth / Sarcasm
30 - Dossa

JANUARY 1995
7 - The Auxiliary Of Real Men / Dead Sex / Motherfist
12 - Dog On A Rope / Contempt / The Tenants
14 - Manfat / Needlestick / Zoopsta
21 - Zoviet France
28 - Bob Tilton / Baby Harp Seal / Manrae / Stretch / Des Man De Amblo / Diablo
31 - Blind Mole Rat / Alianz / Witch World

FEBRUARY 1995
12 - Blyth Power / Witchknot
24 - Funkfish / New Level

MARCH 1995
18 - The Bullets / The Auxiliary Of Real Men / Beer Beast
22 - Gonzo
25 - Whitehouse
26 - Poison Sisters / Curll
29 - Maggot Slayer Overdrive / Muckspreader
30 - Elsie Moon / Boy Racer

APRIL 1995
1 - Lord Skaman And The Magnificent Seven / Swimming Horse
8 - Dropdead / Doom / Extinction Of Mankind / Stalingrad / Voorhees / State Of Filth
14 - Funkfish
20 - WORM / Bug
27 - Oi Polloi / Bloodshot
29 - Naked Aggression / Slumgang / The Nerves

1 IN 12 CLUB GIGS 1995

MAY 1995
5 - Mapp / Virtual Reality
6-7 Two Day Punk Festival
6 - Trbute / Baby Harp Seal / Stretch / Spithead / Pig Pile / Smog / Des Man Diablo
7 - Bob Tilton / Shutdown / Stamping Ground / Blood Sucking Freaks / Suffer / Haywire / ABC Diablo / Offset
18 - Psycho Duck / Naked Eye
27 Monster Festival - Funkfish / Northern Rage / Trip & Stumble / Dub Kitchen / Longkinfillie / Witchknot / Delicate Vomit / Love Chips And Peace

JUNE 1995
1 - Kitten Kineval / Shrug / Hulmanoids / Golden Startlett
3 - Dirt / Final Warning / Woodhouse Rejects / Scatha / Substandard / Headache
18 - Kava Kava / Slur
29 - Scum Of Toytown

JULY 1995
1-2 Two Day Hardcore Festival 4
1 - Oi Polloi / Chaos UK / Policy Of Three / Malva / Manrae / Ex-Cathedra / Marker
2 - Bob Tilton / Tribute / Schema / Baby Harp Seal / Broccoli / Above All / Withdrawn
4 - Baby Harp Seal / Polaris
9 - Attwenger
11 - RDF / Iowaska
15 - Dieter Muh / Suicidal Flowers
19 - Dischange / Extinction Of Mankind / Aftermath
29 - The Cherries / Witchknot

AUGUST 1995
4 - Scatha / Headache / Suffer / Love Chips And Peace
12 - Smell And Quim / Con-Dom
19 - Backbone / Chevonne / Bonafied
25 - Scorn

SEPTEMBER 1995
8 - Curll / Underclass
18 - Zoviet France
22 - Bob Tilton / Schema
23 - Grover / Underclass / Doubleday
29 - Suicidal Flowers / God's Little Monkeys / Raindogs

OCTOBER 1995
6 - Unique Freak / Mash-M / Dog On A Rope
7 - Guilt Trip / Eggbread
11 - Sabot / Troggy
15 - Glue / Broccoli / Apple Orchard
19 - Morbid Symphony
26 - Sleepy People / Heart Of Darkness / Dub Kitchen
27 - Defiance / Substandard / Haywire / Combat Shock
28 - 108 / Abhinanda / Stamping Ground

NOVEMBER 1995
3 - Masskontrol / Blood Sucking Freaks
4 - Whirling Pig Dervish / Sparta
10 Hardore Festival 5 - Tribute / Stalingrad / Marker / Kosjer D / Polaris / Stampin' Ground / Schema / Manfat / Doubleday / Underclass / Beacon / Baby Harp Seal / Bob Tilton / Withdrawn / Hard To Swallow / Dead Fall / Revolt
11 - Manrae
12 - Bob Tilton
17 - Skull Flower / Grey Wolves
18 - Tofu Love Frogs / Kava Kava

DECEMBER 1995
8 - Bonafide / Virtual Reality
9 - Beer Beast / Heart Of Darkness / State Of Filth
14 - The Haters / Smell And Quim / Con - Dom
16 - Scum Of Toytown

1 IN 12 CLUB GIGS 1996

JANUARY 1996
14 - Spanakorzo / Polaris
19 - Baby Harp Seal / Stalingrad / Tribute

FEBRUARY 1996
16 - Scanner
17 - Suicidal Flowers
?? - Auxilliary Of Real Men
19 - PAIN
26 - Eugene Chadbourne / Kenny Process Team

MARCH 1996
3 - Stamping Ground / Above All / Bob Tilton / Baby Harp Seal / Unborn / Schema
15 - Ex-Cathedra / Newtown Grunts / Active Minds
29 - Carol / Curll / Ebola / Tribute / Hard To Swallow

APRIL 1996
3 - UK Subs / Clockwork Zombi
6 - Cress / Witchknot / Scatha / Quarantine / Bloodsucking Freaks / Suffer
12 - Bus Station Loonies / PMT / Filth
19 - Zona Rosa / Bullweek / Spank / Earwig
20 - Splintered / Bilge Pump / Husk
19 - Spite / Four Letter Word
28 - Stalingrad / Unborn / Withdrawn / Schema

MAY 1996
2 - Black Horizon
17 - Bodychoke / Bige Pump
23 - The Bullets / Right Hand Action
25 - Undone / Portobello Bones / Ananda / Congress
26 - Liar / Unsilent Majority / Unborn / Lifer / Area Effect

JUNE 1996
6 - Love Chips And Peace
8 - Suicidal Flowers
12 - Hiatus / Headache / Doom / Urko

JULY 1996
5 - Black Horizon
12 - Gaza Strip / Termite Club
21 - Polaris / Kito / Suffer / Manfat / Hard To Swallow / Systral / Baby Harp Seal
25 - Dawnraiser
26 - Dumbfucks / Mark Jones / Newtown Grunts
28 - Gin Goblins / Rumorosa

AUGUST 1996
1 - PAIN / GFA / Solanki
2 - Swing Kids / Grover / Revolt / Hessel
9 - Gaza Strip
10 - Fleas And Lice / Gruff / Extinction Of Mankind

SEPTEMBER 1996
6 - Quarantine / Newtown Grunts / Bonejack
13 - Poisoned Electric Head
27 - Avail / Voorhees / Barcode Biopsy

OCTOBER 1996
3 - International Strikeforce / Witchknot / Delicate Vomit / Hiphuggers
5 - Citizen Fish / Smell & Quim
19 - Los Crudos / Ebola / Voorhees / Diminished / State Of Filth / Barcode Biopsy / Bloodsucking Freaks
25 - Dead & Gone / Stalingrad / Unplugged Dicky
27 - Chamberlain / Yummy Fur / Polaris / Hiphuggers

NOVEMBER 1996
9 - Damnation / Battery / Dropdead / Feeding The Fire / Sherry / Voorhees
10 - Bob Tilton / Tribute / Stalingrad / Kneecapped / Hard To Swallow
14 - Apartment 3G
15 - Schimpfluch Gruppe / Bilge Pump
16 - Tribal Stance
23 - Fog H.C. / Kava Kava
24 - Scatha / State Of Filth

DECEMBER 1996
7 - Tofu Love Frogs
14 - Strife / Unborn / Canvas / Area Effect / Knuckledust / V55 / Bob Tilton / 3rd Estate
31 - Hard To Swallow

CHAPTER 6   1994 - 1996

In early March, the Club played host to an evening called *Vampire Nite,* seemingly where goths dressed up in role-playing, these nights eventually became regular extravaganzas over the years under the banner of Carpe Noctum, which featured also the odd goth/darkwave/industrial band.

In early April 1994, local Keighley Labour MP Bob Cryer died. He was a fearless left wing activist, his wife Ann won his seat at the subsequent by election.

LOCAL 'EXTRAS' FOR THE FILM ID

On April 20 /21, twenty odd members of The 1 In 12 Club were part of 2,000 Bradford folk who played football supporter extras, filming terrace fight scenes at Bradford City's Valley Parade ground. Extras were paid £25 per day and all meals were provided, it was great fun for everyone involved over the two days.

The basic premise of the film was an undercover investigation of hardcore football gangs by a team of young 'coppers', concentrating on the fictional London team Shadwell Town, known as 'The Dogs'.

In the film, the police believed that a crime syndicate was using the terraces as a recruiting ground, and the police team were to track down the 'generals', shadowy figures who orchestrated the violence. The film starred Reece Dinsdale, Sean Pertwee, Saskia Reeves and Warren Clarke, and was directed by the actor Phil Davis who had a small cameo appearance as a police sergeant.

The football crowd and terrace scenes were filmed in London, Hamburg, Rotherham and Bradford and all the stunts were arranged by one Andy Bradford and Roy Alon.

I.D. was originally made as part of BBC2's *Screen Two* series, and came out on Video and DVD later.

HANNAU TOURNAMENT

During the second and third weeks of June 1994, the 1 In 12's football team were invited to take part in a tournament in Germany.

It was held in the small town of Hanau, just outside the city of Frankfurt, and was jointly organised by supporters of St. Pauli and Werder Bremen.

The whole weekend's atmosphere was wonderful; hot sunshine, great games, good comradeship and plenty of beer in the post-game cool downs. The 1 In 12 Club team got into the quarter finals and were

the tournament's highest scorers, and afterwards enjoyed the local hospitality of German comrades in their squat in the nearby woods (they lived in old railway carriages!) before returning to Blighty.

In the summer months of 1994, the Club played host to more foreign bands, like Where's Rachel, from Germany, and the intense US hardcore band Iconoclast from New Jersey, whose self titled CD had come out on the Ebullition label.

CRISIS #2

The second financial crisis hit The 1 In 12 Club in August, as the UK's economy continued under the Tories of John Major in recession. But enthusiasm was high and everyone pulled together and many efforts were made to fundraise, like benefits, raffles etc. Donations came from all over the UK and the world, from individuals, bands and Record labels, such as Smack In the Mouth Records who released a benefit 7" single with the bands Revolt, State of Filth, Spite and Suffer.

In the end, the debts were finally settled, with the help of another brewery loan and in May 1995 everyone was paid off and the Club made a profit that year.

THREE-DAY HARDCORE & PUNK FESTIVAL

From Friday 7 to Sunday 9, October, The 1 In 12 Club held a three-day festival. Headlining on Friday was the crunching hardcore of Lash Out from Norway, supported by Neckbrace, Kito and State Of Filth, from Preston. Two French bands Jasmine and Undone from Paris, headlined on Saturday with Bob Tilton, Spithead, Will To Power, Voorhees and The Nerves as support. Sunday was an all UKHC affair with Dead Wrong, Tribute, Above All, Stalingrad, Baby Harp Seal and Extinction Of Mankind.

ANARCHY IN THE UK

Over ten days in October, from 21-30, 1994, anarchists from all over the UK and elsewhere descended on London for a series of activist conferences and debates on various topics, gigs, parties, gatherings, exhibitions and a football tournament billed as *Anarchy In The UK - Ten Days That Shook The World*.

The 1 In 12 sent a delegation of members and also their football team to play in the tournament. The 1 In 12 team was beaten in the final by rivals and comrades from Bristol Easton Cowboys 1-0, played on a rain-soaked 5-a-side pitch, somewhere in Hackney.

The US punk zine *Profane Existence* reviewed the whole ten days in an article the following month.

Over the weekend of November 26-27, 1994, Surehand Records and *How We Rock* zine supremo Nick Royales booked two shows at the 1 In 12 for US metalcore band Earth Crisis.

Paying from his own pocket, he flew in the band from Syracuse, New York state to play back-to-back gigs and promote their Victory Records release *Destroy The Machines* album. The first night was rammed with punters travelling from all over the UK, but not so many attended the following night, so unfortunately Nick lost money on the overall promotion.

In the first months of 1995, many local bands graced the stage at the 1 In 12, from local indie-pop artists Elsie Moon (pictured), Keighley's Mapp, Auxiliary Of Real Men, Mash-M, Dub Kitchen and hardcore punk chaps Beer Beast.

DUB KITCHEN

Bradford's own dub reggae band started as a collective, playing dub/ska/reggae in guitarist Pogz's kitchen.

Dub Kitchen's life as a performing band was quite short-lived, starting in January 1994 and ending around Christmas of the same year. During this time they were quite busy, performing over twenty gigs in the Bradford area, and releasing three albums on cassette, including *Green & Pleasant*.

They had over 400 people dancing at the Queen's Hall when they played at the Bradford Festival Finale, with songs such as *Criminal Justice*, *Living On A Giro*, *Don't Watch TV* and *Special Brew*. With three singer-song-writers in the band (Pogz, Fran and Min) they were quite prolific. Along with Pogz on bass was John Martin on guitar, a Roland drum machine and Deb Bong on percussion. Sam

replaced John for the last couple of gigs before band politics saw their sad demise.

Highly regarded exponents of their ambient dubplate style, likened to, *'PIL meets Black Slate via PJ Harvey mixed with The Clash's Sandanista style bass-heavy dub.'*

Fran went on to record as Frantic with former New Model Army duo Rob Heaton and Stuart Morrow at Rob's Righteous Sound Studio. Her track *Move Me* appeared on the Mutiny 2000 compilation *White Abbey Road* in 2000.

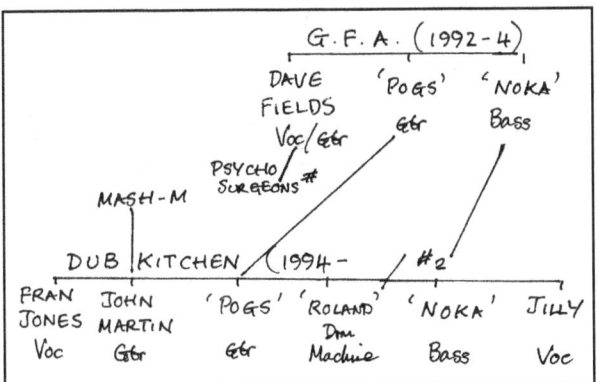

Bassist Pogs also played in the band #Crime (hash-crime) who played at Club Rio on July 25, 1991, with Pogs's other band, GFA, and The Bomb Circle. #Crime played at Treadwell's Arts Centre in 1999.

As well as the usual UKHC (United Kingdom Hard Core) bands, electronic noise merchants Zoviet France and Whitehouse played at The 1 In 12 Club, plus ska outfits Funkfish and Lord Skaman & The Magnificent Seven.

In April, US bands Dropdead and Naked Aggression came over on tour for the first time to play the Club

SPIES AT WORK

In early, 1995, 1 In 12 Publications produced its latest book, *Spies At Work: The Rise & Fall Of the Economic League*, by Mike 'Dirk Spig' Hughes.

The book was an expose of the far-right organisation that, since its inception in and around 1926 after that year's General Strike, had played an important role in British political and industrial life by compiling lists of leftists and trade unionists on a blacklist for sale to employers, in the struggle to halt the growth of left-wing activism.

the Zapatistas of Mexico

THE ZAPATISTAS

Mexico's Zapatista Army Of National Liberation (EZLN) hit the world's headlines on January 1, 1994, when, in simultaneous actions, they took over seven municipal townships in the south-eastern state of Chiapas, declaring war on the federal government and proclaiming for democracy, freedom and justice for all Mexicans. Inspired and named after Emiliano Zapata, the historic hero of the Mexican Revolution, the indigenous men and women (one-third of combatants are women) of the Chiapas region, led by Sub-comandante Marcos (El Sub) built camps and trained in the jungle. They survived the repression and lies of the Federal government, its estimated 73,000 troops and the unknown number of para-military gangs in this 'medium-intensity' war.

Their international presence was enhanced by the insurgent's novel use of the internet to promote their struggle, helping form world opinion and bringing donations of food and clothing from human rights organisations, the Red Cross and many other smaller groups across the world. (6)

While military and politically encircled for more than twenty years, they continued to bravely struggle for their rights and culture, demanding dignity and they constructed a way of living based on direct democracy and cooperation.

CHAPTER 6 — 1994 - 1996

ENDLESS STRUGGLE.
THE WORST OF THE 1 IN 12 CLUB VOL.12/13

In March 1995, the eighth vinyl release by 1 In 12 Records came out. It was a split benefit for The Zapatistas and the UK's Anarchist Black Cross (ABC). (7)

A double album with a booklet, it featured 24 bands who had played the Club between July 1990 and July 1992, including tracks from Cluster Bomb Unit (Germany), Scraps (France), Protest (Switzerland), Hiatus (Belgium) and Contropotere (Italy).

> V/A - "Endless Struggle - 1 In 12 Vol 12/13" 2xLP
> This double LP is a benefit for Class War Prisoners and the Zapatistas, and contains tracks from many of the British and European bands who have played at the legendary 1 In 12 Club in Bradford in the last few years. There's 24 bands on here, with standout tracks from the mighty DISAFFECT, SEDITION, ONE BY ONE, OI POLLOI, SCRAPS and WAT TYLER. The 28 page booklet has lyrics and info on the bands and the benefit causes. A rad package and well worth your support. Shame they don't mailorder veggie burgers. (AM)

Reviewed in US zines *MRR*, *Heartattack* and *Profane Existence*, as well as many UK zines. It even got four Ks in *Kerrang!*

The album was playlisted by two of *MRR*'s staff writers in their top tens, came in at No. 3 in Italian radio station Attaco Sonoro's chart and reached No. 27 on the US College radio WHRB 95.3FM.

VARIOUS
'The Worst Of The 1 In 12 Club'
(1in12 12012/13)
KKKK
Anarchist benefit compilation. Some of the (live) recordings are rough, but this is a great value double LP featuring the likes of Voorhees, Doom, Scraps and the brilliantly named Beer Beast. £8 from: *1in12 Records*

The LP sold out in just over six months and was the first 1 In 12 release to be repressed. It raised around £250 for the ABC and £500 for the Zapatistas. (8)

> VARIOUS "Endless Struggle: Worst Of The 1 in 12 Club Vol 12/13" double LP-Probably the most "together" 1 in 12 Compilation. Everything from the cover to the choice of bands is thematically linear and uh...like full of fuckin sense. Fans of hardcore and punk will no doubt have a field day blasting out the likes of TERMINUS, SEDITION, SORE THROAT, DOOM, IRONSIDE, ONE BY ONE, OI POLLOI, WAT TYLER, VOORHEES, CONTROPOTERE, CONCRET SOX, SCRAPS, HIATUS & a whole lot more. Not much in the way of guitar solos so I'm personally a little distressed but hey, thats just me & is in no way meant as a criticism.

```
PLAYLIST OCTOBER '95

1. RECHARGE    "SILENT SCREAMS"    12"
2. '77 SPREADS  7"
   THE SICKOIDS/CRUNCH SPLIT  7"
3. ENDLESS STRUGGLE. THE WORST OF THE 1 IN 12 CLUB VOL.12/13
   DOUBLE LP COMPILATION
4. MISERY  "WHO'S THE FOOL..."  LP
5. THE CHOICE  "LOOKING OUT MY WINDOW"  7"
   ACTIVE MINDS  "DIS IS GETTING PATHETIC..."  7"
```

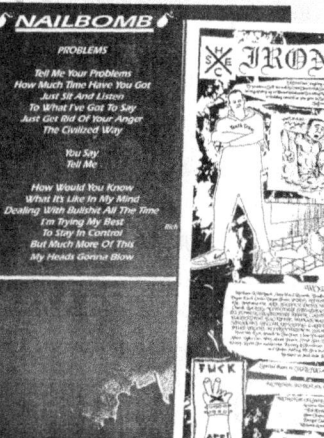

In May 1995, another two-day Hardcore/Punk festival was organised at The 1 In 12 Club, with German band ABC Diablo headlining. Also playing were Des Man DeAblo (ex-members of Dead Wrong), Baby Harp Seal, Nottingham's Bob Tilton, who played crazy ass emo, Smog, Tribute, PigPile, with Shutdown and Stamping Ground, (both based in Ledbury), Blood Sucking Freaks and Bradford's newest Club band Suffer.

```
              2 day
   HARDCORE & PUNK FESTIVAL
       Sat 6th & 7th MAY 1995
    Sat 7pm til late, Sun 2pm onwards
     16 BANDS IN 2 FUCKING DAYS
Saturday - VOORHEES, SUFFER, BABY HARP SEAL,
 BLOOD SUCKING FREAKS, PIG PILE, TRIBUTE,
       STRETCH , and ABOVE ALL
Sunday - ABC DIABLO, BOB TILTON, DES MAN De
ABLO, SMOG SHUTDOWN, HAYWIRE , STAMPING
         GROUND & OFFSET.
at THE 1 IN 12 CLUB, ALBION ST, BRADFORD.
  Tel 01274 734160 for sleeping places at club
       Band info 01274 392518 (nick)
```

Starting in July 1995, 1 In 12 Publications produced a series of DIY pamphlets, the first was entitled *What Is The 1 In 12 Club?*

The pamphlet explained the 1 In 12's history and development, how it was managed, etc and its long-term aims, accompanied by a profile of the fifteen autonomous collectives that worked within the Club.

One such collective, the *Peasants* (who worked an allotment to produce vegetables for the cafe) organised themed three-course meal nights, like the Mexican, Spanish, Italian etc for a modest fee.

Another collective, the 1 In 12 footy team, returned to play in the tournament in Hannau, Germany that June. This time, out of ten teams, they reached the final and beat the German team FC Banana 3-0 to win the cup. (9)

Unfortunately, one potential collective called Project X (an experimental dance/theatre group) initially suggested by member Rachel Minsul in September 1995, didn't spark enough interest to proceed, but within a few years, the Club would have its own drama collective, more of which later.

SUFFER

When Mandy left Health Hazard, the remaining trio of Sned, Alec and Chris carried on as Suffer, playing their own distinctive style of thrash-punk.

In late 1995, they released a self-titled *Suffer* 7" six track EP on Flat Earth Records, recorded at In A City Studios after touring Europe and the US with Drop Dead. While in the US they got interviewed for a feature article in Minniapolis's *Profane Existence* zine.

That same year Alec, with his partner Sarah of Witchknot, had provided an interview about the 1 In 12 Club for a book that came out, published by Eviltwin a joint Dutch/American enterprise,

Not For Rent: Conversations With Creative Activists In The UK by Stacy Wakefield & Grrt was a series of articles on projects including The 1 In 12 Club, 120 Rats in Leeds, Brixton and Hackney Squatters, Scottish activists and renegade sound system collectives around at the time.

CHAPTER 6 — 1994 - 1996

COWBOYS VISIT

Over the weekend of December 8-10, the Club's Bristol comrades, the Easton Cowboys, came up for a visit, to get pissed, socialise and play football.

The Friday night kicked off with a gig by VR, on Saturday, after the Club's football team had played their Grattan league fixture there was another gig and curry night, with Beer Beast and Heart Of Darkness. (Paul of The Cowboys pictured above.)

On the Sunday, the Cowboys took on the Club football team in a friendly match, amongst many a hangover... There is no record of the score, must have been a draw!

The Cowboys had a great weekend and vowed to return soon, if the Club didn't visit them first.

From July to December, some of the most memorable gigs at the Club were by Attevenger (Austria), RDF, Smell & Quim, Zoviet France (again!), Sabot (US/Czech), Defiance (US), 108/ Abhinanda, Masskontrol, Whirling Pig Dervish (Scotland), Bob Tilton, and rounding the year off nicely in December, local heroes VR, Beer Beast and Heart of Darkness.

The first gig of 1996 was a benefit for the Zapatistas, with visiting US band Spanakorzo and Leeds group Polaris.

LAUNCH OF 1 IN 12 LIBRARY

ANARCHIST GATHERING
1 in 12 Club
Saturday January 20th

Black Flag Benefit
with
"The Auxiliary of Real men"
Black Flag Readers' Meeting

Northern Book Launch of Albert Meltzer's Autobiography "I Couldn't Paint Golden Angels"

On Saturday, January 20, veteran British anarchist Albert Meltzer officially opened The 1 In 12 Club's library at the top of the building with the launch of his autobiography, *I Couldn't Paint Golden Angels*.

Wednesday, January 17, 1996
Telegraph & Argus

Anarchy rules at library do

A new "anarchist" library will be unveiled in Bradford at the weekend.

It will be opened at the 1 in 12 Club in Albion Street, Bradford, by veteran anarchist writer Albert Meltzer.

The library will contain anarchist and libertarian material as well as the club's archives.

The opening at 8pm on Saturday will double as the northern launch of 75-year-old Meltzer's autobiography I Couldn't Paint Golden Angels, which tells the story of his involvement in anarchism in Britain and Spain.

Tony Grogan, who is organising the event, said: "Albert, the grandfather of British anarchism, was a great inspiration to a number of us who helped start the 1 in 12 Club in 1981.

"We are therefore particularly pleased to have him at the club 15 years on."

That evening there was a benefit gig by local act The Auxiliary Of Real Men.

Sadly, later that year in May, Albert died aged 76. His funeral in London was well attended by many activists and, as he'd requested, the sound of Marlene Dietrich singing was heard as his coffin slid into the incinerator.

Between, March and June 1996, gigs at the Club included visits by regulars Bob Tilton, Ex-Cathedra, Carol (from Bremen, Germany), UK Subs (their fourth gig since the Club opened in 1988), Cress, Scatha, the atmospheric guitar noise of Bodychoke (ex-Whitehouse) and Belgian band Hiatus who played their umteenth gig at the 1 In 12.

A group of new local bands

played that spring and summer, such as indie-rockers Bullweek, Heavy-Rockers Dawnraiser, The Bullets,

Right Hand Action and a young band of sixteen/seventeen years olds called Black Horizon, who played twice.

CHAPTER 6   1994 - 1996

SURE HAND RECORDS

The label was started by ex-Sore Throat / Ironside drummer Nick Royles in August 1992, initially to release Ironside's cassette single *Neutered Innocence.*

It then lay dormant till 1995 when it re-emerged with two 7" single releases (one a flexi) by Southend's Above All, followed by the 1996 Unborn six-track EP *Ancestral Pagan Roots.*

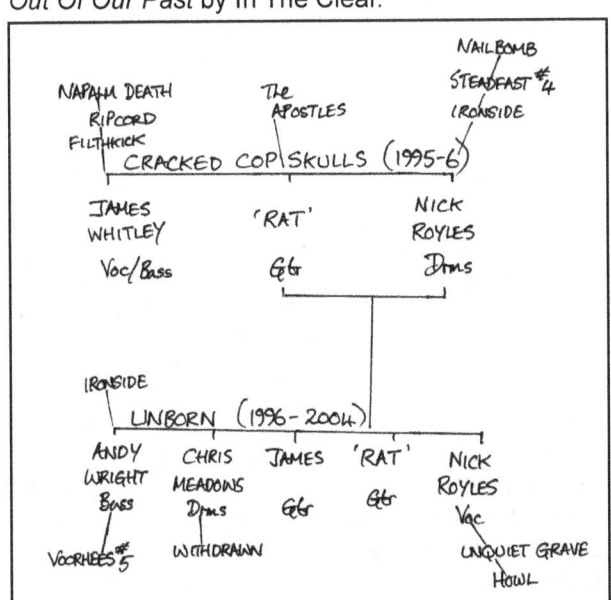

Prior to forming Unborn, Nick had been in Cracked Cop Skulls who never played live, but did release two 7" singles, *No Fucking Tears For The Pieces Of Shit* in 1995 on Days Of Fury and later, *Why Pussyfoot, When You Can Kill.* The trio of CCS were helped out in the studio by Decadence Within members Ian 'Slug' Glasper and Mobs.

Besides running the label and doing the fanzine *How We Rock*, Nick was instrumental with Richard of AWA Records in organising at least two or three hardcore festivals a year at the 1 In 12 between 1993-98, such as the one on May 25/26, 1996 which had twenty bands playing. French bands Portobello Bones and Peu Etre, Germany's Unsilent Minority and Nick's band Unborn all appeared.

Sure Hand's last three releases were a 7" by Liverpool's Withdrawn in 1997, then two CDs in 1999, the compilation *Justice For The Enslaved* and *Out Of Our Past* by In The Clear.

MAYDAY IN BARCELONA

Following a suggestion made at a cafe-themed Spanish meal night, members of The 1 In 12 Club organised a trip to Barcelona in Spain to celebrate May Day.

On April 28, forty-three members set off from Gatwick airport for seven days in Barcelona, which involved meetings with Spanish comrades, exhibitions, talks on organisation at the social centre La Vakeria, other debates at El Lokal and general sightseeing. The highlight of the trip was when 1 In 12 members joined the CNT May Day parade through Barcelona, ending up at Cuatro Paso which was an Anarchist-run bar.

Most nights before either gigs or meetings and as all Club members were vegetarian or vegan, they all ate at the Escondite (an anarchist-run cafe) where meals were cooked especially for them.

The 1 In 12 Club members were impressed by their Spanish comrades who worked so hard to prepare for the visit, showed such warm and friendly hospitality and inspired them with their skills in overall organisation.

This trip was an inspiration to organise regular 1 In 12 Club *May Day Festivals* which began in 1997.

ARMED WITH ANGER RECORDS BENEFIT LP

Armed With Anger Records released the *A Means To An End* benefit compilation LP in aid of The 1 In 12 Club during 1996. It featured ten bands who were all regular visitors to the Club stage; Voorhees, Manfat, Hard To Swallow, Unborn, Solanki, Stalingrad, Tribute, Schema, Baby Harp Seal and Bob Tilton (pictured), it also contained a booklet of the band's artwork.

As Richard Corbridge of AWA Records stated, *'To an extent, the Club does get taken for granted by the hardcore scene, at times even neglected. I thought it important to specifically choose bands who do actually support the Club itself and it's values. The opportunity to partially document the scene and help give something back to the Club by such a release couldn't be more obvious. There's not many places in the world like the 1 In 12 Club... I honestly don't know what would happen if the place ever closed down. It would certainly leave a huge gap that would unlikely to be replaced.'*

Between July and December, more top gigs took place at the 1 In 12, such as Systral from Germany, the two-day Monster Fest, a *Club Ugly* gig with Bradford's *Battle Of The Bands 1989* winners Poisoned Electric Head, another two-day Hardcore Festival in early November and

more touring bands from Europe and the USA; Fleas & Lice (Holland), Gruff (Germany) and San Deigo's Swing Kids, from Virginia, Avail, from Chicago the political hardcore band Los Crudos, San Francisco's Dead & Gone and the Californian metalcore band Strife.

BAD WISDOM TOUR

On October 24, 1996, the former KLF members Bill Drummond and Mark Manning, aka Zodiac Mindwarp, appeared at the 1 In 12 on their short six-venue tour to promote their book *Bad Wisdom*. The evening involved spoken word and readings from the book about their strange adventure together to the North Pole to sacrifice an icon of Elvis Presley.

The support act on the night was local lad Chris Brook with his performance piece Pitch Blend Congress. Chris was then based in London and was a writer/performer who moved from the parameters of performance projects towards text-based solo excursions.

During 1996, the old Wool Exchange was converted and refurbished into a Waterstones Book shop (downstairs) and a Starbuck's coffee shop (upstairs).

IN YER FACE RECORDS

This label was formed in July 1996 by Billy Allen, of Fagley, as a platform for up-and-coming talent.

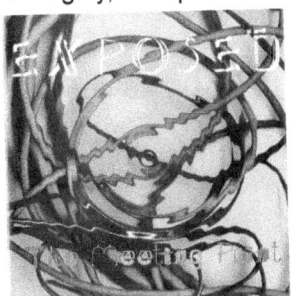

The first release was the compilation CD *Exposed: The Meeting Point* which contained eighteen unsigned bands including Vochi, Blade and Clouded Fish, from Bradford, The CD gained some airplay on Radio 1 and two bands who appeared on the compilation, Symptom and Blessed Rain, got signed to record labels.

In Yer Face's next release was another compilation, *Create From Beyond,* a seven band affair, which again got some airplay and reviews in rock magazines.

Two more compilation CDs followed in the next year, *Anarchy Reign* and *Expo '97*. The last one had tracks by Blade, Blister Factory and Stipetic Project all from Bradford.

BLADE - "Twisted Religion"
In Yer Face Record (IYFCD18)

The first single to follow on the heels of last years album *"Always"* (sold 12,000+ copies). A throbbing trigger slappy high tempo melodic slab of rock/hardcore industrial mayhem. Chainsaws and laithes would not be out of place. the lyrics are naturally heavily influenced by time spent in Croatia and Bosnia - the battle zone for real upon which the spirit of *Twisted Religion* seems to have been lifted. A snap shot of observations and emotions of the time would seem to be an apt statement.
Info: 01274 643030
Panic Rating : 89%

IN YER FACE RECORDS PRESENTS
COSMIC JOKER
+ BLADE
Live at Rio Rokz - Friday April 4th

IN YER FACE RECORDS
49 Fagley Lane, Bradford
01274 643030

EXPO 97
(iyfo2cdi)
OUT NOW!
Only £4.99 inc P&P, payable to
IN YER FACE RECORDS
at 49 Fagley Road, Bradford, W/Yorks.
Featuring : Velma, Blessed Rain, Redcard, Laughland, Hedgepig, Blade and more!
16 BAND CD ALBUM,
CHECK IT OUT!

The debut album *Life, As One* by Cosmic Joker was released in April 1997 and promoted by a gig at Rio's where Cosmic Joker were supported by Blade on Friday, April 4.

Blade was Billy Allen's own band, who released the album *Always* on CD that September, followed by the CD single *Twisted Religion* from the album. The band received admiring letters from listeners as far afield as Japan and got a management deal with a company called Flick based in Luton.

Two new young local bands formed around this time;

FACELIFT

Facelift were a young indie outfit who produced a couple of demos during their short lifespan.

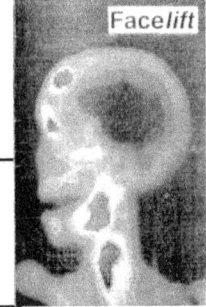

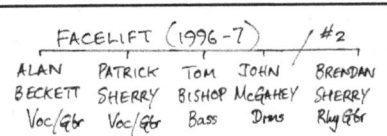

FACELIFT (1996-7)				#2
ALAN BECKETT	PATRICK SHERRY	TOM BISHOP	JOHN McGAHEY	BRENDAN SHERRY
Voc/Gtr	Voc/Gtr	Bass	Drms	Rhy Gtr

MUNDANE

Mundane were a rock act with an average age of fifteen. They released a six-song demo in late 1996, which received some interest from EMI Records. The band's main spokespersons were Ross Elliot and Michael Jones They made an appearance on BCB's *Bradford Beat* radio show.

SLACK ELVIS

This trio of Bradford/Leeds musicians, which included former members of La Costa Rasa, were playing gigs around the local scene at the time.

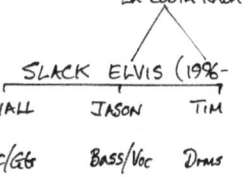

LA COSTA RASA		
SLACK ELVIS (1996-		
NIALL	JASON	TIM
Voc/Gtr	Bass/Voc	Drms

DRAGSTER

This Leeds/Bradford-based indie band garnered a big local following and major record company interest, which led to singer Craig Brauns being signed to Island Records.

After initial demo sessions, Craig recruited former Dragster members Dave Ledgard and Jake Riley, his brother Greg Brauns and Sean Dillon (all four were performing as Elvis Taxi at the time) to form a new band, Zico, named after the Brazilian footballer of the 1970s.

Zico went on to tour with bands like Terrorvision and recorded a complete album in London and South Wales for Island Records in 2002 which was unfortunately never released.

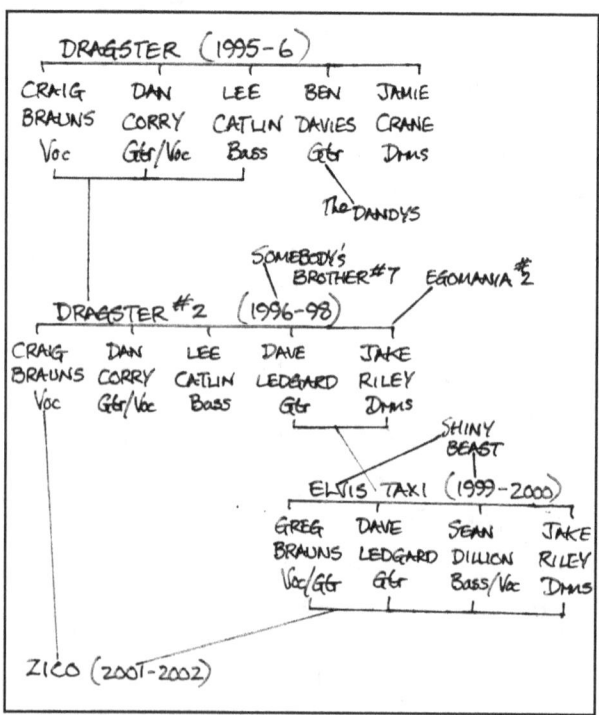

BRADFORD FESTIVAL 1996

The tenth Bradford Festival ran from June 28 to July 13.

The programme featured the tagline *'Bradford By The Sea'* which was the bizarre obsession of various councillors and town planners and has led to various ideas which have bemused local folk ever since, from plans to make a false beech to excavating a large stagnant, pool in the middle of the city centre.

The Festival was the usual mix of street entertainment and events taking place at venues all around the city, including *The Infamous Circus Of Horrors* which took place on the infirmary Fields from Thursday, June 27 to Sunday, July 7.

Local pubs and clubs like MacRory's Bar, New Beehive, the Spotted House and the Windsor Baths all put on gigs and events, featuring live bands poetry and comedy.

Events were covered on BCB - *Your Festival Radio* and Bradford Festival TV, which was on air for the duration.

The Bradford Mela took place over the weekend of July 6-7 at Lister Park.

The big gig on the middle Sunday was Gregory Isaacs at The Windsor Baths.

The Festival closed with a firework display at Peel Park.

MUSIC AT MYRTLE

The free concert at Bingley's' Myrtle Park that year was Suzi Quatro supported by The Steve Gibbons Band and local band Made In Milwaukee.

LOST WEEKEND

A sort of NWOBHM 'supergroup' consisting of former members of Rhabstallion, Krakatoa and Voyager UK. In 1996, they released a four-track mini-CD, that was recorded at the Academy Studios, Dewsbury. Two further CDs followed, then in 2005 they released a CD of all three releases entitled *The Story So Far*.

GREEN

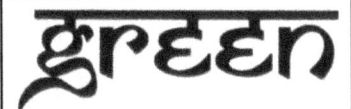

When local band Peached Out split up, Dominic Sheard formed Green in 1996. They then began to play many local gigs including 1996's *Bands On The Beck* at Bradford University. The band recorded a couple of demos and later produced a three-track CD in 2007.

HOMESICK

One of the local bands managed by Andy Farrow's *Northern Music*, they included ex-members of Bomb Circle and Dawnraiser/Neckbrace. The band's second demo was recorded at the Engine Rooms Studio and was financed by Epic Records.

They played many local shows, headlining Rio's on December 11, 1996, and later played at Camden Falcon, London.

TROTWOOD'S SUNDAY SUNDAY

Roger 'Trotwood' Nowell, former bassist with Keighley's Skeletal Family, published a book on the local Keighley Sunday league football teams called *Sunday Sunday*, in October 1996.

It took Roger two years to complete, while he worked as a guitar tech for Paul 'Guigsy' McGuigan, bassist of rock band Oasis, travelling all over the world.

Roger had played for the Boltmakers Arms FC since they were founded in 1991, and during the 1995-96 season managed to get Oasis to sponsor the team's kit for the next five years.

BANDS ON THE BECK

On Saturday, June 15, 1996, there was an open-air gig outside the University. *Bands On The Beck* was organised by Andy Barnet.

For What, Slick 50, Rent, GFA, Green, The Auxiliary Of Real Men, The Bullets, Bodyjar, Dub Kitchen, UB IK and Homesick played at the all-day event.

OFF THE WALL

Starting in 1996, this bunch of very talented musicians, with years of experience in local bands, played for the first time at The Ring 'O' Bells, Queensbury.

Within a short space of time, Off The Wall would become one of Europe's best Pink Floyd tribute bands, out-growing the smaller pub/club venues.

Their mastery of the intricacies of the music of Floyd from *Dark Side Of The Moon* through to *The Wall*, punctuated by their stunning light show gained them critical acclaim.

Besides touring the UK and Europe regularly over the years, they always fitted in a local gig, at either St George's Hall or Halifax's Piece Hall Yard.

By the end of their career, they were playing sell-out gigs like the outdoor event at Ripley Castle in July 2007.

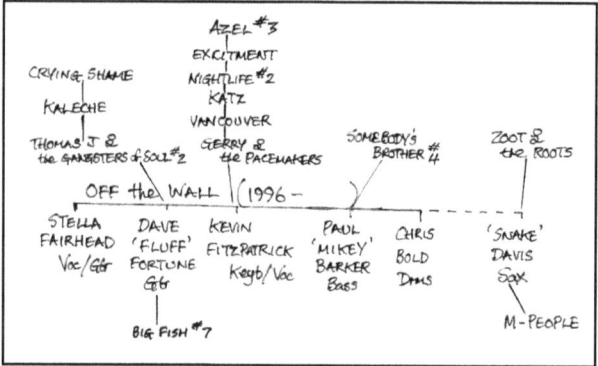

Finally, two Keighley bands emerged during this period:-

DEAD CELEBS

From the ashes of the local thrash metal band Mr Meana, came the Keighley based Dead Celebs.

Their new musical direction was a far cry from the metal-edged rock of their previous incarnation, more pop-friendly chart-type material.

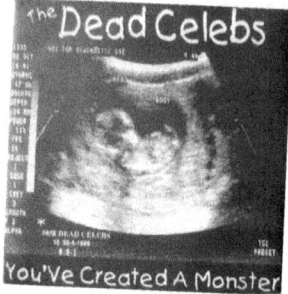

One track, *You've Created A Monster*, was recorded and broadcast on Sky TV. It later resurfaced as the title track on their debut four-track 12" single, with *No One Cares*, *Cycling To Pluto* and *Head Grenade* being the other tracks, in June 1997.

These four slices of pop-friendly tunes were released on the My Records label and they were recorded at the legendary Abbey Road Studios in London, made universally famous by The Beatles.

GARDEN OF REMEMBRANCE

Keighley's doom-metal specialists Garden Of Remembrance played their first-ever gig supporting American thrash metallers Xentrix at Rio's. The band headlined at Rio's and supported My Dying Bride, Serenity and Cradle Of Filth.

They recorded three demos, *Imposter*, *Mourner's Cry* and *A Sickening Sun*, which was recorded at Ash Mount Studios in Heaton, and comprised six of their own compositions.

When the band split up, their vocalist Jaxon and guitarist Iceman formed the band Aftermath in 2004.

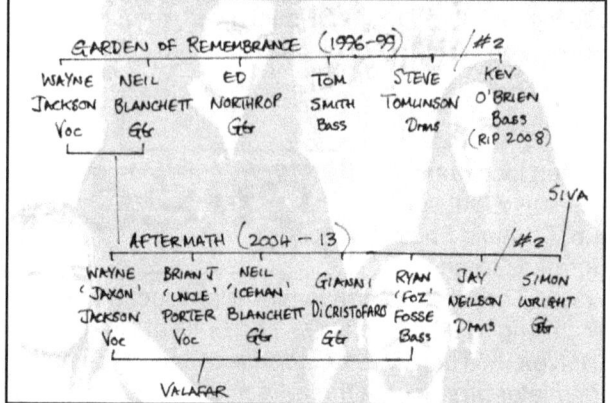

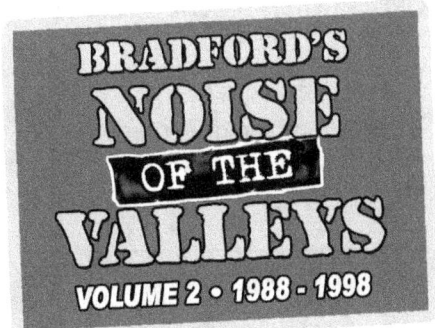

CHAPTER 7: 1997 - 1998

Hardly a year went by in the 1990s when the Bradford music scene didn't keep producing as many new bands and artists as previously. So, the years 1997-98 were no different, as a new crop of local musicians continued to form new combos and perpetuate the city's musical heritage.

Two new potential music venues opened at this time too, The Love Apple and Delius Lived Next Door, which would help to accommodate with existing music venues this fresh bunch of artists wanting gigs.

THE LOVE APPLE

This cafe/bar, opposite the car park that was the old Bradford College Alexandra Building, was opened by a group of ex-Buttershaw Upper School students, Parvez Iqbal, Mazzafer Hussain and Victoria and James Brett. Within a year or so it would be playing host to gigs and dance nights in the larger room within the complex.

In later years the became a regular venue for local bands and events including *Fresh Milk* recording and promotion nights in the early 2000s..

DELIUS LIVED NEXT DOOR

This new bar opened at No 8 Claremont (off Great Horton Road, near the University) and aimed at catering for the area's student population.

Again, within a short period of time, this would become one of Bradford's newest music venues. (1)

The pub later became a more regular venue for local bands and also took over hosting the annual *Ginger Fringe Festival* after MacRory's bar closed in 2004.

BRADFORD'S FIRST ASIAN LABOUR MP

In February, Marsha Singh became Bradford's first Asian Labour MP as he replaced Max Madden in the Bradford West seat. Over the next seventeen years, Marsha effectively represented his constituents in Parliament for the Labour Party before tragically passing away in 2012.

On March 27, HRH The Queen arrived in the city to mark and celebrate Bradford's 100 years as a City by opening the newly constructed open space called Centenary Square, which put a pedestrianised area in front of the City Hall's steps

CECIL ZINYUKU

Cecil had been the bassist for Somebody's Brother between 1986-87 and had worked with local act New Musical Testament. In 1995, he appeared on *Top Of The Pops* with American outfit De'Lacy when they played their No 9 hit *Hideaway*.

In 1997, he put a demo album together with the help of Inder 'Goldfinger' of Detrimental which impressed music industry scouts. They hoped to land a deal with a major label.

ZED AGAIN

After the demise of their band Grim, bassist Jont and drummer Matt Webster continued the spirit of the project with a new band featuring former Western Dance/Primate guitarist Steve Andrews and later Crispian Baker.

After toying with a few names, they decided to resurrect the name Zed and combine some of their old songs with a whole album's worth of new songs.

The band took over part of the top floor, which also housed Griff's Magic Theatre, of what later became known as The Mill.

After initial gigs at The Peel and MacRory's Bar, Steve left. The new Zed continued as a trio to record an album, taped by engineer Nick Horton, at Ali Briggs's Blue Noise Studios, which was also based in the same building.

The band played a gig at the *Sussex Art Festival* in June 1997 under the banner of an anti-racism *Unity 1997* concert. Former Nowt/Grim guitarist Adam Bennett was playing live guitar with the band but turned up late for the gig, making it on stage just in time to play tambourine on the last encore! Liverpudlian and Amsterdam party organiser Bone jokingly referred to the event as *'Mutiny 1997'*, a title that was adapted for the title of Zed's new album, *Mutiny 2000*.

They opened the *Bradford Centenary Music Week*, headlining a gig at Queen's Hall on June 2, 1997.

After guitarist Crispian left Zed due to health issues, Matt and Jont decided to put their energies into building a studio and record label, named *Mutiny 2000*.

Zed
Mutiny 2000
(Mutiny 2000 ZED2001)

It's long been a mystery to me why Zed have never been snapped up by record company talent scouts.

They have been around long enough for their brand of mystical punk to have been in and out of fashion any number of times and it's difficult to pinpoint why they missed the boat.

The Zed blueprint is a muscular variety on alternative rock, taut and driven by the rhythm section of bassist Jont and drummer Matt.

Zed's distinctive vocal harmonies are another key component of their sound and at their best — as they do on Summer Rain or All Uneven — they sound as urgent as anything else around today.

Although the bass and drums axis is central in most songs on Mutiny 2000, there is also plenty from guitarist Crispian to keep those happy who like their rock seasoned with plenty of gutsy riffing, notably on opener White Knuckle Ride.

There's rarely a let-up in the intensity of Zed's sound but they prove they can successfully take it down a notch or two on the slightly more laid-back Velvet Revolution.

SIMON ASHBERRY

THE HORTON CARPETS

This collaboration was formed by former members of Zed and other Bradford bands in 1997/98 and were named after a carpet shop opposite the flat at which most of the band had lived, on Great Horton Road.

They played a semi-acoustic set around local venues like MaCrory's and The Melborn. A version of the band later recorded the tracks *Driven* and *Summer Rain* which appeared, along with some older, recordings on their CD album *Underlay* in 2002.

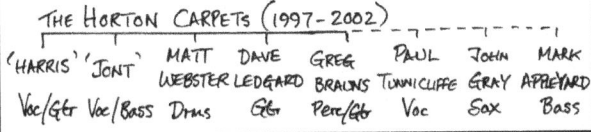

MUTINY 2000

The idea behind the Mutiny 2000 studio/label was to be a collective of local musicians combining their various talents to create an environment where bands and artists could rehearse, record and release material.

The combined talents could provide full recording, mixing and mastering facilities along with artwork, press releases, recordings and live sound to cover every base for new and already-established bands.

Jont and Matt were joined in the project by local musicians, songwriters, and engineers in a core which included singer-songwriter Harris, producer and Rob Heaton (drummer with New Model Army), dance DJ Chad Meade and singer/songwriter Mark 'Moota' Appleyard who oversaw the building of the walls and floors and electrics of the studio, with aid and assistance from Harris, former Slammer singer Paul Tunnicliffe and Bradford punk legend Johna Johnson.

The top floor of The Mill, which was already the home of Griff's Magic Theatre saw the building of the Mutiny studio, followed by purpose-built studios by New Model Army and Chumbawamba and became a vibrant hub of activity for local music.

Mutiny 2000 began regular Thursday night jam sessions to test recording facilities, attended by the core members and other local musicians, including John Gray, Bela Emerson, Sean Dillon, Jez Farrar, Simon 'Nogsy' Nolan, Nat Brewer, Rob Rhodes and others.

From these sessions, an industrial set was formulated and later performed by the Mutiny 2000 collective in the new venue based in the cellar of The Mill on several occasions, featuring soundtrack-style music with tape loops of iconic clips from classic films and TV shows, put together by Rob Heaton.

Chad Meade and Harris in the Mutiny control room

Mutiny 2000 released a compilation of all the contributing bands, called *White Abbey Road*, in 2000, and put on a gig at The Mill to launch the album.

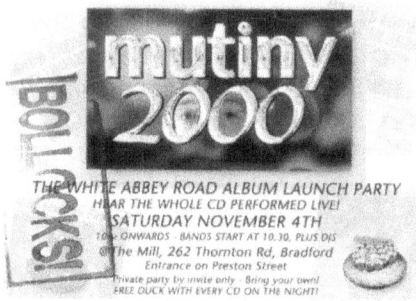

This mammoth gig included every band who had tracks on the album including The Gardeners Of Eden (their only live appearance), Shiny Beast, Angelo Palladino, Year Dot, Supersonic, Moota, Elvis Taxi, and Frantic.

Rob Heaton and Matt Webster were the main producers of the albums and sessions at Mutiny 2000 Studios, followed by Simon 'The Guvnor' Mawson and, later, guitarist James Atkinson who continued to run the studio and record new music.

A second compilation album, *Soup Bowl Press*, was recorded and released in 2002, as were albums by bands including Moota, Angelo Palladino, Transu and Kwai Chang Caine, all on Mutiny 2000 Records.

There was also a re-release album catalogue produced, with the re-mastering of Bradford bands including, Zed, Psycho Surgeons, Requiem, Western Dance, Primate and Nick Toczek onto CD.

After various core members emigrated, moved cities died (Rob Heaton, RIP 2004) or moved on, the project splintered. It continued as a recording studio, with James 'Atko' Atkinson at the helm, until 2018.

Mutiny 2000 Records went on to release new vinyl and CD albums by the likes of Signia Alpha, Nick Toczek, Harris, The Mainline (Jont's band).

GARDENERS OF EDEN

Rob Heaton's studio project, The Gardeners Of Eden, recorded a full album. It featured Rob, Stuart Morrow, Rob Rhodes, Harris, John Gray, Lianne Hall and others. Although tracks appeared on the Mutiny 2000 compilations, the full album was never released. Rob was busy playing and recording his other projects, Jazz Mutiny and Loose Furs, and then started the *Fresh Milk* project.

DAILY MUTINY

1998 also saw the first few issues of the *Daily Mutiny*, Matt Webster's humorous half-true reports on the ongoing adventures of members and friends of the bands that helped to set up Mutiny 2000 or were regulars at pubs like MacRorys, The Melborn and The Peel.

BLUE NOISE STUDIOS

This 8-track recording studio was based in what became known as The Mill. It was called Blue Noise Studios because it was housed on the same floor as the Blue Print printing company, and both were run by Ali Briggs. The studio was also the site of many jams and recordings by local musicians who worked or hung around in the building.

Engineer Nick Horton recorded tracks for a compilation that remains unreleased, featuring local acts Siren, Zed and Paul Tunnicliffe.

Sadly, Nick Horton passed away in the early 2000s.

'Terrible' Nic Darby, Marki 'Moota' Appleyard with Nick Horton (right) outside MacRory's Bar.

CHAPTER 7 — 1997 - 1998

BIAS

A Bradford/Batley-based band who, when they played at The 1 In 12 Club on February 8, 1997, were still going out under the name Liberty Scream. By April, they had changed their name to Bias and released a six-track demo in the musical style of US grunge-rock bands.

TV EYE

In early February 1997 members of the 1 In 12 Club approached the local Council about the extent of the City's CCTV surveillance scheme.

Concerned Club member Matt Hannam

A Club spokesman said, *'Once cameras go up they will never come down. There is currently no legal constraints at all on CCTV. The blanket coverage of our public space has huge implications for us all. We want to know how the scheme is being monitored and by whom and what happens to the films.'*

The chairman of the council's community safety committee said he had received no other complaints about the system which has made huge inroads into crime.

RADIUS

Former Stax Wheelright and Bullweek drummer Jay Barraclough in this local group. They played some gigs around the pub circuit, like Queensbury's Ring 'O'Bells, but concentrated on honing their material in the studio, producing demos.

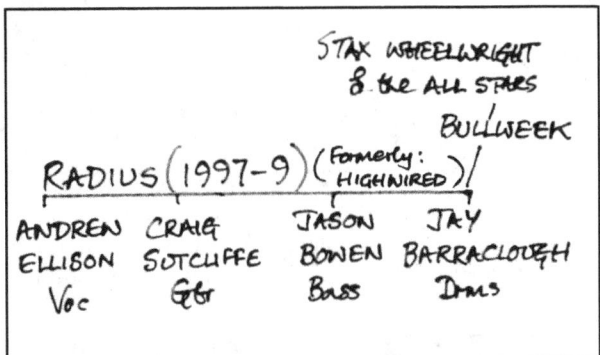

BENWAY

This local rock quartet headlined a concert at The Duchess Of York in Leeds, supported by Slack Elvis and Slick 50.

THE BLISTER FACTORY

Twister 5 guitarist Rusz Petcher moved onto bass guitar to be part of this local five-piece band.

They released a cassette EP *The Blister Factory* in 1996.

The tape included the track *Coming Good* which is featured on the *Bradford's Noise Of The Valleys - The Music 1988 -1998* box set that accompanies this book.

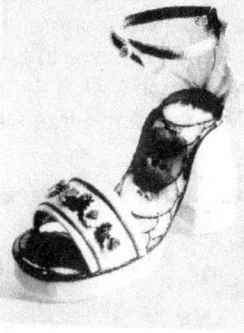

STORM PROMOTIONS

During April, a new band management company called *Storm* was operating in West Yorkshire and had a few Bradford bands belonging to their stable of artists.

One was the band Damn Nation who had been going since 1991, gigging all over the UK and had supported on tour the likes of Faith No More, FM and Magnum.

Another Bradford based-band was Blackout (pictured below) who had done some extensive gigging in the local area since forming around 1994. They received some record company interest from Europe and Japan.

Meanwhile, at The 1 In 12 Club, the first four months of 1997 saw some fine gigs by loads of the usual suspects like Blyth Power, Voorhees, Stalingrad, Hard To Swallow and Scotland's Scatha, plus more visiting foreign bands in early February; To Live And Shave In LA (US), Japanese band Conclude on March 6, Locust / Jenny Piccolo (US) on March 8 and State Of Fear (US) on the 23rd.

FEBRUARY — EVENTS FOR:

THUR 6th - It's JUKE BOX JURY - Episode 2. Bring your favourite hoppin' tunes, and put 'em to the vote!!!

FRI 7th - Never mind Trainspotting - here's BLYTH POWER - Roots and culture folkpunk tales from beyond the end of the platform, support from acoustic bearded man - MOUNTAINEERING DICKIE, also URJE - bass driven tunes and power from Preston. £2.50 / £3

SAT 8th - LIBERTY SCREAM and guests..

FRI 14th - TO LIVE AND SHAVE IN L.A (ex PUSSY GALORE) forgot how Rich described them, also the extremely hard 'n' heavy HARD TO SWALLOW. £2.50 / £3.50.

FRI 21st Blinkey Blinkey Blimey it's.... Noel & Matt's LOVELY KNEES UP - A traditional East end night around the old Joanna. Pie, Mash and Vegan Eels, Pearly Kings and Queens. Luvly Jubbly!

SAT 22nd - "STIMULATIONS" - Dance Event (Members Only)

MARCH

THU 6th - A night of good ol' Punk rock with bands from as far afield as Sheffield, Leeds and Wisbech: namely - WORM, DOG ON A ROPE and COMBAT SHOCK.

SAT 8th - "Slender Means" presents: a benefit for the National Abortion Campaign featuring - SHUTDOWN, MONTH OF BIRTHDAYS, BEACON, VENGEANCE OF GAIA, CECILLE. £2.50 / £3. Hardcore as in Hardcore Punk. First band on at 7.15.

SUN 16th - WITCHKNOT and others to be confirmed.

SAT 22nd - 'FLOATING BONG' BIRTHDAY BASH! - Dance Music (Members Only)

SAT 29th - "STIMULATIONS" - Dance Event (Members Only)

....AND ON THE TOP FLOOR....

FROM NOON TIL 3PM, THURSDAY TO SATURDAY EVERY WEEK THE CAFE IS OPEN - SERVING DELICIOUS, GOOD VALUE, VEGAN QUISINE. IN ONE CORNER THERE'S THE FLAT EARTH SHOP - SELLING PRODUCT FROM THE D.I.Y COUNTERCULTURE - BOOKS, ZINES, RECORDS ETC. IN THE OTHER CORNER IS THE ALBERT MELTZER MEMORIAL CYBER LIBRARY. FEEL FREE TO BROWSE. THE CAFE NEEDS PEOPLE TO HELP COME, HANG OUT & GET INVOLVED!

ALL AT THE: **1 IN 12 CLUB, ALBION ST, BRADFORD 1.** £2 / £2.50 (MEMBERS / GUESTS)

1 IN 12 CLUB GIGS 1997/1998

JANUARY 1997
31 - Seal Team 6 / The Sprawl

FEBRUARY 1997
7 - Blyth Power / Urje / Mountaineering Dickie
8 - Liberty Scream /
14 - To Live And Shave In LA (ex- Pussy Galore) / Hard to Swallow
22 - Stimulations

MARCH 1997
6 - Worm / Dog On A Rope / Conclude / Combat Shock
8 - Locust / Jenny Piccolo
9 - Shutdown / Month Of Birthdays / Beacon / Vengeance Of Gaia / Cecille
23 - State Of Fear

APRIL 1997
5 - Hard To Swallow / Voorhees / Stalingrad / Revolt
5 - Scatha / Imbiss / Scrofula
6 - State Of Fear / State Of Filth / Sawn Off

MAY 1997
1 at Centenary Square. Free Allday Gig (daytime) - the first time the new Square was used to hold a concert - Heart Of Darkness / Suitable Hooligans / Blyth Power / James Brookes / Stridemanwide
1 at Bradford University Communal Building (evening) - Chmbawamba / Blyth Power
5 - Frodus / Nine / Canvas
? - Oi Polloi / Kito / Doom
21 - Forca Macabra / Konstruct / Sarcasm

JUNE 1997
16 - Scatha / Bloodshot / The Jockney Rejects / Ebola / Ur

JULY 1997
? - Bob Tilton / Shaft / Month Of Birthdays / Imbalance / Polaris
? - Dystopia / Revolt / Extinction Of Mankind / Stalingrad
? - Archbishop Kebab / Dominic Waxing Lyrical / Witchknot / Red Monkey / Hip Huggers

AUGUST 1997
16 - Unhinged / Scatha / Bloodshot / The Jockney Rejects / Ebola / Urko / Cress
22 - Half Man, Half Biscuit

NOVEMBER 1997
Two Day Hardcore Festival 8 - Kodak / Hari Kiri / Kill For Christ / Voorhees / Red Monkey / Polaris / Scatha / Kito
9 - Minute manifesto / Imbiss / Canvas / Imbalance / Beacon / Stalingrad / The Sin-Eaters / The van Pelt
13 - Judy Small
28 - The Groundhogs
29 - Oi Polloi / Doom / Luddgang / Pete The Poet

DECEMBER 1997
20 - Cress / Active Minds / Scuym Of Society / Kreosote / Scrofula
?? - Dick Gaughan

1 IN 12 CLUB GIGS 1998

FEBRUARY 1998
27 - Martin Stephenson & The Toe-Rags

APRIL 1998
8 - Brendon Croker & Roy Wyke

MAY 1998
1 at Centenary Square (daytime) - UK Players / Lianne Hall / Little Brother / Hessel
1 at Bradford university Communal Building (evening) - Fundamental / The Underground Set DJs
3 - Rory McLeod
15 - The Men They Couldn't Hang
18 & 19 - Iron Monkey / Hard To Swallow / Voorhees / Month Of Birthdays / Imbiss / Quarantine / Scalplock / Ebola / John Holmes / Canvas / Kill For Christ / Urko / Active minds / Slain / Number One Son / Western Union / Rydall / Crawl Space / Rauschen
20 - Refused / Ink & Dagger / Cath O'Conner Sound / Canvas

JUNE 1998
3 - His Hero Is Gone / Hard To Swallow / Ebola / John Holmes
17 10th Anniversary of The 1 In 12 Club - Logical Nonsense / Medula Nocte
? - Ambush / Bilge Pump / DDI

AUGUST 1998
30 - Ambush / Bilge Pump / DDI

SEPTEMBER 1998
4 - Seized
11 - SDS / Hellkrusher / Luddgang
12 - Detestation / Doom / Sawn Off / Urko / Cress / Kito

OCTOBER 1998
10 - Submission Hold / Red Monkey / Wichknot / Solanki / Ebola
28 - Drop Dead / Reiziger / Kito / 666 Dead
29 - Cress / Eradicate / John Holmes / Sawn Off / Bilge Pump / Black Rag

NOVEMBER 1998
28-29 Two Day Hardore Festival
28 - Drop Dead / Reiziger / 666 Dead / Step Back / Out Cold / Diesel Vs Steam / Sunfactor / 30 Seconds Until Armageddon
29 - Braid / Burning Airlines / Stalingrad / Imbalance / Spy Versus Spy / Kill for Christ / DBH / Hernandez

This is as full a list of 1 In 12 Club gigs we can find at time of going to press. Anyone who knows any of the missing dates please contact us via bradfordnoise.com and we will update the list in a future edition.

CHAPTER 7 — 1997 - 1998

RECLAIMING MAY DAY 1997

Inspired by the sense of community spirit and solidarity from their trip to Barcelona the previous year, The 1 In 12 Club was determined to revive May Day in Bradford. Many members worked very hard in preparations leading up to the five days of events and produced a free programme that was distributed around the city.

'Five days of May Day action included The Haymarket Incident, a play about the origins of May Day, written and performed by local people, most of whom had never acted before. The University's Theatre In The Mill had its busiest week for years as people crammed in to see the performance.'

'A radical book fair was organised attracting people from across the country, Public meetings on a variety of issues (CCTV, the Zapatista Uprising, Community Resistance, etc) were held in pubs for five consecutive nights. A month-long film

Club banks on holiday switch

Gig-goers will have the chance to enjoy a traditional May Day music celebration next week.

Bradford's 1 in 12 Club is organising a Music Mayfest on Thursday, which will feature top bands Chumbawamba and Blyth Power.

Organiser Gary Cavanagh said the club was fed up with the traditional people's holiday being sidelined to the nearest bank holiday and had decided to return to a day of celebration on May 1 itself.

The event will kick off with a free outdoor festival in Centenary Square featuring Blyth Power, Heart of Darkness, The Blarney Bunch, Stridemanwide, Australian singer-songwriter James Brook and others. Comperes will be Wild Willi Beckett and Little Brother.

Blyth Power will then dash up to Bradford University where they are supporting Chumbawamba for the main event in the evening.

"With the demand for tickets there could be some disappointed fans. This way they can enjoy the free gig in Centenary Square," said Gary.

1/2/3 May Thur/Fri/Sat
The Haymarket Incident By Noel L Batstone
1 IN 12 DRAMA COLLECTIVE IN ASSOCIATION WITH THEATRE IN THE MILL

Never mind bank holidays – this is where it all began.

Chicago 1886. Murder, perjury, conspiracy, state corruption, anarchy! Four men hanged, but who is guilty?

Penned by local writer Noel Batstone and performed by members of the community, *'The Haymarket Incident'* tells the story of the origins of May Day and the early labour movement.

As the workers come out on strike to protest against working conditions, the authorities crack their knuckles and prepare to contain the rebellion.

From teartful love scenes to courtroom drama and from intense loyalty to betrayal, it is the fast-moving and passionate story of workers fighting against injustice.

festival was held at the Pictureville cinema. A walk retraced the history of West Yorkshire's machine-wrecking Luddites. Football teams from as far away as Norwich and Bristol battled to become Bradford's May Day champions. Folk, pop, and punk gigs kept people going during the evenings.'

'On May Day itself, a small but noisy parade wound its way through town towards a full afternoon of music in Centenary Square, enjoyed by around a thousand people. Chumbawamba saw events off with a memorable performance on May Day evening at Bradford University's Communal Building.'

'During the May Day events, hundreds of pounds were collected for the striking Liverpool Dockers. All of this was achieved without a penny of funding.'

(Taken from an article in *After The Break #1* February 1998, a quarterly **Bradford Arts Forum** magazine)

On Thursday, May 1, the May Day parade joined up in Centenary Square. The afternoon's free gathering of music (2) began with Stridemanwide (pictured), a six-piece grunge-rock band from Chesterfield (North Derbyshire), followed by visiting Australian singer/guitarist James Brookes, then Irish folk outfit The Blarney Bunch, trainspotters Blyth Power and two Bradford bands, Suitable Hooligans and headliners Heart Of Darkness.

That evening, at the Communal Building, Club stalwarts Chumbawamba and Blyth Power (pictured right) played again after their afternoon gig in Centenary Square - an excellent sold-out benefit for the 1 In 12 to top off the day.

Over the next few days, there were packed meetings all over town, a two-day Hardcore Festival and a two-day Football Tournament, which, out of six teams, from Norwich, Bristol and Leeds, produced an entertaining final between the Leeds team Republica and 1 In 12 AFC, who lost 2-1 to Republica.

On Monday, May 5, after a final *Grand May Day Picnic* in Lister Park during the afternoon and an early evening meeting on the *Grand National Holiday*, there was a hardcore gig by Frodus (US) Nine (Sweden) and Leeds' Canvas to end an eventful five days.

NOTICE of a PUBLIC MEETING

William Bembow's
GRAND NATIONAL HOLIDAY

Monday 5 May, 1997
The Diplomat Hotel, Sunbridge Rd,
Bradford. 7.30 pm start.

Presented by Steve Bushell (of Pelagian Press and Here & Now)

In January 1840, forty armed citizens of Bradford descended on Green Market and attempted to instigate a National Holiday and Congress of the Productive Classes. Unsurprisingly, those with the most to lose from such an undertaking unleashed a savage response and the uprising was crushed.

The idea of a Grand National Holiday, advocated William Bembow, borrowed heavily from biblical texts and ancient notions of the Jubilee, was also attempted in Tyneside.

Over 150 years later, what do these ideas and actions have to say to us, what can be learned, and is there a case for a Grand National Holiday today?

ADMISSION FREE.

Reclaiming May Day - Liberty • Equality • Solidarity

THE TRAGIC DEATH OF KEITH NAREY

May Day 1997 coincided with the General Election. The result ended the eighteen-year rule by the Tories, with a Labour landslide victory for their leader Tony Blair, with a majority of 179 MPs.

On the night of Labour's landslide victory, local socialist and activist Keith Narey had been out celebrating at a jazz night at the Midland Hotel. On returning home, somewhat the worse for wear, he had fallen badly outside the security fence that surrounded Thorald House, the block of flats where he lived in Thorpe Edge. By the time the watching security guard called an ambulance, it was too late to save Keith's life.

Keith had a long association with the far-left group *Militant* and had been expelled from the Labour Party in September 1989.

Keith began writing and set up the Phoenix Theatre Company in 1991 after the death of Pat Wall, the Labour MP for Bradford North, with whom he had worked closely.

His first play was *The Union Man*, which premiered at The Theatre In The Mill.

The second in his trilogy was called *Promised Land*. The third, *A Party That Will*, was about the Independent Labour Party and the Manningham Mills Strike. In that production, Keith played the Scottish socialist MP Keir Hardie.

In October 1997, as a mark of respect, the *Phoenix Theatre Company* renamed itself *The Keith Narey Players* and performed *A Party That Will* at the Alhambra.

After completing a radio production course at Bradford Community Broadcasting in 1994, he presented regular political shows on the station.

Keith was also involved in the local CAMRA group and was a regular at the Brewery Tap in Idle, where he worked behind the bar.

Keith's obituary appeared in The Guardian.

PURITY CRIES

Formed in May 1997, this local group were an experimental electronic-rock outfit. They incorporated face and body paint, costumes, projected animation, electronic soundscapes and weird effects into their live shows.

Purity Cries released two demo CDs, *Vast* and *Interim Why2K*. They also recorded two tracks for the Voltage Studios compilation *Aural Quagmire* before splitting up in early 2002.

CYBER CIRCUS

This metal band was formed by former Foul Play/ Khang bassist Darren Miah in 1997.

CRIME (HASH CRIME)

Another Bradford band active during the 1990s was this indie combo, formed around 1988 by Simon 'Quinch' Carter and future GFA/Dub Kitchen members Pogs and Steve 'Noka' Bruzzese. The changing line-up over the years included Adrian Lloyd-Owen, Debbie Turner and Craig Shepherd.

BRADFORD MUSIC WEEK

This week long event was organised by Wild Willi Beckett and Malcolm Hanson.

The line-up for Bradford Music Week so far...

QUEENS HALL CELLAR BAR
June 2 - Zed, Parisman, Tangerine
June 3 - Scratch, Cream River, The Underworld
June 4 - Far Fetched, 5th Wheel, 49 Reliever
June 5 - Percy, Pond Skaters Screaming Abdabs
June 6 - Warm, Slack Elvis, Cheesie

ESCAPE BAR
June 2 - Dub Kitchen, Litle Reata, Lopez
June 3 - Sugarfiend, Smokescreen, Tangerine
June 4 - Entire, The Sprawl, Astralux
June 5 - Facelift, 5th Wheel, Cream River
June 6 - Looking Glass, Boston Tea Party, Bullweek

THE SOUND GALLERY
June 2 - The Big Bang, Decoy, Calm
June 3 Capour Trail, Old Man Stone
June 4 - Real Life, Collide, Tangerine
June 5 - Lydian Dream, Emba, Lapdog
June 6 - Blim, The Blister Factory, Saturn 5

THE UNDERWORLD
June 2 - My Inside Kisser, Justray
June 3 - Proof
June 4 - Orphiachus, Neophyte, Liquid Head
June 5 - Tangerine, Crying Shame
June 6 - Privilege, Psyclozine, Urban Guru

UNDERWORLD: *Urban Guru*

Dozens of bands from Bradford and beyond are lined up to celebrate the city's Centenary.

They will be taking part in a music marathon organised by Psycho Surgeons frontman Wild Willi Beckett.

The event, called Bradford Music Week, will take place simultaneously at four venues in the city from June 2 to 6.

Fifty-six bands have been booked so far to play at the Queens Hall Cellar Bar, the Escape Bar (formerly the Subway Bar) in Bradford University, the Underworld in Great Horton Road and the Sound Gallery, also in Great Horton Road.

Entry to all gigs will be by Bradford Music Week pass, available from the bands taking part and the venues. Passes are £3 each and are valid for all venues every night of Bradford Music Week.

Among the groups performing are familiar names from the Bradford rock music scene including reggae rabble-rousers Dub Kitchen, The Big Bang (recently reformed again) and indie popsters The Blister Factory, Bullweek, 49 Reliever and Facelift.

Veterans Zed will also be appearing after recently getting back together to take part in the Brighton Fringe Festival.

The band, whose reconstituted line-up features Jont on bass and vocals, Crispian on guitar and vocals and Matt on drums, also play an open air gig at The Peel on June 13 with Dragster and Slack and a charity gig at Todmorden Centre Vale Park on June 15, before heading south for further dates in London and Brighton.

Other bands taking part in Bradford Music Week include Holmfirth rockers Urban Guru, who are pencilled in for the week's closing set at the Underworld and punk metal outfit Liquid Head, who are supporting Theatre of Hate next month.

One band are even coming from Germany for the event. Tangerine, formerly the Tragic Comics, hail from Hamm and have previously played in Bradford as part of a twin-town exchange.

● Any bands interested in filling vacant slots at Bradford Music Week should contact Willi on (01274) 502402 as soon as possible.

WORM

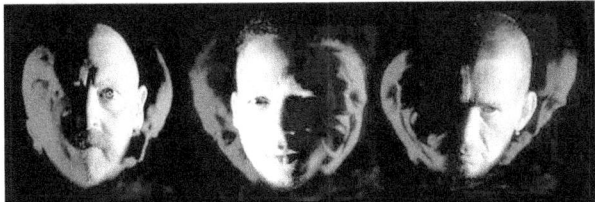

Worm were formed in late 1995 by Tim Walker and Carl Arnfield as an experimental dance project for music publishers Sherlock Holmes.

Although their music was considered too dark for the company, the pair continued writing and recording sporadically. In 1997, they were approached to submit two tracks for Hal 2000, a compilation album by new Leeds label, Jerusalem Records.

A live performance for the album's launch

at Leeds' Duchess Of York inspired the guys to add more guitars to their sound. They added hip-hop vocalist Sacha Martin Luther King to their lineup.

Worm recorded two full-length albums for Voltage Records, to critical acclaim, *Integral Virus* in 2002 and *Hate* in 2005.

US

This Bradford rock band formed in 1997. Rob Moore and Ricky Howard of Blood Orange/Happiness Ad on vocals and drums teamed up with Tim Walker and Steve Willow, previously guitarist and bassist of Architect.

Their *Two Gods* demo received a lot of attention in the music industry and the band had interest from Gut Records and One Little Indian.

They recorded a full-length album entitled *It* at Revolver Studios, which was released in 1999 on Voltage Records, and made a promo video for *Two Gods,* but split up in 2000 without having secured a record deal.

As part of the 1997 Bradford Festival, the bizarre Japanese vocal duo Frank Chickens gave a performance in Centenary Square.

A meeting of the environmental group, *The Bradford District Permaculture Group*, was held at The 1 In 12 Club on Thursday, July 31.

It gave updates on the ongoing projects (such as *Paradise Green*'s organic vegetable and herb garden at Brackenhill Park in Lidget Green), and future challenges aimed at providing a sustainable regeneration of Bradford's green areas.

Memorable gigs at the 1 In 12 during July and August included visits from Bob Tilton, US band Dystopia and old favourites, the quirky Edinburgh outfit Archbishop Kebab.

In August, Belgian hardcore band Unhinged topped the bill on the 16th and on the 22nd the Wirral-based comedy-indie group Half Man, Half Biscuit played to a packed room.

CHUMBAWAMBA HIT TOP SPOT (IN AUSTRALIA)

In late August 1997, Chumbawamba's latest single, the novelty pop song *Tubthumping*, with its infectious chorus chant, shot straight to number 2 in the UK singles chart.

It was only denied the top spot by Will Smith's *Men In Black* - the theme the summer's hit comedy sci-fi movie.

Tubthumping stayed in the charts for twenty weeks, eleven of those in the top ten.

It also reached No 6 in the US Billboard Hot 100 and topped the charts in Canada and Australia!

It has since been sampled for TV ads, various TV shows (*The Simpsons*), video games (including *FIFA 98*) and used on film soundtracks.

Tubthumping was the UK's eleventh best selling single in 1997, in a chart topped by Elton John's reworking of Candle In The Wind after the death of Diana, Princess Of Wales.

Originally formed in Burnley, Lancashire in 1981, these anarcho-punk vegans moved to Leeds in 1982 and lived communally at Southview House, Armley. Their early gigs were a mixture of performance theatre (costumes, banners, TV sets and a sweeping brush as props) and a raucous noise with ranting vocals.

From 1983, the band became long-time comrades of The 1 In 12 Club, playing regularly over the years, including at benefits such as the *Not The International Garden Festival* outdoor concert in 1984, and when the Club got its own building, Chambawamba were actively involved in its renovation.

After producing some early cassettes and having a track on the Crass-backed compilation *Bullshit Detector #2*, the band self produced and released their debut 7" single *Revolution* in 1985.

It came out on their Agit-Prop label at £1.20 and got to No 4 in the indie charts, while their full LP, *Pictures Of Starving Children*, reached No 2 in the Indie charts the next year.

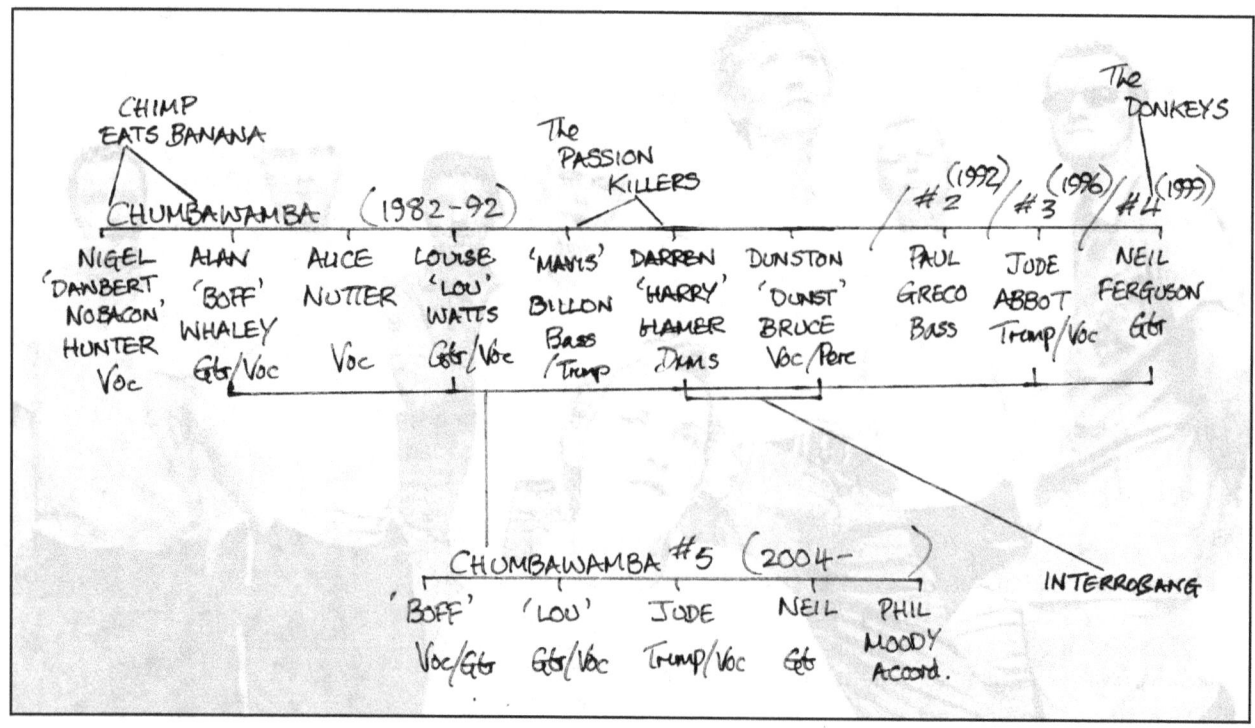

They continued to release influential albums like *Slap* (1990) and *Shhh* (1992) before signing to indie label One Little Indian for their 1994 album *Anarchy*.

They signed to EMI in Europe in 1997 and released their *Tubthumper* album from which the famous single came.

They continued to release albums up to 2004 after which some members moved on to other projects although the band continued as a stripped-down acoustic five-piece.

LOCAL JAZZ VIRTUOSO GUITARIST

Local Bradford lad Allan Holdsworth, the well-respected virtuoso guitarist in jazz circles, made one of his perennial UK visits from his US base in California to play two dates at London's Jazz Cafe in late October 1997.

He had started with his group 'Igginbottom in 1968 with fellow Bradford lads before moving down to London and playing with some of the UK's best jazz-fusion ensembles of the 1970s, like Nucleus, Soft Machine, UK and Bruford.

Allan then relocated to America, went solo and soon became the in-demand guest guitarist on many top US jazz artists' albums.

More key gigs at the 1 In 12 during November and December included another two-day hardcore festival over the weekend of November 8-9. On November 27, legendary UK blues-rock guitarist Tony McPhee with his band The Groundhogs stunned everyone present with material from his 1970s albums such as *Split*.

On the 29th, Scotland's Oi Polloi joined Doom for a noisy night's gig and Lancashire's Cress played out the year on December 20.

THE EMPRESS

The Empress pub on Sunbridge Road (now a Tesco's) began putting on metal gigs during 1997, like the one on October 31 by Nottingham's Iron Monkey and Leeds' Canvas.

THE BAND MAGAZINE

In issue #5 of this new magazine, subtitled *Gigging, Recording And Making It*, their 'set-list' had articles and features on The Lightening Seeds, Chumbawamba, the biz: distribution, tricks of the trade and digital decisions.

The magazine also ran a competition called *The Great £250 Cash Advance* and December's winners were the Bradford/Leeds young trio Neon, who were all pupils at Benton Park School in Rawdon and

'hoped to play their first gig before Christmas'

The band's drummer, Daniel, who was the son of Jon Binns, former drummer of Radio 5, The Word and Poppy Factory, went to drum for the band Vertical Smile.

INARCADIA

Over in the town of Keighley, another local super group formed called Inarcadia.

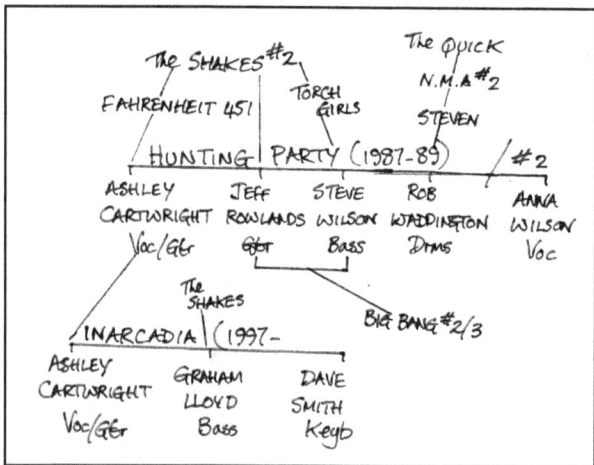

In early February, 1998, the world's largest mountain bike manufacturer, US company Huffy, named its latest 18-speed model *Bradford*.

Tyler Scott, their production manager, who was responsible for the naming, said, *'I was lucky enough to study at Bradford University for a year in the 1980s. And I've never forgotten the city's character, not to mention the curries, rugby league and Tetley's bitter.'*

The $150 midnight blue bike was aimed at the lower end of the mountain-riding market in the US, and the *Bradford* was not on sale in the UK, where Huffy has no market penetration. Mr Tyler did send one machine to his old university, for a raffle in aid of the Lord Mayor of Bradford's charity appeal. (3)

DRENCH WARFARE / ICE COOL BRITANNIA

The Brits (British Music Industry Awards) in February 1998, saw an ill-fated publicity stunt by Labour's Deputy leader John Prescott. By ignoring the large demonstration of sacked Polygram packers, he took his £500 seat and hobnobbed with the rich and famous.

As the Club's KDIS source at the event stated, *'The evening kicked off with Chumbawamba performing Tubthumping with a revised chorus "New Labour sold out the Dockers, just like they'll sell out the rest of us." As Prescott sat visibly squirming, several striking Polygram workers smuggled in by the band earlier in the evening, set about reminding those present of how they had been sacked from their £3 per hour jobs for trying to establish a union.*

'As the evening wore on the sense that the whole event was being hijacked by the Mandelsonian New Labour media machine

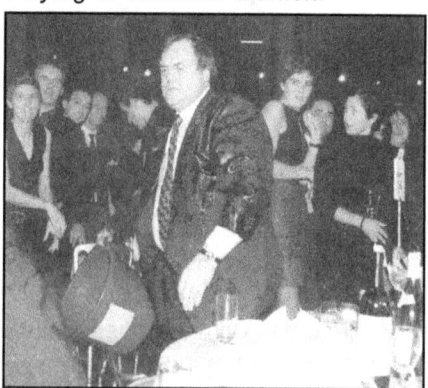

became increasingly widespread. The feelings of anger went way beyond those seated with Chumbawamba. Frustration and resentment finally came to a head when several of the band briefly escaped the attentions of the bouncers and approached Prescott's table.

'Danbert Nobacon got in first, climbing on the table and pouring the contents of a champagne ice bucket over the Deputy leader. Prescott struck out at several of the band and members of the audience in a fit of fury, exhorting the gathered throng to a 'F**k Off'. As bouncers quickly moved in, Danbert was arrested by police, then soon released uncharged.' (4)

Two local Keighley-based bands who formed in 1998 were:

SASQUATCH

This four-piece rock outfit played distinctive homages to hard rock bands of the previous three decades.

SOULFISH

This eight-piece soul covers band have been gigging extensively around the local area, and after a few line-up changes was still playing up to the mid-naughties.

After a gap of six years, they made a comeback to live performance in 2013.

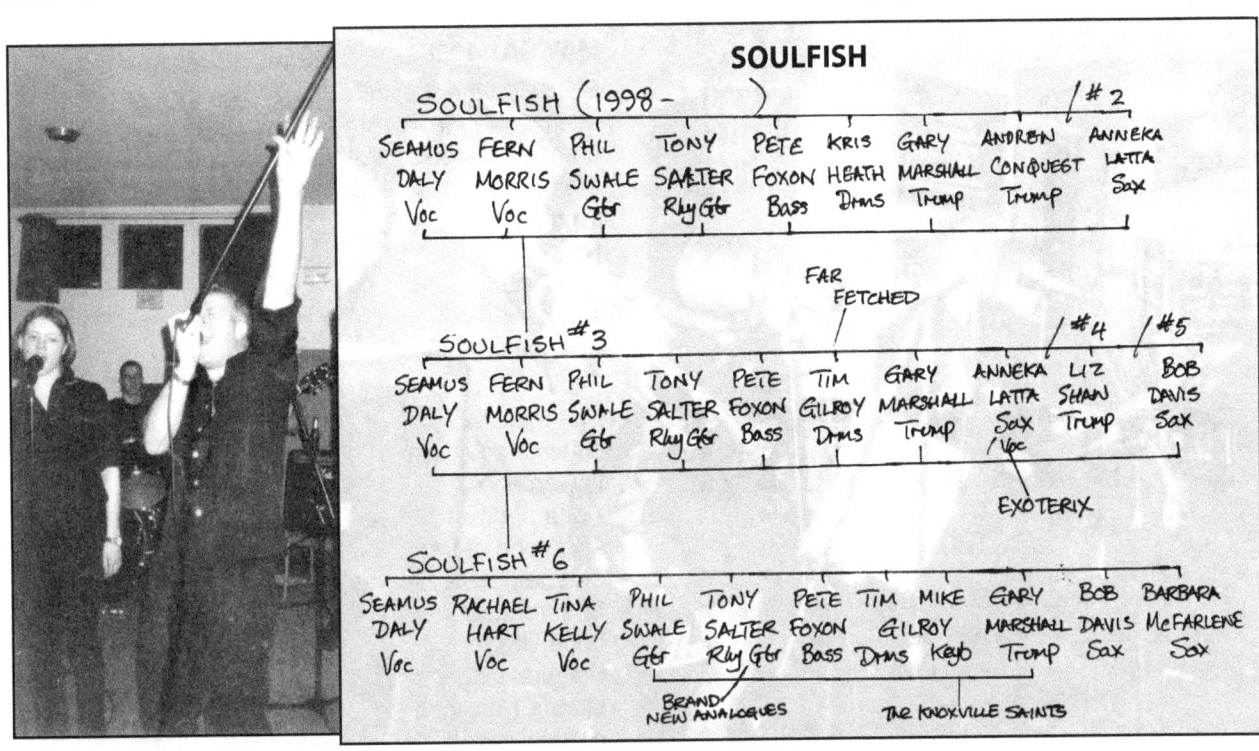

Leading up to that year's May Day week, was a two day benefit hardcore fest on April 18-19.

Red & Black bitter, specially brewed for the 1 in 12 Club by local brewers Marston Moor, went on sale in time for May Day. The Ale was brewed to mark the Clubs 10th year at Albion Street.

"It's a light, full flavoured 4.5 ale" said club steward Pete Chapman. "we've only got 4 barrels. I just hope it sees us through May Day".

ON THE BALL: *Chumbawamba's Danbert NoBacon — who drenched Labour's Deputy Prime Minister at the Brit Awards— swapped tub-thumping for a spot of bingo in aid of Bradford's May Day celebrations. Danbert, real name Nigel Hunter, attracted a full house when he tried bingo calling at the 1 in 12 Club in Albion Street where he has been a member for 15 years. The event raised £100. Leeds-based Chumbawamba played regularly at the member-run club before they broke into the charts last year with the anthem Tubthumping*

MAY DAY 1998

Following the previous year's highly successful events, the *May Day '98* week started with another parade headed by the sacked Magnet workers and their 'Delboy Trotter' yellow Robin Reliant, which had successfully highlighted their campaign.

The march culminated again in Centenary Square for an afternoon of free entertainment from reggae band UK Players, singer Lianne Hall, jazz group Hessel

and Salsa dancing with the Cuba Solidarity Group.

That evening, the 1 In 12 footie team hosted a disco at the Club, while earlier in the evening, upstairs in the Club's library, a night of rebel songs from over 200 years was enjoyed.

At various venues around town that weekend, meetings, exhibitions and film shows took place, including the book launch of *Taking Sides: Against Ethnic Cleansing In Bosnia* by Geoff Robinson and John Davies at the Saathi Centre.

On Saturday, the 1 In 12 held a punk all-dayer from one o'clock and in the evening, at the Bradford University Communal Building, radical dance band Fundamental (ex-Southern Death Cult's drummer Aki's group which had in its lineup revered Dhol drummer Johnny Kalsi) and guest DJs The Underground Set also performed.

Over the weekend, a total of 350 delegates from all over the UK attended a three-day libertarian conference entitled *Struggle For Social Change* at Bradford's McMillan College.

As part of a radical dialogue on the nature and effects of capitalism on people and social control,

the conference had four themed discussions, *Away From The Margins*, *Land, Ecology And Environment*, *All Worked Up?*, and *Dream Time*.

Also running in tandem, was the second May Day Football Tournament with eleven teams from Bristol, York, Norwich, Leeds,

Hebden Bridge and from Hannau, Germany. Also, in tandem, was another play by the 1 In 12 Drama Collective at the Playhouse (Priestley Centre), off Leeds Road, called *Durruti* - the story of the life of Buenaventura Durruti and the 1936-39 Spanish Revolution.

On Sunday, May 3, Dave Stockell (aka Little Brother) led a free walkabout/ herb history tour, while at the Diplomat Hotel, there was a discussion on May '68 (Paris and Prague) then an evening folk concert by troubadour Rory McLeod at The 1 In 12 Club.

Key gigs at the 1 In 12 from the end

of May through to Christmas started with a visit from the highly regarded Swedish band Refused, supported by US band Ink & Dagger and Leeds' Cath O'Connor and Canvas on May 20.

During June, US band His Hero Is Gone with Ebola and John Holmes played on the 3rd and a special gig, celebrating the 10th anniversary of the Club at its own building gig, took place on the 17th with

Logical Nonsense and Medula Nocte. German noise merchants Ambush played on August 30, US band Detestation on September 12, two Canadian bands, Submission Hold on October 10, and Seized on November 4, with Japan's SDS on the 11th.

Another 2-day hardcore festival was held during the weekend of November 28-29, with four American bands, including Drop Dead, whose vocalist, Ben relocated to Bradford for a year or so (pictured), Reiziger from Belgium and eleven UK acts.

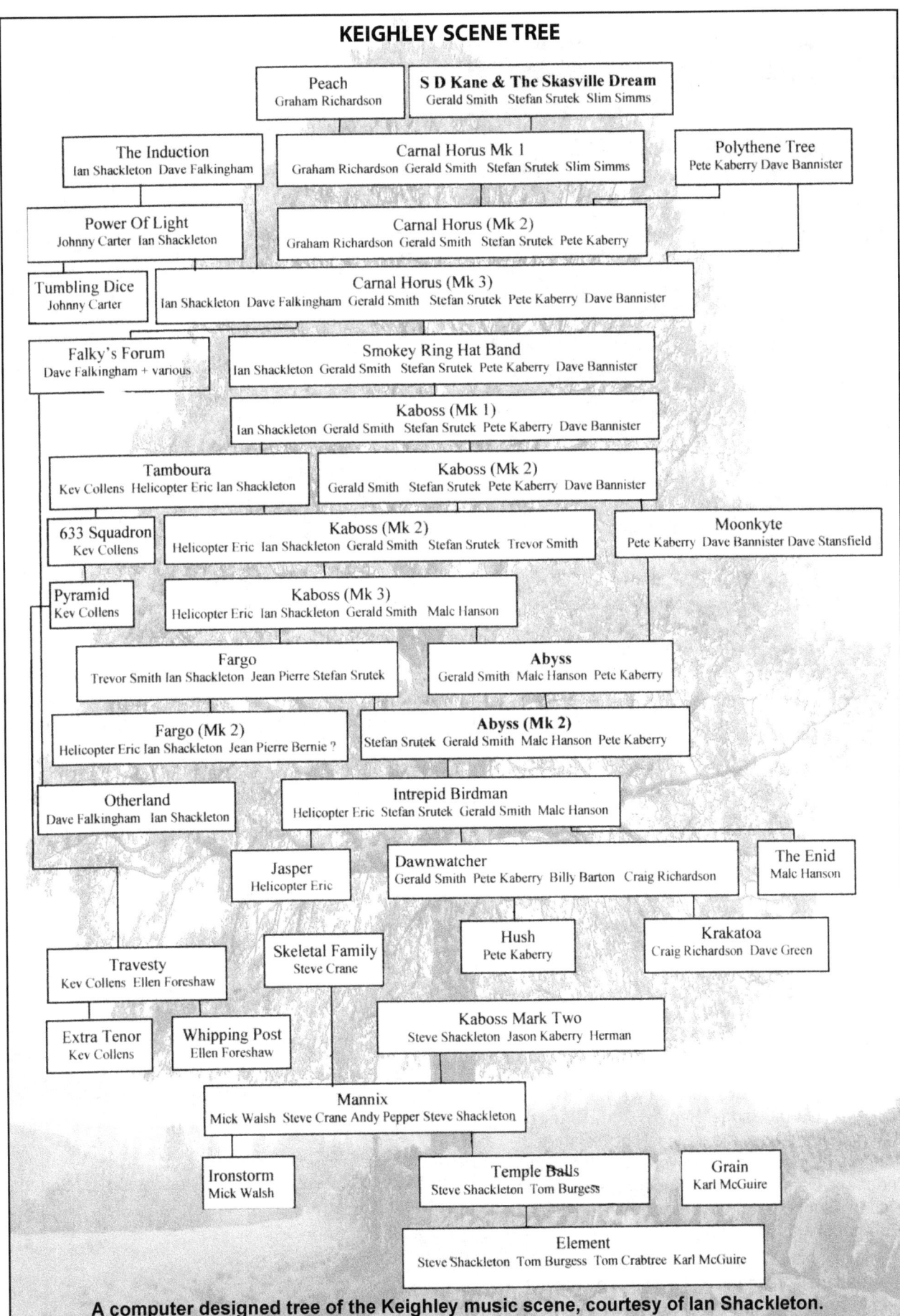

A computer designed tree of the Keighley music scene, courtesy of Ian Shackleton.

JOHN HOLMES

A quartet collaboration by members from Manfat, Suffer and Hard To Swallow, who released the *El Louso Suavo* CD/LP on their own Devil Rock label in 1999, supported with backing from DIY distributors Flat Earth and Active.

A further split CD with Dublin-based Irish band Kabinboy was released, with each band contributing four tracks.

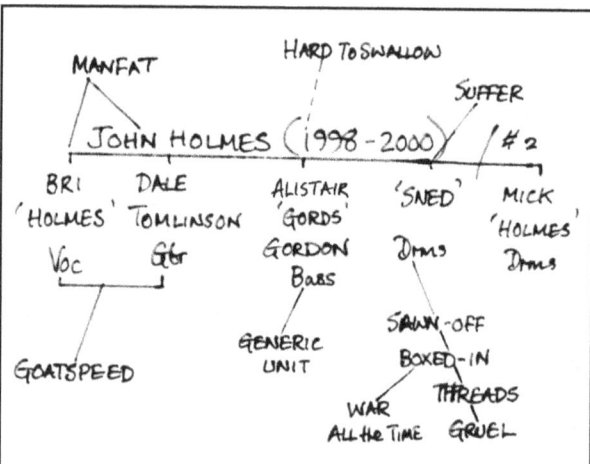

INFEST

In August 1998, at Bradford University, three students, Garth 'Gadge' Harvey, Chris 'Crusty' Molyneux and Max 'Maxi Slag' Niblock, started with the idea of a one-day West Yorkshire Goth/Industrial/Dark Synth Pop electronic noise event, with the support and the help of the then Student Entertainments Manager, Floyd Peltier.

The event spiralled into the three-day, annual internationally recognised festival of bands of this genre, and took place for over fifteen years.

AFTER THE BREAK

Printed in February 1998, *After The Break #1: Regeneration* was a free arts paper by Bradford Arts Forum. It was produced as a quarterly paper by a voluntary editorial group consisting of Ken Sparne, Alan Marks, Robert Galeta and Geoff Robinson from the Art Forum. They hoped to see it develop into a sustainable paper that would be the voice for the views and ideas of young people from different communities in Bradford.

Partly funded by A4E and Bradford Council, the paper had articles on Community Arts by Albert Hunt, on the Golden Jubilee of the Polish Community (1948-98), Shipley Glen, Bradford Festival, the late Bradford Community Print Shop on Thornton Road, Reclaiming Mayday and a nostalgic article on the local music scene by Midnight Train vocalist / Bradford College music tutor Grom Kelly.

OTHER BANDS ON THE SCENE

Bands from Bradford and its Metropolitan District who are known to have existed during the period 1988-1998 but are not profiled or listed in the Index Of Bands On Trees, are listed below.

1988: And As Above So Below, Albericoque, The Emotionalists, Food For Worms, Fnrr Fnrr, Imagination Lost, Infant Vision, Spellsinger, This Concern.

1989: Boilerhouse, Metal Merchants, Realm, Sex Flowers, Skinchoir, Slyk Kutt.

1990: Big Talk, New Morning, Kibbutz, Roberta Junk (Halifax).

1991: Bassa Bassa, Loveland, Obsession, Pink Elephants, Screaming Option, Killing Beat.

1992: Dead Dogs, Idle Prophets, Persuasion, Spectrum, Arbuckle.

1993: 1:1, Chris Sharp Project, Crossing, Henry's Cat, Imago, I Think So, Psychic, Soul Concern.

1994: De Cabeza, Silver Screen.

1996: Kitanna, Surge.

1997: 49 Reliever, Eternity, Greener Grass, Scratch, Urban Guru.

1998: The Seen, Krawl.

To be continued...

REFERENCES

The local Bradford newspaper the *Telegraph & Argus* provided a lot of the material for the research in this book, the rest was gleaned from many other local sources, some of which are listed below, and the personal recollections of some of the people involved in the Bradford music scene during the relevant period.

CHAPTER 1

1. Strummercamp Flyer

2. *The Observer*

3. Battle Of The Bands 1988 entrant Lord Crucifier were an Italian metal band who had settled in Sowerby Bridge, they released an LP The Focus of Life.

4. T&A 1.4.1988

5. *Kerrang!* review: The rock magazine Kerrang! first appeared in June 1981, at the height of the NWOBHM revival. During the 1980s and early 1990s it developed as the only Metal magazine, but adapted later to the more eclectic rock scene with coverage of the pop/Emo too. New magazines like Terrorizer, Metal Hammer etc, developed a more detailed coverage of the emerging darker metal of Doom, Speed, Death and Grindcore styles of crossover metal

6. *T&A* 6.1989

7. The first Bradford Asian Mela was held at the (Al Haq) field on Woodhead Road

8. The album's conductor and orchestral arranger was David Bedford who also worked with many artists on the Virgin label in 1970s

9. *T&A* 12.1988

10. Mike and Pat published their book later that year - *The Blake Escape: How We Freed George Blake And Why* (1989) Harrup

11. In July 2005, in answer to a query regarding the single in the *Record Collector's Value Added Fax* column, it was valued at £200

12. Titan is the moon of the planet Saturn, discovered by Christian Huygens in 1655, who through the telescope theorised what made up the mysterious 'Orange world of Titan'

13. *T&A* 1.1988

14. The old Mecca Ballroom of the 1960s on Manningham Lane had changed to Dollar's in the 1980s and was at this point (1989) Ceasar's Palace

15. Tim Booth, the lead singer of the Manchester based group James, was born in Bradford in 1960. The group had a No 2 hit with *Sit Down* in march 1991

16. *T&A* 25.10.91

17. The songs were recorded in the cellar of Bell House, Hebden Bridge, the former home of David Hartley, the infamous vagabond and King of the Cragg Vale Coiners, who was hanged at York for murder in 1770

CHAPTER 2

1. Checkpoint is the home of the West Indian community in Bradford and is based at the lights on Westgate, behind Albion Street. The 1 In 12 Club had strong links since the mid 1980s and had put on many benefits and the odd gig, as it was a larger venue.

2. A quote from an anonymous member on the opening night

3. The EX were the first foreign band ever to play the Club, they became good comrades and played many times before the building opened, so it was fitting that they were the first foreign band to play after opening.

4. In Ian Glasper's *Trapped In A Scene: UK Hardcore 1985-89* he documents the whole scene in a extremely detailed way, and of the 83 bands profiled 52 had played at the Club between 1985 and 1992.

5. p 238-239 Glasper *Trapped In A Scene: UK Hardcore 1985-89*

6. p 45 *Terrorizer #180* February 2009

7. After leaving Bradford council, Eric Pickles was offered a safe Tory seat down south and became an MP. He then became chairman of the Conservative Party and is at present (2013) the Communities Minister-Local Government Secretary. In November 2011, Eric failed to report and declare a luxury Savoy dinner enjoyed with lobbyists for the public relations firm Bell-Pottinger. The meal he claimed was eaten privately, not ministerially, a loop hole some Labour MPs suggest needs closing

8. The 1 In 12 Club's booking collective had traditionally been responsible for gigs and events but over the next years more gigs were organised by members in their own promotion teams and groups like Metal Faeces

9. Malise Ruthven - *A Satanic Affair: Salman Rushdie And The Wrath Of Islam* (1991) Hogarth Press

10. A full list of 1 In 12 gigs from 1981 onwards is available on the Club's website, 1in12.com

11. Inky Pig were made up of ex-members of Chinese Gangster Element, who featured on Volume 3 of the *Worst Of The 1 In 12 Club* album series and were given a John Peel session after he raved about their track *World's On Fire*.

12. Ramsey, of Political Asylum, set up AK Press; a radical publishing and distribution operation selling books/pamphlets/periodicals initially from his Edinburgh home. Over the years he expanded his catalogue to include audio releases, badges and T-shirts and even opened an office in Oakland, California, USA

13. Key Madchester band The Stone Roses sent one of their early 12" to the Club in 1986 in the hope of a gig, unfortunately someone on the booking collective forgot to arrange one for them.

14. The Swedish born, New York raised rap singer had four top ten hits between 1988-96, after she settled in London in the 1980s. Neneh had previously been in the great indie/jazz funksters Rip, Rig & Panic and was the step-daughter of Jazz trumpeter Don Cherry

15. The LP *Volnitza* (it means 'free life' in Russian) contained on it's back cover the following quote in Russian: '*Your revolution was undermined by Lenin And Trotsky, Ours continues to strive towards a true Social Revolution.*' A copy of the LP was sent to Tony Wilson's Factory Records in Manchester, he or someone must have listened to it, as later they signed Edinburgh band The Wendies whose track *Do Anything* was the closer on side three

16. Councillor Pickles took such exception to Sore Throats little ditty that he demanded an investigation into 1 In 12 Records. (see right) Extracts from the secret report by Bradford Council were passed to the club by a council worker/member of the Club

17. We now (2013) have an enlarged European Union (EEC) with eight former communist bloc countries being part of the third largest economic entity on the planet

18. *The Guardian* 12.2.1990

19. Barrister Cherie Blair QC, wife to future PM Tony Blair, made some of her barrister's income by acting for local council's against Poll Tax defaulters, sending one penniless non-payer back to jail

20. *Poll Tax Riot: 10 Hours that Shook Trafalgar Square* (1990) ACAB Press

21. The Club's veggie burgers became world famous when a MRR reviewer stated that it was '*...a shame they don't mail order their veggie burgers.*'

City of Bradford Metropolitan Council

EMPLOYMENT INITIATIVES DIVISION

5th September, 1989

Dear Mr. Anderson,

ONE IN TWELVE CLUB URBAN PROGRAMME 1989/90 CP6-12

In response to your letter of the 22nd August 1989 the points made have been investigated and the findings are as follows:

1. A record has been produced under the name of '1 in 12 Records'. This is a business in its own right with a separate legal status. The individual who owns the record label and who produced the record is currently funded by the Government's Enterprise Allowances Scheme.

2. As the 1 in 12 Club do not have copyright of their name, it can be used by anybody. The use of their name does not give them control over the content of any records or publications with that name on.

4. Since the approval in February 1986 a progress report was sent to P. Pickles in October 1986 detailing the building work to that date. The visit to the project had to be cancelled; this has not been rearranged. The Club also invited the Department to their official opening, but this was not attended.

Enclosed are the progress reports previously submitted to your Department on the building work from October 1986 to December 1987 when the building work was virtually complete. Most of the work after this date was done by the Brewery and volunteers.

There is no doubt that the 1 in 12 Club are successfully achieving these aims. On my last visit to the Club there were 12 volunteers involved in cleaning, repainting and maintaining the building. Their evening venues are well attended and they continue to offer performance facilities for new bands.

I hope this clarifies the situation. If you require any further information, please contact me.

Yours sincerely,

22. After months of waiting the US and its allies started the Gulf War on January 17, 1991. Allied bombers targeted Baghdad and other targets as the liberation of Kuwait began. President George Bush (snr) stated that he intended to wreck Saddam's war ability

23. The track is based on the real life story of Harry Goldthorpe, who wrote the book *Room At The Bottom* in 1959

24. *Leeds Other Paper* was founded in 1973, as a collective and was published once a week. It published local and radical news as well as listings for theatre, exhibitions, gigs, etc. By 1991, it had changed its name to the *Northern Star* in memory of the Chartist paper which was based in Leeds during 1837-52. The paper finally ceased production due to financial difficulties in 1994

CHAPTER : 3

1. p *The Nineties: What the F**k was that all about?* John Robb (1999) Embury Press

2. p 33 *Energy Flash* Simon Reynolds (1998) Picador

3. p 417 Reynolds

4. E's cost around £20 in the late 1980s, by 1997 they were about £10, the effect *'...severely 'cabbage' youth who began to take 3-6 tablets per session, sometimes 10-20 over the course of a three day weekend.'* p 113 Reynolds

5. *T&A* 18.8.1989

6. p 98 Reynolds

7. Karin Minott was the daughter of Bibi owner of the Capricorn Club.

8. Westrex was an audio electrical phonograph company.

9. p 17 *Stork* #11 May 1993

10. p 16 *Stork* #7 November 1992#

11. p 135-140 Reynolds

12. p 139-140 Reynolds

13. p 147-150 Reynolds

14. Stimulations nights carried on into the new century, and will be covered in *Volume 3 1999-200*

15. Taken from the Insert in MOB 12" Glamorous Hooligan's first release *Research & Destroy*

16. Quote from the sleeve notes by Dean Cavanagh on the CD *International Language Of Dub*

17. E-mail via Richard Brass

18. *T&A* 23.11.96

19. *T&A* 3.3.97

20. *T&A* 17.2.97

CHAPTER 4

1. The word 'Mela' means 'gathering', from the Sanskrit word and is used to describe all manner of cultural and religious celebrations. In Britain the term encompasses the earliest bazaars, fairs, family days and festivals organised by the South Asian diaspora. p 10 *Coming Of Age* (2009)

2. p 17 Coming of Age

3. MDB's vocalist Aaron also turned his hand to on-line digital art and photography

4. The author, who was associated with the band, videoed their gig at Queens Hall on May 23, 1992

5. *T&A* 25.8.95

6. Tasmin, consciously or not, gave the same title of her debut LP as fellow Bradford songtress Kiki Dee, who had released hers on Motown in 1970. Great Expectations was also the title of New Model Army's second single, in 1984.

7. The gig at Bradford University's Communal Building was on December 8, 1993, with support from Cop Shoot Cop and Understand

8. The Wedding Present kindly donated all the monies raised on the night from sales of t-shirts, CDs etc on their stall to The 1 In 12 Club

9. Huffty was last seen on the BBC3 programme *Geordie Finishing School For Girls* in 2011

10. Tez of Full Circle said Dead Kennedy's vocalist Jello Biafra ordered all the *Worst Of The 1 In 12 Club* releases from his distro

11. Quote by bassist Chris in Glasper *Armed With Anger* (2012)

12. The 'kidz' sure did stage-dive, some bouncing off the Club's ceiling and this is clearly seen in the video footage of the gig

13. Lecky moved down to Bradford and helped set-up Wisdom skate shop, originally situated above System Records on Barry Street, before moving to Leeds

14. In a *MRR* (US magazine) interview with members of Voorhees, Stalingrad and Richard Corbridge of AWA Records, Lecky added this obscure remark, *'Don't you think Gary looks like the guy (the comic actor Paul Whitehouse) in "in't milk brilliant"*, not realizing that most American readers would not have seen this TV advert at that time

15. The MDC gig was videoed by the author on a borrowed hand-held camera from Bradford College, ironically standing next to some youth recording with the latest 'state of the art' palm corder

16. Quoted from the article *Can Women Rock?* by Lucy O'Brien in the current affairs magazine *Everywoman*, October 1993

17. Quoted by Bikini Kill an article in the free music magazine *The Stool Pigeon*, November 2012

18. Ian Glasper's Cherry Red published books include; *Burning Britain: UK Punk Scene 1980-1984*; *The Day the Country Died: UK Anarcho-Punk 1980-4*; *Trapped In A Scene: UK Hardcore 1985-1989*; *Armed With Anger*

19. 1 In 12 AFC's first ever game was on December 15,1992 against Werder Woodhouse, losing 7-1 on Scholemoor's all weather pitch

20. In one game the son (Michael) substituted the father (Gary), a first for the team. Cavanagh snr played over sixty games in all competitions (league, cup, tournaments, friendlies) over these years and scored ten goals

DIVISION TWO						
Local Hygiene	7	6	0	1	39	19	18
Fagley	7	4	1	2	23	15	13
Ravenscliffe Celtic	6	4	0	2	26	8	12
Jeromes	5	4	0	1	20	10	12
Dudley Hill Rgrs	7	3	1	3	26	14	10
Smiling Mule	6	3	0	3	14	26	9
One in Twelve	7	2	1	4	20	25	7
Ajax Windhill	5	2	0	3	19	25	6
Ambler Thorn	6	2	0	4	16	21	6
Brook Hansen	5	1	1	3	9	14	4
Bradford Deaf	5	0	0	5	7	41	0

In the Second Division, One In Twelve could afford the luxury of a missed penalty in a 2-0 win over Ravenscliffe Celtic B. Gary Kavanagh missed the first half spot kick, but second half goals from Andy Lee and Shiz Yousaf spared his blushes.

Leaders Local Hygiene increased their lead at the top to seven points despite a below par performance in a 4-2 win over visitors Smiling Mule.

CHAPTER 5

1. Email via Dave Foster

2. For those who may not know, Cleckheaton is a small township (BD 19) on the edge of the Bradford district near the boundary with Kirklees

3. *Northern Star* #7 13 December 1991

4. p 13 C Richardson *The Irish In Victorian Bradford* (1971) Bradford Antiquary

5. The Chartists (1838-50) were the first working class movement of social and political protest in the UK, their six point charter proposed universal suffrage, annual parliaments, payment for MPs and equal electoral areas. p 42 DG Wright *The Chartist Rising In Bradford* (1987) Bradford Libraries

6. op. Cit. Richardson

7. *T&A* 27.7.94

8. via Wikipedia

9. via Wikipedia

10. Quote from George Melly *Owning Up* (1960) Penguin

11. *T&A* 22.6.94

12. *T&A* 11.5.96

13. *T&A* 5.7.96

CHAPTER 6

1. *T&A* July 1994

2. *T&A* 13.6.95

REFERENCES 1988 - 1998

3. p 66 Glasper, *AWA* (2012) Quoted by Karl of the band Canvas

4. p 66 Quoted by Andy of the band Dead Wrong

5. p 166 Quoted by 'Gords' of the band Hard To Swallow

6. In 2004, Argentinian Javier Zanetti, captain of Italy's Inter Milan, donated his football shirt, valued at 5,000 euros, as a gesture of solidarity with the Zapatistas

7. The Anarchist Black Cross is an international network of autonomous anarchist prisoner support groups

8. The Zapatistas received the money via our Spanish comrades who made regular trips and we were later told it helped build a library in one of their townships

9. The Hannau Cup trophy is housed with all the other trophies from the quiz and games leagues in a glass case at the end of the Club's top bar on Albion Street

CHAPTER 7

1. Number 6, Claremont (off Great Horton Road, near the university) was the birthplace of Bradford's world famous classical composer, Frederick Delius (1862-1934)

2. Bradford Council's City Centre Management Team allowed the May Day organisation team to use Centenary Square as the first event in this new open space

3. *The Guardian* 4.2.98

4. P 3 *KDIS* May 1998

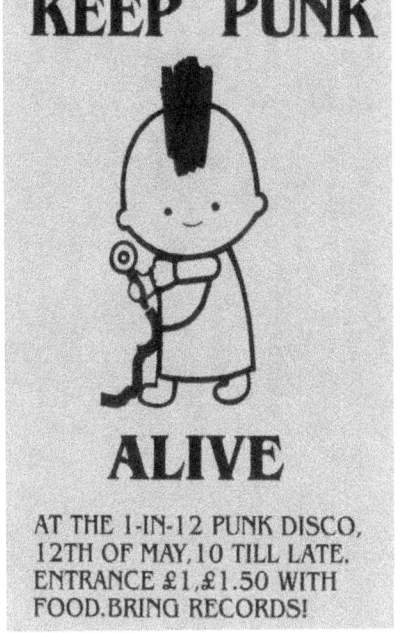

BIBLOGRAPHY

Other invaluable reference material includes the following publications:

Record Collector's Rare Record Guide (2010, 2012, 2014)

Clay, John *Black Dyke : An Inside Story* (2005) Jagrins

Glasper, Ian *The Day The Country Died* (2006) Cherry Red

Glasper, Ian *Trapped In A Scene UKHC 1985-1989* (2009) Cherry Red

Glasper, Ian *Armed With Anger* (2012) Cherry Red

Gordon, Alistair *The Authentic Punk: An Ethnography Of DIY Music Ethics* (2005) Loughborough University (Doctoral Thesis)

Grogan, Tony *The Pickles Papers* (1989) 1 In 12 Publications

MacMillan, Malc T*he NWOBHM Encylopedia 2nd Edition* (2005) Iron Pages

Melly, George *Owning Up* (1960) Penguin

Reynolds, Simon *Energy Flash* (1998) Picador

Ruthven, Malise *A Satanic Affair: Salman Rushdie & The Wrath Of Islam* (1991) Hogarth Press

Coming Of Age: Celebrating 21 Years of Mela In The UK (2005) CMS (Bradford)

Sometimes, Bradford is overshadowed by its near neighbour Leeds, but we have beaten them in the pop stakes to date! Bradford comes joint tenth (with Leicester & Stoke) in the UK's top musical cities with the city's artists achieving six number one singles (four by Gareth Gates!) while Leeds comes joint eleventh with five number ones!

p 66 *The Observer Book Of Rock & Pop* (2007) Observer Books

INDEX OF BANDS ON TREES

A

Abiosis 133, 231
Abyss 194
Abraxas 19
Adolescants 221
Affluence Of Incahol 131
Afteritsm 246
Aftermath 260
Agnosy 95
Agog 161
Aim 188
Albeit 144, 147
Alan Wormald Band 238
Alehammer 162
All About Eve 26
Ambertone 131
Analog Bombs 11
Anathema 133, 135
Angeles 118
Angelo Palladino 203
Anjana 205
Animal Day Sessions 144, 162
Anita Madigan Band 47
Anti-System 41, 91, 229
Annihilater 95
Another Burn Zero 135
Anything But That 83
Ape 131
Apes, Pigs & Spacemen 147
Apple Moths 55
Apostles 255
Archers 145
Architect 26, 51
Arcromnia 198
Arise 39, 84, 227
Argy Bargy 229
Asha Brewer Trio 214
Asylum 60
Atavist
Ataxia 84
At Least We Got Shoes 9
At The Gates 69
Attic 75
Aurora 24
Auxillary Of Real Men 180
Avalanche 19, 49
Azel 260
Azores 246

B

Bbc 53
Baba Yaga 161, 179
Baby Harp Seal 135, 243
Baby Tuckoo 19
Bad Habits 9
Bad Rep 26
Bad Wolf 127
Balls To The Wall 49, 54
Bantus 45
Barcode Biopsy 161
Barbarellas 212
Bartail-Goodwit 194
Bastard Son Of Toranaga 67
Battle Royale 243
Beckoning 76
Bedlam 23, 47, 54
Beer Beast 93, 161, 240
Beggars Bones 24
Beginning Of The End 95
Belonging 137
Berlin 20, 25
Best Way To Walk 198
Beyond The Veil 55
Bias(Liberty Scream) 265
Big Bang 47, 48, 59, 61, 189, 276
Big Electric Cat 43
Big Eyed Beans 202
Big Fish 12, 27, 29, 41, 51, 231, 260
Big Love 144
Big Stone Culture 90
Bill Presley's Coat 10
Billy Reubin 246
Bio-Hazard 71, 83, 84
Birdog 180
Bittersweet 11
Black Falcon 147
Black Lace 241
Black Lanterns 131, 162
Black Star Liner 37
Blade 12
Blister Factory 232
Bloodbath 69
Blood Orange 7, 43, 51
Blood Robots 83
Blood Sucking Freaks 95
Bloodstream 147
Bluesbite 130
Blunderbuss 127, 275
Bob Got Shot 139
Bobby Charltons 29
Bolyne 198
Bomb Circle 8, 41
Bomb Disneyland 8, 135
Bomb Everything 8
Boston Crabs 127
Bottleneck Boogie Band 57, 202
Box 27, 29
Boxed-In 95, 280

Brand New Analogues 275
Breene 189
Brendan Croker & The 5 O'Clock Shadows 138
Bridge 49
Brody 135
Broomdusters 148, 194
Bugeyed 83
Bullets (Jam Band) 231
Bullweek 55, 129, 229, 265
Burning Bridges 21
Burning Flag 162
Bush Pilot 131, 162
Butch Campi 83
Buzzcocks 212
Byte The Bullet 25, 47

C

Cabbage Head Kids (Atomic Leds) 90
Cardiacs 55
Carrera (Taboo) 21, 23, 49
Cajun Aces 198
Cameras In Cars 37
Camp Boyz 51
Canadidates 56
Capt. Haddock & The Fishy Fingers 39
Captain Hotknives 131
Carbomb 245
Car Boot Cowboys & The Sidekicks 198
Carnage 8
Catharsis 243
Catch 22 21
Cath O'Connor Sound
Chainsaw 20, 25
Challenger 19
Chaos 61, 189
Charles Dickens & The Great Expectations 9
Chest 131, 162
Chi 209
Child's Play 189
Chimp Eats Banana 274
China Doll 232
Choice 61
Chorus Of Ruin 8, 135, 147
Chronic 37
Chumbawamba 274
Chutzpah 91
Circle Of Nine 62
Circles 51
Circulus 135
Civilised Society 71, 137
Class Type Bees 188
Classique 47

INDEX

Clocks & Clouds 33
Cobalt 67
Cockfight 169
Cocktail Shakers 45
Coda 27
Cold War 243
Collen's Fancy 196
Colour Of Money 12
Comic Book Heroes 17, 236
Convulsions 91
Cool Jerx 9, 130
Coping Saw 179
Corrosive Uk 71
Corvus 95
Coup De Grace 76
Cracked Cop Skull 135, 255
Cradle Of Filth 69, 137
Creation's Tears 69
Criminal Damage 221, 229
Critical Mass 8
Crone 216
Cry Freedom 8
Crying Shame 260
Cud 45
Curse Of Eve 179
Cut-Out Shapes 5, 36
Cyber Circus 20, 231
Cyrka 19, 20, 21

D

Damien Wolfe 43
Damned 5
Damn Nation 147
Dan 83
Dandys 258
Dark Embrace 147
Das Tor 26
Dave Arran & The Belairs 194
Dave Arran & The Crusaders 237
Dave Lee Sound 130, 148
Dawnraiser 84, 147
Dawnwatcher 20, 194
Dead Celebs 49
Dead Pets 233
Dead Resurrected 23
Dead Wrong 243
Death Brew 83
Delirium 231
Delius Myth 26, 48
Demonix 187
Detrimental 209, 215
Deuteronomy 51
Devil's Child 189
Devils 95, 242
Dhol Foundation 209
Diagnosis? Bastard! 135
Diamond Light 7, 21, 23
Dignity 145
Dillion & Gibbons 212

Dijibouti Blue (Party Dress) 32
Dirt 95, 242
Disaffect 95
Disaster 83
Discontrol 84
Distorted 242
Doctor & The Inmates 48
Dodger 138
Donkeys 272
Doom 71, 83, 95, 162, 235, 242
Dragon Rapide 243
Dragster 258
D: Ream 219
Drench 162
Dr.sarcophagus 162
Dubh Chapter(Alchemists) 36
Dub Kitchen 161, 249
Duffy Gibbons 212
Dv8s 10, 27

E

Early Riders 62
Earthquake Johnson 194
East 10, 209
Eaten Alive By Insects 10
Easy 11
Eazy Street 57
Ebola 83
Echo & The Bunnymen 75
Edge 9, 141, 147, 202
Edible Marquetry 10
Eggy Bread 162
Egomania 212, 258
Eiger 144
Elected 17
Electric Love 23
Electric Wizard 231
Element 187
Elements 27, 59, 105
Eleven 18 231
Elizabethans 241
Ellison's Hogline 194
El Loco 17, 231
Elsie Moon 39
Elvis Taxi 179, 258
Embrace 45, 220
End 57
Enchanted 135, 147
Endless Grinning Skulls 135
Endtimes 235
Escapement 8
Ethel & The Heroes 21
Everly Sisters 131
Excalibur 20, 43, 47, 127
Excel 6
Excitement 260
Exoterik 57, 188, 275
Extreme Noise Terror 95, 242
Extinction Of Mankind 162

F

FKM 19
Fabians 26, 189
Facelift 257
Face The Unknown 67
Fahrenheit 451 276
Falconetti 131, 162
Fallacy 8, 55, 135
Fallen Horses 62
False Claims 202
False Face 169
Far Fetched 57, 277
Fatal Joy 189
Fear 23, 49, 54
Fever Hut 37
Filthkick 255
Firefive 10
Fishwives 188
Five Previous Owners 59
Flange 56, 227
Flashpoint 49
Flat Back Four 232
Flori 21
Ford Prefects 9
Forest Of Stars 133
For What 8
Foul Play 21, 23, 57, 231
Four Beats Behind Bars 9
Four Fighters 135
Four Horsemen 198
Freaks Union 229
Freaky G's 240
Fred Oyster 57
Fresh Garbage 238
Frontrunner 24, 277
Fuckin' Glorious 233
Full Colour 139
Fundamental 209

G

GBH 8
GFA 249
Galaxians 246
Garden Of Remembrance 260
Gardeners Of Eden 43
Gary Kaye & The Libertines 61
Gary Whitfield's Big Secret 9
Generic 71
Generic Unit 280
Genesis 55
Genital Deformities 95
Gentlemen's Pistols 169
Geoffrey Oi-Cott 233
Gerry & The Pacemakers 260
Getting The Fear 209
Ghostdance 37
Give Up All Hope 95

INDEX

Glam Nation 20
Glamorous Hooligan 103
Goatspeed 280
Goderrhorea 83
Godfathers 5, 36
Gods Of Hellfire 55, 147
Gorgeous 48, 51
Gorgeous Wham Boys 9
Grace Notes 204
Grain 187
Granny Thompson's Big Bald Head 9
Graven Image 137
Green 144, 162
Grim 41, 129
Grip 57, 129, 202
Gruel 282
Guido 9, 29
Guild 162
Gypsy 17

H

HDG 83
HX2 62
Hacksilver 246
Haircut 100 6
Halo 180
Halstead Clan 201
Handful Of Dance 41
Happiness Ad 43, 51
Hardland 19
Hard To Swallow 35, 280
Hardware 43
Harlequyn 19, 51
Harsh Words 29
Haters 169
Haxan 95
Headache 161, 180
Headmen 33
Headstone 187
Health Hazard 71, 83, 84, 242
Hedgehog Pie 201
Height 37
Hellkrusher 95, 162
Help Yourself 194
Herbal Remedy 11
Hiatus 83
Hidden Warfare 60
Hi-Fly 148
High Z 17
Highway To Hell 187
Himself 144
Hip Huggers 179
Hollow Earth 235
Hollow Horse 189
Hollow Men 37
Hollywood Blondes 59
Hokupayshun 194
Homesick 41, 43, 84, 144, 147
Hong Van 189

Hooligans 241
Hormones 131
Horror 135, 169
Horton Carpets 263
Hot Spiced Bananas 141, 206
Howl 255
Huighin Quintet 10, 27, 130
Human Wreckage 162
Hump 139
Hunting Party 59, 61, 274
Hush 57
Hyacinth House 45

I

Ian Brown Band 209
Idiot Box 55, 129, 169, 221, 233
Idle Rich 5, 36
Inarcadia 274
Indiqa 39
Info-Zany 57
Innadaze 103
Insect 54
Instigators 71
Interrobang 272
Interstate 21, 57
In-Touch 169
Immortal Dead 161
Importance Of Else 26
Iron Monkey 135, 235
Iron-On Maiden 135
Iron Rat 84, 187
Ironside 84, 133, 135, 169, 246, 255
Ironstorm 187
Isotope 204
It's Amazing/ Drink 11

J

Jab Jab 9
Jacacanda 138
Jackals 8
Jack Bentley Blues Band 194
Jack The Lad 201
Jaded Hart 23, 49
James 105
Jan Dyl & Joe 148
Jasper 20
Jayver 27, 59, 105, 206
Jed's Blues Band 12, 27, 231
Jigsaw Culture 147
Jj's Bones 27, 41, 224
Joe's Cafe 216
Joe Gallagher 231
John Holmes 83, 246, 280
Johnny & The Poorboys 29, 61
John Sheppard Set 203
John Verity Band 241
Joy 209

Juke Joint 27, 48, 51
Ju-Ju 51
Jumping The Gun 11
Juratory 233

K

KGB 20, 25, 231
Kaboss 194
Kaleche 9, 25, 260
Karrion 84, 137
Katz 29, 260
Keep 8
Keyside Strike 233
Khang 20, 21, 95, 133, 135, 235, 242
Khayn 131
Kick 57
Kill Ii This 8, 43, 147
Kindness 237
King Booty 39
Kiss My Axe 20
Kissing The Pink 47
Kitsch 45, 220
Kito 135, 246
Knoxville Girls 198
Knoxville Saints 275
Kool Jerx 9
Krakatoa 19, 20, 235
Kudos 51
Kwai Chang Caine 41, 55, 129

L

Laboratory Noise 144
La Costa Rasa 257
Lady Vic 9, 27
Laika Dog 127
Lamp Of Thoth 137
Largactil 95, 131
Last In The Brain Q 146
Lazarus Blackstar 95, 135, 137, 235, 245
Leafeater 127
Legend 9, 47, 54
Lemathus 35
Lemon Enema 233
Lemoniod 24
Let 'Em Burn 275
Liberty Ship 56
Lifting The Veil 17
Lionel Blairs 225
Lipsbury Pinfold 17
Liquidate Brains 71
Lithium 6 95
Little Egypt 20, 25, 43, 47, 241
Lively Arts 57, 188
Living Legends 83
Livingston Daisy 26, 43, 51
Lizgizzard 83
Liz Wright Band 25

Loco Mosquito 227
Loobie 216
Loom 180
Loose Furs 43
Lost Patrol 56
Lost Weekend 19
Los Zimmos 204
Lot 49 (Motel Chronicals) 146
Loud 26, 43, 51, 103
Lounge 84, 187
Love, Chips & Peace 93, 161
Loved Ones 138
Love Room 145
Lowlife UK 55, 84, 129, 169, 233, 229

M

M People 260
M62 Goddam 10, 27, 130
Macaxe 59
Magna Carta 35
Malibu Stacey 127
Mammoth 45
Manfat 280
Mannix (Sacrement) 187
Mapp 188
Marshall Law 69
Mash-M 161, 249
Mask 48
Masquerade 17
Matt Black & The Emulsions 7, 51
Me & My Emu 55, 76
Meanstreak 23, 54
Meatlocker 169
Melt 7
Middle 8 17
Midnight 49
Midnight Train 148, 194, 202, 203
Mighty Wah! 75
Milan Lad Octet 209, 215
Milan Lad Jazz Fuse 215
Milestone 201, 205
Minefield 84, 233
Minute Manifesto 83, 243
Minx Grill 179
Miozan 246
Miracle Mile 6
Misdemeanor 20
Mission 43
Moist 32
Momentum 103
Monolith Cult 133, 187, 231
(Funky)Monorail 141
Montage 27, 61, 105
Month Of Birthdays 179
Moon 141, 179
Moonkyte 148, 194
Moota 41
Morbid Humour 41, 221
Morrissey-Mullen 215

Morrowdawn 135
Mother's Son 21
Motley Crudos / Losing The Battle 240
Motorvators 221
Mouldy Warp 25, 148
Mountain Ash 204
Mourn 137
Mr E 19
Mr. Giblet / Red Bean Game 56, 227
Mr Mak / Daisy Cutter 221
Mr Meana 49, 60
Mugwamp 93, 161
Murderpuss 265
Mwstard 83, 179, 189
My Dying Bride 133, 135, 137, 231
My Psychedelic Uncle 39
Mysterious Footsteps 45

N

Nnn 55
Nailbomb 84, 229, 255
Nail Keg Nellie 198
Napalm Death 71, 95, 255
Natural Rhythm (Spars) 11, 12, 238
Navaho UK 221
Neckbrace 84, 147
Necromancer 147
Necroxist 137
Negatives 7, 221
Negativz 91
Nelson's Column 39, 56, 84, 227
Never Forever 45, 57
New Model Army 5, 8, 27, 43, 48, 59, 147, 212, 227, 276
New Musical Testament 27, 105, 212
Next World 95
Nexus 135
Nightlife 9, 29, 206, 260
Nightmares On Wax 103
Nightmare Visions 231
Nightshift 9
Noisegate 20, 127, 231
No Way Out 169
Nowt 27, 41, 129
Nursery 131, 144, 162

O

Ocean 29
Oceansize 69
Oddfellow & Sampler 103
Off The Wall 9, 206, 260
Oisin 216
Old Joe Zydeco 198
Old School 238
Old School Enemy 147
Oktober 209
One By One 83
One Deaf Ear 36

One Zone 243
Optic Nerve 58
Orange World Of Titan 35
Otis & The Elevators 141, 202
Out From Animals
Outlander 20
Outrider 24, 144, 277
Ozbest 24, 275

P

PADD 43
Palladinos 203, 212
Panama Jack 20
Pappa Brittle 209
Paradise Lost 69
Pariah 27
Paris Effect 57
Passion Killers 274
Passmore Sisters 37
Peached Out 144
Peppa Junction 17, 236
Pepperjam 27, 138
Perfume Fish 11
Phil Gilbert Band 206
Phosphene 180
Pilot 231
Pink Turds In Space 71
Placebo 105
Planet Soul 130
Pleasant Valley Children 83
Pleasure Seekers 27, 130
Pockets/ White Soul 47
Polaris 147
Police Bastard 95
Pool's Winner's From Kent 33
Pondskaters 57
Poppy Factory 45, 220
Popular Fiction 5, 36
Popzene 10
Powder Monkey 10
Preacher's Dream 194
Pregnant 58
Premiere 57, 105
Press 25
Pride 25, 47
Primate 41, 91, 129, 202
Private Dicks 9, 62
Private Eyes 25
Pro Patria-Mori 240
Prophecy Of Doom 39
Psyche 17
Psychedelic Singh 11
Psychic Peace Machine 43
Psycho Surgeons 41, 48, 51, 60, 189, 249
Pulse 9, 47, 54
Purity Cries 135, 147
Push Button Technology 105

INDEX

Q

Quick 276
Quickening 21, 49
Quiet Life 27
Quireboys 61

R

Radio 5 45
Radius (High Wired) 265
Rattlesnake Shake 48, 49, 60, 127
Raw 233
Raw Deal 62
Razorback 162
Realeyz 12
Really 204
Recussant 161, 179
Red Room 144
Reefer 7, 21, 39
Reeved 147
Rent 212
Repo Brothers 54
Resonance 135
(Mighty) Resonators 33
Rhabstallion 19
Rhino 19, 20
Rhombus Of Doom 83
Rhythm Cruisers 9
Rhythm Seeds 27, 138
Rhythm Sisters 21
Ribena Men 27
Ridgerunner 23
Right To Silence 146
Rio 241
Ripcord 225, 255
Ripsnort 7, 23
Risky Business 45
Rock 19
Rockheads 57
Rocksolid ('Angabout) 9, 130
Rodeo Jones 27, 105
Roger Higgins Band 202
Rollin' Joan 27, 130, 231
Rot-In-Hell 169
Royce 139
Rudimentary Youth 83, 240
Ruin 95, 245

S

69 Ways 238
Sad Cypress 51
Salvation 37, 43, 206
Sansaar 205
Saracen 49
Sasquatch 24, 275
Sawn Off 83, 95, 243, 280

Saw Throat 71
Scaramanga 225
Scarlet Heights 201, 205
Scatter (2) 39
Scene 5
Screaming Jellyfish 198
Screaming Life 24
Screaming Lord Sutch 9
Screamachine 49
Screaming Plastic Turtles 141
Score 91, 129
Seal Team Six 131, 162
Seaton Sisters (Screaming D-Cups) 31
Second Coming 7, 55
Secret People 17
Seer's Tear 71, 133, 137
Seige 54
Seldom Red 25
Sensei 24
September Kitchen 11, 12
Serenity 137, 229
Seven Antelopes 51
Seven Dead Americans 8
Severed Heaven 133
Sex Gang Children 26
Sex Maniacs 169
Sex Patels 235
Shack 51
Shanghai 57
Shahkaar 10, 27, 206
Shark 19
Shakes 59, 276
Sheds 202
Sheepskin Children 7
Shiny Beast 10, 41, 179, 212, 258
Ship Of Fools 137
Shirts 62
Shit 242
Shogun 29
Shrine 67
Sickfuckino 169
Sicko 179
Sidewinder / Sidewynder 21
Sid Presley Experience 5
Sigmund Void 103
Silas Warthelmet's Battering Ram 194
Silverburn (Burn Horizon) 135, 231
Silvergrass 194
Silverwing 59
Simply Red 215
Since The Accident 57, 188
Siva 260
Six Feet Under 91
Skeleton Crew 8
Skeletal Family 61, 187, 188, 189
Sketch 204
Skidmarks 91
Skin Huk 48
Slack 27, 41, 179
Slack Elvis 257

Slam 60, 127
Slammer 23, 43, 51, 103
Slick 50 246
Slipstream 215
Sloan Square East 11
Sludgelord 71
Skidoo 27
Smart Arse 25, 57 141
Smokie (Smokey) 25, 237
Smokescreen 139
Snake Arms 27, 130
Sniffa 25, 231
Snuff Rock 141, 229
Social Sin 121
Sofa Head 243
Soggy Biscuits 39
So It Goes 49, 61
Solstice 84, 133, 135, 137, 231
Sonando 10, 130, 206
Sons Of Liberty 189
Son Of Sam 209
Somebody's Brother 27, 41, 145, 179, 201, 212, 258, 260
Sore Throat 71, 83, 95
Soricide 246
Sounds Of Swami 189
Soulfish 57, 188, 277
Southern Death Cult 209
Space Hog 37
Spectre 12
Spiral Highway 194
Sponge 51
Sprawl 147
Spurs 62
Stacks 6
Stagefright 20
Stagnant Era 83
Stalingrad 93, 95, 242
Stampede 186
Stamping Ground 84
Stand-Ins 25
Stranded 11
Station West 60
Stax Wheelwright & The All Stars 84, 129, 229, 243, 265
Steadfast (McDonalds) 135, 169, 255
Steven 27, 59, 276
Stipetic 206
Stone 146
Stoney Mountain Boys 9
Stormin' Normans 20, 25
Stormtrooper 23
Street Regal / Albion St 12
Strongpoint 103
Strutz 25
Studebaker 201
Stutta 7
Subsonics 154
Subverters (Religious Vomit) 95
Sudden Impulse 25
Suede 105

INDEX

Suffer 83, 95, 280
Sugarland 47
Suicide By Cop 147
Sully's Heroes 238
Summon Bonum 225
Sunfish Doo 55, 129, 228
Sunflowers 29
Super 8 37
Supercollider 135
Surreal Estate 11
Swing Parisienne 214
Sword In The Stone 196
Sybil 58
Sybil Beats 10
Symphony In X 17
Syndicate 9,12

T

22 Blue 189
309s 198
TNT 59
Talk To Angels 45
Talulah Gosh 10
Tasmin Archer Band 145
Tea House Camp 36
Temple Balls 187
Teenage & The Wildlife 188
Teresina 118
Terrorvision (Spoilt Bratz) 127
Then The Third Half 131
Thighslapper Three 198
Thin 75
Third Season 26, 51
This Et Al 55
This Ritual 24
Thomas J & The Gangsters Of Soul 9, 11, 47, 130, 138, 260
Those Frayed Edges 48
Threads 127, 135, 231, 243, 280
Three Men & A Bass 27, 138
Threshold Shift 91, 129
Tropicana 206
Thundering Hearts 27, 59, 61
Tibet 194
Ticklish 90
Timeless Thoughts 186
Timelife 145
Timeout(Stop The Clock) 9, 130
Tiny Monroe 224
Titan 35
Tony 'Guitar' Sound 57
Too Many Chiefs 91
Too Much 231
Tooth Fairy 179
Toranaga 67
Torch Girls 61, 276
Tortoise Waltz 147, 229
Tour De Force 17
Toyz 45

Tranquility 7, 23
Transatlantic Alien 179, 189
Trashed 83
Treachery 21
T.rex Tribute Band 47
Trip & Stumble 39
Turbo 9, 62
Turnpike 194
Tuxedo 19, 54
Twice Around The Houses 27
Twilight 60
Twister 55
Twister 5 (Paris Twist) 228
Two Sandwiches Please 7
Tyger Of Pan Tang 25

U

Unborn 135, 169, 255
Underground Swing 105
Unholy Trinity 5
Unicorn Love 240
Uninvited Guests 17
Union Wireless 131
Unique 3 103
Universal(Crayon Face) 58
Unquiet Grave 255
Unsuitable Footwear 58
Urban Originals 131
Us 51
Usurpa 117
UXL 57, 105

V

VDMC 71, 137
VR 95, 231, 242
Valafar 260
Vallenfyre 69, 133, 137
Vancouver 260
Vanishing Point 17
Varukers 240
Vegetable Section 141
Vendetta 84, 162
Vengeance Of Gaia 169
Verity 19, 241
Violent Carsons 7, 23
Vochi 11
Voorhees 55, 135, 169, 229, 255
Voyager UK 19
Voyce 139

W

Wally 194
Walk The Plank 169
Wankys 243
Want 51
Ward Brothers 237

War All The Time 243, 282
Warfare 71, 84
Wartorn 71, 84
Waste 83
Wasteland 48
Weird Emotions 25
Western Dance 129, 141, 202, 238
Wharf Rats 146
When Idols Fall 135
While Heavens Wept 137
Whipper Snapper 189
Whirlwind 9
Whiskey Priests 169
White Hot & Blue 20, 25
Wicked Rich 21, 23, 61
Wild Geese 201
Wild Trash 147, 221
Wild Willi Beckett & Jont 48
Windy Mills 55
Wipeout 9, 130
Witchknot 161, 179, 189
Withdrawn 255
Without Prejudice 10, 130
Withstand 71
Witness 21, 23
Woodhouse Rejects 83
Wolf Unit 39
Wolves In Winter 103
Wonderful Thing Called Tiddles 76
Word 45
Worm 51

X

Xentrix 51

Y

Year Dot 129

Z

Zed 8, 27, 41, 48, 129, 147
Zico 27, 212, 258
Zippy Deph 24, 277
Zippy Noise 24, 277
Zoopsia 131, 162
Zoot & The Roots 35, 62, 260
Zounds 95, 240
Zubop 9
(Zydeco) Funk Butchers 198
Zy-Tyr 17
ZX Plectrum 24

AFTERWORDS

When's the next bloody book coming out?

After the publication of *Bradford's Noise Of The Valleys Volume One* we had barely a break before continuing with this, the second volume. In fact, the front cover was almost finished before the first book hit the shelves.

Once again, we both had various bits and pieces that we had accumulated, inherited or collected over the years and so set about the time-devouring task of researching and discovering all the bits we didn't know and hopefully we have even got some of it right!

So, meeting up every week or so with what we had come up with, we started piecing together this volume, word by word, image by image, page by page, chapter by chapter, leaving gaps along the way that we filled in when we could.

Once again the painstaking trawl through old copies of the *Telegraph & Argus* began at Bradford Library until the library building was closed in 2013 when, thankfully, we got permission from the *T&A* to have weekly access to the newspaper's own archives.

This time round, apart from the usual face-to-face meetings with various band members, we had various interweb search engines and resources like *Facebook* to track down friends and friends of friends who were able to send information.

But the inevitable question was asked many times over the four and a half years since Volume One was originally published in summer 2009; *'When's the next bloody book coming out?'*

Four and a half years may seem like a long time but count the number of bands mentioned, names drawn on family trees, pictures scanned in, recordings tracked down and packed into these 300 or so pages and you might appreciate how long it takes to find out and document all this information!

But don't think it will stop there. Within a few weeks of this book hitting the shelves, the question is sure to be asked again, *'When's the NEXT bloody book coming out?'*

Ok, so we admit it, it took a while for *Volume 3* to make an appearance. *Volume 3 Part 1* was published in 2025, along with improved, expanded and updated editions of *Volumes 1 & 2*. And *Volume 3 Part 2* is on its way soon... promise!

Gary Cavanagh was born in Clayton, Bradford, and is a founder member of Bradford's 1 In 12 Club, a former university tutor in history and politics, and a local historian and archivist.

He has been a lifelong Bradford City supporter and one-time City Junior. If it hadn't been for that niggling knee injury....

Former vocalist with legendary local rock gods Phobia, he has been involved in the local music scene since the mid 1970s and was instrumental in the production of the 1 In 12 Club compilation LP series.

Since the publication of *Volume One*, Gary has appeared on ITV's *Calender* news programme and local radio stations including Radio Leeds and BCB to promote the book, as well as giving talks on local music history at various seats of learning.

Matt Webster hails from Thackley, Bradford, and has been a drummer in numerous local bands since the early 1980s, including The Convulsions, The Nerve Agents, Swamp Flower, Western Dance, Primate, The Bottleneck Boogie Band, Nowt, Grim, Zed, The Horton Carpets and Kwai Chang Caine. Also known as Matt Nazgul and Pete, Matt is a graphic designer and recording engineer/producer, and co-founder of Mutiny 2000 Studios/Records.

He was an occasional music reviewer for the *Bradford Star* in the early 1990s during his time working in the Pre-Press Department at the *Telegraph & Argus* where he also used to sneak various bits onto the *Rock On* page when no-one was looking.

He was the editor of the non-existent *Daily Mutiny* and was also the original co-presenter of the *Bradford Beat* show on BCB from 1995 to 1999.

Acknowledgements

Thanks to Tim Walker for his forward.

We are grateful to the following for permission to reproduce certain articles: Telegraph & Argus; Perry Austin-Clark, Peter Orme, Jim Greenhalf, Emma Clayton, Odele Ayres, Keighley News (David Knights) and Record Collector's Rare Record Guide.

This book would never have happened without the contributions of information, support, photos, rare music and other memorabilia from the following people:

Lee Baines, Kath Canoville, Jonathon Gregson, Graham Scaife, James Bordass, Jonjo McCoglan, Tim Walker, Paul Cunningham, Mick Sugden, Matt Jennings, Mick Birdsall, Craig Sheehan, Jago Ibbotson, Gill Parrett, Ian Buxton, Clive Hughes, Gordon Wilkinson, Liz Narey, Alec Marlow, Dave Stockell, Dave Friend, Sally Stone, Robb Philpotts, Rich Savage, Malcolm Manning, Steve Narey, Graham Bancroft, Rich 'Militia' Walker, Malcolm Hanson, Gary Holdsworth, Russ Snell, 'Sned', Susan Kasher, Richard Brass, Tony Brennan, Leigh Stothard, Craig Williams, Anita Madigan, Titus Toiletseat, Steven Bentley, John Thornton, Paul Solynskyj, Neil Roddis, Jon Binns, Simon Ashberry, Darren Miah, Ian 'Tosh' Ward, Roger Mitchell, Tony Boyce, Andy 'Tiddy' Wells, Hannah & Kev Poppleton, John & Mark Higgins, Jez Farrar, Kendra Pashley-Farrar, Norman Hill, Steve Tandy, 'Trog', Ciaran Hafferty, Giuseppe Lambertino, Richard Fanthrope, Bryan Outlaw, Martin Sturdy, Darren Dowson, Gary Quinn, Johnny Lorrimer, Carl Stipetic, Dom Sheard, John Bolloten, Les Hall, Rob Holden, Nigel Broadbent, Fritz The Cat, Michael Fryer, Hayden Berry, Ian 'Griff' Griffiths, Lianne Hall, Rich Fawthrop, Andy Farrow, Rory Cavanagh, Chris 'Hotknives' Smith, Nagbea, George Quinn, Noel Bateson, Richard Bolton, Stuart Firth, Andy Abbott, Tony Grogan, Danny Whittingham, Darron Ward, Bri 'Doom' Talbot, Matt Fortune, Ken Waller, Richard 'Gilly' Gill, Frances Hollins, Enzo Annecchini, Sinead Minott, Lindsay Burns, Mark Kershaw, Ian Austin, Tom Chapman, Ian 'Lecky' Leck, Sean Dillion, Steve Ward, Britt Jagger, Maya Jagger, Marie Bennett (pics), Tony Woolgar, Lorna Eastwood, Anthony Tretton, Nick Toczek, Pete Burns, 'Scoot', Nick Royles, David James, Margery Webster, John Rigby, Mangal Singh, Satpal, Kalvin Singh, Bela Emerson, Jon Gibbons, Neil Blanchett & Wayne Jackson, Simon 'Nogsy' Nolan, Dave Fields, John Rhodes, Paul Denman, Fran Jones, Paul 'Harris' Hennessy, Fern Morris, Martin Hawthorn, Jay Barraclough, Rob Rhodes, Simon Denning, Ade Clark, Liam Sheeran, Mark Cranmer, Peter Finan, Richard Ingham (pics), Jont 'Dr Watson', Dave Ledgard, John Duffy, Dave Malt, Phil Hey, Tony Fox, Michael Dean, Steve Walsh, Lindsey Teale, Tracy Teale and anyone else who has sent us stuff or contributed in any way!

From Keighley: Gary Kaye, Daz Robb, John Gow, Tony McCoglan, Tony Tronnolone, Joe McEvoy, Kurt Wood, Mick Walsh, Roger 'Trotwood' Nowell, Steve Wilson, Ian Shackleton, John - Landlord of The Cricketers.

Special Consultants on Chapter 3:
Clive Hughes, Richard Brass, Richard Gill, Enzo Annecchini, John Bolloten.

Bridgit Izod for guidance on proof reading

All the DJs, presenters and staff at BCB Radio (106.6 FM) for all their support.

Thanks for the kind help of Rachel Helliwell for box set slipcases.

Big thanks to Maeve Crawford at Scarborough Library and finally, Sue Caton, Mick, Alison and all the staff at Bradford Central Library's Local Studies.

BRADFORD'S NOISE OF THE VALLEYS
VOLUME 2
THE MUSIC 1988-1998
6 CD BOX SET

The 6 CD set that accompanies this book features over eight hours of music from over a hundred local bands and acts. It covers a massive range of musical styles from pop and rock to folk and blues to indie and punk to hardcore and doom metal to the dance scene.

The Music 1988-1998 is available from various local outlets or to order from

bradfordnoise.com

or

mutiny2000.com

Visit our Facebook page **Bradford's Noise Of The Valleys - The Book**
for updates and news of upcoming releases

1988 - 1998   BRADFORD'S NOISE OF THE VALLEYS VOLUME 2 THE MUSIC

BNOTVCD007 1988-1996

1. *The Godfathers* - **Birth, School, Work, Death** (Coyne/Coyne/Dollimore/Mazur/Gibson) © 1988 SM Publishing (UK) Limited
2. *Seven Dead Americans* - **Night Of The Living Dead** (Wood/Lyon/Clarke/Hooper) © 1988 Copyright Control
3. *The Spurs* - **Soldier** (Horsfall) © 1988 Horsfall
4. *Thundering Hearts* - **Caught Red Handed** (Thundering Hearts) © 1988 Copyright Control
5. *Little Brother* - **SS Spies** (Stockell/Austin/Stockell) © 1988 Sixty Three
6. *Symphony In X* - **Dreams Never Die** (Cattlin/Cass) © 1989 Madigan/King/MacDonald
7. *Pride* - **Mercenary Man** (Madigan/MacDonald/King) © 1989 Madigan/King/MacDonald
8. *Kage Engineering* - **Whistling** (Binder/Binder/Shaw/Saddington) © 1989 Artlos Music
9. *The Hollow Men* - **White Train** (Hosein/Taylor/Roberts/Owen/Cragg) © 1989 Hollow Men
10. *Dubh Chapter* - **Touch And Go** (Mann/Quinn/Staunton/Staunton) © 1990 Universal Music MGB Ltd
11. *The Wonderful Thing Called Tiddles* - **Where Has Everybody Gone?** (Wonderful Thing Called Tiddles) © 1990 1 Noise 12 Pub Inc
12. *The Miracle Mile* - **What Became Of Monty** (Nemes/Jones) © 1990 Nemes/Jones
13. *The Orange World Of Titan* - **Big Baby** (Whittaker) © 1990 Whittaker
14. *Poppy Factory* - **7x7** (Cotton/Binns/Dale) © 1991 Universal Music Publishing
15. *The Headmen* - **Reach The Sky** (Eskriett/Pattern/Slater/Keene) © 1991 Copyright Control
16. *For What* - **Clear** (For What) © 1994 Voltage
17. *Summum Bonum* - **Exploding Raindrops** (Mitchell) © 1994 Copyright Control
18. *Comic Book Heroes* - **Changing** (Comic Book Heroes) © 1995 Copyright Control
19. *Monorail* - **Like I Do** (Fewtrell) © 1996 Copyright Control
20. *Dead Celebs* - **Nobody Cares** (Dead Celebs) © 1996 Copyright Control

BNOTVCD008 1988-1998

1. *Jane Harrison* - **If You Leave Me Now** (Cetera) © 1988 Universal Music Pub/Spirit Music Pub
2. *Kevin Young* - **Hello Little One (Song For Adam)** (Trad./Young) © 1988 Young
3. *Old Joe Zydeco* - **Zydeco Gris Gris** (Trad./Tothill) © 1989 1 Noise 12 Publishing Inc
4. *The Everly Sisters* - **Inside/Outside** (Harris) © 1989 1 Noise 12 Publishing Inc
5. *Heart Of Darkness* - **The Storm** (Jackson/Ram) © 1989 1 Noise 12 Publishing Inc
6. *Uncle Ted Grundy* - **Sacred Cow** (Chapman) © 1989 1 Noise 12 Publishing Inc
7. *Not Precious* - **Nightmares** (Hill/Bayliss) © 1989 1 Noise 12 Publishing Inc
8. *Mary & Chris* - **Dam(n) Your Eyes** (Halliwell) © 1990 Oval Music Ltd
9. *Natural Rhythm* - **Bluebeat & Ska** (Boyce) © 1991 Kassner Associated Pub
10. *Roger Higgins* - **Take Me Back To Mississippi** (Higgins) © 1994 Higgins
11. *Cajun Aces* - **Chere Joues Roses** (Trad/Cajun Aces) © 1994 Copyright Control
12. *Crone* - **Rain** (Crone) © 1994 Crone Music
13. *Scarlet Heights* - **The Scarcity Prayer** (Sherry/Broadbent) © 1995 Scarlet Music
14. *Shiny Beast* - **Ed Wood** (Hennessy) © 1996 Mutiny 2000
15. *Milan Lad* - **Witch Hazel** (G Stewart) © 1995 Swall World Records Limited
16. *Loobie* - **It Fascinates Me** (Maclean) © 1996 Limetree Arts & Music
17. *Phil Gilbert* - **Gideon Here** (Gilbert) © 1997 Second Chance Music
18. *Grace Notes* - **The Quiet Land Of Erin** (Traditional) © 1998 Copyright Control

BNOTVCD009 1990-1998

1. *Tasmin Archer* - **Sleeping Satellite** (Archer/Beck/Hughes) © 1992 Beck/Nettwerk One Music Ltd
2. *Psycho Surgeons* - **Panic On!** (Beckett/Gambles/Hoey/Kirkley) © 1990 QTA/Mutiny 2000
3. *Bomb Everything* - **Just Like Mine** (Cooper/Prytherch) © 1990 Imagem London Limited
4. *Slammer* - **What's Your Pleasure?** (Annecchini/Gagic/Tunnicliffe/Zivanovic) © 1991 Slammer
5. *Station West* - **Love Calling** (Station West) © 1991 T-Bone Records
6. *Threshold Shift* - **Cardboard City** (Threshold Shift) © 1992 Threshold Shift
7. *Egomania* - **Cool, Calm And Collected** (Gibbons) © 1994 Copyright Control
8. *Paul Mother* - **Till Dawn** (Bolan) © 1993 Spirit Music Publishing Limited
9. *Grim* - **Grim** (Watson/Bennett) © 1995 Mutiny 2000
10. *Screaming Life* - **Away** (Screaming Life) © 1995 Copyright Control
11. *Rollercoaster* - **Modern Man** (Rollercoaster) © 1995 Copyright Control
12. *Far Fetched* - **Clumsy** (Cichy) © 1994 Copyright Control
13. *Chest* - **Angels** (Chest) © 1996 Copyright Control
14. *Lional Blairs* - **Wishing Your Life Away** (Stubbs/Pickard) © 1996 Copyright Control
15. *Blister Factory* - **Coming Good** (Blister Factory) © 1996 Copyright Control
16. *Vochi* - **Please** (Vochi) © 1996 Naracen Musik
17. *Embrace* - **All You Good Good People** (McNamara/McNamara) © 1997 EMI Music Pub Ltd
18. *The Auxiliary Of Real Men* - **Brown Love** (Bateson) © 1998 Copyright Control
19. *Fundamental* - **Godevil** (Qureshi) © 1998 Copyright Control

This compilation © 2013 Bradford Noise. Licensed by MCPS.
All tracks used courtesy of the original artists and copyright of the original recordings belongs to their individual owners.
All rights of the producer and the owner of the recorded works reserved. Unauthorised copying, hiring, public performance and broadcasting of this record prohibited.

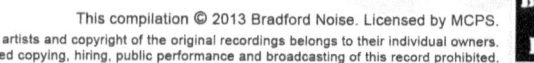

BRADFORD NOISE RECORDS

BRADFORD'S NOISE OF THE VALLEYS VOLUME 2 THE MUSIC — 1988 - 1998

BNOTVCD010 1990-1998
1 *Zed* - **Easy Does It** (Watson/Nolan/Farrar) © 1990 QTA/Mutiny 2000
2 *Loud* - **D Generation** (McLaughlin) © 1990 Universal Music Publishing Ltd
3 *Primate* - **Break My Fall** (Andrews) © 1992 Mutiny 2000
4 *Bobby Charltons* - **Bastard Town** (Quinn) © 1991 Copyright Control
5 *The Big Bang* - **Gangland** (Big Bang) © 1990 Copyright Control
6 *Wicked Rich* - **Rebel** (Wicked Rich) © 1990 Copyright Control
7 *Mr Meana* - **Social Elite** (Mr Meana) © 1991 Mean Music
8 *Architect* - **Set Me On Fire** (Cunningham/Walker) © 1992 Voltage Records
9 *Krakatoa* - **Poison** (Krakatoa) © 1992 Copyright Control
10 *New Model Army & Tom Jones* - **Gimme Shelter** (Jagger/Richards) © 1993 Abkco Music Ltd/Onward Music Ltd/Westminster Music Ltd
11 *Tiny Monroe* - **VHF855V** (Wilow) © 1994 Wilow
12 *Psyche* - **Skimming Stones** (McKendrick/Chrisanthou) © 1994 Flux Music
13 *Blood Orange* - **Why** (Blood Orange) © 1995 Copyright Control
14 *Ripcord* - **You (Anytime, Anyplace, Anywhere)** (Ripcord) © 1995 Copyright Control
15 *Facelift* - **It's Alright** (Facelift) © 1996 Copyright Control
16 *Twister 5* - **Barbara** (Twister 5) © 1996 Copyright Control
17 *Terrorvision* - **Perseverance** (Marklew/Shuttleworth/Wright/Yates) © 1996 Touch Tones Music Ltd
18 *Bullweek* - **Superglue Star** (Sheeran) © 1996 Copyright Control
19 *Slack* - **In Our World** (Nolan) © 1996 Copyright Control
20 *Nowt* - **Another Bloody Blustry Day In Bradford** (Hennessy/Bennett) © 1998 Mutiny 2000

BNOTVCD011 1988-1998
1 *Toranaga* - **Bastard Ballads** (Toranaga) © 1988 Copyright Control
2 *Sore Throat* - **Eric Pickles Is A Fat Tory Bastard** (Sore Throat) © 1989 1 Noise 12 Inc
3 *The Next World* - **Respect The Earth** (Ward/Roue) © 1989 1 Noise 12 Publishing Inc
4 *One By One* - **Shop Me** (One By One) © 1990 1 Noise 12 Publishing Inc
5 *Health Hazard* - **Not Just A Nightmare** (Health Hazard) © 1992 1 Noise 12 Publishing Inc
6 *Wartorn* - **Armed Response** (Wartorn) © 1992 1 Noise 12 Publishing Inc
7 *Paradise Lost* - **Gothic** (Mackintosh/Holmes) © 1991 Imagem London Limited
8 *Chorus Of Ruin* - **Dreaming Of Indigo** (Chorus Of Ruin) © 1993 Avantegarde Music
9 *Solstice* - **The Revenant** (Solstice) © 1993 Copyright Control
10 *Ironside* - **Skincrawl** (Ironside) © 1993 Copyright Control
11 *Witchknot* - **Pianist Envy** (Witchknot) © 1994 Copyright Control
12 *Dark Embrace* - **Dark Embrace** (Dark Embrace) © 1995 Copyright Control
13 *Dawnraiser* - **Holy Lies** (Dawnraiser) © 1996 Copyright Control
14 *Serenity* - **The Way I Bleed** (Serenity) © 1996 Holy Records
15 *Doom* - **(We Hate The) Brew Crew** (Talbot/Dickens/Croft/Gladock) © 1996 1 Noise 12 Pub Inc
16 *VR* - **Intolerance** (Ward/Roue/Talbot) © 1995 1 Noise 12 Publishing Inc
17 *Voorhees* - **Fucker** (Leck/Readman/Rogman-Jones/Nichols/Gillham) © 1996 1 Noise 12 Publ Inc
18 *Stalingrad* - **The Politics Of Ecstacy** (Allison/Claxton/Snell/Wood) © 1996 1 Noise 12 Publ Inc
19 *Hardware* - **What Race Are You?** (Hardware) © 1996 Copyright Control
20 *Purity Cries* - **Division** (Purity Cries) © 1998 Copyright Control
21 *Bryan Outlaw* - **Sunday's Pleasure** (Outlaw) © 1998 1 Noise 12 Publishing Inc

BNOTVCD012 1990-1998
1 *Unique 3* - **Rhythm Takes Control** (Brown/Collins/Parke/Cargill) © 1990 Int Mus Network
2 *Push Button Technology* - **Just 4 U** (PBT) © 1992 Copyright Control
3 *Rodeo Jones* - **Shades Of Summer** (Copland/Plato/Tretton) © 1993 Tretton/Plato/Copeland
4 *Monument* - **I Like It (Guitar Mix) (Edit)** (Annecchini/Cargill/Khan) © 1994 Copyright Control
5 *Mystic Light* - **In Casa Bella (Funk Mix) (Edit)** (Annecchini/Cargill/Khan) © 1994 Copyright Control
6 *Glamorous Hooligan* - **New Age Pension** (Annecchini/Cavanagh) © 1995 Universal Music Publishing
7 *Detrimental* - **Babylon** (Detrimental) © 1994 Copyright Control
8 *Dayiah* - **Storm Clouds** (Dayiah) © 1995 Thrd Eye Music
9 *Sansaar* - **Bind Us Together (Global Scale Mix)** (Bolloten/Rootsman) © 1995 Third Eye Music
10 *King's Highway* - **Temple Of Light (Low Rider Mix)** (Rootsman/Davemet) © 1995 Third Eye Music
11 *Strongpoint* - **Perilous Time (Stop The War Mix)** (Rootsman/Monument) © 1995 Third Eye Music
12 *Rootsman* - **Old Pan Killer** (Rootsman) © 1995 Third Eye Music
13 *Doctor Man* - **Comin' In Style** (Doctor Man) © 1996 DMP
14 *Pianoman* - **Blurred** (Albarn/Coxon/James/Rowntree/Dabney) © 1996 Universal/MCA Music Ltd/Garber Music Ltd
15 *Angeles* - **Hi Horse (Edit)** (Welsh/Cartledge) © 1998 Cartledge/Proof Songs Limited

This compilation © 2013 Bradford Noise. Licensed by MCPS.
All tracks used courtesy of the original artists and copyright of the original recordings belongs to their individual owners.
All rights of the producer and the owner of the recorded works reserved. Unauthorised copying, hiring, public performance and broadcasting of this record prohibited.

BRADFORD NOISE RECORDS

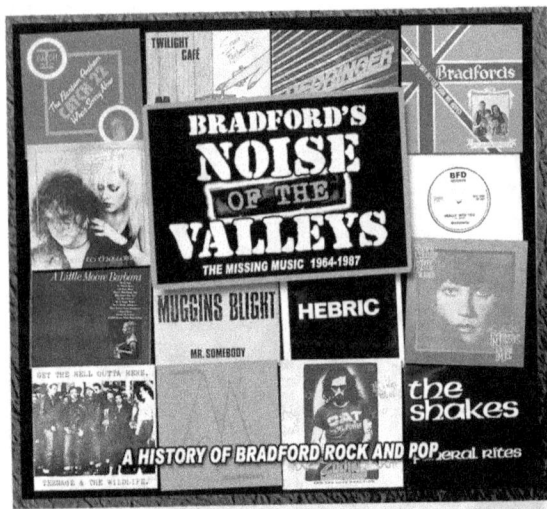

Also available are the two *Missing Music* CDs which capture some of the tracks we didn't have access to when *Bradford's Noise Of The Valleys Volume One* was originally published in 2009.

These CDs form the bridge between *Volume One* and this book. Both CDs and *Bradford's Noise Of The Valleys Volume One 1967-1987* are available to order from **bradfordnoise.com**

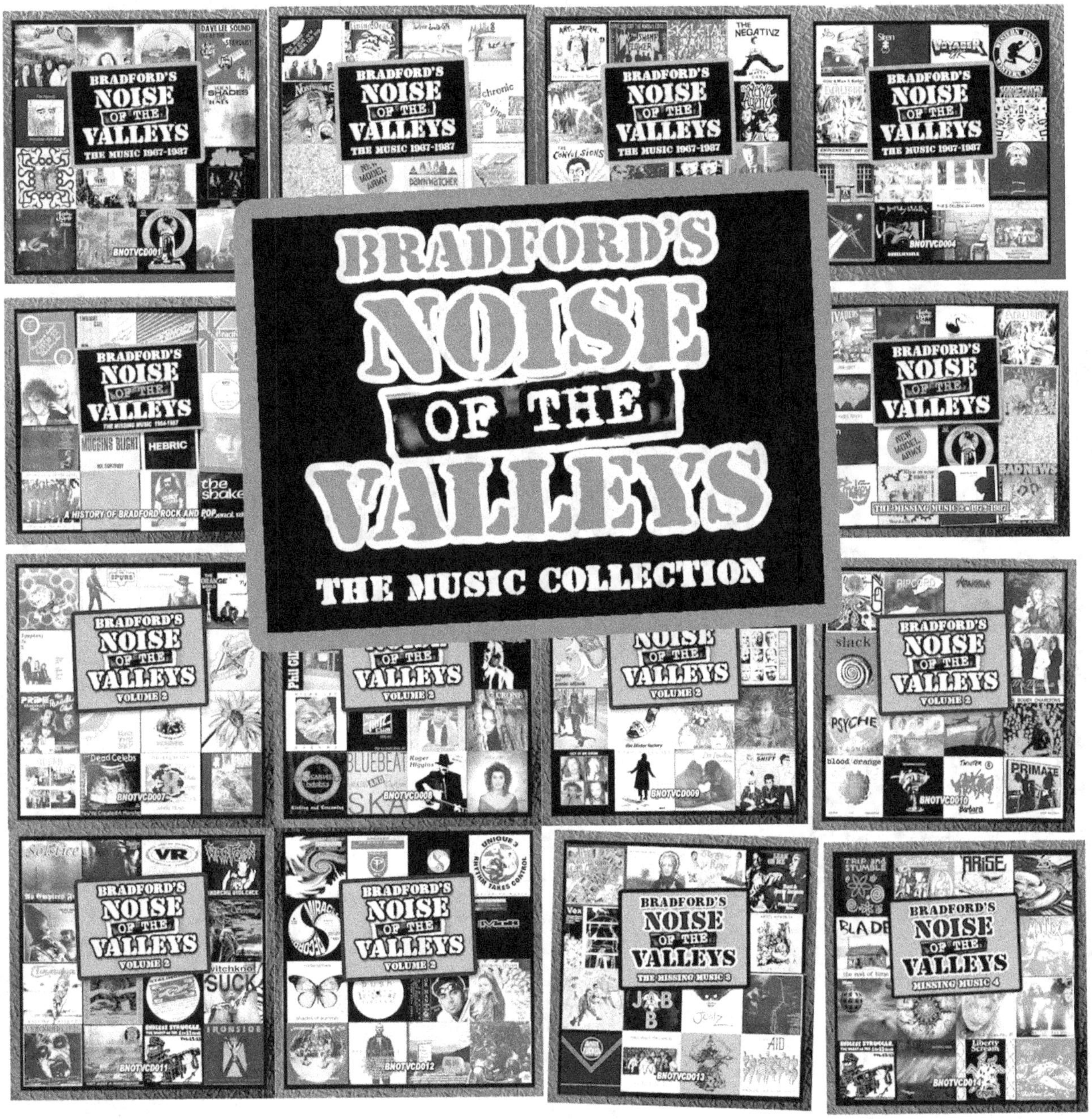
BRADFORD'S
NOISE
OF THE
VALLEYS
THE MUSIC COLLECTION

BRADFORD'S NOISE OF THE VALLEYS
THE MUSIC 1988-1998
BRADFORD'S
NOISE
OF THE
VALLEYS
VOLUME 2

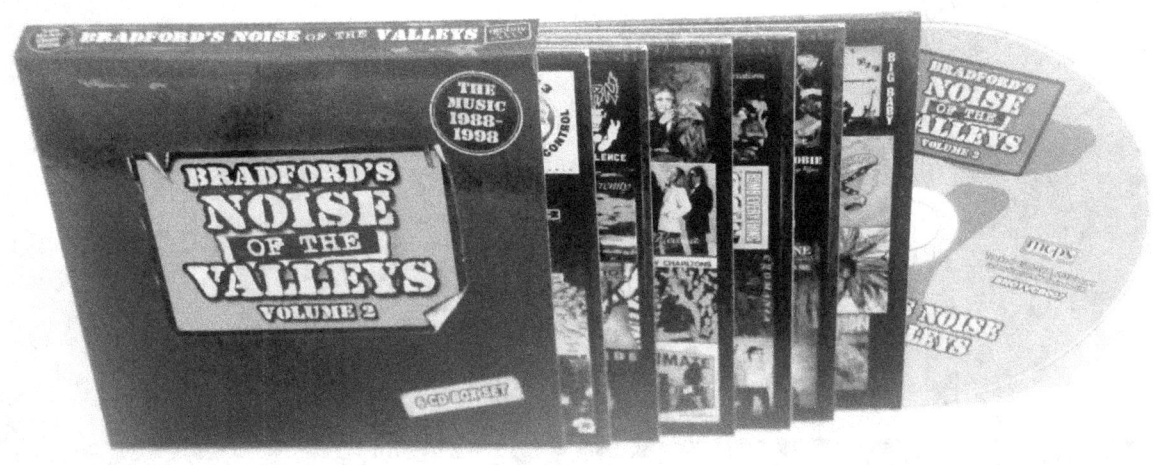

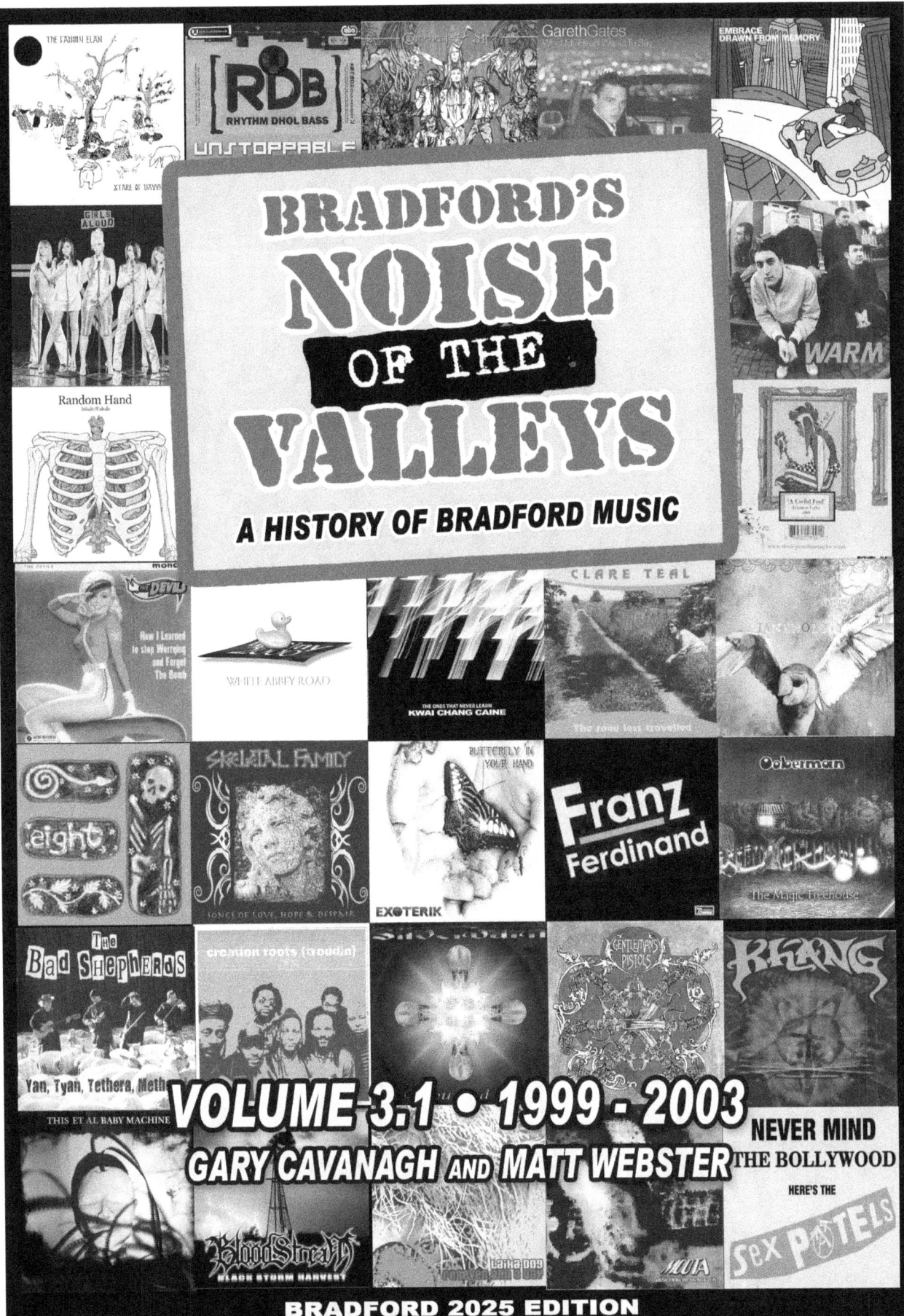